Revised Second Edition

Masterplots

1,801 Plot Stories and Critical Evaluations
of the World's Finest Literature

Revised Second Edition

Volume 12
Unf – Z
6869 – 7382
Indexes

Edited by
FRANK N. MAGILL

Story Editor, Revised Edition
DAYTON KOHLER

Consulting Editor, Revised Second Edition
LAURENCE W. MAZZENO

SALEM PRESS

Pasadena, California   Englewood Cliffs, New Jersey

Editor in Chief: Dawn P. Dawson
Consulting Editor: Laurence W. Mazzeno   *Managing Editor:* Christina J. Moose
Project Editors: Eric Howard   *Research Supervisor:* Jeffry Jensen
Juliane Brand   *Research:* Irene McDermott
Acquisitions Editor: Mark Rehn   *Proofreading Supervisor:* Yasmine A. Cordoba
Production Editor: Cynthia Breslin Beres   *Layout:* William Zimmerman

Library of Congress Cataloging-in-Publication Data
Masterplots / edited by Frank N. Magill; consulting editor, Laurence W. Mazzeno. — Rev. 2nd ed.
    p.   cm.
Expanded and updated version of the 1976 rev. ed.
Includes bibliographical references and indexes.
1. Literature—Stories, plots, etc. 2. Literature—History and criticism. I. Magill, Frank Northen, 1907-   . II. Mazzeno, Laurence W.
PN44.M33   1996
809—dc20   96-23382
ISBN 0-89356-084-7 (set)   CIP
ISBN 0-89356-096-0 (volume 12)

Revised Second Edition
First Printing

PRINTED IN THE UNITED STATES OF AMERICA

LIST OF TITLES IN VOLUME 12

MASTERPLOTS

LIST OF TITLES IN VOLUME 12

MASTERPLOTS

Revised Second Edition

THE UNFORTUNATE TRAVELLER
Or, The Life of Jack Wilton

Type of work: Novel
Author: Thomas Nashe (1567-1601)
Type of plot: Picaresque
Time of plot: Mid-sixteenth century
Locale: England and Europe
First published: 1594

Principal characters:

JACK WILTON, a page for King Henry VIII and a soldier of fortune
DIAMANTE, a rich widow and later Jack's wife
THE EARL OF SURREY, Jack's friend and benefactor
HERACLIDE DE IMOLA, the hostess of Jack and Diamante in Rome

The Story:

Jack Wilton was a page serving in the army of King Henry VIII of England when his adventures began. While the English troops were encamped near Turwin in France, Jack pretended that he had overheard the king and his council planning to do away with a certain sutler and convinced the sutler that he ought to give away all of his supplies to the soldiers and then throw himself on the king's mercy. Completely fooled, the sutler did just that. The king, enjoying the prank, gave the sutler a pension and forgave Jack.

Shortly after the escapade, Jack befriended a captain who forced Jack to help him get rich by throwing dice. Jack tired of his subservience to the captain and persuaded the officer that the best means of getting ahead in the army was to turn spy and seek out information valuable to the king. The gullible captain entered the French lines and was discovered by the French and almost killed before he was hustled back to the English camp.

The campaign over, Jack found himself back in England once more. When the peacetime duties of a page began to pall, he left the king's household and turned soldier of fortune. After crossing the English Channel to find a means of making a livelihood, he reached the French king too late to enter that monarch's service against the Swiss. He traveled on to Münster, Germany, where he found John Leiden leading the Baptists against the duke of Saxony. He observed a notorious massacre, in which the Baptists were annihilated because they refused to carry the weapons of war into battle. After the battle, Jack met the earl of Surrey, who was on the Continent at the time.

Surrey had been acquainted with Jack at court and now was glad to see the page. He confided to him his love for Geraldine, a lovely Florentine woman. Surrey proposed that Jack travel with him to Italy to find her. Since Jack had no immediate plans, he readily consented to accompany the earl.

Jack and Surrey proceeded southward into Italy. As they traveled, Surrey proposed to Jack that they exchange identities for a time, so that the nobleman could behave in a less seemly fashion. Pleased at the prospect of being an earl, even temporarily, Jack agreed.

Upon their arrival in Venice, they were taken up by a courtesan named Tabitha, who tried to kill the man she thought was the earl of Surrey, using the true earl as her accomplice. Surrey and Jack turned the tables on her, however, and caused her and her pander to be executed for attempting to conspire against a life. In the process, however, Jack had unknowingly come into possession of counterfeit money. When they used the coins, Jack and the earl were seized as counterfeiters and sentenced to death.

While in prison, Jack met Diamante, the wife of a goldsmith, who had imprisoned her because he suspected her of infidelity. The page made her his mistress after assuring her that thereby she revenged herself on a husband who did not believe in her chastity.

After a few weeks, Jack and the earl were released through an English gentleman who had heard of their plight and had secured the efforts of the poet Aretine to prove to the court that Tabitha and her procurer had been the counterfeiters. Aretine also saw to it that Diamante was released from prison. She continued to be Jack's mistress, and within a few weeks, after her husband died of the plague, Jack married her. He decided to travel.

He left the earl of Surrey in Venice, but he took such pleasure from bearing the nobleman's title that he continued to do so. After some time, Surrey heard that there was another earl by the same name and went to investigate. Learning that the double was Jack, Surrey forgave him, and they once again resumed their interrupted trip to Florence. Upon arriving there, the earl issued a challenge to all the knights and gentlemen of the city; he hoped thereby to prove his love for Geraldine. The tourney was a great success, and Surrey carryed off all the honors of the day. After that, Surrey and Jack parted company, and Jack, still accompanied by Diamante, went on to Rome.

There they lived with Johannes and Heraclide de Imola. During the summer, Signor de Imola died of the plague. Shortly after his death and before his corpse could be removed from the house, bandits broke in and raped Heraclide de Imola and Diamante. Jack was overpowered by the bandits and unable to help the women. Heraclide killed herself after the attack. When police broke into the house, they blamed Jack for what had happened. He was unable to clear himself because the only other witness was Diamante, whom the bandits had kidnapped.

A banished English earl, appearing in time to save Jack from the hangman's noose, produced witnesses to show that one of the bandits had made a deathbed confession, which cleared the page of any complicity in the crimes. Jack was released and went in search of Diamante. While searching for her, he fell through an unbarred cellar door into the house of a Jew, where he found Diamante making love to an apprentice. The Jew, roused by the noise of the fall and Jack's anger at Diamante, came into the cellar and accused them both of breaking into his house and corrupting his apprentice. Under the law, they became the Jew's bond servants. Jack was turned over to another Jew, the pope's physician, to be used in a vivisection.

He was saved from horrid death when one of the pope's mistresses fell in love with him and used her influence to secure him for herself. Diamante also fell into the woman's hands. Jack and Diamante kept their previous relations a secret and hoped in that way to be able to escape from the house. One day, when the woman went to a religious festival, they escaped, taking with them as much loot as they could carry.

Traveling northward, Jack went to Bologna, where he saw a famous criminal executed. The assassin, Cutwolfe, had confessed to murdering the bandit who had led the assault on Heraclide de Imola and Diamante months before. Moving on into France, Jack found the English armies once again in the field and returned to King Henry's service.

Critical Evaluation:

Following the example of Robert Greene, one of his predecessors at St. John's College, Cambridge, Thomas Nashe overcame whatever religious scruples might have been bred into him as a preacher's son and set out with profane determination to become one of the first "professional writers" in England, and one of the most controversial. As a member of the

University Wits, he distinguished himself by the diversity of his authorial talents, unashamedly plying the writers' trade as polemical pamphleteer, poet, dramatist, and reporter. He said of himself, "I have written in all sorts of humours more than any young man of my age in England." When he died, still a young man in his thirties, Nashe left behind a veritable grab bag of miscellaneous literary pieces. Later critics have often concluded that Nashe's explosive productivity was more comparable with the effect of a scattergun than with that of the big cannons wielded by such contemporaries as William Shakespeare, Ben Jonson, and Philip Marlowe. Nashe has been accused of superficiality, of both thought and style, and he richly merits the accusation. Nevertheless, all would agree that at least two of his works deserve the continued attention of all of those interested in the development of English literary style—*The Unfortunate Traveller: Or, The Life of Jack Wilton* and *Pierce Penniless, His Supplication to the Devil* (1592), which received three editions in the first year of publication alone. *Pierce Penniless*, Nashe's most popular and wide-ranging satirical pamphlet, is a harsh, graphic indictment of the follies and vices of contemporary England, seen from the perspective of one of the first indisputable forerunners of yellow journalism. Nashe's ready talent for immediately distilling the fruits of his observation and experience into gripping firsthand reports served him well in the complicated narrative of Jack Wilton.

The Unfortunate Traveller was written almost one hundred and fifty years too early to be classified as a novel. It is, however, an important forerunner of the English novel as it was to develop in the eighteenth century. *The Unfortunate Traveller*, along with Sir Philip Sidney's *Arcadia* (1581), was one of the high points of the literature of the last years of the sixteenth century. The level of realism is high in this work, yet Nashe also catered to the Elizabethan taste for the romantic and farfetched, especially in dealing with Italy and the Italians. Seldom has a work, even in later centuries, described in such detail the horrors of public torture and execution and the incidents of a rape and a looting.

Rambling narrative, travelogue, earthy memoirs, diary, tavern yarn, picaresque adventure, political, nationalistic, and religious diatribe, *The Unfortunate Traveller*, although impossible to classify generically, is nevertheless clearly one of the seminal starting points in the development of the English novel. The critics are in general agreement with H. G. Wells, who declares that the work "has no organic principle; it is not a unified work of art," yet it definitely has an organic wholeness. That wholeness is as much external as internal, provided more by the author's pen than by the ephemeral events in the life of the main character. The lack of unity accurately reflects the mind of its author, who had a mind as chaotically diverse as the narrative it produced. The structure of the book, a recounting of Jack's travels through Great Britain, the Low Countries, Germany, France, and Italy, seems entirely arbitrary. It is a structure ideally suited to Nashe's always changeable purpose and varying interests. The reader will look in vain for a balance between one part of Jack's travels and another; there is none, since Nashe sees contemporary life as completely unbalanced. Like Jack, the author stays where he likes as long as he likes and especially as long as he senses the reader can still be interested. Nashe's sense of his audience is one of his most charming assets, and it is highly appropriate that this tale is set up in the guise of a barroom brag on the part of Jack, lately returned from Bologna. Nashe's structural nonchalance almost certainly influenced Sterne's *Tristram Shandy* (1759-1767).

Sterne also must have been intrigued by the ambiguity of viewpoint found in *The Unfortunate Traveller*. There are times when it is almost certain that the author forgets about Jack entirely, setting off on his own to denounce, castigate, ridicule, or expound on one thing or another. At other times, Nashe can be most subtle in his handling of the complicated relationship between narrator and fictive reader, as when Jack quotes a Latin phrase to justify his actions, mistranslating it for his ignorant victims and leading readers to wonder whether the mistranslation is also intended to poke fun at them ("Tendit ad sydera virtus," for example, which Jack renders as, "there's great virtue belongs, I can tell you, to a cup of cider"). If Lawrence Sterne in *Tristram Shandy* overlooked the neat narrative distinctions Dante and Chaucer had drawn between their naïve pilgrim and narrator-pilgrim, he was able to do so with the comfortable knowledge that Nashe had done it first and had succeeded brilliantly.

Nashe's style reaches its finest and most characteristic expression in this book: with the vivacity of an undiminishing *sprezzatura*, brilliantly uneven, uncontrolled, and disorganized. *The Unfortunate Traveller* walks a precarious line between the realistic and romantic perspectives and frequently, as Nashe did in his own mind and life, gains its appeal from its inability to prevent one aspect from overflowing into the other. The journalistic nature of Nashe's prose is marked both positively and negatively: positively, for its unprecedented precision of detail, proving the author's considerable powers of observation (equalled only by his lack of discipline); negatively, for his inability to separate objective narration from personal viewpoint—indeed, his unwillingness to see the value of such a separation. The result is a work as prodigious for its literary faults as it is for its virtues.

Why the work continues to be read, lies to some extent in the character of Jack Wilton himself, the semifictional counterpart of Nashe's own personality. In his ambivalence between ambition and cowardice, the desire for adventure and the need for security, aggressiveness and passivity; in his switch from awestruck observer to cantankerous prankster, innocent victim to devious culprit; in his love of acting and enjoyment of performance, passionate enthusiasms, and vicious hatred; in all of these Jack is an earthy Everyman with whom every new reader can identify. He is as typical of the Renaissance English spirit as he is universal. In him, Nashe has depicted brilliantly what is so rarely successful, a mixture of opposites. *The Unfortunate Traveller* is a mixture of the devout and the debauched, the sacred and the profane, the scholarly and the vulgar, the delicate and the brutal, the aristocratic and the common, the explorer and the patriot that made Elizabethan and Tudor England an era quite different from any other before or since. The singularity of an age, after all, can be found only in its tensions, in the peculiar coupling of opposing forces. *The Unfortunate Traveller*, in the unforgettable crudity and refinement of its humor, and in its instantaneous leaps from highly serious didacticism to profoundly trivial farce, is a kind of template both shaped by and reproducing the shape of its times.

"Critical Evaluation" by Kenneth John Atchity

Bibliography:
Barbour, Reid. *Deciphering Elizabethan Fiction*. Newark, N.J.: University of Delaware Press, 1993. Barbour summarizes the narrative's action and examines the motif of decipherment in it. Jack Wilton's world cannot be simply explained, for chaos rules it and the past's glosses have failed.
McGinn, Donald J. *Thomas Nashe*. Boston: Twayne, 1981. This work is intended as an introduction to Nashe's life and art: It includes a meaty chapter on *The Unfortunate Traveller*. McGinn summarizes the work's complicated plot and then examines critics' estimation of its place in the history of the novel.
Simons, Louise. "Rerouting *The Unfortunate Traveller*: Strategies for Coherence and Direction." *Studies in English Literature, 1500-1900* 28, no. 1 (Winter, 1988): 17-38. Simons argues that the work has a "novelistic coherence" in its plot and rhetoric: Its plot shows us the education of Jack Wilton, and its images reinforce that theme.

Stephanson, Raymond. "The Epistemological Challenge of Nashe's *The Unfortunate Traveller*." *Studies in English Literature, 1500-1900* 23, no. 1 (Winter, 1983): 21-36. Stephanson examines the work's "enigmas," its preoccupation with ugliness and mutilation, its erratic plot line, and Nashe's excessive prose style, noting that part of the problem lies in the modern reader's artistic expectations.

Suzuki, Mihoko. "*Signiorie Ouer the Pages*: The Crisis of Authority in Nashe's *The Unfortunate Traveller*." *Studies in Philology* 81, no. 3 (Summer, 1984): 348-371. Suzuki examines the problem of unity and violence in *The Unfortunate Traveller*, suggesting that Nashe is interested in ineffectual authority—whether political, social, moral, or religious—which results in a world in chaos.

THE UNNAMABLE

Type of work: Novel
Author: Samuel Beckett (1906-1989)
Type of plot: Absurdist
Time of plot: Mid-twentieth century
Locale: Indeterminate
First published: L'Innommable, 1953 (English translation, 1958)

> *Principal characters:*
> THE UNNAMABLE
> MAHOOD, an Irishman
> WORM

The Story:

The Unnamable, although he never called himself that, seems to have been an old male who was not certain of where he was, who he was, or if, in fact, he actually existed. Intelligent, loquacious, and sometimes very funny, he constantly bemoaned his odd situation. He believed that he had been used for some unknown reason by some unknown persons who put words in his mouth, although he was not sure that he had a mouth. He was certain that the constant talk that flowed through him was, in part, some kind of punishment. He believed that until he did his "pensum" (a term for a school assignment for misbehavior), he could not get on to his lesson and satisfy his tormentors, who he hoped would let him go so that he could fall silent and cease to exist. However, he had no idea what his pensum was, nor what his lesson was. Instead, he presumed that in time, in constant babbling, he would by chance utter the right words or phrases and be allowed his freedom. He had trouble trying not to give in to his urge to talk about things about which he knew little or nothing.

All that he actually was prepared to accept as true was the fact that he was sitting in some unknown, dim place; he could feel the pressure on his backside from some kind of seat without a back, and he could feel the pressure of his arms resting on his thighs. He also thought that certain male figures were passing in front of him on a kind of circular path, but since he could only look forward, he was not certain of where they came from.

An early tale initially concerned a character named Mahood but then slid into being a tale about the Unnamable himself, who had returned from a long trip abroad and was trying to get back to his family. He was disabled and having difficulty in reaching them. He took so long, in fact, that they were all dead on his entrance into their home. He had to be content to stamp about on their putrid corpses. The Unnamable habitually rejected the possibility of these incidents being true or having anything to do with him. A later tale again involved Mahood. On that occasion, legless, armless, and speechless, he was living in a large jar across from a small restaurant in a Paris side street close to the slaughterhouse. The proprietor of the restaurant took some desultory care of him, feeding him scraps, cleaning out his jar, covering his head in inclement weather, and using the surface of the huge jar to display her menus. She did not speak to him, and no one looking at the menu seemed to notice him, although his rigidly clamped head protruded over the lip of the jar. It was a kind of life, but the Unnamable was not fooled: It was not his life.

Later on, another character appeared, since Mahood seemed to have exhausted his power to convince. This one, called Worm, was less than human; it had a single, unlidded eye but no other physical features, save for the coiled body of a serpent. It never managed to become anything more than a failed attempt to exist in any active manner. The Unnamable suspected that it was just another attempt to convince him that he had a life.

These bizarre tales are interspersed among the Unnamable's long, sometimes confused but always lively considerations of his situation. Ultimately, the Unnamable was where he started, with tears running down his face and the constant flow of grotesque, sometimes offensively vulgar ideas running unbidden through his mind. Occasionally, it seemed that he just might have escaped the clutches of his tormentors. There were occasional moments of silence, but inevitably the babble began anew and the Unnamable knew that the misery would continue, perhaps forever.

Critical Evaluation:

Samuel Beckett's *The Unnamable* can be read in at least three different ways or combinations of ways. The work is the final volume of a trilogy of novels beginning with *Molloy* (1951) and *Malone Dies* (1951), and it can be read in conjunction with those texts. It might be suggested that the character in *The Unnamable* is, in fact, Malone, who apparently dies in the second novel. It might be that the complaining voice of this novel is all that is left of Malone after death—a cruel joke of continuing existence after departure from the corporeal world. This might go some way toward explaining why the character has no body but is living in a kind of miserable limbo. The matter of interpretation is complicated by the fact that so many of the names of supposed imaginary characters mentioned by the speaker are, in fact, characters in previous Beckett novels, and not only to those of the trilogy. The possibility therefore arises that the novel is autobiographical, above all because there is considerable talk about the Unnamable having invented these characters.

The best way to deal with the novel is to take it at face value as a factual account of an absurd experience in the late twentieth century. The idea of the absurd is, quite simply, that something means what it says. Beckett's work in general is a literary representation of the proposition that life is meaningless and absurd in the sense of not making any sense, a conclusion reached on the basis of the twentieth century loss of social, political, and religious certainties. The novel may thus be read as a metaphor for the chaotic nature of the human condition during that time. The work can also be interpreted philosophically, given Beckett's interest in the problem of how human beings know not only themselves but others and their relations with those others. How do people know things? It is an old problem for philosophers, and it is a question that shows up regularly in Beckett's work.

The Unnamable is a long account narrated in the first person by someone, supposedly a man, who does not know who or where he is but has strong suspicions that he is being manipulated. He is prepared to talk about this situation and complain about it in terms not only of the past but of the present. The complaints make sense as a psychological representation of that sort of problem, and there is considerable credibility in how the narrator acts and reacts. There is further confirmation of reality in the way Beckett explores the way the mind goes on and on even when a human being might want to stop that mind, particularly in times of stress. In that sense, *The Unnamable* is a sensible study of an odd but not uncommon human predicament.

The narrative voice is subject to quick changes, not only of subject, but of opinion, and a fact established at one moment is denied in the next. The form of the work is, in fact, a dramatic monologue in prose form. The dramatic monologue as a poetic form was perfected by Robert Browning, but it was already used in William Shakespeare's soliloquys and later with considerable success by poets such as T. S. Eliot and W. H. Auden. In all these cases, the narrator has a problem, sometimes trivial, sometimes very serious, and speaking about it usually leads to some sort of solution that is apparent either in a new understanding or in action. Sometimes, however, the act of consideration leads to failure, as it does in T. S. Eliot's *The Love Song of J. Alfred Prufrock* (1917). Much the same thing happens in *The Unnamable*. The speaker neither learns the truth of his situation nor is able to escape from it, despite his determined attempts to consider the matter from all angles. However odd or absurd the situation may be, it has its basis in the human condition. This is particularly true in the twentieth century, a time that was characterized by skepticism, disbelief, and sheer destructiveness. Beckett's characters may be physically impoverished, but intellectually they are formidable, sometimes foul-mouthed but astringently clever and blessed with the gift of saying things wittily and with flashes of graveyard humor. It is possible to read the novel as a realistic representation of a man who has lost touch with reality and is living within his own mind in paranoid terror. Certainly, there is a gritty reality about him, despite his denial of corporeal proportion. A more valid reading, however, interprets the novel as absurdist. The absurd is, in fact, not simply content that does not make ordinary sense: It is a literary genre that demands to be accepted as it is presented. Like many of the arts, literature in the twentieth century occasionally attempted to disassociate itself from meaning in the realistic sense. Music and the visual arts were often successful in this endeavor. Literature, however, wedded as it is to words that have fixed meaning, a fixed form in sentences and paragraphs, has been hard pressed to become "meaningless" in the artistic sense. Beckett made this attempt. His greatest ambition was to write on nothing, and in later works he goes even further in his attempt to get beyond sense. *The Unnamable* can be considered to represent the midpoint of this development.

Charles Pullen

Bibliography:
Alvarez, A. *Beckett*. London: Fontana Collins, 1973. Short, lively, sensible discussion of Beckett's entire career, including his work on the trilogy.
Esslin, Martin. *Samuel Beckett: A Collection of Critical Essays*. Englewood Cliffs, N.J.: Prentice-Hall, 1965. Essays by several scholars on various aspects of Beckett's career. Discussions cover his work as a novelist.
_____. *The Theatre of the Absurd*. Rev. ed. New York: Anchor Books, 1969. Points out that Beckett, who is sometimes considered the finest novelist of the last half of the twentieth century, is also sometimes considered to be the finest playwright of the period. His plays are valuable because they represent a simpler version of his work. Also puts his work in the intellectual and social context of the period.
Kenner, Hugh. *A Reader's Guide to Samuel Beckett*. London: Thames and Hudson, 1973. Deals with individual texts, including *The Unnamable*. Excellent source and a pleasure to read.
_____. *Samuel Beckett: A Critical Study*. Rev. ed. Berkeley: University of California Press, 1968. A study by one of the best commentators on Beckett. Witty, idiosyncratic, but blessed with an understanding of the experimentalist mind, and of Beckett in particular.
Mercier, Vivian. *Beckett/Beckett*. New York: Oxford University Press, 1977. A study by an Irish scholar with understanding of the Irish mind, absurdist literature, and Beckett. Offers helpful insights into all the novels, particularly into the trilogy ending with *The Unnamable*.

THE UNVANQUISHED

Type of work: Novel
Author: William Faulkner (1897-1962)
Type of plot: Bildungsroman
Time of plot: Mid-1860's
Locale: Mississippi and Alabama
First published: 1938

Principal characters:
JOHN SARTORIS, a colonel in the confederacy
ROSA MILLARD (GRANNY), his mother-in-law
BAYARD SARTORIS, his son
RINGO, Bayard's companion, the son of slaves on the Sartoris plantation
DRUSILLA HAWK, Colonel Sartoris' second wife
AB SNOPES, a neighbor of the Sartoris family

The Story:

In the midst of the Civil War, Colonel Sartoris came home for a day to warn his family that the Yankee soldiers were close and to help build a stock pen to hide his animals from the Yankees. A few days later, Bayard and Ringo, twelve-year-olds, shot at a Yankee soldier who rode onto Sartoris land. They hid under Granny's skirts while soldiers searched the property for them. Granny denied that any children lived on the property, and a colonel ordered the rest of the men off the land while eyeing Granny's skirts. A family man himself, he left after telling Granny his name and saying he hoped she would suffer nothing worse from the Yankees. Later, advised by Colonel Sartoris, Granny left for Memphis because of the dangers of the war. Joby, the Colonel's servant, drove the wagon carrying Granny, Ringo, Bayard, and a trunk filled with silver that had been buried in the yard for safekeeping. During the journey, Yankee soldiers stole their mules, and Bayard and Ringo chased them unsuccessfully on a "borrowed" horse. Colonel Sartoris found the boys and took them home, capturing a Yankee camp on the way. Joby and Granny also made it back home with the help of "borrowed" horses, and the trunk containing the silver was again buried in the yard. Yankee soldiers came to capture Colonel Sartoris. True to a dream of Granny's, Loosh, Ringo's father, showed the Yankee soldiers where the trunk was buried. They took it and burned the house, but Sartoris escaped. Loosh and Philadelphy, his wife, left because the Yankee soldiers told them they were free.

Granny, Ringo, and Bayard drove six days to Hawkhurst, Alabama, to recover their trunk, mules, and Loosh and Philadelphy. On the journey, they passed hundreds of former slaves who were following the Yankee troops to freedom. At Hawkhurst, Granny's niece, Drusilla Hawk, joined them and the four traveled to the river where Yankee soldiers built a bridge. After crossing, the soldiers hurried to destroy the bridge so that the people who had followed them to freedom could not cross. The Sartoris wagon got pushed into the river and the four from the Sartoris family made it to the other side, where the Yankee troops were then stationed. Granny asked to speak with Colonel Dick, the man who did not pursue Bayard and Ringo when they hid after shooting at the Yankee soldier. She asked for the return of her mules, her trunk, and Loosh and Philadelphy. Colonel Dick gave Granny a written statement from the General dated August 14, 1863, which validated the return of 10 chests, 110 mules, and 110 former slaves who were following the troops. The document allowed them to pass safely through any Yankee troops they would encounter and also to petition them for food during the journey home.

Once home, Granny, with the aid of Ringo and Ab Snopes, forged papers similar to the document given to her by Colonel Dick in order to requisition mules from various Yankee regiments in the area. She kept the mules in the hidden pen on Sartoris property until she either sold them to other Yankee units or gave them to local poor people. Near the end of the war, just before the Yankee troops left the South, they discovered Granny's activities. The Yankees, acting on information from Ab Snopes, took back all the mules still in the Sartoris pen. Ab Snopes then talked Granny into one last deal, getting valuable horses from Southern raiders. Although Ringo and Bayard tried to stop Granny, she went to the raiders and was killed. After Granny's funeral, Uncle Buck McCaslin rode with Ringo and Bayard to find Grumby, the man responsible for Granny's death. For months they tracked the raiders. When they were close, Uncle Buck left the boys because of a gunshot wound he suffered during the chase. In a fight, the boys killed Grumby; they then nailed his body to the compress where Granny was killed and brought Grumby's right hand back to put on Granny's grave.

Drusilla, having fought with Sartoris and his troops, returned from the war with the Colonel and worked with Ringo, Bayard, and Joby to regenerate the land while Sartoris worked in Jefferson four miles away. Drusilla's mother and the women of Jefferson were outraged that Drusilla camped with the widower Sartoris during the war and returned to live on his land. They insisted Drusilla and Sartoris marry and unknowingly set election day for the wedding. Drusilla set out for Jefferson to meet Sartoris and marry him but got involved in the politics of election day. Sartoris killed two men who were trying to get a black man elected marshall; he appointed Drusilla voting commissioner, and, with Drusilla, the white men returned to the Sartoris land to vote against the black candidate. In the excitement, Drusilla forgot to get married.

About eight years later, Bayard was in his third year studying law in Oxford, Mississippi. Ringo came to him reporting that John Sartoris had been killed by his rival, Ben Redmond. On the forty mile ride home, Bayard reflected on the last few years: his father's marriage to Drusilla and the code of violence to which they adhered, his father's railroad venture with Redmond, their run against each other for political office, his father's humiliating taunting of Redmond, and his father's recent decision to turn against killing and meet Redmond unarmed. Bayard knew Drusilla and the men in Jefferson would expect him to avenge his father's death. Bayard, who could not forget the death of Grumby, realized that killing was not a satisfactory solution. Determined not to kill or to be a coward, he went to Jefferson the next day to meet Redmond unarmed. Redmond shot twice, intentionally missing Bayard, and left town. Bayard returned home and found Drusilla had gone to live with her brother but had left behind a sprig of verbena for him.

Critical Evaluation:

One of America's greatest writers, William Faulkner was awarded the Nobel Prize in Literature in 1949. A prolific writer, he published through five decades, from the 1920's into the 1960's. Faulkner's major subject matter is the complicated history of the American South, and his fiction deals with it with humor, irony, and sympathy. Fifteen of his twenty novels are set in Yoknapatawpha County, a fictionalized version of the land around Oxford, Mississippi, where Faulkner lived. Yet his novels and short stories reverberate so that it is not just the South or the United States about which Faulkner writes but of all people concerned with what he called in his Nobel Prize acceptance speech the "old verities and truths of the heart . . . courage and honor and hope and pride and compassion and pity and sacrifice."

Faulkner's tenth novel, *The Unvanquished*, set in Yoknapatawpha County, deals with the

Civil War years and the Reconstruction era. The novel has seven titled chapters, six of which were published in magazines as independent stories before being revised for publication in the novel. The last chapter, "An Odor of Verbena," was written specifically for the novel. A sense of honor, the importance of family, and race relations are themes that dominate this novel as they do many of Faulkner's other works. Although the same themes, setting, characters, and some stylistic devices of this novel appear in other Faulkner works, *The Unvanquished* highlights adventure, sacrificing some of the complexity that comes with Faulkner's greater novels.

The style of *The Unvanquished* makes it one of the least difficult of Faulkner's novels. Known for their complicated shifts in point of view and chronology, Faulkner's novels are often demanding. *The Unvanquished*, on the other hand, is narrated by a single character, Bayard Sartoris. His age and intelligence, a bright twelve-year-old when the novel begins, also simplify the novel for the reader. The plot is presented almost entirely in chronological order. The reader is able to follow the life of the Sartoris family during the Civil War and through the months following the surrender, with the last chapter jumping ahead about eight years into Reconstruction. Only the last chapter uses extended flashbacks which break the chronological order of the novel. In the first six stories, Bayard ages from twelve to his midteens; the last chapter, covering two days, begins and ends with him at twenty-four, but flashbacks present him at twenty and again at twenty-three.

Two rather typical Faulkner stylistic devices, delayed information and repetition with variation, allow the novel to work well although comprising seven separate stories. Delayed information connects chapters while adding suspense to the novel. In the first chapter, the Yankee colonel who allows Granny to hide Bayard and Ringo tells her his name, which is not revealed to the reader until chapter 3. Climactic scenes are sometimes told first obscurely, only to be revealed in more detail later. For example, the reader is left uncertain at first as to the fate of the ambushed Yankee in chapter 1 and of Grumby in chapter 5. Later passages clarify that the Yankee was not hit but that Grumby was killed and mutilated.

Repetition with variation also helps connect the different stories of the chapters. The stock pen built in the first chapter plays a crucial role in a number of the chapters; the prayer and the soap used by Granny as an antidote for sin and swearing help provide humor and continuity of character throughout the novel; the odor of the Civil War soldier sensed as "powder and glory" in the first chapter becomes transformed into the odor of the raider Grumby senses as "sweat" and "grease" in the fifth chapter and is then transformed again into the odor of verbena, a symbol of victory and peace, in the last chapter. Parallel scenes help knit the novel and develop characterization. Bayard, the narrator, eagerly shoots at—but misses—a Yankee soldier in the first chapter, feels confused when he kills Grumby in the fifth chapter, and refuses to kill in the last chapter. The development of the novel parallels this character development as the reader sees the society of the South changing in the character of Bayard, who moves beyond the violence of the past to break the chain of killing.

Marion Boyle Petrillo

Bibliography:

Brooks, Cleanth. *William Faulkner: The Yoknapatawpha Country.* New Haven, Conn.: Yale University Press, 1963. Presents a favorable discussion of the novel, remarking on strong characterization and the importance of the female characters. Finds the last chapter strong as a coda for the novel's themes.

Hoffman, Daniel. *Faulkner's Country Matters: Folklore and Fable in Yoknapatawpha*. Baton Rouge: Louisiana State University Press, 1989. Contains a clear synopsis of the novel's plot as well as discussions of Bayard's maturity and his relationship with Ringo.

Roberts, Diane. "A Precarious Pedestal: The Confederate Woman in Faulkner's *Unvanquished*." *Journal of American Studies* 26, no. 2 (August, 1992): 233-246. Notes that the novel does not endorse the more masculine roles of Granny or Drusilla.

Taylor, Nancy Dew. "'Moral Housecleaning' and Colonel Sartoris's Dream." *Mississippi Quarterly* 37, no. 3 (Summer, 1984): 353-364. Concentrates on the last speech between the Colonel and Bayard; believes that only the methods, not the aggressive nature and goals, of the Colonel change.

Walker, William E. "*The Unvanquished*: The Restoration of Tradition." In *Reality and Myth*, edited by William E. Walker and Robert L. Welker. Nashville: Vanderbilt University Press, 1964. Deals with the maturation of Bayard Sartoris, the theme of the novel. Suggests that Bayard restores the Southern tradition by eschewing violence. Explores the different ways Bayard is influenced by Granny, Colonel Sartoris, Drusilla, and other characters.

UP FROM SLAVERY

Type of work: Autobiography
Author: Booker T. Washington (1856-1915)
First published: 1901

Booker Taliaferro Washington's best-selling autobiography, *Up from Slavery*, translated into at least fifteen languages around the world, is part of an African American literary tradition that has found its place among the American classics. The book's fifteen chapters give a progressive historical account of the author's life as it began on a plantation in Franklin County, Virginia, in 1858. The poverty and human misery of Washington's early years are documented with unusual candor in the first two chapters. He did not know his father, had very little recollection of his extended family, never slept on a bed before the Emancipation Proclamation was issued, never ate a family meal with knives and forks around a table as a child, and had a trying ordeal wearing his first pair of heavy and hard wooden "brogans" on his feet. After his family moved to Malden, West Virginia, to work at the salt furnace and coal mine, they lived in the most derelict of conditions, surrounded by unreconstructed African Americans who were given over to excessive "drinking, gambling, quarrels, fights, and shockingly immoral practices." Washington worked very long, hard, and lonely hours, and was exploited by his stepfather, but he never lost the "intense longing to learn to read and write."

Washington learned to read from an old copy of Webster's spelling book that his mother got for him. Since African American teachers were rare, any black person who could read and write almost always became an educator. After a young black soldier from Ohio moved into Malden, he was immediately pressed into establishing "the first school for Negroes." The people were so poor, the teacher got his support from "boarding around"—sleeping and eating with a different family each day. Washington comments, "Few people who were not right in the midst of the scenes can form any exact idea of the intense desire which the people of my race showed for education. . . . It was a whole race trying to go to school. Few were too young, and none too old, to make the attempt to learn."

When Booker himself went to register at his first school, he chose the name Washington so he could have two names like the other students. He had such a passion for education, no obstacle could deter him from going to college. He traveled over eighty miles on foot, slept under (wooden) sidewalks, and worked on a shipping dock just to earn enough to buy breakfast and pay his way to Hampton, five hundred miles from home. Matriculation at Hampton was the dream of a lifetime. There, Washington met General Samuel C. Armstrong, who had the greatest impact on Washington's life. The ideology of industrial education taught at Hampton fashioned Washington's career. Following graduation in 1875, Washington assisted in a successful campaign to move the capital of West Virginia from Wheeling to Charlestown. His rhetorical ability in the campaign brought him many speaking engagements, and he seriously considered a career in public service. He also taught for a year in West Virginia before spending a year as a student at Wayland Seminary in Washington, D.C. In 1878, Armstrong recruited him to teach Native Americans in Indian territory, and he won the complete confidence of his students there. Washington noted that Indians were served at restaurants and admitted to motels but that he was not.

Chapter 7 begins the epoch in Washington's life for which he is most well known. In the spring of 1881, General Armstrong called him to Alabama, where he would begin his life's work building Tuskegee Institute. There, Washington said he found "hundreds of ignorant" and uncultured "hungry, earnest black souls who wanted to secure knowledge" and who had not "degraded and weakened their bodies by vices such as are common to the lower class of people in the large cities." Encouraged by local blacks and a $2,000 allocation from the state legislature to pay a teacher to start a college, Washington opened the institute in an "old dilapidated shanty near the colored Methodist church" in June, 1881. The building was in such deplorable disrepair that a student had to hold an umbrella over Washington's head as he taught in the leaking, unheated shack. For the first few months, Washington supported himself by "boarding around." Often the people had nothing to eat except "slave food"—fat pork, corn bread, and black-eyed peas. The poor people of the area were so anxious to demonstrate their freedom and share in the "American culture" that they allowed plantation owners to dupe them into buying expensive furniture on credit with extremely heavy premiums.

Against all odds, Washington pursued his goal of establishing industrial education for blacks. Desperate for funds and proper support, he found his task as hard as that of the early Israelites who had to "make bricks without straw." On one occasion, he pawned his ring in order to obtain $15 to purchase supplies to make bricks. He was convinced, however, that the students who were involved in brick making and building construction were not only getting practical education but were also building moral character. Brick making was inseparably tied to morality and became a required course on the curriculum for all students. In return, the institute's brick industry encouraged whites to do business with blacks at Tuskegee and provided much needed patronage.

Chapters 13 and 14 narrate some personal as well as nationally significant events in Washington's life. He mentions his marriage to Olivia Davidson only as an afterthought. As if the romantic was forbidden territory for this black industrial educator, the only paragraph in the book in which he gives a hint that he was interested in companionship is used to discuss "Miss Davidson's" untiring work at Tuskegee, and their sons' early mastery of brick making. Washington got on the popular lecture circuit because "there was no word of abuse" of the South in any of his addresses, and they rarely dealt with the question of race. He said, "I determined never to say anything in a public address in the North that I would not be willing to say in the South." Hence in his address to the National Education Association at Madison, Wisconsin, Washington argued that "the policy to be pursued with reference to the races was, by every honorable means, to bring them together and to encourage the cultivation of friendly relations, instead of doing that which would embitter." Washington contended that African Americans must put the interests of their community over individual voting rights. The Madison speech to the National Education Association introduced him to a very wide audience in Boston and other cities of the North. In 1893, he gave a five-minute address to about 2,000 Southern and Northern whites of the Christian Workers in Atlanta, Georgia, and was hailed a "friend of the white race." The speech that really catapulted Washington into the national spotlight, however, was the address to the Atlanta Cotton States and International Exposition on September 18, 1895. As the representative of the black race, he said "I knew . . . that this was the first time . . . a member of my race had been asked to speak from the same platform with white Southern men and women on any important national occasion." Washington's speech lasted only twenty minutes but it sent ripples throughout the continental U.S. and around the world, and its impact was felt in America for almost a century.

Washington used the speech to show that white-black cooperation could be of concrete (or brick) benefit, increasing production. He appealed to Congress to support the rebuilding of the South in the interests of both ethnic groups. He argued that "while the Negro should not be deprived by unfair means of the franchise, political agitation alone would not save him, and that back of the ballot he must have property, industry, skill, economy, intelligence, and character." Washington told African Americans to cast down their buckets in agriculture, mechanics, commerce, and domestic service in the South. He said the greatest danger for his people is that they would despise manual labor and misuse freedom. Washington also told whites to cast down their buckets among the 8,000,000 blacks in the South "without strikes and labor wars, tilling your fields, clearing your forest, building your railroads and cities." Whites should cast down their buckets in African American education for the benefit of the nation.

Many whites did not hear his plea to them to cast down their buckets of opportunity among black people. Most whites saw the speech as primarily a call for African Americans to remain subservient to whites. Governor Bullock of Atlanta ran out to congratulate Washington, and the media said that Washington was profound. President Grover Cleveland received a copy of the speech with delight and opened a line of communication from the White House to Washington. President D. C. Gilman of The Johns Hopkins University, Baltimore, invited Washington to serve on the "Judges of Award in the Department of Education at Atlanta." As far as African Americans were concerned, in turn, Washington's view that "the agitation of questions of social equality is the extremist folly" was preposterous. They felt that the idea of sacrificing civil rights for supposed good relations and meager wages was untenable. Months after the speech, black ministers and religious bodies continued their condemnation of the Tuskegee president. W. E. B. Du Bois labeled the speech the Atlanta Compromise and saw it as another sellout to the white community at the expense of justice, freedom, equality, and integration. Washington's fame spread in Europe, Africa, Canada, and the Caribbean. Letters poured in from Paris and London with both praise and condemnation. Washington received many honorary degrees and awards. He was regarded as the spokesperson for black America, and the financial support for Tuskegee flowed in with the letters of congratulation and recognition.

The autobiography ends describing various events. There is the work of Washington's second wife Margaret James Murray and their children. He recounts his meeting in Boston with Du Bois, Paul Lawrence Dunbar, and other prominent African Americans when he went to give a speech. Washington describes his successful tour of Europe and especially his experience in England. The last chapter chronicles the complimentary correspondence Washington received. The book offers several surprises. Washington claims that "the ten million Negroes inhabiting this country . . . are in a stronger and more hopeful condition, materially, intellectually, morally, and religiously, than is true of an equal number of black people in any portion of the globe." Paradoxically Washington constantly portrays African Americans as primitive and lacking the "good morals and culture" found among whites. He even claims that the black teachers in the South were just as miserably poor in their preparation for teaching as in moral character. For Washington, good race relations were more desirable for African Americans than civil rights and justice. These controversial ideas will continue to generate condemnation and praise every time Booker T. Washington's name is mentioned.

N. Samuel Murrell

Bibliography:

Appiah, Anthony, ed. *Early African-American Classics*. New York: Bantam Books, 1990. Four of the most outstanding slave autobiographies.

Harlan, Louis R. *Booker T. Washington: The Making of a Black Leader, 1856-1901*. New York: Oxford University Press, 1972. Scholarly and extensive work on Washington as a leader.

Low, W. Augustus, and Virgil A. Clift, eds. "Washington, Booker T." In *Encyclopedia of Black*

America. New York: McGraw-Hill, 1981. A brief but important essay on Washington's life.

Riley, B. F. *The Life and Times of Booker T. Washington*. New York: Fleming H. Revell, 1916. Provides information on Washington's era.

Washington, Booker T. *The Story of My Life and Work*. With an Introduction by J. L. M. Curry. Naperville, Ill.: J. L. Nichols & Co, 1900. Curry's introduction is insightful.

U.S.A.

Type of work: Novel
Author: John Dos Passos (1896-1970)
Type of plot: Historical
Time of plot: 1900-1935
Locale: United States
First published: 1937: *The 42nd Parallel,* 1930; *1919,* 1932; *The Big Money,* 1936

Principal characters:
FAINY "MAC" MCCREARY, a labor organizer
JANEY WILLIAMS, a private secretary
JOE WILLIAMS, her brother
J. WARD MOOREHOUSE, a public relations executive
ELEANOR STODDARD, an interior decorator
CHARLEY ANDERSON, an airplane manufacturer
RICHARD ELLSWORTH SAVAGE, Moorehouse's assistant
EVELINE HUTCHINS, Eleanor Stoddard's partner
ANNE ELIZABETH "DAUGHTER" TRENT, a relief worker
BEN COMPTON, a radical
MARY FRENCH, a labor worker
MARGO DOWLING, a film star

The Story:

The Spanish-American War was over. Politicians with mustaches said that America was now ready to lead the world. Mac McCreary was a printer for a fly-by-night publisher in Chicago. Later he worked his way to the West Coast. There he got work as a printer in Sacramento and married Maisie Spencer, who could never understand his radical views. They quarreled, and he went to Mexico to work in the revolutionary movement there.

Janey Williams, growing up in Washington, D.C., became a stenographer. She was always ashamed when her sailor brother, Joe, appeared in her life, and even more ashamed of him after she became secretary to J. Ward Moorehouse. Of all Moorehouse's female acquaintances, she was the only one who never became his mistress. J. Ward Moorehouse's boyish manner and blue eyes were the secret of his success. They attracted Annabelle Strang, the wealthy nymphomaniac he later divorced. Gertrude Staple, his second wife, helped to make him a prominent public relations expert. His shrewdness made him an ideal man for government service in France during World War I. After the war, he became one of the nation's leading advertising executives.

Eleanor Stoddard hated the sordid environment of her childhood, and her delicate, arty tastes led her naturally into partnership with Eveline Hutchins in the decorating business and eventually to New York and acquaintanceship with J. Ward Moorehouse. In Europe with the Red Cross during the war, she lived with Moorehouse. Back in New York in the 1920's she used her connections in fashion and became engaged to a member of the Russian nobility.

Charley Anderson had been an aviator in the war. A successful invention and astute opportunism made him a wealthy airplane manufacturer. He married a wife who had little sympathy for his interest in mechanics. In Florida, after a plane crash, he met Margo Dowling, an actress. Charley Anderson's series of drunken escapades ended in a grade crossing accident.

Joe Williams was a sailor who had been on the beach in Buenos Aires. In Norfolk he met Della, who urged him to give up seafaring and settle down. Unable to hold a job, he shipped out again and almost lost his life when the ship he was on was sunk by a German submarine. When Joe got his third mate's license, he and Della were married. He was ill in the East Indies, arrested in New York for not carrying a draft card, and torpedoed once more off the coast of Spain. Della was unfaithful to him. Treated coldly the few times he looked up his sister Janey, he shipped for Europe once more. One night in St. Nazaire he attacked a huge Senegalese who was dancing with a girl he knew. His skull was crushed when he was hit over the head with a bottle.

Teachers encouraged Dick Savage in his literary talents. During his teens, he worked at a summer hotel, and there he slept with a minister's wife who shared his taste in poetry. A government official paid Dick's way through Harvard, where Dick cultivated his estheticism and mild snobbery before he joined the Norton-Harjes ambulance service and went to Europe. There some of his letters about the war came to the attention of censorship officials, and he was shipped back to the United States. His former sponsor got him an officer's commission, and he returned to France. In Italy, he met a relief worker named Anne Elizabeth Trent, who was his mistress for a time. When he returned to the United States, he became an idea man for Moorehouse's advertising agency.

Eveline Hutchins, who had a small artistic talent, became Eleanor Stoddard's partner in a decorating establishment in New York. All her life she tried to escape from boredom through sensation. Beginning with the Mexican artist who was her first lover, she had a succession of affairs. In France, where she was Eleanor's assistant in the Red Cross, she married a shy young soldier named Paul Johnson. Later she had a brief affair with Charley Anderson. Dissatisfied, she decided at last that life was too dull for endurance and died from an overdose of sleeping pills.

Anne Elizabeth Trent, known as Daughter, was the child of moderately wealthy Texans. In New York, she met Webb Cruthers, a young anarchist. One day, seeing a policeman kick a woman picketer in the face, Daughter attacked him with her fists. Her night in jail disturbed her father so much that she returned to Texas and worked in Red Cross canteens. Later she went overseas, met Dick Savage, became pregnant by him, and learned that he had no intention of marrying her. In Paris, she went on a drunken spree with a French aviator and died with him in a plane crash.

Benny Compton was the son of Jewish immigrants. After six months in jail for making radical speeches, he worked his way West through Canada. In Seattle, he and other agitators were beaten by deputies. Benny returned East. One day police broke up a meeting where he was speaking. On his twenty-third birthday, Benny went to Atlanta to serve a ten-year sentence. Released after the war, he lived for a time with Mary French, who was also politically active.

Mary French spent her childhood in Trinidad, where her father, a physician, did charity work among the native miners. Mary, planning to become a social worker, spent her summers at Jane Addams' Hull House. She went to Washington as secretary to a union official and later worked as a union organizer in New York City. There she took care of Ben Compton after his release from Atlanta. While working with the Sacco-Vanzetti Committee, she fell in love with Don Stevens, a fellow party member. Summoned to Moscow with a group of party leaders, Stevens returned to New York with a wife assigned to him by the party. Mary went back to her committee work for laboring men's relief.

Margo Dowling grew up in a rundown house in Rockaway, Long Island, with her drunken father and Agnes, her father's mistress. At last, Agnes left her lover and took Margo with her.

In New York, Agnes became the common-law wife of an actor named Frank Mandeville. One day, while drunk, Mandeville raped Margo. Margo ran off to Cuba with Tony, an effeminate Cuban guitar player, whom she later deserted. She was a cheerful companion for Charley Anderson, who gave her a check for five thousand dollars on his deathbed. In Hollywood, she met Sam Margolies, a successful producer, who made a star of her.

Jobless and hungry, a young hitchhiker stood by the roadside. Overhead droned a plane in which people of the big money rode the skyways. Below, the hitchhiker with empty belly thumbed cars speeding by. The haves and the have-nots—that was America in the Depression-era 1930's.

Critical Evaluation:

John Dos Passos' statement at the beginning of *U. S. A.*—that America is, more than anything else, the sounds of its many voices—offers several insights into the style and content of the trilogy. The style, for example, reflects the author's attempt to capture some sense of characteristically American voices, not only in the narration but also in what are called the Newsreel, Biography, and Camera Eye modes as well. These last three narrative modes reflect, respectively, the public voice of the media and popular culture, the oratorical and eulogistic voice of the biographies, and the personal and private voice of the artist. The most important voices in the trilogy, however, are those of the chronicles in which Dos Passos introduces a cross-section of American voices ranging from the blue-collar worker to the professional and managerial classes, and representing a variety of regional and ethnic backgrounds. As Walt Whitman does, who profoundly influenced Dos Passos, Dos Passos takes all America as his subject matter as he tries to capture through the sounds of the many voices that characterize its people.

Many people have associated the social, political, and economic views expressed in *U. S. A.* with Marxism. Leftists in the 1930's liked to believe this important author had a common cause with them. It is really the American economist, Thorstein Veblen, rather than Marx, who seems to have shaped Dos Passos' thinking about the economic and political situation in the United States during the first part of the twentieth century. Dos Passos had read Veblen's *The Theory of the Leisure Class* (1899), *The Theory of Business Enterprise* (1904), and other writings, and it was from these sources that his attack on the American business economy stemmed. In *The Big Money*, Dos Passos offers a biography of Veblen in which Dos Passos summarizes this economist's theories of the domination of society by monopoly capitalism and the sabotage of the workers' human rights by business interests that are dominated by the profit motive. According to Dos Passos, the alternatives Veblen saw were either a society strangled and its workers destroyed by the capitalists' insatiable greed for profit or a society in which the needs of those who do the work would be the prime consideration. Veblen held out hope that the workers might yet take control of the means of production before monopoly capitalism could plunge the world into a new dark age. Dos Passos further developed the idea that any such hope died with World War I and that the American dream of democracy was dead from that time forward.

Against the background of Veblen's ideas, *U. S. A.* can be seen as a documentary chronicling the growing exploitation of the American worker by the capitalist system and a lamentation for the lost hope of Veblen's dream of a society that would make the producer the prime beneficiary of the producer's own labor. The best characterization of the blue-collar worker is Mac McCreary—a rootless laborer constantly searching for some outlet for his idealistic hope of restoring power to the worker. Certainly one of the most sympathetic characters in *U. S. A.*, Mac dramatizes the isolation and frustration of the modern worker, who is only a human cog in the industrial machine, unable either to take pride in his work or to profit by it. Other characters as well fit within the pattern of the capitalist system as Veblen described it, or else, like Mac, revolt against the injustice of the system. There are the exploiters and the exploited, and there are some few, like Mary French and Ben Compton, who make opposition to the system a way of life. Equally prevalent are those characters who dramatize Veblen's theory of conspicuous consumption by serving as playthings (Margo Dowling), lackeys (Dick Savage), or promoters (J. Ward Moorehouse) for those who control the wealth and power.

Throughout the trilogy, the essential conflict is that between the business interests who control the wealth and the workers who produce it. Dos Passos is almost equally concerned with the way in which the system of monopoly capitalism exploits and destroys even those of the managerial class who seem to profit most immediately from it. Dick Savage, for example, starts out as a talented young writer only to be corrupted by the system. Charley Anderson, who early could be seen as typifying the American Dream of success through ingenuity and imagination, dies as much a victim of the system as any of its workers. J. Ward Moorehouse, on the other hand, makes nothing and produces nothing, but his is the talent that can parlay nothing into a fortune and the mentality that can survive in the world of *U.S.A.*

The two national historical events to which Dos Passos gives most attention are World War I and the execution of the anarchists Nicola Sacco and Bartolomeo Vanzetti. The war, as Dos Passos saw it, under the pretense of making the world safe for democracy, gave the capitalists the opportunity they needed to solidify their power. For Dos Passos, democracy was dead in America from World War I, and the Sacco and Vanzetti case proved it. The death of these two immigrant Italian radicals on a trumped-up charge of murder was, in Dos Passos' eyes, the ultimate demonstration of the fact that traditional freedoms were lost and that monopoly capitalism had usurped power in America. When, in his later and more conservative years, Dos Passos was accused of having deserted the liberal positions of his youth, he maintained that his views had not shifted from those he argued in *U.S.A.* The evidence of the novel would seem to bear him out. The *U.S.A.* trilogy is a more nostalgic than revolutionary work. It looks back to that point in American history before the options were lost rather than forward to a Socialist revolution. Dos Passos' finest work shows Dos Passos as a democratic idealist rather than as a Socialist revolutionary.

"Critical Evaluation" by William E. Grant

Bibliography:
Hook, Andrew, comp. *Dos Passos: A Collection of Critical Essays.* Englewood Cliffs, N.J.: Prentice-Hall, 1974. Explores political and social influences, theme, technique, and Dos Passos' contradictory stylistic blend of romantic individualism and radical history.

Landsberg, Melvin. *Dos Passos' Path to "U.S.A.": A Political Biography, 1912-1936.* Boulder, Colo.: Associated University Press, 1972. Begins with Dos Passos' parents' background, describing the development of his political and social attitudes and tracing his literary influences.

Ludington, Townsend. *John Dos Passos: A Twentieth Century Odyssey.* New York: E. P. Dutton, 1980. Connects contradictions in Dos Passos' personality and writings to his illegitimacy and to his role as an outsider. Includes planning notes for *U.S.A.*, showing its historical influences.

Pizer, Donald. *Dos Passos' "U.S.A.": A Critical Study.* Charlottesville: University Press of Virginia, 1988. Relates the novel to Dos Passos' life and times. Examines theme and technique, using work plans, character lists, tables, and typescripts. Detailed analysis of the four modes: Camera Eye, Biography, Newsreel, and narrative.

Wagner-Martin, Linda. *Dos Passos: Artist as American.* Austin: University of Texas Press, 1979. Discusses use of shifting panoramic view to re-create history, evaluating the effect of this technique on characterization. Traces the effect of American mythology and American political and economic realities on *U. S. A.*

UTILITARIANISM

Type of work: Philosophy
Author: John Stuart Mill (1806-1873)
First published: serial, 1861; book, 1863

One of the geniuses of the modern era, John Stuart Mill coined the term "utilitarianism," the subject of this brief, five-part essay. By doing so, he reaffirmed and redefined the philosophical doctrine espousing the practical, useful idea that the rightness of an action may be measured by whether it achieves the greatest possible good for the greatest possible number. It was a doctrine around which a small but influential group of English radical reformers—utilitarians—rallied, Mill among them. All of his intellectual activities were calculated to effect changes in British society. When *Utilitarianism* was published in 1863, Mill already enjoyed international recognition as a distinguished political economist. He was a precocious polymath, however, and his fame rested equally on his contributions to political theory and to political philosophy. *On Liberty*, for example, which he published in 1859, just a few years before *Utilitarianism*, stands as one of the greatest expositions on civil liberty and endures as an assertion of cultural freedom.

John Stuart Mill imbibed his utilitarian philosophy and his extraordinary education from his father, James Mill. James Mill, in turn, had been a companion to, and a devoted disciple of Jeremy Bentham. Although Bentham acknowledged intellectual debts to various European thinkers, including Claude-Adrien Helvétius, Cesare Beccaria, Voltaire, and Jean Le Rond Alembert, he nevertheless rightly has been considered the founder of the British utilitarian movement.

Britain's utilitarians premised their philosophy on Bentham's remarkable *Introduction to the Principles of Morals and Legislation* (1789), a reformist document that sought to bring scientific analysis to bear upon ethics, legislation, and law. The opening chapter of Bentham's landmark work furnishes utilitarians with the basis of their beliefs, namely that humanity is the servant of two absolute masters that govern all of its actions: pleasure and pain. The principle of utility, therefore, lay in approving or disapproving of every action according to its tendency to augment or to diminish the individual's, or society's, happiness. Utility itself Bentham identified as "that property in any object" that tended to produce "benefit, advantage, pleasure, good, or happiness," or conversely, that prevented "mischief, pain, evil, or unhappiness." Around such principles and definitions, Bentham elaborated the philosophy to which John Stuart Mill adhered for many years.

By the 1860's, however, reassessments of utilitarian philosophy seemed in order. Previously the beneficiary of wide exposure among educated people in Great Britain as well as in Europe, utilitarianism had lost its original force. Utilitarians were disturbed that their precepts were being confused with the merely expedient behavior by which they often characterized a flourishing new generation of industrialists and entrepreneurs. They worried that the literature about utilitarian doctrines had become so abundant that understanding of them was being diluted. In addition, John Stuart Mill had begun a reevaluation of his own thought, and thus of Bentham's ethical concepts. James Mill's death made John Stuart's work easier; the elder Mill had censored his son's writings, particularly those dealing with utilitarian beliefs. Thus, the importance of *Utilitarianism* lay in its reflections of changes in John Stuart Mill's intellectual position. While the essay does not rank among Mill's greatest works, it nonetheless became the best-known essay on the subject.

The "General Remarks" with which John Stuart Mill prefaces his essay are significant chiefly because Mill, unlike Bentham, makes no pretense of using the scientific method to justify his principles. Bentham and Mill alike employed deductive reasoning. Each based his discussions on assumptions, or first principles, that were not susceptible to scientific proof. It may be true intuitively, for instance, that all humanity acts to maximize pleasure and to minimize pain. It is a matter of common sense. It cannot be proven, however. Scientific reasoning, on the contrary, draws no conclusions from intuition, common sense, innate ideas, or first principles premised on assumptions. Science has general laws, to be sure, but they are arrived at through step-by-step proof, generally mathematical. Mill insisted that the morality of individual action was not solely a question of commonsensical observation. The morality of individual action also could be tested by applying moral laws to those actions and to their consequences. Mill, in short, tries to demonstrate how close together those who reasoned inductively were to the utilitarian position arrived at deductively.

Explaining in Chapter 2 "What Utilitarianism Is," Mill introduces his famous qualitative distinctions to the orthodox Benthamite position. Mill departs from Bentham's view that the superiority of mental over physical pleasures is due to the greater permanence, safety, and uncostliness of mental activity over the physical. For Bentham the differences are merely quantitative. Mill also derides prevalent depictions of utilitarian ideas as vulgarly hedonistic. It is absurd, for example, to say that the pleasure that a drunk derives from breaking crockery is equal to the pleasure an individual derives from listening to Mozart.

Mill argues that there are qualitative distinctions between, say, the drunk's pleasure and the intellectual's pleasure drawn from thought, from feelings, from play of the imagination as well as from the moral sentiments. In fact, he reminds readers that every Epicurean or hedonistic theory of life has assigned higher values to the more enduring pleasures attending the cultivation of the mind or efforts to ennoble one's character. Even if it were demonstrable that a noble person is not invariably happier because of his nobility, still, Mill declared, the world in general benefits immensely from the example of noble and virtuous character.

Friends and critics alike note Mill's inconsistency in taking this position. The inconsistency is: If good things are good in proportion to the amount of pleasure they bring, one cannot add that pleasure itself is more or less desirable in terms of something else—say, of human dignity—that was not pleasure. Mill, however, is not primarily concerned about remaining logical. Rather, he is interested in adding Stoic and Christian elements to utilitarianism in order to transform what many people considered a barren, godless, and inhumane philosophy into a humane one that agrees with the ethics of their religions or other ethical systems.

While addressing further critical attacks on utilitarian beliefs, Mill proceeds in his third chapter to explain of what the "ultimate sanction" of utilitarian ethics consists. Bentham and early utilitarians had taken an extreme dualistic approach. They viewed the result of an individual's action, and the motive that informed it, as different. After all, an individual can only will his or her own happiness, not ensure it. Subsequently, critics had complained that utilitarian standards were too demanding, that people could not be expected always to act so as to promote society's general interest: that is, to act out of a sense of duty.

In rejoinder, Mill points to the mistake of confusing a standard of morals, which furnishes a test of what one's duties are, with the requirement that a sense of duty must always inform one's actions. Once the general happiness principle is recognized as the ethical standard, Mill explains, the sanction for an individual to act in accordance with that standard arises from the "natural" or "social feelings of mankind." Another natural motivator would be the pain produced in the individual's conscience when that person's actions contravened such natural, social feelings. The ultimate sanction, therefore, lay with an individual's subjective desire to see that his or her duty and the "conscientious feelings of mankind" were in harmony.

In the fourth chapter Mill seeks to demonstrate "of what sort of proof the principle of utility is susceptible." He acknowledges that questions of ultimate ends—the greatest good, for example—cannot be proved in the ordinary sense. He argues, however, that while no reason can be given as to why the general happiness is desirable, it is still a fact that all people desire their own happiness. Since each person's happiness is good to that person, the general happiness therefore is a good to the aggregate of all persons. To explain why virtuous people might not will happiness for themselves, that is, to show why the desire for happiness is not the sole canon of morality, Mill draws a psychological distinction between will and desire. Will, he suggests, is amenable to habit, and out of habit individuals might will something they do not desire; or, conversely, might desire something because they will it. Since on historical grounds Mill locates the source of will in desire for happiness, it seems clear to him that the Benthamite pleasure-pain criterion is still valid. That pleasure and pain, from the beginning of one's life experiences, respectively act in accord with, or against, tendencies of the will regardless of how they are explained, Mill simply declares to be facts.

Mill's final chapter, the lengthiest portion of *Utilitarianism*, originally was written, according to his stepdaughter, as a separate essay that, with cosmetic changes, he appended to the book. The argument Mill presents, while conventional in utilitarian terms, nevertheless became familiar to a large audience and was cited frequently. This was chiefly because, from Bentham's day onward, one of the major goals of the utilitarians was to banish the outworn traditions and fictions that cloud understanding of British law. The utilitarians sought to supplant them with scientific definitions and classifications of the entire body of law. An important objection to such utilitarian efforts, and to the approach to law that was associated with them, stemmed from popular impressions that justice was something absolute, immutable, and independent of public or private opinions and influences.

Responding to the charge that utilitarians perceived justice as a matter of expediency, not as an absolute, Mill denied that utilitarian sentiments had their origins in any ideas of expediency. He declared boldly that while utilitarian sentiments about justice were not founded in expediency, whatever was moral in those sentiments was. Justice, in sum, is not an absolute. After defining attributes ordinarily attached to justice, he proceeded to demonstrate, by evoking specific cases, that in actuality the concept of justice historically has not only been filled with ambiguities but has also been the subject of constant disagreement.

The nature of justice being thus controverted, what is required, Mill asserts, is some practical, external, or objective standard by which to measure it. That standard, he suggests, is to be found in the utilitarian concept of "social utility." Justice, from his utilitarian perspective, is another name for certain social utilities continuously reassessed in the light of what produced the most good for the larger number of people within a community or society. Such social utilities, he acknowledges, are far more important, absolute, and imperative than others as a class. Furthermore, they are distinguishable from the "milder feeling which attaches to the mere idea of promoting human pleasures or conveniences" by the definite nature of their commands and the sterner character of their sanctions.

The logical inconsistencies in *Utilitarianism* have long been known. Blending elements of older utilitarian precepts with his new ones—and not ignoring difficult philosophical problems along the way—Mill humanizes hedonistic utilitarianism and lends impetus to its modernization.

Clifton K. Yearley

Bibliography:

Albee, Ernest. *A History of English Utilitarianism.* Winchester, Mass.: Allen & Unwin, 1957. An excellent, readily available survey that discusses Mill's essay at length.

Halevy, Elie. *The Growth of Philosophic Radicalism.* Translated by Mary Morris. Winchester, Mass.: Faber & Faber, 1928. A brilliant analysis of the subject by a distinguished historian that includes extensive discussion of Mill and *Utilitarianism.*

Lyons, David. *Form and Limits of Utilitarianism.* Oxford, England: Clarendon Press, 1967. This respected study provides context and direct commentary on Mill's position in *Utilitarianism.*

Sher, George, ed. *Utilitarianism.* Indianapolis: Hackett, 1979. A brief but useful introduction to Mill and other utilitarians.

Stephen, Leslie. *The English Utilitarians.* London: Duckworth, 1900. This is one of the best studies on the subject.

UTOPIA

Type of work: Social criticism
Author: Sir Thomas More (1478-1535)
Type of plot: Utopian
Time of plot: Mid-fifteenth century
Locale: Antwerp, England, and Utopia
First published: 1516

How to make a better world in which to live has fascinated the minds of thinkers in every age. From Plato to the present, people have been thinking and writing about what the world would be like if people could create an earthly paradise. One of the most famous pieces of such thought and writing is Sir Thomas More's *Utopia*, a work so famous that its title has come to mean an ideal state. Originally written in Latin, the international language of medieval and Renaissance Europe, the book was widely read, and as early as 1551 a translation into English was made by Ralph Robinson, a London goldsmith.

The book is in two parts, with the second part (curiously enough) written first, in 1515, and the introductory half written in the following year. The book begins with a fictional frame story in which More tells how he traveled to Antwerp on a royal mission and there met Peter Giles, a worthy citizen of Antwerp, who in turn introduced him to Raphael Hythloday, whose name means in Greek "a talker of nonsense."

Hythloday proves to be more than a mariner, for in his conversation he appears to More to be a man of ripe wisdom and rare experience. Hythloday was supposedly a companion of Amerigo Vespucci when that worthy was supposed to have made his voyages to America. It was on one of his voyages with Vespucci that Hythloday, according to his own account, discovered the fabled land of Utopia, somewhere in the oceans near the Western hemisphere.

The first part of *Utopia* does not deal with the legendary island; rather, Hythloday visits England, converses with Cardinal Morton, and suggests to that churchman (who was Henry VII's chancellor) some reforms that might benefit England. Among the reforms the fictional Hythloday suggests are the abolition of the death penalty for theft, the prevention of gambling, less dependence upon the raising of sheep for wool, discontinuance of use of mercenary soldiers, cheaper prices for all commodities, and an end to the enclosure of the common lands for the benefit of great and wealthy landlords. Although Cardinal Morton listens intently to Hythloday's suggestions, a lawyer objects that Hythloday's reforms cannot be undertaken and that they would not be deemed desirable by anyone who knows the history and customs of England.

In this first part of *Utopia*, More is pointing out some of the social and economic evils of sixteenth century European life. More than that, he is suggesting that only an outsider can see the faults with an objective eye. The introduction of the lawyer's objections, which are cut short by Cardinal Morton, suggest also that More discerned in sixteenth century society persons who opposed reform and who had reasons—not necessarily edifying ones—for doing so. Part 1 of *Utopia* is More's way of preparing the reader, through contrast, for the section in which his ideal realm is delineated.

In the second part, Hythloday expounds at length about the culture of the land of Utopia (Latin for "nowhere"), which he visited during his travels. Hythloday describes Utopia as an island kingdom that is crescent shaped and about five hundred miles in perimeter, separated from other lands by a channel constructed by its founder, the fabulous King Utopus, who saw that the Utopian experiment, if it were to succeed, must be isolated and protected from the encroachments of warlike and predatory neighbors. The island is divided into fifty-four shires, or counties, each with its own town, no town more than a day's walking journey from its neighbors. The central city, Amaurote, is the capital, the seat of the prince who is the island's nominal ruler.

The government of Utopia is relatively simple and largely vested in older men, in patriarchal fashion. Each unit of thirty families is ruled by one man chosen by election every year. Each ten groups of families elects a member of the island council. This council in turn elects the prince, who serves throughout his lifetime unless deposed because of tyranny. The council meets every three days to take up matters of consequence to the people, and no decision is made on the same day the problem is advanced, lest undue haste cause mistakes.

It is not in government alone that More introduces suggestions for reform in his *Utopia*. In this ideal state everyone works, each man having a trade or craft, except the unusually talented, who are selected for training and service in the academy of learning. The workday is six hours long, with the time divided equally between the morning and the afternoon. Each man spends a two-year period working as a farmer in the shire outside the city in which he resides. Since everyone works, there is more than enough food and all other commodities for the inhabitants. All goods are community-owned, with each person guarding what is given him for the benefit of the commonwealth. The tastes of the people are simple; having enough individually, no one desires to have more than others. Even the prince of Utopia is designated only by the symbol of a sheaf of grain, a symbol of plenty. Each person is garbed in durable clothing of leather, linen, or wool. Jewelry is given to children to play with, so that everyone associates such baubles with childishness. Gold and silver are despised, being used for chamber pots, chains for slaves, and the marks of criminal conviction.

In the dialogue Sir Thomas More interjects some objections to the communal idea, but this is the only point on which he seems to have reservations; yet even on this point Hythloday's answers to his objections satisfy him.

Violence, bloodshed, and vice, says Hythloday, have been done away with in Utopia. Lest bloodshed of any kind corrupt the people, slaves are required to slaughter the cattle. Dicing and other forms of gambling are unknown. The people choose instead to labor for recreation in their gardens, improve their homes, attend humanistic lectures, enjoy music, and converse profitably with one another. The sick are provided for in spacious hospitals erected in each quarter of each city. In the event of a painful and incurable illness, the priests consult with the patient and encourage him to choose death administered painlessly by the authorities. Although no one is required to do so, everyone eats in mess halls where slaves prepare the meals under the supervision of the wives of the family group. At mealtime young and old eat together, except for children under five and enlightening, pleasant conversation is encouraged.

The Utopian criminal is enslaved, rather than put to death, as he was in sixteenth century England. Adultery is regarded as a crime and punished by slavery. Marriage for love is encouraged, but also prudence in selecting a mate. Males must be twenty-two and women eighteen before marriage is permitted. The welfare of the family is a state matter, since the family is the basic unit of the Utopian state. The people are anxious for the commonwealth to be rich, for the Utopians buy off their enemies and use their wealth to hire foreign mercenary soldiers; they hope in this manner to encourage potential enemies to murder one another instead of attacking Utopia.

The Utopians are described as a religious people who practice toleration, which was almost unknown in Tudor England. Some are Christians; others worship God in other ways. Atheism and militant sectarianism alike are forbidden.

If to a contemporary reader much of what More cites as an ideal to be reached seems not idealistic enough, then such a reaction may be considered a sign of great hope, in that people have improved over time and that they may continue to do so. Two additional points should be made in connection with Sir Thomas More's work. One is that his borrowings from Plato and other earlier authors did not prevent him from adding much that was his own in theory and practice. The second point is that, in the time since the writing of *Utopia*, some of the author's ideas have been, in England and elsewhere, put into effect—unlikely as they may have appeared to his contemporaries. Human society may never come to the utopian ideal, but some credit should go to Sir Thomas More for the existence of the urge to attempt improvement in the human condition.

Bibliography:
Baker-Smith, Dominic. *More's "Utopia."* New York: HarperCollins, 1991. A complete study of *Utopia* that balances analysis of its contents as a literary work and as a treatise on political theory. Includes information about the history of *Utopia*'s composition, the Renaissance humanism that permeates More's thought, and the sources that influenced its ideas and literary style.
Hexter, J. H. *More's "Utopia": The Biography of an Idea.* New York: Harper & Row, 1965. Examines *Utopia* for evidence of its stages of composition. This sequence forms the basis for analyzing More's intentions in writing *Utopia* and the ideas he wanted to express in his work.
Johnson, Robbin S. *More's "Utopia": Ideal and Illusion.* New Haven, Conn.: Yale University Press, 1969. An essay interpreting *Utopia* based on an honors thesis by a Yale undergraduate. Presents More's *Utopia* as a continuing discourse on the balance between ideal and reality in society and government.
Logan, George M. *The Meaning of More's "Utopia."* Princeton, N.J.: Princeton University Press, 1983. Interprets *Utopia* in the context of Renaissance humanism. Situates More's work in the tradition of classical and Renaissance political theory, and demonstrates how More's critique of some humanist political views gives *Utopia* a modernity of outlook.
Marius, Richard. *Thomas More: A Biography.* New York: Alfred A. Knopf, 1984. A complete biography of Thomas More. Three chapters are devoted to *Utopia* and its place in the context of More's life, religious beliefs, and thought.

V.

Type of work: Novel
Author: Thomas Pynchon (1937-   )
Type of plot: Satire
Time of plot: 1898-1956
Locale: Italy, France, Egypt, German Southwest Africa, Malta, Virginia, and New York
First published: 1963

> *Principal characters:*
> BENNY PROFANE, "a schlemihl and human yo-yo"
> HERBERT STENCIL, an adventurer on a quest for V.
> SIDNEY STENCIL, his father, a spy for the British Foreign Office
> PAOLA MAIJSTRAL, the wife of Profane's ex-shipmate, Pappy Hod
> FAUSTO MAIJSTRAL, her father, a Maltese poet
> HUGH GODOLPHIN, an explorer and the discoverer of Vheissu
> EVAN GODOLPHIN, his son, a World War I pilot
> THE WHOLE SICK CREW, a group of decadents in 1950's New York
> RACHEL OWLGLASS, Paola's roommate and Profane's sometime girlfriend
> McCLINTIC SPHERE, a jazz saxophonist
> V., the object of Stencil's quest, possibly a woman, a place, or a paranoid
>   fantasy

The Story:

At the end of 1955, Benny Profane drifted off the street and into the Sailor's Grave, a Norfolk tavern, and found his old shipmate Pig Bodine. Pig had abandoned his military duty. He had abandoned ship, driven crazy by Pappy Hod, whose wife, Paola, had left him to become a barmaid at the Sailor's Grave. After a wild New Year's Eve party, Profane and Paola took a bus to New York. Profane began to worry that Paola was becoming dependent on him, so he dumped her off on Rachel Owlglass, his occasional girlfriend. Freed of Paola, he traveled across town on the subway until he met the Mendoza family, who helped him get a job hunting albino alligators under the streets in New York's sewer system.

Meanwhile, Rachel paid her roommate Esther's financial debt to Dr. Schoenmaker, the plastic surgeon who had performed Esther's nose job. Esther's surgery reminded the doctor of his original motivation to practice reconstructive surgery. As a mechanic in World War I, Schoenmaker's hero, the ace aviator Evan Godolphin, had a horribly disfiguring accident. A quack surgeon experimented with grafting ivory, silver, and other inert matter into Evan's face. This material later decayed and destroyed the young, once-handsome Godolphin's appearance.

Haunted by his father's death in Valletta in 1919, Herbert Stencil materialized in New York in 1956 at a party thrown by the Whole Sick Crew. He was tormented by a passage in his father's diary which referred to a mysterious "V." When he read that passage, Stencil began his quest for V.

For Sidney Stencil, Herbert's father, V.'s history began with the assassination of the British spy, Porpentine, in Cairo in 1898. There, Sidney first encountered Victoria Wren, a beautiful young tourist with a penchant for espionage. They were both in Florence a year later when Hugh Godolphin and his son, Evan, were drawn into a revolutionary conspiracy and an absurd plot to steal Sandro Botticelli's *Venus*.

The theft failed, but the enigmatic figure resurfaced in a story Herbert heard in the Rusty Spoon, a place frequented by the Crew. According to Stencil, Vera Meroving was a guest at "Foppl's Siege Party," a depraved romp held in 1922 in the African fortress of a German official who fondly recalled Luther von Trotha's annihilation of the native population. Later, in New York, Paola gave Stencil a copy of her father's "Confessions," which documented the appearance of V. in Valletta during World War II. V., who was disguised as the Bad Priest, was attacked by the local children, who "disassembled" her. They removed her glass eye, her artificial foot, and other inanimate parts her body had accumulated. She then died. Finally, Stencil received information about a lesbian affair between an unnamed woman, possibly V., and a young ballerina in 1913 Paris. After the dancer's onstage death, the mysterious woman was rumored to have fled to Valletta.

In New York, Profane avoided making any commitment to his adopted family and returned to Rachel. He reminded Rachel that he was a schlemihl, incapable of living in peace with inanimate objects. Still, she found him a night watchman's job at Anthroresearch Associates, where he had imaginary conversations with SHOCK (Synthetic Human Object, Casualty Kinematics) and SHROUD (Synthetic Human, Radiation Output Determined), two test dummies.

Esther became pregnant by her plastic surgeon, and the Whole Sick Crew hosted a party to raise money to send her to Cuba for an abortion. Profane and Rachel, who saw herself as Esther's protector, followed her to the airport, but Profane literally tripped over the Mendoza family and allowed Esther to escape. Dejected because he thought he had lost two women, Profane decided to leave Rachel. He blamed his schlemihlhood for their doomed relationship and thus evaded responsibility for his inability to care.

At the same time, McClintic Sphere, a jazz musician, visited a prostitute. They went for a drive outside the city. Paola, who had been impersonating a prostitute, confessed her identity to Sphere. She also announced her intention to return home to Malta. Outside New York, Sphere arrived at the conclusion that a person must learn to "keep cool, but care."

Stencil knew he too must return to Valletta. Apprehensive about his visit to the country where his father had died and afraid that his quest was ending, Stencil invited Profane to accompany him to Malta.

Paola, Stencil, and Profane sailed to Valletta. After they arrived, Paola saw Pappy Hod and told him that she was going to wait for him in Norfolk. Stencil met Fausto but chose not to believe the story about the death of the Bad Priest. He followed a clue to Stockholm, where his quest continued. Alone, Profane fell in with Brenda Wigglesworth, an American tourist. He admitted he had not learned anything, and they disappeared together into the night.

During Malta's June Disturbances of 1919, Sidney Stencil had an affair with Veronica Manganese, a Fascist spy, who was accompanied by Evan Godolphin. After the violence, V. abandoned Sidney. As he departed the island, a random waterspout capsized his boat and killed him. From the shore, the mutilated Evan watched as the small boat vanished beneath the surface of the sea.

Critical Evaluation:

The publication of *V.*, winner of the prestigious William Faulkner Foundation's award for the year's best first novel in 1963, signaled the arrival of a major American novelist. While a few readers find Thomas Pynchon's work to be as elusive as the author himself (an intensely private person who has allowed little biographical information to surface), others marvel at his labyrinthine plots and astounding erudition. The range of Pynchon's writing, including *The*

Crying of Lot 49 (1966), *Gravity's Rainbow* (1973), *Slow Learner* (1984), and *Vineland* (1990), invites inevitable comparisons to François Rabelais, Laurence Sterne, James Joyce, Edgar Allan Poe, Herman Melville, Walt Whitman, T. S. Eliot, William Faulkner, and Vladimir Nabokov, securing Pynchon's place, along with John Barth, William Gaddis, Robert Coover, and Joseph McElroy, among the top echelon of contemporary authors.

A common criticism of Pynchon is that he is a difficult writer. It is this difficulty, however, which makes novels like *V.* and *Gravity's Rainbow* so rewarding to read and reread. Pynchon's texts are not easily comprehensible, because he intends to do nothing short of reinventing the way people interpret their experiences.

Much of the difficulty of *V.* stems from Pynchon's focus on the epistemological uncertainty of human experience in the twentieth century. The Antarctic explorer Hugh Godolphin laments his inability to penetrate the surface of Vheissu, describing the unknown land as a tattooed woman whose skin "would begin to get between you and whatever it was in her that you thought you loved." Tourists, he feels, only want the surface of a strange land, while an explorer wants to reach its heart. Godolphin's revelation that he has been to the South Pole and witnessed "Nothing" echoes Marlowe's discovery in Joseph Conrad's *Heart of Darkness* (1902) and reflects Sidney Stencil's view of the "Situation." For Stencil, "no Situation had any objective reality: it only existed in the minds of those who happened to be in on it at any specific moment . . . a sum total or complex more mongrel than homogeneous."

In the novel's present, Benny Profane, the "human yo-yo," moves around like a tourist, finally admitting at the end of the book that he never learned "a goddamn thing." On the other hand, Herbert Stencil diligently pursues traces of V. as they appear around the world, but it is impossible to know whether the plots he detects are real or if he is projecting "cabals" onto "the world's random caries." Pynchon's sophisticated narrative technique subtly displays how the events of the past are "Stencilized." The Egyptian episode is generated from "veiled references to Porpentine" in his father's journals, alluding to an incident that occurred before Stencil was born. "Mondaugen's Story," the reader is told, took "no more than thirty minutes" when Stencil heard it in the Rusty Spoon, but when he retold it to Dudley Eigenvalue "the yarn had undergone considerable change." The section "V. in love" is told to Stencil secondhand by the composer Porcepic. All of Stencil's information, in fact, comes to him secondhand. Because Stencil is not present at any of the events he recounts, the reader must ask if these are caries or cabals. To his credit, Pynchon does not afford the reader any solid ground from which to survey what is real and what is illusion.

Stencil's sections reproduce V.'s "obsession with bodily incorporating little bits of inert matter" as he incorporates people into his narrative of the quest for V. The theme of the inanimate asserts Pynchon's distress at the progressive dehumanization of contemporary life, whereby people are becoming more like objects every day. Profane turns himself into an object by retreating into his role as a schlemihl, which lets him experience only the "cool" surface of life while he avoids any of the potential dangers involved in caring about another person. Rachel Owlglass, who is overly fond of her car when Profane meets her, begins to act overprotective of people she imagines as victims. The jazz player McClintic Sphere offers a third possibility that is "the only way clear of the cool/crazy flipflop": "Love with your mouth shut, help without breaking your ass or publicizing it: keep cool, but care. . . . There's no magic words."

Sphere's philosophy cannot sum up Pynchon's; however, it offers a reference point in the text from which the reader can examine Pynchon's analysis of history and imperialism, his use of entropy and other scientific metaphors, and his original moral vision for the twentieth century. In any case, readers should be able to agree with the elder Stencil that "there is more behind and inside V. [and *V.*] than any of us had suspected."

Trey Strecker

Bibliography:
Hite, Molly. "Duplicity and Duplication in *V.*" In *Ideas of Order in the Novels of Thomas Pynchon*. Columbus: Ohio State University Press, 1983. Challenges view of V.'s intrusive, enigmatic recurrence as a "puzzle." Argues that metaphoric relations or repetition replace conventional linear narration.
Levine, George, and David Leverenz, eds. *Mindful Pleasures: Essays on Thomas Pynchon*. Boston: Little, Brown, 1976. An essential work of Pynchon criticism. Analyzes problems of identity that center on the desire to avoid randomness and the paranoid tendency to create order. Includes essays on women, apocalypse, language, and entropy in *V.* and an appendix with useful biographical data.
New, Melvyn. "Profaned and Stenciled Texts: In Search of Pynchon's *V.*" In *Thomas Pynchon: Modern Critical Views*, edited by Harold Bloom. New York: Chelsea House, 1986. Notes the reader's role in creating systems of organization in artistic texts. Employs a generic distinction between the romance and the novel to examine how Pynchon's text defies closure.
Patteson, Richard. "What Stencil Knew: Structure and Certitude in Pynchon's *V.*" *Critique* 16, no. 2 (1974): 30-44. This study of point of view and narrative technique in Stencil's pursuit of V. illustrates Pynchon's thematic concern with the limitations of human knowledge.
Slade, Joseph W. *Thomas Pynchon*. New York: Warner Paperback Library, 1974. The first book-length discussion of Pynchon's fiction serves as an excellent introduction to this complex author. Traces dominant themes, motifs, allusions, and tensions in *V.* A helpful chronological approach unravels the novel's time scheme.

THE VAGABOND

Type of work: Novel
Author: Colette (Sidonie-Gabrielle Colette, 1873-1954)
Type of plot: Psychological realism
Time of plot: Early twentieth century
Locale: France
First published: La Vagabonde, 1911 (English translation, 1954)

Principal characters:
RENÉE NERÉE, a music hall mime
MAXIME DUFFEREIN-CHAUTEL, an admirer
BRAGUE, a mime
HAMOND, a friend of Renée
ADOLPHE TAILLANDY, Renée's former husband

The Story:

Renée Nerée was musing. She had applied makeup to her face in the French music-hall dressing room and looked into the mirror at her own reflection as it began to speak to her. Her image asked her why she was seated there, all alone. Renée, seated in her dressing room, waited to go onstage for her act and listened to the voice of her double in the mirror, all the while wondering who or what would appear at her dressing room door to change her state of solitude. Renée wished for something that would release her from the life of solitude she had created for herself through her life on the stage. She also feared any change.

She performed her act and returned to her dressing room to find a note from the Marquis de Fontanges (Maxime Dufferein-Chautel). The Marquis expressed his admiration for her talents on the stage, and inquired whether Renée had other talents. He invited her to dine with him that evening. Renée refused.

Alone again in her dressing room, she reviewed her eight years of marriage and three years of separation from Adolphe Taillandy, a pastelist. He had lied to her and had been a womanizer. Renée had been a jealous and tormented young wife and had turned to literature as an outlet. She had written four books, which obtained varying levels of success, but once she had separated from Taillandy, she was shunned by their middle-class friends, at which point she had taken a ground floor flat for herself in Paris and turned to the music hall to earn her living.

Meanwhile, Brague had set up an evening performance at a private home where the two of them were to perform their act of mime. Renée arrived at the residence of a wealthy Parisian to dance before an assembled audience, and she spied several of her former husband's mistresses in the audience. Aware of the shock in their eyes, she danced before them unabashed, but aware of the pain of her past. It was not she, Renée reflected, who had done any wrong.

As the winter progressed, Hamond brought Maxime, uninvited, to dinner at Renée's flat. She was not impressed with him as a suitor, and laughed him off. The show at the music hall closed. Renée wondered what she would do next. Maxime continued to visit Renée, which caused her to acknowledge her desire for companionship. When Maxime told her he loved her, she did not respond. She told Hamond, however, that she would never love anyone again after the devastating experience of her marriage to a liar and a cheat. She signed a contract to leave Paris for a forty-day tour of provincial theaters with Brague. Laughing, she happily told Maxime and Hamond about her forthcoming tour. Maxime visited her at her apartment to ask her to stay in

Paris, and while there, he approached her and kissed her. Renée resisted, but then gave in to the kiss and experienced a sensual reawakening. The reawakening gave rise to a conflict in her mind. To give in to sexual impulses meant a return to her former humiliation with her unfaithful husband, a reenactment of the painful state of submission to a man.

She refused to give herself to Maxime. Her experience with her former husband kept her from trusting Maxime or her own impulses. By the time she embarked on her tour, however, her love for Maxime had blossomed. They came to an understanding that they would live together as a couple when she returned. She would give herself to him fully. Renée left Paris in high spirits, after having promised to start a life with Maxime upon her return from the tour. Renée left Maxime a love letter upon her departure. It proclaimed that she would return tired of solitude. She would, she wrote, be ready to begin her life with him fully and completely. Upon leaving Paris, she began an exchange of passionate letters with Maxime.

Gradually, as she traveled by train further south from Paris during the following days and nights and into the regions of her childhood, doubts assailed her and grew until a letter arrived for her in Avignon. Maxime, afraid of losing her, sensed that Renée was drifting away emotionally during her extended tour of provincial France, so he wrote to her with a proposal of marriage. Renée's conflict increased. She reflected to herself that marriage was a form of confinement, although it had its positive sides, while her vagabond existence, although lonely and hard, allowed her to live as an independent soul.

As she left the south and embarked on the return leg of her trip, she began to psychologically separate herself from Maxime. Once back in Paris, she furtively entered her apartment alone. In the early morning light she left Maxime a note in her apartment. It told him that she would not see him again. She returned to her life as the traveling artist, on her way to South America on a tour.

Critical Evaluation:

Considered by many critics to be one of the greatest of French fiction writers, Colette was the first woman member of the Académie Goncourt. The author of more than fifty books, she began her writing career at the insistence of her first husband, Henri Gauthier-Villars, known as Willy. At the age of twenty-seven, her first novel, *Claudine at School* (1900), was published under her husband's name. That novel was the beginning of the highly popular *Claudine* series. After her divorce from Willy, Colette supported herself as a music-hall mime and continued to write, publishing the acclaimed novels *The Vagabond* (1911), *Chéri* (1920), and *The Last of Chéri* (1926). Many more novels followed, and her fame became renown.

In *The Vagabond*, Colette treats the theme of a woman's conflicts between love and independence. Colette's probing analysis of the psychological states that give power to these conflicts, and her lyrical, rhythmic prose style, give voice to the struggles women have with society and with their own desires. Analytical, harsh, lyrical, and honest in its examination of a woman's choices, *The Vagabond* is one of Colette's most important novels.

The novel's theme may be stated as the difficulty in reconciling sensual love with a woman's need for independence. This dilemma is posed by Renée, who, wounded by the memory of her past with her former husband, cannot give in to her temptation for a physical and emotional relationship with a man. Rather, she must choose a life of independence and solitude, marked by hardship and freedom.

The novel is divided into three parts and is told in the first person. In the arena of the music hall, individuals—though facing a difficult, lonely life—reach out to help one another. Renée, however, must choose between a relationship with a man and her own freedom in negotiating the world on her own terms. There is, it seems, no other choice. For the heroine, there is the individual female life, fraught with solitude and hardship, but with a degree of freedom, or there is the life in relationship to a man, which may bring fulfillment, but is, in the heroine's view, confining.

Renée Nerée is thought to be the most autobiographical of Colette's heroines. Colette had suffered from the infidelities of her first husband, and was able to portray the emotional effects of betrayal through her heroine, Renée. Colette's earlier works, especially those of the *Claudine* series, portray young women who settle for love as a state of physical desire and a social and psychological state of submission to men. Colette's later, more mature heroines ask, as did Colette, for a love that can encompass more than just the physical. Renée is one such example. A thirty-three-year-old divorcée who supports herself as a music-hall artist, she parallels many aspects of Colette's earlier years. Unlike Colette, Renée is unable to break away from the effects of her past. When she does become involved with Maxime, she is obsessed with preoccupations of aging.

The past and its effect on the present is an underlying motif in *The Vagabond*. In the opening paragraph of *The Vagabond*, the heroine faces herself in a mirror and holds a conversation with herself. The figure prompts Renée to examine where she is and where she has been. The heroine's consciousness is also a mirror that reflects her past in such a way that Renée cannot embrace a life that holds sensuality, a relationship with a man, and freedom all at once. The mirror held up to the past reveals the heroine's struggle against society, which demands the submission of women to men. Renée's struggle is also with herself. Colette poses the question, through the conflicted Renée Nerée, of whether it is possible for woman to accept her natural desires while remaining independent.

The Vagabond can be seen as an extended conversation that Colette had with herself on the themes of sexuality and freedom. Colette's superb novel about this major theme is masterfully written.

R. C. S.

Bibliography:

Cottrell, Robert D. *Colette*. New York: Frederick Ungar, 1974. Discusses and evaluates *The Vagabond* with emphasis on themes of freedom and sexuality. Important starting place for the reader of Colette's works.

Phelps, Robert, ed. *Earthly Paradise*. New York: Farrar, Straus & Giroux, 1966. Delves into the myths created by Colette in her life and in her works. Chapters on her early marriage and her music-hall years, which were the basis for *The Vagabond*.

Sarde, Michele. *Colette: A Biography*. New York: William Morrow, 1980. Quotations from *The Vagabond* illuminate Colette's life. Reflects on the major themes of that fictional work. Bibliography.

Stewart, Joan Hinde. *Colette*. Boston: Twayne, 1983. Places *The Vagabond* in the context of Colette's career as a major writer. A good starting place.

Ward, Nicole Jouve. *Colette*. Bloomington: Indiana University Press, 1987. Analyzes structures, tropes, themes, and characters in Colette's work and has illuminating sections on *The Vagabond*.

VANITY FAIR

Type of work: Novel
Author: William Makepeace Thackeray (1811-1863)
Type of plot: Social satire
Time of plot: Early nineteenth century
Locale: England and Europe
First published: serial, 1847-1848; book, 1848

Principal characters:
    BECKY SHARP, an adventuress
    AMELIA SEDLEY, her friend
    JOSEPH SEDLEY (JOS), Amelia's brother
    RAWDON CRAWLEY, Becky's husband
    MISS CRAWLEY, Rawdon's wealthy aunt
    OLD SIR PITT CRAWLEY, Rawdon's father
    YOUNG SIR PITT CRAWLEY, Rawdon's brother
    GEORGE OSBORNE, Amelia's husband
    CAPTAIN WILLIAM DOBBIN, Amelia's friend

The Story:

Becky Sharp and Amelia Sedley became good friends while they were students at Miss Pinkerton's School for girls. It was proof of Amelia's good, gentle nature that she took as kindly as she did to her friend, who was generally disliked by all the other girls. Amelia overlooked the indications of Becky's selfishness as much as she could. After the two girls had finished their education at the school, Becky accompanied her friend to her home for a short visit. There she first met Joseph Sedley, Amelia's older brother, called Jos, who was home on leave from military service in India. Jos was a shy man, unused to women, and certainly to women as designing and flirtatious as Becky. His blundering and awkward manners did not appeal to many women, but Becky was happy to overlook these faults when she compared them with his wealth and social position. Amelia innocently believed that her friend had fallen in love with her brother, and she discreetly tried to further the romance.

To this end, she arranged a party at Vauxhall. Becky and Jos, along with Amelia and her admirer, George Osborne, were present. There was a fifth member of the group, Captain Dobbin, a tall, lumbering fellow, also in service in India. He had been in love with Amelia for a long time, but he recognized that dashing George Osborne was much more suitable for her. All the maneuvering of the flirtatious Becky and the amiable Amelia, however, was not sufficient to corner Jos, who drank too much punch and believed that he had made a silly figure of himself at the party. A day or so later, a letter delivered to the Sedley household announced that Jos was ill and planned to return to India as soon as possible.

Since there was no longer any reason for Becky to remain with the Sedleys, she left Amelia, after many tears and kisses, to take a position as governess to two young girls at Queen's Crawley. The head of the household was Sir Pitt Crawley, a cantankerous old man renowned for his miserliness. Lady Crawley was an apathetic soul who lived in fear of her husband's unreasonable outbursts. Becky decided that she would have nothing to fear from her timid mistress and spent most of her time ingratiating herself with Sir Pitt and ignoring her pupils.

Becky also showed great interest in Miss Crawley, a spinster aunt of the family, who was exceedingly wealthy. Miss Crawley paid little attention to Sir Pitt and his children, but she was fond of Rawdon Crawley, a captain in the army and a son of Sir Pitt by a previous marriage. She was so fond of her dashing young nephew that she supported him through school and paid all of his gambling debts with only a murmur.

During Becky's stay, Miss Crawley visited Sir Pitt only once, at a time when Rawdon was also present. The handsome young dragoon soon fell prey to Becky's wiles and followed her about devotedly. Becky also took care to ingratiate herself with the holder of the purse strings. Miss Crawley found Becky witty and charming and did not attempt to disguise her opinion that the little governess was worth all the rest of the Crawley household put together. Becky, therefore, found herself in a very enviable position. Both Sir Pitt and his handsome son were obviously interested in her. Miss Crawley insisted that Becky accompany her back to London.

Becky had been expected to return to her pupils after only a short stay with Miss Crawley; but Miss Crawley was taken ill and refused to allow anyone but her dear Becky to nurse her. Afterward, there were numerous other excuses to prevent the governess from returning to her duties. Certainly, Becky was not unhappy. Rawdon Crawley was a constant caller and a devoted suitor for Becky's hand. When the news arrived that Lady Crawley had died, no great concern was felt by anyone. A few days later, however, Sir Pitt himself appeared, asking to see Miss Sharp. Much to Becky's surprise, the baronet threw himself at her feet and asked her to marry him. Regretfully, she refused his offer. She was already secretly married to Rawdon Crawley.

Following this disclosure, Rawdon and his bride left for a honeymoon at Brighton. Chagrined and angry, old Miss Crawley took to her bed, changed her will, and cut off her nephew without a shilling. Sir Pitt raved with anger. Amelia's marriage had also precipitated a family crisis. Her romance with George had proceeded with good wishes on both sides until Mr. Sedley lost most of his money through some unfortunate business deals. Then George's snobbish father ordered his son to break his engagement to a penniless woman. George, whose affection for Amelia was never stable, was inclined to accept this parental command; but Captain Dobbin, who saw with distress that Amelia was breaking her heart over George, finally prevailed upon the young man to go through with the marriage, regardless of his father's wishes. When the couple arrived in Brighton for their honeymoon, they found Rawdon and Becky living there happily in penniless extravagance.

Captain Dobbin also arrived in Brighton. He had agreed to act as intercessor with Mr. Osborne. Nevertheless, his hopes of reconciling father and son were shattered when Mr. Osborne furiously dismissed Captain Dobbin and took immediate steps to disown George. Captain Dobbin also brought the news that the army had been ordered to Belgium. Napoleon had landed from Elba. The Hundred Days had begun.

In Brussels, the two couples met again. George Osborne was infatuated with Becky. Jos Sedley, now returned from India, and Captain Dobbin were also stationed in that city; Captain Dobbin was in faithful attendance upon neglected Amelia. Everyone was waiting for the next move that Napoleon would make; but in the meantime, the gaiety of the Duke of Wellington's forces was widespread. The Osbornes and Crawleys attended numerous balls. Becky, especially, made an impression upon military society, and her coquetry extended with equal effect from general to private. June 15, 1815, was a famous night in Brussels, for on that evening the Duchess of Richmond gave a tremendous ball. Amelia left the party early, brokenhearted at the attentions her husband was showing Becky. Shortly after she left, the men were given orders to march to meet the enemy. Napoleon had entered Belgium, and a great battle was impending.

As Napoleon's forces approached, fear and confusion spread throughout Brussels, and many of the civilians fled the city, but Amelia and Becky did not. Becky was not alarmed, and Amelia refused to leave while George was in danger. She remained in the city some days before she heard that her husband had been killed. Rawdon returned safely from the Battle of Waterloo. He and Becky spent a merry and triumphant season in Paris, where Becky's beauty and wit gained her a host of admirers. Rawdon was very proud of the son she bore him.

Amelia also had a child. She had returned to London almost out of her mind with grief, and only after her son was born did she show any signs of rallying. When Becky grew bored with the pleasures of Paris, the Crawleys returned to London. There they rented a large home and proceeded to live well with little money. By this time, Becky was a master at this art, and so they lived on a grander scale than Rawdon's small winnings at cards would warrant. Becky had become acquainted with the nobility of England and had made a particular impression on rich old Lord Steyne. At last, all society began to talk about young Mrs. Crawley and her elderly admirer. Fortunately, Rawdon heard nothing of this ballroom and coffeehouse gossip.

Through the efforts of Lord Steyne, Becky eventually achieved her dearest wish, presentation at Court. Presented along with her was the wife of the new Sir Pitt Crawley. The old man had died, and young Sir Pitt, his oldest son and Rawdon's brother, had inherited the title. Since then, friendly relations had been established between the two brothers. If Rawdon realized that his brother had also fallen in love with Becky, he gave no sign, and he accepted the money his brother gave him with good grace; but more and more, he felt himself shut out from the happy life that Becky enjoyed. He spent much time with his son, for he realized that the child was neglected. Once or twice he saw young George Osborne, Amelia's son.

Amelia struggled to keep her son with her, but her pitiful financial status made it difficult to support him. Her parents had grown garrulous and morose with disappointment over their reduced circumstances. At length, Amelia sorrowfully agreed to let Mr. Osborne take the child and rear him as his own. Mr. Osborne still refused to recognize the woman his son had married against his wishes, however, and Amelia rarely saw the boy.

Rawdon was now deeply in debt. When he appealed to Becky for money, she told him that she had none to spare. She made no attempt to explain the jewelry and other trinkets she bought. When Rawdon was imprisoned for a debt, he wrote and asked Becky to take care of the matter. She answered that she could not get the money until the following day. An appeal to Sir Pitt, however, brought about Rawdon's release, and he returned to his home to find Becky entertaining Lord Steyne. Not long afterward, Rawdon accepted a post abroad, and he never returned to his unfaithful, scheming wife.

Amelia's fortunes had now improved. When Jos Sedley returned home, he established his sister and father in a more pleasant home. Mrs. Sedley had died, and Jos resolved to do as much as he could to make his father's last days happy. Captain Dobbin had returned from India and confessed his love for Amelia. Although she acknowledged him as a friend, she was not yet ready to accept his love. It was Captain Dobbin who went to Mr. Osborne and gradually succeeded in reconciling him to his son's wife. When Mr. Osborne died, he left a good part of his fortune to his grandson and appointed Amelia as the boy's guardian.

Amelia, her son, Captain Dobbin, and Jos Sedley took a short trip to the Continent. This visit was perhaps the happiest time in Amelia's life. Her son was with her constantly, and Captain Dobbin was a devoted attendant. Eventually, his devotion was to overcome her hesitation and they were to be married. At a small German resort, they encountered Becky once more. After Rawdon left her, Becky had been unable to live down the scandal of their separation. Leaving her child with Sir Pitt and his wife, she crossed to the Continent. Since then, she had been living with first one considerate gentleman and then another. When she saw the prosperous Jos, she vowed not to let him escape as he had before. Amelia and Jos greeted her in a friendly manner, and only Captain Dobbin seemed to regard her with distrust. He tried to warn Jos about Becky, but Jos was a willing victim of her charms.

Becky traveled with Jos wherever he went. Although she could not get a divorce from Rawdon, Jos treated her as his wife, and despite Captain Dobbin's protests, he took out a large insurance policy in her name. A few months later, his family learned that he had died while staying with Becky at Aix-la-Chapelle. The full circumstances of his death were never established, but Becky came into a large sum of money from his insurance. She spent the rest of her life on the Continent, where she assumed the role of the virtuous widow and won a reputation for benevolence and generosity.

Critical Evaluation:

When critics call William Makepeace Thackeray's characters in *Vanity Fair* lifelike, they are using that term for a subtler meaning than it usually conveys. His people are not true to life in the sense of being fully rounded or drawn with psychological depth. On the contrary, readers sometimes find their actions too farcical to be human, as in Jos Sedley's ignominious flight from Brussels after the battle of Waterloo, or too sinister to be credible, as in the implication that Becky poisons Jos to collect his insurance—totally out of keeping with what readers learned about her in the previous sixty-six chapters. She may be a selfish opportunist, but she is not a murderess. Thackeray's characters are lifelike if "life" is defined as a typological phenomenon; when readers shrug their shoulders and say "that's life," readers are indulging in a kind of judgment on the human race that is based on types, not individuals; on the common failings of all men and women, not on the unique goodness or evil of some. Insofar as all people share one another's weaknesses, everyone is represented in *Vanity Fair*. Human banality levels all. That is the satirical revelation that *Vanity Fair* provides; that is the way in which its characters are lifelike.

Thackeray's general approach is comic satire; his method is that of the theatrical producer, specifically, the puppeteer. In his prologue, he calls himself the "Manager of the Performance" and refers to Becky, Amelia, and Dobbin as puppets of varying "flexibility . . . and liveliness." Critics usually interpret this offhanded way of referring to his principal characters as a vindication of his own intrusions and asides; as a reminder to the reader that he, the author, is as much involved in the action as any of his characters. Nevertheless, readers should probably take a harder look at Thackeray's metaphor: He is a puppeteer because he must be one; because his people are puppets, someone must pull the strings. The dehumanized state of Regency and early Victorian society comes to accurate life through the cynical vehicle of Thackeray's puppeteering. Sentimentality and hypocrisy, closely related social vices, seem interchangeable at the end of the novel when Thackeray gathers all the remaining puppets: Amelia and Dobbin, a "tender little parasite" clinging to her "rugged old oak," and Becky, acting out her newfound saintliness by burying herself "in works of piety" and "having stalls at Fancy Fairs" for the benefit of the poor. "Let us shut up the box and the puppets," concludes Thackeray, "for our play is played out."

Despite the predictability of all the characters' puppetlike behavior, they often exhibit just enough humanity to make their dehumanization painful. Thackeray wants readers to feel uncomfortable over the waste of human potential in the vulgar concerns of *Vanity Fair*. George Osborne lives like a cad, is arrogant about his spendthrift ways, is unfaithful to his wife, and dies a hero, leading a charge against the retreating French at Waterloo. The reader is left with the impression that the heroism of his death is rendered irrelevant by the example of his life. Such satire is demanding in its moral vision precisely because it underscores the price of corruption: Honor becomes absurd.

Rawdon Crawley's love for his little son slowly endows the father with a touch of decency, but he is exiled by the "Manager of the Performance" to Coventry Island where he dies of yellow fever "most deeply beloved and deplored." Presumably the wastrel, separated from his son, dies in a position of duty. Or are readers to pity him for having been forced, by his financial situation, to accept the position at Coventry as a bribe from Lord Steyne? Thackeray is elusive; again, the suggestions of pathos are touched on so lightly that they hardly matter. The indifference itself is *Vanity Fair*'s reward. For all of his jocularity and beef-eating familiarity, the "Manager of the Performance" sets a dark stage. *Vanity Fair* is colorful enough: the excitement at Brussels over Waterloo, the gardens at Vauxhall, the Rhine journey; but it is a panoply of meretricious and wasteful human endeavor. Readers really do not need Thackeray's moralizing to convince them of the shabbiness of it all.

Astonishing is the fact that, despite the novel's cynicism, it also has immense vitality. Readers sense the very essence of worldliness in its pages. It is difficult to deny the attractiveness of *Vanity Fair*. John Bunyan made that perfectly clear in *The Pilgrim's Progress* (1678), and Thackeray simply updates the vision. What was allegory in Bunyan becomes realism in Thackeray; the modern writer's objectivity in no way detracts from the alluring effect achieved by Bunyan's imaginary Vanity Fair. Bunyan still operates in the Renaissance tradition of Spenserian façade; evil traps man through illusion, as exemplified in the trials of the Knight of the Red Crosse. Thackeray drops the metaphor of illusion and shows corruption bared—and still it is attractive.

Becky Sharp is described as "worldliness incarnate" by Louis Kronenberger, but the reader cannot deny her charms. Thackeray calls his book "A Novel Without a Hero," but readers and Thackeray know better. Becky's pluck and ambition are extraordinary; her triumph is even more impressive because of the formidable barriers of class and poverty she has to scale. When she throws the Johnson dictionary out of the coach window as she leaves Miss Pinkerton's academy, readers are thrilled by her refusal to be patronized; her destructive and cruel manipulations of the Crawleys have all the implications of a revolutionary act. Thackeray actually emphasizes Becky's spirit and power by making virtuous Amelia weak and sentimental. Although readers are tempted to see this as a contradiction of Thackeray's moral intention, they must remember that he understood very clearly that true goodness must be built on strength: "Clumsy Dobbin" is Thackeray's somewhat sentimental example of this point. The human tragedy is that most men and women cannot reconcile their energies with their ideals and that in a fallen world of social injustices, people must all sin in order to survive. It is ironic that precisely because Becky Sharp is such an energetic opportunist, readers almost believe her when she says, "I think I could have been a good woman if I had 5000 a year."

"Critical Evaluation" by Peter A. Brier

Bibliography:
Bloom, Harold, ed. *William Makepeace Thackeray*. New York: Chelsea House, 1987. Contemporary critical anthology brings together essays on Thackeray's main novels. Excellent starting place for discussion of Thackeray's major works.
Harden, Edgar F. *The Emergence of Thackeray's Serial Fiction*. Athens: University of Georgia Press, 1979. Discussion of the serial structure of five novels, including *Vanity Fair,* with

focus upon the manuscripts and process of composition as the novels evolved. Explains how the fact that the novel was written in serial installments shaped its form.

Ray, Gordon N. "Thackeray: 'The Newcomes.'" In *The Age of Wisdom (1847-1864)*. New York: McGraw-Hill, 1958. The authoritative biography of Thackeray, authorized by the Thackeray family. The two volume set contains an in-depth study of Thackeray as well as an excellent study of the novel.

Sundell, M. G., ed. *Twentieth Century Interpretations of "Vanity Fair."* Englewood Cliffs, N.J.: Prentice-Hall, 1969. Comprehensive collection of six essays on such topics as characters, form, theme, and content. Eight short viewpoints give concise focus to various elements of the novel.

Tillotson, Kathleen. "Vanity Fair." In *Thackeray: A Collection of Critical Essays*, edited by Alexander Welsh. Englewood Cliffs, N.J.: Prentice-Hall, 1968. Discusses Thackeray's plan and purpose. The book contains two other excellent essays: "On the Style of *Vanity Fair*" by G. A. Craig and "Neoclassical Conventions" by John Loofbourow.

VATHEK
An Arabian Tale

Type of work: Novel
Author: William Beckford (1760-1844)
Type of plot: Gothic
Time of plot: The past
Locale: Arabia
First published: English translation, 1786; original French edition, 1787 as *Vathek*

Principal characters:
VATHEK, an Arabian sultan
THE GIAOUR, a magician and a prince of darkness
CARATHIS, Vathek's mother
EMIR FAKREDDIN, a noble prince
NOURONIHAR, his daughter
GULCHENROUZ, her betrothed

The Story:

Vathek was an Arabian caliph whose reign had been marked by turbulence and unrest. A sensuous person, he had built five palaces, each devoted to the enjoyment of one of the five senses, and his fondness for food and women consumed much of his time. In addition to the gratification he found in the life of the senses, he also tried to master the sciences and the deep, unfathomable secrets of the world beyond. To this end, he built a huge tower where he pursued his studies in astronomy and astrology. There Carathis, his mother, burnt refuse and live bodies to appease the dark powers.

One day, Vathek obtained several mysterious sabers from a hideous, repulsive stranger. These sabers bore letters the caliph was unable to decipher. He offered great rewards to anyone who could read them; but because the punishment for failure was also great, few accepted the offer. At last, an old man appeared and read the inscriptions. The next morning, however, Vathek discovered that the inscriptions had changed. From that time on, the letters on the sabers changed daily.

Vathek was in despair. He begged the stranger to return and explain the inscription to him, for he was sure that the letters were the key to the dark kingdom and the riches Vathek hoped to find there. The stranger, who was the Giaour, finally reappeared and told Vathek that only a sacrifice would put the powers in a receptive mood. On a journey with his court, Vathek threw fifty young children into a chasm as a sacrifice for the bloodthirsty Giaour. The people were angered by his cruelty and began to hurl execrations at Vathek, but his guards returned him safely to his palace.

Carathis continued her own sacrifices in the tower, to the disgust and anger of the people, who increasingly objected to Vathek's defiance of Mahomet and the Muslim creed. Obeying a message written on a mysterious piece of parchment, Vathek and his court set out on a pilgrimage in search of the mountains of Istakhar, where the secrets of the dark world were to be revealed to him. On the way, they met the messengers of Emir Fakreddin, a deeply religious prince. For some time, Vathek was Fakreddin's guest. Although he loathed the prayers and religious ceremonies observed by his host, he was attracted to Fakreddin's daughter, the lovely Nouronihar. She had long been betrothed to her cousin Gulchenrouz, and their mutual devotion had the approval of the emir and his people.

Nouronihar so attracted Vathek that he plotted to seize her by force. Fakreddin, already scandalized by Vathek's behavior, was informed of the plot. He and his court determined to outwit Vathek. He administered a drug to the young lovers, and when Vathek saw them in their deathlike trance, he was convinced they were dead. Nouronihar and Gulchenrouz were secretly taken to a safe retreat and looked after by Fakreddin's servants. When the young people awakened they believed that they had really died and that they were now in Paradise.

One day, however, Nouronihar strayed from the hidden retreat and was discovered by Vathek. She finally yielded to his entreaties and became the favorite of his harem. After Vathek and his wives and followers continued their journey, Nouronihar came to share her lord's ambition; she, too, wished to enjoy the pleasures of that strange other world and, like Vathek, she was willing to resort to the most unscrupulous behavior to realize those desires.

At last, after a long journey, the entourage arrived at the mountains of Istakhar and entered the secret retreat of Eblis, dread lord of darkness. There they found all the beautiful and strange wealth they had desired. They were given permission to roam through the palace and to enjoy its treasures to their hearts' content. In the vast domed hall of the palace, they saw creatures whose hearts were continually devoured by fire, and they learned that a like fate was to be theirs, for they had sought knowledge that no mortal should know.

Carathis had also been summoned to the abode of Eblis. Transported on the back of an evil monster, she came at once to the mysterious palace and was overjoyed to view its secrets at last. Then, before the eyes of Vathek and Nouronihar, her heart caught fire and a consuming flame burst forth to punish her eternally for her crimes. A moment later, flames began to burn in the hearts of Vathek and Nouronihar. The fifty children whom Vathek had sacrificed were miraculously returned from death and, along with Gulchenrouz, carried to an earthly paradise. For them, life was perpetual happiness. Not having sought evil, they achieved goodness.

Critical Evaluation:

William Beckford's *Vathek* is usually classified as a gothic novel, and it does indeed contain many of the same elements as the gothic novels more typically set in Europe, including a defiant and charismatic villain, a submerged but obsessive interest in perverse sexuality, and a diabolical bargain that ultimately leads to damnation. *Vathek* is, however, a highly idiosyncratic example of the gothic genre, not only in the overblown exoticism of its Oriental setting but also in its near-comedic grotesquerie. As if the text's inherent eccentricities were not enough, the familiar English version of it is an unauthorized translation of an unpublished manuscript of Beckford's text, which he had written in French, by a clergyman named Samuel Henley. Beckford seems to have disapproved of the translation beyond the fact that it preceded publication of his original version.

The most obvious debt *Vathek* owes is to *The Arabian Nights' Entertainments* (fifteenth century), which had been translated into French by Antoine Galland 1704-1717. A more direct influence, however, was Voltaire, whom Beckford met in Paris in 1777, the year before Voltaire's death. Voltaire had borrowed materials from Galland to construct a series of extended satirical works he called *contes philosophiques* (philosophical tales); these included *Zadig* (1732) and *The Princess of Babylon* (1768), as well as *Candide* (1759). It was probably the rumor that Voltaire had composed *Candide* at a single sitting that prompted Beckford to boast (falsely, according to his biographers) that he had written *Vathek* in a single session of something less than seventy-two hours.

If *Vathek* was intended to be a *conte philosophique*, it is a peculiar example. Such tales are supposed to have clear and explicit morals, though philosophical reasoning often proceeds doggedly to dreadful inconclusiveness. As *Candide* demonstrates—the philosophical tale can be more a powerful devastator of hopeful systems than a supporter of them. Voltaire, however, subjected his corrosive skepticism, mocking sarcasm, and phantasmagorical imagination to a strict discipline, whereas Beckford plainly saw no reason not to give free rein to imagination, which is what he allows his character Vathek to do. Five years before the publication of the first of the Marquis de Sade's elaborately extended *conte philosophique*—which proposes that morality is an arbitrary and hollow sham, and that nothing in nature can deny the powerful the right to indulge to the full in perverse pleasures—Beckford's Caliph Vathek had gone forth in search of similar extremes.

That great figure of diabolical bargains, Doctor Faust, had bargained with the devil for enlightenment, pleasure, and profit, but Vathek desires what is beyond mere pleasure and profit, some final and absolute evil. The dreadful fate that claims him at the end is not the kind of trivial damnation that was later to claim such gothic villains as Matthew Gregory Lewis' monk. Instead, Beckford devises the awful revelation that the archfiend Eblis has no absolute to offer. Vathek's hell is the realization that his boundless desires must remain forever unsatisfied. One of the great triumphs of the text is the image that encapsulates this fate: the limited hellfire that cages but never consumes the heart. This fire does not merely singe the flesh and rack the body with pain; it is a metaphysical flame that leaves all the yearnings of the flesh intact while mocking all ambition, emotion, and enlightenment. The image of the eternally burning heart remained unsurpassed throughout the subsequent centuries when legions of writers delved in search of the ultimate horror.

William Beckford inherited an immense fortune from his erratic father, which included the neo-Gothic monstrosity of Fonthill Abbey, which was repeatedly burnt to the ground and rebuilt at vast expense and ever greater expansiveness. Beckford turned the abbey into a fabulous palace, fully equipped for the contemplation of absolutes. The life he led there was rumored to be debauched, at least in its latter phases. Certainly he was well-placed to dream of such desires as those that consumed Vathek.

Beckford seems to bow to conventional morality in his novel's last paragraph, in which he describes the fate of "the humble and despised Gulchenrouz" as that of passing "whole ages in the undisturbed tranquillity and the pure happiness of childhood." He must have known (through Galland if not otherwise) that the paradise promised by the Qur'an to the faithful followers of Allah bears no more resemblance to this imagined fate than do orthodox visions of hell to the novel's Halls of Eblis. It can be assumed that, as a loyal follower of Voltaire, Beckford meant his concluding observation sarcastically, and that he intended to imply that paradise is a place fit only for children, bliss fit only for the ignorant, and peace fit only for the mindless. The final irony of Vathek's paradoxical damnation is that there is no alternative that anyone blessed with freedom of desire could possibly want. That conclusion entitles *Vathek* to be considered an authentic *conte philosophique*, for it represents a braver display of authentic horrors than all the gothic novels that trailed in its wake.

Brian Stableford

Bibliography:
Alexander, Boyd. *England's Wealthiest Son: A Study of William Beckford*. London: Centaur Press, 1962. Includes chapters on the origins of *Vathek* and its connection with the three supplemental episodes that Beckford wrote in the 1820's, which did not appear in print until 1912.

Day, William Patrick. *In the Circles of Fear and Desire: A Study of Gothic Fantasy*. Chicago: University of Chicago Press, 1985. One of many studies of gothic fiction that include a discussion of *Vathek*. Links the work to the "apocalyptic vision" of literary modernism.

Frank, Frederick. "*Vathek: An Arabian Tale*." In *Survey of Modern Fantasy Literature*, edited by Frank N. Magill. Englewood Cliffs, N.J.: Salem Press, 1983. A useful essay on the work, which draws interesting comparisons between *Vathek* and the works of Edgar Allan Poe.

Mahmoud, Fatma Moussa, ed. *William Beckford of Fonthill 1760-1844: Bicentenary Essays*. Port Washington, N.Y.: Kennikat Press, 1972. Includes Mahmoud's essay, "Beckford, *Vathek* and the Oriental Tale," which offers a comprehensive analysis of *Vathek*, and Mahmoud Manzalaoui's "Pseudo-Orientalism in Transition· The Age of *Vathek*," a useful account of the work's literary-historical context.

Varma, Devendra P. "William Beckford." In *Supernatural Fiction Writers: Fantasy and Horror*, edited by Everett F. Bleiler. New York: Scribner's, 1985. A brief essay that provides information and interesting speculations about the origins of *Vathek* and its connections to Beckford's own life.

VENICE PRESERVED
Or, A Plot Discovered

Type of work: Drama
Author: Thomas Otway (1652-1685)
Type of plot: Tragedy
Time of plot: Renaissance
Locale: Venice
First performed: 1682; first published, 1682

Principal characters:
JAFFEIR, a young Venetian, formerly Priuli's servant
PRIULI, Jaffeir's father-in-law, a senator
BELVIDERA, Priuli's daughter and Jaffeir's wife
PIERRE, the friend and fellow conspirator of Jaffeir
RENAULT, another conspirator
ANTONIO, a senator
AQUILINA, a courtesan

The Story:

Jaffeir, formerly the servant of Priuli, a senator of Venice, had secretly wooed and married Belvidera, Priuli's daughter. For three years the couple lived comfortably and blissfully, despite the father's antagonism; then Jaffeir lost his fortune. When he went to ask Priuli for aid, in the name of Belvidera, the old senator refused to help in any way, and he swore that his ungrateful daughter and her equally ungrateful husband would have to make their way as best they could. Jaffeir, after reminding Priuli that it was he who had saved Belvidera from a shipwreck after which she had fallen in love with him, left the senator's home in a most unhappy frame of mind.

Soon afterward Jaffeir met Pierre, a friend who had given long and faithful, though unrewarded, service to Venice. Pierre, sympathizing with Jaffeir, offered him the means of getting revenge on Priuli and striking, as he put it, a blow for liberty against the bad government of the senate. Jaffeir agreed to meet Pierre that night and to become a member of the band of conspirators. When he arrived home, Jaffeir was also comforted by Belvidera, who claimed that she was rich as long as she had his love, no matter how little fortune they possessed.

Meanwhile Pierre had gone to visit Aquilina, a courtesan whom he loved. He was extremely incensed with the woman because she had given herself for money to old Antonio, a senator. Antonio's theft of his mistress made Pierre more eager than ever for revenge. He made Aquilina, who loved him, swear to extract all the information she could from Antonio and pass it on to the conspirators, who were meeting that night in Aquilina's house.

When midnight came, Jaffeir was sadly bewailing his fate on the Rialto. There Pierre met him and conducted him to the conspirators' meeting place. Because the plotters were unwilling to take Jaffeir into their number, he brought Belvidera and offered her as hostage for his honesty. The leader of the plotters, Renault, and the Spanish ambassador, who also had a hand in the plot to ruin the government, accepted her as hostage. She was to be killed if Jaffeir failed them in any way.

The next day Jaffeir's hopes for revenge and his confidence in his fellow conspirators were shaken when he learned that Renault had offered violence to Belvidera and had been driven off only by her screams. Belvidera swore that she would bear anything, if only she knew why she had been offered as a hostage. Jaffeir, seeing her predicament, and thinking it only fair that she know the truth, revealed the plot to assassinate the senate and take over the city. Because the mass assassination would include her father, Belvidera, greatly shocked, tried to convince her husband that terrible wrongs would be committed against innocent people in the mass slaughter that was planned.

In the evening, the conspirators met to complete plans for the uprising, which was to take place that same night. At the meeting Jaffeir was seized with revulsion for the plot and the conspirators; he slipped away from the meeting and went to Belvidera. The two started toward the chamber where the senate council was meeting. On the way they were taken prisoners by the ducal guard and escorted to the council. To the senators and the duke Jaffeir admitted his part in the plot and prevailed on their fear to gain a general amnesty for his friends in exchange for information preventing the overthrow of the government. Within a matter of minutes, the other conspirators were brought in as prisoners. They, including Pierre, were furious with Jaffeir for revealing the plot. Pierre, refusing to listen to Jaffeir, much less to forgive him, slapped Jaffeir's face.

The senators, although they had given their word that the conspirators would be permitted to live, broke their promise and sentenced the prisoners, including Pierre, to death on the wheel. Jaffeir's rage knew no bounds when he learned of that perfidy. He offered to stab Belvidera, who had been pledged as hostage for his faithfulness to the plot. When his love prevented his actually killing her, he persuaded her to go to her father and seek his aid in rescuing the conspirators, lest her own life be forfeit for their deaths. Priuli, overcome at last by his love for his daughter, agreed to help Belvidera. His promise, however, was made too late.

When Jaffeir arrived at the scene of execution, he learned that all of the conspirators except Pierre had already been killed by the public executioner. Pierre had been saved until last because he had been granted a request to speak to Jaffeir. On the scaffold Pierre apologized for slapping Jaffeir's face and asked him a boon. Jaffeir readily assented and Pierre whispered to him. He asked that Jaffeir save him from an ignominious death by stabbing him instead. Jaffeir immediately complied and then turned his dagger into his own breast. He died within seconds of his friend.

Aquilina, hoping to save Pierre's life, had gone to seek the aid of Antonio. When the senator refused to help her, she stabbed him and left him to die. In the meantime Belvidera, overcome by her fears, had become distraught in her father's house. In spite of Priuli's efforts and those of his servants, she became steadily worse. She quickly went mad, even before she knew of her husband's death by his own hand; he had told her when she saw him last that they would never meet again. Before the messenger arrived to tell of Jaffeir's death, her husband's ghost appeared before her. Shortly after the messenger came and left, the ghosts of Jaffeir and Pierre appeared briefly. Following their appearance she went into a frenzy and died. Her father, sick of the bloodshed, plotting, and violent death, begged his attendants to take him away to a lonely place where the sun never shone, so that he might mourn in solitude and darkness the loss of his daughter and her unhappy fate.

Critical Evaluation:

Thomas Otway's career as a dramatist lasted only eight years (his first play, *Alcibiades*, was performed in 1675; his last, *The Atheist*, in 1683), but during that brief period he was able to establish himself as one of the leading playwrights of his day. *Venice Preserved* secured Otway a more lasting reputation. Acted 337 times during the eighteenth century, it continued to be popular during the nineteenth century and remains one of the more frequently anthologized plays from the period.

Otway lived and wrote during the turbulent reign of Charles II (1600-1685). A popular but troubled monarch, Charles was plagued by a long series of political crises. One such crisis, known as the Popish Plot, involved an alleged attempt by the Catholic church to overthrow the English government. Though a hoax, the Popish Plot played on deep-seated national fears, inciting considerable furor and helping bring to a head the long-standing conflict between the king's supporters (the Tory party) and his opponents (the Whig party). Otway's loyalty lay staunchly with the king, and *Venice Preserved*, his best-known play, with its portrait of a Venice racked by political strife and double-dealing, can be seen in part as a celebration of Charles's political victory over the Whig opposition.

How appreciative the initial audience of *Venice Preserved* was of its political dimension is amply suggested by the extent of royal patronage: King Charles attended the play's third night (the profits of which traditionally went to the author), and two months later the king's brother, James, duke of York (later King James II), and James's wife, the duchess of York, attended special performances. The royal brothers no doubt took particular relish in the savage personal satire against their foremost political opponent, Anthony Ashley Cooper, first earl of Shaftesbury, portrayed by Otway in the characters of Antonio and Renault as a corrupt, debauched sensualist without moral or political principles. (Soundly defeated and in fear for his life, Shaftesbury had fled England several months before the play opened.) It is unlikely, however, that either Charles or James was able to discern any grander satirical scheme at work. Though clearly anti-Whig in its sentiments, *Venice Preserved* does not effectively "reduce" to a coherent political allegory, and no historical counterparts exist for the three lead characters, Jaffeir, Pierre, and Belvidera. In fact, except for the personal attack against Shaftesbury and a general parallel between the murky world of Venetian politics and the conspiracy-laden England of Otway's day, *Venice Preserved* can best be viewed not as a political satire at all but rather as an especially effective example of the serious Restoration drama known as "pathetic tragedy."

In pathetic tragedy, the playwright is most concerned with fashioning a dramatic vehicle that will arouse powerful emotions in his audience. Pity, not surprisingly, is the principal emotion targeted, and the elements of plot, character, and theme are arranged in ways that will help maximize an emotional response. In *The Orphan* (1680), Otway had already proved himself something of a master in this form, and *Venice Preserved*, with its loftier theme of the conflicts between love and honor, personal loyalty and public duty, set against the background of Europe's most notoriously decadent and corrupt city, was a hit with audiences, critics, and actors alike.

If one sets aside one's modern prejudices against overblown, bombastic melodrama, one can readily see what made *Venice Preserved* such a long-lived, popular entertainment. First, and perhaps most important, from an acting perspective, there is the play's "openness" to dramatic interpretations. The three lead roles (Jaffeir, Pierre, and Belvidera) permit a wide range of equally valid interpretive choices. Pierre, for example, has been variously portrayed as a heroic idealist and as a Machiavellian schemer, while one noted eighteenth century actress (Susanna Cibber) played Belvidera as delicate and passive, and another (the beautiful and gifted Sarah Siddons) made her the virtual center of the play. Against earlier interpretations of Jaffeir as a pathetic weakling, the great David Garrick offered an interpretation of Jaffeir marked by a violent and stormy nature. Important staging considerations also include the notorious "Nicky-Nacky" scenes between Aquilina and Antonio. They have been presented in some productions as almost farcical in tone and in others as sordid and repulsive. Rather than confront the problem of which presentation to choose, most eighteenth century acting companies simply cut out the scenes altogether. On a performance level, then, *Venice Preserved* is truly protean, open to any number of staging and interpretive possibilities.

This openness, taken together with the play's obvious "pathetic" objectives, creates problems for the critic who would like to treat *Venice Preserved* principally as a literary text. Even the major elements of character and theme are difficult to interpret. Any reasonable analysis, for example, must take Jaffeir as the play's central character—his two decisions, after all, first to join the conspiracy and second to betray it, provide what little plot there is. Neither decision, however, seems either intelligently or nobly motivated. He joins the conspirators mainly to seek revenge against his father-in-law for denying him financial assistance and then betrays them to the Venetian senate after one of the conspiracy leaders sexually assaults his wife. Both moves are dramatically plausible, of course, but neither seems likely to increase Jaffeir's heroic stature. The disaster that ensues therefore seems thematically opaque. The conclusions one can legitimately draw from Jaffeir's plight are that it is bad to join conspiracies but even worse to betray them. Even Jaffeir's one arguably authentic heroic act—killing Pierre and then turning the dagger upon himself—though undoubtedly impressive theater, seems in retrospect to suggest pathetic desperation more than heroic defiance.

Equally problematic is Otway's portrayal of the Venetian senate and the conspirators who plot against it. The senators are venal and unscrupulous; the conspirators, with the exception of Pierre, are no better. Certainly Otway means to place Jaffeir within a classic "double-bind" situation, caught between what appear to be equally compelling demands (friendship and loyalty to one's country). When the choice is between two evils, however, rather than two "goods," one is led inevitably to question the hero's intelligence rather than to admire his heroism. Perhaps, as several critics have suggested, Otway's ultimate intention is to reveal not humanity's potential nobility but its tragic inadequacy.

"Critical Evaluation" by Michael Stuprich

Bibliography:
Brown, Laura. *English Dramatic Form, 1660-1760: An Essay in Generic History.* New Haven, Conn.: Yale University Press, 1981. An interesting discussion, within the context of "affective" tragedy, of Otway's two best-known plays, *The Orphan* and *Venice Preserved.*

Kelsall, Malcolm. Introduction to *Venice Preserved,* edited by Malcolm Kelsall. Lincoln: University of Nebraska Press, 1969. Kelsall's is the best modern edition of *Venice Preserved.* His introduction is first-rate in its discussion of Otway's main source, the many problems attendant upon viewing the play as a political satire, and its long life on the English stage.

Milhous, Judith, and Robert D. Hume. *Producible Interpretation: Eight English Plays, 1675-1707.* Carbondale: Southern Illinois University Press, 1985. Highly recommended for anyone interested in Restoration drama. The chapter on *Venice Preserved* provides a lucid and interesting introduction to the play, as well as a fascinating history of the many different stagings Otway's play received over the course of the eighteenth and nineteenth centuries.

Stroup, Thomas B. "Otway's Bitter Pessimism." In *Essays in English Literature of the Classical Period Presented to Dougald MacMillan.* Chapel Hill: University of North Carolina Press, 1967. A classic general study of Otway. Stroup sees all of Otway's dramatic works as cynical and frustrating and finds *Venice Preserved* to be a moral chaos marked by "broken oaths and curses."

Taylor, Aline MacKenzie. *Next to Shakespeare: Otway's "Venice Preserv'd" and "The Orphan" and Their History on the London Stage.* New York: AMS Press, 1966. Though originally published in 1950, this remains the most exhaustive and most reliable account of *Venice Preserved* and its stage history.

VENUS AND ADONIS

Type of work: Poetry
Author: William Shakespeare (1564-1616)
Type of plot: Erotic
Time of plot: Antiquity
Locale: Greece
First published: 1593

> *Principal characters:*
> VENUS, goddess of love
> ADONIS, a handsome youth loved by Venus

The Story:

In all the world there was no more beautiful figure, no more perfectly made creature, than young Adonis. Although his beauty was a delight to the sun and to the winds, he had no interest in love. His only joy was in hunting and riding over the hills and fields after the deer and the fox. When Venus, the goddess of love, saw the beauty of young Adonis, she came down to Earth because she was filled with love for him.

Meeting him one morning in the fields as he rode out to the hunt, she urged him to dismount, tie his horse to a tree, and talk with her. Adonis had no desire to talk to any woman, even the goddess, but she forced him to do as she wished. Reclining by his side, she looked at him with caressing glances and talked passionately of the wonder and glory of love. The more she talked, the more she begged him for a kind look, a kiss, the more anxious he became to leave her and go on with his hunting. Venus was not easily repulsed, however, she told him how even the god of war had been a willing prisoner of her charms. She numbered all the pleasures she could offer him if he would accept her love. Blushing, Adonis finally broke from her arms and went to get his horse.

At that moment, his stallion heard the call of a jennet in a field nearby. Aroused, he broke the leather thong that held him and galloped to her. At first the jennet pretended to be cold to the stallion's advances, but when she perceived that Adonis was about to overtake his mount, she gave a neigh of affection and the two horses galloped away to another field. Adonis was left behind.

Dejected, he stood thinking of the hunt that he was missing because his horse had run away. Venus came up to him again and continued her pleas of love. For a while he listened to her, but in disgust he turned finally and gave her such a look of scorn that the lovesick goddess fainted and fell to the ground. Thinking he had killed her with his unkind look, Adonis knelt beside her, rubbed her wrists, and kissed her in hope of forgiveness. Venus, recovering from her swoon, asked him for one last kiss. He grudgingly consented before turning to leave. When Venus asked when they could meet the next day, Adonis replied that he would not see her, for he was to go boar hunting. Struck with a vision, the goddess warned the youth that he would be killed by a boar if he hunted the next day, and she begged him to meet her instead. She threw herself on the boy and carried him to the earth in her arms in a last attempt to gain his love, Adonis admonished the goddess on the difference between heavenly love and earthly lust. He left her alone and weeping.

The next morning found Venus wandering through the woods in search of Adonis. In the distance, she could hear the noise of the dogs and the voices of the hunters. Frantic because of her vision of the dead Adonis, she rushed through the forest trying to follow the sounds of the hunt. When she saw a wounded and bleeding dog, the fear she felt for Adonis became almost overpowering. Suddenly she came upon Adonis lying dead, killed by the fierce wild boar he had hunted. Venus' grief knew no bounds. If this love were taken from her, then never again should man love happily. Where love was, there also would mistrust, fear, and grief be found.

The body of Adonis lay white and cold on the ground, his blood coloring the earth and plants about him. From this soil there grew a flower, white and purple like the blood that spotted his skin. With a broken heart, Venus left Earth to hide her sorrow in the dwelling place of the gods.

Critical Evaluation:

Venus and Adonis and *The Rape of Lucrece* (1594), two of William Shakespeare's most famous nondramatic works, were probably composed during the period between June, 1592, and May, 1594, while the theaters were temporarily closed because of the plague. *Venus and Adonis*, the earlier of the two poems, was entered at the Stationers' Register on April 18, 1593, and was printed shortly thereafter by Richard Field, who, incidentally, had originally come from Stratford-on-Avon. *Venus and Adonis* was the first work of Shakespeare ever to be printed.

It should not be supposed from the date of composition that *Venus and Adonis* was merely a way of passing time while the theaters were closed. All indications are that Shakespeare thought of this poem as the public commencement of his serious literary work as distinct from his quotidian employment as a dramatist. Indeed, Shakespeare never bothered to see his plays into print, a fact that has proved the bane of editors ever since. *Venus and Adonis*, however, was handsomely printed with an ornate dedication to the earl of Southampton in which Shakespeare speaks of the poem as his first serious literary effort. In subject and style, it is a kind of poetry that occupied most of Shakespeare's serious contemporaries.

Although the poem has been transmitted in only a few manuscripts, there is ample evidence that it was extremely popular in its own day. By 1600, it had become one of the most frequently quoted poems of the period, and many of Shakespeare's contemporaries referred to it with admiration. Even Gabriel Harvey, fellow of Cambridge and stern arbiter of critical taste, noted the great fame that the poem enjoyed among undergraduates, although he did add reservations about the erotic nature of the poem. In that eroticism, *Venus and Adonis* reflected a vogue for such poetry, which appeared in profusion in the 1590's. Like Shakespeare's, these narrative or reflective poems generally drew on classical or pseudoclassical sources.

Shakespeare derived the story of *Venus and Adonis* from Ovid's *Metamorphoses* (before 8 B.C.E.), the main difference being that in his poem Adonis becomes a coy and reluctant lover. This variation may be the result of accidental or intentional conflation of the tale with Ovid's story of Hermaphroditus and Salmacis or that of Narcissus. It could also be the result of the influence of stories in book 3 of Edmund Spenser's *Faerie Queene* (1590), in Thomas Lodge's *Scyllae's Metamorphosis* (1589), or in Christopher Marlowe's *Hero and Leander* (1598). In any case, the change brings it in line with other late sixteenth century poems that stress male beauty. Regardless of the source, the substance of the poem is almost entirely conventional.

The few original additions that Shakespeare seems to have made—the digressive episode of the jennet and the stallion and the descriptions of the hunting of the fox and the hare, for example—are notable more for the conventional beauty of their style than for their narrative power. The entire poem is, in fact, an excellent example of stylistic decoration, an ornate work for a sophisticated audience more interested in execution than originality. The poetry is on the surface, in the ingenious handling of commonplaces and in brilliant flourishes of image and phrase.

Virtually nothing happens in the poem. The bulk of it is taken up with the amorous arguments of Venus interspersed with objections from Adonis. There is no forward movement, merely a debate that results in no conclusion. The characters do not develop; they simply are what they are and speak in accord with their stylized roles. The plot does not move from event to event by means of internal causality. Indeed, the only movement, that from the debate to the final scene in which Venus comes upon Adonis' body, is occasioned more by the emotional necessities of the poem than by demands of plot.

It is tempting to see the poem, especially the debate, as a moral allegory in which Adonis represents rational control over sensual excess, while Venus represents not only passion but also the enduring love that can triumph over mutability. It is hard, however, to support this interpretation very far. Neither view prevails and the interdeterminacy suggests that the allegory is merely another ornament, not the heart of the poem. Moreover, the tone of the speeches and the tone of the narrator's commentary do not support moral earnestness. The many puns and erotic innuendos provide a suave distance, true both to Ovid and to Elizabethan taste.

The poem is a compendium of the themes that recurred in the amatory poems and sonnet sequences of the age. The arguments proposed by Venus, for example, are familiar appeals to the desire for immortality. *Carpe diem* is prominent, as is the appeal to survival through procreation, and both are themes that Shakespeare exploited in his sonnets. Similarly, Adonis' rationalistic view of sex is reminiscent of Shakespeare's Sonnet 129 and many poems by Philip Sidney.

The poem is also a storehouse of the rhetorical figures and imagistic techniques of Elizabethan lyric style. Balance and antithesis, alliteration and assonance, produce a pleasing aural effect not so much to underline the meaning as to call attention to their own beauty. The imagery is sharply and brilliantly visual with bright reds and whites being the dominant, and highly conventional, colors. Images are there to embellish, not to explain, and even Adonis' fatal wound is gorgeous. The six-line stanza provides a supple medium for the gentle rhythms and sound patterns. The whole is an elegantly decorated blend of common themes into a pathetic-ironic showpiece.

"Critical Evaluation" by Edward E. Foster

Bibliography:

Beauregard, David N. "*Venus and Adonis*." In *Shakespeare Studies*. Vol 8. Edited by J. Leeds Barroll. New York: Burt Franklin, 1975. Considers critical studies of the story that range from classical interpretations of the original myth to twentieth century analyses of Shakespeare's poem.

Bullough, Geoffrey, ed. *Narrative and Dramatic Sources of Shakespeare*. New York: Columbia University Press, 1966. Part of a six-volume series of critical essays on the sources of Shakespeare's works. Included in the discussion of *Venus and Adonis* is a 1575 translation of Ovid's *Metamorphoses* by Arthur Golding.

Jahn, J. D. "The Lamb of Lust: The Role of Adonis in Shakespeare's *Venus and Adonis*." In *Shakespeare Studies*. Vol. 6. Edited by J. Leeds Barroll. Dubuque, Iowa: William C. Brown, 1970. An intense study of the personality of Adonis that Shakespeare creates in his poem.

Muir, Kenneth. "*Venus and Adonis*: Comedy or Tragedy?" In *Shakespearean Essays*. Vol 2. Edited by Alwin Thaler and Norman Sanders. Knoxville: University of Tennessee Press, 1974. Considers the way in which the myth of Venus and Adonis has been interpreted by various authors and how Shakespeare's own audience might have interpreted the poem.

Prince, Frank Templeton. Introduction to *The Poems*, by William Shakespeare. London: Routledge, 1990. Provides more than forty pages of introductory material, in which Prince discusses the text and provides critical interpretations of the works. Also includes appendixes with information about the sources of the Shakespeare's poems, with particular emphasis on *Venus and Adonis*.

THE VICAR OF WAKEFIELD

Type of work: Novel
Author: Oliver Goldsmith (1728 or 1730-1774)
Type of plot: Domestic realism
Time of plot: Eighteenth century
Locale: Rural England
First published: 1766

> *Principal characters:*
> DR. PRIMROSE, the vicar of Wakefield
> DEBORAH, his wife
> GEORGE, the oldest son
> SOPHIA, the younger daughter
> OLIVIA, the older daughter
> MR. BURCHELL, in reality, Sir William Thornhill
> SQUIRE THORNHILL, Dr. Primrose's landlord and Olivia's betrayer
> ARABELLA WILMOT, George's fiancée

The Story:

Dr. Primrose and his wife, Deborah, were blessed with five fine children. The two daughters, Olivia and Sophia, were remarkable for their beauty. The Primrose family lived in a quiet rural community, where they enjoyed both wealth and good reputation. The oldest son, George, fell in love with Arabella Wilmot, the daughter of a neighbor, and the two families made mutual preparations for the wedding. Before the wedding, however, Dr. Primrose and Miss Wilmot's father quarreled over the question of a man's remarrying after the death of his wife. Dr. Primrose stoutly upheld the doctrine of absolute monogamy. Mr. Wilmot, who was about to take his fourth wife, was insulted. The rift between the two families widened when news came that Dr. Primrose's broker had run off with all of his money. Mr. Wilmot broke off the wedding plans, for the vicar was now a poor man.

George departed for London to make his fortune, and the rest of the family prepared to go to another part of the country, where Dr. Primrose had found a more modest living. On the way, they met a man who won the admiration of Dr. Primrose by a deed of charity to a fellow traveler. The man, Mr. Burchell, rode along with them. Suddenly, Sophia was thrown from her horse into a stream, from which Mr. Burchell was able to save her. The gratitude of Deborah assured Mr. Burchell of a warm welcome whenever he should choose to call on them.

Their new home was on the estate of wealthy Squire Thornhill, a young man known for his attentions to all the young ladies in the neighborhood. Deborah thought that either of her daughters would make a good match for the young squire. Soon afterward, a fortunate meeting drew the squire's attention toward Olivia, and her mother's scheming made Squire Thornhill a steady caller at the Primrose home, where Olivia blushingly protested that she thought him both bold and rude. Mr. Burchell also called frequently, but his interest seemed to center upon Sophia, who did not deny her pleasure at his attention. Dr. Primrose, however, could not approve of Mr. Burchell, for he had lost all of his fortune and seemed to live in relative poverty, which revealed an indifference to his fallen condition.

Two noble ladies from the city met the Primrose family in their rustic retreat, and Sophia and Olivia became charmed by talk of city ways. When the women spoke of their need for companions in their households, Deborah immediately suggested that Olivia and Sophia be selected. The two daughters were pleased at the thought of going to the city, despite Mr. Burchell's vigorous objections. All was set for the journey, however, when Deborah received a letter stating that a secret informant had so slandered Olivia and Sophia that the city ladies would not consider them as fit companions. At first, Deborah and her husband could not imagine who the slanderer could have been. When they learned that Mr. Burchell had been the informant, Dr. Primrose ordered him from the house. Mr. Burchell left with no signs of remorse or shame.

Olivia began to insist that Squire Thornhill's repeated visits meant only that he intended to marry her. Dr. Primrose did not believe that the squire really would marry Olivia and suggested to his daughter that she consider the offer of a neighboring farmer, Mr. Williams. When the squire still failed to ask for her hand, Olivia agreed to marry the young farmer, and the wedding date was set. Four days before her wedding, Olivia ran away. With the help of Squire Thornhill, Dr. Primrose learned that it was Mr. Burchell who had carried the girl away.

Saddened by his daughter's indiscretion, the resolute father set out to find her and to help her. On his journey, he became ill and lay in bed in an inn for three weeks. On his recovery, he gave up all hope of finding Olivia and started home. On the way, he met Miss Arabella Wilmot, who inquired about George. Dr. Primrose assured her that George had not been heard from since he had left his family to go to London. Squire Thornhill, who was courting Arabella, asked about Olivia, but the father could give him no news. Fortune brought George, impoverished and in ill luck, back to his father at that time. Pitying the bad fortune of the young boy, Squire Thornhill gave him a commission in the army and sent him away. Arabella promised to wait for her former sweetheart to make his fortune and to return to her.

Dr. Primrose started for home once more. At a roadside inn, he found his dear Olivia, who told him her terrible story. The villain with whom she had run away was not Mr. Burchell. It had been Squire Thornhill, who had seduced her after a mock ceremony by a false priest. The squire had then grown tired of her and had left her. Dr. Primrose took the girl home with him. Bad luck, however, had not forsaken the vicar. As he approached his house, he saw it catch fire and burn to the ground. His family escaped, but all of their belongings were destroyed.

Kindly neighbors helped the penniless Primroses to set up living quarters in an outbuilding on the estate. News came that Squire Thornhill intended to marry Arabella Wilmot. This report angered Dr. Primrose; then to add to his indignation, Squire Thornhill came to see him and offered to find a husband for Olivia so that she could stay near the squire. The doctor was enraged at this offer and ordered him away. The squire then demanded Dr. Primrose's quarterly rent payment which, since the disaster of losing his home, the vicar could not pay.

Squire Thornhill had Dr. Primrose sent to debtors' prison. Soon after being lodged in prison, the vicar encountered his son, George, who, having learned of the squire's cruelty, had attacked him and had been sentenced to hang for attempted murder. Dr. Primrose felt that the happiness of his life was completely shattered. Next, he learned that Sophia had been kidnapped.

Nevertheless, virtue and honesty were soon rewarded. Sophia had been rescued by Mr. Burchell, who turned out to be the squire's uncle, Sir William Thornhill. With the squire's treachery exposed, the Primrose family was released from its misery. Arabella and George were reunited. Even Olivia was saved from shame, for she learned that the priest who had married her to the Squire had been a genuine priest. Sophia married Sir William, and Arabella married George. Dr. Primrose looked forward to his old age with happiness and joy in the good fortune of his children. In the end, even he was rewarded for his virtue. The broker who had run away with his money was apprehended, and Dr. Primrose was once again a wealthy man.

Critical Evaluation:

Two themes dominate Oliver Goldsmith's story of domestic tragedy and joy: The first is a satiric look at the insidious workings of vanity, even on such unpretentious people as Dr. Primrose and his family; the second is the instability of fortune, which ensures that happy people must expect disaster and miserable people may expect relief.

The first theme is the more significant. As the novel's narrator, Dr. Primrose portrays himself as a man committed to intellectual pursuits and charitable actions, one who rejects the world's vanities. His self-evaluation is not inaccurate. He has assigned his income to the relief of the poor (although he has done so unwisely, as he learns), and he has certainly committed himself to rarefied intellectual activities, although his subjects—specifically his promotion of a religious dogma of monogamy that disallows second marriages even on the death of one's spouse—are of only minor interest to the world.

What Dr. Primrose does not understand, however, is his own naïveté, and that blindness is the source of the novel's ironic humor. While Primrose tells his story through the filter of his own innocence, Goldsmith arranges that the reader will understand—or at least suspect—the things that Primrose ignores. This disparity between the narrator's limited vision and the reader's insight creates an ironic point of view that allows the reader to laugh at Dr. Primrose even while sympathizing with him.

The irony of Primrose's limited self-understanding colors much of what he does. He fails to imagine that his family might come to need the income he has signed over to charity. He fails to imagine that financial advisers might be dishonest. Most important, he fails to recognize the difference between the honest values of Mr. Burchell and the false values of the attractive Squire Thornhill and his flashy companions.

As a result of the vicar's limited understanding of the world, his responses to it are frequently wrong. They are often the result of his own vanity, particularly of his intellectual capabilities, which are not nearly so penetrating as he imagines. These limitations lead him to various errors. His intense commitment to the minor doctrine of monogamy leads him to offend his son George's future father-in-law and thus to spoil the prospects for his son's marriage. His reverence for the classics and the limitations of his ability in disputation lead him to confuse the flimflam of the deceitful Jenkinson for real learning, again with disastrous results for his family.

It would be wrong simply to dismiss Primrose as a fool, however, for Goldsmith underscores that Primrose's understanding may be limited, but his heart is golden. Primrose is quick to offer aid to those who need it; he is quick to forgive Olivia in her disgrace and devastated at the news of her death; he is genuinely devoted to his family and finds their presence enough to give him courage even in debtors' prison. Goldsmith never suggests that shrewdness is to be preferred to love as a value to live by.

Primrose's innocence and his vanities are shared by his family; they too mistake things that glitter for true gold. No one in the family seems able to see beyond the glamorous clothes and pretentious talk of the town ladies whom Thornhill brings to the house. No one recognizes the virtue of Burchell's offering unpopular opinions about the family's actions. No one suspects that his damning letter might be interpreted as a condemnation of the town ladies rather than of the Primrose daughters. Olivia is quick to be attracted to Thornhill, even though she has every reason to believe in his reputation as a rake.

Olivia's situation demands closer examination. Her elopement with Thornhill on his false promises of marriage, his betrayal of her with what seems to be a fraudulent wedding ceremony, and her subsequent decline because of her shame—all are common elements of eighteenth and early nineteenth century fiction. Similar events occur in Samuel Richardson's *Pamela* (1740) and *Clarissa* (1747-1748), and in Jane Austen's *Pride and Prejudice* (1813). The values of the age demanded that respectable women be virgins when they married, and custom assumed that any woman who eloped surely had been involved in sexual relations with her partner. The rakehell young man who would go to any lengths to seduce women who attracted him—even arranging false marriages—is another conventional character in fiction of the period. Goldsmith never challenges these conventions; like the Primroses, he assumes that marriage, even to one who has proven himself to be a scoundrel, is a satisfactory solution to Olivia's disgrace.

The eighteenth century saw a vogue for sentimental fiction, and *The Vicar of Wakefield* is an example of that fashion. It is characterized by the idealized pictures of rural family life that appear throughout this novel, as well as in the pathos of the disasters that befall Primrose and his family. The family's lost income, the fire, the disgraced daughter, Primrose's unjust imprisonment, all exemplify the taste of the age for exercising one's tender emotions. Olivia's sad song, which asserts that "when lovely woman stoops to folly" the only fate appropriate to her is to die, offers another example of this sentimentality. That such fiction is not intended to be realistic can be seen from this novel's use of coincidences and disguise.

Through all the family's disasters, however, Dr. Primrose remains faithful in his belief that better things are surely in store for them all, just as he continues to assert that the loving presence of his family can make up for any losses. Along with its gentle humor, this theme must be the source of much of this novel's appeal. For all of their follies, the Primrose family clings to love as a main strength for enduring adversity, feeling certain that the fortunes of the miserable must surely rise if they only endure.

"Critical Evaluation" by Ann Davison Garbett

Bibliography:
Adelstein, Michael E. "Duality of Theme in *The Vicar of Wakefield.*" *College English* 22 (February, 1961): 315-321. Argues that Goldsmith changed his theme in the course of writing this novel, shifting from the theme of providence to that of fortitude, thus changing Dr. Primrose from an innocent simpleton to a resolute hero.
Church, Richard. *The Growth of the English Novel.* New York: Barnes & Noble Books, 1961. Analyzes the novel and sees its tone as characteristic of the national style, praising particularly the ease of his writing.
Dahl, Curtis. "Patterns of Disguise in *The Vicar of Wakefield.*" *English Literary History* 25 (June, 1958): 90-104. Dahl addresses the issue of the novel's coherence; its coincidence and improbabilities are counterbalanced, he asserts, by the unifying effects of the disguise theme. Characters disguise themselves both literally and figuratively and exhibit their growth by their ability to see through deceptions.
Jeffares, A. Norman. *Oliver Goldsmith.* London: Longmans, Green, 1965. Discusses how the novel's theme of Primrose's submission to adversity joins with Goldsmith's gentle irony, which emerges from the straight-faced style of the vicar-narrator. Notes the similarity between Goldsmith's vicar and Fielding's Parson Adams.
Phelps, Gilbert. *A Reader's Guide to Fifty British Novels, 1600-1900.* New York: Barnes & Noble Books, 1979. Offers a brief biography, a summary of the novel's plot, and a section of critical commentary. Faults the novel's proportions but praises its clarity of style.

VICTORY
An Island Tale

Type of work: Novel
Author: Joseph Conrad (Jósef Teodor Konrad Nałęcz Korzeniowski, 1857-1924)
Type of plot: Psychological realism
Time of plot: Early twentieth century
Locale: East Indies
First published: 1915

Principal characters:
AXEL HEYST, an idealist
LENA, a woman whom Axel befriends
MR. SCHOMBERG, a hotel owner
MR. JONES and
MARTIN RICARDO, gamblers
PEDRO, their servant
DAVIDSON, a sea captain
WANG, Heyst's servant

The Story:

After the Tropical Belt Coal Company went into liquidation, Axel Heyst continued to live at the No. 1 coaling station on Samburan. Strange in his manners and desires, he was a legend among the islanders; they called him a Utopist. The coal company had come into existence after Heyst had met an Englishman named Morrison in a Portuguese seaport, where the man was about to lose his trading ship, *Capricorn*, because of an unpaid debt. Heyst had been sympathetic and had offered him a loan. Because Heyst was anxious to keep his generosity a secret and Morrison eager to conceal his shaky finances, the two men pledged secrecy, with the understanding that Heyst would thereafter have a share of the *Capricorn*'s shipping business.

Schomberg, the owner of a hotel in Sourabaya, heard of the partnership and discovered that Heyst maintained some kind of hold over Morrison. Morrison established the coal company and then died in England. After that, Schomberg, who hated Heyst, constructed a mysterious kind of villainy around him and was gleeful when the coal company liquidated.

After Axel Heyst retired from the human society of the islands, Davidson, a ship's captain, came upon him living alone on Samburan. Worrying over Heyst's welfare, Davidson adopted the habit of sailing ten miles out of his way around the north side of Samburan in case Heyst were in need of aid. At one point, Davidson brought Heyst to Sourabaya, where he stayed at Schomberg's hotel. Later, Davidson heard bits of a story that Heyst had run off with a girl who was at the hotel with a troupe of entertainers. He was baffled that the shy, quiet Heyst would take a girl back to Samburan with him. Mrs. Schomberg had pitied the girl and had helped Heyst escape with her. The affair caused quite a bit of gossip on the island because it concerned Heyst.

When Heyst came to the hotel, he had been unaware of Schomberg's hatred. The entertainers were not very attractive to Heyst's fastidious mind, but one girl wearing white muslin seemed younger than the others. Noticing her distress at being ordered to join a guest at a table, Heyst was prompted by the same instinct that had led him to help Morrison. He invited the girl to sit with him. The girl, Lena, told Heyst about herself. Growing up in England, her father had taught her to play the violin. After his death, she had joined the group of entertainers with whom she now worked. Schomberg had been stalking her ever since the troupe had come to the hotel. The contrast between Heyst and the other men she had met was enough to cause the girl to be attracted to her new friend, and she welcomed his promise of help. After Heyst had taken Lena away, Schomberg's hatred was tremendous.

Three strangers then came to Schomberg's hotel: Mr. Jones, Martin Ricardo, and a beastlike, hairy creature whom they called Pedro. Before long, these men had transformed Schomberg's hotel into a professional gambling house. Schomberg's obsession for Lena was increased by his belief that, if he had her at his side, he could rid his hotel of the gamblers. One afternoon, Ricardo told Schomberg that he had been employed on a yacht where he was first attracted by Jones's polished manners. The two had stolen the captain's cash box and jumped the ship. Later, Pedro became attached to them. Schomberg decided that these thieves might leave his hotel if he could arouse their greed by the prospect of richer plunder. He offhandedly told the men of Heyst's alleged wealth and mentioned that Heyst lived on a lonely island with a girl and a hoard of money. Together, Ricardo and Schomberg began to plan their pillage of the island on which Heyst lived.

On his island, Heyst had lived with his Chinese servant, Wang, until Lena joined him. She told him that he had saved her from more than misery and despair. Heyst told her the story of his own background. His father had been a cynical, domineering man whom he disliked. After his death, Heyst had drifted, searching for some meaning in life, a meaning never glimpsed until he met Lena.

One evening, Wang announced that he had seen a boat drifting offshore; Heyst went to investigate. He discovered Ricardo, Jones, and the beastlike Pedro perishing of thirst in a boat moored beside a small jetty. Heyst helped the men to shore and took them to an abandoned bungalow for temporary quarters. That night, Heyst found that his gun was missing from his desk; Wang, frightened, had taken it. Meanwhile, Ricardo and Jones speculated about locating Heyst's money.

Early in the morning, Ricardo stole into Heyst's bungalow and saw Lena combing her hair. He jumped at her hungrily, but she was able to defend herself. When the struggle was over and the repulsed man saw that she raised no outcry, his admiration for her increased. She asked him what the men wanted on the island. Surprised that they had come for money which she knew Heyst did not possess, she was determined to protect Heyst from Schomberg's evil plan. She loved Heyst and knew she could repay his kindness by leading Ricardo and his partners on to their destruction.

Observing Ricardo's attack on Lena, Wang had decided to withdraw from this confusion of white people's affairs; he fled to the forest. When Heyst reported the loss of his servant to Jones and Ricardo, they offered him the service of Pedro. Because their manner made it impossible for him to refuse, Lena and Heyst knew that they were lost. Davidson would not sail past the island for three more weeks. Their only weapon had been stolen, and they were left defenseless. When Heyst mentioned their helpless position without any weapon of defense, Lena recalled that, during their scuffle, she had glimpsed the knife Ricardo wore under his trouser leg.

That night, Ricardo came to the bungalow for dinner with Heyst and Lena. During the evening, Ricardo indicated that Jones wanted Heyst to visit him. Before he left, Heyst insisted that Pedro be sent out of the way, and Ricardo ordered the brute to go down to the jetty. After Heyst had gone, Lena allowed Ricardo to make love to her so that she could take possession of his knife. Meanwhile, Heyst mentioned Lena's presence to Jones. Jones, who suffered a pathological hatred for women, had not even known of Lena's existence. Heyst convinced him that Schomberg had lied about the existence of a cache of money on the island to get rid of the gamblers and to inflict revenge upon Heyst, a revenge that Schomberg was too cowardly to inflict himself. Enraged by what he considered a conspiracy on the part of Ricardo and Schomberg, Jones suggested that they go to Heyst's bungalow.

Meanwhile, Lena had taken Ricardo's knife. As the two men entered the bungalow, Jones fired over Heyst's shoulder, and the bullet pierced Lena's breast. Ricardo sprang through the doorway. Jones followed his partner outside and shot him in the darkness. Heyst carried Lena to the bed, and, as she lay there, deathly pale in the candlelight, she demanded the knife, her symbol of victory. She died as Heyst took her in his arms, speaking, for the first time, words that came from the depths of his heart.

Critical Evaluation:

It is tempting but potentially incorrect to see *Victory* as a melodramatic morality play in which good battles evil and love wins in the end. For one thing, all the kind and compassionate characters are killed by story's end. If death is "the wages of sin," then Conrad seems to be suggesting that death is the wages of virtue and loyalty as well—hardly the makings of a very convincing morality play. Joseph Conrad is a master of relating ambiguous motives and moral choices. In other stories, such as *Heart of Darkness* (1899), *Lord Jim* (1900), *The Secret Agent* (1906), and *The Secret Sharer* (1910), the propriety of an action is all too often based on one's point of view, and Conrad's narrative techniques frequently make the moral parameters of an event very unclear.

In *Victory*, for example, much of Heyst's story is told by, or at least seen through, the eyes of Davidson. This distancing technique, whereby one slowly learns the truth of a story, makes it impossible to read *Victory* as a simple commentary on love, embodied in Lena and represented by the otherwise ineffectual Heyst. These two are present in a world that is dominated by scoundrels like Ricardo and Schomberg, brutes like Pedro, and unredeemably sinister figures like "plain Mr. Jones." A sentimental and allegorical reading will render meaning, but that meaning will not admit the moral complexities which Conrad has built into the novel through the characterization of his protagonist, Axel Heyst.

Those complexities are best represented in Heyst's relationship not so much with his father, as with his father's ideas. The younger Heyst has been "passing through life without suffering . . . invulnerable because elusive," having made himself strictly a spectator, an astute but aloof observer of the human scene. Surely, this is Conrad's Heyst, and, despite a critical tradition to the contrary, this Heyst is no Christ figure; if anything, he is more of an Antichrist, a person convinced after the fiasco of his involvement with Morrison that "all action is bound to be harmful . . . devilish. That is why this world is evil upon the whole." He will tell the stunned Davidson, who could never fathom the real reason behind Heyst's beliefs, "now I have done with observation, too."

When Conrad reveals how much the elder Heyst's ideas had shaped his son, his point becomes clear. Heyst's father had been "the most uneasy soul that civilization had ever fashioned to its ends of disillusion and regret . . . unhappy in a way unknown to mediocre souls," the narrator reveals early on, and Heyst himself will later confess to Lena, "after listening to him, I could not take my soul down into the street to fight there. I started off to wander about, an independent spectator — if that is possible." This is the very point Conrad is making; this isolated observation is not possible. So Heyst, self-described as "a man of universal scorn and unbelief," is, rather than a positive foil to Jones's evil, very much the same kind of character as Mr. Jones, for both imagine that there is no worthwhile human action. The only difference is, instead of taking advantage of people as Jones and his sort do, Heyst has removed himself from all human company, too scornful, disdainful, and disillusioned to be bothered—but too much a gentleman to say so.

It is no more possible, however, for Heyst to avoid the dilemma of making a moral choice than it is for anyone else, and it is not a melodramatic touch on Conrad's part, given the extent to which he has established and exposed Heyst's philosophical underpinnings, to present love as the force that draws Heyst not only out of his isolation but out of his inaction as well. That the choice ends tragically is hardly proof that Heyst's earlier detached cynicism was the more correct attitude. For the real lesson that he learns from the experience, as Davidson later reports, is "woe to the man whose heart has not learned while young to hope, to love — and to put its trust in life!" For Heyst, the tragedy is that he has learned this too late. Because this bold statement of the novel's theme comes at the end of Conrad's long process of meticulously working out the details of this philosophical and ethical struggle, he earns the right to be so bold.

Victory is not a melodrama, or a morality play, or a psychological thriller, but it is, in the best sense of the phrase, a philosophical novel that explores the theme of human moral involvement in an indifferent, if not outrightly absurd, universe. Conrad achieves this in an entertainingly suspenseful story that does not preach, but does state its case in clear and obvious terms expressing Conrad's view that action is always morally ambiguous, even though humans beings are always called upon to act.

"Critical Evaluation" by Russell Elliott Murphy

Bibliography:

Gillon, Adam. *The Eternal Solitary: A Study of Joseph Conrad*. New York: Bookman Associates, 1960. Explores the key role that isolation played in Conrad's life and work. Presents *Victory* as a melodrama that effectively discusses, in symbolic terms, the nature of solitude and its consequences.

Johnson, Bruce. *Conrad's Models of Mind*. Minneapolis: University of Minnesota Press, 1971. Explores Conrad's continual readjustment of his fictions to fit changing philosophical models of human behavior and motivation. Discusses the way *Victory* reassesses the individual's need for human solidarity and community.

Meyers, Jeffrey. *Joseph Conrad: A Biography*. New York: Charles Scribner's Sons, 1991. A highly readable critical biography. Discusses *Victory* as Conrad's most misunderstood, underrated, and controversial novel, its theme being the failure of love in an idyllic setting.

Moser, Thomas. "Conrad's 'Later Affirmation.'" In *Conrad: A Collection of Critical Essays*, edited by Marvin Mudrick. Englewood Cliffs, N.J.: Prentice-Hall, 1966. Explores the role chance plays in later novels, particularly *Victory*, and how it makes the novels' apparent affirmations more evasive.

Sherry, Norman, ed. *Conrad: The Critical Heritage*. Boston: Routledge & Kegan Paul, 1973. An impressive collection of the responses of the time to Conrad's work, the section devoted to *Victory* gives insight into Conrad's critical reputation and the novel's reception in the midst of World War I.

VILE BODIES

Type of work: Novel
Author: Evelyn Waugh (1903-1966)
Type of plot: Satire
Time of plot: Twentieth century, between the two world wars
Locale: England
First published: 1930

Principal characters:
ADAM FENWICK-SYMES, a young writer
NINA BLOUNT, his fiancée
COLONEL BLOUNT, her eccentric father
AGATHA RUNCIBLE, one of the Bright Young People
MILES MALPRACTICE, another of the Bright Young People
LOTTIE CRUMP, the proprietress of Shepheard's Hotel
CAPTAIN EDDY (GINGER) LITTLEJOHN, Nina's beloved
MRS. MELROSE APE, a female evangelist
FATHER ROTHSCHILD, a Jesuit
A DRUNKEN MAJOR

The Story:

During the rough English channel crossing, almost everyone was in some stage of seasickness. Some became tipsy and took to their berths. The Bright Young People, led by Agatha Runcible and effeminate Miles Malpractice, strapped themselves with sticking plaster and hoped for the best. A few hardy souls gathered in the smoking room where Mrs. Melrose Ape, a famous female evangelist traveling with her troupe of singing angels, bullied them into singing hymns. Father Rothschild, S.J., contemplated the sufferings of the saints.

Adam Fenwick-Symes, a young writer, was hurrying home to marry Nina Blount. To his dismay, the Dover customs authorities confiscated and burned the manuscript of the autobiography he had written while in Paris, France. Almost as bad was the case of Agatha Runcible, who was stripped and searched after being mistaken for a notorious jewel smuggler.

In London, Adam's publisher offered him a contract to write a novel, but with no advance in royalties. With only ten shillings to his name, Adam wondered how he was going to get married. Luckily, he was staying at Shepheard's Hotel. Lottie Crump, the proprietress, who bullied kings and advised members of Parliament, was careless about bills if she liked her guests. Most of her guests were drunk. One young man made a foolish bet with Adam and lost a thousand pounds. Adam called Nina and told her they could get married immediately, but before he left the hotel a drunken major persuaded him to put the money on the horse, Indian Runner, in the November Handicap. Then the major disappeared, and Adam was forced to call Nina again and tell her that their marriage would have to be postponed.

Adam and Nina went to Archie Schwert's costume party. Finding the affair dull, some of the Bright Young People went off to Lottie Crump's for a drink. Judge Skimp, an American guest, was entertaining. One young woman had fallen while swinging on a chandelier; she died, despite the champagne used to bathe her forehead.

The party was about to break up when Miss Brown invited the group to her house, which happened to be No. 10 Downing Street, for her father was Sir James Brown, the prime minister. Agatha Runcible stayed all night because she had forgotten the key to her own house. The next morning, still in her Hawaiian grass skirt, she found reporters and photographers waiting when she went out the front door. Reports of midnight orgies at No. 10 Downing Street caused a change of government, and Mr. Outrage, whose dreams were filled with visions of nude Japanese ladies, became the new prime minister.

On Nina's advice, Adam called on Colonel Blount to ask if the eccentric gentleman could finance his daughter's wedding. The colonel generously gave him a check for a thousand pounds. Adam was jubilant and took Nina to a country hotel where they stayed overnight. He was so happy that she waited until the next morning to tell him that her father, an absentminded movie fan, had signed Charlie Chaplin's name to the worthless check. The wedding was postponed once more.

At Lady Metroland's party for Mrs. Ape, Baron Balcairn, a gossip columnist known as Mr. Chatterbox, showed up in disguise after the hostess had refused to send him an invitation. Suspected of spying on a secret political conference between Lord Metroland, Father Rothschild, and Mr. Outrage, he was exposed. Deciding to give his paper the scoop of scoops, he reported a sensational but false account of indiscreet confessions made by aristocrats whom the evangelist had converted. Then he went home, turned on the gas, put his head into the oven, and quietly died.

Adam became Mr. Chatterbox. In the meantime, Balcairn's hoax had swamped the courts with libel suits against the *Daily Excess*. Mrs. Ape confirmed the story in a special interview and then departed with her angels to pep up religion at Oberammergau, Germany. Because Adam was forbidden to mention the names of those suing the paper, he was forced to invent fictitious people for his column. Among his creations was a man named Ginger, a model of fashion and a popular figure in society.

He was rather surprised when he finally encountered Captain Eddy Littlejohn, a man whom everyone called Ginger. Adam and Nina met him at the November Handicap, where Indian Runner came in first, paying thirty-five to one. A few minutes after the race, Adam spied the drunken major, but he disappeared before Adam could push his way through the crowd to collect his winnings.

Adam promised Nina that he would speak to her father again. He found the colonel making a film based on the life of John Wesley and too busy to pay any attention to Adam. During his absence, Nina wrote his column and mentioned green bowlers, a fashion item that was taboo in the *Daily Excess*. As a result, Adam lost his job, and Miles Malpractice became Mr. Chatterbox. Miles took the post because he needed the money. His brother, Lord Throbbing, had returned unexpectedly from Canada and thrown Miles, along with his disreputable boxing and racing friends, out of Throbbing House.

Adam, Agatha, Miles, and Archie Schwert went to the auto races where, in order to get into the pits, they wore brassards indicating that they belonged to the crew of car 13. Between heats, Adam again met the drunken major, who, after assuring him that his thirty-five thousand pounds were safe in the bank, borrowed five pounds to make a bet.

When the driver of car 13 was disabled by an Italian rival, Agatha, who wore a brassard designating her as a spare driver, took the wheel. Careening madly, she established a course record for the lap before she left the track and drove across country until she crashed the car into a monument. She was found wandering about in a dazed condition and died in a nursing home, still thinking that she was driving in a spinning world of speed and sound.

Adam had no money to pay Lottie Crump's bill for seventy-eight pounds sixteen and twopence. Meeting Ginger Littlejohn, he borrowed that amount and promised in return that Ginger could marry Nina. Shortly after Ginger and Nina returned from their honeymoon,

Ginger was called up for military service. Adam and Nina spent Christmas with Colonel Blount. The Wesley film had been finished, and the colonel, planning to show it as a Christmas treat, was too preoccupied to notice that his supposed son-in-law was a writer he had met previously as Fenwick-Symes. On Christmas night, they heard that war had been declared.

Adam met his drunken major again on a blasted battlefield during a lull in the fighting. The officer, who insisted that he was now a general, announced that he had lost his division. Adam was not quite so badly off; he had lost only one platoon. The general offered to pay the thirty-five thousand pounds on the spot, but Adam thought the money would be useless. They did find the general's car and in it a case of champagne and Chastity, who had been one of Mrs. Ape's singing angels. Adam drank some of the wine and fell asleep, leaving the general and Chastity to entertain each other.

Critical Evaluation:

The element of *roman à clef* is much stronger in Evelyn Waugh's first novel, *Decline and Fall* (1929), than in his second, *Vile Bodies*. A few characters reappear in the second novel but very briefly, and none is crucial to the plot or theme. The supposed similarity of *Vile Bodies* to *Decline and Fall* is, upon close examination, found to be somewhat superficial and based mostly on the reappearance of the victim as hero.

Adam Fenwick-Symes, the protagonist of *Vile Bodies*, is in a sense a man of the world: a novelist, recently returned from Paris, and one of the Bright Young People. Yet during much of the novel he is a passive figure, an antihero, a man to whom things happen. Because the world in which he moves is one lacking any order or stability, the things that happen to him often make no sense. Before the novel ends, however, Adam changes from victim to trickster and turns Ginger into the clown of the piece. When Adam sells Nina to Ginger and carries off the Great Christmas Imposture at Doubting Hall, some critics see him as a precursor to Basil Seal, the rogue of later novels.

In *Vile Bodies*, the narrator frequently becomes a sort of camera's eye, which cuts from scene to scene, revealing dialogue and external behavior only, and often leaving Adam to wander about. The result is a collection of many short scenes, snatches of conversation, and bits of farce, all of which combine to create a pastiche effect. Since the narrator, during these montage passages, does not go inside the minds of any of the characters, he seems very distant from them. Events that should strike the reader as horrible are thus rendered merely funny.

There are three deaths in the novel. During a drunken party at Shepheard's Hotel, Miss Florence (Flossie) Ducane is killed when she falls from a chandelier, which, as the *Evening Standard* delicately puts it, "she was attempting to mend." Simon Balcairn, who is both the last Earl of Balcairn and Mr. Chatterbox of the *Daily Excess*, sticks his head in the oven after Margot Metroland has blackballed him from society. Agatha Runcible never comes out of shock following a misadventure in a runaway racing car; from her bed in the nursing home to which she has been taken, she says portentously, "How people are *disappearing*, Adam."

These deaths elicit no sympathy from the reader, not because the reader (or Waugh) is a monster but because the characters are. They are grotesqueries. Cruel and terrible things do indeed happen to them, yet they are like circus performers called out by the ringmaster, Evelyn Waugh, to run through their paces. Their various acts may contain a latent tragedy, but it is well disguised behind the gaudy costumes and painted faces.

Waugh is always interested in religion, and the religious element is prominent in *Vile Bodies*, although it serves to furnish the subject matter for burlesque. The action of the novel occurs primarily during a Christmas season (between November 10 and Christmas Day) in the "near future," as the author is at some pains to point out in his foreword. The first character to appear is Father Rothschild, S.J. This ubiquitous Jesuit possesses in profusion those qualities that most excite British prejudice: he is a plotter in international affairs; he knows everything about everybody, even the location of the prime minister's love nest in Shepheard's Hotel; and he is of the fabulously wealthy banking family, thus exuding the double menace of wily Jesuit and crafty Jewish financier. Another ecclesiastic, a rector, plays a small comic role as Colonel Blount's neighbor and reluctant chauffeur. The second half of the novel features the making of a bogus film of the life of John Wesley at Doubting Hall, known to the locals as "Doubting 'All."

The embodiment of "modern" religion in the novel is the rum-drinking revivalist, Mrs. Melrose Ape. She is clearly a caricature of Aimee Semple McPherson and is one of only two characters in the novel whose models can be definitely identified (the other being Lottie Crump, the champagne-swigging proprietress of Shepheard's Hotel in Dover Street, who is the famous Mrs. Lewis of the Cavendish Hotel in Jermyn Street). The lesbianic Mrs. Ape is accompanied by a band of angels, who carry their wings in violin cases and sing her famous hymn "There Ain't No Flies on the Lamb of God." The irrepressible Margot Metroland proselytizes two of the proselytizer's angels, Chastity and Divine Discontent, for her Latin American Entertainment Company, a white slavery ring.

The slippery Mr. Isaacs and the Wonderfilm Company of Great Britain demean Doubting Hall at the behest of the dotty Colonel Blount. In the film, John Wesley is wounded in a duel, nursed back to health by his lover, Selina, Countess of Huntingdon (played by Effie La Touche), and later, in America, rescued from Red Indians by the same Lady Huntingdon disguised as a cowboy.

The novel is highly episodic; what plot movement there is emanates from two rather mild conflicts: Establishment disapproval of the Younger Generation and Adam's desultory quest for the means to marry Nina. The plot is both less fantastic and less skillfully constructed than that of Waugh's first novel, *Decline and Fall*, an opinion with which Waugh himself agreed.

Some critics have compared Waugh's early novels, especially *Vile Bodies*, to the work of the American novelist F. Scott Fitzgerald. After all, Waugh was writing about the Bright Young People not long after Fitzgerald had written about the flappers of the Jazz Age. However, when an American cinema agent suggested in 1946 that Waugh must have been greatly influenced by Fitzgerald, Waugh responded that he "had not then read a word of his."

"Critical Evaluation" by Patrick Adcock

Bibliography:

Davis, Robert Murray. "Title, Theme, and Structure in *Vile Bodies*." *Southern Humanities Review* 11 (Winter, 1977): 21-27. Davis argues that both the structure and theme of *Vile Bodies* is written from a Christian perspective. Waugh's novels were "religious" long before they became "Catholic" with the publication of *Brideshead Revisited* (1945).

Jervis, Steven A. "Evelyn Waugh, *Vile Bodies* and the Younger Generation." *South Atlantic Quarterly* 66 (Summer, 1967): 440-448. Examines Waugh's portrayal of the Bright Young People, Britain's equivalent of the Jazz Age flappers, and argues that Waugh's disgust with their chaotic and pointless lives helped turn him toward the Roman Church.

Kleine, Don W. "The Cosmic Comedies of Evelyn Waugh." *South Atlantic Quarterly* 61 (Autumn, 1962): 533-539. Focuses on Waugh's early comedies, *Decline and Fall* and *Vile Bodies*, and the fact that many critics have ignored Waugh's essential seriousness of purpose.

Phillips, Gene D. *Evelyn Waugh's Officers, Gentlemen, and Rogues: The Fact Behind His Fiction*. Chicago: Nelson-Hall, 1975. In chapter 2, "Exile from Eden: The Early Satires," Phillips connects the escapades in *Vile Bodies* with Waugh's own experiences as a Bright Young Person. He cites Waugh's diaries, his nonfiction travel books, and newspaper accounts of the period.

Walker, Julia M. "Being and Becoming: A Comment on Religion in *Vile Bodies* and *Brideshead Revisited*." *Evelyn Waugh Newsletter* 16, no. 2 (Autumn, 1982): 4-5. Discusses the fact that *Vile Bodies* was published in the year of Waugh's conversion to Roman Catholicism and that the book to some extent reflects this. Argues that Waugh the satirist approaches religion obliquely in *Vile Bodies*, exposing its gross vulgarization in the modern world, whereas in *Brideshead Revisited* he affirms his belief in the religious life more directly.

THE VILLAGE

Type of work: Novel
Author: Ivan Alexeyevich Bunin (1870-1953)
Type of plot: Social criticism
Time of plot: Early twentieth century
Locale: Russia
First published: Derevnya, 1910 (English translation, 1923)

Principal characters:
>TIKHON ILITCH KRASOFF, a self-made landowner
>KUZMA ILITCH KRASOFF, his imaginative brother
>THE BRIDE, a peasant woman employed by Tikhon
>RODKA, a peasant and the husband of the Bride

The Story:

The ancestors of Tikhon and Kuzma Ilitch Krasoff were nothing to be proud of: Their great-grandfather had been hunted from Durnovka with wolfhounds; their grandfather had distinguished himself by becoming a thief; and their father, a petty huckster, had died early in life as a result of overdrinking. The sons, after serving for a time as clerks in town stores, took to the road as itinerant peddlers. After they had traveled together for many years, the partnership was mutually dissolved during an argument over the division of profits. The two parted very bitterly.

After the partnership was broken, Tikhon took over a posting station a few miles from Durnovka, the little village where his ancestors had lived for many generations. Along with the station, he operated a liquor dispensary and general mercantile establishment. Tikhon, determined to become a man of some consequence, began to build up his fortune when he was already in his forties. His plan was to follow the tax collectors and buy land at forced sales, and he paid the lowest possible prices for what he purchased.

Tikhon's private life was anything but rich. He lived with his cook, a dumb woman, who became the mother of his child. The child, however, was accidentally smothered, and soon afterward Tikhon sent the woman away and married a waiting woman to a noblewoman, by whom he tried to have children. His efforts, however, were fruitless, for the children were always premature and dead. As if to make up, temporarily at least, for his wife's failure to present him with children, fate gave Tikhon the opportunity of finishing off, economically speaking, the last member of the family that had held his own ancestors in serfdom through the previous centuries.

Life was not easy for Tikhon. A government order closed all the dramshops, including his, and made liquor a state monopoly. Tikhon also continued to be disturbed over the fact that he had no children; he felt that it indicated a failure in life.

The summer following the government order closing his liquor business proved to be a bad one. There was no rain and a great deal of heat, and so the grain harvest on his lands was only a fraction of what it should have been. During that fall, Tikhon went to a fair to do some horse trading; while he was there, he became disgusted with himself and with life in general, for life suddenly seemed pointless to him. He began drinking heavily, downing immense quantities of vodka, although not enough to interfere with the conduct of his business.

Tikhon's life was little affected by the war with Japan that broke out soon afterward; he was more affected by persistent rumors of an attempt at a Socialist revolution in the Russian legislative body. When he learned that the great landowners, those who owned more than a thousand acres of ground, were likely to have their estates taken from them for redistribution, he even began to agitate a little for the new laws. Soon, however, he changed his mind when he discovered that the peasants on his own land were plotting against him. One Sunday he heard that they were meeting at Durnovka to rise in rebellion against him. He immediately drove over to the village, but the peasants, refusing to listen to him, drove him away with force. The uprising, however, was short-lived, and within a few days the peasants were back to deal with him again. Yet he no longer trusted them and thought of them as little better than treacherous animals.

One of the workers on Tikhon's land was a young peasant named Rodka, married to a young girl of some beauty who was always called the Bride. The girl was a source of annoyance to Tikhon because she aroused him sexually. On several occasions she resisted his unwelcome attentions, but finally he had his way with her. The Bride did not complain; she simply endured, much as she endured the terrible beatings that her husband administered to her with a whip. The beatings made Tikhon afraid of Rodka, and so he plotted to do away with the man. Such scheming, however, proved unnecessary, for the Bride herself poisoned her husband. Tikhon, at least, was sure that she had poisoned her husband, although no one else thought so.

Chance brought to Tikhon's perusal a volume of poems written by his brother Kuzma. Stirred by the knowledge that his brother was still alive and also an author, Tikhon wrote a letter telling Kuzma that it was high time they buried past differences and became friends again. Kuzma went to Durnovka, and the two brothers became, at least on the surface, friendly. Tikhon offered his brother the overseership of the estate at Durnovka, and Kuzma accepted because he had no other prospects for earning a living.

Kuzma Krasoff had done nothing with his life. Following the dissolution of the partnership with Tikhon years before, he had worked here and there, as a drover, a teamster, a general worker. Then he had fallen in love with a woman at Voronezh and had lived with her for ten years, until she died. In that decade, he busied himself by trading in grain and horses and by writing occasionally for the local newspaper. All of his life he had wanted to become a writer. He had never been educated, except for short periods of instruction at the hands of an unemployed shoemaker and from books he had borrowed occasionally. He considered his life a complete waste, for he had never been able to settle down to writing seriously.

In his maturity Kuzma blamed all of his troubles, and the troubles of Russians in general, on a lack of education. He believed that education was the answer to every problem confronting him and his fellowmen, and he claimed that the Russians, whom he regarded as little better than barbarians with a wide streak of hatred in their makeup, would have been better folk if they had been educated.

Kuzma's life as overseer on his brother's estate was not a happy one. He felt that the position was a last resort, and he disliked the people with whom he had to deal, including Tikhon. He was also perturbed by the Bride, who had been sent by Tikhon to cook and keep house for him. She did not arouse him as she had Tikhon, but Kuzma was bothered by her presence, and he felt extremely sorry for her because, a few years before, a group of men had raped her. The incident, Kuzma felt, lingered like a cloud over her existence. When at last he spoke to Tikhon about the matter, Tikhon, supposing that Kuzma had been sampling the same favors that the owner had enjoyed in the past, laughed at his brother's scruples. Nevertheless, he did arrange to marry off the woman, and the Bride became the wife of a peasant on the estate. On the wedding day only Kuzma realized that the prospect of a husband was but a makeshift in the Bride's mind, and that she, like himself, would never really be happy.

Critical Evaluation:

Born of a noble though impoverished family in 1870, Ivan Alexeyevich Bunin was reared on his father's country estate and educated by tutors. After a time at the University of Moscow, he traveled as a journalist and began writing poetry. By 1901, his poetry received some acclaim, and in 1903 his translations of Lord Byron and Henry Wadsworth Longfellow brought him the Pushkin Prize. His stories also brought him wide attention. *The Village*, in 1910, made him internationally famous.

In the years preceding World War I, Bunin traveled widely, especially in the Middle East. At the time of the Russian Revolution, Bunin sided with reactionary groups. He left Moscow in May, 1918, and the following February he fled the country, spending most of the rest of his life in France. His literary output, never large, maintained a high quality. In 1941, the seventy-year-old Bunin and his ailing wife fled Paris after the Nazi conquest and lived destitute in unoccupied France. The Tolstoy Foundation solicited funds for the relief of the winner of the 1933 Nobel Prize in Literature. Later, it was revealed that he sheltered a Jewish journalist for the length of the occupation. In 1951, he published a brief autobiography, which included his memories of such friends as Ivan Turgenev and Leo Tolstoy. He died in semiobscurity, at the age of eighty-three, at his home in Paris.

Bunin, in an autobiographical introduction to the American edition of this novel, stated that it was one of a series of novels written to portray the character of the Russian people. In the series, said Bunin, he attempted to lay bare the Russian soul in all of its complexity and depth and in its invariably tragic state. Bunin also stated that no one who knew the Russian people as he did could have been surprised by the beastliness of the Russian Revolution and its effect on Russia. Some critics have called Bunin cruel in his portrayal of the Russian people, for he showed them as vicious, egocentric, hatred-filled individuals who cared little for anyone but themselves. Bunin himself stated that he was content to have painted a more realistic picture of the Russian people than the idealized conception usually given in the literature of his land, a land from which he was an exile after the revolution.

Bunin's novel *The Village* presents a grim picture of life in pre-Soviet Russia. It is a world in which people are known by nicknames or crude labels: the Bride, the Goat, Duckhead, the Fool. The villagers do not even know how to acknowledge one another's humanity. These country folk, uneducated and brutalized by hard lives, are stimulated only by disasters; they revel in wife beatings and the thrashing of small children, and they gather around to watch fights or fires. Violence provides their only entertainment, their only break in the monotony of living. The Russia of this novel is a violent, primitive land, where poor men lash their beasts and women equally.

Bunin wrote with the care of a historian or a sociologist describing a kind of life doomed to extinction because of its rottenness. Dirt, filth, and manure seem to cling to everything and everyone in the village. At times, it is difficult to distinguish the human beings from the animals. Bunin does not romanticize the old ways or the country life. His precise, elegant prose pictures with vivid images and skillful, merciless irony the truth as he saw it.

The superstition-ridden peasants led wretched lives, struggling merely to subsist. People who had to struggle to exist got into the habit, so that even after the need ceased, they continued struggling, and their lives became bounded by possessions and prices. Tikhon Ilitch (known as Stiff-Leg) tried vainly to find salvation in "business," but neither busy-ness nor business could bring him happiness. After decades of labor, Tikhon Ilitch could only reflect: How brief, how devoid of meaning, is life! Deniska, with his short legs, mouse-colored hair, and earth-hued skin, was one character who might have offered hope for the future. He was bright and self-educated and was known as an agitator. Nevertheless, it was Kuzma Krasoff, Tikhon's younger brother, who represented the aspirations of the self-educated poor man. His life, despite his efforts, had come to nothing, and he was reduced to working for his brother and to vague desires for writing about how he came to be a failure. True, he was born in a country with more than a hundred million illiterates, but he had hoped to make something of himself. He read, he wrote, he studied, but all to no avail. He despaired of both himself and his country. What kind of nation, his friend Balashkin cried, would seek to destroy all of its best writers? They killed Alexander Pushkin and Mikhail Lermontov, imprisoned Taras Shevchenko for ten years, dragged Fyodor Dostoevski out to be shot. Nikolai Gogol went mad. Balashkin recounted the destruction of many other writers. Kuzma, however, clung to the belief that Russia was a great nation—that it must be great, and so must he. Kuzma was the kind of man who rushed from enthusiasm to enthusiasm, embracing the philosophy of Tolstoy, then patriotism, then something else. Perhaps, Bunin seems to suggest, his shallow idealism and lack of tenacity were characteristic of the Russia of that day. "All Russia is nothing but village," remarks one of the characters. Kuzma also quotes Gogol: "Russia! Russia! Wither art thou dashing?," and, "Vain Babblers, you stick at nothing!"

Like most of the greater Russian novelists who preceded him, Bunin was a craftsman who set forth the incidents in his narrative with an ease that added to the lifelike quality of his characters. Also like most Russian writers, he threaded a somber symbolism through this novel. At times, Bunin's prose possesses the sadness and poetic enchantment of Anton Chekhov's stories; his realism is tempered with an aristocratic dedication to art and style. There are moments when Russian village life seems almost too terrible to bear, yet it all rings true. Beneath the hues of gray and the careful objectivity, a deep understanding seems to radiate through, almost like a touch of sympathy.

Bunin's art was rooted in Turgenev, Chekhov, and Tolstoy. He always felt an aversion to Dostoevski's work. Bunin did not, however, attempt the psychological novel which dominated nineteenth century Russian fiction. Some readers might even hesitate to call *The Village* a novel. When the book first appeared in Russia, many critics condemned its bleak vision, even while admiring its art and the blending of realism with poetry. Most readers even now prefer Bunin's short stories, especially the famous long tale, "The Gentleman from San Francisco" (1922), certainly the writer's masterpiece. Nevertheless, *The Village* presents a memorable picture of a place and a time, an invective against the cruelty and stupidity of Russian peasant life.

"Critical Evaluation" by Bruce D. Reeves

Bibliography:

Connolly, Julian. *Ivan Bunin*. Boston: Twayne, 1982. An analytical survey of Bunin's major works, with a special emphasis on the evolution of Bunin's views on human existence. Examines the treatment of Russian society in *The Village* against the background of Bunin's perceptions on the inevitable decline and fall of major cultures and civilizations.

Kryzytski, Serge. *The Works of Ivan Bunin*. The Hague: Mouton, 1971. The first monograph on Bunin published in English. Contains a detailed description of Bunin's work and its critical reception. Compares Bunin's treatment of Russian peasant life in *The Village* to that found in the work of his contemporaries.

Marullo, Thomas G. "Ivan Bunin's *Derevnja*: The Demythologization of the Peasant." *Russian Language Journal* 31, no. 109 (1977): 79-100. Outlines the way in which Bunin's exploration of Russian village life contrasts with traditional portraits of the peasantry in Russian literature.

Poggioli, Renato. *The Art of Ivan Bunin.* Cambridge, Mass.: Harvard University Press, 1953. Assesses Bunin's place in Russian and world literature. Its examination of *The Village* draws attention to the structure of the work and to the relationships that Bunin establishes among the central characters.

Woodward, James B. *Ivan Bunin: A Study of His Fiction.* Chapel Hill: University of North Carolina Press, 1980. A stimulating discussion of Bunin's work that analyzes the role that nature plays in Bunin's fiction. Also focuses on the way that human attitudes toward nature shape the experience of Bunin's characters.

THE VILLAGERS

Type of work: Novel
Author: Jorge Icaza (1906-1978)
Type of plot: Social realism
Time of plot: Twentieth century
Locale: Ecuador
First published: Huasipungo, 1934 (English translation, 1964)

> *Principal characters:*
> ALFONSO PEREIRA, a debt-ridden landowner
> BLANCA, his wife
> LOLITA, his daughter
> DON JULIO, his uncle
> POLICARPIO, an overseer
> ANDRES CHILIQUINGA, an Indian laborer
> CUNSHI, his wife
> PADRE LOMAS, the village priest
> JUANCHO CABASCANGO, a well-to-do Indian tenant farmer

The Story:

Alfonso Pereira was an Ecuadoran landowner plagued by domestic and financial troubles. His wife, Blanca, nagged him, and he was worried about his seventeen-year-old daughter Lolita, who wanted to marry a man who was part Indian. Don Julio, his uncle, added to his difficulties by demanding repayment of a loan of ten thousand sucres, a debt already three months overdue.

When Pereira confessed that he was unable to pay the loan, Don Julio suggested that his nephew try to interest Mr. Chapy, a North American promoter, in a timber concession on Pereira's mountain estate. Privately, the old man suspected that Mr. Chapy and his associates were on the lookout for oil and used their lumber-cutting activities in the region as a blind. In order to interest the North Americans, however, it would be necessary to build fifteen miles of road and to get possession of two forest tracts. Also, the Indians had to be driven off their *huasipungos,* the lands supplied to them in return for working on the master's estate.

Pereira assured his uncle that such a course would be difficult. The Indians, having a deep affection for their lands along both sides of the river, would never willingly relinquish them. Old Julio ridiculed Pereira's sentimentality and told him to return to the estate at Tomachi and build the road. Back home, Pereira discussed his problem with Padre Lomas, the village priest. The padre agreed to persuade the Indians to work on the road: He would tell them that the labor was the will of God. They also tried to determine how many *mingas,* parties in which Indians were plied with drink to make them willing to work, would be necessary before the road could be completed. Jacinto Quintana, proprietor of the village store and saloon, promised that he and his wife, Juana, would make the home brew for the first of the *mingas.*

Andres Chiliquinga, an Indian workman, was unhappy because Pereira had returned. Chiliquinga had gone against his master's and the priest's wishes by taking Cunshi as his wife. He was one of thirty Indians sent to start cutting wood and clearing the roadbed.

To find a wet nurse for her baby, Blanca Pereira examined some of the Indian mothers. Their undernourished babies were diseased, some with malaria or dysentery; others were idiotic or epileptic. Policarpio, the overseer, finally chose Cunshi, mother of the healthiest child in the village, and took her to the Pereira house. The master, seeing the young Indian woman, forced her to sleep with him.

One night, Andres made the long trip home to see his wife. Finding no one in their hillside shack, he became suspicious and angry. The next day, he deliberately let his ax fall on his foot. The Indians treated the cut with spiderwebs and mud, but when the bandage was removed, three days later, the foot was so badly infected that Andres was sent home. A medicine man who poulticed the sore saved Andres' life, but the wound left him lame.

One day, while Pereira and the priest were at the Quintana store discussing the building of the road, they sent Jacinto on an errand. After his departure, both men forced Juana to sleep with them.

Pereira gave Padre Lomas one hundred sucres for a big Mass. Then he held a *minga* and work on the road was accelerated. Storms made life miserable for the Indians, unprotected as they were in their camps. Some died when they tried to drain a swamp. Others perished in quicksand. Pereira, choosing to risk the Indians rather than follow a longer, safer route, kept the workmen drunk and entertained them with cockfights. The ignorant laborers continued to toil.

The priest went to Juancho Cabascango, an Indian with a prosperous *huasipungo* beside the river, and asked for one hundred sucres to pay for another Mass. When the Indian refused, Padre Lomas cursed him. A short time later, a flash flood drowned some of the Indians and their cattle. Blaming the disaster on Juancho, his superstitious neighbors beat him to death. The priest declared the affair the will of God and easily collected several hundred sucres for his Mass.

At last, the road was completed, but the Indians received none of the benefits Padre Lomas had promised. He bought a bus and two trucks that took all transportation work from those who used to drive mule teams into Quito with the products of the region. Young Indians rode the bus to the city and, there, became criminals and prostitutes.

As a result of easy transportation and the possibility of a profitable sale in Quito, Pereira decided not to give the Indians their customary grain from his plentiful harvest. Policarpio's protests did no good. When the hungry Indians went to Pereira's patio and begged their master to relieve the hunger of their families, he told them that their daily pay of fifty centavos was generous enough. Besides, the ton and a half of corn needed to feed the Indians would help considerably in reducing his debts. He did, however, heed his overseer's warning and asked that guards for his estate be sent from Quito.

Hunger stalked the region and babies and old people perished. When one of Pereira's cows died, the famished Indians begged for the carcass. He refused, because they might be tempted to kill other cows, and ordered Policarpio to bury the dead animal. Desperate, Andres uncovered it; after he and his family ate some of the meat, the tainted flesh killed Cunshi. Padre Lomas demanded twenty-five sucres, more than the Indian could ever earn, in payment for burying the dead woman. That same night, Andres stole one of his master's cows and sold it to a nearby butcher. Tracked down by dogs, the Indian was captured and flogged in Pereira's patio. There was no one to protest except his small son, who was almost killed by the white men when he tried to help his father.

A score of foreigners arrived in Tomachi. The Indians welcomed them timorously, thinking that these new white men could certainly be no more cruel than their Spanish masters. Mr. Chapy's first act, however, was to order the Indians driven from their *huasipungos* to make room for company houses and a sawmill.

When Andres' son brought news of the order, the Indians rebelled. They had stoically accepted the cruelty of the whites, even the lechery of the white men toward the Indian women, but the Indians felt that the land was theirs. Jacinto vainly tried to stop them when they marched on the village. The enraged Indians killed six of the white men. The others, including Mr. Chapy, fled in their automobiles.

They returned, over the road the Indians had built, with three hundred soldiers under a leader who had killed two thousand Indians in a similar rebellion near Cuenca. Troops hunted down and machine-gunned Indians of all ages and sexes. The few survivors, taking refuge in Andres' hillside shack, rolled rocks down on the soldiers and shot at them with birdguns. Finally, the soldiers set fire to the thatched roof. When the Indians ran from the burning house, the troops shot them without mercy.

Critical Evaluation:

This brutal novel flows swiftly. Technically, it is one of the better Spanish American novels. Its virtues are legion, as are its defects, and among the former are interesting dialogue, bitter irony, sardonic humor, interesting plot, effective use of detail, exposure of social injustice, and crispness of style with short sentences that get to the point. *The Villagers* presents the Ecuadoran Andes so clearly that readers see them in stark detail. Even the sounds of the sierra are heard, while the odors, temperature changes, and direction of the night wind are experienced. *The Villagers'* crowning virtue is its defense of Ecuador's oppressed Indians. For this reason it has been considered Jorge Icaza's most significant novel. It helped launch the cycle of so-called *indianista* novels, which are devoted to telling the story of the Indians. The novel's protagonist is not only an Indian but also the Indian, who is characterized collectively but clearly, even to the peculiar flavor of his Spanish.

Decay is a prominent and depressing note in *The Villagers*; images of garbage, filth, mold, slime, and rotten meat are frequent. Trash, dirt, and profanity are always present; everything is sloppy and unkempt, reflecting life's hopelessness. Depression is thus a constant note, accentuated by dismal mountain fogs, clammy cold, foul speech, and superstition. *Soroche* (altitude sickness) occasionally strikes, as do other afflictions. Alcoholism is the Indian's bane, for the *huasipunguero* abandons everything—chickens, corn, potatoes, children—for alcohol.

The characters in the novel generally fail to change or develop. At the novel's end, they are almost the same personalities and characters that they were at its start. The principal exception is the Indian community itself, for "from all corners of the soul, from every pore, grow the secret rebellions of a slave." Icaza also implied that the mestizo or mulatto suffers from a psychological inferiority complex in Ecuador, as is exemplified by Juana la Chola's (Juana the Half-breed) inert submission to rape by a landowner and a cleric. The latter villains, unfortunately, are crudely drawn. Don Alfonso Pereira is a second-rate Simon Legree, a consistent rascal, self-server, hypocrite, and uncomplicated brute from start to finish of the novel. He snarls, curses, and brutalizes Indians but cringes from those above him. The priest is worse; he is so utterly depraved as to be comical. He extorts money from hungry Indians, sells passages out of purgatory or burial plots "close to Heaven" at alarming prices, builds a lucrative trucking business on ill-gotten money, and commits ridiculous rascalities too numerous to mention, including the drunken rape of Juana. Referred to as "the Cassocked One," the priest is a symbol of Icaza's disenchantment with religion, and it is puzzling that this caricature has not aroused disdain or even criticism from many generations of students and professors.

Other ogres in *The Villagers* are wealthy people, businessmen, whites, property owners, and gringo capitalists. The gringos career about in Cadillacs, oblivious to Indians; they relish money and lack human feelings. It is possible that they were grotesquely overdrawn by Icaza to appeal only to readers blinded by prejudice, but it should also be recalled that the novel was intended as a tirade against the social injustice that then blighted Ecuador. Icaza possibly had the illusion that his novel would bring a better life to the Indians, but initially his work was better received and lauded abroad than it was in his own country. In any event, Icaza exposed the plight of Ecuador's peons and also the decay of the rural aristocrats, who had left the work of their ancestors to live luxuriously in the city. The novel also promotes the conflict of red race against white. White aristocrats are portrayed as hard, unfeeling, and cruel. They are contemptuous of Indians and exploit the poor. Some critics feel that Icaza's work had political motivations; others compare him to John Steinbeck and consider him a social reformer.

No one in *The Villagers* apparently wishes to live in the country, since life in Quito is much richer. The countryside is backward, isolated, and uncomfortable; the city is cultured and far superior. Nature is unattractive; its beauties are unmentioned and unextolled. Nature's dangers are stressed, however, such as the scene in which a man dies horribly by drowning in mud. Little interest is shown in animals, birds, and plants. The novel is almost devoid of color. Tints of sunrises, sunsets, mountains, skies, fields, or towns are generally lacking, and even the grayness of the constant mountain mist is assumed rather than described. The author's treatment of color is a deliberate stylistic device to increase the feeling of dismal hopelessness.

Although of Spanish blood and comfortable background, Icaza decided as a youth to champion Ecuador's poor of all races. Having attracted international attention, his novel eventually won acceptance in Ecuador and undoubtedly helped the Indian. It has therefore helped to implement some social reform and to attract attention to the cause of the Indian. Thus, as have other novels written with the intention of provoking reform, the novel has succeeded, through its literary readability, in making considerable impact on its society.

"Critical Evaluation" by William Freitas

Bibliography:
Flores, Angel. "Jorge Icaza." *Spanish American Authors: The Twentieth Century*. New York: H. W. Wilson, 1992. Survey of Icaza's works. An excellent starting point. Stresses Icaza's contributions to modern Ecuadorian literature.
Foster, David William, and Virginia Ramos Foster, eds. "Icaza, Jorge." *Modern Latin American Literature*. New York: Frederick Ungar, 1975. Excerpts from critical studies. An excellent starting point to Icaza's works.
González-Pérez, Armando. *Social Protest and Literary Merit in "Huasipungo" and "El mundo es ancho y ajeno."* Milwaukee: University of Wisconsin-Milwaukee, Center for Latin America, 1988. Indicates that Icaza is an important pro-Indian spokesperson in Ecuadorian political circles. His works often explore themes pertaining to economic exploitation of native populations.
Jones, Cyril. *Three Spanish American Novelists: A European View*. London: Hispanic & LUSO Brazilian Councils, 1967. Comparative study of works of Latin American novelists. Places emphasis on the tendency toward realism as a means of political empowerment.
Vetrano, Anthony Joseph. *Imagery in Two of Jorge Icaza's Novels: Huasipungo and Huairapamushcas*. Tuscaloosa: University of Alabama Press, 1972. Icaza's social concerns for the indigenous Ecuadorian population inspired realistic scenes well-known for their portrayal of the physical abuse of the Indian worker. Analyzes such images in Icaza's two best-known novels.

VILLETTE

Type of work: Novel
Author: Charlotte Brontë (1816-1855)
Type of plot: Bildungsroman
Time of plot: Nineteenth century
Locale: Belgium
First published: 1853

> *Principal characters:*
> LUCY SNOWE, a young teacher
> JOHN GRAHAM BRETTON, a physician
> MRS. BRETTON, his mother
> POLLY HOME, Bretton's beloved
> GINEVRA FANSHAWE, a schoolgirl
> MONSIEUR PAUL EMANUEL, a teacher of literature
> MADAME BECK, the mistress of a girls' school

The Story:

As a young girl, Lucy Snowe visited her godmother, Mrs. Bretton, about twice each year. It was a warm, active household, and Lucy loved Mrs. Bretton. During one of Lucy's visits, young Polly Home, whose widowed father was leaving England for the Continent, came to stay with the Brettons. Polly was mature and worldly for her years, and she developed a tender, almost maternal, fondness for Mrs. Bretton's son Graham. Since Lucy shared a room with the young visitor, she became the recipient of her confidence. Polly's father had originally intended to send his daughter to Mrs. Bretton's home for an extended stay, but he became lonely for her and returned to take his daughter back to Europe with him. Lucy's visits with the Brettons came to an end when they lost their property and moved away. After that, Lucy lost track of her godmother.

As a grown woman, Lucy earned her living by acting as a companion to elderly women. Tiring of her humdrum existence, she went to France. There an unusual chain of circumstances led her to the city of Villette and to a boarding school run by Madame Beck and her kinsman, Monsieur Paul Emanuel. Lucy's calm disposition, ready wit, firm character, and cultivated intellect soon led to her appointment as instructor of English.

Attending the school was Ginevra Fanshawe, a pretty but flighty and selfish girl, whose relations with Lucy took the form of a scornful friendship. Madame Beck was a clever schoolmistress. She conducted her pension by a system of spying that included occasional furtive searches among the personal possessions of others and also a constant stealthy watching from her window. Despite Madame Beck's behavior, Lucy felt a firm respect for her. Her system was steady and unflagging. Monsieur Paul was a voluble and brilliant instructor. He always seemed to be at Lucy's elbow admonishing her, tantalizing her intellect, attempting to lead her. Often, Lucy attributed the peculiar notions of the pair to their Catholicism, which Lucy abhorred. Dr. John, a handsome, generous young practitioner who attended the children, was a general favorite at the institute. Although she did not betray her knowledge, Lucy recognized him as the John Graham Bretton whom she had known as a child.

In her characteristically scornful and triumphant manner, Ginevra Fanshawe confided that she had a pair of ardent suitors, Isidore, who Ginevra claimed was madly in love with her, and

Colonel de Hamal, whom Ginevra herself preferred. One night in the garden, Lucy found a letter intended for someone in the school. Dr. John appeared in time to assist Lucy in disposing of the missive before the spying Madame Beck could interfere. The young doctor apparently knew the person for whom the letter was intended. Some time later, Lucy learned that Ginevra's Isidore was Dr. John himself, and that the nocturnal letter had been sent by de Hamal; Dr. John had been trying to protect his beloved. Dr. John confessed that he hoped to marry the schoolgirl.

Alone at the pension during a vacation, Lucy was overcome by depression. She had been haunted in the past by the apparition of a nun, and the reappearance of this specter so exacerbated the already turbulent emotions of the young teacher that she fled into the streets of the town. There she wandered, driven to despair by her inner conflicts, until she came to a Catholic church. Under a strange compulsion, she was led to make a confession to the priest, but she later regretted her action. While trying to find her way back to the school, she fainted. Upon regaining consciousness, she found herself in a room with familiar furnishings. She was in a Villette chateau occupied by her godmother, Mrs. Bretton, and Graham Bretton. Graham, who was giving Lucy medical attention, was the Dr. John whom Lucy had recognized at the pension. For the first time, he recognized her as the young girl who had so often stayed in his home in England.

Lucy became a frequent visitor in the Bretton home. Before long, she realized that she was in love with Dr. John. The warm friendship between the two young people was the subject of constant raillery by the sarcastic Monsieur Paul. While at a concert one evening with Dr. John and Mrs. Bretton, Lucy noticed Ginevra Fanshawe in the audience, who began to mimic Mrs. Bretton. The older woman was unaware of the young girl, but Dr. John was not. Quite suddenly, he realized the weakness and selfishness of Ginevra, who could so irreverently make fun of a woman as good as his mother. His infatuation for Ginevra ended in disgust.

At another concert he was attending with Lucy, Dr. John rescued a young girl named Paulina Bassompierre from a rough crowd. Upon bringing her home, he discovered that she was in reality Polly Home.

Repeated meetings between Polly, who was now called Paulina, and Dr. John fostered the doctor's love for the girl who had loved him since childhood. Lucy, closing her eyes and ears to this grief, believed that Dr. John was lost to her. Fortunately, a new phase of life began for her at the school. Madame Beck gave her greater freedom in her work, and Monsieur Paul showed a sincere interest in her mind and heart. The only flaw in Lucy's tranquillity was the reappearance of the apparition of the nun.

Once Madame Beck sent Lucy on an errand to the home of Madame Walravens. There Lucy was told a touching story about Monsieur Paul. In his youth, he had loved a girl, Justine Marie, but cruel relatives had refused his suit and Justine had subsequently died. Filled with remorse, Monsieur Paul undertook to care for Justine Marie's relatives. There survived old Madame Walravens and a priest, the same man to whom Lucy had confessed. The priest, Father Silas, had been Monsieur Paul's tutor and he was anxious to keep his former pupil from succumbing to the influence of Lucy, a heretic. Lucy's affection for Monsieur Paul grew, but her hopes were suddenly dashed when the truculent professor announced that he was leaving France for the West Indies. Madame Beck, always present when Monsieur Paul and Lucy met, kept the distraught young woman from talking to him. Ginevra Fanshawe had meanwhile eloped with de Hamal. A letter from the runaway girl explained Lucy's ghostly nun. De Hamal had thus attired himself when making nocturnal visits to Ginevra. On the eve of his sailing, Monsieur Paul arranged a meeting with Lucy to explain his sudden forced departure and recent silence.

Surrounded by his possessive relatives, he had occupied his time with secret arrangements to make Lucy mistress of the school. To avoid the temptation of telling Lucy about his plans before they were consummated, he had remained apart from her. Upon his return, in three years, he promised to rid himself of all his encumbrances, so that he would be free to marry her.

Margaret McFadden-Gerber

Critical Evaluation:

Charlotte Brontë's *Villette*, which is loosely based on the author's time as a student in Brussels, Belgium, is a first-person narrative of development, with Lucy Snowe at its center, both as protagonist and as a sometimes unreliable narrator. In the course of the novel, Lucy grows from a shadowy, self-effacing adolescent into an independent, self-possessed woman, learning to live her own life and tell her own story. She narrates that story from within the framework of the conventional female narratives of domestic or romantic love even while her story critiques those conventions.

The novel's first two scenes, which are centered on other characters, reveal Lucy as passive, virtually invisible, and cynical. At the Bretton home, Lucy exists on the margin, and she observes and describes the household's domestic activities rather than participating in them herself. The lives and loves of Mrs. Bretton, her son Graham, and little Polly Home are the central focus. After Lucy leaves the Brettons and is orphaned by the deaths of her own family, she again experiences life vicariously through Miss Marchmont, a wasted woman for whom Lucy is a companion and nursemaid. In neither place does Lucy feel a part of the scene, and in both places she is treated as little more than a hand to serve and an ear to listen. Lucy is defined, and she defines herself, within the narrow confines of her duties to others.

It is at Madame Beck's school in Villette that Lucy's struggle for independence and self-definition begins. Here, despite the restrictions of being female, she first encounters the opportunity to distinguish herself in opposition to those conventional restrictions. Adamantly Protestant and unable to speak French, Lucy is isolated in the bustling, strange world of foreign Catholics, under the supervision of a woman who silently patrols her school and searches its inmates' possessions. Lucy is appalled by this "woman's world" of well-tended but lazy, cunning females, and to some extent she keeps herself separate from that world. She is however also attracted to these women, who represent dimensions of Lucy's own characteristics and desires—Madame Beck with her independence and authority, Paulina with her magnetic delicacy, and Ginevra with her narcissistic beauty. Lucy experiences contradictory impulses. Proud of her calm detachment, she is also pained by being deprived of the traditionally feminine joys of motherhood and romance. Lucy is caught in the conflict between her desire to stand outside conventional feminine roles and her attraction to those same conventions.

The men in the novel play an important part in Lucy's struggle for self-definition as a woman. Lucy at first cherishes a strong, and secret, passion for Graham Bretton, and hopes that he will someday return her love. Graham however views her as an "inoffensive shadow," and, blithely telling her to "cultivate happiness," he unknowingly tortures her by confessing to his love first for Ginevra and then for Paulina. In contrast to Graham, who sees Lucy as devoid of passion, Monsieur Paul sees Lucy as a woman of just barely contained emotions. He reprimands her for her "finery" when she wears a simple pink dress and for her "flirtatiousness" when she jokes with Graham. On the other hand, Monsieur Paul encourages her to cultivate her intellect and her emotions, and as their friendship (and later romance) ripens, she becomes more assured and self-confident.

From the moment that Madame Beck commands Monsieur Paul to define Lucy's character by "reading" her face when she arrives, those around Lucy attempt interpret exactly who she is. Much of what they do is to misread her, for Lucy leads a double life: the constrictive life of the body and the free life of the intellect and imagination. In the former, she is limited by her social position and her physical appearance. In the latter, she is free to explore her desires for love and independence. Her letters to Dr. John reveal this dichotomy: She begins by writing letters full of passion, which she destroys, and only then writes the calm, friendly notes that give nothing away, which she sends; when she receives letters from him, however, she buries them under a tree so that no one else will find them.

Brontë's imagery and symbolism reflect this doubleness in the descriptions of Lucy's narrow bed, her visits to the attic, and her buried letters. The nun who haunts her solitude is also emblematic of passions buried in an appearance of cold hauteur (hence the name Lucy Snowe, fire and ice). We see images of Lucy's passion in the novel's frequent storms, and in her enjoyment at playing and acting during Madame Beck's birthday celebration. The frequent but private tears that she sheds further show her pent-up emotions. The scene at the city-wide celebration brings together these images, for here is a microcosm in which she encounters virtually all of the significant people in her life and experiences the various emotions that have accompanied her life until then, including feelings of detachment, love, jealousy, contempt, and anger. In releasing, exploring, and finally accommodating herself to these emotions, she becomes a whole woman.

Lucy's story recounts her attempts to find a place for herself within the limited and constrictive range of acceptable Victorian womanhood that she encounters, which ranges from the heartless flirt or domestic homebody to the sexless schoolmistress or self-sacrificing nun. Even as she rejects each of those in turn, she learns to adapt parts of those roles fit her own desires. She wants for herself the peaceful domesticity of Mrs. Bretton and Polly Home, the romantic adventures of Ginevra Fanshawe, and the power of Madame Beck. In the end, she does get this combination when Monsieur Paul gives her a little school of her own (combining the world of domesticity and the world of work). Brontë creates domestic bliss for Lucy without domestic responsibilities, for Monsieur Paul leaves immediately after having declared his love and given Lucy her school. Lucy is thus able to live and work in an atmosphere combining romantic anticipation and independence. These years are, as she says, the happiest of her life. In *Villette*, Brontë thus rewrites the typical woman's story and the typical romance ending, and the novel concludes ambiguously as Lucy, again the unreliable narrator, refuses to give a definitive account of her and Monsieur Paul's fate.

Judith Burdan

Bibliography:

Allott, Miriam, ed. *The Brontës: The Critical Heritage*. London: Routledge & Kegan Paul, 1974. Fascinating collection of sixteen reviews and comments from 1853, the year of *Villette*'s publication. William Makepeace Thackeray is admiring, if condescending, for example, whereas Matthew Arnold finds the novel "disagreeable."

_____, ed. *Charlotte Brontë: "Jane Eyre" and "Villette": A Casebook*. London: Macmillan, 1973. Various writings about *Villette*, including several opinions from the year the novel was published, as well as later Victorian assessments and critical views from the 1950's and 1960's. Allott's introduction includes biographical information and a brief review of Brontë's critical reception. Includes a dated but helpful annotated bibliography.

Martin, Robert Bernard. *Charlotte Brontë's Novels: The Accents of Persuasion.* New York: W. W. Norton, 1966. In this very readable study of Brontë's four novels, Martin proposes *Villette* as the most mature and representing a synthesis of ideas and techniques explored in the earlier works. Detailed examination of the language, plot, character development, and structure.

Nestor, Pauline. *Charlotte Brontë.* Totowa, N.J.: Barnes & Noble Books, 1987. Examines Brontë's life and fiction from a feminist perspective and devotes one chapter to each of the novels. Nestor sees *Villette* as the story of a woman's development from weakness to strength, from dependence to self-sufficiency. Includes many quotations from other critics, and a bibliography.

_____, ed. *"Villette."* New York: St. Martin's Press, 1992. Offers nine essays and extracts written after 1970. Several of the analyses present sophisticated yet accessible feminist interpretations. Also includes an editor's introduction and a list of sources for further reading.

A VINDICATION OF THE RIGHTS OF WOMAN

Type of work: Social criticism
Author: Mary Wollstonecraft (1759-1797)
First published: 1792

Mary Wollstonecraft's *A Vindication of the Rights of Woman* is considered by many to be the manifesto of feminism, the first expression of these ideas. Although others had written about the need for women's rights before its publication, *A Vindication of the Rights of Woman* is the first comprehensive statement about the need for women to be educated and for philosophical treatises on the nature of gender differences. Like many late eighteenth century essays, this text may seem to later readers to ramble and repeat ideas when the point has already been made. Mary Wollstonecraft was expressing new and radical concepts that shocked many, and which were connected to the ideas fueling the French Revolution, an event that so frightened the English government that it suspended most political and many civil liberties during this time. Her repetitions and careful, sometimes overstated, logic can be explained as the natural reflex of anyone who introduces revolutionary notions to a culture.

Wollstonecraft's primary concern is with the education of women. This essay is, in large part, a rebuttal to Jean-Jacques Rousseau's ideas, expressed primarily in his novel *Emilius and Sophia: Or, A New System of Education* (1762), concerning the proper education of men and women. Rousseau contends that civilization has debased humanity, which would be better off in what he calls the "state of nature." He argues that women should be educated to be the solace and companions of men when men wish to turn from serious pursuits and be entertained and refreshed. Accordingly, the guiding principles of a woman's education should be to teach her to obey and to please.

The title of this collection also reflects that of another work, *A Vindication of the Rights of Men* (1790), which Wollstonecraft wrote in response to English conservative philosopher Edmund Burke's criticisms of the French Revolution, which he expressed in *Reflections on the French Revolution* (1790). Burke rejects not only the revolution's violence, but also the premise that all men could and should govern themselves. Wollstonecraft's critique points out the flagrant problems among the working classes in England, effectively disputing Burke's claims.

Mary Wollstonecraft bases much of her argument in favor of women's education on the fact, which had only recently been agreed on, that women do have souls. She asserts that because women are immortal beings who have a relationship to their creator, they must be educated in the proper use of reason. She believes that the quality that sets humans apart from animals is reason, and the quality that sets one human apart from another is virtue. Rousseau argues that emotion is the preeminent human quality; Wollstonecraft contends that humans have passions so they can struggle against them and thereby gain self-knowledge. From God's perspective, the present evil of the passions leads to a future good from the struggle to overcome them. The purpose of life for all humans, not just men, is to perfect one's nature through the exercise of reason. This leads to knowledge and virtue, the qualities God wishes each person to gain. It is, therefore, immoral to leave women in ignorance or formed merely by the prejudices of society. An education that develops the mind is essential for any immortal creature.

The essay argues that both wealth and gender roles create major problems in society, because both tend to create unequal relationships among humans. Inequality leads either to slavery or to despotism, both of which warp the human character. Wollstonecraft contends that all humans have a will to exert themselves and will do so. Dependence on a father or husband, which was woman's lot at the time in which Wollstonecraft wrote, creates cunning and deceit just as slavery did. Wollstonecraft argues that women's typical education in the home is a common knowledge of human nature, the use of power in indirect ways (cunning), a soft temper, outward obedience, a "puerile propriety," and an overemphasis on beauty. This type of education does not develop a good person, but one who is immature, incapable of sustained, orderly thought, and, therefore, easily influenced. Yet this person will still exert her will indirectly. Such an education does not produce a good citizen, Wollstonecraft argues, and it would be for the good of the society to educate women's reason.

This type of education does not produce good wives or mothers either, she argues, and these are the primary human (not female) duties of women. A woman is taught to earn her way by charming and flirting, fascinating a man. Wollstonecraft is quick to point out that love does not last: The cornerstone of any good marriage is friendship. A woman would do better to inspire respect rather than sensual fascination. Furthermore, a woman who is constantly concerned with pleasing men does not make a good mother. She does not have the character to guide her own children, and sometimes views her daughters as rivals rather than becoming their mentor and friend. This can be damaging to the family, particularly if she is left a widow, and, in turn, damages society. Here she employs her most famous image, stating that this current miseducation produces women much like hothouse flowers, which are artificially induced to bloom too early and, therefore, are weak.

Wollstonecraft argues that having too much power over another human also damages human character. Monarchs, she points out, are frequently put on the throne through treachery and crime. How can a man be properly educated in reason and morality when he is surrounded by such activity? Wealth, in fact the entire aristocratic system, produces abuses of power and cripples the human character, she contends. All military branches are based on inequality, on obeying without understanding. Not only the monarch, the aristocracy, and the military, but also priests and husbands rely on blind obedience for their power. She contends that as the divine right of kings has been rejected through reason, the divine right of husbands over their wives should end as well. Society should work to develop well-educated, moral citizens. To that end, society would do well not to develop professions that produce warped human beings, since all human character, not just women's, is formed by the habits of one's occupation and society at large.

Wollstonecraft's views show the influence of the Enlightenment. Enlightenment philosophy developed alongside the scientific revolution that followed the Spanish Inquisition, witch burnings, and the Protestant Reformation. The Inquisition and witch burnings came from a worldview based on tradition and dogma. Persons who did not obey the Church or king without question were tortured and murdered; many women who were burned were accused of disobeying their husbands, the Church, or the monarch. The Reformation, and the subsequent period now called the Enlightenment, can be viewed as a reaction against the extremes of this time. Reason was emphasized above dogma; the Reformation gave each individual direct access to God, whereas before one had to approach the divine through the priesthood. The structure of European government, the divine right of kings, was also called into question. If individuals could approach God themselves, they could also govern themselves. These ideas, in addition to the Iroquois Federation system of government found among Native Americans, fueled the American and French revolutions and subsequently spread until the United States and most of Europe adopted forms of democracy as the primary system of government.

Mary Wollstonecraft concedes that men are superior to women in physical strength, but writes that this is a superiority of degree, not kind. Women and men are similar in the kind of virtues they should and do possess, if not in the amount. Therefore, women should be educated in a manner similar to that of men and be treated as human beings, not a special subspecies called "feminine." Having made this concession, Wollstonecraft states that since a natural physical superiority exists, men should feel no need to produce unnatural weakness in women. She argues for natural exercise for girls, rejects feminine garments that restrict and damage the body, and encourages girls to express themselves naturally rather than developing simpering, weak ways to entice men.

This essay often argues directly with Rousseau, John Milton, and other poets and philosophers. It also addresses itself to a variety of books and manuals written as advice on how women should conduct themselves and raise young girls. The same points underlie these direct critiques: Women should be encouraged to be reasonable, not simply feminine; girls should be allowed healthy exercise and play; an overemphasis on being feminine rather than human is harmful not only to women but also to men and society in general.

Wollstonecraft anticipates psychological models of human development in her discussion of the source of gender differences. While the authors she critiques argue that girls naturally have a fondness for dress and appearance, or love to play with dolls or listen to gossip because it is their nature, Wollstonecraft points to the everyday circumstances of little girls' lives to explain their predilections. She also points out, anticipating Virginia Woolf in her feminist essays, that men also have a fondness for dress. Just observe military men, judges, or priests. In this same vein, in her critique of some male professions, Wollstonecraft argues that miseducation can produce foolish men. The foolishness of women that men often criticize has been produced by society through women's miseducation. Foolishness is not a sexual characteristic, but a trait that comes from miseducation, a condition that can be remedied.

The essay concludes with recommendations on how to correct the problems it has outlined. First, women should be properly educated. Women must be able to support themselves in case a husband or family member cannot do so. Giving women access to the professions will reduce prostitution and other social problems. Women also should have the legal rights of citizens—the rights to own property, have custody of their children, and participate in government.

Wollstonecraft's essay produced a great stir, both critical and favorable. Public opinion, however, was scandalized after her death when her husband, William Godwin, published the frank facts of her life—sex outside of marriage, an illegitimate child, and a suicide attempt. Feminist ideas were branded as immoral and dangerous, apt to lead other women to live such a life. Nevertheless, whenever concerns for women's rights rise in the public consciousness, *A Vindication of the Rights of Woman* is pulled from the shelf, dusted off, reread, republished, and discussed with a great stir, both critical and favorable.

Theresa L. Crater

Bibliography:

Falco, Maria J. *Feminist Interpretations of Mary Wollstonecraft*. University Park: Pennsylvania State University Press, 1996. A good collection of essays looking at Wollstonecraft's ideas in the light of subsequent developments in feminism.

George, Margaret. *One Woman's "Situation": A Study of Mary Wollstonecraft*. Champaign: University of Illinois Press, 1970. Discusses Mary Wollstonecraft's life and ideas.

Kelly, Gary. *Revolutionary Feminism: The Mind and Career of Mary Wollstonecraft*. New York: St. Martin's Press, 1992. A careful analysis of Wollstonecraft's major ideas and her influences.

Sapiro, Virginia. *A Vindication of Political Virtue: The Political Theory of Mary Wollstonecraft.* Chicago: University of Chicago Press, 1992. Excellent analysis of Wollstonecraft's contribution to both feminism and Western political thought.

Wollstonecraft, Mary. *A Vindication of the Rights of Woman*, edited by Carol H. Poston. 1st ed. New York: W. W. Norton, 1975. Contains the authoritative text of this essay, a section on background materials to which Wollstonecraft was responding, selections from the debate sparked by this text, and excellent critical essays.

THE VIOLENT BEAR IT AWAY

Type of work: Novel
Author: Flannery O'Connor (1925-1964)
Type of plot: Psychological realism
Time of plot: 1952
Locale: Tennessee
First published: 1960

> *Principal characters:*
> FRANCIS MARION TARWATER, a fourteen-year-old boy trained to be a
>   prophet
> GEORGE F. RAYBER, his uncle
> MASON TARWATER, Francis' great-uncle
> BISHOP RAYBER, Francis' cousin
> BERNICE BISHOP RAYBER, Francis' aunt, George's wife
> BUFORD MUNSON, a neighbor
> T. FAWCETT MEEKS, a traveling salesman
> LUCETTE CARMODY, a child evangelist

The Story:

Mason Tarwater, great-uncle of Francis Marion Tarwater, died at the breakfast table one morning. The old man had spent years training his nephew, with whom he lived in a backwoods spot called Powderhead, how to bury him properly. As young Francis Tarwater began to prepare for the burial, he recalled events from his life with Old Tarwater and the various reasons he did not want to follow in the old man's footsteps. Young Tarwater recalled that the old man had kidnapped him from the home of his uncle, George F. Rayber, and provided a fundamentalist education quite different from that which the boy would have received in public school. Young Tarwater also recalled the old man's stories about his life as a prophet and his failed attempts to save relatives other than his great-nephew, notably Rayber, whom Old Tarwater kidnapped at age seven; Rayber rejected the old man's preaching and later tried to get young Tarwater back. Old Tarwater would tell his great-nephew that he shot Rayber in the leg and ear to prevent the boy's being taken away by Rayber and the woman who became his wife, Bernice Bishop. Old Tarwater was pleased that Rayber and Bernice had only one child and that the child, Bishop Rayber, was an idiot, for idiocy would protect young Tarwater from the foolish ideas of Rayber, just as the boy had escaped public school by pretending to be an idiot. Young Tarwater remembered that he had been ordered by Old Tarwater to accept the mission of baptizing little Bishop. He also remembered a trip to the city with Old Tarwater, who found out from lawyers that he could not take Powderhead from Rayber and give it to the boy; it was on this day that young Tarwater got the only glimpse of both Rayber and Bishop that he could remember while living with Old Tarwater.

As Tarwater started to dig the old man's grave, he heard a stranger's voice. When two black people, a woman and Buford Munson, interrupted Tarwater's digging to have him fill their jugs with liquor, Tarwater went to Old Tarwater's still and got drunk. The stranger's voice encouraged young Tarwater to go his own way. After being scolded by Buford, Tarwater fell asleep. Buford buried Old Tarwater in accordance with the old man's wishes. When young Tarwater awoke, he burned the house, thinking Old Tarwater was in it, and ran off toward the city.

A traveling salesman, T. Fawcett Meeks, picked up the hitchhiking Tarwater on the highway, lectured him about loving customers, hard work, and machines, and delivered Tarwater to the home of Rayber. While being transported by Meeks, Tarwater remembered Old Tarwater's stories of Rayber's life, especially how Rayber arranged for his sister to take a lover and give birth to Tarwater and how Rayber once betrayed Old Tarwater by writing up their conversations as a case study for a magazine. Old Tarwater's kidnapping of Tarwater followed his reading of Rayber's article. When Rayber took Tarwater into his home, they seemed very strange to each other. Tarwater saw Rayber's hearing aid as a sign that Rayber was a mechanical man; Rayber saw the old man's influence all over Tarwater. Rayber's son Bishop was immediately friendly, but Tarwater rejected the little boy. Rayber set out on a campaign to introduce Tarwater to the city and the modern world. Tarwater was thoroughly unimpressed with the modern world, but he did sneak out of the house one night, and Rayber followed to see what Tarwater liked. They ended up at a Pentecostal church where a child evangelist, Lucette Carmody, started to direct her sermon at the astonished Rayber. The next day, Rayber tried taking Tarwater to the city park. While there, Rayber remembered how he had once tried to drown Bishop. Then Rayber noticed Tarwater was about to baptize Bishop in the park's fountain and stopped him. Later, Tarwater's memory of the park trip revealed Tarwater's encouragement by his stranger/friend to drown Bishop. After the trip to the park, Rayber next tried to get through to Tarwater by taking him fishing. When Rayber took Tarwater out in a boat, Rayber's analysis of Tarwater's mind caused Tarwater to vomit, jump from the boat, and swim to shore. Rayber planned to surprise Tarwater with a visit to Powderhead to make him confront feelings about his past, but when Rayber went to Powderhead in advance to prepare, he realized that he could not bear to return with Tarwater. After returning to the lake, Rayber allowed Tarwater to take Bishop out in a boat; Rayber collapsed as, back in his cabin, he sensed Tarwater was drowning his son. Fleeing from the lake, Tarwater planned to take possession of Powderhead, as he told the sleepy truck driver who gave him a ride. Tarwater admitted to baptizing Bishop but denied it had any significance. After being dropped off, Tarwater was picked up by a man who gave him a smoke, drugged him to sleep with liquor, and raped him.

When Tarwater awoke, he burned the woods around where the rape had occurred, then headed toward Powderhead. He burned more woods when he heard his stranger/friend's voice again. When he reached Powderhead, he encountered Buford, who explained that Old Tarwater was properly buried after all. Now Tarwater had a vision of his own role as a prophet, and instead of remaining at Powderhead, he headed back toward the city.

Critical Evaluation:

Flannery O'Connor is widely considered one of America's greatest short-story writers as well as one of the best religious writers of the modern era. Although her collected works comprise little more than two dozen stories and two novels, and although many of her works replay similar plots using similar sets of characters, she did a masterful job of investigating the specific issues that obsessed her. O'Connor's fictions are filled with humor as well as with profound insights into the eccentric, sometimes tortured strategies human beings use to create meaning.

O'Connor's people are sometimes considered flat, almost cartoonish, but *The Violent Bear It Away* uses several devices for emphasizing the complexities of psychology. For example, the conflicting sides to Francis Marion Tarwater's mind are given voices in the form of strangers and friends who talk to him. Although Tarwater consistently refuses to confess his thoughts to other, real characters, he does carry on conversations with parts of himself, allowing O'Connor to analyze his simultaneous attraction to and rejection of the religious and nonreligious paths his various parental figures have planned for him. In addition, O'Connor draws numerous parallels among Old Tarwater, Rayber, Francis Tarwater, and even Bishop, encouraging us to assume that what one character thinks or feels, the others might experience in some form. Each of these characters arguably contains parts of the others. Although Old Tarwater is dead when the novel begins, the reader receives so much information about the old man's stories and opinions and the other characters are so haunted by him that Old Tarwater seems clearly alive. When Tarwater marches off toward the city at the novel's end, the reader knows that he carries the other characters with him. Even at times when O'Connor's intent may seem to be to distinguish between characters, as when Rayber and Tarwater remember in separate chapters their trip to the city park, the reader can assume that each character feels much of what the other feels. In general, the novel's numerous flashbacks leave the reader with the impression that at least three characters are here collaborating on the creation of a family mythology and that they all exist beyond time, whether alive or dead.

One of O'Connor's major themes is the power of mystery. The kind of rationality promoted by such characters as Rayber and Meeks, with its intelligence testing, its laws, and its economy tied to the machine, is consistently ridiculed by the novel. In O'Connor's world, almost anything is valuable if it turns off the common sense of the brain. Idiocy is good as a protection from education. Liquor may be endorsed as a way to shut down consciousness. Violent acts are essentially unreasonable, but they may be necessary to break through the mind's reasonable defenses.

O'Connor's love of mystery also relates to the religious themes in the novel. Tarwater and Old Tarwater both have problems with forming overly sensible expectations about what a moment of religious insight would be. They expect elaborate visions of exotic divinity; what they get is much more homespun—revelation through images of water and fire, fish and bread. One of the major tasks O'Connor sets for herself in this novel is to make interesting for the modern reader the sacrament of baptism, a ritual in danger of becoming boring through familiarity. To force the reader to investigate the meaning of baptism, she makes it new by having it performed on an idiot by an unenthusiastic Tarwater, who kills at the same time he baptizes. O'Connor makes religion intellectually interesting by making it painful rather than comforting. Old Tarwater says, "The world was made for the dead," a sentiment O'Connor seems to endorse. O'Connor is also interested in making fresh for modern readers the idea of the prophet. Her prophets are individualistic, anti-intellectual, destructive, suicidal, so driven by unconscious forces as to seem insane.

One of the paradoxes of the novel is that while the characters pursue intensely eccentric personal paths, they ultimately seem remarkably similar. For all its rejection of the city, O'Connor's novel hints at the possibility of building a good community. Although the four main characters are white, there are indications that Tarwater at the end of the novel will also minister to blacks, and the black man Buford Munson is arguably the novel's most religious character. There may be less reason to be confident that Tarwater will someday bring women into his community; he has been taught to consider women whores, and the acquaintance of Lucette Carmody, the female who most fascinates Tarwater, may do little to move Tarwater out of his adolescence. Another of the novel's surprises is how little family seems to have to do with the building of community. Relations between parents and children are always strained and sometimes violent in O'Connor's work, and the conscious rejection of family often seems necessary for an O'Connor character to find the right path.

Marshall Bruce Gentry

Bibliography:

Asals, Frederick. *Flannery O'Connor: The Imagination of Extremity*. Athens: University of Georgia Press, 1982. A frequently cited study of O'Connor's attraction to polar oppositions. Emphasizes the Christian sacramentalism, psychology, and use of doubles in *The Violent Bear It Away*, as well as the differences between O'Connor's novels. Treats the novel's ending as both comic and tragic.

Bacon, Jon Lance. *Flannery O'Connor and Cold War Culture*. New York: Cambridge University Press, 1993. Treats O'Connor as a Southern critic of nationalistic Cold War culture in America. *The Violent Bear It Away* becomes a rejection of cultural pressures to conform in terms of politics, public education, consumerism, and religion.

Gentry, Marshall Bruce. *Flannery O'Connor's Religion of the Grotesque*. Jackson: University Press of Mississippi, 1986. Distinguishes between O'Connor and her narrator in an effort to answer the claim that O'Connor wrote from the devil's point of view. Discusses O'Connor's typescripts and emphasizes Rayber's similarity to other characters.

Hendin, Josephine. *The World of Flannery O'Connor*. Bloomington: Indiana University Press, 1970. A controversial but important early study that generally downplays religious explanations. Treats the novel as an examination of a failed initiation into manhood, in which the protagonist finally reverts to a painfully childish role.

Johansen, Ruthann Knechel. *The Narrative Secret of Flannery O'Connor: The Trickster as Interpreter*. Tuscaloosa: University of Alabama Press, 1994. Emphasizes the structures in O'Connor's texts and examines the apocalyptic nature of those texts as well as the role of the trickster figures. Compares O'Connor's novels to one another and to biblical narratives.

THE VIOLENT LAND

Type of work: Novel
Author: Jorge Amado (1912-   )
Type of plot: Social realism
Time of plot: Late nineteenth century
Locale: State of Bahia, Brazil
First published: Terras do sem fin, 1942 (English translation, 1945)

Principal characters:

COLONEL HORACIO DA SILVEIRA, a cacao planter
COLONEL SINHÔ BADARÓ, another planter
DOÑA ESTER DA SILVEIRA, Colonel da Silveira's wife
DOÑA ANA BADARÓ, Colonel Badaró's daughter
CAPTAIN JOÃO MAGALHÃES, in love with Doña Ana
DR. VIRGILIO CABRAL, Doña Ester's lover and da Silveira's lawyer
MARGOT, a prostitute
JUCA BADARÓ, Colonel Badaró's younger brother

The Story:

In the minds of most Brazilians, the São Jorge dos Ilhéus was a semibarbarous country ruled by a handful of rich planters who styled themselves colonels. These men had risen, almost without exception, from humble origins by means of courage, bravado, and murder. The two most important planters were Colonel Horacio da Silveira and Colonel Sinhô Badaró. Between their lands lay a large forest, upon which both men had long cast covetous eyes. The forest, actually a jungle, could be cleared to uncover an almost fabulous cacao-growing soil.

Among the strangers who poured into the region in search of wealth at the time were several people who were to range themselves on one side or the other in the coming struggle. Dr. Virgilio Cabral, a cultured and talented lawyer, was to ally himself with da Silveira. With the lawyer came Margot, a beautiful prostitute who had fallen in love with him and become his mistress while he was a student. Another arrival was Captain João Magalhães, a professional gambler and a courageous opportunist who called himself a military engineer. Among his admirers were Juca Badaró, Colonel Badaró's younger brother, and Doña Ana Badaró, the colonel's daughter, who was also the heiress to the Badaró fortunes.

Soon after his arrival, Cabral fell in love with Ester, da Silveira's beautiful wife. The woman, who hated her semibarbarous husband, quickly returned the affection of the more cultured man. When she became his mistress, both knew that they would be killed if the husband found them out. As his ardor for Ester da Silveira increased, the lawyer's affection for his former mistress waned, and soon Margot found herself unwanted by her lover. In retaliation, and because she needed someone to support her, Margot became the mistress of Juca Badaró. Out of spite, she also furnished him with scandal about the opposition, gossip that he turned to account in the newspaper which favored the Badarós.

Professionally, as well as amorously, Cabral was a success, for he found an old survey of the contested lands and registered the title in da Silveira's name after he had bribed the registry officials. The Badaró family quickly retaliated by burning the registry office and all the records on file. In addition, the Badarós hired Magalhães to run a survey for them. He made the survey, even though he lacked the proper knowledge to do so. His presence at the Badaró plantation earned him the respect of the Badaró brothers and the love of Doña Ana Badaró. The self-styled captain, always an opportunist, permitted himself to fall in love with the woman and pay court to her.

The Badaró family was the more powerful of the two factions, so da Silveira went to several small planters and promised to let them divide half of the forest land if they, as a group, would help him hold it against the Badarós. There was bloody fighting on both sides of the forest and within it, for both factions hired many assassins and bodyguards to back up their interests with bullets. The Badarós controlled the local government, and the state government was in opposition to the federal government of Brazil.

Juca Badaró was assassinated by a hired gunman after he had insulted Cabral. Juca had found the lawyer dancing—at the woman's request—with Margot and had insulted the lawyer for daring to do so. On the other side, too, there were disappointments and deaths. Cabral and da Silveira were deterred in their plans when the colonel fell ill with a fever. The planter recovered, but his wife, the lawyer's mistress, became ill as a result of nursing her husband. Her death removed one incentive in the efforts of both her husband and her lover, but they stubbornly continued the fight.

As the struggle in the courts and in the fields continued, the Badarós spent more and more money. They not only sold their current crop of cacao pods but also sold their next year's crop in order to raise funds. Before his assassination, Juca Badaró had seen to it that his niece, Doña Ana, was married to the gambler, for he saw in Magalhães an ambitious man willing to fight for money and power. So tempting was the proposal the Badarós made that the captain agreed to take his wife's name, her father insisting that he do so in order to carry on the Badaró line.

At first, by tacit consent, the contending parties did no damage to one another's cacao trees, but as the Badarós became desperate, they instructed their desperadoes to burn the cacao groves. Their opponents saw that the matter had to be settled at once, lest both parties be irretrievably ruined and become victims of someone stronger than they. Colonel da Silveira and his henchman, along with their paid gunmen, attacked the Badaró plantation in force and drove off the family, after killing all the men except a handful led by Magalhães.

Da Silveira and his men thought that the women of the Badaró household had been sent away, but the attackers were greeted by gunfire from Doña Ana herself as they entered the house. When she ran out of ammunition, she gave up, expecting to be killed. The attackers let her go, however, because she was a woman. The Badaró rout was completed by an announcement from the Brazilian capital that the political party favoring da Silveira had come into power and was sending troops and government agents to the district to quiet the violence. The jungle lands were ceded to the da Silveira faction by the government's action. Da Silveira was forced to stand trial for the murder of Juca Badaró, but the trial, having been staged more to clear the colonel than to find him guilty, was a mere formality.

The district quickly settled down after the great feud had ended and the new government had started its operations, but there was to be one more assassination. While going through his dead wife's effects, da Silveira discovered the letters Cabral had written to her. He was horrified and embarrassed to learn of her infidelity, which he had not suspected, and his lawyer's duplicity. After thinking about the matter for some time, he sent a gunman to clear his honor by killing the man who had made him a cuckold.

To symbolize the new peace that had come into the frontier district, the church made the city of Ilhéus the seat of a newly created diocese and sent a bishop to officiate as its representative there. As if to show the value of the former jungle land, the cacao trees planted there produced a crop in the fourth year, a full twelve months earlier than usual.

Critical Evaluation:

Jorge Amado's novel is titled *Terras do sem fin* (the endless lands) in Portuguese. This story is the standard-bearer of the cacao cycle in Brazilian literature, a series of novels exposing exploitation of cacao workers. Brazilian novelists have long been making a huge mosaic of Brazil with their novels, each novel being a tiny stone in the literary mosaic of that subcontinent, and Amado's work is a worthy one and his masterpiece.

The Violent Land (first published in English in 1945) is the story of Bahia's Panhandle, where a balmy climate, fertile soil, and lack of high winds make it one of the few areas on earth well suited for chocolate trees, whose weak stems and heavy pods need heat but cannot stand strong winds. Amado's characterization is particularly representative of the raw frontier that the Panhandle of Bahia (a narrow strip stretching southward toward the mountains of Espírito Santo) has been for so long. The reader thus sees not only an area where the "colonels" and their heavily armed cohorts oppress the weak, but also the Bahian *sertão* (backlands) in general, brimming with blood, old feuds, religious messianism, and fanaticism. Amado's characters are thus not larger-than-life but authentic, flesh-and-blood realities from rural Bahia. His principal characterization flaw is an error of omission, for the warmly human types so common everywhere in Brazil, including Bahia, are lacking in the pages of *The Violent Land*.

This novel refreshingly explodes the oft-heard myth that Brazil, unlike Spanish America, is a bland and frivolous land not given to violence. Amado's novel bristles with the violence and mystery endemic to the *sertão*, and it is for this reason that Amado's true title of *The Endless Lands* has been changed for the book's English translation into *The Violent Land*. Amado paints a land fertile with blood, as his preface indicates. Set about the end of the nineteenth century, when cacao was power, wealth, and life, the novel's action portrays the enslavement of everything and everyone to the cacao pod. The shadow of cacao darkens every heart. It smothers finer instincts and levels all characters from aristocratic Colonel Horacio da Silveira to the more common Badarós. Nothing washes away the cacao stain. Workers in the orchards have a thick crust of cacao slime on their boots, while everyone from colonels to lawyers, merchants, and *jaguncos* (hired killers) have cacao slime in their hearts.

The Violent Land reflects progress, however, for the colonels are drawn as a crude but civilizing force in Brazil's historic "march to the west" that opened up the once trackless *sertão*. Amado was born on a cacao plantation in 1912 and admired the *fazendeiros* (ranchers), such as his own father, who settled the raw Panhandle, crossed lands, built roads, and founded towns, all this through heroic strength and what Amado terms "the poetry of their lives." The novel's first scene, symbolically enough, is aboard a ship drawing away from the black-tile roofs of the baroque city of São Salvador de Bahia. The passengers aboard are immigrants to the rich but violent lands of the Panhandle and are discussing lands, money, cacao, and death. They sing a sad song that presages disaster, but that night, in their staterooms and steerage quarters, they dream of laden cacao trees.

Landscape is an important factor in *The Violent Land* and reflects Brazil's intrinsic beauty. Amado paints the golden mornings dawning over green palms, the red soil under the cacao trees, the blue-green waves of the sea, and indigo skies. One also sees stormy nights, wild Brahma cattle, birds, and snakes. Trees are almost idolized, especially the cacao. Above all, Amado lyrically paints the forest in the uninterrupted sleep that it enjoyed before the colonels came. Days and nights pass over the virginal expanses of trees, along with winter rains and summer suns. The waiting forest is like an unexplored sea, locked in its own mystery: virginal, lovely, and radiant. Amado also presents the varied Bahian racial types from Scandinavian-like blonds to Latin brunettes and Hamitic blacks. One also sees the colonels in khaki trousers, white hats, and gun belts, as well as the leather-clad *jaguncos*, legendarily ferocious *oncas* (wild cats), ranch tools, and folklore.

Fear is an additional element in the story. The forest's mysteries incite fear—Ester hysterically fears snakes and is haunted by the phobia that they will one night invade her house en masse. The backlanders tell many snake stories, while dogs howl at night, rain clouds are dark, and nights are jet-black; but the violent Badaró family and the *jaguncos* do not know fear. The Badarós even read the Bible daily for they, like the endless lands that they are so ruthlessly penetrating, are many-sided.

Lamentably, the storied and colorful old city of São Salvador de Bahia does not loom in *The Violent Land*. Little, pastel São Jorge dos Ilhéus, "a city of palms in the wind," is, however, well depicted. Its streets are lined by palms, but it is dominated by the cacao tree, for the scent of chocolate is in every conversation, and each colonel's fortune can be measured by the size of his mansion. Inland from the pastel town, on every red-dirt road leading into the cacao lands, are crosses without names.

Brazilian novelists complained for decades that the harsh, nasal, Germanic-sounding Portuguese language in which they wrote was "the Graveyard of Literature," a literary cul-de-sac. *The Violent Land*, however, was translated into more than twenty languages, and translations of other novels into foreign languages have since been opening Brazilian literature to the world. Amado's masterwork also helps reveal that the key to Brazilian literature is not chronology, nor style, nor study of influences, but geography. *The Violent Land* is to be read and regarded as a work of the land of Bahia.

"Critical Evaluation" by William Freitas

Bibliography:
Chamberlain, Bobby J. *Jorge Amado*. Boston: Twayne, 1990. A study of aspects of Amado's major novels. Places the author's fiction in a biographical and bibliographic context, offers critical analysis, and lays the groundwork for a reevaluation of the author's novelistic output. Discusses *The Violent Land* as the forerunner of the later novels. Chronology and annotated bibliography.
Ellison, Fred P. *Brazil's New Novel: Four Northeastern Masters*. Berkeley: University of California Press, 1954. Insightful study examining style, theme, and characterization in Amado's early fiction. Includes a discussion of *The Violent Land*. One of the earliest studies in English of Amado.
Lowe, Elizabeth. *The City in Brazilian Literature*. Madison, N.J.: Fairleigh Dickinson University Press, 1982. Characterizes Amado's depiction of Salvador, Bahia, as "picturesque exoticism," and his portrayal of the urban poor as "carnivalization."
Pescatello, Ann, ed. "The Braziliera: Images and Realities in Writings of Machado de Assis and Jorge Amado." In *Female and Male in Latin America: Essays*. Pittsburgh: University of Pittsburgh Press, 1973. Compares Amado's female characters (including those in *The Violent Land*) with those of Machado de Assis. Detects a preoccupation with class and race in both writers' female characterizations.
Schade, George D. "Three Contemporary Brazilian Novels: Some Comparisons and Contrasts." *Hispania* 39, no. 4 (December, 1956): 391-396. Compares the structure, theme, and characterization in *The Violent Land* with Graciliano Ramos' *Anguish* (1936) and Rachel de Queiroz's *The Three Marias* (1939).

THE VIRGINIAN
A Horseman of the Plains

Type of work: Novel
Author: Owen Wister (1860-1938)
Type of plot: Western
Time of plot: Late nineteenth century
Locale: Wyoming
First published: 1902

Principal characters:
THE VIRGINIAN, a cowboy
JUDGE HENRY, the Virginian's employer
TRAMPAS, a cowboy and the Virginian's enemy
STEVE, a cowboy friend of the Virginian
SHORTY, a cowboy at Judge Henry's ranch
MOLLY WOOD, a young schoolteacher at Bear Creek, Wyoming

The Story:

The Virginian had been sent by his employer, the owner of the Sunk Creek Ranch, to meet an Eastern guest at Medicine Bow and escort him the 260 miles from the town to the ranch. While the Virginian and the guest awaited the arrival of the Easterner's trunk on the next train, the cowboy entered into a poker game. One of the players, a cowboy named Trampas, accused the Virginian of cheating. The man backed down before the Virginian's gun, but it was clear to everyone that the Virginian had made an implacable enemy.

A few months later, in the fall, a schoolmistress came West from Vermont to teach in the new school at Bear Creek, Wyoming. All the single men—and there were many of them in the territory—eagerly awaited the arrival of the new teacher, Molly Wood. The Virginian was fortunate in his first meeting with her. A drunken stage driver had tried to ford a creek in high water and marooned his coach and passenger. The Virginian, who was just passing, lifted the young woman out of the stage and deposited her safely on the bank of the stream. After he had ridden away, Molly missed her handkerchief and realized that the young cowboy had somehow contrived to take it.

The next time the Virginian saw Molly, she was a guest at a barbecue. He had ridden his horse for two days for the opportunity to see her, but she coquettishly refused to notice him. Piqued, the Virginian and another cowboy got drunk and played a prank on all the people who had brought babies to the barbecue; they switched the babies' clothing, so that many of the mothers carried off the wrong children. Before returning to Sunk Creek, the Virginian warned Molly that she was going to love him eventually, no matter what she thought of him then.

During the next year, the Virginian began to read books for the first time since he had left school in the sixth grade. He borrowed the books from Molly, which gave him the opportunity to ride to Bear Creek to see her at intervals. In the meantime, he had risen high in the estimation of his employer. Judge Henry put him in charge of a party of men who were to escort two trainloads of steers to the Chicago market.

On the trip back to the ranch, the Virginian's men threatened to desert the train to go prospecting for gold that had been discovered in the Black Hills. The ringleader of the insurgents was Trampas. The Virginian saw that the best way to win over the men was to make a fool of Trampas. His chance came when the train stopped near a bridge that was being repaired. Since there was no food on the train, the Virginian went out and gathered a sackful of frogs to cook. Then he began to tell a tall story about frogs that completely took in Trampas. When the other cowboys saw how foolish Trampas appeared, they were willing to return to the ranch, much to the discomfiture of their ringleader.

The Virginian returned to Sunk Creek to find a pleasant surprise awaiting him: The ranch foreman had had to leave because of his invalid wife, whereupon the judge had made the Virginian his foreman. Trampas expected to be discharged from his job as soon as the Virginian became foreman, but the Virginian decided it was better to have his enemy in sight, so Trampas stayed on, sullen and defiant.

The following spring, the Virginian made a trip to a neighboring ranch. On the way back, he was attacked by Indians and severely wounded. He managed to escape from the Indians and make his way to a spring. There he was found, half dead, by Molly Wood. The Indians were still in the vicinity, but the young woman stayed with him at the risk of her life. She bound his wounds, took him back to her cabin, and called a doctor.

Molly, who had been preparing to return to her home in the East, had already packed her possessions. She had to postpone her return to care for the Virginian, and by the time he had recovered sufficiently to go back to work, she had changed her mind. She was sure by then that she was in love with the cowboy foreman, and when the Virginian left her cabin for Sunk Creek, Molly promised to marry him.

Upon returning to work, the Virginian found that his enemy, Trampas, had disappeared, taking another of the cowboys, Shorty, with him. About the same time, the ranches in that territory began to lose cattle to rustlers. A posse was formed to track down the cattle thieves. After several weeks of searching, two of the thieves were caught. Since the rustlers had somehow managed to gain control of the local courts and had already been freed on one charge, the posse hanged both of them. It was a terrible experience for the Virginian, especially since one of the men, Steve, had been a close friend. The Virginian hated to think he had hanged his friend, and the hurt was worse because the condemned man had refused to say a word to his former companion. On his way back to Sunk Creek, the Virginian came across the trail of the remaining two rustlers, Trampas and Shorty. Because they had only one horse between them with which to escape, Trampas murdered Shorty.

When Molly Wood heard of the lynching and of the Virginian's part in it, she at first refused to marry him. After a conversation with Judge Henry, however, she realized that the Virginian had done no more than his duty. She and the Virginian were reconciled, and a date was set for their wedding.

On the day before their wedding, Molly and the Virginian started to ride to Medicine Bow. On the way, they met Trampas, who galloped ahead of them into the town. Molly questioned the Virginian about the man and discovered the enmity between the two. When they arrived in town, they were warned that Trampas had said he would shoot the Virginian if he were not out of town by sunset. Molly told him that she could never marry him if he fought with Trampas and killed him. The Virginian, knowing that his honor was at stake, left her in the hotel and went out to face his enemy. Trampas fired first and missed. Then the Virginian fired and killed Trampas.

When the Virginian returned to the hotel, Molly was too glad to see him alive to remember her threat. Hearing the shots, she had been afraid that the Virginian had been killed. They were married the following day, as they had planned, and spent two months of their honeymoon high in the Rocky Mountains.

Critical Evaluation:

The Virginian is based on Owen Wister's experiences in the cattle country of Wyoming during the 1880's and 1890's, and he used that personal knowledge to create the model for all future Western novels. The setting for the story is the cattle business of Wyoming Territory during the late 1880's, when tension was growing between large cattle ranchers and smaller stock raisers. In April, 1892, wealthy cattlemen organized an expedition to arrest or kill all those in northern Wyoming who were suspected of being rustlers. The Johnson County War that ensued became one of the most notorious episodes of frontier violence. As an aristocratic visitor from Pennsylvania, Wister knew many of the men who were involved on the side of the large ranchers, and he used the people and events of the range war as a backdrop for the rivalry between the Virginian and his enemy, the rustler Trampas. He modeled Judge Henry on Frank Wolcott, a leading participant in the Johnson County violence.

Beyond describing the frontier situation, the novel had a larger artistic purpose. Wister had traveled to the West to recuperate after a nervous breakdown and to experience a change from the spreading industrialism and social tension of the Eastern United States where he had grown up. In *The Virginian*, Wister deals with the way the Eastern narrator and the Virginian's future bride respond to the rough life in the West during the heyday of the range cattle industry. By the time Wister wrote his novel two decades later, the open range and the free life that the cowboys and ranchers had known was already vanishing. *The Virginian* reflects his sense that something valuable was lost with the spread of civilization, a feeling shared by many Americans in the early part of the twentieth century. Wister's book evokes the spirit of the West and laments the passing of that spirit in the face of modern progress and economic development. In novel form, Wister expresses many of the same ideas that Frederick Jackson Turner discusses in his 1894 essay "The Significance of the Frontier in American History" and his 1920 book *The Frontier in American History*.

The Virginian is actually more a series of separate episodes and encounters than a fully realized novel. Some of these moments became classics of the Western genre. The first confrontation, for example, between the Virginian and Trampas—including the response "When you call me that, smile"—was based on an actual encounter Wister had seen, which with his skill as a writer he transformed into so memorable a moment that it has been duplicated on motion picture screens and television programs ever since. The final shoot-out between hero and villain in town just after sunset likewise became the model for countless repetitions of that confrontation in other Western novels, motion pictures, and television episodes.

What gave *The Virginian* its classic status in the literature of the American West were the larger themes Wister developed within the framework of the novel. With his ability to handle all the challenges he encounters in his rugged environment, the Virginian represents the strength and power of the frontier. He emerges as a true gentleman because of the instinctive rightness of his behavior. He only kills Trampas after having given him the first shot. In his depiction of the Virginian's courtship of Molly Wood, Wister depicts the underlying virtues of the West and its codes of manliness, honor, and self-reliance. In his depiction of the Virginian's confrontation with Trampas and the practice of cattle rustling, Wister even manages in Judge Henry's words to Molly Wood to make an argument for frontier lawlessness and lynching as a necessary response to the untamed conditions of the West.

At the same time, the East and its values are shown to have a civilizing effect on the Virginian and his world. He responds to Molly Wood's gentility and learning by beginning to read books and extend his rudimentary education. He forsakes the lonely and doomed life of the average young cowhand to become a trusted foreman and eventually a prosperous ranch owner in partnership with his patron. At the end of the book, he has evolved into a model of the frontier capitalist supervising many businesses. The Virginian is shown to be equally at his ease in the East with Molly's straitlaced relatives and in the West as an honest man who succeeds in the individualistic world of the frontier.

The Virginian achieved instant best-seller status when it was published in 1902 because it captured so well the American fascination with the frontier and with the people who had tamed the West in the nineteenth century. Readers responded to the laconic competence of the hero, the implicit violence of the rivalry with Trampas, and the romantic love story with the Eastern schoolteacher. The book also struck a chord because of Wister's skill in evoking an era that was so recently past.

Owen Wister never repeated the popular success of *The Virginian* with any of his other works. The character he created went on to be the subject of four motion pictures and a long-running television series. While Wister knew that he had touched a chord in the national psyche with his fictional creation, he did not succumb to the temptation to exploit his book's success with a sequel or related novels. The Virginian remains what he was in Wister's book. He is the Western hero with an obscure past that prepared him for the dangers he had to face. He passes through the story, righting wrongs, illuminating character, and doing justice. At the end, he finds happiness and personal fulfillment as do, vicariously, Wister's readers.

"Critical Evaluation" by Lewis L. Gould

Bibliography:

Cobbs, John L. *Owen Wister*. Boston: Twayne, 1984. Argues that Wister was a good writer whose works deserve more attention. Devotes one chapter to a discussion of *The Virginian* and provides a good survey of other secondary sources on the book through the early 1980's.

Etulain, Richard W. *Owen Wister*. Boise, Idaho: Boise State College, 1973. A brief survey of Wister's career and a good introduction to his writings. Includes some perceptive comments about *The Virginian*.

Lambert, Neal. "Owen Wister's Virginian: The Genesis of a Cultural Hero." *Western American Literature* 6 (Summer, 1971): 99-107. A perceptive analysis of the development and meaning of the central figure of Wister's novel by one of the leading students of his work.

Payne, Darwin. *Owen Wister: Chronicler of the West, Gentleman of the East*. Dallas, Tex.: Southern Methodist University Press, 1985. The best available biography of Wister, which draws on extensive research in his papers at the Library of Congress and other manuscript collections. Contains an abundance of material on the history of *The Virginian* and the response it evoked during Wister's lifetime.

White, G. Edward. *The Eastern Establishment and the Western Experience: The West of Frederic Remington, Theodore Roosevelt, and Owen Wister*. New Haven, Conn.: Yale University Press, 1968. Examines the way in which Wister interacted with the West and the historical circumstances that led him to write *The Virginian*. White deals with Wister's links with participants in the Johnson County War of April, 1892.

THE VIRGINIANS
A Tale of the Last Century

Type of work: Novel
Author: William Makepeace Thackeray (1811-1863)
Type of plot: Historical
Time of plot: Late eighteenth century
Locale: England and the Colony of Virginia
First published: serial, 1857-1859; book, 1858-1859

> *Principal characters:*
> GEORGE and
> HARRY WARRINGTON, the Virginians
> RACHEL ESMOND WARRINGTON, their mother
> GEORGE WASHINGTON, a family friend
> LORD CASTLEWOOD, an English kinsman
> MARIA ESMOND, Lord Castlewood's sister
> BARONESS BERNSTEIN, Rachel Warrington's half sister and formerly
>   Beatrix Esmond
> COLONEL LAMBERT, a friend
> THEO LAMBERT, Colonel Lambert's daughter and George's wife
> HETTY LAMBERT, Colonel Lambert's other daughter
> FANNY MOUNTAIN WARRINGTON, Harry's wife

The Story:

Although Harry and George Warrington were twins, George was declared the heir to their father's estate by virtue of having been born half an hour before his brother. Both were headstrong lads, greatly pampered by their widowed mother, Rachel Esmond Warrington, who managed her Virginia estate, Castlewood, much as she would have managed the mansion in the old country. She never let her sons forget their high birth, and she herself had dropped the name of Warrington in favor of her maiden name, Esmond, so that everyone would remember her noble rank. Rachel was a dictator on her plantation, and although she was respected by many, she was loved by few.

Harry and George were trained according to the place and the time. They learned to ride, shoot, and gamble like gentlemen, but they had little formal education other than a small knowledge of Latin and French. Their mother hoped they might pattern themselves after Colonel George Washington, who was their neighbor and her close friend. Harry worshiped Washington from his youth to his death, but George and Colonel Washington were never to be friends.

When General Braddock arrived from England to command the English troops in the war against the French, Washington and George Warrington joined his forces. Although Harry was a better soldier, George represented the family because of his position as elder son. Braddock was defeated, and George was reported captured and killed by the French. George's mother blamed Colonel Washington for not guarding her son, and Washington was no longer welcome at Castlewood.

Upon George's death, Harry became the heir, and his mother sent him to visit his relatives in England. There he met his mother's kinsman, Lord Castlewood; her half sister, Baroness

Bernstein; and Will, Maria, and Fanny Esmond, his cousins. Of all of his relatives, only Baroness Bernstein was fond of him. Harry and Will were enemies from their first meeting, and the rest of the family thought him a savage and tolerated him only because he would some day inherit the estate in Virginia. Harry thought he was in love with Maria, who was his mother's age, and sent her many gifts and passionate letters declaring himself hers and asking for her hand in marriage.

Harry was the toast of the country. He spent money lavishly on fine clothes and horses and at first won thousands of pounds at cards; but when his luck turned and he lost all of his money, most of his former friends had only unkind words for him. Matters became so desperate that he was jailed for his debts, and Baroness Bernstein was the only one of his relatives who offered to help him. Nevertheless, there was a string attached to her offer. She was violently opposed to his intended marriage to Maria and would pay his debts only if he promised to break his word to that lady. Although Harry was tired of Maria, he felt it was beneath a gentleman of his position to break his word, and he refused the Baroness' help under her conditions. He would rather remain in prison.

There his brother George found him. George had escaped from the French after eighteen months in prison and had returned to his home in Virginia, where he and his mother had decided that he, too, should visit England. He paid his brother's debts, and the two boys had a joyful reunion. Harry now had to return to his status as younger brother, and George assumed his place as heir to Castlewood in Virginia.

Before Harry's imprisonment and George's arrival in England, Harry had made the acquaintance of Colonel Lambert and his family. There were two daughters, Theo and Hetty, whom the twin brothers found charming. Theo and George fell in love, and after overcoming her father's objections, they were married. At first, they lived in poverty, for George had spent all of his money to rescue Harry from debtors' prison and to buy for him a commission in the army. For a time, George's only income was from two tragedies he had written, one a success and the other a failure.

Shortly after Harry received his commission, he joined General Wolfe and sailed for America to fight the French in the Colonies. Maria had released him from his promise to her, and he gladly took leave of his English relatives. About this time, George inherited a title and an estate from an unexpected source. Sir Miles Warrington, his father's brother, died; and young Miles Warrington, the only male heir, had been killed in an accident; therefore, the title and the estate fell to George. He and Theo now lived in comparative luxury. They traveled extensively, and one day they decided to visit George's mother and brother in Virginia.

When they arrived in America, they found the Colonies to be in a state of unrest. The colonists were determined not to pay all the taxes that the British Crown levied against them, and there was much talk of war. There was also trouble at Castlewood. Harry had married Fanny Mountain, the daughter of his mother's housekeeper, and his mother refused to accept the girl. Harry had moved to his own smaller estate, but there was a great tension between the members of the family. George and Theo and their mother were loyal to the king. Harry became a true Virginian and followed General George Washington into battle. Despite their different loyalties, the brothers remained friends.

Shortly before the end of the war, George and Theo returned to England. Although they were grieved at the outcome of the war, it made little difference in their lives. Harry visited them in England after the death of his wife, but their mother never again left her native Virginia. George and Theo tried to persuade Hetty to marry Harry, whom she had once loved deeply, but she refused to leave her widowed father. The only departure from their quiet life came when Lord

Castlewood tried to steal Castlewood in Virginia from their mother after her deed and title were burned during the war. George, however, was able to prevent the fraud and save the estate. Intending never to leave England again, he renounced his right to the Virginia land. Harry returned to Virginia, where he was made a general, to live out his life at Castlewood in the company of his mother. The brothers were destined never to meet again, but their love for each other went with them throughout their lives.

Critical Evaluation:

William Makepeace Thackeray is popularly believed to have conceived the idea for *The Virginians* after seeing two swords, mementos of the Battle of Bunker Hill, mounted in the manner described in the opening of the novel in the library of a contemporary historian named Prescott. While such anecdotes are often false, Thackeray did visit Prescott and later outlined to American novelist John Esten Cooke a plan for the novel which is, indeed, strongly suggested by the opening of the work. The story was to take place during the Revolution and was to include two brothers as the predominant characters who would take different sides in the conflict and who would be in love with the same woman. The war itself was to be given major emphasis. Obviously, Thackeray failed to adhere very closely to this plan, and the significant shortcomings of the work are probably chargeable to that regrettable fact. Thackeray faced two problems in the writing of *The Virginians* that well may have been mutually responsible for his seemingly pointless deviation from a sound, organized plan. One of the problems is inherent in the writing of a sequel novel: The author is faced with the twin constraints of fidelity to previous characterizations and compatibility with an established history. Such constraints, as other authors have proved, are almost invariably detrimental to artistic achievement. The second problem arose from Thackeray's commitment to write the novel in serial form, which placed him under a compulsion to provide regular monthly installments that could wait neither for adequate historical research nor for proper artistic attention. Whether these problems were, in fact, the cause of Thackeray's abandoning many of the details of his original plan is, of course, mere speculation and is deserving of no more consideration than speculation warrants. What is clear, however, is that the compelling opening of the work suggests a promising study in comparative values and conflicting loyalties in a novel of epic scope. This promise is in no way delivered. What readers are given instead is a largely shapeless work that begins promisingly enough but dawdles through stretches of irresolute composition and culminates in a series of major events that are crammed into a hasty denouement.

In *The Virginians*, as in most of Thackeray's works, readers must bestow what critical acclaim they might feel inclined to give it principally on the artful characterizations it contains and on the value of its social commentary. Thackeray's settings somehow never quite emerge as definitive places, in marked contrast to later Victorians Thomas Hardy and Joseph Conrad, whose settings are so powerfully conceived that they become virtual characters in their own right and often influence events directly. Thackeray's descriptions of physical environment seem somehow deficient, as if he painted with temperas too much mixed with water. He succeeds in rendering only a faint impression of some sort of vague precincts in which his characters move, the nature and mood of which might well be appropriate to those characters and to their activities if only the setting could be clearly discerned. Furthermore, the scantness of the settings cannot be well defended by the argument that the environment in which Thackeray's characters pursue their thoughts and actions is of significantly less importance to his purpose than are the motivations and social interfaces of those characters. In a novel entitled, *The Virginians*, character and setting ought to have been inextricably bound. The central theme of the work—insofar as one can be said to exist—is the contrast between the innocence and simplicity of the New World and the corruption and sophistication of the Old. This contrast was, ultimately, the cause of the revolt in the colonies and no small contributor to the success of that revolt. Furthermore, it is the very hub about which the central conflict was surely intended to revolve; it, however, does not achieve this function. Included among the reasons why must be the lack of delineation of a physical as well as a societal identity, for the New Eden engendered the altered values that finally made the separation of England and the colonies a matter of more than mere distance.

The Virginians, however, does contain a relatively effective contrast of social life in England and Virginia, but the predominance given to English society is excessive and at the expense of a complete treatment of plantation life in America. Furthermore, the effectiveness of the contrast is frustrated by Thackeray's failure to provide a parallel contrast between the twins. An attempt is apparent, but it is ineffectual because of the lack of structure of the work. The novel becomes not so much a story of conflict between brothers who respond to the sound of different drums but separate stories of characters who only incidentally are twins. The motivations are not fully developed; the brothers seem to move independently rather than in opposition to each other, and, as a consequence, the conflict that should have been the very core of the novel is essentially nonexistent.

If there are major failures in the work, there are major triumphs as well. Numbered among the foremost of these is the singular and fascinating portrait of the Baroness Bernstein, the former Beatrix of *The History of Henry Esmond, Esquire, a Colonel in the Service of Her Majesty Q. Anne* (1852), now an old woman. The Baroness is a minor masterpiece of characterization in a period of literature when authors did not yet consciously employ the subtlety of psychological motivation. Sapped by satiety of all interest and emotion except a single passion for cards, the Baroness' capacity for humanity appears to be as shriveled as her body. Nevertheless, under the stimulus of Harry and George Warrington and the memories of their grandfather that they invoke in her, the Baroness briefly regains the capacity for human feeling with which she was endowed before a life of decadence and wealth displaced it with selfishness and callous indifference. The Baroness' final scene, in which she falls asleep over her cards during a visit of George and rouses to a lost contact with reality, possesses a vivid reality and an impressively dramatic impact.

The secret of Thackeray's most successful characterizations seems to lie in the deft and subtle touches of inner conflict with which he invests them, and this is true of the better-drawn members of the cast of *The Virginians*. Beatrix displays a strength of character that is less incipient than it is suppressed by the society in which she moves. Parson Sampson's betting, card playing, dicing, drinking, and telling of "lively" jokes, despite his moral convictions, "humanizes" the unreverend reverend and serves to suggest that all men are susceptible to corruption, regardless of calling.

Although less captivating than the Baroness and less skillfully drawn than either she or Parson Sampson, Mrs. Esmond Warrington nevertheless stands out as a notable characterization as well. What makes her role in the novel significant, however, is the careful juxtaposition of her and the Baroness, her half sister. The effectiveness of the contrast points to the intended but unachieved parallel effect with George and Harry. Additionally, the central protagonists are emphatic failures. Harry's weaknesses do not fit him either for sympathy or for the interest a villain would generate, and George's benevolent nature is of the smug, self-satisfied kind that alienates rather than endears.

The novel contains much that is interesting, much that is delightful, and some social comment worthy of the making. The novel offers as much or more to the social historian of Thackeray's era as it does to the reader who wishes to know about Virginia in the eighteenth century.

"Critical Evaluation" by Terrence R. Doyle

Bibliography:

Colby, Robert Alan. "*The Virginians*: The Old World and the New." In *Thackeray's Canvass of Humanity*. Columbus: Ohio State University Press, 1979. Contextual analysis of the novel focusing on its origin and the stage it represents of Thackeray's development as a writer. Interesting discussion of the author's portrayal of George Washington.

Harden, Edgar F. *The Emergence of Thackeray's Serial Fiction*. Athens: University of Georgia Press, 1979. Discusses the serial structure of five novels, including *The Virginians,* with focus upon manuscripts and the composition process. Explains how the novels were shaped in view of the fact that they were written in serial installments.

Monsarrat, Ann. "*The Virginians*." In *An Uneasy Victorian: Thackeray the Man*. New York: Dodd, Mead, 1980. Engaging and lucid account of Thackeray's painstaking work to bring back past heroes of his previous novels in *The Virginians*. For the researcher who already has some knowledge of Thackeray's works.

Ray, Gordon. *Thackeray*. 2 vols. New York: McGraw-Hill, 1955-1958. Biography of Thackeray includes thoughtful essays on the novels. The era and background of the author also is discussed.

Williams, Joan M. *Thackeray*. New York: Arco, 1969. Brief but lucid exposition of the novel. Excellent starting point for a beginning study of Thackeray's writings. Gives a straightforward and very readable account of the novel.

THE VISIT

Type of work: Drama
Author: Friedrich Dürrenmatt (1921-1990)
Type of plot: Tragicomedy
Time of plot: Mid-twentieth century
Locale: Güllen, a town somewhere in Central Europe
First performed: 1956; first published, 1956 as *Der Besuch der alten Dame: Eine tragische Komödie* (English translation, 1958)

> *Principal characters:*
> CLAIRE ZACHANASSIAN, a former local girl, now a multimillionaire
> TOBY and
> ROBY, gum-chewers, part of Claire's retinue
> KOBY and
> LOBY, both blind, part of Claire's retinue
> ALFRED ILL, Claire's former lover
> TOWNSPEOPLE, identified by occupation or number
> MISS LOUISA, the only townsperson identified by name

The Story:

Claire Wascher had left Güllen in disgrace forty-five years before the action begins. Now rich, she had announced her intention to return to her impoverished native town. The townspeople, who hoped that she might wish to help them out of the poverty they had endured for years, awaited her return with considerable anticipation. They hoped that Claire's emotional tie to Alfred Ill, her former lover, would induce her to be financially generous to her former town; Alfred Ill knew that if she were to make the expected gift he would be a sure victor in the next mayoral contest. As the townspeople, who served the function the chorus did in classical Greek plays, awaited Claire's arrival, they were a model of community cohesiveness and congeniality. Poor as they were, they were united by the seemingly indestructible bonds that traditionally hold tightly knit communities together.

Claire arrived amid much celebration. Claire greeted the townspeople and Alfred Ill, amused by their transparent cordiality. At a festive banquet she made it clear that they had been correct in their assumption: She was prepared to give the town a gift of 500 million marks. As with most large gifts, however, this one carried a stipulation.

Claire had left Güllen forty-five years earlier after naming Alfred Ill in a paternity suit; he had denied responsibility for her pregnancy and prevailed by bribing two witnesses to give false evidence. Claire was driven out of Güllen by its upstanding, self-righteous citizens, and after she left, Alfred Ill married a well-to-do woman who set him up in a business. Claire had gone to Hamburg, where she was forced to become a prostitute before eventually marrying the multimillionaire Armenian oil tycoon Zachanassian and becoming rich. Zachanassian, whose name she kept despite many subsequent marriages, left her the bulk of her fortune.

Claire now dangled the dazzling prospect of the huge sum of money before the townspeople on the condition that they right the wrong they and Alfred Ill had inflicted on her and her child, who lived for only one year: She would make the gift in return for the murder of her former lover. She wanted, as she put it, to purchase justice. She introduced to the townspeople her butler, who was the former magistrate of Güllen who had decided the paternity case against her, and two blind, castrated old men in her retinue, who were the two perjuring witnesses. Alfred Ill tried to assure her that the past was forgotten and forgiven, but Claire insisted that nothing was forgotten, and that she would await the town's decision.

During the weeks that Claire waited she married three more times. She watched grimly as the insidiousness of her offer became increasingly apparent. Before long, the townspeople began to buy things on credit. At first, when Alfred Ill thanked them for standing by him, they responded loyally. Then it occurred to him that they would not be buying expensive things on credit if they were not expecting their financial position to change. Gradually, attitudes toward him changed. Those who had supported him now began to blame him for his indiscretion with Claire and revile him for the way he had handled the paternity suit.

Alfred Ill vainly sought protection from the mayor, the police, and the church. When he tried to flee Güllen, he was detained by the townspeople. Finally, he faced up to his guilt and publicly accepted responsibility for his misdeeds. The townspeople called for his suicide, but he refused to give them this satisfaction. If they wanted Claire's money, they would have to kill him and bear the guilt that came with his murder. In a somber assembly, a group of townspeople murdered him collectively so that no one person would have to bear the guilt. The doctor pronounced death by heart failure. Claire Zachanassian collected the corpse, presented the check, and left the town with her full retinue. At the newly refurbished train station, the prosperous townspeople silently watched Claire leave.

Critical Evaluation:

In *The Visit*, Friedrich Dürrenmatt poses the basic question of what inroads money, or the promise of it, makes upon the morality of people who are not inherently bad. The citizens of Güllen are average, with average strengths, weaknesses, and foibles. Claire has early been made aware of the consequences of greed, since Alfred Ill's two bribes determined the outcome of her paternity suit.

On the surface, *The Visit* is a play about vengeance, but beyond that it is a tragicomedy that explores human motivation and morality. In the play, Dürrenmatt examines the dark underside of a community unified in its poverty that disintegrates with the prospect of riches. Claire's plan of vengeance is not only directed against the man who had dishonored her but against the community that also defined her disgrace.

Dürrenmatt's sparing use of names helps his audience realize that the community is an aggregation of types rather than individuals. Only Claire and Alfred Ill emerge as individuals. The rest of the townspeople act as a chorus and come to represent the collective ideals of the community. Among those who are identified by occupation rather than number, the priest, the schoolmaster, the policeman, and the physician come in for particularly harsh treatment. They are respected members of the community who should fight to uphold its highest ideals but do not.

As is typical in Dürrenmatt's works, the antihero, Alfred Ill, comes from a low societal class. As the play progresses, however, it is Alfred Ill who finds some degree of salvation, achieving a separate peace with himself before his neighbors succumb to Claire's temptation and murder him.

As the townspeople gradually become aware of how money could change their lives, they increasingly begin to use language more to conceal than to express their thoughts. Claire stands in sharp contrast to this. She is Medea-like in her furious outbursts against the professional people in town who failed to offer the sort of moral leadership that might have saved Güllen from its own nightmarish avarice.

The play opens and concludes with a chorus, giving it a symmetry that serves to heighten the irony of what transpires during the three acts. By play's end, Güllen is much improved materially, but the price is a collective guilt that will plague them in the years to come. Dürrenmatt's audiences easily grasp the message that Güllen was a kind of Everytown meant to represent the twentieth century materialistic dilemma in the starkest terms.

As Dürrenmatt presents her, Claire, who has suffered from an unjust society, has permitted the injustice to consume her utterly. Her emotions have long ago been snuffed out to the point that she is unable to grow, whereas Alfred Ill, the small-time, petty, unimportant man, undergoes a transformation that allows him to face his fate with composure and equanimity.

It is not surprising that *The Visit* is Dürrenmatt's most enduringly popular and successful play and that it has been translated into most major languages. The work is appropriate to its time, striking a responsive chord in those who struggle with the question of how to achieve an equilibrium between the material and the ideal in society.

R. Baird Shuman

Bibliography:
Bogard, Travis, and William Oliver, eds. *Modern Drama: Essays in Criticism.* New York: Oxford University Press, 1965. Adolf D. Klarmann's contribution, "Friedrich Dürrenmatt and the Tragic Sense of Comedy," remains one of the most significant appraisals of the playwright.
Hammer, Carl, ed. *Studies in German Literature.* Baton Rouge: Louisiana State University Press, 1963. Includes F. E. Coenen's extended essay on modern German theater, which makes interesting observations about Dürrenmatt and places him within the broad context of recent German drama.
Heilmann, Robert B. "The Lure of the Demonic: James and Dürrenmatt." *Comparative Literature* 13 (1961): 346-357. One of the most insightful comparative articles on Henry James and Friedrich Dürrenmatt, this essay will help readers to understand some of the origins of *The Visit.*
Peppard, Murray B. *Friedrich Dürrenmatt.* New York: Twayne, 1969. Peppard's analysis of *The Visit* is penetrating and sensitive. Peppard provides an excellent overview of the play, comments on elements of its composition, and interprets it in understandable terms. Perhaps the best source for those just beginning to read Dürrenmatt.
Shaw, LeRoy, ed. *The German Theater Today.* Austin: University of Texas Press, 1963. A valuable collection of essays drawn from a symposium on modern German theater. The material on Dürrenmatt's early plays provides useful background to those unfamiliar with the playwright.
Whitton, Kenneth S. *Dürrenmatt: Reinterpretation in Retrospect.* Providence, R.I.: Berg, 1990. Whitton's understanding of Dürrenmatt is impressive. His material on *The Visit* brings together a considerable amount of interpretive theory on the play.

VOLPONE
Or, The Fox

Type of work: Drama
Author: Ben Jonson (1573-1637)
Type of plot: Social satire
Time of plot: Sixteenth century
Locale: Venice
First performed: 1605; first published, 1607

Principal characters:

VOLPONE, a knave
MOSCA, his servant
CORBACCIO, an old gentleman
CORVINO, a merchant
VOLTORE, an advocate
LORD POLITIC WOULD-BE, a knight
LADY POLITIC WOULD-BE, his wife
BONARIO, Corbaccio's son
CELIA, Corvino's wife
PEREGRINE, a gentleman traveler

The Story:

Volpone and his servant, Mosca, were playing a cunning game with all who professed to be Volpone's friends, and the two conspirators boasted to themselves that Volpone acquired his riches not by the common means of trade but by a method which cheated no one in a commercial sense. Volpone had no heirs. Since it was believed he possessed a large fortune, many people were courting his favor in the hope of rich rewards after his death.

For three years, while Volpone feigned gout, catarrh, palsy, and consumption, valuable gifts had been given to him. Volpone was in truth quite healthy and able to enjoy various vices. Mosca's role in the grand deception was to assure each hopeful would-be friend that he was the one whom Volpone had honored in an alleged will.

To Voltore, one of the dupes, Mosca (which means "fly") boasted that particular attention was being paid to Voltore's interests. When Voltore ("vulture") left, Corbaccio ("crow") followed. He brought a potion to help Volpone ("fox"), or so he claimed. Mosca knew better than to give his master medicine from those who were awaiting the fox's death. Mosca suggested that to influence Volpone, Corbaccio should go home, disinherit his own son, and leave his fortune to Volpone. In return for this generous deed, Volpone, soon to die, would leave his fortune to Corbaccio, whose son would benefit eventually.

Next came Corvino, who was assured by Mosca that Volpone, now near death, had named him in a will. After the merchant had gone, Mosca told Volpone that Corvino had a beautiful wife whom he guarded at all times. Volpone resolved to go in disguise to see this woman.

Sir Politic Would-Be and his wife were traveling in Venice. Another English visitor, Peregrine, met Sir Politic on the street and gave him news from home. While the two Englishmen were trying to impress each other, Mosca and a servant came to the street and erected a stage for a medicine vendor to display his wares. Volpone, disguised as a mountebank, mounted the platform. While he haggled with Sir Politic and Peregrine over the price of his medicine, Celia appeared at her window and tossed down her handkerchief. Struck by Celia's beauty, Volpone resolved to possess her. Meanwhile Corvino brutally scolded Celia and told her that henceforth he would confine her to her room.

Mosca went to Corvino with news that physicians had recommended a healthy young girl to sleep by Volpone's side and that other men were striving to be the first to win Volpone's gratitude in this manner. Not to be outdone, Corvino promised that Celia would be sent to Volpone.

Mosca also told Bonario, Corbaccio's son, that his father was about to disinherit him. He promised to lead Bonario to a place where he could witness his father's betrayal.

When Lady Politic Would-Be came to visit Volpone, she was so talkative Volpone feared she would make him sick in truth. To relieve Volpone's distress, the servant told the lady that Sir Politic was in a gondola with a young girl. Lady Would-Be hurried off in pursuit of her husband. Volpone retired to a private closet while Mosca led Bonario behind a curtain so the young man could spy on Corbaccio. At that moment, eager to win favor with Volpone, Corvino arrived with Celia, and Mosca had to send Bonario off to another room so he would not know of her presence. Meanwhile Corvino, who intended to deceive Celia about what he thought was the true purpose of her lying with Volpone, had told Celia what she had to do to prove her chastity. To quiet her fears, and to guarantee the inheritance from Volpone, Corvino assured his distressed wife that Volpone was so decrepit he could not harm her.

When they were alone, Volpone leaped from his couch and displayed himself as an ardent lover. As he was about to rape Celia, Bonario appeared from his hiding place and saved her. While Mosca and Volpone, in terror of exposure, bewailed their ruined plot, Corbaccio knocked. Volpone dashed back to his couch to assume his role of an invalid. As Mosca was assuring Corbaccio of Volpone's forthcoming death, Voltore entered the room and overheard the discussion. Mosca drew Voltore aside and assured the lawyer that he was attempting to get possession of Corbaccio's money so that Voltore would inherit more from Volpone. Mosca further explained that Bonario had mistaken Celia's visit and had burst upon Volpone and threatened to kill him. Taken in by Mosca's lies, Voltore promised to keep Bonario from accusing Volpone of attempted rape and Corvino of villainy; he ordered Bonario (who, unlike Volpone, Mosca, Corvino, Corbaccio, and Voltore, was innocent) arrested.

Mosca proceeded with his case against Celia and Bonario. He had assured Corvino, Corbaccio, and Voltore, independently, that each would be the sole heir of Volpone. He added Lady Would-Be as a witness against Celia. In court Voltore presented Celia and Bonario as schemers against Corvino, and he further showed that Bonario's father had disinherited his son and that Bonario had dragged Volpone out of bed and had attacked him. Corvino and Corbaccio testified against Celia and Bonario, while Mosca whispered to the avaricious old gentlemen that they were helping justice. To add to the testimony, Mosca presented Lady Would-Be, who told the court she had seen Celia beguiling Sir Politic in a gondola. Mosca promised Lady Would-Be that as a reward for her testimony her name would stand first on Volpone's list of heirs.

When the trial was over, Volpone sent his servants to announce that he was dead and that Mosca was his heir. While Volpone hid behind a curtain, Mosca sat at a desk taking an inventory of the inheritance as the hopefuls arrived. The next step in Volpone's plan was to escape from Venice with his loot. Mosca helped him disguise himself as a commodore. Mosca also put on a disguise.

Having lost his hopes for the inheritance, Voltore withdrew his false testimony at the trial, and Corbaccio and Corvino trembled lest their own cowardly acts be revealed. The court ordered Mosca to appear. Suspecting that Mosca planned to keep the fortune for himself, the disguised Volpone went to the court. When the dupes, learning that Volpone was still alive, began to bargain for the wealth Mosca held, Volpone threw off his disguise and exposed to the court the foolish behavior of Corbaccio, Corvino, and Voltore, and the innocence of Celia and Bonario. The court then sentenced each conspirator according to the severity of his crime. Bonario was restored to his father's inheritance, and Celia was allowed to return to her father because Corvino had attempted to barter her honor for wealth. The court announced that evil could go only so far before it killed itself.

Critical Evaluation:

Written during a period in which Ben Jonson had turned his hand largely to the making of entertaining masques and satirical antimasques, *Volpone*'s success did something to make up for the failure of his tragedy, *Sejanus His Fall* (1603). *Volpone* was performed by the King's Men in London, and at the two universities to which Jonson later dedicated the play in his prologue. The play also led to Jonson's most fertile dramatic period, that of the great comedies, which include *Epicœne: Or, The Silent Woman* (1609), *The Alchemist* (1610), *Bartholomew Fair* (1614), and *The Devil Is an Ass* (1616). Jonson was preeminent among the Elizabethans and Jacobeans as that rare combination of the academic and creative genius. He was a serious classicist who criticized William Shakespeare's "little Latin and less Greek," modeling his own plays on the Romans. As a humanist he brought classical control and purity to English forms. More than anyone else at the time, Jonson followed critical prescriptions of his own time and of the classical era. Jonson believed that the poet had a moral function in society; he viewed drama as a means of social education. This attitude paved the way for the great English satirists of the eighteenth century. His diverse artistic character makes Jonson both representative of his own age and a predecessor of the more rigorous classicism of the Augustans.

Jonson's style, as might be expected, is disciplined, formal, balanced, and classically simple and unembellished—a style that foreshadows the Cavalier School (who called themselves the sons of Ben). His dramatic verse is highly stylized, vibrant, and fast-moving; readers are hardly aware they are reading poetry. Rarely does Jonson allow himself the lyrical excursions of Shakespeare or the rhetorical complexity of Christopher Marlowe, although he was capable of both. There is a solidity, firmness, and straightforward clarity in his comedies only equaled by the classical French comic theater of Molière. In *Volpone* Jonson follows the Aristotelian unities of time, place, and action. The action of the play takes in only one day (the unity of time); it occurs entirely in Venice (place); and, with the exception of some of the exchanges between Peregrine and Sir Politic Would-Be, the action is unified structurally, all centered on the machinations of Volpone, his follower, and the greedy dupes.

The theme of the play is greed, the vice that dominates the actions of all the characters. Family bonds, marriage, and legal justice are not merely disregarded by Corbaccio, Corvino, and Voltore; they are also made the means by which the characters' inhuman avarice destroys them. Jonson implies that their greed is all too human; these characters may be exaggerations but they are not aberrations. It is ironic that the Politic Would-Bes, though they, too, want Volpone's money, seem less offensive and morally corrupt simply because they do not sell their souls for a hope of lucre. They are idiotic but they are not vicious. The passages in which they appear are a kind of relief. Although *Volpone* is a comedy it is so serious that it is almost equally tragic; as a satire, it accomplishes the difficult feat of being funny and morally incisive at the same time. *Volpone* may be a comedy insofar as it deals with particular figures in a particular situation, but its social moral is earnest. Jonson succeeds brilliantly in combining the stereotyped characters of Latin comedy, the Renaissance characters of humors (which he himself used in his first comedy, *Every Man in His Humour*, 1598), the popular tradition of beast fables (from which he derived the names of his characters), and astute psychological insight to make them all come alive onstage. Although the plot of *Volpone* is original, it is based on a common Roman fortune-hunting theme dealt with by Horace, Juvenal, Pliny, Lucian, and Petronius. Jonson turns his fortune-hunters loose in contemporary Venice—chosen, no doubt, because the English of the time regarded Italy as a country of crime and rampant passions. By using a setting roughly contemporary to that of his original audience, Jonson makes the point that con artists and greedy dupes are part of every age. Such is the high moral purpose of comic satire, which Jonson points out in his preface to the play.

Another important theme is that of imitation, as a distortion of normal reality. Sir Politic Would-Be seeks to imitate Volpone, an imitation of a dying man. Characters are constantly assuming either literal or figurative disguises; Mosca, for example, fascinates the audience with his ability to make what his dupes see before their eyes conform to whatever fabrication he has led them to accept. Lady Would-Be attempts to cover her mental deformities with physical cosmetics, and her dressing scene is one of the most pathetic in the play. Carrying imitation even further, Volpone pretends to be a mountebank (something he actually is) in a complicated and convincing scene that leads to the question of how one can distinguish between a real imitator and an imitation imitator. Volpone and Mosca are actors throughout. They are also directors, leading the fortune hunters, one by one, to give their best performances; in the process, they reveal how close to the surface lies the actor's instinct in all people. Any strong desire, such as greed, can activate the attempt at deception. Gilded lies and rampant desires create chaos, confusing notions of species, class, sex, and morals.

Volpone is the exuberant guiding spirit of misrule who takes constant pleasure in his mental agility and showmanship. Mosca is equally forceful; his only motive seems to be a delight in perpetrating perversities, and he accepts his inheritance only because it allows him to continue to be perverse. The three birds of prey, Corbaccio, Corvino, and Voltore, stumble over one another in their haste to devour the supposed carcass. They are hideous caricatures, and they are, ironically, caricatures of themselves—as the development of the play from the first scene demonstrates. Mosca and Volpone simply bring out the worst in them; they do not plant it. The sham trial in Act IV is the dramatic triumph of Jonson's career. When Corvino calls Voltore "mad" at the very point at which the old man has become sane again, the audience sees that it, too, has been beguiled by the terrible logic of greed.

"Critical Evaluation" by Kenneth John Atchity

Bibliography:
Barish, Jonas A. "The Double Plot in *Volpone*." In *Ben Jonson: A Collection of Critical Essays*, edited by Jonas A. Barish. Englewood Cliffs, N.J.: Prentice-Hall, 1963. Analyzes the play's structure to defend the relevance of the subplot concerning Sir Politic and Lady Politic Would-Be, which he sees as a caricature of the main plot.

Cave, Richard Allen. *Ben Jonson*. New York: St. Martin's Press, 1991. Devotes a chapter of analysis to the play's plot, themes, and characters. Includes some discussion of the play's production history.

Dessen, Alan C. *Jonson's Moral Comedy*. Evanston, Ill.: Northwestern University Press, 1971. Dessen devotes one chapter to a discussion of *Volpone*, which he sees as pivotal, marking a shift in Jonson's perceptions away from the influences of the old morality plays such as *Everyman* and toward a satiric comedy that examines the moral implications of human failings.

Miles, Rosalind. *Ben Jonson: His Craft and Art*. New York: Barnes & Noble Books, 1990. Discusses *Volpone* with particular attention to the techniques of Jonson's satire, noting that nothing is exempt from his dark vision of human beings as jungle animals, quick to prey on one another.

Summers, Claude J., and Ted-Larry Pebworth. *Ben Jonson*. Boston: Twayne, 1979. A general introduction to Jonson and his work. Includes a discussion of *Volpone* that concentrates on the play's satiric themes and structure.

VOLUPTÉ

Type of work: Novel
Author: Charles-Augustin Sainte-Beuve (1804-1869)
Type of plot: Psychological
Time of plot: Early nineteenth century
Locale: France
First published: 1834

Principal characters:
AMAURY, the narrator and a man of sensibility
THE MARQUIS DE COUAËN, a royalist
MADAME DE COUAËN, his wife
AMÉLIE DE LINIERS, a woman in love with Amaury
MADAME R., the wife of a royalist sympathizer

The Story:

On the ship that was taking him to the United States, probably forever, Amaury undertook to tell the story of his life to a young friend. Having renounced his past life to live a new one abroad, he was afraid that he might find more pleasure than he should in those past memories; but he felt that his experience could prove useful to the young man, in whom he had recognized so many of his own tendencies.

Amaury, having lost his parents, had been reared by an uncle in Brittany. In his youth he had been sheltered from the world outside his house, which at that time was slowly recovering from the effects of the French Revolution. He spent most of his time studying, and, prone to dreaming, he was actually more concerned with the adventures of Cyrus, Alexander, and Constantine than he was with the men and events of his own day. His Latin teacher was Monsieur Ploa, a man absolutely devoid of personal ambition; only a misinterpretation of Vergil or Cicero could momentarily get him excited. Monsieur Ploa had Amaury translate the voluptuous passages of the *Aeneid* (c. 29-19 B.C.E.) or the *Odes* (23 B.C.E., 13 B.C.E.) of Horace with a complete candor that his disciple did not share.

When Amaury was about fifteen years old, he spent six weeks at a neighboring castle. His life there, no longer checked by his regular schedule, helped to develop his tendency to melancholy; he would disappear into the woods reciting poetry with tears in his eyes, and he would forget to come back for meals.

At the age of eighteen, he began visiting friends in the neighborhood. He would often visit Monsieur and Madame de Greneuc, in whose household lived two granddaughters orphaned during the revolution. The older, Amélie de Liniers, was a charming woman who soon considered herself engaged to him. Amaury, however, did not feel like settling down in life without first learning something of the world.

During a hunting party, Amaury met the Marquis de Couaën, an influential figure in royalist circles, who invited the young man to his castle. There Amaury met Madame de Couaën, the Irish wife of the marquis. One day, Amaury wandered in the woods, lost in his thoughts. As he emerged from the woods, Madame de Couaën called to him from the window and asked him to pick up an ivory needle she had lost. When he took it up to her, she asked him if he would, in the absence of her husband, accompany her to the little chapel of Saint-Pierre-de-Mer before the sun set. As they were walking along, she explained to Amaury that she was making a pilgrimage for her mother in Ireland, from whom she had received bad news.

That walk was more or less the beginning of a hopeless love relationship between Amaury and Madame de Couaën, an affair in which his respect for the marquis and the true love of Madame de Couaën for her husband left him with the sole possibility of platonic adoration. To escape such a situation, he attempted to retire as a hermit on a nearby deserted island which once had been inhabited by Druids, but after spending only one night there, he abandoned that project. He then decided to go to Ireland on a boat that had brought the marquis some secret dispatches; he would see Madame de Couaën's mother and possibly establish some useful political connections for the marquis. As he was embarking, having left a letter of explanation in his room, Madame de Couaën came running to the beach with word that her mother had just died. While he was trying to comfort her she tearfully begged him never to get married but to stay with them, help her husband, and understand her as no one else could.

The Marquis de Couaën had to go to Paris for some political meetings and took his wife, son, and daughter with him in order to avoid raising suspicions. Amaury accompanied them to Paris. When they returned to Couaën, they found the coast occupied by soldiers.

Amaury went to see Amélie, who was preparing to follow her grandmother to Normandy. When he insisted that they ought to delay for two years before making a decision concerning their future, Amélie simply asked him to be prudent.

On his way home, Amaury learned that the marquis had been arrested in Paris; he rushed immediately to Couaën to destroy some papers before the police officers would arrive there. Without objection or thanks, Madame de Couaën accepted his help, and the next day they left for Paris with the two children. There Amaury communicated with Monsieur D. and Monsieur R. in an effort to secure their help.

Meanwhile, the marquis was allowed to receive visitors, and his wife went to see him every day. Amaury spent every evening with her. At the same time, he was beginning to feel attracted to Madame R., a lonely and disillusioned woman who often visited Madame de Couaën. Amaury had also decided to experience physical love with a prostitute, but he accomplished his purpose with no real pleasure.

In the midst of these circumstances, Amaury could see no future for himself. He became involved in a royalist conspiracy, more in an effort to find self-fulfillment in a chivalric cause than to satisfy any political convictions. Faced with imminent action, he realized that his position might endanger the future of the marquis, bring grief to Madame de Couaën, and show ingratitude toward Monsieur R. and Monsieur D. Fortunately, his secret political involvement was never disclosed.

When the marquis was sent to Blois, Amaury did not accompany his friends, although they had wanted him to come with them. Left in Paris, he visited Madame R. and wrote to Blois, where the royalist political leaders were being tried. Madame R., while refusing to become his mistress, liked to be seen with him in public and demanded the most foolish proofs of his attachment. They never really trusted each other, and she was always jealous of his love for Madame de Couaën.

A letter from the marquis arrived, announcing the death of his son and the alarming state of his wife's health; the nobleman further asked for a two-week pass to bring her to Paris for medical attention. Madame de Couaën, who considered the death of her son a punishment for her own weakness, was unhappy to discover the relationship between Amaury and Madame

On a day when Amélie came to visit Madame de Couaën, Madame R. was also present. Amaury realized that his instability had caused the unhappiness of three women. Caus youth in the web of illegitimate love, he had been unable to choose either true virtue or carefree disorder. He never saw Amélie again.

Back in Blois, Madame de Couaën sent him a medallion of her mother and a souvenir of her son. Shortly afterward, he ended his affair with Madame R. Years later he was to hear that Monsieur R. had received a post of importance and that Madame R. had become the mother of a son. Having thus reached the bottom of a moral abyss, Amaury enlisted in the army with the idea of finding death on the battlefield; he arrived at Austerlitz only after the battle had been won. Convinced that there was no place for him in society, he decided to become a priest.

Several years later, after he had taken holy orders, he decided to visit again his uncle's farm and the castle at Couaën. He had received no news from Blois for several weeks, and he was afraid that Madame de Couaën's health had not improved. On his arrival at Couaën he was surprised to find a flurry of activity; his friends had returned the day before. Although Madame de Couaën was very weak, she welcomed him warmly, adding that someone might soon need his assistance. As her condition became worse, Amaury administered the rites of absolution and extreme unction. Madame de Couaën died soon afterward and was buried in the chapel of Saint-Pierre-de-Mer.

This experience and the emotions it called forth proved extremely trying to Amaury, who immediately left Brittany and, a short time later, France. He hoped to find abroad some peace in obscure but useful activities.

Critical Evaluation:

The fame of *Volupté* is the result, in part, of its transposition of real events to the fictional plane. The relationship between Amaury and Madame de Couaën depicts some elements of the affair between Charles-Augustin Sainte-Beuve and Victor Hugo's wife, Adèle. In the novel, however, their relationship is purely platonic. The admiration, friendship, and subsequent enmity of Sainte-Beuve and Hugo appear in the relationship of Amaury and the Marquis de Couaën. The fictional characters reconcile; however, Sainte-Beuve and Hugo did not reconcile. Sainte-Beuve's childhood in Picardy becomes Amaury's in the poetically appropriate Brittany, a land of strong religious traditions, a mythic aura, and a history of royalist conspiracies. Although Sainte-Beuve made his novel credible by basing it on actual events, the themes generated from the story are larger in scope. Through the interaction of spiritual, erotic, and political intrigue, Sainte-Beuve explores the various nuances of memory, the struggle between the spirit and the flesh, divine and human love, the role of the great individual in history, and the conflict between fame and obscurity.

The main plotline traces Amaury's moral disarray and spiritual strivings and, generally, the moral duality of all people. Amaury's spirit is dominated by *volupté*, or a combination of indolence, apathy, self-indulgence, and indecisiveness. Amaury seeks sensual gratification, and he repudiates his responsibilities as a member of the community. The cult of sensuality reveals itself as a stage in the development of every generation. In youth, desire is confused with sacred love. Later, sublime love separates from sensual pleasure. With age, humans realize that without ___ for the soul or intellect, beauty and pleasure are impermanent. Without this realization, ___ replaces moral solicitude and intellectual lucidity. Amaury takes pride in his ___ nse of revolt against God. When he realizes that he has sacrificed the ___ the process of his own spiritual disintegration, he turns inward and ___ th prayer. Since Amaury examines his own emotional and intellectual ___ iveness and subtlety, and since he takes pleasure in recalling his ___ on seems incomplete.

Most of the major characters are presented as mysteries. Madame R. personifies passionate love. Like Amaury, she pursues appearance rather than interior depth. Madame de Couaën represents sublime love, ironically out of her indifference and her inability to understand Amaury's advances. She does not have an affair with Amaury, but she nevertheless views the death of her son as divine punishment. She seeks spiritual solace from Amaury. Madame de Couaën inspires intellectual infidelity, and she motivates Amaury's turn against the marquis. The Marquis de Couaën represents the proud, ambitious people who shape history. His frustrated political ambition, like the repressed physical desire between Amaury and Madame de Couaën, drives him to self-destruction. Despite the differences of the Marquis and Amaury, they reconcile after the death of Madame de Couaën. Sainte-Beuve's humbling of Victor Hugo in the character of the marquis was likely the product of envy, even though the proud conspirator finally emerges as a figure of considerable tragic stature.

For the most part, the story is told chronologically, with occasional flashbacks. Only at the beginning of part 2 does the narrator reflect on his current circumstances. The novel's disorganization conveys the aimlessness of the hero. The theme of flight predominates, and it is expressed through continual changes of scene. The idyllic charm of Amélie's home and Madame de Couaën's chateau are contrasted to the corruption of Paris. The narrator also moves easily between real and imaginary—or metaphorical—landscapes, such as paths of salvation and stormy seas of the soul. Despite the haphazard action, the exploration of ambition, love, and faith from a single point of view provides thematic unity. Amaury's continual wanderings and self-exile suggest an allegory of humanity's estrangement from God; however, Amaury's complex quest does not have a clear goal, and it does not result in a simple truth.

Like Amaury, Sainte-Beuve, who projects his present circumstances thirty years into the past, emphasizes memory over currency. Since the novel concerns events from memory, it examines the inner truth of emotional and intellectual perception, rather than external events. Even though dialogue is rare, and conversations are related secondhand, the interaction of viewpoints plays a decisive role in the action. Speech hides as much as it reveals. The profusion of subordinate and parenthetical clauses, and the deliberate interruption of syntactic flow, are suited to the narrator's own indecision. Silences, or long-delayed responses, instead, communicate more effectively.

Beneath apparent motives and outward events of the novel, lie the secret impulses of the subconscious. Throughout the novel, desire conflicts with performance. Amaury dreams of ideal love, but he pursues promiscuous satisfaction, instead. Madame de Couaën's forgetfulness and anxieties cloud her perception. The dreamlike atmosphere of the novel simulates the thin veil separating conscious from unconscious perception. The vague descriptive passages, filled with mirrors, water, and reflections, are flavored by memory. Physical appearances are merely sketched in, and images of erosion dominate the novel. The ornamental style, complete with archaic words, extended and often outrageous metaphors, incomplete sentences, and breaks in logical sequence, veils the narrative in unreality. Sainte-Beuve prefers to suggest meaning rather than expound.

Critics recognized that the prolix language of the novel departed radically from the established traditions of French prose. The majority of Sainte-Beuve's contemporaries found the language needlessly obtuse and the episodic nature of the plot and the moralizing passages clumsy. The experimental qualities of Sainte-Beuve's novel, however, inspired several famou[s] contemporaries. Charles Baudelaire defended the attempt to communicate through associat[ion] rather than direct statement. Gustave Flaubert found inspiration in the attempt to [?] boredom and futility, and Honoré de Balzac continued to explore the theme of di[s]

Sainte-Beuve, on the other hand, never again wrote fiction; he turned, instead, to literary criticism.

"Critical Evaluation" by Pamela Pavliscak

Bibliography:

Barlow, Norman. *Sainte-Beuve to Baudelaire: A Poetic Legacy*. Durham, N.C.: Duke University Press, 1964. Analyzes the influence of Sainte-Beuve's elaborate style and thematic preoccupations on Baudelaire's poetry. The chapter on *Volupté* examines Amaury's exploration of sensual and spiritual love. Although Barlow traces the spiritual journey, his didacticism is distracting.

Chadbourne, Richard. *Charles-Augustin Sainte-Beuve*. Boston: Twayne, 1977. A survey of Sainte-Beuve's life and works. Reappraisal of Sainte-Beuve's fiction and poetry. Discusses his literary criticism. The chapter on *Volupté* analyzes innovations in narrative technique and genre.

Lehmann, A. G. *Sainte-Beuve: A Portrait of the Critic, 1804-1842*. Oxford, England: Clarendon Press, 1962. Overview of the novel, emphasizing its failure to create convincing characters or to use dialogue effectively. The criticism is unbalanced, however, since Lehmann judges *Volupté* as a realist novel rather than as a Romantic confession.

Mulhauser, Ruth. *Sainte-Beuve and Greco-Roman Antiquity*. Cleveland: Press of Case Western Reserve University, 1969. Traces the classical sources of Sainte-Beuve's literature and criticism. Greek and Roman culture combine Romantic revery and intellectual curiosity. Discusses Sainte-Beuve's Hellenism, or love of physical beauty.

Nicolson, Harold. *Sainte-Beuve*. London: Constable, 1957. Surveys Sainte-Beuve's work. The chapter on *Volupté* considers the novel as a representation of the love triangle of Sainte-Beuve, Adèle Hugo, and Victor Hugo, but also analyzes the prose style and thematic unity of the work.

THE VOYAGE OF THE BEAGLE

Type of work: Nature writing
Author: Charles Darwin (1809-1882)
Locale: South America and the South Seas
First published: serial, 1832-1836; book, 1839

The Voyage of the Beagle shows the English naturalist Charles Darwin's brilliant mind already at work on the problems that led to his seminal theory of evolution. The work's title is somewhat misleading, for the author actually has little to say about the voyage. The original title of the serialized version—*Journal of Researches into the Geology and Natural History of the Various Countries Visited by H. M. S. Beagle*—is a better reflection of the scope of the work.

Not only is *The Voyage of the Beagle* an important book in the history of modern thought, it is also a highly significant one in the life of Charles Darwin. As a young man, Darwin had little sense of vocation or direction. When he was sixteen, he began a career of medicine at Edinburgh University. Discovering, however, that he was unfit for the profession, he entered Christ College, Cambridge, three years later in 1828 to prepare himself as a clergyman. Having failed to take honors or to distinguish himself in any way, he accepted the offer of Captain Fitz Roy of the *Beagle* to sign on as a naturalist on a voyage around the world that eventually took five years. During that time, Darwin not only discovered himself and his career but also began making those observations that he later developed into the theory of evolution expounded in *On the Origin of Species* (1859). This work, together with the work of Karl Marx and Sigmund Freud, constituted a powerful influence on twentieth century scientific thought and values.

In December, 1831, the brig *Beagle* of the Royal Navy set sail from Devonport, England, to begin a series of surveys of Patagonia, Tierra del Fuego, Chile, Peru, some of the islands of the Pacific, and Australia. In addition, chronometric measurements were to be made while the ship circumnavigated the earth. Darwin kept a detailed record of the journey that included observations in natural history and geology. It was in particular his observations on the relationships between animals segregated geographically (those living on islands and those on the mainland) and on the relationships between species separated by time (those living forms and those recently extinct ones) that forced him to reconsider the standard, scientific view of the fixity of species. He was also impressed by "the manner in which closely allied animals replace one another in proceeding southwards" in South America.

The *Beagle* began the voyage by sailing to the coast of South America by way of the Canary Islands, the Cape Verde Islands, and the island of St. Paul's Rocks. From the first American seaport the ship touched, Rio de Janeiro, Darwin went on an inland excursion, and upon his return he made natural history observations near Botofogo Bay. From there the expedition went southward to the mouth of the River Plate, where Darwin remained several weeks collecting animals, birds, and reptiles. On his journeys to the interior, he met gauchos and witnessed their skill with the lasso and the bolas in capturing horses and cattle.

From the next anchorage at Rio Negro, Darwin decided to go to Buenos Aires by land under the protection of the Spanish Army, who had declared war on various Indian tribes. On this journey, he was able to observe the habits of the South American ostrich.

After a stop in Buenos Aires, Darwin set out for Santa Fe by means of a slow bullock wagon. He returned by boat down the Parana River to the seacoast and joined the *Beagle* at Montevideo. On an excursion inland from that seaport, Darwin observed herds of sheep that were watched only by dogs who had been brought up with the flocks. On the coast of Patagonia, a land where

Spanish settlement had been unsuccessful, Darwin observed the guanaco, or wild llama, which he found to be extremely wary but easily domesticated after capture. From Patagonia, the *Beagle* went to the Falkland Islands, where Darwin found horses, cattle, and rabbits thriving on the seemingly desolate land. In Tierra del Fuego, the natives existed in an utterly savage state, with barely enough food and clothing to maintain a miserable existence.

On board the *Beagle* were three Fuegians, who had been taken to England to be educated and taught the Christian religion and who were now to be returned to their own tribes, accompanied by a missionary. The ship anchored in Ponsonby Sound, and four boats set out to carry the Fuegians home. All the natives gathered on shore wherever they landed and asked for gifts. When their wants were not entirely satisfied, they became hostile. The missionary decided that it would be useless for him to stay among them.

Once the *Beagle* arrived in Valparaiso, Chile, Darwin set out to observe the geological formations of the base of the Andes Mountains. On that journey he saw copper and gold mines.

While at anchor in a harbor of the island of Chiloe, all aboard were able to observe the eruption of a volcano on the Chilean mainland. About a month after the *Beagle* had sailed north again, a great earthquake shook parts of the coast and the nearby islands. Darwin saw the damage caused by the earthquake in the harbor city of Concepción, where almost every building had been demolished. Part of the town had also been swept by a tremendous tidal wave.

After the *Beagle* returned to Valparaiso, Darwin procured guides and mules and set out to cross the Andes to Mendoza. Proceeding eastward through the Portillo Pass and returning through the Uspallata Pass, he reported beautiful scenery and collected much interesting geological and natural history data. When the *Beagle* sailed up the coast of northern Chile and continued northward to Peru, Darwin saw a saltpeter works and visited Lima. The city did not impress him, for it was dirty and ugly, having suffered from many revolutions and an almost continual state of anarchy.

Lima was the last point at which the *Beagle* touched on the western coast of South America. The ship proceeded next to the Galápagos archipelago, where the most interesting feature was the prevalence of great tortoises. The inhabitants often killed these reptiles for their meat. Most of the birds on the islands were completely tame, for they had not yet learned to regard man as their enemy. The ship proceeded on to Tahiti, where Darwin was impressed by the swimming ability of the Polynesians. He explored the mountains of the island with the help of guides.

From Tahiti, the *Beagle* went south to New Zealand, New South Wales, and Australia. There Darwin first saw the aborigines' social greeting of rubbing noses, the equivalent of the European custom of shaking hands.

After leaving this group of islands, the ship headed back to Brazil in order to complete chronometric measurements. On the way, Darwin visited the island of St. Helena. It was on this last part of the journey that Darwin began to record in his journal his theories about the formation of coral reefs, many of which he had observed during his stay in the South Seas. Darwin was glad to leave Brazil for the second time, for the practice of slavery in that country sickened him. In October, 1836, the *Beagle* returned to England.

As important as *The Voyage of the Beagle* is to the understanding of the genesis of Darwin's theory of evolution and of an appreciation of his own struggle for self-discovery, the book's most significant aspect is the insight it provides into the Victorian mind. Darwin shares many characteristics with other Victorian intellectuals of his generation, among them Thomas Carlyle, John Stuart Mill, John Henry Newman, and Alfred, Lord Tennyson. Principally, this generation of the 1830's was motivated by a conviction of personal destiny and a sense of being at the beginning of a new era in which the old ways of viewing matters would no longer apply. With the exception of Newman, they all came to embrace an idea of progress, either spiritual or social. Darwin found in nature a reason to assert that there was biological progress. Indeed, he provided Tennyson, for example, with metaphoric proof, in his theory of natural selection, of the poet's own concept of ethical evolution. *The Voyage of the Beagle* reflects the combination of zest for adventure and sense of mission that identifies Darwin clearly with his age and generation.

Most impressive perhaps about Darwin is his capacity for experiences of all kinds. From the start, he exhibited immense energy and thoroughness. Yet despite his commitment to naturalistic data, he remained responsive to the human dimension, and his observations were not untouched by sentiment, indeed, at times, outrage. His description of the sheepdogs could only have been written by an animal lover, and he does not hold back his outrage and disgust when he sees the conditions of anarchy and poverty in Lima.

One of the most salient aspects of nature, which Darwin faced with unceasing honesty, particularly in the Galápagos islands, was that of cruelty. About twenty years after the return of the *Beagle*, he wrote, "What a book a devil's chaplain might write on the clumsy, wasteful, blundering, low, and horribly cruel works of nature." In a sense, it is the other side of the coin of natural selection. If Darwin's theory of evolution points to a general progress of a species, it also reveals the indifference of nature to individuals within the species. It is precisely Darwin's openness to nature that allowed him to perceive this duality, and it was his scientific honesty—which necessitated his acceptance of his observation—that lay behind the final development of his thought. Both of these attributes are already reflected in Darwin's first book, *The Voyage of the Beagle*.

David L. Kubal

Bibliography:
Farrington, Benjamin. *What Darwin Really Said*. New York: Schocken Books, 1982. A basic elucidation and analysis of Darwin's achievement, with a chapter devoted to discussion of Darwin's composition of *The Voyage of the Beagle*.
Keynes, Richard Darwin, ed. *Charles Darwin's "Beagle" Diary*. Cambridge, England: Cambridge University Press, 1988. Provides the raw material on which Darwin drew for his narrative. Also includes useful biographical glossary of persons referred to in the work and connected with it.
Moorehead, Alan. *Darwin and the "Beagle."* London: Hamish Hamilton, 1969. An illustrated and well-detailed introduction to the historical details of Darwin's voyage, including information about his contemporaries and companions, where he went, and what he saw.
Porter, Duncan M. "The *Beagle* Collector and His Collections." In *The Darwinian Heritage*, edited by David Kohn. Princeton, N.J.: Princeton University Press, 1985. A historical discussion of the notebooks Darwin kept on the voyage and of his intellectual preparation for accompanying the *Beagle* as the ship's naturalist and for writing his work.
Sulloway, Frank J. "Darwin's Early Intellectual Development: An Overview of the *Beagle* Voyage." In *The Darwinian Heritage*, edited by David Kohn. Princeton, N.J.: Princeton University Press, 1985. A thorough, critical analysis of all the documents—including notebooks and sketches—from which Darwin composed his narrative.

THE VOYAGE OUT

Type of work: Novel
Author: Virginia Woolf (1882-1941)
Type of plot: Psychological realism
Time of plot: Early twentieth century
Locale: London, mid-Atlantic, and South America
First published: 1915

Principal characters:

RACHEL VINRACE, an inexperienced young woman of twenty-four
HELEN AMBROSE, Rachel's aunt
RIDLEY AMBROSE, Rachel's uncle, a scholar
WILLOUGHBY VINRACE, Rachel's father and owner of the *Euphrosyne*
MR. PEPPER, an old friend of Willoughby Vinrace
RICHARD DALLOWAY, a wealthy gentleman and former parliamentarian
CLARISSA DALLOWAY, Richard's wife
TERENCE HEWET, a novelist, twenty-seven years old
ST. JOHN HIRST, a brilliant twenty-four-year-old intellectual
SUSAN WARRINGTON, a companion to her elderly aunt
ARTHUR VENNING, a barrister with a passion for airplanes
MRS. THORNBURY, the consummate matron
EVELYN MURGATROYD, an impassioned, straightforward young woman
MR. and MRS. FLUSHING, who buy and sell for great profit native artifacts

The Story:

In London, Helen and Ridley Ambrose boarded the *Euphrosyne*, which would take them to Santa Marina in South America, where they planned to vacation. On board ship, the Ambroses met their niece, Rachel, whose father owned the ship and whom they had not seen in several years, and Mr. Pepper, an old family friend. The ship was soon under way, and as it sailed, Helen studied her companions. She judged Rachel to be unformed, a character defect she attributed to her sheltered existence; Pepper she considered somewhat of a bore.

Rachel was indeed an unformed young woman. Her mother was dead, and she lived with her aunts and was seldom in society. She knew virtually nothing of the relations between men and women and had no confidants; questions such as "are you fond of your sister?" were judged inappropriate by her aunts and left unanswered. The things she did hear her aunts discuss seemed to Rachel to have nothing to do with life. She deduced that "no one ever said a thing they meant, or ever talked of a feeling they felt." By the age of twenty-four, Rachel was confused but wondering and inarticulate about her feelings and observations. Unable to express her inner life through language, she instead played the piano, believing that music expressed all the things one meant and felt but could not talk about.

When the ship called at Lisbon, Willoughby Vinrace, ashore on business, learned that an English couple had overwhelmed his clerk with their persistence and won a short passage aboard the *Euphrosyne*. The presence of the Dalloways introduced quite a change into the group. Clarissa energetically and skillfully fostered conversations and showed interest in everyone; Richard enthusiastically and sincerely discussed his political ideals.

The short time spent with the Dalloways affected Rachel profoundly. The couple talked with her about art, sexism, suffering, and making the world better for the poor. One day, during a storm, Richard kissed Rachel while they were alone together. Rachel had never been kissed, and the experience bewildered and terrified her. Soon after this incident, the Dalloways departed. Helen had perceived a change in her niece and was determined to learn the cause, suspecting that it had something to do with the Dalloways. When Rachel blurted out that Richard had kissed her and the effect it had had on her, Helen realized the depth of Rachel's ignorance about sexual matters and attempted to illuminate her.

In her new, self-appointed role as Rachel's mentor, Helen asked Willoughby to leave Rachel with her and Ridley in Santa Marina rather than take her with him. He consented and shortly afterward left them and Mr. Pepper at their destination.

Helen and Rachel developed a ritual they called "seeing life," an evening walk through Santa Marina. On one of these walks, they found themselves at the hotel that housed foreign travelers, among them two young Englishmen named Terence Hewet and St. John Hirst, who befriended Rachel and Helen. Helen was glad of this connection and hoped that the young men would contribute to Rachel's education. Hirst's prejudices against women led him to offend Rachel, but Terence believed that people could break through divisive boundaries and he and Rachel quickly formed a solid friendship. Rachel was encouraged to enquire, speculate, and articulate her thoughts and feelings. She pondered existence, self, and truth.

When Susan Warrington and Arthur Venning, two of the other English travelers at the hotel, became engaged, Rachel wondered what it was to be in love. She and Terence talked at great length about the subject and about men and women in general: their separate spheres; their respective perceptions and powers; women's suffrage; and the changes marriage brought to people, creating wives and husbands where there had once been individuals. They watched such changes come over Arthur and Susan.

Rachel and Terence wondered about their own relationship and wondered whether they felt love for each other. With Hirst, Helen, and Mr. and Mrs. Flushing, the two took an excursion up the river, away from civilization and toward remote villages. Having disembarked in order to explore the terrain, all but Rachel and Terence were too oppressed by the heat to do so. Leaving the others, they followed a trail into the growth, and while they walked they talked about their feelings and decided that they did love each other. Significantly, at this moment they became uncertain of the way back to their friends, although they were sure of the direction in which the river lay. They eventually found their way back.

The couple dreamed of a unique marriage, but Helen had a presentiment of disaster which was realized when Rachel became ill shortly after the river expedition. Her illness diminished her memory and separated her from the ordinary world, and as the fever worsened this distance widened until she was unable to bridge it. She seemed to be at the bottom of the sea. After many days of fever, she died. Terence, who was with her when she died, perceived for an instance that in death they had achieved perfect union. Then he realized that he would never see Rachel again and became distraught; his cries of "Rachel, Rachel!" sounded throughout the villa.

As news of Rachel's death spread at the hotel, the people who had known her responded variously. They wondered whether there was any reason or meaning to it. Mrs. Thornbury wondered whether there is order, equating it, characteristically, with happiness. Mrs. Flushing was furious with death, refusing to submit. Arthur and Susan did not wish to discuss death and tried to steer the conversation in a different direction, while Evelyn Murgatroyd could talk of nothing else. They wondered what had caused the illness and how it might have been prevented. They pondered the immortality of the soul. Life quickly returned to normal, however. People were planning to leave for home, and there were good-byes to be said and packing to be done.

While Hirst lay back in a chair in the large common room and listened to their noise, the hotel guests picked up their books and their knitting and climbed the stairs to bed.

Critical Evaluation:

The Voyage Out is Virginia Woolf's first novel. It is also one of her more accessible novels, as it employs a fairly traditional structure and narrative style and very little of the sometimes difficult, lyric, and highly idiosyncratic style that marks her other novels. In this work, Woolf explores questions about sex and gender, human relationships, civilization and social convention, class and power, social responsibility, existence, reality, and knowledge. This exploration takes place within the structure of a *Bildungsroman*, a work that recounts the education of a single character, in this case, Rachel. Significantly, Rachel learns her lessons through a series of relationships with and observations of a diverse lot of human beings that includes Clarissa and Richard Dalloway, Helen Ambrose, Terence Hewet, St. John Hirst, Susan Warrington and Arthur Venning, Mr. and Mrs. Flushing, Evelyn Murgatroyd, and Mrs. Thornbury.

Each of these characters represents a type of human being, a point Hirst makes early in the novel. He believes that certain types of people find themselves sharing the same inscribed circles and are therefore capable of enjoying relationships with only those people. Different types find themselves within different circles, inhabiting space with others who are like them. There is no fraternizing among different types, and for this reason he believes that men and women cannot have real relationships. They are simply too different from each other.

Hewet, on the other hand, represents the desire to connect with others, and he argues about this with Hirst. It appears that Hewet achieves some success in his belief that people can cross boundaries and connect: It is he who organizes the picnic that brings together disparate groups, "putting virgins among matrons," and it is he who provides Susan and Arthur the opportunity to become engaged and plans the successful ball in honor of the engaged couple. He is also able to establish an easy dialogue with the reticent Rachel. The tragic outcome of their relationship, however, casts a shadow on such optimism. Some critics interpret Rachel's death as possibly an allegorical dictate that all attempts at authentic human connection are doomed.

Woolf's use of the powerful symbol of water—as embodied in the ocean; in a young woman's embarking on an adventure aboard her father's ship; and in a river excursion away from civilization and toward the primitive—also enriches the novel's statements about human relationships. It is little wonder that Woolf's first female protagonist, Rachel Vinrace, can begin her education and growth toward self-knowledge and articulation only after separating herself from her father's sphere of control, for the author had a problematic relationship with her own overbearing father. Rachel must learn to navigate and stay afloat on her own. Indeed, throughout the novel, Woolf describes Rachel and her inner processes in terms of water, rivers, streams, and the sea. When she and Terence first meet, Rachel is stooping to put her hands in a stream; she does not shake hands with him because hers are wet. This detail illustrates not only Rachel's preoccupation with water and self-knowledge; it also suggests that, because of the rules of social decorum, immersion in the self can make people unfit for human interaction.

The Voyage Out suggests that Rachel is ultimately unable to negotiate between her inner world, represented in terms of water, and the outer world of social convention and relationships. Seduced by her own inner life, she retreats farther from others, deeper into the water, until, during her illness, there was such a "gulf between her world and the ordinary world [that] she could not bridge" it. Rachel has achieved the total embrace of the self, leaving the others behind to make what sense they can of her death.

Julie Thompson

Bibliography:

DeSalvo, Louise. *Virginia Woolf's First Voyage: A Novel in the Making.* Totowa, N.J.: Rowman & Littlefield, 1980. Discusses the novel's inception, drafts, inspirations for characters and events, and themes. Detailed comparisons of drafts offer insight into Woolf's creative process. An accessible source.

McDowell, Frederick P. W. "'Surely Order Did Prevail': Virginia Woolf and *The Voyage Out.*" In *Virginia Woolf: Revaluation and Continuity,* edited by Ralph Freedman. Berkeley: University of California Press, 1980. Clearly explicates the novel's psychological complexity, darkness, and questioning of meaning and reality.

Paul, Janis M. *The Victorian Heritage of Virginia Woolf: The External World in Her Novels.* Norman, Okla.: Pilgrim Books, 1987. Paul's chapter on *The Voyage Out* considers the novel within its aesthetic and historical context and pays particular attention to Woolf's struggle between Victorian and modernist conventions, both in life and literature. Also discusses Woolf's experimentation with form.

Rose, Phyllis. *Woman of Letters: A Life of Virginia Woolf.* New York: Oxford University Press, 1978. Offers in one chapter on *The Voyage Out* a compelling discussion that focuses on Woolf's use of character to explore social and philosophical issues.

Rosenthal, Michael. *Virginia Woolf.* New York: Columbia University Press, 1979. Includes an excellent chapter devoted to a thorough discussion of the plot and ideas of Woolf's first novel.

WAITING FOR GODOT

Type of work: Drama
Author: Samuel Beckett (1906-1989)
Type of plot: Absurdist
Time of plot: Indeterminate
Locale: A country road
First published: 1952; first performed, 1953 as *En attendant Godot* (English translation, 1954)

Principal characters:
VLADIMIR, a tramp
ESTRAGON, another tramp
POZZO, a success-blinded materialist
LUCKY, Pozzo's servant
A BOY, a messenger from Godot

The Story:

Estragon tried to take off his boot but failed. Vladimir agreed with him that it sometimes appeared that there was nothing one could do. They were glad to be reunited after a night apart. With Vladimir's help, Estragon succeeded in removing his boot, which was causing him pain. Vladimir, also in pain, could not laugh in comfort; he tried smiling instead but it was not satisfactory.

Vladimir mused on the one gospel account that said Christ saved one of the thieves. Estragon wanted to leave. They could not leave because they were waiting for Godot. They became confused about the arrangements and wondered if they were waiting at the right time, in the right place, and on the right day. They quarreled briefly but were, as always, reconciled.

They considered hanging themselves but decided that it would be safer to do nothing until they heard what Godot said. They did not know what they had asked Godot for. They concluded that they had foregone their rights. Vladimir gave Estragon a carrot, which he ate hungrily. They decided that although they were not bound to Godot, they were in fact unable to act. Pozzo entered, driving Lucky, who was laden with luggage, by a rope around his neck. Estragon and Vladimir mistook him for Godot but accepted him as Pozzo. Although he attempted to intimidate them, he was glad of their company. After ordering Lucky to bring him his stool and his coat, he gave Lucky the whip. Lucky obeyed automatically. Vladimir and Estragon protested violently against Pozzo's treatment of Lucky. Pozzo deflected their outburst and the subject was dropped.

After smoking a pipe Pozzo rose. He then decided he did not want to leave, but his pride almost prevented him from reseating himself. The tramps wanted to know why Lucky never put down the luggage. Pozzo said that Lucky was trying to make Pozzo keep him. When Pozzo added that he would sell Lucky rather than throw him out, Lucky wept; but when Estragon tried to dry his tears, Lucky kicked him away. Then Estragon wept. Pozzo philosophized on this and said that Lucky had taught him all the beautiful things he knew but that the fellow had now become unbearable and was driving Pozzo mad. Estragon and Vladimir then abused Lucky for mistreating his master.

Pozzo broke into a monologue on the twilight, alternating between the lyrical and the commonplace and ending with the bitter thought that everything happened in the world when one was least prepared. He decided to reward Estragon and Vladimir for praising him by making Lucky entertain them. Lucky executed a feeble dance that Estragon mocked but failed to imitate.

Estragon stated that there had been no arrivals, no departures, and no action, and that everything was terrible. Pozzo next decided that Lucky should think for them. For this Vladimir replaced Lucky's derby hat. Lucky's thought was an incoherent flood of words that resembled a dissertation on the possible goodness of God, the tortures of hellfire, the prevalence of sport, and the vacuity of suburbs. He desperately upset his listeners, who attacked him and silenced him by seizing his hat. Having restored Lucky to his position as carrier, Pozzo and the tramps said many farewells before he and Lucky finally left.

The Boy called to Vladimir and Estragon. He came with a message from Godot, who would come the next evening. The Boy, a goatherd, said that Godot was kind to him, but that he beat his brother, a shepherd. Vladimir asked the Boy to tell Godot only that he had seen them.

By the time the Boy left, night had fallen. Estragon decided to abandon his boots to someone else. Vladimir protested and Estragon said that Christ had gone barefoot. Once again they considered and rejected the idea of separating. They decided to leave for the night. They stayed where they were.

The following evening the boots were still there and the tree had grown some leaves. The tramps had spent the night separately. Vladimir returned first. When Estragon came back he said he had been beaten again and Vladimir felt that he could have prevented such cruelty. Vladimir began to talk of the previous day, but Estragon could remember nothing but being kicked. Then they were overwhelmed by the thought of the whispering voices of the dead around them. They tried to break their silence but succeeded only in part. By a great effort Estragon recalled that the previous day had been spent chattering inanities. He reflected that they had spent fifty years doing no more than that.

They discovered that the boots left behind by Estragon had been exchanged for another old pair. After finding Lucky's hat, which assured them that they had returned to the right place, they started a wild exchange of the three hats, shifting them from hand to hand. Finally Vladimir kept Lucky's hat and Estragon kept his own.

Once more Estragon decided to leave. To distract him, Vladimir suggested that they "play" Pozzo and Lucky. Puzzled, Estragon left, but he returned almost immediately because some people were coming. Vladimir was jubilant, convinced that Godot was arriving. They tried to hide, but there was nowhere for them to go. Finally Lucky entered with Pozzo, who was now blind. Lucky fell and dragged Pozzo with him. Pozzo cried for help. Vladimir passionately wished to act while there was the opportunity—to do one good thing as a member of the human race, a species that appalled him. Pozzo was terrified, and Vladimir also fell in his attempts to raise him. Estragon fell too while trying to lift Vladimir. As they fought and argued on the ground, they called Pozzo "Cain" and "Abel." When he responded to both names they concluded that he was all humanity. Suddenly they got up without difficulty.

Pozzo prepared to leave, but Vladimir wanted Lucky to sing first. Pozzo explained that Lucky was dumb. They wanted to know when he had been afflicted. Angry, Pozzo said that all their lives were merely momentary and time did not matter. He left with Lucky.

While Estragon slept, the Boy entered to say that Godot would come, not that night but the next. The message for Godot was that the Boy had seen Vladimir. The Boy left and Estragon awoke. He immediately wanted to leave. Vladimir insisted that they could not go far because they must return the next night in order to wait for Godot, who would punish them if they did not wait.

Estragon and Vladimir remarked that only the tree in the landscape was alive and considered hanging themselves again. Instead, they decided that if Godot did not come to save them the next night, they would hang themselves. At last the tramps decided to go. They remained immobile.

Critical Evaluation:

Waiting for Godot is a landmark in modern drama. When it premiered in Paris, its originality stunned audiences: No one had seen or heard anything like it before. Initially, some were disgusted, some were puzzled, and some were wildly enthusiastic. Within a short time, however, audiences came to the theater prepared for a wholly new dramatic experience and went away with praises for Samuel Beckett. The play ran for more than three hundred performances in Paris, other productions were mounted in London and major cities on the Continent, and it was widely translated and performed around the world. After a disastrous United States premiere in Miami, *Waiting for Godot* went on to a successful New York run, suggesting that the play was best received by an audience of sophisticated intellectuals.

Nevertheless, audience enthusiasm has not been matched by unalloyed critical acclaim. To be sure, many critics as well as eminent playwrights have paid high tribute to the play. Several other critics have been repelled or baffled by *Waiting for Godot*, their reactions most often stemming from a misunderstanding of the play. In order to avert such misunderstanding, it is necessary to examine two crucial aspects of the play: its language and its philosophical orientation.

First of all, the language of the play is intimately connected to Beckett's own background in language studies and literary influences. Beckett was born in Dublin, Ireland, and took his bachelor's degree in French and Italian at Trinity College. After teaching English in Paris for two years, he returned to Trinity to teach and complete his master's degree in French. Next, he traveled in England and on the Continent, and he wrote poems, short stories, and novels in English. He at last settled permanently in Paris, except for a brief hiatus during World War II, and began writing in French in the late 1940's. *Waiting for Godot* was originally written in French but translated into English by Beckett himself. The play is full of verbal and linguistic play; it is the work of a master of words and wordplay.

Second, during Beckett's first sojourn in Paris, from 1928 to 1930, he met James Joyce, a meeting that launched a long and mutually satisfying friendship between the two Irish expatriates and language experts. The philosophical influence of Joyce on Beckett's work is evident in the language play in *Waiting for Godot*. Puns, allusions, and linguistic tricks abound. Joyce and Beckett had little respect for literary convention, including, to an extent, the convention that everything in a book should make perfect sense or be perfectly clear.

Great effort has been expended, for example, in trying to decipher the word "Godot." Beckett himself declined to explain, but critics, undeterred, continue to speculate. The most common view sees Godot as God with the *-ot* as a diminutive suffix. The French title *En attendant Godot* seems to lend support to this interpretation. Another suggestion is the analogy between Godot and Charlot (both utilizing the diminutive suffix), the latter being the French name for Charlie Chaplin's little tramp. The kind of hat that the little tramp wears, a derby, plays a significant part in the stage business of *Waiting for Godot*. Some readings inevitably deteriorate into the preposterous—that Godot represents Charles de Gaulle, for example. A much more likely explanation involves an allusion to a highly obscure source: Honoré de Balzac's comedy, *Le Faiseur* (1851; also known as *Mercadet*). Balzac's play revolves around a character named Godeau who strongly influences the action of the play but who never appears on stage. The parallels between the Balzac work and *Waiting for Godot* are too close to attribute to mere coincidence. Beckett, like Joyce, has a marked fondness for the esoteric literary allusion. It is possible, of course, to circumvent these literary contortions and simply view Godot as a state of being: the waiting, bracketed by birth and death, that we call life.

In addition, Beckett plays other word games in *Waiting for Godot*. Estragon, for instance, begins a sentence which Vladimir then finishes. Yet the overwhelming monotony of the dialogue, reflecting the monotony in the characters' lives, is reminiscent of the exercise drills in old language texts of the "*La plume de ma tante est sur la table*" variety, further suggesting the debasement of language and the consequent breakdown of communication. The non sequiturs that emerge from rapid-fire exchanges in the dialogue echo the music-hall comedians of Beckett's youth. Beckett's penchant for wordplay reveals the influence of his language training and of his friend James Joyce.

The philosophical orientation of *Waiting for Godot* is another matter, however, for the years of Beckett's residence in France coincided with a period of great ferment in existential philosophy, most of it centered in Paris. Beckett is not a formal or doctrinaire existentialist, but he could hardly avoid being affected by existentialism, for such ideas were part of his cultural milieu. There is no systematically existential point of view in *Waiting for Godot*—as there is in, for example, the plays of Jean-Paul Sartre and the novels of Albert Camus. Yet a generally existential and absurdist view of the human condition comes through very clearly in the play. Vladimir and Estragon, and Lucky and Pozzo are psychically isolated from one another; despite physical proximity, they are alienated and lonely, as indicated by their failure to communicate meaningfully. In that state of mind, each despairs, feeling helpless in the face of an immutable destiny. Unlike the formal existentialists, however, Estragon and Vladimir hope, and it is that hope that sustains them through their monotonous and immobile existence. They wait. They wait for Godot, who will surely bring them words of comfort and advice, and who will intervene to alter their destinies. By maintaining this hope, by waiting for Godot to come, Vladimir and Estragon avoid facing the logic of existential philosophy, which postulates hopelessness followed by a sense of futility, reducing humankind to absurdity. In this way, Vladimir and Estragon attain truly heroic proportions; they endure.

Beckett's play has been criticized, even by Estragon, because, as the tramp puts it, "Nothing happens." In fact, however, a great deal does happen: There is a lot of action, much coming and going. However, action in this sense is quite superficial, for all of it is meaningless. That very action assumes a rhythm and a pattern that constitute the structure of the play. The repetitious movements and dialogue reinforce the existential theme of the play: that life is a meaningless and monotonous performance of endlessly repeated routine. The pattern established in the first act is recapitulated in the second act, with only slight variation. Obviously the action in *Waiting for Godot* is not the action of conventional drama, but it is this unique fusion of theme and structure that accounts for the startling originality of the play and that rightly earns Beckett a place as one of the few genuine innovators in modern drama.

"Critical Evaluation" by Joanne G. Kashdan

Bibliography:
Andonian, Cathleen Culotta. *Samuel Beckett: A Reference Guide*. Boston: G. K. Hall, 1989. A comprehensive, annotated bibliography, well indexed. The critical reception of *Waiting for Godot* can be traced through its listings.
Bair, Deirdre. *Samuel Beckett*. New York: Harcourt Brace Jovanovich, 1978. Original, full-

length biography, drawing on hundreds of interviews with Beckett's friends and acquaintances. Provides much interesting circumstantial information on the genesis of the play, its controversial early productions, and its translations.

Bloom, Harold, ed. *Waiting for Godot: Modern Critical Interpretations.* New York: Chelsea House, 1987. The eight representative selections by leading interpreters of Beckett's work (including Ruby Cohn, Martin Esslin, John Fletcher, and Hugh Kenner) consider the theatrical, religious, and philosophical implications of *Waiting for Godot.*

Connor, Steven, ed. *"Waiting for Godot" and "Endgame."* New York: St. Martin's Press, 1992. Four of the eleven interrelated essays deal with *Waiting for Godot* in terms drawn from contemporary theory. They range from the liberal humanist reading of Andrew Kennedy on action and theatricality to Jeffrey Nealon's definition of a postmodernist culture that validates the self through the playing of serious games.

Cousineau, Thomas. *"Waiting for Godot": Form in Movement.* Boston: Twayne, 1990. A theoretically informed student guide to the play. Contends that concrete scenic language and physical movement displaces narrow notions of text. Also contains discussions of various themes and techniques. Annotated bibliography.

Esslin, Martin. *The Theatre of the Absurd.* 3d ed. New York: Penguin Books, 1987. Highly influential for its famous definition and its lucid study of the movement of which *Waiting for Godot* is a classic part. Focusing on existential elements, the analysis attempts to account for the complexity of the effect of the play.

WALDEN

Type of work: Essays
Author: Henry David Thoreau (1817-1862)
First published: 1854

Early in the summer of 1845, Henry David Thoreau left his family home in the village of Concord, Massachusetts, to live for two years by himself in a rude house that he had constructed beside Walden Pond, in a far corner of Concord township. While there, he wrote in his journal about many of the things he did and thought. He was not the owner of the land on which he settled, but he had received the owner's permission to build his house and to live there. His objective was really to live simply and think and write; in addition, he proved to himself that the necessities of food, clothing, shelter, and fuel could be rather simply obtained for a man who desired only what he needed.

As early as March, 1845, Thoreau went out to Walden Pond and cut the timber he needed for the framework of his house, doing all the labor himself. When that was done and the framing in place, Thoreau bought a shanty from an Irish railroad worker. He then tore down the shanty and used the boards for the sidings of the house, even making use of many of the nails already in the boards. By July, then, the house was ready for his occupancy. Before the advent of cold weather the following fall, Thoreau also built himself a fireplace and a chimney for cooking and heating purposes. He also lathed and plastered the interior of the one-room house, in order that it would be warm and comfortable during the cold New England winter.

Having done all the work himself, and having used native materials wherever possible, he had built the house for the absurdly low cost of twenty-eight dollars. In addition to providing himself with a place to live, Thoreau believed he had taught himself a great lesson in the art of living. He was also vastly pleased that he had provided himself with a place to live for less than a year's lodging had cost him as a student at Harvard College.

In order to get the money needed to build the house, Thoreau had planted about two and a half acres of beans, peas, potatoes, corn, and turnips, which he sold at harvest time. The land on which they were grown was lent by a neighbor who believed, along with everyone else, that the land was good for nothing. In addition to selling enough produce to pay his building expenses, Thoreau had enough yield left from his gardening to provide himself with food. He did not spend all of his time, however, working on the house or in the garden. One of his purposes in living at Walden Pond was to live so simply that he might have plenty of time to think, to write, and to observe nature, and so he spent only as much time in other labors as was needed. He had little respect for possessions and material things. He believed, for example, that most people were really possessed by their belongings, and that such a literary work as the *Bhagavad Gita* (c. fifth century B.C.E.) was worth more than all the towers and temples of the Orient.

Thoreau was quite proud of how little money he needed to live comfortably while at Walden Pond. The first eight months he was there, he spent only slightly more than a dollar a month for food. In addition to some twenty-odd dollars he received for vegetables that he had raised, his income, within which he lived, was slightly more than thirteen dollars. His food consisted almost entirely of rye and Indian meal bread, potatoes, rice, a little salt pork, molasses, and salt. His drink was water. Seldom did he eat large portions of meat, and he never hunted. His interest in the animals that lived in the woods and fields near Walden Pond was the interest of a naturalist. Although he spent some time fishing, he felt that the time he had was too valuable to spend in catching fish to feed himself. For the small amounts of cash he needed, Thoreau worked with his hands at many occupations, working only so long as was necessary to provide himself with the money his meager wants required. He kept as much time as possible free for thinking and studying. His study consisted more of people and nature than of books, although he kept a few well-selected volumes about him at all times.

While at Walden Pond, summer and winter, Thoreau lived independent of time. He refused to acknowledge days of the week or month. When he wished to spend some time observing certain birds or animals, or even the progress of the weather, he felt free to do so. About the only thing to remind him that people were rushing chaotically to keep a schedule was the whistle of the Fitchburg Railway trains, which passed within a mile or so of his dwelling. Not that he disliked the railroad; he thought it, in fact, a marvel of human ingenuity, and he was fascinated by the cargoes which the trains carried from place to place. He was glad, however, that he was not chained to the commerce those cargoes represented. As much as he sometimes enjoyed the sound of the train, he enjoyed far more the sounds of the birds and animals, most of which he could recognize, not only as a country dweller knows them but also as the naturalist knows them. The loons, the owls, the squirrels, the various kinds of fish in Walden Pond, the migratory birds, all of these were part of his conscious existence and environment.

People often dropped in to visit with Thoreau, who frankly confessed that he did not consider people very important. He failed, in fact, to tell who his most frequent visitors were. He preferred only one visitor, and that a thinking one, at a time. Whenever he had more visitors than could be accommodated by his small house and its three chairs, he took them into his larger drawing room, the pine wood which lay about his home. From what he wrote about his treatment of all but a very few of the people who came to visit him, it is very probable that he was an unfriendly kind of host, one who, if he had nothing better to do, was willing to talk, but who usually had more to occupy him than simple conversation.

During the winter months, Thoreau continued to live comfortably at Walden Pond, though his activities changed. He spent more time at the pond itself, making a survey of its bottom, studying the ice conditions, and observing the animal life which centered on the pond, which had some open water throughout the year.

After two years of life at Walden, Thoreau left the pond. He felt no regret for having stayed there or for leaving; his attitude was that he had many lives to live and that he had finished with living at the pond. He had learned many lessons there, had had time to think and study, and had proved what he had set out to prove twenty-six months before, that living could be extremely simple and yet highly fulfilling to the individual.

Critical Evaluation:

Few contemporaries of Henry David Thoreau would have predicted the enormous popularity his small volume, *Walden*, would eventually win. Author and work were virtually neglected during Thoreau's lifetime. Locally, he was considered the village eccentric; even his great friend and mentor Ralph Waldo Emerson was disappointed because his young disciple seemingly frittered away his talent instead of "engineering for all America." After Thoreau's death in 1862, his works attracted serious critical attention, but unfavorable reviews by James Russell Lowell and Robert Louis Stevenson severely damaged his reputation. Toward the turn of the century he began to win favorable attention again, mainly in Britain. During the Great Depression of the 1930's, when most people were forced to cut the frills from their lives, *Walden*, whose author admonished readers voluntarily to "Simplify, simplify, simplify!" became something of a fad. In the 1960's, with new awareness of the environment and emphasis on nonconformity, Thoreau was exalted as a prophet, and *Walden* as the individualist's bible.

Walden can be approached in several different ways. It can be viewed as an excellent nature book. During the Romantic era, many writers, such as William Wordsworth, Percy Shelley, Ralph Waldo Emerson, and Walt Whitman, paid tribute to nature. Thoreau, however, went beyond simply rhapsodizing natural wonders. He was a serious student of the natural world, one who would spend hours observing a woodchuck or tribes of battling ants, who meticulously sounded and mapped Walden Pond, who enjoyed a hilarious game of tag with a loon. Like Emerson, he saw nature as a master teacher. In his observations of nature, Thoreau was a scientist; in his descriptions, a poet; in his interpretations, a philosopher and psychologist. Certainly he was an ecologist in his insistence on humanity's place in (not over) the natural universe, and on the need for daily contact with the earth.

Walden may also be considered as a handbook for the simplification of life. As such, it becomes a commentary upon the sophistication, "refinement," frequently distorted values, and devotion to things of civilized society. Thoreau admits the necessities of food, shelter, clothing, and fuel, "for not till we have secured these are we prepared to entertain the true problems of life with freedom and a prospect of success." He then illustrates how people may strip these necessities to essentials for survival and health, ignoring the dictates of fashion or the yearning for luxury. "Most of the luxuries, and many of the so called comforts of life," he asserts, "are not only not indispensable, but positive hindrances to the elevation of mankind." With relentless logic he points out how making a living has come to take precedence over living itself; how people mortgage themselves to pay for more land and fancier clothing and food than they really require; how they refuse to walk to a neighboring city because it will take too long—but then must work longer than the walk would take in order to pay for a train ticket. He questions the dedication to "progress," noting that it is technological, not spiritual. "We are in great haste to construct a magnetic telegraph from Maine to Texas; but Maine and Texas, it may be, have nothing important to communicate."

Perhaps the most serious purpose of *Walden* and its most powerful message is to call people to freedom as individuals. One looks at nature in order to learn about oneself; one simplifies one's life in order to have time to develop that self fully; and one must honor one's uniqueness if one is to know full self-realization. It is this emphasis on nonconformity that has so endeared Thoreau to the young, who have adopted as their call to life these words from the final chapter of *Walden*: "If a man does not keep pace with his companions, perhaps it is because he hears a different drummer. Let him step to the music which he hears, however measured or far away."

There is an ease, a clarity, a concreteness to Thoreau's prose that separate it from the more abstract, eloquent, and frequently involuted styles of his contemporaries. The ease and seeming spontaneity are deceptive. Thoreau revised the book meticulously during the five years it took to find a publisher; there are five complete drafts which demonstrate how consciously he organized not only the general outline, but every chapter and paragraph. For an overall pattern, he condensed the two years of his actual Walden experience into one fictional year, beginning and concluding with spring—the time of rebirth.

Pace and tone are also carefully controlled. Thoreau's sentences and paragraphs flow smoothly. The reader is frequently surprised to discover that sentences occasionally run to more than half a page, paragraphs to a page or more; syntax is so skillfully handled that one never feels tangled in verbiage. Tone varies from matter-of-fact to poetic to inspirational and is spiced with humor—usually some well-placed satire—at all levels. Even the most abstract topics are handled in concrete terms; Thoreau's ready use of images and figurative language prepares one for twentieth century Imagist poetry.

Taken as a whole, *Walden* is a first-rate example of organic writing, with organization, style, and content fused to form a work that, more than one hundred years after its publication, is as readable and perhaps even more timely than when it was written. In *Walden*, Thoreau reaches across the years to continue to "brag as lustily as Chanticleer . . . to wake my neighbors up."

"Critical Evaluation" by Sally Buckner

Bibliography:
Bloom, Harold, ed. *Henry David Thoreau's "Walden."* New York: Chelsea House, 1987. A representative selection of some of the best criticism of Thoreau's *Walden* published since Stanley Cavell's *The Senses of "Walden"* (1972). Although primarily a celebration of Thoreau, some essays question his solipsism and his debt to Emerson.
Cavell, Stanley. *The Senses of "Walden."* New York: Viking Press, 1972. The prelude to the contemporary reading of Thoreau's masterpiece. Cavell argues that *Walden*'s mysteries can be learned by giving the fullest attention to all Thoreau said.
Myerson, Joel, ed. *Critical Essays on Henry David Thoreau's "Walden."* Boston: G. K. Hall, 1988. Contains a very complete record of critical reaction to *Walden* beginning with early reviews by Horace Greeley, George Eliot, and several anonymous reviewers of the day. The book also contains reprints of more than a dozen twentieth century essays examining such topics as the structure of *Walden* and its language.
Ruland, Richard, ed. *Twentieth Century Interpretations of "Walden": A Collection of Critical Essays*. Englewood Cliffs, N.J.: Prentice-Hall, 1968. An excellent source of discussion for *Walden*. Nine short essays and twelve shorter viewpoints by critics and writers offer a coherent reading of Thoreau's book. Contains a brief chronology of Thoreau's life.
Shanley, J. Lyndon. *The Making of "Walden."* Chicago: University of Chicago Press, 1957. A detailed study of how Thoreau wrote the first version of *Walden* while living at Walden Pond and how he rewrote it between 1848 and 1854. Contains the text of the first edition of *Walden*.

A WALK ON THE WILD SIDE

Type of work: Novel
Author: Nelson Algren (Nelson Ahlgren Abraham, 1909-1981)
Type of plot: Picaresque
Time of plot: 1930's
Locale: Texas and New Orleans
First published: 1956

> *Principal characters:*
> DOVE LINKHORN, hobo, con artist, and sexual athlete
> TERASINA VIDAVARRI, owner of the café in Arroyo, Texas, and Dove's
> lover
> KITTY TWIST, Dove's hobo companion and later a prostitute in the
> whorehouse in New Orleans where he works
> OLIVER FINNERTY, a New Orleans whorehouse operator
> ACHILLES SCHMIDT, a legless strongman
> HALLIE BREEDLOVE, a classy prostitute who is in love with him

The Story:

Fitz Linkhorn barely managed to make a living pumping out cesspools, but his consuming vocation was preaching from the courthouse steps in Arroyo, a small town in the Rio Grande Valley of Texas. He denounced all sins except drinking, because he was drunk as often as possible. Fitz had two sons, Byron, who was weak and sickly, and Dove.

Dove had no education because his father had not wanted to send him to a school with a Catholic principal. Instead, he was supposed to see movies with Byron to learn about life, but Dove never got to go—his brother did not have the price of a ticket. Dove got his education from the hoboes who hung around the Santa Fe tracks, telling one another what towns, lawmen, jails, and railroad bulls to avoid.

Dove began hanging around the La Fe en Dios chili parlor in the ruins of the Hotel Crockett on the other side of town. The hotel was the place where Fitz had met the mother of his sons. The hotel was closed, but the café was run by Terasina Vidavarri, a wary woman who had been raped by a soldier and who ran a seldom-visited café. She continued Dove's education by teaching him how to read from two books. One of the books was a children's storybook; the other was about how to write business letters. Dove and Terasina eventually became lovers, and once Dove took Terasina by force outside by the clothesline.

Byron stole from the café, and Terasina mistakenly blamed the crime on Dove. She was so angered that she threw him out, and Dove left Arroyo on a freight train. Dove took up with a girl named Kitty Twist, a runaway from a children's home, and saved her life when she was about to fall under the wheels of a train. When they attempted a burglary in Houston, Kitty was caught. Dove got away on a freight to New Orleans. One of the first things he saw in New Orleans was a man cutting the heads off turtles that were to be made into turtle soup and throwing the bodies into a pile. Even with the heads cut off, the bodies tried to climb to the top of the pile. One turtle was able to reach the top of the pile before it slid back to the bottom.

In the port city, with its many different influences and cultures, Dove experienced his most interesting adventures. He worked as a painter on a steamship (but did not paint anything), fooled a prostitute who was trying to rob him, sold coffeepots and "beauty certificates" (which supposedly entitled the bearer to a treatment at a beauty shop) while seducing the women to whom he was selling, and, in his most memorable escapade, worked in a condom factory. The condoms, which were called O-Daddies and bore interesting names and colors, were made in a house by a mom-and-pop firm, Velma and Rhino Gross.

Dove's lengthiest stay was with the people who inhabited the twin worlds of Oliver Finnerty's brothel and Doc Dockery's speakeasy. In the brothel he found, in addition to his old friend Kitty Twist, who had become a prostitute, Hallie Breedlove, a onetime schoolteacher who was the star of Finnerty's string of girls. Hallie was in love with Achilles Schmidt, a former circus strongman whose legs had been cut off by a train. Schmidt's upper body was still powerful and every day he surged into Dockery's bar with the air of one who could beat up anyone there—and he could. Dove's main job at Finnerty's was to couple with the girls in the place, who were pretending to be virgins being deflowered, while customers watched through peepholes. Hallie, who still retained vestiges of her former life as a teacher, was interested in Dove's mind and helped him to continue to learn to read. Dove's closeness to Hallie angered Achilles, who assaulted Dove in Dockery's bar. Schmidt beat Dove until Dove was blind, and a gang of people then descended on Schmidt and killed him. Dove managed to make his way back to Texas and Terasina's café.

Critical Evaluation:

Nelson Algren, all of whose works are about characters from the lower levels of life—tramps, con artists, prostitutes, petty criminals, and drug addicts—is often considered to be a naturalistic novelist in terms of both philosophy and style. Literary naturalism is a viewpoint that emphasizes that human life is materialistic (based on the struggle for the acquisition of money, prestige, and property and without a spiritual component). Naturalistic novelists concentrate on earthy, even sordid subjects; their style involves the presentation of many physical details. *A Walk on the Wild Side* is so full of physical details that it appears to have no plot at all. The reader is deep into the novel before he or she realizes that there is no specific conflict, and no challenges to be met other than the conflict and challenge of life itself. Although it appears at first glance that Nelson Algren's works fit neatly into the naturalistic pattern, he is actually using the naturalistic elements of his works to make points about the spiritual nature of his characters. Algren signals to the reader that he is not exclusively concerned with material existence. One signal is his use of a lyrical, almost rhapsodic, style.

The scene in which the beheaded turtle crawls to the top of the pile of other decapitated creatures is central in understanding Algren's outlook. The turtle is slow and odd-looking, hardly a likely animal to be chosen as a symbol of indomitability, as might be an eagle or a lion. Through his use of the turtle, Algren reminds the reader that even the lowly people he writes about have dreams and higher yearnings. A horrible death is the turtle's fate, but even after death he keeps going, straining to reach the top of the pile, like Schmidt after his mutilation and Dove after his blinding. When the dead turtle finally slithers to the bottom of the pile, Algren reminds the reader that the ultimate fate is defeat—at least in this life and in this world. Algren presents many other clues in *A Walk on the Wild Side* that he is concerned with the spirit and not simply the body.

Dove Linkhorn's father, Fitz, insists on presenting his own religious view of life regardless of who is listening and regardless of the consequences. The name of his son, Dove, is associated with peace, and Dove never loses his self-possession and control even when he does not understand the crazy world through which he wanders. The café that Terasina operates is called the La Fe en Dios (faith in God), and the characters move about on a railroad called the Santa

Fe (holy faith). Finnerty's brothel and Dockery's bar are located on Perdido (lost) Street. Algren believes that the place to look for spiritual richness is among the downtrodden and the poor. A life in which one is obliged to do without leads one, sometimes without one's knowledge, to a life within, a life of the spirit. It is a spiritual verity that the less one has, the better off spiritually one is, because material possessions tend to tie one down to a life centered on the pointless acquisition of more possessions. Algren implies that if one is to keep one's soul, one must walk through the wild side of human behavior. Algren also draws on another ancient spiritual lesson—from pain and suffering come the growth of the spirit.

As well as exploring spiritual development, Algren draws heavily on two literary traditions, those of the picaresque and the innocent. The picaresque story, which originated in Spain in the sixteenth century, tells the story of a rogue (*pícaro*) who moves from place to place, living by his wits, conning people, and staying one step ahead of the law. Dove is a picaro, and the relative formlessness of the novel is an inheritance from the picaresque tradition. At the same time, he is an innocent, a person whose naïveté and wonder about life serve as foils to the corruption and venality of those around him. Even after he is beaten blind by Achilles Schmidt (himself an icon of spiritual triumph), Dove returns, still himself and still ultimately unbroken, to Terasina Vidavarri, who operates the café and whose name means "true life."

A Walk on the Wild Side differs from most of Algren's other work, which also features low characters caught in desperate circumstances, because in those other works the characters are finally defeated and even destroyed by a world in which everything works against them. In *A Walk on the Wild Side*, however, although there is the usual collection of grotesque characters, wild settings, and violent actions, everyone, good and bad, keeps bouncing back. Dove, for example, seems to take his beating from Schmidt and his blindness as simply another condition with which he must live. He does not descend into despair or self-pity. Algren is too familiar with life's wild side, however, to give his novel a happy ending. At the end of the novel, Dove stands in front of Terasina's café, but he has not gone inside, and it is not clear if she will accept him. The novel's conclusion is not happy, but it is hopeful.

Jim Baird

Bibliography:
Algren, Nelson. *Conversations with Nelson Algren*. Interviews by H. E. F. Donohue. New York: Hill & Wang, 1964. A series of interviews in which Algren discusses his life and writings, including *A Walk on the Wild Side*.

Bluestone, George. "Nelson Algren." *Western Review* 22 (Autumn, 1957): 27-44. Bluestone was the first to identify Algren as not only a naturalistic writer but also one with broader themes than tragic realism. Discusses *A Walk on the Wild Side*.

Cox, Martha Heasley, and Wayne Chatterton. *Nelson Algren*. Boston: Twayne, 1975. A book-length discussion of all of Algren's work up to 1975, with a chapter on *A Walk on the Wild Side*. Contains a biography and bibliographies.

Giles, James R. *Confronting the Horror: The Novels of Nelson Algren*. Kent, Ohio: Kent State University Press, 1989. Discusses *A Walk on the Wild Side* as an example of absurdist comedy and notes the influence of Louis-Ferdinand Céline.

Lipton, Lawrence. "A Voyeur's View of the Wild Side: Nelson Algren and His Reviewers." In *Chicago Review Anthology*, edited by David Ray. Chicago: University of Chicago Press. Evaluates those who have commented on *A Walk on the Wild Side* and adds further critical comments.

WALLENSTEIN

Type of work: Drama
Author: Friedrich Schiller (1759-1805)
Type of plot: Historical
Time of plot: Thirty Years' War (1618-1648)
Locale: Germany
First performed: Wallensteins Lager (Wallenstein's Camp), 1798; *Die Piccolomini (The Piccolominis),* 1799; *Wallensteins Tod (The Death of Wallenstein),* 1799; first published: 1800 (English translation, 1800-1846);

Principal characters:
> WALLENSTEIN, the duke of Friedland, generalissimo of the imperial
>   forces in the Thirty Years' War
> OCTAVIO PICCOLOMINI, a lieutenant general
> MAX PICCOLOMINI, the general's son, a colonel
> COUNT TERZKY, Wallenstein's brother-in-law
> BUTLER, an Irish soldier of fortune
> DUCHESS OF FRIEDLAND, Wallenstein's wife
> THEKLA, Wallenstein's daughter

The Story:

Wallenstein, the duke of Friedland, had once been dismissed from the service of Emperor Ferdinand, but during the Thirty Years' War, in which the countries of central Europe battled to prevent their annihilation by the forces of Gustavus Adolphus of Sweden, the emperor had recalled Wallenstein and given him extraordinary powers to create an army to drive the Swedes out of central Europe. Wallenstein had raised such a powerful army, but both its leaders and its rank and file felt that they owed allegiance to their commander rather than to the emperor.

Wallenstein's army won many victories, and the situation in central Europe became less tense. The threat to his dominions having decreased, the emperor wished to curtail Wallenstein's powers, lest the conquering hero should attempt to dictate to the crown. Wallenstein in turn became suspicious of the emperor and his government, and he wavered on the verge of declaring himself for the Swedes.

The emperor made arrangements to have Wallenstein removed from his post, and as a first step he sent a war commissioner, Von Questenberg, to Wallenstein's camp. The commissioner found the army so sensitive to its leader's wishes that the soldiers were ready to follow him should he turn traitor. The commissioner shared his fears with Lieutenant General Piccolomini and gave him the emperor's secret commission to take over the armies and to arrest Wallenstein. Wallenstein, who believed that General Piccolomini was his trusted friend and brother officer, did not suspect that General Piccolomini was more loyal to his monarch than to him.

General Piccolomini wished to have the help of his son, Colonel Max Piccolomini, in his plans, but the son, who had grown up under Wallenstein's tutelage, refused to believe that Wallenstein could ever be anything but virtuous. Moreover, Max Piccolomini was in love with Wallenstein's daughter, Thekla, and had high hopes that the great general-duke would permit them to marry. Young Piccolomini did not know that Wallenstein, fired with ambition and filled with suspicion of the Emperor Ferdinand, was actually plotting to go over to the Swedes with his army in return for the kingship of Hungary. Wallenstein regarded his daughter a future queen, not the wife of a colonel.

Worried by the arrival of Von Questenberg, Wallenstein gave one of his trusted henchmen the task of seeing that all his great leaders signed a vow to follow him wherever he might lead, even if he led them away from the emperor. The henchman planned a great banquet to accomplish the deed. Before the banquet he showed the officers a document that he refused to let them sign. After the banquet, when the men were drunk, another document containing a pledge of loyalty to Wallenstein was substituted. All the leaders signed except Max Piccolomini, who had remained sober and realized that he could not take a vow against the emperor without forfeiting his honor.

Wallenstein believed that the leaders would be compelled to follow him after signing the document, a paper that would compromise them in the emperor's eyes, regardless of how the signatures were obtained. General Piccolomini signed the document, wishing to let Wallenstein proceed far enough to expose his traitorous hand. General Piccolomini knew it would be easier to turn the army away from Wallenstein after it became clear that he was a traitor.

A crisis arose when Wallenstein received orders to send a large part of his army to a distant point under the command of another leader. The same messenger also brought news that an army from Spain, not under Wallenstein's command, was due to arrive in a matter of days. Seeing that his powers were threatened, Wallenstein refused to break up his army and began to push forward his negotiations with the Swedes in the hope that he could complete his arrangements within a few hours. While Wallenstein prepared to move his army, General Piccolomini set his own plan in motion. First he went to all the officers and convinced them, with the exception of the colonels of two regiments, one of them his own son, that Wallenstein was ambitious and a traitor. The commanders agreed to move their troops and, under General Piccolomini, remain loyal to the emperor.

The Swedes, through their envoy, were making inordinate demands on Wallenstein. Among other things, they wished to have control of Prague and the fortress at Egra, to ensure that Wallenstein would not turn traitor against them. At first Wallenstein refused to turn over the fortifications, but at last he agreed. Shortly afterward his brother-in-law, Count Terzky, informed him that various regiments had marched away. Wallenstein realized what had happened when the count told him about General Piccolomini's negotiations with Von Questenberg and the emperor's commission authorizing General Piccolomini to relieve Wallenstein of his command.

Although his grand design was collapsing, Wallenstein resolved to go ahead with his plan to join the Swedes. He was still busy with his preparations when his daughter came to him with Colonel Max Piccolomini, who was still loyal to his commander. The couple asked to be allowed to marry, but Wallenstein refused. During the interview, Max Piccolomini realized the extent of Wallenstein's ambitions for himself and his daughter and the fact that the duke intended to turn traitor. The young officer thereupon decided to join his father in the plan to arrest Wallenstein. When Wallenstein tried to keep Colonel Piccolomini prisoner, the colonel's regiment rescued him from Wallenstein's soldiers.

Wallenstein fled with his few remaining troops and his family to Egra, where he had planned to meet the Swedish forces. With him was Colonel Butler, an Irish soldier of fortune. Because Wallenstein had dissuaded the emperor from making Butler a count, the Irish adventurer took his revenge by contriving Wallenstein's murder at Egra. Word came to Egra, shortly before Wallenstein's assassination, that Max Piccolomini had met his death in a wild attack on the Swedish forces. Shocked by these events, Thekla fled from Egra.

When General Piccolomini arrived at Egra, he was horrified to learn that the duke had been murdered just moments previously. Butler, confused by the turn of events, fled to the emperor to explain his actions. After his departure, a messenger arrived to inform General Piccolomini that the emperor had elevated him to the rank of prince.

Critical Evaluation:

On February 25, 1634, Albrecht Wallenstein, the duke of Friedland, was murdered in Eger. He had had an astonishing career, rising to power first as the savior of the Holy Roman Emperor. The emperor had, after initial success in putting down a Protestant uprising, found himself facing an army led by King Christian IV of Denmark and financed by England and The Netherlands. This was the second stage in the Thirty Years' War, which would sap the strength of the empire in a series of confrontations between 1618 and 1648. Wallenstein offered the emperor nothing less than an army—twenty thousand men, raised at his own expense—and his success was stupendous. He pursued the enemy across Europe and finally defeated Christian IV in his own kingdom. The forces of his jealous rivals, however, succeeded in persuading the emperor, who was in fact alarmed by the extent of Wallenstein's success and power, to dismiss the duke, who retired quietly, knowing that he would again be needed. In 1630, Sweden entered the war and decisively defeated the imperial forces. At that point Wallenstein was recalled to service. He accepted, but on his own terms, and he led an army of about forty thousand men with virtual autonomy. After initial victories, his thoughts turned to a negotiated peace, and again the emperor began to entertain fears. Friedrich Schiller's great trilogy is the record of the downfall of a man who had created history and seemed above petty intrigue, a man who could have been the harbinger of a new era of peace.

Schiller knew well that the historical Wallenstein was not a suitable figure for tragedy. As a professor of history at Jena, Schiller had written a history of the Thirty Years' War in the early 1790's, and he had at that time pointed out that the duke was in fact an unsympathetic character. It was less his personal magnetism than his money that had held the army together, as well as the prospect of the spoils to come with success. His fall was a product of his own miscalculations, and he lacked nobility of character. As a dramatist, however, Schiller saw the possibility of creating a tragedy that would rival those of William Shakespeare and the Greeks. He developed both the character of Wallenstein and those of his principal associates, invented the idealized figures of Max and Thekla, and shaped the events to create a coherent vision of conflicting loyalties, duty, guilt, and tragic expiation. All the while he yet remained remarkably faithful to the historic events.

In the first section of the trilogy, *Wallenstein's Camp*, Schiller creates the milieu of the time and presents both the visible sign of the general's greatness and an intimation of the divisions within his army, divisions that reflect the tensions that will destroy Wallenstein himself. In a prologue, Schiller explains that this portrait of the camp is an essential part of the work: It is Wallenstein's power that misleads his heart; his camp alone explains his crime. This symbolic representation is meant to place the individual Wallenstein in the nexus created by the diverse forces at play, the expectations of his soldiers, Wallenstein's own power and its limits, and the potential for its misuse. The army is his creation, but it had also come to have its own independent existence. Wallenstein may have been the creator of historical forces, but he is also carried by those forces and ultimately becomes their victim.

The second section of the trilogy, *The Piccolominis*, presents the political intrigue that precipitates the tragedy. When Wallenstein first appears, the movement against him has already begun and the forces leading to his destruction set in motion. He is unaware of this, however, and imagines himself still to be a free agent. Indeed, one of his main characteristics is that of keeping his options open, putting off decisions, as though he were the sole factor involved in directing the course of history. He has breadth of vision, and ranks far above his less imaginative subordinates, and yet he is guilty of a kind of hubris, expressed primarily in his readiness to betray his emperor. Octavio Piccolomini, whom Schiller elevates to a major role in the plot, is unswervingly loyal to the emperor, but betrays his commander. Thus Schiller has established a field of tension in which each figure in the plot experiences divided loyalty and is forced to make a choice. The agony of decision has been intensified through the addition of the character of Max—Octavio was actually childless—a young man who, in the midst of mutual betrayals, insists upon honesty and the authority of the heart over pragmatism. His father argues necessity, but he argues simple right and wrong. He is one of the most radiant of Schiller's creations, an idealist who cannot accept a breach of honor and who is torn between his loyalty to his father and that to Wallenstein, whom he regards as a second father. Schiller realized that this figure might well become the central focus of the play, and in fact for some readers this interpretation seems natural. Yet in the last section, *The Death of Wallenstein*, Schiller passes from a focus on the conflict of those around Wallenstein and from details of plot to focus upon Wallenstein himself. Johann Wolfgang von Goethe observed that in this last section the purely human aspects are dominant. Wallenstein becomes an increasingly tragic figure as the plot against him moves inexorably forward.

Yet the tragedy is more than that of Wallenstein alone; all the figures are caught in a movement of history, which is in part Wallenstein's own creation and yet also something independent that moves by its own laws. Insofar as he is a creator, Wallenstein is responsible for his own destruction; yet every character is forced by history to make a choice that compromises his integrity. All are stricken. Even Max, the only pure soul, is destroyed by the intolerable conflict in which the net of betrayals has placed him, and for Octavio, the bereaved victor, it must be a hollow triumph when he is elevated to the rank of prince.

"Critical Evaluation" by Steven C. Schaber

Bibliography:
Garland, H. B. *Schiller.* Westport, Conn.: Greenwood Press, 1976. Contains biographical information and interpretation of the major plays. Explains the construction of *Wallenstein* and mentions Johann Wolfgang von Goethe's suggestions. Interpretation and criticism of characters and plot with many German quotes.
Graham, Ilse. *Schiller's Drama: Talent and Integrity.* New York: Barnes & Noble Books, 1974. A study that provides a reading for many Schiller plays. Discusses special issues of *Wallenstein*; includes a chapter about the connections between *Wallenstein* and Goethe's *Laokoön*.
Sharpe, Lesley. *Friedrich Schiller: Drama, Thought, and Politics.* Cambridge, England: Cambridge University Press, 1991. Extensive chronology, bibliography, notes, and index to Schiller's works. Includes a full chapter on *Wallenstein*, which examines Schiller's sense of tragedy, melancholia, charisma, characterization, and style.
Simons, John D. *Friedrich Schiller.* Boston: Twayne, 1981. Contains an extensive chronology and bibliography. Discusses Schiller's aesthetics and examines his poetry and dramatic works. Explains *Wallenstein*, with emphasis on historical background and the political, social, economic, and military situation of the time.
Thomas, Calvin. *The Life and Works of Friedrich Schiller.* 1901. Reprint. New York: AMS Press, 1970. Examines the works of Schiller in remarkable detail. Gives commentary and criticism of *Wallenstein* and compares it to the earlier works. Includes biographical information and an examination of the characters and Schiller's method.

THE WANDERER

Type of work: Novel
Author: Alain-Fournier (Henri-Alain Fournier, 1886-1914)
Type of plot: Psychological
Time of plot: Nineteenth century
Locale: France
First published: Le Grand Meaulnes, 1913 (English translation, 1928)

> *Principal characters:*
> AUGUSTIN MEAULNES, the wanderer
> FRANÇOIS SEUREL, his friend
> FRANTZ DE GALAIS, a young aristocrat
> YVONNE DE GALAIS, his sister
> VALENTINE BLONDEAU, Frantz's fiancée

The Story:

François Seurel's father was head of the middle school and one of the higher elementary classes at Saint-Agathe's School, and his wife taught the infants. François lived in the school with his parents and his sister Millie and attended classes with the other pupils. He never played much with the village boys, however, because of an infection in his hip.

When François Seurel was fifteen years old, Augustin Meaulnes entered the school. With his arrival, a new life began for François, for Meaulnes banished his contentment with his family and his love for staying home. As his hip continued to improve, Seurel began to spend more time with Meaulnes in the village. Even the school became livelier, for Meaulnes always drew a crowd of people around him in the evenings.

The adventure began one Christmas Day when Meaulnes set out for the railroad station to meet Seurel's grandparents, Monsieur and Madame Charpentier. When the grandparents arrived, Meaulnes had disappeared. Three days later, he casually took his seat in the classroom where Monsieur Seurel was conducting a lesson. No one knew where he had been, and he claimed when questioned that he himself did not know. Sometimes at night, in the attic room they shared, Seurel awakened to find Meaulnes pacing the floor, fully clothed, eager to reenter a mysterious world he had once glimpsed briefly. Meaulnes promised to take Seurel along the next time he left on a journey.

At last, Meaulnes told Seurel the story of his adventure when he ran off from the school. It had been a very cold December day, and Meaulnes had lost his way and found that his horse was lame when darkness was falling. He had wandered to a cottage, where he was fed. Then he had stumbled on until he had found a barn in which, cold and lost, he had fallen asleep. The next day he wandered a long distance, until that night he had come to a manor where small children and old people were merrily planning a wedding feast. Tired and cold, Meaulnes had crawled through a window and climbed into a bed, where he had slept all night. The next day, thinking that he was one of the guests, some strolling players invited him to eat with them. Then Meaulnes discovered the reason for the feast. Frantz de Galais, the son of the man who owned the manor, had gone off to fetch his fiancée for the wedding.

All that first day, Meaulnes danced and played with the other guests. The next day, he met a beautiful girl with whom he fell in love. Although she declined to see him again, she promised to wait for his return to the manor. Inquiring about the strange girl, Meaulnes learned that she was Yvonne de Galais, Frantz's sister. When Frantz returned to the manor without his bride, he dismissed all the guests. Meaulnes had joined the crowd of children and old people as they dejectedly walked or rode away from the manor. He fell asleep in a cart and when he awoke he had found himself near Saint-Agathe's School.

Meaulnes's story would have seemed too unreal to young Seurel if the arrival of a strange boy at Sainte-Agathe's had not brought the story to reality. The boy, who was dressed as a gypsy and reminded Meaulnes of the Bohemians he had seen at the manor, stole the map Meaulnes had been making to find his way back to the manor. Meaulnes and Seurel learned that the gypsy was young Frantz de Galais, who in a fit of despair after losing his sweetheart had run away with a band of gypsies. The boys promised that they would help Frantz if they could, but one night Frantz disappeared. Meaulnes finally went to Paris, from where he wrote only three letters to Seurel.

Months passed. Seurel finished his school days and went to visit relatives in another village. There he heard that a mysterious manor was not far off. Seurel eagerly took up his friend's quest. His cousins, he learned, knew Yvonne. The manor had been razed after Frantz's disappearance, but his sister often came to visit Seurel's cousins. One night, she arrived. He told her that Meaulnes hoped someday to find her again. Seurel learned from his aunt that Frantz's fiancée had feared to marry him because she was certain that such great happiness could not come to her because she was the daughter of peasants. She was now in Paris working as a dressmaker. Seurel recalled his promise to Frantz to help him if he could. First, however, Seurel intended to find Meaulnes and bring him to Yvonne de Galais.

When Seurel found Meaulnes, the adventurer was packing his clothes to go on a journey. He abandoned his plans, and he and Yvonne were married, but there was something mysterious in their lives that kept them from being as happy as Seurel had expected them to be. One night, Frantz appeared near the village. Seurel met him and listened to his complaint of loneliness and sorrow. The following morning, Meaulnes left Yvonne to go on another adventure.

Seurel was now a teacher at Sainte-Agathe's. For months he and Yvonne awaited Meaulnes's return. After her baby was born, Yvonne died, leaving Seurel with an untold sadness. He searched through his friend's old papers and found a diary that told him why Meaulnes had been so troubled before his disappearance. While Meaulnes was living in Paris, he had met Valentine Blondeau, who became his mistress. Valentine often spoke of her former lover, whom she had deserted because she feared to marry him. When she showed Meaulnes her lover's letters, he realized that Valentine was the fiancée for whom Frantz de Galais had never stopped searching. In anger, Meaulnes told her that he would leave her, and Valentine cried that she would then return to Paris to become a streetwalker. After returning to his mother's home, where Seurel had found him, Meaulnes began to feel remorse for his treatment of Valentine.

Seurel, reading the diary, realized that Meaulnes must have been packing to go in search of Valentine when Seurel brought the news that Yvonne had been found. He decided that Meaulnes had deserted Yvonne to go on the same quest.

As Yvonne's daughter grew into a lovable, pretty child, Seurel often went to play with her, but she did not allow him to possess her affections completely. She always seemed to be waiting for someone. One afternoon, while playing with the little girl, Seurel noticed a burly stranger approaching. As the man neared him, Seurel recognized Meaulnes. He told Seurel that he had brought Valentine and Frantz together at last. With tears in his eyes at the news of his wife's death, Meaulnes took his daughter into his arms.

Seurel watched the father and daughter play together, and the schoolmaster smilingly imagined that he could envision Meaulnes arising in the middle of the night, wrapping his daughter in a cloak, and silently slipping off with her on some new adventure.

Critical Evaluation:

"The novel that I have carried in my head for three years," Henri-Alain Fournier wrote in 1905, "was at first only me, me, and me, but it has gradually been depersonalized and enlarged and is no longer the novel that everybody plans at eighteen." That novel, *The Wanderer*, written and revised over a period of six more years, is the major work of the author, who fell in battle at Saint-Remy in 1914. Although *The Wanderer* is surely more than a romantic autobiography, aspects of the author appear in the three important male characters: the meditative, passive François Seurel; the adventurer Augustin Meaulnes; and the despairing lover Frantz de Galais. Like each of them, Alain-Fournier was a romantic idealist, a dreamer, a child-man not entirely able to come to terms with adult responsibilities. Precisely for this reason, his childlike vision of reality gives the story a psychological dimension beyond its trappings of sentimental fantasy.

Seurel, the narrator, is the most timorous of the three heroes; he experiences life vicariously through the more intense activities of the others. Yet when he must act to assist his beloved friend Meaulnes he does so decisively. "Admiral" Meaulnes is bold in dreams but indecisive when he needs to act, and his will is paralyzed by guilt. While living in Paris, he betrayed Valentine Blondeau (as in real life Alain-Fournier deceived Jeanne B.), and for that reason—and because he had betrayed Yvonne's brother, who had truly loved Valentine—he cannot accept the pure love of Yvonne de Galais. Toward the end of the novel, after reconciling Frantz with Valentine, Meaulnes partly eases his own guilt feelings and becomes free to accept the love of his young daughter. Yet it is questionable whether there is happiness in store for Frantz, the most idealistic and shadowy of the three hero-wanderers, for he is pursued by a child's dream of perfection that he cannot possibly realize. For Seurel, the passive sympathizer, love is a dream that only other, stronger souls can hope to attain; for Meaulnes, the adventurer, love is a quest, never a conquest; for Frantz, the hopeless searcher, love may be the final tragic deception.

As for Yvonne and Valentine, they are merely projections of the idealized dreams, or guilty passions, of the male child-heroes. Apart from their lovers, they have no lives of their own. Indeed, it is the heroes' peculiar childlike fantasy concerning women and love that unifies the novel and provides its psychological insights. The three male heroes are drawn to one another in a friendship so devoted that it resembles a ritual of brotherhood: protective, empathetic, nearly mystical. At the same time, they are half-maddened by love for "pure" women. This love is overpoweringly sudden, threatening (even when the object is as frail and delicate as Yvonne), and absolute. Once they have fallen in love, the child-heroes are victims of their fate: Their bond of brotherhood is shattered, their lives fragmented.

To express this story of a child's fascination with, and fear of, love and sexuality, Alain-Fournier effectively uses a symbolist-impressionist style. Like Maurice Maeterlinck, he is a master of pauses and sudden breaks in the narrative that underscore the sense of tension and menace. He subtly shifts between scenes of realistic detail presented with perfect clarity (the wedding feast, for example) and scenes of haunting, ambiguous, hallucinatory mystery (Meaulnes' meeting with Yvonne). At his best, Alain-Fournier writes passages of touching simplicity. At other times, he loses artistic restraint and allows his characters to declaim romantically bombastic speeches. Some of his symbolic passages, too, tend to be murky, the prose childish instead of childlike. Yet such lapses are rare. Alain-Fournier is justified in saying of his one great novel, "If I have been childish and weak and foolish, at least I have, at moments, had the strength in this infamous city to create my life, like a marvelous fairy-tale."

Bibliography:

Blair, Fredrika. Introduction to *The Wanderer*, by Alain-Fournier, translated by Françoise Delisle. Garden City, N.Y.: Doubleday, 1953. An analysis of Alain-Fournier's style that connects it to the impressionist and symbolist movements in art and literature. The translation of the work has been superseded by later ones.

Fowles, John. Afterword to *The Wanderer*, by Alain-Fournier, translated by Lowell Bair. New York: New American Library, 1971. A well-known British novelist explains his enthusiasm for the novel and shows why he thinks the work must be read on its own terms and why it resists conventional critical analysis.

Gibson, Robert. *The Land Without a Name: Alain-Fournier and His World.* London: Paul Elek, 1975. A thorough, dense, yet accessible study that reviews all previous scholarship on Alain-Fournier as well as his posthumously published correspondence. Uses the theme of the lost paradise as its organizing principle.

Gurney, Stephen. *Alain-Fournier.* Boston: Twayne, 1987. A complete introduction to the writer and his work. Relates *The Wanderer* to Alain-Fournier's poems and letters, especially the ones he wrote to his brother-in-law, who was a literary and psychological soulmate. Contains a good selected bibliography.

Jones, Marian Giles. *A Critical Commentary on Alain-Fournier's "Le Grand Meaulnes."* New York: St. Martin's Press, 1968. Reviews many important themes of the novel in detail and provides a good starting point for further discussion. Not as comprehensive as Gibson but easier to use in an analysis of the novel.

THE WANDERING JEW

Type of work: Novel
Author: Eugène Sue (1804-1857)
Type of plot: Melodrama
Time of plot: 1831-1832
Locale: France
First published: Le Juif errant, 1844-1845 (English translation, 1868)

Principal characters:
  RODIN, an ambitious Jesuit
  MONSIEUR L'ABBE D'AIGRIGNY, the provincial of the Jesuits
  BLANCHE SIMON,
  ROSE SIMON,
  FRANÇOIS HARDY,
  PRINCE DJALMA,
  JACQUES DE RENNEPONT or COUCHE-TOUT-NUD,
  GABRIEL DE RENNEPONT, and
  ADRIENNE DE CARDOVILLE, the descendants of Marius de Rennepont
    and the heirs to his legacy
  SAMUEL, the Wandering Jew
  HERODIAS, a woman who demanded the head of John the Baptist

The Story:

A solitary figure stalked down a bleak hill in Poland. He was an old man, his face gentle and sad. His footsteps left in the soil imprints of a cross made by the several large nails in his shoes. He was hurrying, for he had to be in Paris on the thirteenth of February, 1832, when the surviving descendants of his sister would gather in that city—the last members of that family over which he had watched for eighteen centuries. The lonely traveler was the Wandering Jew, that artisan of Jerusalem who mocked Christ on the day of the Crucifixion, the sinner condemned to wander undying through the centuries over all the world. Far in the wilds of America a woman also turned toward Paris, driven by that same power that guided the Wandering Jew. She was Herodias, who had demanded the head of John the Baptist on a charger, also condemned to live through the centuries of sorrow.

François Baudoin, called Dagobert, a faithful friend of Marshal Simon and an old Bonapartist hero, never faltered in his loyalty toward the Simon family. Years before, he had followed the marshal's Polish wife into Siberia, where she was exiled, and after her death he set out with her twin daughters, Blanche and Rose, for Paris, where, on a certain day in February, 1832, a legacy awaited the two girls. This was the legacy of Marius de Rennepont, an ancestor who, despoiled by the Jesuits, had salvaged out of his ruined estate a house and a small sum of money. He had placed the money in the hands of a faithful Jewish friend named Samuel, who had promised to invest it profitably. A hundred and fifty years later the descendants of this ancestor were to gather at a house where each was to receive a share of the legacy. Blanche and Rose Simon were only half-aware of the fortune awaiting them, for they were too young to understand what Dagobert told them about their inheritance.

If these heirs of Marius de Rennepont did not know of the legacy, others nevertheless did.

For many years the Jesuits, masters of an intricate and diabolical conspiracy, had plotted to prevent the descendants from acquiring the money. They were responsible for Marshal Simon's exile and for his wife's banishment to Siberia.

The plotters had been so meticulous and so thorough in their scheming that they had persuaded young Gabriel de Rennepont to become a priest and a member of the Society of Jesus. Through Gabriel they hoped to acquire the tremendous fortune; for by preventing the other heirs from reaching Paris—and the society had agents all over the world who would do its bidding under any conditions—Gabriel would inherit the legacy. Then, since he was forbidden by his vow of poverty to possess money, the funds would revert to the society. With that money the Jesuits would be able to reestablish their supremacy over the French people and would be able once more to govern countries and guide the destiny of Europe.

As soon as Dagobert and the two girls arrived in Paris, the Jesuits arranged to have them spirited away to a convent. Adrienne de Cardoville, another descendant of the de Rennepont family, was declared insane and committed to an asylum. Jacques de Rennepont, a good-hearted sensualist named Couche-tout-Nud, was jailed for debt. Prince Djalma, who had left India despite the efforts of the Jesuits, was drugged. François Hardy, a benevolent manufacturer, was sent out of town through the treachery of a friend who was a Jesuit spy.

As a result of that Jesuit conspiracy, on that fateful day in February, 1832, only the priest, Gabriel de Rennepont, went to claim the legacy at the house of an old Jew known as Samuel. With Gabriel were Monsieur l'Abbe d'Aigrigny, Provincial of the Jesuits, and Rodin, his secretary. Before the reading of the will, Gabriel was persuaded to sign a paper in which he renounced all claims to the legacy. When the bequest was announced, the Jesuits were astounded at the incredible sum of the inheritance, which had grown from 150,000 francs to a fortune of 212,175,000 francs. Just as the money was being handed over to the priests, however, a strange woman appeared and produced a codicil to the will, a document suspending its execution for three months. The woman was Herodias, but none then called her by that name. The priests were enraged, and they feared that their conspiracy would be exposed. Adrienne de Cardoville was certain to be released from the asylum. General Simon was reported to be on his way back to France to claim his daughters. Couche-tout-Nud would borrow money from his friends to pay his debts. Prince Djalma would soon awaken. François Hardy would return to Paris from his fruitless errand.

Rodin immediately produced a paper that placed him in complete charge of the Jesuit cabal. He proclaimed that they had not lost, that they could and would win by employing psychological methods instead of violence. He would let each heir destroy him or herself by his or her own desires, passions, or vices.

During the following three months, Rodin pretended that he had left the service of the Abbe d'Aigrigny and passed himself off as a friend of the de Rennepont heirs. He secured the release of the Simon girls and Adrienne, and by those acts he became known as a good, unselfish man. Shortly before her death, one of Adrienne's servants confessed that she had been blackmailed into spying for the Jesuits, and she revealed the whole sordid, brutal, unprincipled conspiracy. Rodin, however, was not yet willing to accept defeat. At his direction, François Hardy's factory was burned to the ground, his best friend's treachery was revealed, and his beautiful young mistress was spirited away. A broken man, Hardy was taken to a Jesuit retreat, where he accepted the doctrines of the order and died as the result of the penances and fasts imposed upon him. Couche-tout-Nud, separated from his mistress, died a miserable death after an orgy that was arranged by another Jesuit agent. The Simon girls were taken to a hospital during a cholera epidemic and died there of the disease. Prince Djalma, led to believe that Adrienne had become the mistress of Agricola Baudoin, Dagobert's son, attacked Agricola and killed a girl whom he mistook for Adrienne. He discovered his error too late, for in his remorse he had already swallowed poison. Adrienne chose to die with him.

When the time came for the final disposition of the de Rennepont legacy, Gabriel was the only survivor. Just as Rodin was about to claim the inheritance in the name of his churchly office, the casket containing the money and securities burst into flames and the fortune was lost forever. A moment later Rodin fell to the floor and writhed in agony. As he had left a church, shortly before claiming the legacy, he had taken holy water from the fingers of an Indian who had accompanied Prince Djalma from India and who had become a lay member of the Jesuits. Too late, Rodin realized that he had been poisoned in some manner by the Indian. He died a few minutes later.

Gabriel de Rennepont, shocked when he realized the crimes of greed and lust for power that the lost fortune had caused, retired to live out the rest of his brief life with his friends, the Baudoin family. After Gabriel's body had been laid in the de Rennepont tomb, old Samuel went to a secret spot where a great cross was set upon a lonely hill. There Herodias found him. In the dawn's light each saw upon the face of the other the marks that age had put upon them, but they had found peace and happiness at last. Samuel—for he was the Wandering Jew—gave praise that their long punishment was ended, and Herodias echoed his words.

Critical Evaluation:

The Wandering Jew is an enormous novel. It touches several continents, the worlds of religion, economics, the supernatural, politics, medicine, and social protest. There are hundreds of characters on this vast stage and dozens of plots, subplots, and plots within subplots. The novel is in that tradition of French literary Romanticism, which mixes the supernatural with politics and social commentary. Yet its vast scale, reminiscent of *Les Miserables* (1862), also is remindful of the large social tapestry of eighteenth century novels. Further, Eugène Sue loves melodrama. He attempts, at every juncture, to induce the extremes of horror, anticipation, and suspense in his readers through a variety of well-tested literary techniques. The novel is also of interest for the study of genre: It is a precursor of the mystery-detective novel, as well as being an example of the Romantic novel.

It must be said that *The Wandering Jew* is not a successful novel. In terms of theme, action, character, and style, it must be classified as one of those magnificent, towering failures. Central to the novel's difficulties is Sue's inability to connect and unify the vast and complicated action of the work. The intrigues and schemes of the Jesuits and the problem of the legacy, although convenient, simply cannot sustain the ambitious weight of this novel. The world of *The Wandering Jew* is overflowing, without sufficient discipline imposed on the material. Indeed, Sue's Romanticism carries him quite far away from the discipline of some sort of unity, be it of place, of time, or of structure.

In *War and Peace* (1865-1869), another very large novel, the scope is also enormous and the characters and motives are extremely various, but Leo Tolstoy has a firm grasp of his war and peace theme and the processes of history. At the same time, he is able to offer the most vivid and accurate psychological and moral descriptions. The thematic content of *The Wandering Jew* is clouded by Romanticism and idealization; and, in addition to superficial and melodramatic characterizations, Sue offers large doses of the supernatural and mysticism. Weaknesses of characterization, action, and theme are, naturally, reinforced and magnified as the scope of the work increases. Sue's attempt itself, however, is impressive, and there are frequent artistically valid and touching individual scenes. The novel retains its place in the canon of Western literature by virtue of its great accomplishments in the areas of exploration of genre (the mystery-detective novel, the Romantic novel) and engrossing plot.

Bibliography:

Day, James T. "Eugène Sue." In *Nineteenth Century French Fiction Writers: Romanticism and Realism, 1800-1860*. Detroit: Gale Research, 1992. Basic facts about Sue's life and works. A good place to begin research.

Murch, Alma Elizabeth. *The Development of the Detective Novel*. New York: Philosophical Library, 1958. Historical context for considering *The Wandering Jew* as an early detective novel.

THE WANDERING SCHOLAR FROM PARADISE

Type of work: Drama
Author: Hans Sachs (1494-1576)
Type of plot: Farce
Time of plot: Sixteenth century
Locale: Nuremberg, Germany
First performed: 1550; first published, 1880 as *Der fahrende Schüler im Paradies* (English translation, 1910)

> *Principal characters:*
> THE FARMER, a crude peasant
> HIS WIFE, an ignorant, dreaming housewife
> THE STUDENT, a quick-witted young man, more adventurer than scholar

The Story:

A Nuremberg woman claimed to all and sundry that her deceased first husband was still her true love. She dismissed her second husband as being no lover at all and described him as scrimpy, mean, and sour of disposition. One day, while she was voicing her complaints, the wandering Student came by, doffed his hat in a polite gesture, and begged for alms. Rightly guessing that boasts about his successes in Paris would impress the woman, he immediately used the advantage it gave him when the Wife misunderstood him to say that he had come from Paradise.

The Wife's mind was still lost in dreams of her first husband when she asked the Student if he knew the departed one. The Student allowed that he did not, but he thought that on his return to Paradise the acquaintance could perhaps be effected. The Student went on to tell her how ill-clothed, ill-fed, and completely destitute her late husband was, whereupon the Wife accepted his offer to take gifts back to her husband.

As the Student prepared to leave, the Wife inquired when he might come again to bring word of her first love. He assured her that the road was long and difficult and that he would not be likely to pass her way again. Without delay and with a minimum of ceremony, the Student took her gifts and strode off—and none too soon, for the Farmer appeared just as the young man was taking his departure.

The Wife continued to sing the love song that she had been singing just before meeting the Student, but now, as her husband noticed, she sang happily. Naïvely she told him of the visitor who had brought her happiness and of her having sent gifts to her first love. Craftily concealing his anger at her simplicity, the Farmer sarcastically ordered her to prepare more gifts that he might take them to the Student as additional presents to the man who, though dead, retained her devotion. Laden, he went off in search of the Student.

In a rough slough the Student was stuffing his booty into bushes when he heard the Farmer approaching. With cunning and a veil of innocent helpfulness, he directed the Farmer deeper into the furze, where he claimed the culprit was hiding. He also offered to help the Farmer by holding his horse while he went on his search. When the Farmer was out of sight, the Student rode off on the horse, with the Farmer's and the Wife's contributions across the saddle. Meanwhile, the Farmer stumbled through the slough, getting muddier and more scratched with each step in his vain effort to find the offending traveler from Paradise.

At the cottage, the Wife was peering into the distance for some sign of the Farmer. Her chief concern was that her husband might be lost in the mist on the moor and unable to overtake the Student to add to her gifts. Her doubts vanished when she saw the Farmer trudging in slowly and wearily, hoping against hope that his horse had come home on his own. Not seeing the animal, he accepted the fact that he had been duped. What could he do or say to the Wife—the stupid one, the gullible one—whom he had intended to beat for giving away a few farthings and some worn-out clothes? She was indeed a lesser fool than he who had lost his swiftest horse.

Stirred to activity in an effort to ease her husband's anger, the Wife carried in the milk pails and asked about the success of his search. The Farmer mumbled a halting explanation about his altruism; he had decided, he said, to make a gift of his horse to the Student, since the young man was tired and had far to go. The Wife was overwhelmed by her husband's unexpected kindness. For his thoughtfulness in behalf of her first husband, she promised that were he to die that night, she would send him all manner of presents in Paradise. Such a generous husband should have the goodwill of his neighbors, she declared, and she proceeded to circulate the story of her husband's generosity throughout the parish.

The angry Farmer decided that it was bad enough to be burdened with such a fool of a wife; it was unbearable to think that his neighbors considered him the same kind of fool. The moral was that if married people were to get along, they must cover for each other's weaknesses and not let others see a flaw in the bonds of wedlock.

Critical Evaluation:

Hans Sachs gained international fame as the central figure of Richard Wagner's opera *Die Meistersinger von Nürnberg* (1867). Sachs was a *Meistersinger*, or master singer, who plied his trade as a shoemaker in the city of Nuremberg, where he was also the leader and a creative innovator in the local *Singschule*, the guild of poets and musicians. The guild members were mostly artisans, skilled in the composition and singing of rigid technical formulas, who claimed descent from the medieval *Minnesänger*, or courtly poets. To gain the rank of *Meister*, a candidate had to compete in a public contest in which he created and performed a new melody and a new stanzaic form.

Between 1511 and 1516, during the prescribed *Wanderjahre* that completed a craftsman's professional and general education, Sachs the journeyman shoemaker and poet traveled throughout Germany and Austria. An eager student and accomplished writer, he had gained a reputation as a poet before he returned to Nuremberg at the age of twenty-two to marry and settle down. A prolific poet for the rest of his eighty-two years, he left more than two hundred plays; countless fables, epic poems, and anecdotal stories; and more than four thousand master songs. In addition to his writing, he was influential in the stagecraft of his day both as an actor and as a theatrical manager. There was no theater that could be termed professional in Nuremberg, but the Nuremberg *Meistersinger* guild carried on a lively amateur theatrical tradition and performed their plays in churches, convents, and inn yards. The performances were so popular that playgoers were sometimes known to interrupt the church's afternoon religious service in order to obtain seats for an evening's theater performance.

Sachs classified his dramatic works as tragedies, comedies, *Fastnachtspiele* (Shrovetide plays), and, quite simply, plays. Critics are in general agreement that the tragedies and comedies, while exhibiting a wide range of subjects from biblical material to medieval legends and classical mythology, are often plodding in style and technique. It is with his innovations and skill in the Shrovetide plays that Sachs achieved mastery.

The Shrovetide play, essentially a farcical dialogue written in verse and centered on a humorous incident, was meant to amuse theatergoers during carnival time. It generally reflects the life of the peasants and burghers among whom Sachs lived. The early Shrovetide plays were rather formless and full of coarse and obscene humor. Sachs made the humor gentler, tightened the form, and created a theatrical piece that delivered satire and wit together with a moral lesson. His moral stance reflects his vigorous Protestantism; his championship of Martin Luther in 1523 inspired him to compose a poem entitled "Die Wittembergerisch Nachtigall" ("The Wittenburg Nightingale"), which praised the reformer's efforts.

Sachs was a genial storyteller who delighted in human foibles and avoided the pitfalls of cynicism or bitterness; his usual satiric targets were boorish simpletons or shrews. *The Wandering Scholar from Paradise* exhibits much of the best that appears in Sachs's Shrovetide plays. The play pokes good-humored fun at a simple, gullible woman and her more cunning but no less easily fooled husband. As is often the case, the clever trickster in the play is an itinerant student, lacking in goods but not in wit. No doubt Sachs's five years as a wandering journeyman contributed to his knowledge of such characters.

Critics have praised Sachs's ear for the language of the commoner and for achieving harmony between subject and style in plays such as *The Wandering Scholar from Paradise*. He is also credited with imposing solid construction and unity on to the typical rambling structure of the Shrovetide play. One technique he employed was to limit settings. Early plays wandered from locale to locale, making little distinction between them. In his play, Sachs uses only two locales—the farmhouse and the bog, and he indicates in the stage directions that a curtain with a slough painted on it be drawn to mark the change of scene. Sachs also wrote precise stage directions for the actors, instructing them in how to portray certain actions.

Most significantly, Sachs achieves unity through his characterization. The Wife in *The Wandering Scholar* reveals her naïveté from the very opening of the play as she sings a romantic ballad and laments the loss of her first husband. Sachs directs the actor to sob and sigh deeply during the speech. Her excited mistaking of the word Paris for Paradise reveals to the Student, as well as to the audience, not only that she is ingenuous, but that she will be gullible. It is also important to note, however, that she is duped because of her kindheartedness and generosity. She is genuinely concerned for the well-being of her former husband.

When the Farmer realizes how his simpleton wife has been tricked by the Student, he is determined to get revenge and immediately goes after him, not bothering to enlighten his wife as to her witless behavior. Time enough to box her ears when he returns with the goods she has given to the Student. His determined haste leads to his downfall, for he is so intent on capturing the Student that he follows the directions given to him by that very Student pretending to be a doltish peasant. Chagrined by his own gullibility, the Farmer returns home unable to chastise the Wife for her stupidity. To make matters worse, he learns that she has boasted of his generosity to the whole parish, who are vastly amused by the tale.

Although the Farmer has lost his goods and his reputation for cunning tightfistedness in the community, he has gained some humanity and understanding of marital relationships. This is pointed out in Sachs's traditional moral observation at the close of the play:

> Folly in folly must find excuse
> If married folks are to live in truce
> And the bonds of wedlock not show cracks—
> Which is the warning and wish, of Hans Sachs.

It is a temperate warning that has been delivered with humor and good grace.

Hans Sachs's Shrovetide plays represent the pinnacle of sixteenth century German dramatic activity. His achievement must, however, be considered the climax of medieval amateur theater rather than as the harbinger of a new form.

"Critical Evaluation" by Jane Anderson Jones

Bibliography:
Garland, H. B. "The Sixteenth Century." In *A Concise Survey of German Literature*. Coral Gables, Fla.: University of Miami Press, 1971. Places Sachs in the context of the contemporary Protestant burghers of Nuremberg and Augsburg and discusses the prominence given the poet by Richard Wagner's opera. Claims that Sachs's influence has less to do with his writing than with Wagner's famous portrayal.

Liptzin, Sol. "Early German Literature." In *Historical Survey of German Literature*. New York: Prentice-Hall, 1936. Discusses the *Meistersinger* guilds of sixteenth century Germany and points out Sachs's mastery in such Shrovetide plays as *The Wandering Scholar from Paradise*.

Merkel, Ingrid. "Literature of the Sixteenth and Seventeenth Century." In *The Challenge of German Literature*, edited by Horst S. Daemmrich and Dieter H. Haenicke. Detroit, Mich.: Wayne State University Press, 1971. Discusses Sachs's regeneration of the Shrovetide play, claiming that his structure, lively dialogue, and realistic characterizations might have laid the groundwork for German comedy but that he had no successors.

Robertson, J. G., and Dorothy Reich. "The Drama in the Sixteenth Century." In *A History of German Literature*. 6th ed., edited by Dorothy Reich with the assistance of W. I. Lucas et al. Elmsford, N.Y.: London House and Maxwell, 1970. Robertson and Reich declare that Sachs was the most prolific humanist dramatist and created new forms. Conclude that *The Wandering Scholar from Paradise* is one of the best extant Shrovetide plays.

Rose, Ernest. "The Parabolic and Didactic Style: Middle Class Literature." In *A History of German Literature*. New York: New York University Press, 1960. Discusses the strengths and limitations of Sachs's verse and dramas, and concedes that his Shrovetide plays were lively and amusing both to contemporary and modern audiences.

THE WAPSHOT CHRONICLE

Type of work: Novel
Author: John Cheever (1912-1982)
Type of plot: Social realism
Time of plot: 1890's-1950's
Locale: St. Botolphs, Massachusetts; Washington; New York; and a rocket-launching station
First published: 1957

> *Principal characters:*
> LEANDER WAPSHOT, a Yankee skeptic, philosopher, and skipper of the
>   launch *Topaze*
> SARAH WAPSHOT, his brisk, practical wife
> MOSES and
> COVERLY, their sons
> MELISSA, Moses' wife
> BETSEY, Coverly's wife
> HONORA WAPSHOT, a wealthy cousin and the family matriarch
> JUSTINA WAPSHOT MOLESWORTH SCADDON, another wealthy cousin
> ROSALIE YOUNG

The Story:

St. Botolphs had been a bustling, prosperous river port in the days of the Massachusetts clipper fleets. It was currently, however, kept alive by a few small industries and by summer visitors. It was a moribund port town with a tourist center of antique stores, gift shops, and tearooms quaintly decorated by the handcrafted artifacts of an older seafaring and agricultural United States.

Leander's home, West Farm, cluttered with the memories and the possessions of dead and gone Wapshots, was an image of a good past and an uncertain present. The Wapshots, like the village, had come down in the world. The older generations of the family's men had been seafaring wanderers in their youth, and they had come back to St. Botolphs with their manhood seasoned by the hardships and perils of their calling and with their wits sharpened by the strategies of trade in foreign ports. The ancestral Wapshot men had memories of lovely, naked brown women in the islands of the Pacific. Leander had never known adventure in far places or a sultry paradise of love. Failing fortunes and changing times beached him inland, a spiritual castaway on the shores of Wapshot tradition and a dependent on Cousin Honora's charity.

Nominally, he was the head of the family, but the real power was Cousin Honora, a matriarch who spoke and acted with the authority of one who held the purse strings. In her eccentric way, she regarded Leander and herself as the holders of a family trust, Leander because he had fathered two sons, herself because she controlled the fortune, which she intended to pass on to the boys when they married and produced sons of their own. Meanwhile, she paid the bills and bullied Leander. He had never been provident, and now he was old. A man should be useful for something, however, so Cousin Honora bought the *Topaze*, a battered old launch that Leander ferried daily between Travertine and the amusement park at Nangasakit across the bay. In Honora's opinion, the *Topaze* kept Leander out of other mischief and satisfied his taste for romance and nonsense. Leander's wife was Sarah, a brisk, practical woman who indulged her husband, looked after her sons, and, as president of the Women's Club, worked energetically for the civic improvement of St. Botolphs.

In spite of his failings, old Leander, with his regard for ceremony and for the idea of life as a process of excellence and continuity, dominated the family's consciousness. In his zest for life, he was the guardian of tribal rituals and of masculine skills that he hoped to pass on to his sons. What Moses and Coverly absorbed from his examples of parental love and wisdom showed them to be true Wapshots. Although the family fortunes depended on proof of their virility, they could not take ordinary mortals as wives after they had heard of the pagan sirens, singing on distant beaches, of the Wapshot past.

Rosalie, for example, although catapulted into the Wapshot household from a blazing car in which her lover died, was not romantic enough. Rosalie's giving herself to Moses was a gesture of her inner despair. Her brief passage through Leander's world served chiefly as an excuse for Cousin Honora's decision that the time had come for Moses to go out into the world to seek his fortune in the approved Wapshot manner.

When Moses left home, Coverly also ran away. First a government employee in Washington, Moses later found his place in a New York fiduciary house. Coverly's adventures were more varied and included failure to get a job in a carpet factory because the company psychiatrists found him psychologically unstable. Coverly found work as a department store clerk, went to night school, had civilian status in a secret government project in the South Pacific, and found a position on a rocket-launching project in the West. Both brothers, in the end, found what they were seeking. Moses' choice was Melissa, the penniless ward of another Wapshot cousin who was the parsimonious widow of a five-and-dime store tycoon. This rich widow, Justina Wapshot Molesworth Scaddon, lived in ugly baroque discomfort on the Hudson. For Melissa's sake, Moses put up with Cousin Justina's penny-pinching and nagging. Coverly's fate came to him in the person of Betsey, a lonely, unpretentious Southern woman. So the Wapshot fortunes were made secure, for with the birth of sons to Melissa and Betsey, Cousin Honora proved as good as her word and turned her money over to Moses and Coverly.

Meanwhile, Leander's world had fallen apart. He had wrecked the *Topaze*, and Cousin Honora refused to pay for the repairs. When Sarah Wapshot converted the old craft into "The Only Floating Gift Shoppe in New England" and opened the establishment with a gala tea and a sale of Italian pottery, Leander was heartbroken. At first he tried to keep busy writing his memoirs, but remembrance proved too painful for him to continue. At last, disgusted with the ugliness of life, he drowned himself. Moses and Coverly, returning to St. Botolphs to buy their father a new boat, heard instead the burial service for those who have perished at sea. On a later visit home, Coverly found in a copy of Shakespeare a note of advice bequeathed by Leander to his sons, a litany of idiosyncratic personal belief and homely folk wisdom.

Critical Evaluation:

The first thing the reader will notice in *The Wapshot Chronicle* is the novel's paradoxical tone, a mix of comedy and tragedy, darkness and light. John Cheever is intent on imitating the richness and the paradoxical, unpredictable nature of life, full of joy, silliness, humor, love, hate, pain, and frustration in combination.

The lack of structure and logic in people's lives is reflected in the structure of Cheever's novel, where narrative coherence, cause-and-effect, and meaning are subservient to the anecdotal. Just as in one's own life the significance of events is not always immediately clear or indeed remains obscure forever, the interpretation of what befalls Cheever's characters is often left to the reader. The narrator's whimsical, capricious, and arbitrary presence may be seen as analogous to God's role in people's lives—if one thinks of the deity as one who determines the flow of events without reference to justice, logic, or clarity. The narrator in *The Wapshot Chronicle* reports, sometimes with tongue in cheek; the narrator does not steer the characters from one well-structured event to the next.

A central theme of the novel is what life may mean, what people are to learn from the sum of their experiences, and how to react to turns of events that people do not expect and over which people have no control. *The Wapshot Chronicle* ends with the touching description of Leander's funeral, to which his sons have returned to honor him in his hometown of St. Botolphs. Amid his tears, Coverly reads the passage from William Shakespeare's *The Tempest* (1611) that Leander wanted read at his funeral. The passage from Shakespeare emphasizes fragility—that people are all actors in some grand drama, actors made only of dreams. If there is a fundamental message in the novel, it is what Leander affirms in notes he made in a copy of Shakespeare that Coverly finds while going through his father's things after Leander's funeral. These rules to live by, the final words in the novel and apparently the sum of Leander's experience, are simple, very practical guides for the most part. He says never sleep in the moonlight, never make love with one's pants on, and take a cold bath every morning.

The list of rules ends with more general affirmations—that the world is to be admired, that the love of a good woman is to be relished, and that people should trust in God, after all. Hence, the novel ends on a note of positive closure: Moses' and Coverly's wives have given birth to sons, the boys have come home, Honora has honored her promise to endow Moses and Coverly as her heirs (now that they have produced sons), and Moses and Coverly have evidently weathered their trials and learned their own lessons.

The Wapshot Chronicle is presumably a parody of histories, as suggested by the word "chronicle." The novel tells about the distinction between what is apparent and what lies beneath the surface of personalities and events. In this regard, the novel's narrative mocks the stature and dignity of New England and its figures (Honora, for example, is often seen in public in a three-cornered hat). The narrator also remarks that the ladies of the Wapshot clan always eat daintily in public but stuff themselves like animals at home. The history of St. Botolphs is less a story of continuous prosperity than one of decadence. In an image of the novel's skewed tone, Honora heads for Boston shortly after Leander's funeral to take in a Red Sox baseball game. The narrator describes her, in her three-cornered hat, as a pilgrim, gallant and absurd, who is nonetheless confident of her country's noble power and endurance.

"Critical Evaluation" by Gordon Walters

Bibliography:
Bosha, Francis J., ed. *The Critical Response to John Cheever*. Westport, Conn.: Greenwood Press, 1994. Sampler of reviews and critical essays on all Cheever publications. Reprints five reviews of *The Wapshot Chronicle* and includes a new essay by Kenneth C. Mason on "Tradition and Desecration" in the two Wapshot books.
_____, comp. *John Cheever: A Reference Guide*. Boston: G. K. Hall, 1981. Excellent discussion of the inconsistent critical response to the fiction. Provides a comprehensive, fully annotated listing of works about Cheever, including reviews, articles, and interviews.
Collins, R. G., ed. *Critical Essays on John Cheever*. Boston: G. K. Hall, 1982. Good overview of the critical reception of Cheever's fiction. Reprints many of the most important and influential reviews and essays (some in revised form). A new essay by Samuel Coale on Cheever's "Romancer's Art" is especially noteworthy.

Donaldson, Scott. *John Cheever: A Biography*. New York: Random House, 1988. Full, objective, sympathetic account of Cheever's life and work. Discusses the publication and reception of *The Wapshot Chronicle*, in which, Donaldson asserts, "Cheever distilled in one book the accumulated vitality of two decades." Fairminded and richly detailed.

Hunt, George W. *John Cheever: The Hobgoblin Company of Love*. Grand Rapids, Mich.: Wm. B. Eerdmans, 1983. Longer and more detailed, but also more tendentious, than earlier book-length studies by Samuel Coale (1977) and Lynn Waldeland (1979). Useful summaries of plot and criticism and Hunt's critical reading in terms of Cheever's Christian perspective.

THE WAPSHOT SCANDAL

Type of work: Novel
Author: John Cheever (1912-1982)
Type of plot: Social satire
Time of plot: Early 1960's
Locale: St. Botolphs, Massachusetts; Proxmire Manor, a Westchester suburb; and Talifer, a
   missile research base
First published: 1964

> *Principal characters:*
> HONORA WAPSHOT, matriarch of the Wapshot clan, a Yankee
>   individualist, and an anachronism in the modern world
> COVERLY WAPSHOT, her good-hearted, well-meaning cousin, a public
>   relations worker at the Talifer Missile Site
> BETSEY WAPSHOT, his wife, a woman of whims
> MOSES WAPSHOT, another cousin, a stockholder and an alcoholic
> MELISSA WAPSHOT, his wife, a modern Circe disguised as a suburban
>   matron
> EMILE CRANMER, the grocery boy who becomes Melissa's lover
> DR. LEMUEL CAMERON, the atomic scientist in charge of the Talifer
>   Missile Site
> MR. APPLEGATE, the rector of Christ Church in St. Botolphs, also an
>   alcoholic
> GERTRUDE LOCKHART, a Proxmire Manor matron driven to
>   drunkenness, promiscuity, and suicide by the failure of her household
>   appliances
> NORMAN JOHNSON, an agent of the Internal Revenue Service

The Story:

   Honora Wapshot was eccentric spinster and septuagenarian guardian of the Wapshot treasure
trove, oldest living descendant of a family that settled in the town of St. Botolphs, Massachusetts, in the seventeenth century. Honora supervised—but mainly underwrote with quarterly
checks from a trust fund—the lives of her two young cousins, Moses and Coverly Wapshot.
The two brothers had lost both their mother, Sarah, and their father, Leander, who drowned
while swimming.

   After a Christmas visit to Honora, during which Coverly was haunted by the ghost of his
high-minded father, he traveled west. He returned to a world that would have baffled his
father—the Talifer Missile Site. At this top-secret complex of experimental laboratories and
space equipment, some irrevocable error by a personnel-selecting machine had recently placed
Coverly in the department of public relations, although he was trained for computer program-
ming. He lived in Talifer with his wife Betsey and their son Binxey, but their social life in the
community was a little bleak. One day Betsey, after watching with bland indifference as a
neighbor fell to his death on a cement terrace, neglected to notify anyone because of her vague
fear that she might violate security regulations. Coming home one day, Coverly learned that
their garbage pail had been taken by a neighbor, and Coverly and the neighbor's husband came

to blows and bites over the incident. Shortly afterward, Betsey and Coverly attempted to meet their neighbors (who had never called on them since their arrival) by inviting twenty-five people to a cocktail party; the plan was aborted, however, when no one appeared. Betsey was shattered, and her reaction took the form of a lasting resentment of Coverly, whom she blamed for making her live in Talifer.

Through a strange accident in circumstance, Coverly was offered a position on the personal staff of Dr. Lemuel Cameron, the egomaniacal titan of the missile complex. Coverly, however, was entirely at the mercy of Cameron's caprice and soon discovered that he was nothing more than a chauffeur for the great man. Also, beneath the surface of Cameron's brilliance and cultural pretensions (he is capable of quoting a little poetry) lay the viciousness of a man who professed a belief in the blessedness of the universe, but who talked with perfect equanimity of the destruction of the world. Cameron also suffered agonies of lust that could be satisfied only by a mistress in Rome, beat his subordinates in ferocious outbursts of temper, and had driven his son to insanity by practicing hideous extremes of cruelty in the name of discipline. In a short time, therefore, Coverly found that he had hitched his wagon to a rather sinister star. When his security clearance at the missile site was withdrawn because of Honora's delinquency on her federal income tax, Coverly expected that Cameron would get him reinstated. When he went for that purpose to Washington, where Cameron was being questioned by a congressional committee, he was witness to a rather startling phenomenon: As a result of his savage temperament, Cameron's own security clearance was withdrawn.

Moses Wapshot had trouble with his work but far more with his wife Melissa. He worked at a brokerage house (in, presumably, New York), and the couple lived with their son in an affluent suburban cocoon called Proxmire Manor, where the only thing that occupied the police is the memory that once, several years prior to the time of the novel, a woman had been arrested for tearing up a parking ticket. The community made a pretense at maintaining rigid moral standards. Melissa quickly learned, for example, that a certain couple was being expelled from Proxmire Manor because the wife had been flagrantly promiscuous, notably with grocery boys and deliverymen. Melissa was bored with such standards, and she became a little unhinged when she stumbled across evidence of lesbianism at a local dance that evening. Shortly thereafter, she developed a fondness and then a passion for Emile Cranmer, the boy who delivered her groceries. She seduced him without much difficulty. They began with a weekend at her house in Nantucket, followed by rendezvous in Boston, in New York, and eventually, in a little shack outside the town of Proxmire Manor. Emile engaged in the affair with little compunction; Melissa's money bought him food to satisfy an insatiable appetite and supplied him with expensive baubles, such as an eight-hundred-dollar sapphire ring. Melissa paid much more than money to maintain the affair. After meeting Emile for the third time, she was tortured with remorse and sought release in drunkenness. When she went to a doctor for a physical examination, she became so aroused that she ended up having sex with him. As a last resort, she sought the counsel of the minister, who did nothing but refer her to the town psychiatrist. Melissa, however, would not settle for the explanation that she was simply sick (and therefore irresponsible). She had only one place left to go, back to Emile.

Moses learned of his wife's infidelity from Emile's mother. The impact of the news was explosive. He nearly strangled his wife, then left his home and turned to drink and dissipation. By a series of bizarre and elaborate maneuvers, Melissa managed to meet Emile in Italy, where she went with her son. She bought Emile at an auction in Ladros for a hundred thousand lire; they retired to her luxurious villa, and they were last seen together in Rome. For his part, Moses abandoned himself completely to sex and alcohol. On Christmas Eve, at the end of the novel,

Coverly found him in the upstairs room of the St. Botolphs hotel drunkenly wallowing in the embrace of an equally inebriated widow. Moses came home with Coverly to Honora's house, but the next morning he shut himself in a closet full of bourbon.

During all of this, Honora had been steadily losing her grip. She seemed at first incapable of any serious wrong, but then learned that because she had never paid any federal income tax, she faced a criminal indictment. Her friend, Judge Beasley, recommended that she take her money out of the bank and leave the country. She followed his advice and decided on a ship to Europe, but this move was scarcely the end of her troubles. On the ship she was flattered by the attentions of a nice-mannered young man who helped her to get around the decks; when he told her that he was a stowaway, she arranged for him to be fed regularly in her cabin, and she developed enough interest in him to be capable of jealousy when she saw him in the company of another woman. One morning, however, in the early hours, he attempted to steal her money belt, and she struck him over the head with a brass lamp. She thought he was dead, but he survived the blow and pursued his calling elsewhere. Before the ship docked at Naples, he strolled by Honora with another aging victim on his arm. Her only way of releasing her fury was by striking out at the entire ship. She did so by the simple expedient of plugging her curling iron into an outlet in the bathroom of her cabin. This, as she had already discovered, had the effect of blowing out the ship's generators.

Honora entered the Bay of Naples, therefore, on a ship in darkness. In Italy, she found little to brighten her world. She visited the pope in the Vatican, but his rather precarious command of the English language frustrated communication between them and only sharpened her nostalgic yearning for the familiar territory of St. Botolphs. A short time later, her wish to return was satisfied, but in a cruelly unexpected way. Norman Johnson, an agent of the Internal Revenue Service who had visited her first in St. Botolphs, now came to her calmly and politely with extradition papers, a criminal indictment, and an order for the confiscation of all her property. She returned to St. Botolphs immediately and spent the last of her days immured in her old house, consuming nothing but bourbon. Shortly before Christmas, she was pronounced dead of starvation. She left Coverly with a command to hold a Christmas dinner in her house for the inmates of the local institute for the blind. Coverly executed her wish.

Critical Evaluation:

In *The Wapshot Chronicle*, John Cheever tells the story of the eccentric Wapshot clan from the once-prosperous seaport town of St. Botolphs, modeled on Quincy, Massachusetts, where Cheever grew up. Autobiographical to a degree, the novel traces the coming-of-age of the two sons against the many blows their father suffers to his self-esteem in his relations with his wife, who starts her own business, and his cousin Honora, the spinster-matriarch who controls the Wapshot inheritance. *The Wapshot Scandal* takes up the sons' and their elderly cousin's fortunes some years later. Both novels were generally well received; *The Wapshot Chronicle* earned for its author a National Book Award and *The Wapshot Scandal* a Howells Medal. Reviewers and critics, however, continued to wonder whether Cheever the short-story writer possessed the right temperament and talent to write a novel that was more coherent and less episodic. His reputation as a writer of short, relatively realistic fiction depicting generally middle-class, often suburban characters seemed sufficient reason to judge his work according to such standards.

Cheever, however, was not trying but failing to write according to such standards; he was adapting the conventions of nineteenth century novels such as George Eliot's *Middlemarch* (1871-1872), Sarah Wapshot's favorite reading, to meet the demands of life in the mid-twentieth century. Far from proving narrative mismanagement on Cheever's part, the multiple plots of both Wapshot books, *The Wapshot Scandal* in particular, suggest the psychological restlessness of his nomadic characters. Even as he creates a soothing, nostalgic sense of distance and wholeness (for example, by using the phrase, "at the time of which I am writing"), he undercuts it by making this distant past closely resemble the reader's own present and by deploying transitional phrases ("in the meantime" and "at about this time") that suggest randomness rather than causality, comic coincidences rather than cosmic connections. As Cheever undercuts the novel's seeming realism by interjecting elements of farce and fantasy, he undermines the ceremoniousness that figures so importantly in *The Wapshot Chronicle*, which begins with an Independence Day parade and ends with Leander's funeral. Cheever's choosing to frame *The Wapshot Scandal* with two ambivalently described Christmas scenes makes the book's ceremoniousness seem a little too pat, too self-consciously contrived, leaving the novel poised between celebration and satire. Haunted at the beginning by Leander's ghost and sounding more hollow than hallowed at the end, *The Wapshot Scandal* winds down in three progressively shorter parts of 160, 100, and 47 pages.

"Oh Father, Father, Father, why have you come back?" Coverly asks early in the novel. Although this comic Hamlet is not charged with avenging a father's murder most foul, there is something rotten nevertheless. *The Wapshot Chronicle* ends with Leander's "Advice to My Sons," but *The Wapshot Scandal* begins with Coverly wondering whether he has any counsel to give his son at a time when the world "was changing with incomprehensible velocity" and "total disaster seemed to be [so much a] part of the universal imagination" that even the Vatican wants a missile. As in Cheever's 1961 story "The Brigadier and the Golf Widow," fears about nuclear destruction are the outward manifestation of fears of a more inward kind, fears that the modern condition does not so much evoke as exacerbate. No longer a moral touchstone, the old river town of St. Botolphs (the first of Cheever's novelistic metaphors for confinement) has been supplanted by suburban life (his second). Suburbia is represented by Talifer, a security-conscious residential development for twenty thousand people attached to a missile site and research center, and Proximire Manor, an upscale New York suburb where putting up a for-sale sign is considered a subversive act. Cheever's rendering of American social practices is cartoonish, yet full of insights into the mid-twentieth century epidemic of social and psychological malaise.

"Loneliness was one thing, and she knew how sweet it could make light and company seem, but boredom was something else, and why, in this most prosperous and equitable land, should everyone seem so bored and disappointed?" Melissa's question is at the heart of this novel and much of Cheever's fiction, as well as his life. Part of the reason for this disappointment is that the world has grown not only more prosperous but "more and more preposterous," artificial and alienating. Another part of the reason is the immense chasm separating the characters' dreams and their actual existences. Emile, for example, "wanted something that would correspond to his sense that life was imposing; something that would confirm his feeling that, as he stood at the window of Narobi's grocery store watching the men and women on the sidewalk and the stream of clouds in the sky, the procession he saw was a majestic one." Melissa "had wanted to bring into her life the freshness of a journey" but early in her affair with Emile she realizes that she "had achieved nothing but a galling sense of moral shabbiness." What Melissa experiences so acutely Cheever often records in a comically deflating language targeted not at the characters' aspirations per se but at the ways they seek to realize or articulate those aspirations.

Spiritual striving takes various, generally unsatisfying, often debased forms: sex, suburban living, decorum (which can be either a mode of hope or a form of hypocrisy), and shopping. The supermarkets in *The Wapshot Scandal* may not be as Dantesque as the one in "The Death of Justina" (1961) or as massive as the Buy Brite in *Oh What a Paradise It Seems* (1982), but they are pervasive and serve an important thematic function. Melissa figuratively shops for love at the family-owned Narobi's, soon to be driven out of business by "the new market on the hill" (a description which ironically echoes John Winthrop's admonition to his fellow Puritans in 1630 to be "as a city on a hill," "a model of Christian charity"). In Italy, Melissa, "grieving, bewildered by the blows life has dealt her," tries to fight off the "Roman blues" by shopping at the Supra-Marketto Americano. If this modern Ophelia appears "no less dignified a figure of grief than any other," as the narrator contends (only half-facetiously, one suspects), it is because she is engaged in her own oddly angled way in "the engulfing struggle with good and evil." She intuitively understands, as do the other characters in this richly comic yet strangely disturbing novel, what a certain old senator means when he says to Dr. Cameron, "We possess Promethean powers but don't we lack the awe, but humility, that primitive man brought to the sacred fire?"

"Critical Evaluation" by Robert A. Morace

Bibliography:

Bosha, Francis J., ed. *The Critical Response to John Cheever*. Westport, Conn.: Greenwood Press, 1994. Sampler of reviews and critical essays on all Cheever publications. Reprints five reviews of *The Wapshot Chronicle* and includes a new essay by Kenneth C. Mason on "Tradition and Desecration" in the two Wapshot books.

_____, comp. *John Cheever: A Reference Guide*. Boston: G. K. Hall, 1981. Excellent discussion of the inconsistent critical response to Cheever's fiction. Provides a comprehensive, fully annotated listing of works about Cheever, including reviews, articles, and interviews.

Collins, R. G., ed. *Critical Essays on John Cheever*. Boston: G. K. Hall, 1982. Good overview of the critical reception of Cheever's fiction. Reprints many of the most important and influential reviews and essays (some in revised form), including Frederick Karl on pastoral, Beatrice Greene on Cheever's vision as an effect of style, and Frederick Bracher on comedy. A new essay by Samuel Coale on Cheever's "Romancer's Art" is especially noteworthy.

Donaldson, Scott. *John Cheever: A Biography*. New York: Random House, 1988. Fair-minded and richly detailed, this biography offers the fullest and most objective, but nevertheless sympathetic, account of Cheever's life and work, including the publication and reception of *The Wapshot Scandal*.

Hunt, George W. *John Cheever: The Hobgoblin Company of Love*. Grand Rapids, Mich.: Wm. B. Eerdmans, 1983. Longer, more detailed, but more tendentious than the earlier book-length studies by Samuel Coale (1977) and Lynn Waldeland (1979). Hunt offers useful summaries of plot and criticism before offering his own critical reading in terms of Cheever's Christian perspective.

WAR AND PEACE

Type of work: Novel
Author: Leo Tolstoy (1828-1910)
Type of plot: Historical
Time of plot: 1805-1813
Locale: Russia
First published: Voyna i mir, 1865-1869 (English translation, 1886)

Principal characters:
PIERRE BEZUHOV, the illegitimate son of a wealthy count
NATASHA ROSTOVA, the beautiful daughter of a well-to-do Moscow family
NIKOLAY ROSTOV, Natasha's older brother
ANDREY BOLKONSKY, a wealthy Russian prince
HÉLÈNE KURAGINA BEZUHOVA, Pierre's beautiful and immoral wife
ANATOLE KURAGIN, Hélène's brother
PRINCESS MARYA BOLKONSKAYA, Andrey's sister
OLD PRINCE BOLKONSKY, Andrey's tyrannical father
KUTUZOV, commander-in-chief of the Russian Army, appointed in
    August, 1812
NAPOLEON BONAPARTE

The Story:

In 1805, it was evident to most well-informed Russians that war with Napoleon was inevitable. Austria and Russia joined forces at the battle of Austerlitz, where they were soundly defeated by the French. In the highest Russian society, however, life went on as though nothing of tremendous import were impending. After all, it was really only by a political formality that Russia had joined with Austria. The fact that one day Napoleon might threaten the gates of Russia seemed ridiculous. Soirees and balls were held, old women gossiped, and young women fell in love. War, though inevitable, was being waged on foreign soil and was, therefore, of little importance.

The attraction held by the army for the young noblemen of Russia was understandable enough, for the Russian army had always offered excellent opportunities for ambitious, politically inclined young men. It was a wholesome release for their energies. Young Nikolay Rostov, for example, joined the hussars simply because he felt drawn to that way of life. His family idolized him because of his loyalty to the czar, because of his courage, and because he was so handsome in his uniform. Natasha, his sister, wept over him, and Sonya, his cousin, promptly fell in love with him.

By contrast, Pierre Bezuhov, a friend of the Rostov family, was looked upon as somewhat of a boor. He had just returned from Paris, where he had studied at the university, and he had not yet made up his mind what to do with his life. He would not join the army, for he saw no sense in a military career. His father gave him a liberal allowance, and he spent it frivolously at gambling. In truth, he seemed like a lost man. He would start long arguments, shouting loudly in the quiet drawing rooms, and then suddenly lapse into sullen silence. He was barely tolerated at soirees before his father died and left him millions. Then, suddenly, he became popular, although he attributed his rise to some new personality development of his own. He was no longer sullen but loved everyone, and it was quite clear that everyone loved him. His most dogged follower was Prince Vassily Kuragin, the father of a beautiful, unmarried daughter, Hélène, who was recognized everywhere as a prospective leader of St. Petersburg society. Pierre was forced into marrying her by the crafty prince, who knew a good catch when he saw one. The marriage, however, was never a success.

Pierre Bezuhov's closest friend was Prince Andrey Bolkonsky, an arrogant, somewhat cynical man who despised his wife. Lise, the "Little Princess," as she was called, was pregnant, but Prince Andrey could endure the bondage of domesticity no longer. When he received a commission in the army, he left his wife at the family estate, Bleak Hills, in the care of his sister Marya and his tyrannical old father and went off to war. During his absence, Princess Lise bore him a son but died in childbirth. Prince Andrey returned after the battle of Austerlitz to find himself free once more, but he enjoyed no feeling of satisfaction in his freedom. Seeking Pierre, Prince Andrey turned to his friend for answers to some of the eternal questions of loneliness and despair that tortured him.

Pierre had joined the brotherhood of freemasons and through this contact had arrived at a philosophy of life that he sincerely believed to be the only true philosophy. Had Pierre realized that the order had initiated him solely because of his wealth, he would never have adopted their ideals. Pierre restored some of Prince Andrey's lost courage, however, by means of his wild if unreasoning enthusiasm. In the belief that he was now an unselfish, free individual, Pierre freed his peasants and set about improving his estate; having absolutely no sense of business administration, he lost a great deal of money. Finally, with his affairs in hopeless disorder, he left an overseer in charge and retired to Bleak Hills and Prince Andrey's sane company.

Nikolay Rostov was in the thick of the fighting. Napoleon had overcome the Prussian forces at Jena and had reached Berlin in October. The Russians once more had gone to the assistance of their neighbors, and the two opposing armies met in a terrible battle at Eylau in February, 1807. In June, Nikolay entered the campaign at Friedland, and when the Russians were beaten, he naïvely thought the war was over. Napoleon and Czar Alexander signed the Peace of Tilsit, but Napoleon possessed a remarkable gift for flattery and he had promised, with no intention of keeping his word, that Russia would be given a free hand with Turkey and Finland. For two years, Nikolay enjoyed all the privileges of his post in the army without having to endure any of the risks. Napoleon had gone to Spain.

After having served in minor skirmishes as an adjutant under General Kutuzov, leader of the Russian forces, Prince Andrey returned to the country. He had some business affairs to straighten out with Count Rostov, marshal of his district, and so he went to the Rostov estate at Otradnoe. There Andrey almost immediately fell under the spell of Count Rostov's lovely young daughter, Natasha. He fancied himself in love as he had never loved before. Once again, he turned to Pierre for advice. Pierre, however, had experienced an unfortunate quarrel with his wife, Hélène. They were now separated, and Pierre had fought a senseless duel with an innocent man because he had suspected his wife of being unfaithful. At the sight of Prince Andrey, so hopelessly in love, Pierre's great heart was touched. He had always been fond of Natasha, whom he had known since childhood, and the match seemed to him ideal. With love once more flowing through his heart, he took his wife back, feeling very virtuous at his own generosity, and he encouraged Prince Andrey in his suit.

Natasha had ignored previous offers of marriage. When dashing and wealthy Prince Andrey came on the scene, however, she lost her heart to him instantly. He asked her parents for her hand, and they immediately consented to the match, an excellent one from their point of view. When Prince Andrey broke the news to his quarrelsome and dictatorial old father, however, the ancient prince said he would not give his blessing until a year had elapsed. He felt that Natasha had too little money and was much too young to take charge of Prince Andrey's home and his son. Marya, Prince Andrey's sister, also disapproved of the match, for she was jealous of her brother's fiancée.

Natasha was heartbroken but agreed to wait a year; Prince Andrey kept their betrothal a secret, in order, as he said, to let her have complete freedom. Natasha went to visit a family friend in Moscow. There her freedom was too complete. One night, at the opera with Pierre's wife Hélène, who was now recognized as an important social leader, she met Hélène's disreputable brother, Anatole. Unknown to Natasha, Anatole had been forced to marry a peasant girl whom he had ruined. The young rake now determined to conquer Natasha. Aided by his unscrupulous sister, he forced his suit. Natasha became confused. She loved Prince Andrey, but he had joined the army again and she never saw him; and she loved Anatole, who was becoming more insistent every day. At last, she agreed to run away with Anatole and marry him. Anatole arranged with an unfrocked priest to have a mock ceremony performed. On the night set for the elopement, Natasha's hostess discovered the plan. Natasha was confined to her room. Unfortunately, she had already written to Prince Andrey's sister asking to be relieved of her betrothal vows.

When Pierre heard the scandal, he forced Anatole to leave town. Then he went to see Natasha. Strangely, he was the only person whom she trusted and to whom she could speak freely. She looked upon him as if he were an older uncle, and she was charmed with his gruff friendliness. Pierre felt attracted toward Natasha in a way he knew he should not, as he was not free, but he managed to let her know that he would be a friend to her, and she was pleased over his attentions. She soon began to get well, although she was never again the lively, frivolous girl whom Prince Andrey had loved.

Prince Andrey had suffered a terrible blow to his pride, but in the army there were many engrossing matters to take his attention away from himself. By 1810, the Franco-Russian alliance had gradually dissolved. When France threatened to free Russia of responsibility for Poland, the czar finally understood that Napoleon's promises meant little. The dapper little French emperor had forsaken Russia in favor of Austria as the center of his European domination. He married Marie Louise, and in 1812, with his eyes unmistakably fixed on Moscow, crossed the Nieman River. From June to August, Napoleon enjoyed an almost uninterrupted march to Smolensk.

In Smolensk, he found burned and wrecked houses. The city was deserted. That marked the beginning of fierce opposition. Old General Kutuzov, former leader of the army of the East and now in complete charge of the Russian forces, was determined to halt the French advance. His tactics, however, were the very thing that kept the Russians from a decisive victory. If instead of attempting to halt the French he had drawn them deeper and deeper into the country, lengthening their lines of communication and cutting them off in the rear, the Russians might have won their war earlier. It was odd, too, that Napoleon, in attempting to complete his march, also lessened his chances for victory.

Battle succeeded battle, with heavy losses on both sides, before Napoleon finally led his forces to Borodino. There the most senseless battle in the whole campaign was fought. The Russians, determined to hold Moscow, which was only a short distance away, lost nearly their whole army. The French forces dwindled in proportion, but it was clear that the Russians got the worst of the battle. General Kutuzov, bitter and war-weary, decided, against his will, that the army could not hold Moscow. Again a triumphant Napoleon marched into a deserted city.

Prince Andrey was gravely wounded at Borodino. The Rostovs were already abandoning their estate to move into the interior, when many wagons loaded with wounded soldiers were brought to the house for shelter. Among these was Prince Andrey himself. Natasha nursed him and sent for Marya, his sister, and his son, Nikolushka. Old Prince Bolkonsky, suffering from the shock of having French soldiers almost upon his doorstep, died of a stroke. Nikolay managed to move Marya and the boy to safer quarters. Although Prince Andrey welcomed his sister, it was evident that he no longer expected to recover. Natasha nursed him tenderly, and they once more declared their love for each other. When his wound festered, Prince Andrey knew that the end was near. He died one night in his sleep. United in tragedy, Marya and Natasha became close friends; young Nikolay found Prince Andrey's sister attractive.

Pierre Bezuhov had decided to remain in Moscow. Fired with thoughts of becoming a national hero, he hit upon the plan of assassinating Napoleon. He was captured as a prisoner of war, however, when he attempted to rescue a Russian woman, who was being molested by French soldiers.

Napoleon's army completely disintegrated in Moscow. After waiting in vain for peace terms from the czar, Napoleon decided to abandon Moscow and head back to France. A ragged, irresponsible, pillaging group of men, who had once been the most powerful army in the world, gathered up their booty, threw away their supplies, and took the road back to Smolensk. Winter came on. Pierre Bezuhov, luckily, was robust and healthy. Traveling with the other prisoners, he learned from experience that happiness could consist of merely being warm and having enough to eat. His privations aged and matured him. He learned responsibility and gained courage, and he developed a sense of humor at the irony of his plight. His simplicity and even temperament made him a favorite with French and Russians alike.

On the road to Smolensk, the French forces became completely demoralized. Cossacks charged out of the forests, cutting the lines, taking countless French prisoners, and rescuing the Russian captives. Many Frenchmen deserted. Others fell ill and died on the road. Pierre was freed at last and returned to Orel, where he fell ill with fever. Later he learned of the deaths of Prince Andrey and his own wife. Hélène had died in St. Petersburg after a short illness. These shocks, coupled with the news of the defeat of the French, seemed to deprive him of all feeling. When he finally recovered, he was overwhelmed with a joyous sense of freedom of soul, a sense that he had at last found himself, that he knew himself for what he really was. He knew the sheer joy of being alive, and he was humble and grateful. He had discovered a faith in God that he had never known before.

Pierre returned to Moscow and renewed his friendships with Marya Bolkonskaya and the Rostovs. Once more Natasha charmed him, and Pierre suddenly realized that she was no longer a child. He loved her now, as always, and so when the opportunity presented itself, he dutifully asked Natasha's parents for her hand. Natasha and Pierre were married and were very happy. Natasha was an efficient wife who dominated her husband, much to the amusement of their friends, but Pierre loved her and respected her because she knew how to take charge of everything. She managed his estates as well as her household.

Nikolay, though not entirely sure that he loved Marya, knew that to marry her would be a wise thing. The Rostovs were poor now, and the old count had left his affairs in a deplorable state. At the insistence of his mother, Nikolay finally proposed to Marya, and the two families were joined. The union proved happier than Nikolay had expected. They adopted Prince Andrey's son, Nikolushka.

After eight years of marriage, Pierre and Natasha had four fine children, of whom they were very proud. Although society thought that Natasha carried her devotion to her husband and children to an extreme, Natasha and Pierre were happier than they had ever been before, and they found their lives together a fulfillment of all of their dreams.

Critical Evaluation:

Leo Tolstoy's *War and Peace* is a panorama of Russian life in that active period of history known as the Napoleonic era. The structure of the novel indicates that Tolstoy was not concerned with plot, setting, or even individual people, as such, but that his purpose was to show that the continuity of life in history is eternal. Each human life holds its influence on history, and the developments of youth and age, war and peace, are so interrelated that in the simplest patterns of social behavior vast implications are recognizable. Tolstoy wanted to present history as it was influenced by every conceivable human force. To do this, he needed to create not a series of simple, well-linked incidents but an evolution of events and personalities. Each character changes and affects others; these others influence yet others, and gradually, imperceptibly, the historical framework of the nation changes.

War and Peace is a moving record of historical progress, and the dual themes of this vast novel—age and youth, war and peace—are shown as simultaneous developments of history. Both this novel and *Anna Karenina* (1875-1877), two of the greatest works of fiction in Russian literature, were written when Tolstoy was at the height of his powers as a writer. He enjoyed a happy marriage, and he was busy managing his country estate as well as writing. His life had a healthy, even exuberant, balance between physical and intellectual activities. *War and Peace*, in particular, reflects the passionate and wide-ranging tastes and energies of this period of his life—before domestic strife and profound spiritual conversion led him to turn away from the world as well as from art. The novel is huge in size and scope; it presents a long list of characters and covers a splendid variety of scenes and settings. At the same time, however, it is carefully organized and controlled.

The basic controlling device involves movement between clusters of characters surrounding the major characters Natasha, Kutuzov, Andrey, and Pierre. The second ordering device is thematic and involves Tolstoy's lifelong investigation of the question: What is natural? This theme is offered in the first chapter at Anna Scherer's party, where readers encounter the artificiality of St. Petersburg society and meet the two chief seekers of the natural, Andrey and Pierre. Both Andrey and Pierre love Natasha, who is an instinctive embodiment of the natural in particularly Russian terms. Kutuzov is also an embodiment of Russian naturalness; only he can lead the Russian soldiers in a successful war against the French. The Russian character of Tolstoy's investigation of the natural or the essential is the main reason one speaks of *War and Peace* as a national epic. Yet, Tolstoy's characters also represent all people.

Natasha's group of characters centers in the Rostov family, and the novel is, among many things, a searching study of family life. Count Ilya Rostov, a landowning nobleman, is a sympathetic portrait of a carefree, warmhearted, wealthy man. His wife is somewhat anxious and less generous in spirit, but they are happily married and the family as a whole is harmonious. Natasha's brothers and sisters are rendered with great vividness: the passionate, energetic Nikolay; the cold, formal Vera; the youthful Petya; the sweet, compliant Sonya, cousin to Natasha and used by Tolstoy as a foil to her. Natasha herself is bursting with life. She is willful, passionate, proud, humorous, and capable of great growth and change. Like all the major characters, she seeks the natural. She is the natural; her instincts are right and true. All of book 7, particularly chapter 7 when she sings and dances, dramatizes the essential Russianness of her nature. Her nearly consummated love affair with Anatole Kuragin, her loss of Andrey, and her final happy marriage to Pierre show how intensely life-giving she is. One of the great experiences of reading *War and Peace* is to witness her slow transition from slim, exuberant youth to thick-waisted motherhood. For Tolstoy, Natasha can do nothing that is not natural and right.

Kutuzov stands above the generals who cluster about him. Forgotten at the start of the war, he is called into action when all else seems to have failed. Unlike the other generals, many of them German, Kutuzov knows that battles are not won in the staff room by virtue of elaborate planning but by the spirit of the soldiers who actually do the fighting. Kutuzov alone knows that one must wait for that moment when the soldiers' spirit is totally committed to the battle. He knows that the forces of war are greater than any one man can control and that one must wait upon events and know when not to act as well as when to act. His naturalness is opposed to Napoleon's artificiality. A brilliant strategist and planner, Napoleon believes that he controls events. His pride and vanity are self-blinding; he cannot see that if he invades Russia, he is doomed. Kutuzov's victory over Napoleon is a victory of the natural and the humble, for he is, after all, a man of the people. Furthermore, the figure of Kutuzov is very closely related to Tolstoy's philosophy of historical change and necessity.

The characters of Andrey and Pierre probably represent two sides of Tolstoy: the rational-spiritual and the passionate-mystical, although these labels are far too simple. Andrey's group of characters centers in the Bolkonsky family: the merciless, autocratic, but brilliant General Bolkonsky, Andrey's father, and his sister Princess Marya, who is obedient, pious, and loving and who blossoms when she marries Nikolay Rostov. When readers first see Andrey, he is bored and even appears cynical; yet, like Pierre, he is searching for an answer to life, and he undergoes a series of awakenings that bring him closer to the natural. The first awakening occurs when he is wounded at Austerlitz and glimpses infinity beyond the blue sky; the second occurs at his wife's death; the third occurs when he falls in love with Natasha; and the last when he dies. In all of these instances, Andrey moves closer to what he conceives of as the essential. This state of mind involves a repudiation of the world and its petty concerns and passions. In all but one of these instances, death is involved. Indeed, Andrey's perception of the natural is closely related to his acceptance of death. He comes to see death as the doorway to infinity and glory and not as a fearful black hole. Death becomes part of the natural rhythm, a cycle which promises spiritual rebirth.

Pierre's group is composed of St. Petersburg socialites and decadents: the Kuragin family, composed of the smooth, devious Prince Vasily; his son, the rake Anatole, and daughter, the beautiful, corrupt Hélène, Pierre's first wife; the rake Dolokhov; and finally, in Pierre's third or fourth transformation, the peasant Platon Karataev. Unlike Andrey, Pierre's approach to life seems almost strategically disordered and open—he embraces all forms of life passionately and hungrily. Compared to Andrey's rigorous and discriminating mind, Pierre seems hopelessly naïve and chaotic.

Pierre, however, even more than Natasha, is capable of vital and creative change. As Andrey seems fitted to perceive intimations of essences beyond the world, Pierre seems fitted to find his essences in the world. He shucks off his mistaken connection with Hélène and her family and experiences the first of his own awakenings in the conversion to freemasonry (one of several interesting "false" conversions in the novel, one other being Natasha's after she is rejected by Andrey). Pierre, too, learns from death, both in his duel with Dolokhov and in his observations of the battle of Borodino. His two most important awakenings, however, occur in his love for Natasha and in his experience as a prisoner of the French. In the latter instance, he encounters the harmonious, perfectly round (whole) peasant Karataev who teaches him to accept all things—even death—in good grace and composure of spirit. When Natasha encounters Pierre after this experience, she rightly recognizes that he has been transformed. All that is superficial and nonessential is gone from him. Their marriage is a union of two vital human beings tempered by suffering. At the end, there is more than a hint that Pierre is involved in efforts on the part of the aristocracy to modify the ossified system of government under the czars. Life and change go on.

War and Peace, perhaps beyond any other work, shows the advantages of the long novel. After reading the book, the reader feels a sense of space and a sense of change through the passage of time which are impossible to transmit so vividly in shorter fiction. This great novel reveals the beauty and injustice, the size and complexity, of life itself.

"Critical Evaluation" by Benjamin Nyce

Bibliography:
Citati, Pietro. *Tolstoy*. Translated by Raymond Rosenthal. New York: Schocken Books, 1986. Gives a full explanation of Tolstoy's youth and background that led to the writing of his novels. A huge section is devoted to *War and Peace*, with attention to the portrayal of historical Russia. Gives sketches of the major characters of the novel.

De Courcel, Martine. *Tolstoy: The Ultimate Reconciliation*. Translated by Peter Levi. New York: Charles Scribner's Sons, 1988. Explains the research Tolstoy did for writing the historical novel *War and Peace* and his marital situation at the time of writing it. A long and complete study of Tolstoy.

Noyes, George Rapall. *Tolstoy*. New York: Dover, 1968. Connects the many works of Tolstoy and refers to biographical information important to them. Draws heavily on Tolstoy's published writings, diaries, and letters. Discusses the preparations for writing *War and Peace*.

Rowe, William W. *Leo Tolstoy*. Boston: Twayne, 1986. Gives background on the writing of *War and Peace* and includes a thorough discussion of the characters. Other chapters include biographical information and treatments of other novels and stories.

Simmons, Ernest J. *Tolstoy*. London: Routledge & Kegan Paul, 1973. Focus is on Tolstoy as a major thinker of his time, a religious, social, and political reformer. Describes Tolstoy's childhood and life as a writer. Explains the reception of *War and Peace* and early criticism. Includes notes from Tolstoy's diary during the time he wrote *War and Peace*.

THE WAR OF THE MICE AND THE CRABS

Type of work: Poetry
Author: Giacomo Leopardi (1798-1837)
First published: I paralipomeni della batracomiomachia, 1842 (English translation, 1976)

Italians consider Giacomo Leopardi one of the great poets of the nineteenth century, although his work is relatively unknown in the English-speaking world. His life was short and bitter, and he was crippled by disease, usually in need of money, and cut off from the world about him. Most of the poetry for which he is praised is his lyric poetry, which is marked by the beauty, concreteness, and exactness of its language. Leopardi's language is, in itself, an assertion and creation of human value, yet in all of his work, both prose and poetry, he expresses a realistic, pessimistic view of human existence. Leopardi believed that human belief in happiness is an illusion: Happiness is not now, but always to come. This illusion of happiness and good applies not only to individual lives but also to human institutions.

Leopardi, a great scholar, wrote not only lyric poetry but also remarkable philosophic essays and political satires, one of which is the narrative poem, *The War of the Mice and the Crabs.* This work came late in Leopardi's career, and originally even some of his closest supporters disapproved of it; one of them called it "a terrible book." It was so widely criticized because it is a scathing satire not only of the European intellectual and political world of the early nineteenth century but also of the rhetoric, pretensions, and posturings of those Italian patriots who wanted an independent, unified Italy. Italy at that time was a collection of small, often mutually antagonistic, states; most of the north, including Milan and Venice, was directly or indirectly controlled by the Austro-Hungarian empire, which many Italians considered alien and uncivilized.

Leopardi was an Italian patriot, and two of his earliest poems were patriotic. He believed that Italy had been a leader in civilizing the world and perhaps could be again. He hated the emptiness of bluster, however, and thought that certain kinds of patriotism were simply refusals to face realities. He also believed that most political and social theories were intellectual daydreams.

The War of the Mice and the Crabs builds on the ancient Greek poem, *The Batrachomyomachia,* once attributed to the poet Homer. The poem—the title literally means "The War of the Frogs and the Mice"—is a mock epic in the form of a beast fable, using animals in order to satirize the heroic values of the Homeric poems, the *Iliad* and the *Odyssey* (both c. 800 B.C.E.). Leopardi's Italian title can be translated as the additions to (or the things left out of) the war of the frogs and the mice. He modernizes the satire in order to speak of Italy, its warring factions, and the overriding power of the intruding Austro-Hungarian empire. At the same time, he comments on the political, historical, and universal theorizing that asserts order. The political world that Leopardi's poem depicts is essentially chaotic. The only thing that matters in the end is brute force. Yet the natural world is also chaotic, purposeless, leading only to motionless death.

Leopardi's satire was not solely in subject matter but also in form. For example, *The War of the Mice and the Crabs* is in cantos (longer divisions) and octaves (eight-line stanzas)—divisions and stanzas used by the Renaissance Italian writers of romantic epics, such as Ludovico Ariosto's *Orlando furioso* (1485). A number of later mock epic poems deliberately used the same form in order to satirize the elevated tone of the standard romantic epic. Leopardi chooses the form in order to emphasize the satirical note.

In the Greek poem, the mice attacked the frogs to get revenge for the accidental drowning of their prince; they were winning the war when the gods decided that they did not want the frogs to be destroyed and so sent an army of crabs to help the frogs. Leopardi's poem begins with the mice in frightened retreat from the terrible crabs. The king of the mice has been killed, and the mice are utterly demoralized.

The mice obviously represent the Italians, the crabs the armies sent by the Austro-Hungarians, but there is no straightforward allegory here. The history is generalized, and only rarely can the reader identify what exact historical figures Leopardi had in mind in his leaders of the mice and the crabs. This is deliberate, for he is commenting on the political oppression and the foolish hopes common to many times.

The mice finally notice that the crab army has stopped pursuing them. They regroup, elect a new leader, Rubatocchi (Chunk-Stealer), and decide to send an envoy to the crabs, choosing Count Leccafondi (Bottom-Licker) to ask why they have been attacked. There is a long characterization of Leccafondi, who represents the best of progressive thought but who is essentially shallow because that thought is shallow. He arrives at the camp of the crabs, is taken to the headquarters of General Brancaforte (Strong-Claw), and tries to soothe the cruel crabs with his diplomatic skills. Brancaforte consults with his king, Senzacapo (Without-Head, or Headless)—representing Emperor Francis I of Austria-Hungary—who dictates harsh terms, including stationing troops in Rat City, the mice's capital. Indeed, the Austrians had troops in all of the major cities they had occupied. Brancaforte defends the crabs' actions by arguing that the crabs are right because they have power, although he seems to think that this is natural law.

Rat City is based upon Naples, a city that Leopardi despised as corrupt and vicious. Here the poet digresses to a savage attack on the decay of European civilization. Meanwhile, the mice have elected a new king. Surprisingly, Rubatocchi had refused the throne, so the mice turn to Rodipane (Bread-Muncher), the son-in-law of the old king. This was acceptable to the crabs because the new king belonged to an established royal family. Here Leopardi mocks the readiness to believe that virtue resides in certain families.

Rodipane agrees to a constitution, but this is repellent to the crabs. The Austrian emperor and the other rulers of Europe had rejected the idea that a people had the right to elect their king. More important, they thought no king should agree to a constitution. Such acts implied that rulers could be enthroned and dethroned by the people, and had no absolute right to their power.

In the opening of canto 4, Leopardi digresses again with an attack on a priori theories of human behavior, mocking romantic ideas of the natural human being destroyed by civilization and conservative ideas that a golden age was lost through human sinfulness. Leccafondi returns with the crabs' terms, which the mice reluctantly accept. Rodipane gives free cheese and polenta—bread and circuses—to the mice and gains popularity. The crabs set up their garrison, but the mice revive their prosperity and recover their courage. Leccafondi is named minister of the interior, and all seems well. The crabs, however, feel threatened. Emperor Senzacapo sends orders to the head of his garrison, Boccaferrato (Iron-Mouth), to order the mice to abrogate the constitution.

The mice resist and decide to fight, but as soon as the crab army appears, they run away. Leopardi is mocking what he regarded as the Italian impulse to swagger but not to fight. Only Rubatocchi is brave and dies slaughtering crabs.

The crabs seize Rat City with the help of their garrison there. They keep Rodipane as puppet king; their envoy, Camminatorto (Crooked-Walker), rearranges the government in the image of the crab world. Camminatorto is based on a number of people, but in particular Prince Klemens von Metternich (1773-1859), the powerful Austrian minister who led the European reactionaries against all democratic ideas after the final defeat of Napoleon the First of France.

Leccafondi, although hardly a revolutionary, is caught up in intrigues. The crabs exile him, and he wanders the world looking for help for the mice, getting promises but no real help, just as happened to the Italian exiles of the time. One night, he takes refuge in the house of a man named Daedalus. This Daedalus may not be the Daedalus of Greek legend, but he is a great inventor. Wishing to help the mice, he suggests that he and Leccafondi visit the residence of the dead animals. There Leccafondi can consult the dead mice, who are reputed to know more than the living. Daedalus makes wings for Leccafondi, and the two of them fly around the globe until they come to an island in the Pacific, their destination. Leccafondi goes alone to the underground abode of the dead mice and finds them staring silently and blankly ahead: Death itself is neither reward nor punishment for one's actions in this world; religious beliefs concerning the afterlife are false. The dead mice are apparently emotionless, forbidden to laugh. When Leccafondi asks if the mice will get the promised help, there is a great stir as the dead mice repress their laughter.

For the moment they speak, telling him that upon his return he should consult a general named Taster. Taster will tell the mice how to recover their lost honor. Most commentators consider Taster to be Leopardi's image of himself. Leccafondi and Daedalus return to Rat City, where the mouse immediately visits Taster. Taster at first refuses advice because he has no stomach for vain plots. At last he speaks, but the reader never hears his good advice. Leopardi ends his poem with the excuse that the ancient manuscripts he has been "translating" ran out here and that he cannot finish his story. No doubt Leopardi himself had no real solution to the Italian problem. Yet the very abruptness of the ending emphasizes the major themes: The natural and human worlds are morally purposeless, and people must not rely upon empty words.

L. L. Lee

Bibliography:
Barricelli, Gian Piero. *Giacomo Leopardi*. Boston: Twayne, 1986. Complete and intelligent discussion of Leopardi's work, with detailed treatment of individual poems and prose works. A short but useful section on *The War of the Mice and the Crabs*. Notes and references, selected bibliography, index.
Caserta, Ernesto G. Introduction to *The War of the Mice and the Crabs*. Chapel Hill: University of North Carolina, Department of Romance Languages, 1976. Caserta's introduction to his prose translation of the poem and his presentation of the historical situation of the time are useful for reading *The War of the Mice and the Crabs* and for understanding Leopardi as more than a lyric poet. Selected bibliography.
Origo, Iris. *Leopardi: A Study in Solitude*. 2d ed. London: Hamish Hamilton, 1953. The standard introduction to Leopardi, which treats his life and works.
Perella, Nicolas James. *Night and the Sublime in Giacomo Leopardi*. Berkeley: University of California Press, 1970. Superb discussion of Leopardi the poet. A three-stanza quotation from *The War of the Mice and the Crabs* in the original Italian could help those with some knowledge of the language. Perella uses the quotation to discuss Leopardi's use of the sublime. Notes.
Singh, Ghan Shyam. *Leopardi and the Theory of Poetry*. Lexington: University of Kentucky Press, 1964. Thorough discussion of Leopardi's aesthetic ideas and practices. Discusses the ideas and influence of the English Romantics.

THE WAR OF THE WORLDS

Type of work: Novel
Author: H. G. Wells (1866-1946)
Type of plot: Science fiction
Time of plot: Late nineteenth century
Locale: Woking and London, England
First published: 1898

Principal characters:
THE ANONYMOUS NARRATOR, also the story's main character
OGILVY, the first to discover the Martian cylinder
THE ARTILLERYMAN, the only survivor of an assault on the Martians
THE CURATE, the anonymous narrator's companion and victim

The Story:

Although scientists had speculated about intelligent life on Mars, it came as a complete surprise to England when Martians landed, shot to Earth in flaming cylinders. At first the projectiles were taken to be shooting stars or meteorites. Then Ogilvy, the first to discover one of the cylinders, realized that it was hollow and that as it cooled he could hear something inside unscrewing the thing's top.

Ogilvy informed a local journalist, Henderson, and soon a crowd, including the narrator, gathered around a cylinder. The narrator suspected the object had come from Mars, but he did not think it would contain a living being. He and the crowd were shocked when grayish tentacles emerged from the cylinder. The crowd fled as the huge creature appeared, the size of a bear, with a sheen like wet leather, two large dark eyes, and a lipless mouth, heaving and pulsating. Just before the narrator ran away he caught sight of the monster's large inhuman eyes and fungoid mass, which he found disgusting and terrifying.

It was decided to send a deputation (including Ogilvy and Henderson) to parlay with the Martians, since it seemed that the Martians were intelligent, if repulsive looking to human beings. However, the deputation was wiped out in a blinding flash of fire and smoke, which the narrator later learned was the Martians' heat ray. People panicked; the narrator was stunned by the swiftness of the destruction.

The Martians began to terrorize the cities and the countryside, dealing a silent and quick death to everyone in their way. For the first time it occurred to the narrator that the Martians meant to rule Earth, although he assured his wife that it seemed unlikely that they would prevail because Earth's gravitational pull on their bodies was three times what it was on Mars. Returning home, the narrator regained some of his confidence.

In London, the news from Woking seemed so incredible that it was deemed a ruse. Even at Woking junction, where the trains still ran, the Martian invasion was treated as a rumor and a curiosity, not a cause for evacuation. The narrator could hear the Martians hammering and stirring, making some sort of preparations. A company of soldiers was dispatched to form a cordon around the pit where the Martians had landed. The Martians stayed in their pit, but then the narrator, at home, saw one of his chimneys crack, and he realized the power of the heat ray. He sent his terrified wife away to Leatherhead. Out in the road he met people escaping from the area of the pit. The Martians had set fire to everything within range of their heat ray.

The narrator then got his first full view of a walking Martian or Martian machine of glittery metal, swinging its long, flexible tentacles. It came out of the third of ten cylinders the Martians had fired at Earth. On the road the narrator encountered an artilleryman, the only survivor of a clash with the Martians, who described his fallen comrades as burnt meat. The destruction had been indiscriminate and universal and unprecedented in the history of warfare on Earth. The artilleryman decided to try for London to join the horse artillery there; the narrator opted to return to Leatherhead. The third cylinder blocked their way. Although artillery did destroy one Martian, it proved ineffective against the heat ray, which destroyed everything in its path. The narrator just missed death as the foot of a Martian came within yards of his head.

The narrator then realized that the Martians were methodically destroying the country. Every twenty-four hours, another cylinder arrived to strengthen and consolidate their power. Although England sent all of its heavy guns and warships against the Martians, this firepower was destroyed as soon as it came within range of the heat ray.

Unable to return to Leatherhead, the narrator took refuge in a house occupied by a curate, who was devastated by the invasion and depressed that it was a sign of God's judgment. Soon it became clear to the narrator that the curate had become insane. Talking to himself, refusing to listen to the narrator's plea that they must ration their food and make no noise, the curate put both his life and the narrator's in jeopardy. Martian tentacles had already invaded the house and had just missed detecting the narrator's presence. When the curate announced that he was going out to preach the word of God that sanctioned this destruction of the world, the desperate narrator felt he had no choice but to kill the curate, which the narrator did by bashing in his head with the back of a meat cleaver.

After more than two weeks in the house, his food supply exhausted, the ravenous narrator chanced the streets, encountering once again the artilleryman. It now seemed clear to the artilleryman that there was no way of defeating the Martians. He planned an underground life, staying below ground in the city's sewers, and thinking of ways to accommodate himself to the Martian rulers. The narrator revolted against this subhuman existence but also thought that the rule of human beings on Earth was over. They had become merely food for Martians, who fed on human beings by injecting themselves with human blood.

Yet the Martians were defeated. To the narrator's astonishment, he came across the rotting bodies of Martians, and it suddenly occurred to him that they had been destroyed by the lowliest of life forms: bacteria. On Mars there had been no bacteria, and the Martians had no immune systems, which made them prey to organisms human beings had learned to tolerate over thousands of years.

To the narrator, the destruction of the Martians was only a reprieve. Although he had been incredibly fortunate—reuniting with his wife—he now lived with a sense of insecurity, no longer certain of Earth's invulnerability.

Critical Evaluation:

The War of the Worlds is one of H. G. Wells's most riveting stories. Much of its power stems from its first-person narrator. He is a learned man, a writer on scientific subjects, equipped with a precise mind and a formidable ability to describe what he sees. He begins his story calmly, rehearsing the evidence for life on Mars, and explaining the investigations of his contemporaries. At the same time, he brings to his opening words a tone of foreboding, a sense of someone who has been through an ordeal—even though he does not explain what has happened to him. Instead, he re-creates events as he experienced them, enhancing the drama and suspense of the novel.

The narrator intensifies the interest of his story by releasing details about the Martians gradually. This steady but well-paced dispensing of information not only whets the curiosity, it is a realistic device, since the point of the story is that it takes the world some time to understand the ramifications of the invasion. At first, the Martians stay in their pit, a mystery until they begin to range across the country. Their heat ray is not well understood because from a distance it is obscured by the smoke of its destruction. Only when the narrator gets uncomfortably close to the line of fire does he realize what sort of destructive instrument humans are confronting.

Much of the gripping narration centers on the sheer struggle to survive. As the narrator learns about the Martians' awesome power, he must also adapt to the destruction of civilization. He never loses his intelligent and resilient manner, but he does become more desperate. The curate, an irrational man, has to be killed if the narrator is to survive. The narrator shows no remorse for his act, only pity, because the curate had become insane and a danger to himself and to the narrator. Also, the narrator seems to hold little tolerance for the religious point of view. Several critics have commented on Wells's hostility to organized religion in his other work.

If the narrator does not lose his humanity, the artillery man nearly does. When they meet a second time, the artilleryman is guarding his ground and tells the narrator that he must look to some other part of England for food. After the artilleryman recognizes the narrator, he relaxes his guard, and tries to persuade the narrator that the human race is beaten. Although he dreams of somehow outlasting the Martians or at least coming to some sort of compromise with them—he is a defeated man who will settle for living on a level so subhuman that it appalls the narrator.

In addition to the brilliant evocation of the Martian invasion, Wells provides the first description in English literature of modern, mechanized warfare. The images of a city and countryside wiped out with weapons of mass destruction were startling and prophetic. Wells's vision challenged English complacency about their secure and common-sense life. His science-fiction novels heralded a century of unprecedented destruction, the displacement of whole populations of people, and the use of technology to dehumanize people.

Wells enhances the effectiveness of his first person narrator by including accounts of how the Martian invasion was reported in the press. Another theme of the novel is how mass populations get their news and how a modern society copes with disruptions in communication and transportation. Few people actually witness the events of the novel; many more react to what they read in newspapers, sometimes containing inaccurate reports or only partial accounts.

It is quite extraordinary the way Wells provides both the immediacy of firsthand experience and a sense of a whole society mobilizing to comprehend and to defend itself against a foreign menace. Parts of the Martian invasion that the narrator has not witnessed and that are not clarified in the newspapers, are supplied by the narrator's versions of his brother's experience during the invasion. His brother's reports not only help to put the narrator's experience into a context and to fill in gaps, but also to provide another voice that the narrator must absorb and factor into his own account. Consequently, the novel captures a sense of both the immediate events and a retrospective account of them. The novel becomes both the narrator's autobiography and an objective historical account.

The novel's ending, although it includes the narrator's sentimental reunion with his wife, is anything but optimistic. There is an extraordinary feeling of loss—not merely of lives and homes and institutions but of confidence in the human spirit. It is a sobering conclusion, marking an end to the ebullience of the nineteenth century faith in science and human progress, to the idea that human beings were unlocking the secrets of nature. Wells believed, certainly, that twentieth century science and technology would make remarkable discoveries, but he was shortly to write a series of novels predicting devastating warfare as well. *The War of the Worlds* is a warning, probing, brooding look at humankind's place in the universe and a counsel against smugness.

Carl Rollyson

Bibliography:

Costa, Richard Hauer. *H. G. Wells*. Rev. ed. Boston: Twayne, 1985. Praises the novel's vivid imagery, its superb characterizations, its antiutopian theme, Wells's scientific knowledge of life on Mars, and his extraordinary sociological grasp of his own times.

Hammond, J. R. *An H.G. Wells Companion: A Guide to the Novels, Romances, and Short Stories*. New York: Barnes & Noble Books, 1979. Describes Wells's ability to describe startling events happening to ordinary people, his remarkable anticipation of how crowds react to events of mass destruction, his superb evocation of actual settings, and his literary style. Includes a map showing the sites of the Martian invasion.

McConnell, Frank. *The Science Fiction of H. G. Wells*. New York: Oxford University Press, 1981. Compares the novel's themes to Wells's work as a scientific journalist. Discusses the narrative's image patterns, contrasting the novel with other tales of invasion, the uniqueness of Wells's description of the Martians, the role of the curate, and the relationship between realism and fantasy in Wells's fiction.

Mackenzie, Norman, and Jeanne MacKenzie. *The Life of H. G. Wells: The Time Traveller*. Rev. ed. London: Hogarth Press, 1987. Compares the novel to scientific theories of catastrophe and stories of the apocalypse. Emphasizes the moral tone of the novel, written at a time when there was much discussion of a decadent England.

Smith, David C. *H. G. Wells: Desperately Mortal*. New Haven, Conn.: Yale University Press, 1986. Emphasizes that the novel was written at a time when Germany was challenging England as a world power and invasion was on peoples' minds. Explains Wells's scientific knowledge, the precision of the plotting of the Martian invasion and of Wells's descriptions.

THE WARDEN

Type of work: Novel
Author: Anthony Trollope (1815-1882)
Type of plot: Social realism
Time of plot: Mid-nineteenth century
Locale: London and Barchester, a fictitious English cathedral town
First published: 1855

Principal characters:

THE REVEREND SEPTIMUS HARDING, the warden of Hiram's Hospital
ELEANOR HARDING, his young daughter
JOHN BOLD, a young physician
DR. GRANTLY, the husband of Mr. Harding's older daughter
TOM TOWERS, a newspaperman
SIR ABRAHAM HAPHAZARD, Mr. Harding's counsel

The Story:

At the age of fifty, the Reverend Septimus Harding was appointed precentor of Barchester Cathedral, a position that carried with it the wardenship of Hiram's Hospital. For more than four hundred years, this institution had provided a home for twelve men in their old age; since the income had grown to a considerable size, both the warden and the steward received substantial yearly salaries. With his income of eight hundred pounds a year, Mr. Harding was able to provide comfortably for his younger daughter, Eleanor. His older daughter, Susan, was married to Dr. Grantly, the archdeacon of the cathedral.

John Bold, a young physician with a small practice, turned his energies to reform. On investigation, he discovered that the will of John Hiram, the donor of the hospital, made no stipulation that would result in such a discrepancy as existed between the incomes of the warden and the steward and the incomes of the twelve inmates. Bold decided that it was his duty to bring the discrepancy to light. He engaged the interest of a newspaper friend, Tom Towers, and the services of a solicitor named Finney, who explained the situation to the inmates and encouraged them to think in terms of an annual income of as much as one hundred pounds a year. Most of them signed a petition addressed to the bishop, asking that justice be done.

When *The Jupiter*, for which Towers worked, began to publish editorials about the greediness of the Church and unscrupulous clergymen, Mr. Harding was distressed. It had never entered his head that he was living on an income not his by rights, and he began to talk of resigning. Eleanor agreed that if her father were unhappy at Hiram's Hospital, they would be better off at Crabtree Parva, a small parish that belonged to Mr. Harding and that paid an annual income of fifty pounds.

Dr. Grantly, a worldly man, would not hear of Mr. Harding's resignation. He insisted that the warden had an obligation to the church and to his fellow members of the clergy that required a firm stand against the laity and the press. Besides, as he pointed out, the living at Crabtree Parva could not procure a suitable match for Eleanor.

Dr. Grantly came to the hospital and addressed the inmates. He told them John Hiram had intended simply to provide comfortable quarters for old single men who had no other homes. Dr. Grantly's speech had little effect on anyone except John Bunce and two of his cronies. John

Bunce, who was especially close to Mr. Harding, served as the old men's subwarden. The others felt they had a right to a hundred pounds a year.

When Eleanor saw how unhappy the whole affair made her father, she begged him to resign. She also went to John Bold and begged him to give up the suit. After promising to do anything he could for her, Bold declared his love. Eleanor, who had not meant to let matters go so far, confessed that she loved him in return.

Bold went to see Dr. Grantly and told him that for reasons best known to himself he was withdrawing the charges he had made. Dr. Grantly replied that he did not think the defendants wished to have the suit withdrawn. He had been advised that Mr. Harding and the steward were, in effect, servants, and therefore were not responsible and could not be defendants in a suit.

Mr. Harding decided to go to London for a conference with Sir Abraham Haphazard, the counsel for the defense. Eleanor had come home expecting to tell her father all that Bold had told her, but she could not bring herself to discuss her own affairs before those of the wardenship had been settled. Mr. Harding had decided that he had no right to the income from Hiram's Hospital.

Bold also was going to London. When he arrived there, he went to Tom Towers and asked him not to print any more editorials about the Barchester situation. Towers said he could not be responsible for the attitude of *The Jupiter*. Bold then went to the offices of his lawyer and told him to drop the suit. The lawyer sent word to Sir Abraham.

Mr. Harding arrived in London and was given an appointment with Sir Abraham the next night at ten o'clock. He had explained his intention in a note to Dr. Grantly and now was afraid that Dr. Grantly would arrive in London before he had a chance to carry out his plan. He left his hotel at ten in the morning and spent most of the day in Westminster Abbey in order to avoid Dr. Grantly. That night, he told Sir Abraham that he must in all conscience resign his post as warden. When he returned to his hotel, he found Dr. and Mrs. Grantly waiting for him, but their arguments could not sway the warden. Back in Barchester, he wrote a formal letter of resignation to the bishop and sent a copy to Dr. Grantly.

The bishop offered him a position as chaplain in his household. Mr. Harding declined the offer. Then it was suggested that a trade be effected between Mr. Harding and Mr. Quiverful of Puddingdale. Mr. Quiverful, who had ten children, would be glad to double his annual income and would be impervious to any attacks from the press. Nevertheless, this arrangement also met with opposition, for Puddingdale was too far from Barchester for Mr. Harding to attend to his duties as precentor at the cathedral.

As the time for Mr. Harding's departure from Hiram's Hospital drew near, he called in all the inmates and had a last talk with them. They were disturbed—even those who had petitioned the bishop—for they knew that they were being deprived of a friendly and sympathetic warden.

Mr. Harding took lodgings and was given a tiny parish at the entrance to the cathedral close. His daughter Eleanor married John Bold. Mr. Harding's income continued to be ample for his needs. He dined frequently with the bishop and kept his violoncello at Eleanor's house, where he often went to make music. In short, Mr. Harding was not an unhappy man.

Critical Evaluation:

Anthony Trollope, one of the most prolific and popular Victorian novelists, began his successful Barchester series of six novels with *The Warden*, which was published in 1855. Trollope spent many years working for the civil service in the post office division, and only gradually made enough money by his writing to retire and write full-time. *The Warden* was his first financial success.

Trollope owes his success with readers and critics alike in part to his knowledge of ecclesiastical and political mores, his clever writing style, and the sympathy he shows for his characters and, indeed, for the human condition.

The story of *The Warden* is based very loosely on several ecclesiastical inquiries of Trollope's era, in which the Anglican church was accused of diverting monies from ancient endowments to the pockets of idle clergymen, thereby stinting the charitable purposes for which the endowments had been intended. Trollope's novel raises just such an ethical question, then complicates the issue by making the benefitting clergyman, Mr. Harding, the most honest and decent of men. Trollope states his own view of the matter through his narrator when he says, "In this world no good is unalloyed, and . . . there is but little evil that has not in it some seed of what is goodly."

Most of the characters in *The Warden* display this mixed quality. John Bold, the reformer, is zealous to do good but inadvertently injures Mr. Harding, whom he respects, whereas Archdeacon Grantly bullies and insults Mr. Harding, whom he purports to defend. Eleanor Harding assiduously defends her father to John Bold while furthering her own romance. The warden himself, in his humility and honesty, is the most consistent character. Harding, a cello-playing church mouse, ultimately faces down his church-militant son-in-law Grantly and resigns as warden of Hiram's Hospital, but, as Trollope predicted through his narrator, the twelve bedesmen who were his charges are worse off and no one has gained anything.

Trollope uses his knowledge of ecclesiastical minutiae, church and English politics, and journalism to good advantage in *The Warden*, bringing the reader to see that seemingly small points of dispute can matter more and affect more lives than such large events as wars and intrigue.

Trollope employs several chapters of *The Warden* to satirize fellow writers in the figures of Dr. Pessimist Anticant, who is intended to represent Thomas Carlyle, and Mr. Popular Sentiment, who represents Charles Dickens. He criticizes Dr. Anticant for instituting himself "censor of things in general" and being too hard on others, while noting that Mr. Sentiment fights an incredible number of evil practices by making "his good poor people . . . so very good [and] his hard rich people so very hard." He also takes a swipe at the Pre-Raphaelite painters for depicting overly ethereal subjects. Obviously these allusions to well-known figures of Trollope's own time were more easily understood and popular in Victorian England than they have been in subsequent eras.

The Warden is written from a third-person, omniscient point of view that includes many authorial asides to the reader in which Trollope asks the reader's opinion, chides the reader for a probable uncharitable response to happenings in his story, and makes whimsical comments. Trollope also employs a number of rhetorical devices to ironic or comic effect, including euphemism, oxymoron, and grotesque or startling anticlimax. The names of his characters are likewise a source of delight, ranging from Mr. Quiverful, father of twelve, to Sir Abraham Haphazard, Mr. Harding's fancy London lawyer. Like Trollope's other works, *The Warden* also contains many allusions to authors such as William Shakespeare, Dickens, and John Milton.

Trollope's narrator often writes with a divided voice in *The Warden*: He assumes a pseudo-naïve tone in describing one character or situation, then turns the tables by employing a worldly-wise phrase or two to describe the same subject, thereby letting the reader know he is not so naïve as he first appeared. The stylistic, rhetorical, and narrative techniques in the novel create comedy and irony as well as insight into character.

Trollope's interest in character transcended his concern for plot, descriptive detail and locale, although he was quite adept in establishing those as well. There is actually very little descriptive detail of places and things in *The Warden*, yet the reader has a vivid mental picture of the Barchester milieu. Trollope achieves this through his use of characterization. Archdeacon Grantly could expound his Tory, high-church convictions nowhere as well as in Plumstead Episcopi, and Mr. Harding lends descriptive presence to the rectory of Hiram's Hospital.

By studying the environs of Barchester and its denizens, Trollope invests *The Warden* with his central insight and theme, the mixed quality of most human endeavors and choices. Overfunded ecclesiastical preferments are irresponsible on the part of the Anglican church, yet Mr. Harding, who holds one of these sinecures, is a good and honest man. John Bold, Tom Towers, the newspaperman, and Hiram's bedesmen are zealous reformers, yet their reforms serve no useful end and do harm. Dr. Grantly maintains the prerogatives of the Anglican church, but he is little interested in justice within the church. Trollope looks at these creatures he devised with amused tolerance and, through them, warns his reader not to judge their fellows too hastily. *The Warden* instructs and gives insight into the human condition as it delights.

"Critical Evaluation" by Isabel B. Stanley

Bibliography:
Booth, Bradford A. *Anthony Trollope: Aspects of His Life and Art*. London: Edward Hulton, 1958. Contains a study of Trollope's religious beliefs and their impact on *The Warden* and subsequent ecclesiastical novels. Also examines the Church of England and its high and low wings.
Cockshut, A. O. J. *Anthony Trollope: A Critical Study*. New York: New York University Press, 1968. A study of Trollope and his times that gives the author's views on human nature, property and rank, families, religion and the clergy, death, politics, and love, all subjects that inform *The Warden*, the first of his Barchester novels.
Glendinning, Victoria. *Anthony Trollope*. New York: Alfred A. Knopf, 1993. Considered the standard late twentieth century biography of Trollope. Provides insight into the characters of Mr. Septimus Harding and Archdeacon Grantly. Connects the plot of *The Warden* to actual ecclesiastical scandals in the Victorian church.
Sadleir, Michael. *Trollope: A Commentary*. New York: Farrar, Straus, 1947. The author first produced with Frederick Page the uncorrupted Oxford edition of *The Warden*. In this study, Sadleir uses Trollope family papers and letters as well as contemporary reviews of *The Warden* to elucidate some of Trollope's sources as well as the initial reception of the book.
Skilton, David. *Anthony Trollope and His Contemporaries: A Study in the Theory and Conventions of Mid-Victorian Fiction*. New York: St. Martin's Press, 1972. Situates Trollope and *The Warden* in the mid-Victorian world in which they appeared. Shows their relationship to other authors such as Dickens and Thackeray.

WASHINGTON SQUARE

Type of work: Novel
Author: Henry James (1843-1916)
Type of plot: Psychological realism
Time of plot: c. 1850
Locale: New York City
First published: 1880

Principal characters:
DR. AUSTIN SLOPER, a prominent New York physician
CATHERINE SLOPER, his daughter
MRS. LAVINIA PENNIMAN, his sister
MORRIS TOWNSEND, Catherine's suitor

The Story:

Peace, especially of the domestic variety, became increasingly important to Dr. Sloper when he entered his fifties. Intelligent, poised, and distinguished in his profession, he was accustomed to meeting life on his terms. He had suffered the loss of his wife and a young son many years before, but the passage of time had softened this blow. Now he dwelt quietly and comfortably in his mansion on Washington Square with his only remaining child, Catherine, and his widowed sister, Mrs. Penniman.

Neither of his companions inspired the doctor with great fondness. His sister had just the sort of nature, incurably romantic, devious, and feminine, to set his teeth on edge; he saw her presence in his establishment as merely a necessary inconvenience to provide female supervision for his growing daughter. As to his daughter, Dr. Sloper thought Catherine was a good girl, but incurably dull. When she entered her twenties, she had never had a romantic interest or even the prospect of such. She was shyly fond of her father and very much afraid of him, especially when an ironical tone crept into his voice. He was, however, generally kind and courteous to her, though more self-contained than an adoring daughter might wish.

Catherine's taste for ornate dress was one of the characteristics that her father found especially trying. She had long cherished this taste without venturing to express it, but when she reached the age of twenty, she bought herself a red satin gown trimmed with gold fringe. Her father inwardly grimaced at the thought that a child of his should be both ugly and overdressed.

Catherine wore her red gown on the evening when she first met Morris Townsend. The occasion was a party, given by her aunt, Mrs. Almond. Catherine quickly became convinced that she had never met a young man so handsome, clever, and attentive. When his absorption with Catherine attracted notice, Townsend shifted his attentions to Mrs. Penniman, whose romantic sensibilities were soon aflutter with delight and anticipation. Before the evening ended, she had managed to intimate to this agreeable young man that he would be welcome to call in Washington Square.

Soon Townsend was in regular attendance on Catherine. Mrs. Penniman, undertaking the role of a middle-aged Cupid, pressed Townsend's claims and assisted his cause as ardently as she dared. Dr. Sloper, on the other hand, was at first skeptical and then became concerned. An interview with the young man strengthened his conviction that Townsend's charming manner was a mask for irresponsibility and selfishness. He suspected that Townsend was living off the

7045

meager resources of his sister, a widow with five children, and the doctor determined to investigate the matter. Before he could do so, however, Catherine told him that Morris Townsend had proposed to her and that she was anxious to accept him.

When his suspicions were confirmed by a talk with Townsend's sister, the doctor was more than ever convinced that Catherine's suitor was a fortune hunter. For once, however, his objections failed to sway the infatuated girl. As a last resort, Dr. Sloper declared that if Catherine married Townsend he would disinherit her. This measure would not leave her penniless by any means, since an inheritance from her mother would provide her a comfortable income, but it would reduce by two-thirds the amount Catherine would otherwise have been able to expect.

Mrs. Penniman, alarmed, counseled delay, and Townsend agreed to part with Catherine while she accompanied her father to Europe. Both Townsend and Mrs. Penniman hoped that time would soften the doctor's obdurate opposition to the match. Catherine, while agreeing to make the trip, cherished no such illusions. When she and her father returned several months later, the situation remained unchanged. Catherine was determined to go ahead with the marriage, but Townsend kept putting her off. One day, he vanished from New York altogether.

Years passed before she saw him again. By that time, Dr. Sloper had died and, fearful to the end that Townsend might reenter Catherine's life, had left his fortune to charity. One night, while Catherine was sitting quietly at home, there was a ring at the door. Morris Townsend had come back, secretly encouraged by the unwearying Mrs. Penniman. Bearded, heavier, and now forty-five years old, he was still fluent and personable; his manner made it clear that he expected a warm welcome in Washington Square. The lapse of twenty years might have taken much from him, including the European wife of whom Catherine had vaguely heard, but he had not lost the bright assurance with which he now waited for his words to work their old magic on Catherine's heart.

He stood, hat in hand, murmuring warm phrases, but Catherine did not ask him to sit down. She looked at him as if he were a stranger, repelling all advances and brushing off all explanations with a cool imperturbability that would have been worthy of the old doctor himself. For Catherine there was no longer any question of yielding to his charm: She had suffered too much. This time it would be she who sent him away. She dismissed him with a finality he had no choice but to accept and understand.

Critical Evaluation:

Henry James, discussing his novel *Washington Square* in a letter to his brother, stated that "the only good thing about the story is the girl." James, however, underestimated his book. The novel is a masterpiece in the interweaving of the moral and psychological dimensions with the influence of an economy-oriented society on the different characters. Catherine Sloper emerges as a woman who defies her overprotective father, who is a pillar of society, but her victory is a small one, for which she must pay a great price. Dr. Austin Sloper regards his daughter as a dull and unattractive heiress whose major function is to see to his welfare. She, however, awakens to the father's tyranny, to the fortune-hunting motives of her suitor, and to the meddling of her aunt, the three people she had loved and trusted. Catherine Sloper moves from her unthinking acceptance of the idea that as a woman she was inferior to a sense of self-worth that challenges the rigid value system of Washington Square.

Austin Sloper, a scholarly doctor who lives and works in the best society of New York City, is a local celebrity whose path to prosperity was made easier by his marriage. When after the death of his wealthy wife and young son Sloper is left with a disappointing daughter, he leaves her to the care of his widowed sister, Lavinia Penniman, whom he considers to be of "foolish indirectness and obliquity of character." He does not expect much from Catherine except devotion, but his intellectual pride makes him incapable of loving her. His own devotion to business leads him to think of Catherine as a marketable product, which means that she need only be "clever" in womanly ways—knowing how to dress and how to talk to gentlemen, and being efficient in knitting or embroidering.

Sloper is obsessed with his powerful social position and convinced of his intellect. He is proud of his ability to judge and categorize people, and he is convinced that Catherine, whom he considers "abnormally deficient" in intelligence, must be protected from fortune hunters. When Morris Townsend starts calling on her, Sloper is suspicious. His investigation reveals that Townsend is not a gentleman. He lives off his sister and has no money or prospects. Catherine, however, is not led by her father's warnings. Instead, encouraged by Mrs. Penniman, Townsend becomes for her the embodiment of romance. Her infatuation is stronger than her sense of duty to her father, and although Townsend is not romantically sincere, he awakens in Catherine her father's own selfishness. She begins to see that he does not treat her well, especially during the European tour that Sloper intended as a means of cooling her relationship with Townsend. When he abandons his daughter in the Alps, after she refuses to give up her suitor, the doctor goes too far. According to Dr. Sloper's economic view, the trip should make Catherine more valuable in the marketplace, but since she insists that Townsend be the buyer, he changes his will to make her less of a financial asset.

When Catherine observes that her father is a cold man of business and intellectual pride, she accepts her economic loss without regret and resolves to marry Morris Townsend immediately. When Townsend reneges on his promises, Catherine refuses to give her father the satisfaction of knowing that she was jilted. She also refuses to promise Sloper that she will never marry Townsend, but when Mrs. Penniman, not understanding the change in her surrogate daughter, brings Townsend back years later for another chance at marriage, Catherine is morally outraged.

Catherine Sloper wins the battle of money and sex, but it kills her ability to love. Betrayed by the three people she loved, she learns merely to "fill the void." She becomes a "kindly maiden-aunt" to girls who confide in her, and she is an "inevitable figure at all respectable entertainments." She tolerates her meddling aunt, who continues to live with her in the fashionable house in Washington Square. Catherine grows from what her father considered a dull girl into a perceptive woman who does what she thinks is right. Yet, she feels that the "great facts" of her career were that Morris Townsend had trifled with her affection, and that her father had broken its spring. Catherine is not able to break entirely from the confinements of her world, but she does confront the wrongdoings of her father and her suitor. She does not yield to the hypocrisy of society. Though she does not change that society, she is aware of the inner transformation that gives her a sense of accomplishment.

Dr. Sloper is right about Morris Townsend, but he is a victim of his pride. He is so obsessed with his sense of power, including his assumed rationality, that he is able to love only himself. He labels his daughter an inferior product and exults in dominating her. Her rebellion becomes an entertainment for him, but he underestimates her. His confidence in himself and in socio-economic prevalence blinds him to the change in Catherine, and he is unaware of the prejudices that limit him and make him morally inferior to Catherine.

In *Washington Square*, James focuses on Catherine Sloper's efforts to attain an identity in an environment dominated by men like her father. By challenging a value system that protects and promotes male superiority, she proves Dr. Sloper wrong.

"Critical Evaluation" by Noel Schraufnagel

Bibliography:

Hall, Donald. "Afterword." In *Washington Square*, by Henry James. New York: New American Library, 1980. Stresses the moral dilemma represented by Dr. Sloper's role as both protector and antagonist of his daughter.

Hoffman, Charles G. *The Short Novels of Henry James*. New York: Bookman Associates, 1957. Discusses the dramatic structure of the book, which was influenced by its serial publication in *Cornhill Magazine* and *Harper's New Monthly Magazine*.

Hutchinson, Stuart. *Henry James: An American as Modernist*. London: Vision Press, 1983. Treats the book as James's attempt to discover a historical tradition for American literature, which he thought did not share the European sense of belonging to a civilized order.

Samuels, Charles Thomas. *The Ambiguity of Henry James*. Urbana: University of Illinois Press, 1971. An analysis of James's use of irony to illustrate Catherine Sloper's integrity. Compares Dr. Sloper's fascination with observing innocence to that of the governess in James's *The Turn of the Screw* (1898).

Willen, Gerald, ed. *Washington Square: The Crowell Critical Library*. New York: Thomas Y. Crowell, 1970. A casebook with fourteen critical entries, including excerpts from books on James by Joseph Warren Beach, Edwin T. Bowden, Richard Poirier, Leon Edell, and Maxwell Geismar. Also includes four new essays, the most enlightening being Leo Gurko's analysis of the distortion of personality by a dominant trait.

THE WASPS

Type of work: Drama
Author: Aristophanes (c. 450-c. 385 B.C.E.)
Type of plot: Satire
Time of plot: Fifth century B.C.E.
Locale: Athens
First performed: Sphēkes, 422 B.C.E. (English translation, 1812)

> *Principal characters:*
> PHILOCLEON, an Athenian
> BDELYCLEON, his son
> SOSIAS and
> XANTHIAS, slaves of Philocleon
> CHORUS OF WASPS

The Story:

Afflicted with a constant desire to judge and to convict the people brought before the courts of Athens, Philocleon was locked up in his own house by his son, Bdelycleon, who had previously tried all rational means of persuading his father to give up his mania and become a gentleman. Bdelycleon even resorted to a net cast around the house in order to keep his father from leaving. Two slaves, Sosias and Xanthias, were set to guard the house, and Bdelycleon, as an added precaution, watched from the roof.

The three men were kept busy thwarting Philocleon's attempts to escape. He tried to crawl out through the chimney, threatened to chew his way through the net, and, at last, was almost successful when he crawled beneath the belly of his ass, in the manner of Odysseus, and then insisted that the beast be taken out and sold. The ass moaned and groaned so intently, however, that Xanthias noticed the concealed burden. Philocleon was caught and thrust back into the house just before the other jurymen, the Wasps, arrived to escort him to the courts.

When the Wasps arrived, Philocleon appeared at an upper window, told them of his plight, and begged them to help him find some means of escape. Between them they decided that his only hope was to gnaw through the net and then lower himself to the ground. In this manner Philocleon had all but regained his freedom when Bdelycleon, who, worn out with watching, had fallen asleep, awoke and again detained him. Although the Wasps quickly came to the aid of their friend, they were no match for the stones and clubs used against them by Bdelycleon and the two slaves; and they were soon driven back.

In the argument that followed Bdelycleon explained that he simply wanted his father to lead the joyous, easy life of an old man, rather than concern himself constantly with the tyranny and conspiracy of the courts. He argued convincingly enough to force Philocleon into a debate on the merits of his occupation. Philocleon agreed that if Bdelycleon could convince the Wasps, who were to act as judges, that a public career was disreputable, then he would give it up. The old man, speaking first, defended the jury system on the basis of the pleasures and benefits that he personally derived from it. Bdelycleon, on the other hand, proved that the jurists were no more than the slaves of the rulers, who themselves received the bulk of the revenue that should have gone to feed the hungry people.

Philocleon, along with the Chorus, was converted by Bdelycleon's persuasive argument. Philocleon thought that he could not live without judging, however, so Bdelycleon consented to allow him to hold court at their home. Philocleon was to be allowed to judge the slaves and all other things about the house. This solution had the added advantage, as Bdelycleon carefully pointed out, of allowing Philocleon to eat and drink and enjoy all the comforts of home at the same time that he was following his profession.

Philocleon agreed to this solution and all the paraphernalia of a court were quickly assembled and the first case was called. Labes, one of the household dogs, was accused of stealing and devouring a Sicilian cheese all by himself, having refused to share it with any other animal. Bdelycleon himself undertook the defense of Labes and pleaded for mercy, but Philocleon felt it his duty as a judge to convict everyone and everything that was brought into his court. His son, however, tricked his father into acquitting the dog, an act that was foreign to Philocleon's nature.

Philocleon then concluded that he had betrayed the one thing sacred to him—reaching a guilty verdict—and that he was, therefore, no longer capable of judging. Bdelycleon's problems were apparently solved at this point, for his father agreed to live a happy and carefree life. Such a plan, however, entailed changing Philocleon's whole mode of being. His manner of dress, his speech—everything about him had to change; in short, he needed to acquire at least some of the elementary social skills. He was to learn how to walk, how to recline at dinner, what to talk about in order to appear a gentleman of leisure.

After a short period of training Bdelycleon took his father to a dinner party, where Philocleon quickly proved that he was as much a hard-headed old man as ever. He drank and ate too much, he insulted both his host and the other guests, he beat the slaves who waited on him, and, finally, he ran off with a nude flute girl. On his way home with the girl he struck everyone that he encountered.

By the time Philocleon arrived home, he had a large following, all anxious to accuse him and bring him before those courts he had so recently abandoned. He tried to appease the people by telling them stories that he had just learned and by using his other social skills, but to no avail; everyone clamored for justice. Philocleon, paying no attention to their cries, continued to talk and act as if he were far above such plebeian concerns. Bdelycleon, who had hurried after his father, finally caught up with him and again used force to get him into the house. This time Bdelycleon was unable to keep the old man there. Philocleon immediately returned to the streets, now determined to prove his dancing skill, and led off the Chorus in a licentious, drunken dance.

Critical Evaluation:

The Wasps is a brilliant combination of political and social satire. Produced in 422 B.C.E., this play, like Aristophanes' earlier work, is an attack on Aristophanes' personal enemy Cleon, who in Aristophanes' plays is a demagogue and a manipulator of the Athenian people. In this play Aristophanes does not criticize Cleon for advocating continuation of the Peloponnesian War (431-404 B.C.E.), which was in a temporary lull at the time the play was presented. Instead, Cleon's supposed control of the democratic juries is the focus of the playwright's scorn. The poet's criticism reaches beyond the person of Cleon to the whole institution of popular juries, making *The Wasps* an important historical document regarding contemporary attitudes toward this Athenian institution. *The Wasps* is, however, more than a political critique. Its plot revolves around a single elderly juror whose son wishes to cure the old man's addiction to jury service. *The Wasps* is a brilliant social satire, partly as a result of its clever depiction of tensions between young and old and between rich and poor in Athenian society.

The system of trial by popular jury was a hallmark of Athenian democracy and one of Athens' unique contributions to the world. Most lawsuits were heard by large juries, sometimes composed of more than five hundred volunteers, whose only qualifications were to possess Athenian citizenship and to be over thirty years of age. For their service on juries participants received a small sum, too small to make jury service attractive to most, but enough to enlist the very indigent, infirm, or elderly. Juries were therefore largely peopled by such individuals. The Athenians stubbornly maintained the fiction that the popular juries were representative of the people as a whole. The continuing relevance of this issue is clear. From their verdicts there was no appeal, no matter how capricious or unjust the decision. This background is necessary for understanding the thrust of Aristophanes' comedy. The play suggests that Cleon, by promising greater pay or otherwise manipulating the verdicts of popular juries, exercised undue influence over the courts. Cleon claimed that he was merely acting as the watchdog of Athens, but others like Aristophanes apparently saw his activities as another aspect of his vulgar and dangerous political ambition.

One way that Aristophanes makes his topical political satire explicit is by naming his crazed juryman Philocleon ("Cleon-lover") and his son Bdelycleon ("Cleon-hater"). Philocleon, who has retired from working his farm and has handed over his estate to his son, is in some respects a stereotype of the kind of juryman whom Cleon supposedly could control: He is elderly, he counts on his small income from jury service, and most of all he is drunk with the power he possesses as a jury member over rich and poor alike. All the same, Aristophanes does not depict Philocleon, who is the protagonist of the play, as a mindless stooge. He is extremely clever in frustrating the efforts of his son to curb his appetite for jury duty, and as he articulates the pleasures of sitting in judgment, one is inclined to sympathize with him. On the other hand, although Bdelycleon seems perfectly justified in trying to free his father from his unusual obsession, he appears as a staid, personality free, and generally much less sympathetic character than his father. That Aristophanes probably shared the political views of the less attractive character is testimony to his outstanding ability as a comic writer.

The Wasps is unique among the surviving plays of Aristophanes in that it contains all of the formal parts of a Greek comedy that scholars consider to be the traditional constituents of the genre. In particular, the play contains a fully developed contest (*agon*) in which the merits and defects of the Athenian jury system are debated. The appearance of the chorus, dressed as wasps equipped with a fearsome sting with which to strike at litigants, means that Philocleon will have support in his advocacy of the joys of jury service. Like Philocleon, the chorus is composed of poor, elderly men who enjoy the feeling of power that comes with passing judgment over those who stand before them as litigants or defendants. In taking the opposite side in the debate, Bdelycleon can only argue that they are duped by individuals like Cleon. Bdelycleon then openly appeals to their greed and barely manages to win the debate by persuading Philocleon and the chorus that they are poorly compensated for their heroic efforts.

The purpose of the formal debate is to free Philocleon from his obsession; but interestingly enough this object is not accomplished by the end of the contest. Philocleon only agrees to transfer the apparatus of the court to his own home. This is indicative of the strong and stubborn character of Philocleon. At his home the mock trial of the dog by Cuon (Greek for "dog"; the word also sounds like "Cleon") takes place, recalling Cleon's statement that he was the watchdog of Athens and incidentally revealing in the midst of the parody little-known aspects of the workings of the Athenian system of justice. The dog is acquitted of the crime because Bdelycleon sophistically marshals all the manipulative power of oratory in defense of his client, who can only bark. The outcome—it is implied that Philocleon has never before voted for acquittal—is a disturbing revelation. Philocleon is free to give himself to new pleasures that are supposedly more appropriate to his age and status. A rejuvenated Philocleon leaves jury duty behind and indulges in food, drink, and sex to his heart's content. *The Wasps* ends with such a burst of riotous celebration that one may suspect, in the view of the proper Bdelycleon, his father's cure is perhaps worse than the original disease.

"Critical Evaluation" by John M. Lawless

Bibliography:
Aristophanes. *Wasps*. Edited and translated by Alan H. Sommerstein. Warminster, Wiltshire, England: Aris & Phillips, 1983. Provides scholarly introduction, bibliography, Greek text, facing English translation, and commentary keyed to the translation. Sommerstein's translation supersedes most earlier versions.

Dover, K. J. *Aristophanic Comedy*. Berkeley: University of California Press, 1972. Useful and authoritative study of the plays of Aristophanes. Chapter 9 provides a synopsis of the play, discussion of problems with theatrical production, a discussion of the character of Philocleon, and relevant information on the Athenian courts. An essential starting point for study of the play.

Harriott, Rosemary M. *Aristophanes: Poet and Dramatist*. Baltimore: The Johns Hopkins University Press, 1986. A recent study of all the plays of Aristophanes. The plays are discussed not in individual chapters but as each illustrates the central themes and techniques of Aristophanes' work.

Spatz, Lois. *Aristophanes*. Boston: Twayne, 1978. A reliable introduction to the comedy of Aristophanes for the general reader. Chapter 4 summarizes the play and offers discussion of the plot and the major themes.

Whitman, Cedric. *Aristophanes and the Comic Hero*. Cambridge, Mass.: Harvard University Press, 1964. A standard work on the characterization of the Aristophanic protagonist. Chapter 4 discusses *The Wasps*, with special emphasis on the generational conflict depicted by the play.

THE WASTE LAND

Type of work: Poetry
Author: T. S. Eliot (1888-1965)
First published: 1922

Thomas Stearns Eliot, together with Ezra Pound, revolutionized the style and structure of poetry in the early twentieth century. Eliot was a modernist poet who, as Ezra Pound claimed, had modernized himself. His reading of the French Symbolists, especially Jules Laforgue, and such seventeenth century metaphysical poets as John Donne gave him models for the use of precise imagery and complex structures that contrasted with the softness of late Romantic poetry. With his first book of poems, *Prufrock and Other Observations* (1915), a new voice appeared in poetry.

Eliot was very successful as a poet and critic in his early years in London. He completed a Ph.D. dissertation on F. H. Bradley, the philosopher (though he never returned to Harvard to defend it), and in 1915 married Vivienne Haig Wood. The marriage was unhappy, however, and in 1921 Eliot entered a sanatorium in Switzerland to recover from a nervous breakdown. It was during this disturbed period of his life that he wrote *The Waste Land*. Later that year, Eliot gave the poem to Ezra Pound, who cut it by half into its current form. Eliot's original title for the poem was *He Do the Police in Different Voices*, but Pound preferred emphasizing the mythic structure and cut the social satire. Upon publication in 1922, the poem was immediately recognized as a major if very difficult creation. The poet later described *The Waste Land* as "the relief of a personal and wholly insignificant grouse against life; it is just a piece of rhythmical grumbling." It was read by most critics, however, as a social indictment rather than a personal utterance.

The poem begins with an epigraph from Petronius and a dedication to Ezra Pound as *il miglior fabbro* (the better maker), the tribute paid by Arnaut Daniel to Dante in *Purgatory* of *The Divine Comedy* (c. 1320). The epigraph portrays the Cumean Sibyl responding to the question "Sibyl, what do you want?" with the answer "I want to die." This sets the mood of despair and hopeless resignation. In portraying the spiritual, sexual, and social emptiness of the post-World War I world, Eliot drew on Jessie L. Weston's *From Ritual to Romance* (1920), on the medieval quest for the Grail, and James Frazer's *The Golden Bough* (1890-1915), especially the sections on a dying god who is resurrected. From its inception, the poem was centrally concerned with the myth of a dead land that needs to be renewed by a quester or a sacrificial god.

The first section of the poem, "The Burial of the Dead," is a reference to the burial service in the Anglican church. The time is April, but instead of being a period of renewal it is "the cruelest month." The outer renewal of the seasons is not matched by that within the speakers and characters in the poem. The imagery shifts to the dryness of the wasteland, a place

> . . . where the sun beats,
> And the dead tree gives no shelter, the cricket no relief,
> And the dry stone no sound of water.

The imagery of dryness becomes a central motif in the poem and is used to define the spiritual and social aridity of the time.

Knowledge and authority in this decayed world are found in "Madame Sosostris, famous clairvoyante" and her pack of tarot cards rather than in the church or state. One of the cards in that deck, "the man with three staves," represents the Fisher King, the wounded ruler whose disease causes the wasteland; the disease can only be relieved by the quester for the Holy Grail who successfully answers ritual questions at the Chapel Perilous. His answers complete the quest and bring fertility to the land. In the last part of this section, Eliot portrays the "Unreal City," an allusion to Charles Baudelaire, with a crowd of dead crossing London Bridge and a corpse that is planted, which will not bloom or provide relief—a parody of renewal. The world of the wasteland is dominated by the living dead.

In the next section, "A Game of Chess," Eliot explores the social world of the wasteland. First, he shows a nervous society woman who isolates herself among the "glitter of jewels" and "synthetic perfumes." Her social life is a substitute for a meaningful one, her routine consists of "The hot water at ten./ And if it rains, a closed car at four." The social world depicted here is similar to the fearful and frustrated world of "The Love Song of J. Alfred Prufrock."

The section ends with a descent into a London pub where two women from the lower class discuss the return of Lil's husband, Albert, from the war. He "wants a good time" upon his return, but Lil has no teeth, and she is a wreck since she took "them pills to bring it off," a reference to her abortion. The sordid scene of sexual and personal sterility is presented in counterpoint with allusions to Ophelia's farewell in William Shakespeare's *Hamlet* (c. 1600-1601). Eliot consistently juxtaposes the decayed present with the heroic past, using allusions to the Bible, Shakespeare, Richard Wagner, and other great sources of the past.

"The Fire Sermon," the third section, is an allusion to the sermon preached by the Buddha against the fires of lust. Here, Eliot continues his analysis of the arid, meaningless sexuality that fails to bring life or renewal. He begins with negative images of the river Thames:

> The river bears no empty bottles, sandwich papers,
> silk handkerchiefs, cardboard boxes, cigarette ends
> Or other testimony of summer nights. The nymphs are departed.

Eliot juxtaposes the sordid modern river with Edmund Spenser's marriage song, "Prothalamion." He also refers to the Fisher King, who is "fishing in the dull canal" and whom he merges with an allusion to the passage in Shakespeare's *The Tempest* (1611) in which Ferdinand mourns the supposed death of his father. The song by Ariel to Ferdinand suggests a process in which the bones of his father are metamorphosed into beautiful objects such as "pearls." Eliot contrasts these positive images of metamorphosis with the death-in-life of his world.

Positive allusions are also contrasted with the homosexual proposal of Mr. Eugenides and the mechanical sexual scene between the carbuncular clerk and the typist. The sexual scene is mediated by Eliot's use of Tiresias, the blind Greek prophet. Eliot claimed that "Tiresias, although a mere spectator and not indeed a 'character,' is yet the most important personage in the poem, uniting all the rest. . . . What Tiresias *sees*, in fact, is the substance of the poem." What Tiresias sees in that passage is the clerk engaging a "bored and tired" young typist in a sexual liaison that she neither desires nor resists. "His vanity requires no response." At the completion of the meaningless, mechanical act, she says, "Well now that's done: and I'm glad its over."

These scenes are followed by one of the most positive images in the poem: There is music in a bar on Lower Thames Street "where fishmen lounge at noon." Eliot expands the allusion to the Fisher King with a reference to a London church, Magnus Martyr, where the walls "hold/ Inexplicable splendor of Ionian white and gold." This is then contrasted with the recurring images of the river that "sweats oil and tar." Another sexual interlude is contrasted with the glorious past, this time with an allusion to Queen Elizabeth sailing on the Thames with her favorite, Essex. After the sexual act, "He wept, He promised 'a new start.' I made no comment.

What should I resent." The section ends with images of burning and of the fires of lust not purged in the poem, slightly mitigated by an allusion to Saint Augustine, who achieved a purgation of these fires by asking God to deliver him from its ravages.

The fourth section of the poem is as brief as it became controversial. It deals with the death of "Phlebas the Phoenician," who drowns in water rather than being renewed by it, and ends with a warning of the transitoriness of life:

> Gentile or Jew
> O you who turn the wheel to winward,
> Consider Phlebas, who was once handsome and tall as you.

This passage resembles the burial of the body earlier, for this death, too, even though it is by water, brings no renewal.

The last section of the poem, "What the Thunder Said," begins with imagery associated with the Passion of Christ. Eliot chooses to show the death of Christ rather than his resurrection, but even that is preferable to death-in-life.

> He who was living is now dead
> We who were living are now dying
> With a little patience.

This is followed by images of dryness and an allusion to the appearance of Christ to the disciples at Emmaus.

After an allusion to Hermann Hesse's *In Sight of Chaos* (1923), which portrays the situation of Eastern Europe, the poem moves to the "empty chapel" where the quester passes the last test in the search for the Grail. This leads to the change to which the poem has been pointing from the beginning:

> Only a cock stood on the rooftree
> Co rico co rico
> In a flash of lightning. Then a damp gust
> Bringing rain.

The imagery of rain presumably renews the wasteland. Eliot then turns to the renewal of the individual, using allusions from yet another tradition, the Indian *Upanishads*. He cites the three principles of renewal from that text: give, control, and sympathize. Control can be achieved, but the other principles have yet to become a part of the individual's life. Each individual remains locked within himself, unable to give to others or sympathize with their plight.

The poem ends with images of leaving the wasteland behind:

> I sat upon the shore
> Fishing, with the arid plain behind me
> Shall I at least set my lands in order?

The only order that can be brought about is through a baffling series of allusions and the limited assent: "These fragments I have shored against my ruins." The last lines again refer to the principles of individual renewal from the *Upanishads* and to the *Upanishads'* ending, "Shantih," which Eliot translates in a footnote as "The Peace that passeth understanding." This blessing expresses a desire for enlightenment and peace, but in the poem it is only cited, not achieved.

The Waste Land was recognized soon after its publication as a tremendously important work, one that both defined an attitude toward the period and established a model for other poets to follow. It was believed at the time that poetry needed to be complex, difficult, and filled with allusions to earlier writers, that its structure needed to be mythic and its style a dazzling juxtaposition of elements. The expectations and social role of poetry continually change, but *The Waste Land* continues to be regarded as a monumental achievement that challenges and rewards its readers.

James Sullivan

Bibliography:
Bergonzi, Bernard. "Allusion in *The Waste Land*." *Essays in Criticism* 20, no. 3 (July, 1970): 382-385. An important analysis of Eliot's use of both high and low allusions in the poem.
Brooks, Cleanth, Jr. "*The Waste Land*: An Analysis." *Southern Review* 3, no. 1 (1937-1938): 106-136. An influential New Critical reading of the poem that draws out the complexities and the ironic structure.
Canary, Robert H. *T. S. Eliot: The Poet and His Critics*. Chicago: American Library Association, 1982. A thorough bibliography on the poet and his works and a series of bibliographical essays that discuss various critics who have dealt with Eliot's criticism and poetry.
Frye, Northrop. *T. S. Eliot*. New York: Grove Press, 1963. An analysis of Eliot's works primarily the critical perspective of myth. Excellent conclusions on the archetypal aspects of *The Waste Land*.
Kenner, Hugh, ed. *T. S. Eliot: A Collection of Critical Essays*. Englewood Cliffs, N.J: Prentice-Hall, 1962. A useful collection of essays, part of the Twentieth Century Views series. Contains a number of important essays, including three on *The Waste Land*.
Williamson, George. *A Reader's Guide to T. S. Eliot*. New York: Noonday Press, 1953. A close reading of all of Eliot's poems, with a useful introduction to the interpretative problems of *The Waste Land*.

WATCH ON THE RHINE

Type of work: Drama
Author: Lillian Hellman (1905-1984)
Type of plot: Melodrama
Time of plot: Late spring, 1940
Locale: Twenty miles outside of Washington, D.C.
First performed: 1941; first published, 1941

Principal characters:
> FANNY FARRELLY, a dowager matriarch
> DAVID, her thirty-nine-year-old son, a lawyer
> SARA MULLER, her forty-year-old daughter
> KURT, Sara's German husband, an anti-Nazi resistance fighter
> JOSHUA, their fourteen-year-old son
> BABETTE, their twelve-year-old daughter
> BODO, their nine-year-old son
> COUNT TECK DE BRANCOVIS, a ne'er-do-well European refugee
> COUNTESS MARTHE DE BRANCOVIS, his wife and a daughter of Fanny's
>   childhood friend
> ANISE, Fanny's French housekeeper
> JOSEPH, Fanny's African American butler

The Story:

In the aristocratic Farrelly home outside Washington, D.C., Fanny Farrelly, with the assistance of her two servants, was prepared for the arrival of her daughter, Sara, and her husband and children. Sara had not visited her for twenty years, and Fanny had never met the three children. Nervous about the visit, Fanny tried to get her son, David, and her houseguests, the Count and Countess Teck and Marthe Brancovis, to breakfast by nine, as her late husband had decreed. Her gossip with her housekeeper, Anise, revealed that the Count and Countess were heavily in debt and that Fanny was concerned about David's attraction to Marthe. When Fanny and David went to the outside terrace for breakfast, Teck and Marthe argued about money, about his intention to gamble with the Nazis at the German embassy, and about his jealousy that she might be attracted to David.

After the Count and Countess retired to the terrace, the Mullers entered. They had arrived several hours before they were expected because they had taken an earlier and cheaper train. Their reaction to the spacious livingroom made it clear that they were not accustomed to such luxury. Sara, poorly dressed, was delighted by the beautiful things she had not remembered. The family discussed the differences between the lifestyle that Sara remembered from her childhood, with its unlocked doors, plentiful food, and beautiful clothes, and their own bleaker existence.

The reunion was a happy one. The children so impressed Fanny with their maturity that she asked Sara, "Are these your *children*? Or are they dressed up midgets?" Responding to Fanny's and David's questions, Kurt told of his family's travels and revealed that he had not worked at his profession as an engineer since 1933. He confessed that his family has not had "adequate breakfasts" because his new occupation, which he identified as "Anti-Fascist," did not pay well. He had worked as an engineer and had lived a normal, quiet life for twelve years after he and

Sara were married, but this changed when a festival in his home town ended with a street fight and the murder of twenty-seven men by Nazis.

Kurt and Teck were wary of each other. Kurt recognized the Count's name, and Teck probed to find out more about Kurt. When the family went to the terrace for breakfast, Teck examined their luggage, then told Joseph that Fanny wanted him to take the luggage upstairs. When Marthe objected to this lie, Teck threatened her. She was not to interfere and not to make any plans with David.

At the opening of Act II, ten days had passed. The family had become comfortable in the house, and the scene was relaxed, with Sara crocheting, Fanny and Teck playing cribbage, Bodo "repairing" a heating pad for an anxious Anise, Joseph teaching Joshua to play baseball, and Babette making potato pancakes for dinner. When Teck questioned the children in an obvious attempt to learn more about their father, tensions rose and Sara cut him off, saying, "It's an indulgence to sit in a room and discuss your beliefs as if they were a juicy piece of gossip."

Teck revealed that he and Marthe planned to leave in a few days and suggested that the nature of Kurt's work meant that the Mullers would also be moving on. Fanny objected, joking that she planned to keep them there for several years as she took a long time to die. David and Kurt returned from assisting a local farmer, and talk turned to Babette's birthday party and presents for the whole family. When Teck became angry at the suggestion that David had bought jewelry for Marthe, Fanny tried to distract him by confronting him with the rumor that he had won a great deal of money in a card game with Nazis.

Kurt and Teck sparred about Germany and Kurt sang "Watch on the Rhine," a song German soldiers had sung on their return from World War I. He also sang lyrics made up by Germans with whom he had fought against the fascists in Spain. When Teck again started to question the children about Kurt's activities, Kurt told him to address his questions directly to him.

The atmosphere was temporarily lightened when Marthe entered with dresses that Fanny had bought for Sara and Babette, but the pleasant scene was interrupted by a long distance phone call for Kurt. Teck, Marthe, and David argued about David's gift to Marthe. She declared she would not leave with Teck, insisting David did not have much to do with her situation. When Fanny objected to her staying, Marthe informed her that she had been forced by her mother into the marriage with Teck when she was only seventeen and that it had always been an unhappy relationship.

When Kurt returned from the call, saying he must leave for California, Teck confronted him with a news story on the capture of three of Kurt's resistance colleagues in Germany. Teck had learned of the capture at the German embassy the previous evening, and upon reviewing a list of resistance fighters that the Nazis had given him, he had made the connection between Kurt and a man called Gotter, whom the Nazis wanted. Revealing that he had broken into Kurt's briefcase and knew that Kurt had $23,000 in cash, Teck demanded $10,000 of it in blackmail money.

David and Fanny insisted that Kurt not submit to the blackmail because they did not believe Teck could harm anyone in their safe American home. Kurt, however, revealed that he belonged to an organization that had been outlawed by the Nazis and that they had placed a price on his head. As a result he had had problems with his passport and could not go to the American authorities. Sara realized that Kurt had to return to Germany to buy friends out of the German prisons, though this would involve great risks for him. The act ended with her comforting Kurt and clearly supporting his decision.

Act III opened half an hour later, with Kurt, Sara, Fanny, and David waiting anxiously for Teck to return. Kurt used the opportunity to dispute the idea that Nazis were supermen. He told them about his imprisoned friend Max, who at one time had saved Kurt's life. Teck returned with Kurt's briefcase, but when Kurt refused to pay the blackmail money, Fanny and David decided they would do so. With them out of the way, Kurt overpowered Teck and took him outside, where he killed him.

Kurt explained his actions to David and Fanny, who accepted the violence as necessary and admired Kurt's struggle and sacrifices. Emotion-laden farewells followed. Kurt's farewell to his children was especially moving as he spoke of men who loved children and fought to make a "good world" for them. Fanny and David were left alone, "shaken out of the magnolias" and bracing for the trouble they knew would come when Teck's body was discovered.

Critical Evaluation:

Lillian Hellman's *Watch on the Rhine* is generally considered the best of the anti-Nazi plays of the 1930's and 1940's, primarily because Hellman wrapped her political message in a character drama that focuses on several positive and likeable characters. Kurt Muller, her protagonist, is not only a heroic and principled resistance fighter but also a loved husband and father. Hellman has been praised for making her protagonist a German, by which means she could have Muller assess the Nazis from the point of view of one inside the culture that had nurtured both him and them.

Sara and the Muller children appeal to the audience because they share Kurt's idealism and willingness to sacrifice for the long-term good of Germany and the world. Their suffering is anticipated when they bid Kurt farewell not knowing whether they will ever see him again.

The play contains a surprising amount of humor, most of it revolving around Fanny and her attempts at controlling and judging her family and servants. (The stereotyped French maid and African American butler are problematic, but Hellman portrays them as assertive and capable.)

Hellman's purpose in writing this play, which she began in 1939, was to awaken American awareness to the growing Nazi threat. A major theme is the necessity for each person to take responsibility for making and carrying through ethical choices. Hellman clearly believes that the death of fascism is more important than the comfort and well-being of those who hate and fight it. The choice not to act can have devastating effects, and even a country house belonging to a wealthy American family is not safe. Hellman's play argues strongly in favor of action, and she implies that a nonviolent and idealistic person may on occasion have no alternative to violence. Although the issues that Hellman addresses in this play are not likely ever to be completely resolved, she defined the circumstances of *Watch on the Rhine* so narrowly that despite the play's many strengths, it received relatively little critical attention since the close of World War II.

Elsie Galbreath Haley

Bibliography:

Estrin, Mark W. *Critical Essays on Lillian Hellman.* Boston: G. K. Hall, 1989. Contains twenty-three essays discussing three main topics—Hellman's plays, her memoirs, and "the Hellman persona." Of special interest are Jacob H. Adler's essay, in which he discusses blackmail in *Watch on the Rhine* and other Hellman plays, and Timothy J. Wills's article, which examines Hellman's political plays and her attitudes toward war.

Gurko, Leo. *The Angry Decade: American Literature and Thought from 1929 to Pearl Harbor.* New York: Harper-Calophon Books, 1967. Gurko discusses the political influence of *Watch on the Rhine.* He considers Hellman the best dramatic poet of the period.

Holman, Lorena Ross. *The Dramatic Works of Lillian Hellman*. Stockholm, Sweden: Uppsala, 1973. An accessible source for beginners, this book contains a chapter on *Watch on the Rhine* that analyzes characters and structure in detail. Also includes an extensive bibliography with journal and newspaper articles and reviews.

Lederer, Katherine. *Lillian Hellman*. Boston: Twayne, 1979. A detailed overview of Hellman's life, plays, and nonfiction. Includes a selected bibliography of both primary sources (plays, collections of plays, memoirs) and secondary sources. In the discussion of *Watch on the Rhine*, Lederer takes issue with those who see its importance primarily in the character of Kurt Muller, arguing instead that the play concerns multiple characters and as such will remain relevant.

Riordan, Mary Marguerite. *Lillian Hellman: A Bibliography, 1926-1978*. Metuchen, N.J.: The Scarecrow Press, 1980. An extensive annotated bibliography that focuses on the wide variety of Hellman's writing, including her contributions to newspapers and periodicals, and provides an index of letters, manuscripts, and recordings. The detailed index gives numbered references for each play.

WAVERLEY
Or, 'Tis Sixty Years Since

Type of work: Novel
Author: Sir Walter Scott (1771-1832)
Type of plot: Historical
Time of plot: 1745
Locale: England and Scotland
First published: 1814

Principal characters:
EDWARD WAVERLEY, a young English officer
BARON BRADWARDINE, a Scottish nobleman
ROSE BRADWARDINE, the baron's daughter
EVAN DHU MACCOMBICH, a follower of Fergus Mac Ivor
DONALD BEAN LEAN, a Highland bandit
FERGUS MAC IVOR VICH IAN VOHR, the leader of the clan of Mac Ivor
FLORA MAC IVOR, Fergus' sister
PRINCE CHARLES EDWARD STUART, the Young Pretender

The Story:
The English family of Waverley had long been known for its Jacobite sympathies. In 1745, Waverley-Honour, the ancestral home of the family, was a quiet retreat for Sir Everard Waverley, an elderly Jacobite. In an attempt to seek political advantage in London, his brother, Richard Waverley, had sworn loyalty to the king.

Edward Waverley, the son of Whig Richard, divided his time between his father and his Uncle Everard at Waverley-Honour. On that great estate, Edward was free to come and go as he pleased, for his tutor Pembroke, a devout dissenter, was often too busy writing religious pamphlets to spend much time with the education of his young charge. When Edward became old enough, his father obtained a commission in the army for him. Shortly afterward, he was ordered to Scotland to join the dragoons of Colonel Gardiner. Equipped with the necessary articles of dress, accompanied by a retinue of men who had been selected by Sir Everard, and weighed down by the dissenting tomes of Pembroke, Edward left Waverley-Honour in quixotic fashion to conquer his world.

He had been instructed by Sir Everard to visit an old friend, Sir Cosmo Comyne Bradwardine, whose estate was near the village of Tully-Veolan in the Scottish Lowlands. Soon after his arrival at the post of Colonel Gardiner, Edward obtained leave to go to Tully-Veolan. There he found Sir Everard's friend both cordial and happy to see him. The few days spent at Tully-Veolan convinced Edward that Scotland was a wilder and more romantic land than his native England. He paid little attention to Rose Bradwardine, the baron's daughter, his youthful imagination being fired instead by the songs and dances of Davie Gellatley, the baron's servant, and by tales about the Scottish Highlanders and their rude ways. At Tully-Veolan, he was also confronted by a political issue that had been but an idealistic quarrel in his former existence; these Scottish people were Jacobites, and because of his father's politics and his own rank in the army of Hanoverian George II of England Edward ostensibly was a Whig Royalist.

During his stay at Tully-Veolan, an event occurred that was to change Edward's life. It began with the unexpected arrival of Evan Dhu Maccombich, a Highlander in the service of the renowned clan chieftain Fergus Mac Ivor Vich Ian Vohr, a friend of the baron. Since his taste for romantic adventure had been aroused, Edward begged another extension of his leave in order to accompany Evan Dhu into the Highlands. In those rugged hills, Edward was led to the cave that sheltered the band of Donald Bean Lean, an outlaw who robbed and plundered the wealthy Lowlanders. Staying with the bandit only long enough to discover the romantic attachment between Donald's daughter Alice and Evan Dhu, Edward again set out into the hills with his cheerful young guide. His curiosity had been sufficiently whetted by Evan's descriptions of Fergus Mac Ivor and his ancient castle deep in the Highland hills at Glennaquoich.

The welcome Mac Ivor extended to Edward was openhanded and hearty. No less warm was the quiet greeting that Flora, Fergus Mac Ivor's sister, had for the English soldier. Flora was a beautiful woman of romantic, poetic nature, and Edward soon found himself deeply in love with the chieftain's sister. Mac Ivor seemed to sanction the idea of a marriage. That union could never be, however, for Flora had vowed her life to another cause—that of placing Charles, the young Stuart prince, on the throne of England. When Edward proposed marriage, Flora advised him to seek a woman who could attach herself wholeheartedly to his happiness; Flora claimed that she could not divide her attentions between the Jacobite cause and marriage to one who was not an ardent supporter of Charles Edward Stuart.

Edward's stay at Glennaquoich was interrupted by letters carried to him by Davie Gellatley from Tully-Veolan. The first was from Rose Bradwardine, who advised him that the Lowlands were in a state of revolt. Since her father was absent, she warned Edward not to return to Tully-Veolan. The other letters informed him that Richard Waverley had engaged in some unfortunate political maneuvers that had caused his political downfall. On the heels of this news came orders from Colonel Gardiner, who, having heard reports of Edward's association with traitors, was relieving the young officer of his command. Repulsed by Flora and disgraced in his army career, Edward resolved to return to Waverley-Honour. He equipped himself suitably for the dangerous journey and set out toward the Lowlands.

Because of armed revolt in Scotland and the linking of the Waverley name with the Jacobite cause, Edward found himself under arrest for treason against King George. The dissenting pamphlets of Pembroke that he carried, his stay in the Highlands, and the company he had kept there were suspicious circumstances that made it impossible for him to prove his innocence. He was captured by some of the king's troopers and turned over to an armed guard with orders to take him to Stirling Castle for trial on a charge of treason.

Because he was a friend of Fergus Mac Ivor Vich Ian Vohr, however, a quick ambush rescued Edward from his captors, and he found himself once again in the hands of Highlanders. He recognized them as a party of Donald Bean Lean's followers. Indeed, Alice once appeared among the men to slip a packet of letters to him, but at the time, he had no opportunity to read the papers she had given him so secretively.

A few days' journey brought Edward to the center of Jacobite activities at Holyrood, the temporary court of Charles Edward Stuart, who had secretly crossed the channel from France. There Edward Waverley found Fergus Mac Ivor awaiting him. When the Highlander presented Edward to Prince Charles, the Pretender welcomed the English youth because of the name he bore. The prince, trained in French courts, was a model of refinement and courtesy. His heartfelt trust gave Edward a feeling of belonging, particularly because he had lost his commission, his cause unheard, in the English army. When Charles asked him to join in the Scottish uprising, Edward assented. Mac Ivor seemed quite happy about Edward's new allegiance. When the young Englishman asked about Flora, Mac Ivor explained that he had brought her along to the prince's court so that she could help him gain a political foothold once the battle was won. Edward resented this manner of using Flora as bait, but soon he perceived that the court of the Pretender functioned very much like the French court where Charles and his followers had learned statecraft. Mac Ivor pressed Edward to continue his courtship of Flora. The sister of Mac Ivor, however, met his advances coldly. In the company of the Highland beauty was Rose Bradwardine, whose father had also joined the Stuart cause.

Edward was accepted as a cavalier by the women who clustered around the prince. Under the influence of the Pretender's courtly manners, Edward soon became a favorite, but Mac Ivor's sister persisted in ignoring him. He began to compare the two women, Rose and Flora, and Rose gained favor in his eyes as he watched them together.

The expedition of the Pretender and his Highlanders was doomed to failure. As they marched southward to England, they began to lose hope. The prince ordered a retreat to Scotland. Many of the clansmen were killed at the disastrous Battle of Culloden. The survivors escaped to the Highlands to spend their days in hiding from troops sent to track them down. A few were fortunate enough to make their way in safety to France.

Edward managed to get away and to find a friend who helped him to steal back to Scotland, where he hoped to find Rose Bradwardine. By now, Edward had cleared himself of the earlier charges of treachery and desertion, which had been the initial cause of his joining the Pretender. It had been Donald Bean Lean who had deceived Colonel Gardiner with a false report of Edward's activities. The letters Alice had slipped to him had conveyed that information to Edward. Now he hoped to escape to France with Rose and wait for a pardon from England. Richard Waverley had died, and Edward had inherited his fortune.

Fergus Mac Ivor and Evan Dhu Maccombich were executed for their crimes against the Crown, and the power of the Highland clan was broken. Flora entered a Catholic convent in France, the country in which she had been reared. Edward Waverley and Rose were married once Edward had made certain of his pardon. They returned to Tully-Veolan, where the baron's estate was awaiting its heirs.

Critical Evaluation:

Sir Walter Scott's *Waverley* is a striking representative of literature about the Highlanders and Lowlanders of pre-nineteenth century Scotland. Like Maria Edgeworth in her *Castle Rackrent* (1800), Scott intended his novel to be a romanticized sketch of a people and their customs during a time that had faded into history by the time he wrote *Waverley*. A tension exists in the novel between Scott's romanticized description of the Highlanders who fought in the Stuart uprising of 1745 and a story based on historical fact and eyewitness accounts.

Scott romanticizes the story by including various vivid, poetic descriptions of the eerie, rugged Highland terrain to elicit a sense of awe in his readers. Inspired by the success of his long poem *Lady of the Lake* (1810), Scott had intended *Waverley* as a piece of poetic prose. Scott also romanticizes the novel through the plot. Typical of heroes of romances, Edward overcomes many obstacles in pursuit of a valued object. In the course of the novel, a young man whose perceptions had been clouded by the romantic tales of English chivalry and Highland nobility that he read as a child experiences disillusionment and education. An introvert who needs someone to care for him, Edward finds a companion in Rose Bradwardine, a gentle woman more inclined to domestic pleasures than Highland heroics. At one significant point, Rose proves to be Edward's rescuer; gaining the support of Prince Charles, she has Edward rescued from his Lowland captors and returned to the forces of Fergus Mac Ivor. When Edward learns that it was Rose who rescued him, he pledges to marry her.

Edward's romance is made interesting by the nature of his conflict: He is torn in his allegiance between the old Jacobite order, represented by Prince Charles Edward Stuart and Fergus and Flora Mac Ivor, and the new Hanoverian order represented by Colonel Talbut, who ventures into the battle between the Scots and the English to rescue Waverley. Fiercely loyal, the Highlanders supporting Charles Stuart's claim to the English throne are holding on to a way of life that, to Scott, has become archaic. On the other hand, the Hanoverians—and Edward is initially a part of this order as a young British recruit—are more rational, more benevolent. To Edward, this conflict is intensified by Flora Mac Ivor, sister of Highland prince Fergus Mac Ivor. Although Edward falls in love with Flora, he finally accepts that this woman, as politically fanatical as her brother, is not the companion he seeks. Edward's conflict is resolved when he concludes that the warring life of the Highlander is not for him, and Scott creates a traditional ending: Edward marries Rose, characters that had become estranged from the Crown are forgiven, and enmities are placed aside.

A possible contradiction of Scott's romanticizing of the Highlanders is his device of intermingling historical narratives from individuals who had witnessed the Highland uprising of 1745. In the final chapter of *Waverley*, Scott asserts that this work is historically accurate: "The accounts of the battle at Preston, and the skirmish at Clifton, are taken from the narrative of intelligent eye-witnesses, and corrected from the History of the Rebellion by the late venerable author of Douglas." In his preface to the third edition, Scott defends the character of the ruthless Highlander Callum Beg as being "that of a spirit naturally turned to daring evil and determined, by the circumstances of his situation, to a particular species of mischief." Following the defeat of the Highlanders and the trial and execution of Fergus Mac Ivor, the romantic ending is somewhat anticlimactic.

The one element that most contributes to the success of *Waverley* is the character of Fergus Mac Ivor. Fergus is not only the novel's most realistic character but also its one true hero. Fergus is an intensely loyal man who is true to his word and incapable of understanding Edward's doubts about joining the Highland cause. Fergus is a tragic hero, however, because his steadfastness is also his flaw. He remains intensely, even blindly, loyal to the Stuarts, and in the most powerful scene of the novel, Fergus proclaims his loyalty to Scotland and the Stuart cause as he is condemned to execution for his role in the uprising.

The other characters must be judged in relation to Fergus. Edward Waverley, as his name suggests, is not capable of Fergus' unwavering devotion to a political cause. Because of his friendship with Fergus, Edward learns that his is not to be a life of military endeavor. Fergus makes the point to Edward, completely taken by Prince Charles's charisma, that the prince mingles foolish words with his military talk and that he is not the gallant, heroic figure that he might seem to be. The Pretender ultimately abandons his Highland supporters and flees to the Continent, but Fergus remains and is finally beheaded. Even Baron Bradwardine, representative of a heroic past that Scott tries to capture, is pedantic, pretentious, and ridiculous when measured by the realistic and heroic standard of Fergus. The only character who is a match for Fergus' heroism is Colonel Talbut, who also represents the benevolence and rationality of the new Hanoverian order.

The novel's vivid descriptions and high adventure support Scott's purpose in writing this novel. Although not born a Highlander, Scott wrote *Waverley* for "the purpose of preserving some of the ancient manners, of which I have witnessed the almost total extinction."

"Critical Evaluation" by Richard Logsdon

Bibliography:

Daiches, David. "Scott's Achievement as a Novelist." In *Literary Essays*. Edinburgh, Scotland: Oliver & Boyd, 1956. Argues that Scott's achievements as a novelist, overlooked in the twentieth century, make *Waverley* and his other novels worth reading.

Davie, Donald. *The Heyday of Sir Walter Scott*. London: Routledge & Kegan Paul, 1961. Considers some of the factors contributing to the enormous popularity of Scott's novels in the nineteenth century.

Hillhouse, James Theodore. *The Waverley Novels and Their Critics*. New York: Octagon Books, 1968. Contains critical reviews of Scott's novels.

Pearson, Hesketh. *Walter Scott: His Life and Personality*. New York: Harper, 1954. Presents the novels of Scott as a reflection of himself, his family, and his culture.

Scott, Sir Walter. *Waverley: Or, 'Tis Sixty Years Since*. Edited by Claire Lamont. New York: Oxford University Press, 1986. Contains an excellent introduction to the historical and narrative background of *Waverley*, as well as Scott's notes and prefaces to the novel.

Welsh, Alexander. *The Hero of the Waverley Novels*. New Haven, Conn.: Yale University Press, 1963. An interpretation of Scott's hero, whose behavior is determined by class and who is acted upon by outside forces.

THE WAVES

Type of work: Novel
Author: Virginia Woolf (1882-1941)
Type of plot: Psychological realism
Time of plot: Between World Wars I and II
Locale: England
First published: 1931

> *Principal characters:*
> BERNARD, the phrase maker
> NEVILLE, the poet
> SUSAN, the elemental woman
> RHODA, the plain, clumsy misfit
> JINNY, the hedonist
> LOUIS, the self-conscious outcast of his social group
> PERCIVAL, the symbol of the ordinary man

The Story:

The waves rolled shoreward, and at daybreak the children awoke. Watching the sunrise, Bernard, maker of phrases and seeker of causes, saw a loop of light—he would always think of it as a ring, the circle of experience giving life pattern and meaning. Shy, passionate Neville imagined a globe dangling against the flank of day. Susan, who loved fields and seasons, saw a slab of yellow, the crusted loaf, the buttered slice, of teatime in the country. Rhoda, awkward and timid, heard wild cries of startled birds. Sensuous, pleasure-loving Jinny saw a tassel of gold and crimson. Louis, of a race that had seen women carry red pitchers to the Nile, heard a chained beast stamping on the sands.

While the others played, Louis hid among the currants. Jinny, finding him there and pitying his loneliness, kissed him. Suddenly jealous, Susan ran away, and Bernard followed to comfort her. They walked across fields to Elvedon, where they saw a woman writing at a window. Later, in the schoolroom, Louis refused to recite because he was ashamed of his Australian accent. Rhoda was unable to do her sums and had to stay in. Louis pitied her, for she was the one he did not fear.

The day brightened. Bernard, older now, yawned through the headmaster's speech in chapel. Neville leaned sideways to watch Percival, who sat flicking the back of his neck. A glance, a gesture, Neville realized, and one could fall in love forever. Louis, liking order, sat quietly. As long as the headmaster talked, Louis forgot snickers at his accent and memories of kisses underneath a hedge. Susan, Jinny, and Rhoda were in a school where they sat primly under a portrait of Queen Alexandra. Susan thought of hay waving in the meadows at home. Jinny pictured a gold and crimson party dress. Rhoda dreamed of picking flowers and offering them to someone whose face she never saw.

Time passed, and the last day of the term arrived. Louis went to work in London after his father, a Brisbane banker, failed. In his attic room, he sometimes heard the great beast stamping in the dark, but now the noise was that of city crowds and traffic. At Cambridge, Neville read Catullus and waited with uneasy eagerness for Percival's smile or nod. Bernard was Byron's young man one day, Shelley's or Dostoevski's the next. One day, Neville brought him a poem. Reading it, Bernard felt that Neville would succeed and that he would fail. Neville was one person in love with another, Percival. In his phrase making, Bernard became many people—a plumber, a horse-breeder, an old woman in the street. In Switzerland, Susan dreamed of newborn lambs in baskets, of marsh mist and autumn rains, of the lover who would walk with her beside dusty hollyhocks. At a ball in London, Jinny, dancing, felt as if her body glowed with inner fire. Rhoda, at the same ball, sat and stared across the rooftops.

They all loved Percival. Before he left for India, they met at a dinner party in London to bid him good-bye. Bernard, not knowing that Susan had loved him, was already engaged. Louis was learning to cover his shyness with brisk assurance; the poet had become a businessman. Rhoda was frightened by life. Waiters and diners looked up when Jinny entered, lovely and poised. Susan came looking dowdy, hating London. Neville, loving Percival in secret, dreaded the moment of parting that would carry him away. Here, thought Bernard, was the ring he had seen long ago. Youth was friendship and a stirring in the blood, like the notes of Percival's wild hunting song.

The sun passed the zenith, and shadows lengthened. When word came that Percival had been killed in India, Neville felt as if that doom had been his own. He would go on to become a famous poet and scholar, always a lonely man waiting in his rooms for the footstep on the stair of this young man or that whom he loved in place of Percival. Bernard was married by then and his son had been born. He thought of Susan, whom Percival had loved. Rhoda also thought of Susan, engaged to her farmer in the country. She remembered the dream in which she had offered flowers to a man whose face had been hidden from her, and she knew at last that the man had been Percival.

Shadows grew longer over country and town. Louis, a wealthy, successful businessman, planned a place in Surrey with greenhouses and rare gardens. He still kept his attic room, though, where Rhoda often came; they had become lovers. Susan walked in the fields with her children or sat sewing by the firelight in a quiet room. Jinny groomed a body shaped for gaiety and pleasure. Neville measured time by the hours he spent waiting for the footstep on the stair, the young face at the door. Bernard tried to snare in phrases the old man on the train, the lovers in the park. The only realities, he thought, were in common things. He realized that he had lost friends by death—Percival was one—and others because he had not wished to cross the street. After Louis and Rhoda parted, Louis' new mistress was a vulgar cockney actress. Rhoda, always in flight, went to Spain. Climbing a hill to look across the sea toward Africa, she thought of rest and longed for death.

Slowly, the sun sank. At Hampton Court, the six friends met again for dinner. They were old now, and each had gone a different way after Percival had died in India years before. Bernard felt that he had failed. He had wrapped himself in phrases; he had sons and daughters, but he had ventured no farther than Rome. He had not become rich, like Louis, or famous, like Neville. Jinny had lived only for pleasure, little enough, as she was learning. After dinner, Bernard and Susan walked by the lake. There was little of their true thoughts they could say to each other. Bernard, however, was still a maker of phrases. Percival, he said, had become like the flower on the table where they ate—six-sided, made from their six lives.

So it seemed to him years later, after Rhoda had jumped to her death and the rest were old. He wondered what the real truth had been beneath Louis' middle-class respectability, Rhoda's haunted imagination, Neville's passion for one love, Susan's primitivism, Jinny's sensuous pleasures, his own attempt to catch reality in a phrase. He had been Byron's young man and Dostoevski's and also the hairy old savage in the blood. Once he had seen a loop of light, a ring, but he had found no pattern and no meaning, only the knowledge that death is the great adversary against whom humans ride in the darkness where the waves break on the shore.

Critical Evaluation:

In *The Waves*, Virginia Woolf explores the fictional representation of the unconscious and the connection between the unconscious and fluidity, the interplay of which permeates the text. Images and suggestions of fluid elements permeate the text and extend from the book's title through its closing line, "The waves broke on the shore." Bernard invites Susan to explore a new idyllic world of fluid, unshackled communication where "the lady sits between the two long windows, writing." Woolf expresses the idea of fluidity most purely in the interludes. In the first interlude, "Everything became softly amorphous, as if the china of the plate flowed and the steel of the knife were liquid." The fluidity of formerly concrete objects, the liquidity of formerly blunt or sharp ones, constitutes a metamorphosis metaphor throughout the novel, as in the interlude: "A plate was like a white lake." When the sun sinks, in a later interlude, the iron black boot becomes "a pool of deep blue," and the rocks "lose their hardness."

Tellingly, Neville, who hates "dangling" or "dampish things," is the most resistant to the disruption caused by such fluidity. He insists on order. Somewhat ironically, he is the spokesman for the powerless frustration of being appropriated by someone else's language when he says, "We are all phrases in Bernard's story." Neville alludes to the illusory nature of linguistic mastery and critiques allegedly guaranteed meanings: "Nothing should be named lest by so doing we change it."

Bernard, the discriminating phrase maker, uses language in ways that satisfy his ego. When describing how and what he will write to impress his woman friend with his profundity, he acknowledges his ability to appropriate events. After his discussion with Neville, Bernard alludes to the power to create and re-create the self, or selves, that constitute a presence: "I am Bernard; I am Byron; I am this, that and the other. . . . For I am more selves than Neville thinks."

Woolf's idealistic vision of the emerging self is possible only when the feminine and masculine permeate each other. This androgyny is given its most physical manifestation in the most body-oriented of the characters, Jinny, who describes many experiences in terms of fluid interaction between men and women. Jinny, who objectifies herself in the looking-glass, reflects both literally and figuratively on the limitations of language for her. In order to experience the warmth and privacy of another soul, Jinny must first be fluid. She claims in the passage immediately preceding a dance with a melancholy romantic man, "I flutter. I ripple. I stream like a plant in the river, flowing this way, flowing that way."

Conversely, Rhoda expresses, indeed exemplifies, what happens to those who are not fluid or permeable. "What I say is perpetually contradicted. I am to be broken. I am to be derided all my life. . . . The wave breaks. I am also a girl, here in this room." As a girl confined to a certain definable space, both her speech and her very existence are subject to contradiction.

Confined in a way different from Rhoda, Susan makes it her ambition to "have more" than either Rhoda or Jinny has, and she will do so through her children. She personifies the cyclic nature of women's lives and realities: childbearing and rearing, about which she is strangely ambivalent when she declares that "I shall be debased and hide-bound by the bestial and beautiful passion of maternity." Though relegated to this sphere by the dictates of biology, Susan at least imagines an odd sort of self-determination, a self-willed denial and isolation, which Woolf indicates with the repeated phrase "I shall."

Louis, on the other hand, voices the orderly hyperlinear reality of men's lives: "This is life; Mr. Prentice at four; Mr. Eyres at four-thirty." He repeatedly refers to the stability and satisfaction he receives from having this definite schedule, while Susan regards such regularity as insufferable tedium. Though multisensory in her descriptions of this ennui, Susan's senses are muted.

Regulation holds even more complex ramifications for Neville. Evan though being a poet places him in a position to order or not to order life's elements as he sees fit, he feels beset by the gravest responsibilities. He echoes the burden of duties, weights, obligations until it subsides after middle age. Just as Neville acknowledges that they are scarcely to be distinguished from the river—the life-source of creation—Woolf writes in the interlude immediately following that "sky and sea are themselves indistinguishable." This expresses the ultimate permeability of boundaries between human existence and nature. Significantly, this climactic anticlimax occurs only after the "sun had sunk" and thus when darkness (a metaphor for the unconscious) is able to flow: It washes down streets, rolls its waves along grass, blows along slopes, envelops, and engulfs.

Woolf's awareness of unconscious forces becomes clear in her portrayal of inherent contradictions, for this covering darkness must come before humans can be enlightened. Bernard's summation soliloquy epitomizes the eternal struggle of the mind to bring ideas to light and sift the elements of life. Sensation, the subconscious, self-consciousness, sex, and guilt all lead to a sustained inquiry into selfhood. Woolf uncovers the insufferable pain of denying permeability, that is, claiming boundaries, as when the bodies of the novel's six characters become separated. Only among themselves, Bernard reflects, is there a "body of the complete human being." Thus can he speak of them in the first person plural (yet singular) and collective (yet individual): "our life . . . our identity."

The blurring of separateness manifests itself when Bernard contemplates the suicide of one of this body's parts. As he imagines his own attempt to convince Rhoda to wait and not to kill herself, he realizes he is also persuading his own soul: "For this is not one life; nor do I always know if I am man or woman, Bernard or Neville, Louis, Susan, Jinny or Rhoda—so strange is the contact of one with another." Woolf projects her own worldview through Bernard, who sees wholes and unity as illusions. He seeks throughout his life to find something unbroken through language—a perfect unity among phrases and fragments.

At several moments throughout this soliloquy, Bernard is able to see clearly what it is that differentiates the emanations, which Woolf did not intend or perceive as individual characters; what they all have is a "rapture; their common feeling with death." Indeed, *The Waves* was Woolf's elegy to her deceased brother Thoby. Percival was Woolf's creation of a rare complete person who, though a victim of senseless death, is the prime antagonist. Percival's death is a rupture in the lives and sensibilities of the six other parentless peers who make up one whole identity. At the same time, that death functions as their unifying core or nucleus. Death is both a victory and a defeat, a loss of self but at the same time an ecstatic embrace. Percival's death, the novel's transition and transformation point, occurs in the center of the book. The movement is from diffusion in the first half of the book (covering early childhood, school, and separate paths taken according to sex and class) to (e)mergence in the second half, which includes their reactions to Percival's death, middle age and the solidifying or coalescing of identities, nostalgia, the reunion dinner at court, and Bernard's soliloquy.

Bernard defies death, which he deems the enemy, but he is able to do so only by his acceptance of and belief in the "eternal renewal, the incessant rise and fall and fall and rise again." The oscillating waves suggest the undercurrents of Woolf's novel, the undertow that pulls humans into the extension of their selves, the quickening of memory and deepening of perception, and, intermittently, allows them to surface. Given that the early titles for this novel included "The Life of Anybody" or "Life in General," part of Woolf's search may have been for a voiceless, characterless form of expression that could contribute to the work's profoundly surreal quality. A complex part of that quest is, inevitably, an ongoing individuation of self while that self is almost antithetically in communion with the other (or, in this case, others). Rhoda achieves this—as Woolf herself would later—in the ultimate isolation of suicide.

The Waves represents the refinement of Woolf's subjective novels and possibly an attempt to transform the genre. The writing in *The Waves* is generative rather than conclusive, recursive rather than discursive. Woolf demonstrates that, like waves, the experience of being in the world constitutes a fluid, perpetual process of reconstruction.

"Critical Evaluation" by Roseanne L. Hoefel

Bibliography:
Caughie, Pamela. *Virginia Woolf and Postmodernism.* Urbana: University of Illinois Press, 1991. Discusses the artist figure in *The Waves*, using sources from other recent Woolf criticism to discuss her novel.
Hafley, James. *The Glass Roof: Virginia Woolf as Novelist.* New York: Russell & Russell, 1963. Discusses the "creative modulation of perspective" in *The Waves* and argues that the novel is a demonstration of the futility of intellectual analysis and the validity of intuitional perception.
Kaivola, Karen. *All Contraries Confounded: The Lyrical Fiction of Virginia Woolf, Djuna Barnes, and Marguerite Duras.* Iowa City: University of Iowa Press, 1991. A discussion that focuses on Rhoda's relations to language and culture in *The Waves*. Rhoda's exclusion from language suggests the restricted ways women can participate in culture. She has no place, no identity, nothing is fixed for her. She is equally alienated from her body.
Lee, Hermione. *The Novels of Virginia Woolf.* New York: Holmes & Meier, 1977. Includes a thirty-page chapter analyzing *The Waves* and comparing its stream-of-consciousness technique with those employed by Marcel Proust and James Joyce. Lee contrasts the lack of social realism in this novel with Woolf's other novels.
Love, Jean O. *Worlds in Consciousness: Mythopoetic Thought in the Novels of Virginia Woolf.* Berkeley: University of California Press, 1970. Contains a long and detailed analysis of *The Waves* as a movement from diffusion to differentiation and back. Progressive differentiation of the novel's symbolism effectively expresses the growth and development of the characters.

THE WAY OF ALL FLESH

Type of work: Novel
Author: Samuel Butler (1835-1902)
Type of plot: Social realism
Time of plot: Nineteenth century
Locale: England
First published: 1903

> *Principal characters:*
> GEORGE PONTIFEX, a publisher of religious books
> THEOBALD, George's son
> ALETHEA, George's daughter
> CHRISTINA, Theobald's wife
> ERNEST, Theobald's oldest son
> MR. OVERTON, Ernest's friend
> ELLEN, Ernest's wife

The Story:

Mr. and Mrs. Pontifex were middle-aged when their son George was born. When the time came for George to learn a trade, they accepted the offer of Mr. Pontifex's brother-in-law to take George with him to London as an apprentice in his printing shop. George learned his trade well, and when the uncle died he willed the shop to his nephew.

George had married, and five children were born to him and his wife: John, Theobald, Eliza, Maria, and Alethea, at whose birth Mrs. Pontifex died. George considered himself a parent motivated only by the desire to do the right thing for his children. When Theobald proved himself not as quick as John but more persistent, George picked the clergy as Theobald's profession. Shortly before his ordination, Theobald wrote to his father that he did not wish to become a minister. In reply, George threatened to disinherit him. Theobald submitted and was ordained. He then had to wait for an older member of the clergy to die so that he could be given a living.

The Allabys had three daughters, all of marriageable age. After having selected Theobald as a possible husband for one of the daughters, Mr. Allaby suggested to his daughters that they play a game of cards to decide who would become Theobald's wife. Christina won. Without knowing of this, Theobald obligingly courted Christina until he won her promise to marry him. George wrote to Theobald that he objected to his son's marriage into the impoverished Allaby family, but Theobald was too deeply committed to release himself. Five years later, he obtained a decent living in a community called Battersby, where he and Christina settled. Because their first child was a son and the first new male Pontifex, George was pleased. For the first time in his life, Theobald felt that he had done something to satisfy his father. After Ernest came Joseph and then Charlotte. Theobald and Christina reared their children with strict adherence to principles that they believed would mold fine character. The children were disciplined rigorously and beaten when their parents deemed it appropriate. When George Pontifex died, he left seventeen thousand, five hundred pounds to Theobald and twenty-five hundred pounds to the oldest son, Ernest.

From the oppressive existence at home under the almost obsessive rule of his parents, Ernest was sent to Roughborough to be educated under Dr. Skinner, as strict a disciplinarian as Theobald. Ernest was physically weak and mentally morose. He might have succumbed completely to his overpowering environment had he not been rescued by an understanding and loving relative. Alethea Pontifex, Theobald's sister, had retired to London, where she lived comfortably on an inheritance that had been wisely invested. Looking about for someone to whom she could leave her money when she died, Alethea hit upon Ernest. Because she did not wish to bestow her fortune blindly, however, she determined to learn more about the boy. She moved to Roughborough so that she could spend time with him.

From the first, she endeared herself to the lonely youngster. She encouraged him to develop his own talents, and when she learned that he had a passion for music, she suggested that he learn how to build an organ. Enthusiastically, he set about to learn wood construction and harmony. Theobald disapproved, but he did not forbid Ernest's activities because he and Christina were eager that Ernest inherit Alethea's money. Ernest's shrinking personality changed under the benevolent influence of his aunt. When Alethea died, she left her money in the hands of her best friend, Mr. Overton, whom she had appointed to administer the estate that would go to Ernest on his twenty-eighth birthday.

After Ernest completed his course at Roughborough, Theobald sent him to Cambridge to study for the ministry. At Cambridge, Ernest made a few friends and took part in athletics. He was ordained soon after he received his degree and then went to London. Still innocent and unworldly, he entrusted the inheritance he had received from his grandfather to his friend Pryer, who cheated him out of it. Because he could not differentiate between good and evil people, Ernest also became entangled in a charge of assault and battery and was sentenced to a term in the workhouse. Theobald sent word that henceforth Ernest was to consider himself an orphan.

Ernest was twenty-three years old at the time. Unknown to Ernest, Mr. Overton was still holding the estate Alethea had left for him. Mr. Overton began to take an interest in Ernest's affairs. When Ernest was released from prison, he went to Mr. Overton for advice concerning his future, since it was no longer possible for him to be a clergyman.

While Ernest had been at Roughborough, Christina had hired a young girl named Ellen as a maid. She and Ernest had become good friends simply because Ellen was kinder to him than anyone else at home. When she became pregnant and Christina learned of her condition, she sent Ellen away. Fearing that the girl might starve, Ernest had followed her and given her all the money he had. Theobald learned about this from John, the coachman, whom Theobald thereupon dismissed.

Soon after his release from prison, Ernest met Ellen again by chance in a London street. Because both were lonely, they married and set up a small secondhand clothing and bookshop with the help of Mr. Overton, who deplored the idea of their marriage. Unknown to Ernest, Ellen was a habitual drunkard. Before long, she had so impoverished him with her drinking and her foul ways that he disliked her intensely. He could not leave her, however, because of the two children she had borne him.

One day, Ernest again met John, his father's former coachman, who revealed that he was the father of Ellen's illegitimate child and that he had married Ellen shortly after she had left Theobald's home in disgrace. Acting on this information, Mr. Overton arranged matters for Ernest. Ellen was promised an income of a pound a week if she would leave Ernest, and she readily accepted the proposal. The children were sent to live in a family of happy, healthy children, for Ernest feared that his own upbringing would make him as bad a parent as Theobald had been.

When Ernest reached the age of twenty-eight, he inherited Alethea's trust fund of seventy thousand pounds. By that time, Ernest had become a writer. With a part of his inheritance, he traveled abroad for a few years and then returned to England with material for a book he planned to write. He went on to publish many successful books, but he never told his own story. Mr. Overton, who had access to all the Pontifex papers and who knew Ernest well, wrote the history of the Pontifex family.

Critical Evaluation:

Aside from many essays and articles, Samuel Butler wrote fifteen books, among them several travel books and five on science. He had been strongly influenced by Charles Darwin's *On the Origin of Species* (1859), an influence that is reflected in the substance and style of *The Way of All Flesh*. That influence, however, is revealed only gradually in the philosophizing of Overton and Ernest. Butler began the novel in 1873 but interrupted its composition several times to do scientific writing; he finally completed it in 1885. In chapters 8 and 25, for letters from Theobald and Christina to their son Ernest, Butler used letters that had actually been written to him by his parents. Because he had so caustically satirized members of his family, he refused to publish *The Way of All Flesh* so long as any of them were living. It was his literary executor who arranged publication in 1903 despite the fact that Butler's two sisters were still alive.

Those family letters are among the various bits of evidence in *The Way of All Flesh* that Butler uses wittily but relentlessly to persuade the reader that the central character, Ernest, was fortunate to survive, much less surmount, his parents' mid-Victorian Christian tutelage and his formal schooling. Ernest slowly and unsteadily begins to overcome the narrow, stupid, and often cruel values imposed upon him. At last, he dimly perceives what Butler believed human beings would instinctively remember had it not been for the restrictions of Victorianism. Ernest learns mostly by hindsight, in the wake of disastrous involvements with such supposed friends as Pryer and Ellen. Nevertheless, he also learns by naïvely and torturously sifting through the controversial and fashionable religious and scientific issues of his time. Butler gently satirizes Ernest's pursuit of "first causes" or other abstractions, and his fortunes take a decided change for the better when he gives up "abstractions" for the most part, sheds his alcoholic wife, and realizes that because he is the child of his parents he would be unable to be a good father himself. He therefore places his children with good, simple people who can love them and make them happy adults. Like Butler, Ernest at the age of thirty settles into bachelor quarters in London, where until his death he contentedly writes, paints, enjoys music, and reflects upon the folly of much that transpires in the world.

Butler did not go to prison; instead, he went to New Zealand where between 1858 and 1864 he raised sheep profitably. The earlier circumstances of Ernest's life, however, closely parallel those of Butler's through the Cambridge period and, to a lesser extent, following that period. Much of the critical discussion of the novel has, as a result, centered on the author's personal life. Some critics have thought that Butler treats Theobald and Christina unfairly and thereby alienates the reader. Other critics have said of Butler, as Overton says of Ernest in contrasting him to Othello: "he hates not wisely but too well."

Critical comment might also address the quantity of coincidences in the novel. Of perhaps the greatest consequence is Ernest's encounter with John, from whom he learns that John and Ellen are legally husband and wife; this leads to Ernest's being freed from a dreadful marriage. It may also be considered implausible that Overton is so successful in investing Ernest's inheritance that it increases fivefold and allows Ernest to live comfortably for the rest of his life.

Many critics interpret the autobiographical dimension in *The Way of All Flesh* as a literary precedent for parent-son and self-discovery novels such as Somerset Maugham's *Of Human Bondage* (1915), D. H. Lawrence's *Sons and Lovers* (1913), or James Joyce's *A Portrait of the*

Artist as a Young Man (1914-1915). Other perspectives, however, are possible, particularly for readers long familiar with Freudian and post-Freudian psychological approaches to the novel. Readers of Norman Mailer's autobiographical works, for example, may view Butler's work as more than either personal diatribe or overreaction to the excesses of Victorianism. Novelists now thread through mazes of neuroses and attempt to expose the origins of neurotic and self-destructive behavior such as that practiced by Ernest; often, they propose therapeutic solutions to the protagonists' problems. However imperfectly Butler integrated the autobiographical or personal and the theories that underlie his novel, he was doubtless trying to show the causes of Ernest's stunted personality and his path to relative self-respect and happiness.

The narrative of the novel proceeds slowly because only in the course of thirty years of painful experience could Ernest achieve some intellectual objectivity and degree of self-knowledge. He learned that he must totally reject his self-centered parents' pious domination. He learns, according to Overton, that virtue springs from experience of personal well-being—the "least fallible thing we have." When meditating in prison, Ernest decides that a true Christian takes the "highest and most self-respecting view of his own welfare which is in his power to conceive, and adheres to it in spite of conventionality." Nevertheless, circumstances change, as Overton informs the reader, and the self is always changing: Life is nothing but the "process of accommodation," and a life will be successful or not according to the individual's power of accommodation. Overton is doubtless Butler's alter ego, and his detached view of Ernest reveals that "smug hedonism" is more accurately seen as less than a perfect resolution: Ernest is somewhat withdrawn, lonely, bearing ineradicable marks of his heredity and environment.

Butler explores the themes of heredity and environment plurally through telling the histories of four generations of Pontifexes: Only Ernest's great-grandparents led happy, instinctual lives. The title of the novel gives a summarized version of Butler's judgment, that it is the way of all flesh to learn, if at all, by rejecting convention and dogma and to live by self-direction.

"Critical Evaluation" by Mary H. Hayden

Bibliography:
Ganz, Margaret. "Samuel Butler: Ironic Abdication and the Way to the Unconscious." *English Literature in Transition (1880-1920)* 28, no. 4 (1985): 366-394. Charts the novel's many ironic twists of sentimental phrases to show Butler's abrogation of familiar assurances and his anticipation of twentieth century uncertainty.
Guest, David. "Acquired Characters: Cultural vs. Biological Determinism in Butler's *The Way of All Flesh.*" *English Literature in Transition (1880-1920)* 34, no. 3 (1991): 283-292. Discusses Butler's understanding of Darwin; emphasizes the novel's anticipation of pessimistic cultural determinism.
Holt, Lee E. *Samuel Butler.* Rev. ed. Boston: Twayne, 1989. Asserts the book's challenge was to show the near-destruction of a young man by the stupidity of his parents while describing a new type of human fulfillment not reflected in traditional terms of success. To this was added Butler's theories of inherited evolutionary forces.
Rosenman, John B. "Evangelicalism in *The Way of All Flesh.*" *College Language Association Journal* 26 (September, 1982): 76-97. The novel charts the history of the influence of Evangelicalism in four generations of English society. Asserts that Butler's use of scripture surpasses any other writer in English, suggesting that, although he criticizes the practices of Christians, he writes from a deep moral earnestness.

Sieminski, Greg. "Suited for Satire: Butler's Re-tailoring of *Sartor Resartus* in *The Way of All Flesh.*" *English Literature in Transition (1880-1920)* 31, no. 1 (1988): 29-37. Demonstrates how Butler composed his novel as a satirical response to Thomas Carlyle, whom he hated. Ernest does not seek action, but the humiliation of others.

THE WAY OF THE WORLD

Type of work: Drama
Author: William Congreve (1670-1729)
Type of plot: Comedy of manners
Time of plot: Seventeenth century
Locale: London
First performed: 1700; first published, 1700

> *Principal characters:*
> LADY WISHFORT, an aged coquette
> MRS. FAINALL, her daughter
> MRS. MILLAMANT, Lady Wishfort's niece
> FOIBLE, a servant
> SIR WILFULL WITWOUD, Lady Wishfort's nephew
> WITWOUD, his half brother
> MIRABELL, a gentleman of fashion
> WAITWELL, his servant
> FAINALL, Lady Wishfort's son-in-law
> MRS. MARWOOD, Fainall's mistress

The Story:

Mrs. Millamant, who was by far the most beautiful and wittiest of all the fine ladies in London, was sought after by all the beaux in town. The niece of the rich Lady Wishfort, she was also an heiress in her own right and was looked upon with great favor by Witwoud, a kinsman of Lady Wishfort. Millamant's acknowledged preference among her suitors, however, was for young Mirabell, who was the only man in London who could match that lady's devastating wit.

Mirabell himself was as great a favorite among the ladies in the town as Millamant was among the beaux. She was the perfect coquette; he was the perfect gallant. Among Mirabell's jealous admirers was Mrs. Marwood, the mistress of Fainall, Lady Wishfort's son-in-law. In fact, Mirabell had but one real enemy among the ladies, and that was Lady Wishfort herself. On one occasion, in order to further his suit with Millamant, Mirabell had falsely made love to the old lady. Discovering his subterfuge later, she had never forgiven him. She determined that he would never marry her niece so long as she controlled Millamant's fortune. In consequence, Mirabell was hard put to devise a scheme whereby he might force Lady Wishfort to consent to the marriage.

The plan he devised was an ingenious one. Realizing that Lady Wishfort would respond to anything which even resembled a man, he promptly invented an imaginary uncle, Sir Rowland, who, he said, had fallen madly in love with Lady Wishfort and wanted to marry her. He forced his servant, Waitwell, to impersonate this fictitious uncle. To placate Waitwell and further ensure the success of his plan, he contrived his servant's marriage to Lady Wishfort's maid, Foible.

His scheme might have worked had it not been for the counterplans of the designing Mrs. Marwood and her unscrupulous lover, Fainall. Although she pretended to despise all men, Mrs. Marwood was secretly in love with Mirabell, and had no intention of allowing him to marry Millamant. Fainall, although he detested his wife heartily, realized that he was dependent upon her and her mother's fortune for his well-being, and he resolved to stop at nothing to make sure that that fortune was in his control.

While these plans were proceeding, Millamant gave little thought to plots or counterplots. She had not the slightest intention of compromising with life, but insisted that the world's way must somehow be made to conform to her own desires. She had little use for the life around her, seeing through its shallow pretenses and its falsity, and yet she knew that it was the world in which she had to live. She realized that any attempt to escape from it into some idyllic pastoral existence, as her aunt often suggested, would be folly.

Millamant laid down to Mirabell the conditions under which she would marry him, and they were stringent conditions, not at all in conformity with the average wife's idea of her lot. She would have in her marriage no place for the ridiculous codes and conventions which governed the behavior of the people around her. She would be entirely free of the cant and hypocrisy of married life, which were only a cloak for the corruption or misery hidden underneath social custom. In short, she refused to be merely a married woman in her husband's or society's eyes. Mirabell, likewise, had certain conditions which must be fulfilled before he was turned from bachelor into husband. When his demands proved reasonable, both lovers realized that they saw life through much the same eyes. They decided that they were probably made for each other.

However, the world had not come to the same conclusion. Lady Wishfort, still embittered against Mirabell for his gross deception, resolved that Millamant was to marry a cousin, Sir Wilfull Witwoud, a country lout many years her senior, who had just arrived in London. Fortunately for Millamant, Sir Wilfull turned out to be a harmless booby, who, when he was drunk, became the most understanding of men.

There was a greater obstacle, however, in the scheme which Mirabell himself had planned. Waitwell, disguised as Mirabell's imaginary uncle, Sir Rowland, paid ardent court to Lady Wishfort, and would have been successful in inveigling her into marriage had it not been for a letter from Mrs. Marwood exposing the whole scheme. Lady Wishfort's maid, Foible, succeeded in intercepting the letter, but Mrs. Marwood appeared at Lady Wishfort's in person and disclosed the deception.

Lady Wishfort was furious, and more determined than ever to prevent any marriage between her niece and Mirabell. She angrily discharged Foible from her employ. Mrs. Fainall, Lady Wishfort's daughter, was on the side of the two lovers. When Foible informed her that she had tangible proof of the relationship between Fainall and Mrs. Marwood, Mrs. Fainall resolved to prosecute her husband to the limit. Meanwhile, the wily Fainall had taken pains to have all of his wife's property transferred to his name by means of trumped up evidence of an affair between his wife and Mirabell.

In this act, Lady Wishfort began to see for the first time the scheming villainy of her daughter's husband. Mirabell, with the aid of Foible and Millamant's servant, Mincing, exposed the double-dealing Mrs. Marwood and her lover and further proved that, while she was yet a widow, Mrs. Fainall had conveyed her whole estate in trust to Mirabell. Lady Wishfort was so delighted that she forgave Mirabell all of his deceptions and consented to his marriage to Millamant.

Critical Evaluation:

Although born in England, William Congreve was reared and educated in Ireland, thus joining the procession of great Irish comic writers which includes Richard Sheridan, Oliver Goldsmith, Jonathan Swift, Oscar Wilde, and George Bernard Shaw. Returning to England as a young man, Congreve studied at law briefly, wrote a novel, and joined with John Dryden in a translation of some works of Juvenal. His literary rise was rapid, and his first comedies, *The Old Bachelor* (1693) and *Love for Love* (1695), were highly successful. His sole tragedy, *The Mourning Bride* (1697), acclaimed by Samuel Johnson a generation later, was widely applauded. However, *The Way of the World*, now considered the masterpiece of all Restoration comedies, was coolly received. Congreve became involved in a notorious controversy over the morality of the stage and had to defend his plays strenuously from what he felt was misrepresentation. Despite this, he held honorary posts under King William and Queen Anne and was associated with Sir John Vanbrugh in the direction of the Queen's Theatre in Haymarket. He was one of the most admired literary figures during the reign of Queen Anne; the duchess of Marlborough was his patron, and Alexander Pope, John Gay, Swift, Richard Steele, and Voltaire were his friends. When Congreve died in 1729, he was buried with much pomp and ceremony in Westminster Abbey.

Restoration comedy was critical comedy, bringing "the sword of common sense" to bear upon the extravagances of the period. Congreve's works are perhaps as close to those of Molière as the English theater has ever come; his plays brought an ironic scrutiny to the affectations of his age, with a style and perfection of phrase that still dazzles audiences. He has been called the wittiest man who ever wrote the English language in the theater; certainly, his characters speak some of the wittiest dialogue. Without question, *The Way of the World* introduced a new standard of wit and polish to the theater. In Millamant, Congreve created one of the great characters of English drama, a comic heroine at once lovable and laughable. The poetry of the courtly life of the Restoration is summed up in the duet between these two brilliant lovers, Mirabell and Millamant.

The Way of the World is carried forward by the witty speeches of the characters rather than by dramatic reversals. The play is all of one piece, a world of wit and pleasure inhabited only by persons of quality and "deformed neither by realism nor by farce." The plot is confusing, but almost irrelevant, and the situations exist really only for the conversation. Although Congreve seemed almost above such concerns as careful plotting, he was surprisingly artful in some of his stage effects. By delaying the entrance of Millamant until the second act, he arouses intense anticipation in the audience. The fifth act, crowded as it is with activity, flows with continual surprises.

Some critics have held that *The Way of the World* is marred by the artificial contrivances of the plot, but most audiences pay no attention to the complications, relishing instead the characters and dialogue. The design of the play was to ridicule affected, or false, wit. Possibly, the play's original lukewarm reception was a result of its coming too close to the faults of the courtly audience to be wholly agreeable to them. The dialogue is, also, closely woven, and the repartee demands such close attention that it might have exhausted its listeners. *The Way of the World* is now one of the most frequently revived and enjoyed of all of the Restoration comedies.

Apart from the presentation of incidental wit, Restoration comedy had two main interests: the behavior of polite society and of pretenders to polite society, and particular aspects of sexual relationships. The wit varied from a hard, metallic kind that seemed to exist for its own sake, without any relation to anything, to subtle satire. Occasionally, even Congreve falls into a pattern of easy antitheses, monotonously repeated until the sting of surprise is lost. His wit is never as blunt or as ruthless as that of William Wycherley. Considered fairly outspoken for many generations, the comedy seems primarily to consist of titillation, to suggest more than it delivers. However, the best of the Restoration playwrights, such as Congreve, did not rely entirely on titillation to get their laughs. There is also much feeling present in *The Way of the*

World, particularly in the battle of the sexes. Congreve could not view love merely as a gratification of lust, as some of the Restoration playwrights seemed to think of it.

The characters in *The Way of the World* are among the best drawn in any Restoration comedy—or perhaps in any play of the period, comic or tragic. Besides Mirabell and Millamant, one of the most perfect pairs of lovers in any comedy, the play boasts a parade of such personalities as Foible, Witwoud, and Petulant, and particularly Lady Wishfort, who approaches the tragic in her desperate attempt to preserve her youth. No character in the play, not even Fainall, fails to surprise the audience with witty observations. In *The Way of the World*, Congreve penetrated deeper than any of his contemporaries into the mysteries of human nature; he possessed more feeling for the individual, and was subtler in his treatment of human idiosyncrasies.

The Way of the World reflects attitudes concerning sexuality that prevailed for centuries; above all, the play suggests, the most fascinating aspect of sexual relations is that of the chase. The pursuit, usually of the male for the female, although sometimes reversed, dominates Restoration comedy and is both glorified and satirized in *The Way of the World*. The lovely and intelligent Millamant herself expresses her belief in the necessity for a period devoted to such pursuit if a woman is to attract and keep her lover. By playing hard to get, a woman proves her eventual worth. Congreve took these conventional attitudes and fabricated his comedy from them, weaving a complicated and fascinating satire that continues to delight audiences and readers after two centuries.

"Critical Evaluation" by Bruce D. Reeves

Bibliography:
Holland, Norman. *The First Modern Comedies.* Cambridge, Mass.: Harvard University Press, 1959. This remains required reading for any student of English comedy written between the Restoration and the eighteenth century. Holland's discussion of *The Way of the World* does justice to the play's many complexities. Highly recommended.
Muir, Kenneth. *The Comedy of Manners.* London: Hutchinson University Library, 1970. A handy little book that provides an overview of the principal writers of stage comedy in England between the Restoration and the early eighteenth century. The chapter on Congreve contains a fine discussion of one of his best-known plays, *The Way of the World*.
Novak, Maximillian E. *William Congreve.* New York: Twayne, 1971. Probably the best general introduction to Congreve, with an act-by-act discussion of *The Way of the World* and an extensive annotated bibliography.
Powell, Jocelyn. *Restoration Theatre Production.* London: Routledge & Kegan Paul, 1984. A delightful and very readable account of Restoration drama—from a "production" angle. Powell discusses music, acting styles, and scenery, provides many wonderful illustrations, and concludes with a particularly sensitive and informed discussion of *The Way of the World*.
Williams, Aubrey L. *An Approach to Congreve.* New Haven, Conn.: Yale University Press, 1979. Williams stresses the "common ground" of Christian belief shared by Congreve and his audience. Controversial, but clearly and persuasively written. The chapter on *The Way of the World* focuses on Mirabell, the play's hero, whom Williams would exonerate of the charges of Machiavellianism so often brought against him.

THE WAY WE LIVE NOW

Type of work: Novel
Author: Anthony Trollope (1815-1882)
Type of plot: Social realism
Time of plot: February to August, 1873
Locale: London and Suffolk
First published: 1874-1875

Principal characters:
    LADY CARBURY, a writer
    SIR FELIX CARBURY, her son
    HETTA CARBURY, her daughter
    ROGER CARBURY, the squire of Carbury Hall, in love with his cousin
        Hetta
    PAUL MONTAGUE, also in love with Hetta
    MRS. WINIFRED HURTLE, an American, formerly Paul Montague's fiancé
    AUGUSTUS MELMOTTE, financier
    MARIE MELMOTTE, his daughter
    LORD NIDDERDALE, Marie's suitor
    MR. ADOLPHUS LONGSTAFFE, the squire of Caversham Hall
    DOLLY LONGSTAFFE, his son
    GEORGIANA LONGSTAFFE, his daughter
    EZEKIAL BREHGERT, a Jewish banker and Georgiana's suitor
    MR. BROUNE, a newspaper editor
    RUBY RUGGLES, in love with Sir Felix Carbury
    JOHN CRUMB, Ruby's fiancé
    MRS. PIPKIN, Ruby's aunt and Mrs. Hurtle's landlady

The Story:

Lady Carbury was beset by worries about her career and the futures of her son and daughter. She tried to flatter editors into reviewing her new book favorably; she tried to persuade her daughter Hetta to marry her cousin Roger Carbury; and she hoped to find an heiress to marry her wastrel son, Sir Felix.

Roger Carbury was deeply in love with Hetta, but Hetta loved Roger's friend, Paul Montague. Roger had earlier persuaded Paul to break with his American fiancée, Mrs. Hurtle, arguing that her vagueness about her past, coupled with rumors that she had fought a duel with her husband and had shot a man, made her an unsuitable wife for an English gentleman. When Paul fell in love with Hetta, however, Roger felt betrayed.

Sir Felix was a financial drain on his mother; his chief pastime was gambling with other dissolute young gentlemen at their club, the Beargarden. He reluctantly agreed to his mother's plan that he court Marie Melmotte, the only child of the arrogant financier Augustus Melmotte. Melmotte had been in London only for a short time and was dogged by rumors of past shady dealings, but he had established himself as London's leading financial genius. Felix's wooing of Marie lacked spirit, but Marie thought him beautiful and determined to marry him despite her father's opposition and preference for another suitor, Lord Nidderdale, whose family connections were superior to those of Sir Felix. Marie, who knew she had control over money that her father had settled on her in order to make it secure if his speculations failed, devised a plan whereby she and Sir Felix would elope to New York. Melmotte's men seized Marie in Liverpool before her ship had sailed, however, and Sir Felix did not leave London at all, instead spending the night gambling away the money provided him by Marie and his mother. Lady Carbury, in anguish over her son's behavior, turned for help to Mr. Broune, an editor with whom she had flirted and whose marriage proposal she had rejected, but with whom she began to develop a more honest intimacy.

Melmotte had skillfully drawn members of the British upper classes into his financial schemes, the biggest of which involved selling shares in a projected railroad from Utah to Mexico. Paul Montague had been made a partner in the scheme through his association in California with Hamilton Fisker, a wheeler-dealer who had originated the railroad plan. Melmotte organized a toothless board of directors, including English aristocrats with no financial expertise, among them Sir Felix Carbury and Adolphus Longstaffe. Longstaffe was a Suffolk squire; unlike Roger, Longstaffe had social ambitions that had led him to live far beyond his means.

Longstaffe's financial straits had led him to sell one of his properties, Pickering, to Melmotte (and foolishly to give Melmotte the title deeds before Melmotte had paid him), and to suggest that his daughter Georgiana stay with the Melmottes in London. Georgiana despised the Melmottes but thought her only hope of finding a husband was to spend the social season in London. When Georgiana became engaged to the banker Mr. Brehgert, her family was outraged that she would marry a Jew. Her father ordered her to return to Caversham, and she wrote Brehgert such an insensitive letter that he broke off the engagement.

Melmotte's aura of astounding wealth and ever-increasing profits had moved political leaders to sponsor his candidacy for Parliament. The climax of the political campaign coincided with a magnificent dinner Melmotte gave for the visiting emperor of China. Melmotte was elected, but many of the social and political elite of London who had vied for tickets to the dinner failed to attend when rumors arose that Melmotte had committed forgery. Melmotte had indeed forged the signature of Longstaffe's son on a document giving Melmotte title to Pickering. Melmotte entered Parliament but knew he had little chance of saving his reputation and fortune.

While he was courting Marie Melmotte, Sir Felix Carbury had also aroused the interest of Ruby Ruggles, a Suffolk farm woman who had deserted her fiancé, the meal and pollard dealer John Crumb, to run away to London, where she stayed with her aunt, Mrs. Pipkin, and went out to music halls with Sir Felix. Boarding with Mrs. Pipkin was Mrs. Hurtle, who had come to London hoping to resume her engagement to Paul Montague. Montague loved Hetta, but he so hated causing pain to Mrs. Hurtle that he agreed to call on her and even spent a weekend with her in a seaside hotel. After Roger Carbury encountered them on the beach, Paul finally made a firm break with Mrs. Hurtle (he had also withdrawn from the Railroad Board) and became engaged to Hetta Carbury. Sir Felix, coming to Mrs. Pipkin's house in search of Ruby Ruggles, found Mrs. Hurtle there and told Hetta about Mrs. Hurtle's entanglement with Paul. Hetta, distraught, broke off her engagement.

Mrs. Pipkin and Mrs. Hurtle persuaded Ruby to marry John Crumb after Crumb had given Sir Felix a beating. Marie Melmotte, no longer caring whom she married, became engaged to Lord Nidderdale, but the engagement collapsed when Melmotte, having again committed forgery, was found out and killed himself with prussic acid. Marie still had the money her father had settled on her, and she went to California with Mrs. Hurtle, whose former husband now claimed their divorce was invalid, and with Hamilton Fisker, whom Marie married.

At Paul Montague's request, Hetta had gone to Mrs. Hurtle to inquire about her relationship with Paul. Mrs. Hurtle, resisting her desire for revenge, had convinced Hetta that Paul had been faithful to her. Hetta and Paul married, and Roger Carbury, knowing he would never love anyone else, invited them to live at Carbury Hall and promised to make their son his heir. Georgiana Longstaffe settled for marriage to a curate. Lady Carbury married Mr. Broune, and Sir Felix was sent to Germany under the care of a clergyman.

Critical Evaluation:

Although some twentieth century critics regard *The Way We Live Now* as Anthony Trollope's masterpiece, the novel was greeted with disappointment by its first readers. Trollope came to see it as an aberration, going too far in its satirical disgust with the corruption of upper-class British society. His earlier novels had striven for a balance between belief in the virtuous stability of British institutions and the viability of the British class structure, and skepticism about their defects. In *The Way We Live Now*, moral concerns seem nearly to have disappeared from the lives of upper-class characters, who have given themselves over to greed and ostentation.

A key figure in the novel is an outsider of murky origins and shady financial dealings, Augustus Melmotte, whose rapid rise in English society, even to the point of election to Parliament, is supported by members of the ruling class. Those who support him are aware that Melmotte is a fraud but are cynically eager to attach themselves to his power to make money. He represents "the way we live now." The central figure for "the better way we lived in the past" is Roger Carbury, one of the model English gentlemen who appear in many of Trollope's novels. Carbury is an ideal. His modest country estate has been in his family for centuries. He lives within his income, without ostentation, as did his forefathers; he believes "a man's standing in the world should not depend at all upon his wealth" (though it certainly is connected to inherited social standing—Trollope is no democrat). He is absolutely trustworthy, and he "would have felt himself disgraced to enter the house of such a one as Augustus Melmotte."

The Way We Live Now presents Roger Carbury as an anachronism. His social standing in the general estimation—though not in his own—has been eclipsed by that of more ambitious neighboring families such as the Longstaffes, who live beyond their means and are easy prey for Melmotte's investment schemes. Carbury is nearly alone in the world: He has never married, and his sisters go off to India and the American West with their husbands. His cousin Hetta, whom he wants to marry, prefers Paul Montague, who, although not despicable, is morally and socially unanchored. Demonstration of this is his becoming one of the members of the Board of Directors of Melmotte's railroad scheme. Without a son of his own, Roger fears his heir will have to be Hetta's wastrel brother, Sir Felix.

Roger Carbury lacks an immediate family and seems unlikely to acquire one, but many other characters in the novel have dysfunctional families. One of these is Lady Carbury and her two children: Lady Carbury spoils her son, who is incapable of caring for anyone and who threatens to bankrupt her. Lady Carbury seems to have little feeling for her daughter other than anger that Hetta refuses to be married off safely to Roger. Family relations are even worse among the Longstaffes, the Melmottes, and, Trollope leads readers to assume, myriad other upper-class families of the 1870's.

The dominant symbol of the loss of traditional moral values is gambling. The novel parallels a general upper-class eagerness to buy shares in Melmotte's railroad speculation with the nightly card games enjoyed by Sir Felix, the Longstaffes' son Dolly, and other dissolute young gentlemen. The IOUs they exchange when they run out of cash are the equivalent of the worthless pieces of paper representing shares in Melmotte's yet-to-be-built railroad. When it is discovered that one of the young gentlemen habitually cheats, the others are at first shocked but quickly absorb cheating as yet another category of behavior one might as well accept.

Trollope's idealization of Roger Carbury makes it clear that *The Way We Live Now*'s critique of a money-oriented capitalistic world comes from a conservative, aristocratic perspective. Unlike Charles Dickens' *Little Dorrit* (1855-1857), for example, which has a predecessor of Melmotte in the financial schemer Merdle, Trollope's novel is not concerned with the exploitation of the poor.

Despite its stolid conservatism, *The Way We Live Now* becomes in its later sections more complex and open-ended in its depiction of the dilemmas facing Trollope's society. One example of this development is the way in which Trollope's characterization of Melmotte shifts from caricature to a moving, if also horrifying, psychological portrait of a man caught up in a game he can no longer control. A second example is the novel's treatment of its more independent female characters. Lady Carbury, Marie Melmotte, and Mrs. Hurtle all serve Trollope as examples of what was going wrong with London society, but they also emerge as women doing their best to free themselves from the abusive situations life has given them. In the second half of the novel, Roger Carbury, who has no use at all for Mrs. Hurtle and little for Lady Carbury, seems increasingly irrelevant. The novel's broad satire diminishes, and Trollope seems to become increasingly engaged with the emotional complexities of his characters.

Anne Howells

Bibliography:

Barickman, Richard, Susan MacDonald, and Myra Stark. *Corrupt Relations: Dickens, Thackeray, Trollope, Collins and the Victorian Sexual System.* New York: Columbia University Press, 1982. Explores the extent to which Trollope's fiction, like that of some of his contemporaries, moves beyond the sexual stereotypes of the time to recognize the damage these stereotypes did to the lives of women and men.

Gilmour, Robin. *The Idea of the Gentleman in the Victorian Novel.* Winchester, Mass.: Allen & Unwin, 1981. Sets Trollope's gentlemanly ideal in its historical context.

Harvey, Geoffrey. *The Art of Anthony Trollope.* New York: St. Martin's Press, 1980. Thoughtful discussion of *The Way We Live Now*, praising Trollope's combination of "an absolutist moral stance and a high degree of moral relativism."

Levine, George. *The Realistic Imagination: English Fiction from Frankenstein to Lady Chatterly.* Chicago: University of Chicago Press, 1981. The best discussion of Trollope's modes of representation, emphasizing the dependence of Trollope's realism on "an almost cynical acceptance of the necessity for arbitrary and traditional rules."

MacDonald, Susan Peck. *Anthony Trollope.* Boston: Twayne, 1987. Excellent introduction to the complexities of Trollope's fiction; includes an annotated bibliography.

THE WEALTH OF NATIONS

Type of work: Economics
Author: Adam Smith (1723-1790)
First published: An Inquiry into the Nature and Causes of the Wealth of Nations, 1776

The classic statement of economic liberalism, the policy of laissez-faire, was written during a ten-year period by Adam Smith, a Scottish professor of moral philosophy. The book's ideas were useful in encouraging the rise of new business enterprise in Europe, but the ideas could not have taken hold so readily had it not been for the scope of Smith's work and the effectiveness of his style.

As a philosopher, Smith was interested in finding intellectual justification for certain economic principles that he came to believe, but as an economist and writer, he was interested in making his ideas prevail in the world of business. He was reacting against oppressive systems of economic control that were restricting the growth of business; but, although he concerned himself with general principles and their practical application, he was aware of the value of the individual, whether employer or laborer. There is no reason to believe Smith would have sanctioned monopolistic excesses of business, or any unprincipled use of the free enterprise philosophy. To cite him in reverential tones is not to gain his sanction.

Smith began his work with the assumption that whatever a nation consumes is either the product of the annual labor of that nation or what is purchased with the products of labor. The wealth of the nation depends upon the proportion of the produce to the consumers, and that proportion depends partly upon the proportion of those who are employed to those who are not, but even more on the skill of the workers and the efficiency of the means of distribution.

Book 1 of *The Wealth of Nations* considers the question of how the skill of the laborers can best be increased. Book 2 is a study of capital stock, since it is argued that the proportion of workers to nonlaborers is a function of the amount of capital stock available. In book 3, Smith explains how Europe came to emphasize the industry of the towns at the expense of agriculture. Various economic theories are presented in book 4, some stressing the importance of industry in the town, others, the importance of agriculture. Book 5 considers the revenue of the sovereign, or commonwealth, with particular attention paid to the sources of that revenue and the consequences of governmental debt.

In Smith's view, the productive power of labor is increased most readily by the division of labor: If each worker is given a specific job, the worker becomes more skillful, time is saved, and machinery will be invented that further speeds the rate of production. Smith believed that, as a result of the increase in production that followed the division of labor, a well-governed community would enjoy a "universal opulence which extends itself to the lowest ranks of people."

Smith regarded the division of labor as a necessary consequence of the human propensity to trade or exchange one thing for another. He believed that the propensity to trade is a consequence of a more fundamental human trait: self-love. Thus, for Smith, the basic motivating force of any economic system is the self-interest of each person involved in the system.

Money originated as a means of facilitating exchange when the products of those who wish to barter are not desired by those with whom they choose to trade. To use Smith's example, a butcher who has all the bread and beer he or she needs will not accept more bread or beer in exchange for meat. If the person with bread or beer can exchange it elsewhere for "money"— whether it be shells, tobacco, salt, or cattle, or the most favored medium of exchange, metal—

the money can be used to buy meat from the butcher.

Among the most important ideas in *The Wealth of Nations* is Smith's claim that labor is the real measure of the exchangeable value of commodities. Commodities have a value in use, but this value is unimportant to the producer, who seeks to exchange what has been made for something that is needed. The amount of work that can be purchased with a commodity is the real exchangeable value of that commodity. Thus, Smith defines wealth as the power of purchasing labor. The nominal, as distinguished from the real, price of commodities is their money value.

Smith defines natural price as the average price of a commodity in a community, and market price as the actual selling price. He presents the familiar principle of supply and demand by stating that market price increases when the quantity of a commodity brought to market falls short of the demand.

Wherever there is perfect liberty, the advantages and disadvantages of different uses of labor and stock must be either equal or tending to equality, according to Smith. There are counterbalancing circumstances that affect equality: the agreeableness of the job, the cost of learning the business, the constancy of employment, the amount of trust that must be put in the employee, and the probability of success.

Smith makes a distinction between productive and unproductive labor. Labor is productive when it adds to the value of something, unproductive when it does not. The labor of a manufacturer adds to the value of the material that is used, but the labor of a menial servant adds nothing to the value of the employer who is served. This distinction is important, because capital is explained by reference to the proportion of productive to unproductive labor. Capital can be used for purchasing raw materials, for manufacturing, for transportation, and for distribution.

Adam Smith was confident that he could discover the natural order of economic matters. To later critics, however, it has appeared that he was mistaking his own preferred kind of economic situation for that which would prevail if economic relations among people were in no way affected by social habit. His inclination was to regard what would prevail in a civilized community free from governmental restraint as the natural state of affairs. This view is acceptable when he says, for example, "According to the natural course of things, therefore, the greater part of the capital of every growing society is, first, directed to agriculture, afterwards to manufactures, and last of all to foreign commerce"; but the following account of rent is more provocative: "Rent, considered as the price paid for the use of land, is naturally the highest which the tenant can afford to pay in the actual circumstances of the land." Smith appears to have written without any obvious interest in supporting one economic class against another, and his definitions of "natural" price, rent, and other economic factors are couched in neutral terms.

Smith's experiences as a teacher and philosopher are reflected most clearly in his account "Of the Expence of the Institutions for the Education of Youth." He is rather bitter about the quality of education that results when the teacher is not driven by economic necessity to do his or her best. He asserts that professors who are responsible only to their colleagues are likely to allow one another to neglect their duties as teachers. The result is that "In the university of Oxford, the greater part of the public professors have, for these many years, given up altogether even the pretense of teaching." Smith favors giving students a considerable part to play in the selection and retention of teachers, and he warned that if this were not done, the professors would devise ways of giving "sham-lectures" and would force their students to attend regularly and keep silent.

Smith thought that the wealthy and wellborn could see to the education of their young, but that the state should support education for those who could not otherwise afford it. He argued that it was important, particularly in free countries, that the public be educated in order to exercise good judgment.

In considering the revenue of the state, Smith proceeded on the principle that whatever expense was beneficial to the whole society could justly be defrayed by the general contribution of the whole society. Thus, defending the society, supporting the chief magistrate, administering justice, maintaining good roads and communications, supporting state institutions or public works, and, under certain circumstances, defraying the expenses of educational institutions and institutions for religious instruction are all properly supported by general contribution of the whole society.

Support of the institutions and activities of the state must come either from some fund belonging to the state or from the revenue of the people. Smith considers three sources of the revenue of individuals: rent, profit, and wages. His discussion of taxes is based upon four maxims: The taxpayer ought to be taxed according to ability to pay, as determined by revenue; the tax should be certain in the sense that there should be no question as to the time, manner, or quantity of payment; taxes should be levied in a convenient manner, for example, taxes on consumer goods are paid for when the goods are bought; and the tax should be economical in the sense that it should not be expensive to collect.

Adam Smith's *The Wealth of Nations* is a temperate, thorough, engrossing analysis of the economic facts of life in a free industrial society. Insofar as it is, to some extent, a proposal, it is not surprising that it has not won universal approval; but it is a masterpiece of its kind, and its influence on modern thought and practice has been significant.

Bibliography:

Brown, Vivienne. *Adam Smith's Discourse: Canonicity, Commerce and Conscience.* London: Routledge & Kegan Paul, 1994. Discusses the attack on mercantilism in *The Wealth of Nations* and reveals problems with Smith's theories. Examines those theories from political, moral, and economic viewpoints. Discusses inconsistency between *The Wealth of Nations* and Smith's *The Theory of Moral Sentiments* (1759).

Muller, Jerry. *Adam Smith in His Time and Ours.* New York: Free Press, 1993. Describes the basic economic theories in *The Wealth of Nations.* Examines the effect of those theories on the mercantilism of Smith's time, on the growth of capitalism, and on the late twentieth century.

Rae, John. *Statement of Some New Principles on the Subject of Political Economy: Exposing the Fallacies of the System of Free Trade, and of Some Other Doctrines Maintained in "The Wealth of Nations."* Boston: Hillard, Gray, and Company, 1834. Very critical evaluation. Views *The Wealth of Nations* as a philosophy to explain known phenomena, not as an inquiry producing new economic laws.

West, E. G. *Adam Smith: The Man and His Works.* Indianapolis: Liberty Press, 1976. Presents the historical context of *The Wealth of Nations* and its immediate impact on Great Britain. Examines in detail many of Smith's ideas. Discusses misconceptions about *The Wealth of Nations.*

Winch, Donald. *Adam Smith's Politics: An Essay in Historiographic Revision.* Cambridge, England: Cambridge University Press, 1978. Discusses the concepts in *The Wealth of Nations* from the perspective of liberal capitalism. Examines the influence of Smith's involvement in Whig politics on his economic theories in *The Wealth of Nations.*

THE WEARY BLUES

Type of work: Poetry
Author: Langston Hughes (1902-1967)
First published: 1926

The Weary Blues, Langston Hughes's first published volume of poetry, is grounded in a blues aesthetic. Hughes, one of the younger writers of the so-called Harlem Renaissance, had begun publishing his verse in such journals as *Crisis*, *Opportunity*, and *Survey Graphic*, and his landmark poem, "The Negro Speaks of Rivers," appeared in *Crisis* in 1921. His work, as well as that of fellow Harlem Renaissance poets such as Countee Cullen, Claude McKay, and Gwendolyn Bennett, was also published in the short-lived journal, *Fire!!* (1926), edited by Wallace Thurman. *The Weary Blues*, which contains an introduction by Carl Van Vechten, was published during the height of the Jazz Age, when the blues recordings of Mamie Smith, Ma Rainey, and Bessie Smith were in vogue.

Jazz and blues themes underlie Hughes's presentation of Harlem nightlife. Jazz, which provided a stimulus for the poets Carl Sandburg and Vachel Lindsay, was more than an incidental subject for Hughes, too. Although the *aab* pattern of traditional blues songs is not pronounced in *The Weary Blues*, Hughes structured a number of his poems on blueslike formats, and he used vernacular to replicate the vocal patterns of black speech.

The collection of poems treats a primary blues theme, that of the problems encountered in personal relationships. Many critics did not appreciate the blues elements Hughes explored because they thought it represented an area of black life that was not socially uplifting. *The Weary Blues* shows Hughes' determination to present the many sides of black life. He addresses romantic love, African heritage, and the social aspects of race and color. In doing so he raises the experiences of the common people to the level of art. The poems distill Hughes's own experience in locations as varied as Mexico, West Africa, and Harlem.

The collection contains seven sections: "The Weary Blues," "Dream Variations," "The Negro Speaks of Rivers," "Black Pierrot," "Water-Front Streets," "Shadows in the Sun," and "Our Land." Each section is named after the first poem of the group. The book opens with "Proem," in which Hughes defines the "Negro" with references to African heritage, slavery, musical contributions, and oppression.

"The Weary Blues" section consists of fifteen poems that depict Harlem nightlife through images of cabarets, performing artists, and personal relationships. Structured in free verse form, the single poem entitled "The Weary Blues" contains a blues lyric from an actual blues composition. The poem depicts the jazz life through the observations of a persona sensitive to the conditions of performance, who comments,

> Droning a drowsy syncopated tune,
> Rocking back and forth to a mellow croon,
>   I heard a Negro play.
> Down on Lenox Avenue the other night
> By the pale dull pallor of an old gas light.

In these lines, syncopation, the defining rhythmic quality of jazz, is characterized by the word "rocking." The nightclub is the setting in which musicians labor to the point of weariness, and the act of performance is equated with race in the image of "ebony hands." The observer also notes "the sad raggy tune," a reference to ragtime and to the sadness and despair implicit in the blues performance.

"Jazzonia," the second poem in this section, describes an uptown nightclub where jazz artists are accompanied by a sensuous dancer whose movements imply seduction, which is signified by "Eve" or "Cleopatra." Another poem depicting dance, "Negro Dancers," contains black vernacular and representations of jazz rhythms in syllables that suggest future motifs of bebop. "Two mo' ways to do de Charleston!" the closing line of the poem, identifies the highly popular dance style associated with James P. Johnson.

In "The Cat and the Saxophone (2 A.M.)," the lyrics to a popular song—"Everybody loves my baby but my baby don't love nobody but me"—are used to form a call-and-response pattern that parallels the conversation in a cabaret. "Young Singer" and "Cabaret" are other poems depicting jazz venues. In "Cabaret," the persona asks, "Does a jazz-band ever sob?" a question that implies that the observer is somewhat distanced from the blues experience. In "To Midnight Nan at Leroy's," the persona speaks in syncopated black vernacular. The poem portrays African American women and the problematic love relationships often depicted in blues songs.

Using jazz performance as a backdrop, "Harlem Night Club" explores interracial socializing. The poem suggests that nightlife integration does not signify social equality. African American women performers are the subject of "Nude Young Dancer," and in "Young Prostitute" sexual exploitation is suggested in the line "like a withered flower." The withering of the prostitute contrasts with the exotic sensuousness of the dancer in "To a Black Dancer in 'The Little Savoy.'"

The black woman dancer is also portrayed in "Song for a Banjo Dance," which is set in a rural folk context, whereas the ability of the blues to provide a transcendent experience is exemplified in "Blues Fantasy." The closing poem of the section, "Lenox Avenue: Midnight," restates nightlife themes and evokes the cabaret atmosphere.

"Dream Variations," the second section, presents nature and romantic themes. Though these lyric poems primarily focus on such images of nature as the moon and autumn, there are references as well to racial themes. The "Dream" metaphor, central to Hughes's poetic concept, is evident in the title poem, in which black liberation is equated to the end of "the white day." In "Winter Moon," the moon is described as "thin and sharp and ghostly white." "Fantasy in Purple" contrasts musical images of black culture with those of Europe. The drum signifies African American culture and announces tragic social circumstances. The "white violins" are contrasted with the "blaring trumpet" and "darkness." "March Moon" is an ironic lyric poem that personifies the moon as a naked woman "undressed" by the wind. The closing poem, "Joy," uses personification to locate joy in an urban situation.

Section 3, "The Negro Speaks of Rivers," contains one of Hughes's best-known poems. Dedicated to W. E. B. Du Bois, "The Negro Speaks of Rivers" traces African heritage from the perspective of a universal black persona who compares the black legacy with certain major rivers of the world. These rivers, which form the structure of the poem, represent locations where people of African descent have lived: "I've known rivers ancient as the world and older than the/ flow of human blood in human veins." The Euphrates, the Congo, and the Nile represent ancient heritage; slavery in the Americas is symbolized by the Mississippi. The poem also uses "soul" to identify sources of being and spirituality.

"Cross," the second poem in this section, deals with race mixture and the uncertain identity of the mulatto, who is "neither white nor black." "The Jester" questions the dual mask of comedy and tragedy. In "The South," the speaker, angry and embittered by racial persecution, describes the South as "Beast-strong" and "Idiot-brained." Personified as a woman, the South rejects the love of black people. By contrast, the North, although cold, is a "kinder mistress." In "Aunt Sue's Stories," Hughes examines oppression in the South and the legacy of slavery through the oral tradition, and he praises blackness in "Poem," which counters the negative stereotypes of darkness: "The night is beautiful/ So the faces of my people."

In the fourth section, "Black Pierrot," Hughes addresses romantic love and images of black women. In the signature poem, the speaker is troubled by unrequited love. "Color" is used to identify the night, the soul, and hope in "a new brown love." In "Harlem Night Song," cabaret and jazz are the backdrop for a declaration of love. In "Poem," a lyrical praise to black beauty, the black woman becomes a symbolic figure of adoration and "black" is a positive.

> My black one,
> Thou art not beautiful
> Yet thou hast
> A loveliness
> Surpassing beauty.

Using biblical pronouns, the persona redefines beauty through the negative stereotype of darkness. "Songs to the Dark Virgin" and "When Sue Wears Red" elevate black women as timeless representatives of ancestral queenliness. Susanna Jones appears like "an ancient cameo/ turned brown by the ages."

"Water-Front Streets," the fifth section, draws on Hughes' experience as a seaman. The title poem uses the dream motif and traditional British poetic language to suggest the romantic hopes of a sailor destined for places "where the spring is wondrous rare." Other poems in this section, such as "A Farewell" and "Long Trip," use water imagery and the journey motif to portray separation and isolation. "Caribbean Sunset," a four-line poem, describes the sun in startling images of blood. "Natcha" addresses the theme of love for sale, and "Death of an Old Seaman" considers the seaman's soul and afterlife.

In section 6, "Shadows in the Sun," Hughes focuses primarily on women. Isolation, suicide, illness, labor, and alienation are among the themes he covers. "Beggar Boy" describes a lad whose flute song contrasts with his bare existence. "Troubled Woman" presents an image of despair and fatigue by portraying a woman who is "Like a/ Wind-blown autumn flower." "Suicide's Note," a three-line piece, implies death by drowning. "To the Dark Mercedes of 'El Palacio De Amor'" and "Mexican Market Woman" depict, respectively, the young beautiful prostitute and the aged vendor whose labor is timeless. These poems, along with "Soledad: A Cuban Portrait," reflect the poet's treatment of women in the Spanish-speaking world of the Americas. "Young Bride" also deals with a woman's tragic circumstances. The dream motif is developed in "The Dream Keeper," in which the poet sees the escape of dreaming as an alternative to life's realities: "Bring me all your dreams,/ You dreamers."

In "Our Land," the final section, the title poem calls for a natural world of "gorgeous sun" and "tall thick trees" as opposed to a "land where life is cold." Other poems return to political and race-conscious themes. "Lament for Dark Peoples" describes the disruption of Native American and African cultures by European "civilization." The "red" and "black" people are "caged" in "the circus of civilization." "Poem" treats the clash of African and Western civilizations; "Danse Africaine" shows the connection between African dance and a heritage of rhythm. "Summer Night" considers jazz images and musical life. In "The White Ones," the poet uses whiteness to address ambivalent feelings and relative beauty: "I do not hate you,/ For your faces are beautiful, too." Two of Hughes's best-known poems close the collection, "Mother to Son," which develops the metaphor of life as "no crystal stair," and "Epilogue," also known as

"I, Too," which describes the "darker brother" and his resolve to declare his beauty and his rightful place at the "table" of equality.

Joseph McLaren

Bibliography:

Cullen, Countee. Review of *The Weary Blues*, by Langston Hughes. In *Langston Hughes: Critical Perspectives Past and Present*, edited by Henry Louis Gates, Jr., and K. A. Appiah. New York: Amistad, 1993. Questions the merit of Hughes' jazz and blues poems, but praises his more traditional lyrical verse.

Jemie, Onwuchekwa. *Langston Hughes: An Introduction to the Poetry*. New York: Columbia University Press, 1976. One of the first full-length treatments of Hughes' poetry. Discusses both jazz and blues themes and treats *The Weary Blues* in chapter 2, "Shadow of the Blues."

Miller, R. Baxter. *The Art and Imagination of Langston Hughes*. Lexington: University Press of Kentucky, 1989. Examines Hughes' poetry by focusing on the imaginative process. *The Weary Blues* is interpreted in chapter 3, "'Deep like the Rivers,' The Lyrical Imagination," as a work that reveals a diversity of techniques.

Rampersad, Arnold. *1902-1941: I, Too, Sing America*. Vol. 1 in *The Life of Langston Hughes*. New York: Oxford University Press, 1986. A definitive biography of Hughes, which addresses the literary history of *The Weary Blues* in the context of Hughes's relationship to literary figures of the 1920's.

Tracy, Steven C. *Langston Hughes and the Blues*. Urbana: University of Illinois Press, 1988. A comprehensive treatment of blues influences in Hughes's poetry. Includes a substantial definition of the structures of blues songs and corresponding patterns in Hughes' poetry. Examines *The Weary Blues* in chapter 3, "Creating the Blues."

THE WEB AND THE ROCK

Type of work: Novel
Author: Thomas Wolfe (1900-1938)
Type of plot: Impressionistic realism
Time of plot: 1900-1928
Locale: North Carolina, New York, and Europe
First published: 1939

Principal characters:
GEORGE WEBBER, a young writer
ESTHER JACK, his beloved

The Story:

George Webber's childhood was one of bleakness and misery. He was a charity ward who lived with his aunt and uncle. George's father had deserted him and his mother and had gone off to live with another woman. After the death of George's mother, her Joyner relatives took George into their home, where the boy was never allowed to forget that he had the blood of the Webbers mixed in with his Joyner blood. Strangely, all of his good and beautiful dreams were dreams of his father, and often he hotly and passionately defended his father to the Joyners. His love for his father made his childhood a divided one. George hated the people his aunt and uncle called good, and those they called bad, he loved. A lonely child, George kept his thoughts and dreams to himself rather than expose them to the ridicule of the Joyners, but the picture of that happy, joyful world of his father, and others like him, stayed with him during those bleak years of his childhood.

When George was sixteen years of age, his father died, leaving the boy a small inheritance. With that money, George left the little Southern town of Libya Hill and went to college. There he found knowledge, freedom, and life. Like many other young men, George wasted some of that freedom in sprees of riotous and loose living, but he also read everything he could get his hands on, and he was deeply impressed with the power of great writers. George was beginning to feel the need to put some of his thoughts and memories down on paper. He wanted to write of the two sides of the world—the bright, happy world of the people who had everything and the horrible, dreary world of the derelicts and the poor. His college years ended, and George fulfilled the dream of every country boy in the nation; he went to the city, to the beautiful, wonderful "rock," as he called New York.

The city was as great and as marvelous as George had known it would be. He shared an apartment with four other young men; it was a dingy, cheap place, but it was their own apartment, where they could do as they pleased. George, however, found the city to be a lonely place in spite of its millions of people and its bright lights. There was no one to whom he was responsible nor to whom he belonged. He thought he would burst with what he knew about people and about life, and, because there was no one he could talk to about those things, he tried to write them down. He began his first novel.

The next year was the loneliest one George had ever known. He drove himself mercilessly. He was wretched, for the words torturing his mind would not go on the paper as he wanted. At the end of a year, he took the last of his inheritance and went to Europe. He hoped to find there the peace of mind he needed to finish his book. The cities of Europe did not hold his salvation.

He was still lonely and bitter, because he could not find the answer to the riddle of life. He went back to New York, and the city was no longer an unfriendly enemy, for George had found Esther.

They had met on the ship bound for New York. Esther was Mrs. Esther Jack, a well-known and successful stage-set designer. She was fifteen or twenty years older than George, but she was also younger in many ways, for Esther loved people and believed in them. Where George was silent and distrustful, Esther was open and trusting. George sometimes felt that theirs was the greatest love of all times, at once brutal and tender, passionate and friendly, so deep that it could not last. For the next three years, however, he was the king of the world. To Esther, George told all of his dreams, all of his memories, and all of his formerly wordless thoughts about life and people.

At first, George failed to realize that Esther meant more to him than just a lover. Gradually, he came to know that through her he was becoming a new person, a man who loved everyone. For the first time in his life, George Webber belonged to someone. Since he was no longer lonely, the torture and the torment left him. At last, his book began to take shape, to become a reality. George was happy.

Slowly, however, the magic of his affair with Esther began to disappear. He still loved her more than he believed possible and knew that he would always love her, but they began to quarrel, to have horrible, name-calling scenes that left them both exhausted and empty, even the quarrels that ended with passionate lovemaking. At first, George did not know the reason for those scenes, although he always knew that it was he who started them. Slowly, he began to realize that he quarreled with Esther because she possessed him so completely. He had given her his pride, his individuality, his dreams, his manhood. Esther had also unknowingly been a factor in his disillusionment, for through her he had met and known the great people of the world—the artists, the writers, the actors—and he had found those people disgusting and cheap. They had destroyed his childhood illusions of fame and greatness, and he hated them for it.

When George's novel was finished, Esther sent the manuscript to several publishers she knew. After months had passed without his hearing that it had been accepted, George turned on Esther in one final burst of savage abuse and told her to leave him and never return. Then he went to Europe again.

Although he had gone to Europe to forget Esther, he did nothing without thinking of her and longing for her. Esther wrote to him regularly, and he paced the floor if the expected letter did not arrive; but he was still determined to be himself, and, to accomplish his purpose, he must not see Esther again.

One night in a German beer hall, George got into a drunken brawl and was badly beaten. While he was in the hospital, a feeling of peace came over him for the first time in ten years. He looked into a mirror and saw his body as a thing apart from the rest of him. He knew that his body had been true to him, that it had taken the abuse he had heaped upon it for almost thirty years. Often he had been almost mad, and he had driven that body beyond endurance in his insane quest—for what, he did not know. Now he was ready to go home again. If his first novel was not published, he would write another. He still had much to say. The next time he would put it down correctly, and then he would be at peace with himself. George Webber was beginning to find himself at last.

Critical Evaluation:

In *The Story of a Novel* (1936), Thomas Wolfe responded to critics' complaints that he could write only about his own life, and that his Scribner's editor, Maxwell Perkins, was responsible for organizing the material of his first two novels, *Look Homeward, Angel* (1929) and *Of Time and the River* (1935). He promised to write in a more objective, disciplined style, and, to prove that he could structure his sprawling fiction without assistance, he severed his professional association with Perkins. In July, 1938, two months before he died following a brain operation, Wolfe submitted to his new editor, Edward C. Aswell, the manuscript from which his last two novels, *The Web and the Rock* and *You Can't Go Home Again* (1940), were assembled. Although somewhat more objective and more finely controlled than his earlier fiction, the novels continue the supreme subject of all of his work: the story of his own life reshaped into myth.

Critics have said that *The Web and the Rock* is at once the best and the worst novel written by Wolfe. Certainly the first part of the book, that describing George Webber's childhood in a Southern town, is an excellent regional chronicle. Here Wolfe's genius with words reaches new heights. The rest of the novel, however, drags somewhat from overdone treatment of a love story in which similar scenes are repeated until they become monotonous.

George Webber, described as monkeylike, with long arms and an awkward, ambling gait, scarcely resembles the tall, hawklike Eugene Gant of *Look Homeward, Angel*. Nevertheless, he is surely another psychological portrait of Wolfe, the tormented artist among Philistines. In the first part of *The Web and the Rock*, the author attempts to provide for his hero a new family and social background, but the Joyners, despite their vitality, are mere copies of the Pentlands; Libya Hill resembles Altamont; and the moody, romantic Webber recalls the young Eugene. Some of the minor characters, notably the baseball hero Nebraska Crane and Aunt Maw, are brilliantly drawn. The chapter "The Child by Tiger," originally published as a short story, reveals Wolfe's great power to create tragic myth. Above all, the strength of the first part of the book rests upon the author's heroic vision of the townspeople and the mountain folk of North Carolina—a stock of enterprising, stubborn, passionately independent souls. They represent the mysterious web of the earth. Like Webber, a child of the mountain folk, they are tied by threads of destiny not only to the land but also to the seasons, the workings of time. As an artist, Webber understands intuitively the heart of things, the patterns of life and dreams.

In roughly the second half of the novel, Wolfe contrasts the web of the earth with the rock of the city of New York. At this point in his writing, he abandons, for the most part, his scheme of objectivity and deals with the experiences of his own life. Webber meets and falls in love with Esther Jack (the same Esther who first appears to Eugene Gant in the "Faust and Helen" chapter of *Of Time and the River*)—in real life, the stage designer and artist Aline Bernstein. With remarkable frankness, Wolfe describes the tragic course of the affair between these markedly different personalities: the egotistic, brilliant, despotic provincial genius and his mistress, a sophisticated, sensitive, upper-middle-class Jewish wife and mother. As a realist, Wolfe is at his best detailing scenes of lovemaking and eating, of tempestuous quarrels and passionate reconciliations. Throughout the extended part of the book that deals with the love affair—for all of its excesses and absurdities—Wolfe is able to touch the reader: George and Esther truly care about each other and try desperately to make their fragile relationship endure.

The theme of *The Web and the Rock* is the fragility of all dreams. The rock of New York, which George once loved as well as feared, begins to crumble in this novel. The city, founded upon greed and selfish power, has no soul. To escape from his own sense of ruin, George visits pre-Nazi Germany, already ripe for the advent of Adolf Hitler. George hopes to recapture, among the drunken revelers at a Munich Oktoberfest, the sense of joy of his own manhood; but he becomes violent, a savage fighting the beer-hall swaggerers, and is terribly beaten. By the end of the novel, he wishes to return to the United States so that he might establish his dreams once again upon a foundation that will endure: upon the web of his failing sense of the earth, and the rock of an already insecure civilization. In the last chapter, "The Looking Glass," Webber comes to understand the futility of these dreams.

Bibliography:

Evans, Elizabeth. *Thomas Wolfe*. New York: Frederick Ungar, 1984. Excellent introduction to *The Web and the Rock*. Analytically summarizes its episodes and discusses Wolfe's narrative devices.

Idol, John Lane, Jr. *A Thomas Wolfe Companion*. Westport, Conn.: Greenwood Press, 1987. Explains how Wolfe's editor became virtually his coauthor. Identifies as major themes an artist's problems in a hostile environment; loneliness; and personal, social, and religious conflicts. Presents a book-by-book plot summary, an explication of symbols, and analyses of characters, all of whom are identified in a glossary.

Kennedy, Richard S. *The Window of Memory: The Literary Career of Thomas Wolfe*. Chapel Hill: University of North Carolina Press, 1962. Definitively combines biographical data and critical perceptions to fit *The Web and the Rock* into the evolution of Wolfe's career.

Ryssel, Fritz Heinrich. *Thomas Wolfe*. Translated by Helen Sebba. New York: Frederick Ungar, 1972. Shows how Wolfe confronted and partially solved technical and thematic problems resulting from turning to less autobiographical writing in *The Web and the Rock*.

A WEEK ON THE CONCORD AND MERRIMACK RIVERS

Type of work: Memoir
Author: Henry David Thoreau (1817-1862)
First published: 1849

In 1839, two years after his graduation from Harvard College, Henry David Thoreau and his brother John built a riverboat with their own hands and took the leisurely trip that provides the framework for Thoreau's *A Week on the Concord and Merrimack Rivers*. Although the work is based on a real experience, Thoreau molded his material to fit his artistic requirements. Thus, the actual time of the trip is reduced to seven days, each represented by a chapter in the work. The author does not hesitate to introduce observations and references to literary works which occur in his journals years after the actual journey. It is a mistake, then, to consider this work as a travel journal, just as it is a mistake to consider his *Walden* (1854) merely a treatise on domestic economy.

The work includes both prose and poetry and often provides meticulous observations about the flora, fauna, or geography of the area through which the boat passes. So the sight of a fisherman leads the author early in his work to discuss at length the fish in shoals in the stream and the "fish principle in nature" which disseminates the seeds of life everywhere so that wherever there is a fluid medium there are fish. In this respect, the work is somewhat like the scientific data gathering in nineteenth century works such as Charles Darwin's *The Voyage of the Beagle* (1839). The work, however, is neither a naturalist's handbook nor a traveler's guide.

Actually, the geographical journey down the rivers is a metaphor for our journey into the mind of the author. As Thoreau tells us about what he saw and thought as he drifted down the river, the reader enters the flow of ideas in the writer's mind. Just as the current of the stream bears along the boat with Thoreau and his brother, so the current of ideas in his mind bears along the reader by evoking the joy and nostalgia that Thoreau feels for those lost, golden days. As Thoreau says, human life is very much like a river running always downward to the sea, and, in this book, the reader enters for a moment the flow of Thoreau's unique existence.

One must remember that the circumstances of Thoreau's life provide an undercurrent of emotion in this apparently tranquil holiday as he recalled it in the solitude of Walden Pond. Both Henry and his brother John had been deeply in love with the same girl, Ellen Sewall, the daughter of a prominent New England family. John had first proposed marriage to her and had been refused; Henry fared no better. Perhaps their relative poverty was a contributing factor in their rejection. The two brothers are therefore friendly rivals, and their relationship occasions a long discussion of the nature of friendship. When one says that someone is a friend, one commonly means only that he or she is not an enemy. The true friend, however, will say, "Consent only to be what you are. I alone will never stand in your way." The violence of love is dangerous; durable friendship is serene and equable. The only danger of friendship is that it will end. Such was the emotional relationship of the two brothers.

Yet their friendship was to end. Within a year, John died suddenly and horribly. Thoreau could not look back to their vacation on the rivers without realizing that the happiness of those times could never be repeated. In a very real sense, the work is a prose elegy for his dead brother, the true friend, the rival in love. As in all elegies, the reader follows the progress of the mourner's soul as it seeks consolation for the loss, and the consolation comes from the passage of the seasons and the observation of the natural processes of death and regeneration. This unstated elegiac element is the main motive for the composition. Why grieve for a particular lost friend when all the world is subject to decay and change? Every natural object when carefully observed shows the natural process of death and rebirth. If one must grieve, one should therefore grieve for the sadness of all things and the transitory nature of all beauty found in the material world. So if one were to go to a New England village such as Sudbury, one would see in great detail the teeming activity there, but one must not forget that it was settled by people who were once as much alive as the people there now, but who are all gone, their places taken by new people. The Indians are replaced by the white settlers and the settlers in turn by their children. The Concord and Merrimack rivers flow timelessly into the sea; every individual life flows to its conclusion. The passage of the seasons is cyclical in that every autumn implies a future springtime. The voyage on the rivers is circular, and the two brothers return to their point of departure; thus life must pass back into the great body from which it was first drawn.

Thoreau's thinking is strongly conditioned by Romantic ideas. The whole book represents a return to nature. The author sees an accord between nature and the human spirit. He observes that he has a singular yearning for all wildness. He values cultural primitivism. He tells us that gardening is civil and social, but it wants the vigor and freedom of the forest and the outlaw. In fact, there may be an excess of cultivation that makes civilization pathetic. His poetry is plainly in the style of the English Romantics, written in ballad measure and celebrating nature and primitive heroes:

> Some hero of the ancient mold,
> Some arm of knightly worth,
> Of strength unbought, and faith unsold,
> Honored this spot of earth.

Among poets Thoreau praises Homer because he lived in an age when emotions flowed uncorrupted by excessive cultivation. Like William Wordsworth, he has a theory that the world is but a canvas to human imagination. He says that surely there is a life of the mind above the wants of the body and independent of it and that this life is expressed through cultivation of the capacity of the imagination. Like many Romantic writers, Thoreau seems to exalt the emotions at the expense of the rational faculty. He says that people have a respect for scholarship and learning that is out of all proportion to the use they commonly serve and that the scholar has not the skill to emulate the propriety and emphasis of the farmer's call to his team. In Thoreau's mind, act and feeling are to be valued above abstract thought.

Thoreau's work constitutes a major document in Transcendental thought. His observation that a farmer directing his team of horses is as important as a scholar's thought is connected to the theological notion that every person is called to perform a peculiar activity, to fill a particular place in life. This view that life presents a duty for everyone, that music is the sound of universal laws promulgated, and that marching is set to the pulse of the hero beating in unison with the pulse of nature and he steps to the measure of the universe, is characteristic of the pervasive moralism in Transcendental thought. When Thoreau looks at a sunset, he records that he is grateful to be reminded by interior evidence of the permanence of universal laws. In other words, by personal intuition a person watching a sunset is aware of an immanent deity presiding over the universe and providing people with an ethical imperative, a duty to do.

At the end of the week, Thoreau's boat grates once more on the bulrushes of its native port. The trip provides a framework to support a vast weight of Thoreau's thought—direct observation of nature, elegiac sentiment, Romantic and Transcendental notions—all flowing naturally across the mind of a young man as he drifts through the pastoral countryside of nineteenth century New England.

Bibliography:

Drake, William. "A Week on the Concord and Merrimack Rivers." In *Thoreau: A Collection of Critical Essays*, edited by Sherman Paul. Englewood Cliffs, N.J.: Prentice-Hall, 1962. Argues that Thoreau's journey on the Concord and Merrimack rivers is an exploratory journey into thought. Easily accessible.

Fink, Steven. *Prophet in the Marketplace: Thoreau's Development as a Professional Writer.* Princeton, N.J.: Princeton University Press, 1992. Contains a detailed discussion of the structure of *A Week on the Concord and Merrimack Rivers* and how Thoreau composed the book.

Johnson, Linck C. *Thoreau's Complex Weave: The Writing of "A Week on the Concord and Merrimack Rivers."* Charlottesville: University of Virginia Press, 1986. An extensive study of *A Week on the Concord and Merrimack Rivers*. Johnson focuses on both the complete version of the book and its first draft. Contains the text of the first draft.

Thoreau, Henry David. *The Illustrated "A Week on the Concord and Merrimack Rivers."* Edited by Carl F. Hovde, William L. Howarth, and Elizabeth Hall Witherell. Princeton, N.J.: Princeton University Press, 1983. Contains the text of *A Week on the Concord and Merrimack Rivers* complete with photographs by Herbert Wendell Gleason which visually document Thoreau's rivers. Also contains a helpful historical introduction to the book.

THE WELL OF LONELINESS

Type of work: Novel
Author: Radclyffe Hall (1880-1943)
Type of plot: Social realism
Time of plot: Early twentieth century
Locale: England, France
First published: 1928

>   *Principal characters:*
>   STEPHEN GORDON, a young lesbian
>   SIR PHILIP GORDON, her father
>   LADY ANNA GORDON, her mother
>   COLLINS, a housemaid
>   MISS PUDDLETON or PUDDLE, Stephen's governess
>   ANGELA CROSSBY, Stephen's first lover
>   MARY LLEWELLYN, Stephen's principal lover
>   JONATHAN BROCKETT, a playwright
>   VALÉRIE SEYMOUR, an author
>   MARTIN HALLAM, Stephen's friend

The Story:

Sir Philip and Lady Anna Gordon assumed that their firstborn would be a boy, and so when a female arrived they named her Stephen as planned. Schooled happily at Morton, the family's country estate, Stephen endeared herself to her father with her boyish demeanor, which troubled her mother and confused the children of the local gentry. The first sign of her homosexuality emerged at the age of seven, when she became infatuated with a housemaid named Collins, and was enraged one day to find a footman kissing her in a garden shed. Given a new pony, which swiftly replaced the housemaid in her affections, Stephen named it Collins. Riding with her father and hunting with the gentry now became her great passion; her skill won respect despite her unladylike manners, and soon her father presented her with a fine hunting horse, Raftery.

A tall, athletic teenager, Stephen learned to ride, fence, and speak fluent French, but her father wanted to enlarge her learning and so hired Miss Puddleton to be her governess. Under Puddle's exacting tutelage, Stephen resolved to become a writer. At a Christmas party, she at last found a companion, Martin Hallam, her equal in imagination and love for nature, and he soon became her first close friend. On the eve of his return to Canada, he proposed marriage, and Stephen fled from him in horror. Only Sir Philip—and perhaps Puddle—recognized Stephen's true nature, but he proved unable to speak of it, even when, in confusion, Stephen sought his aid. With mother, father, and daughter each concealing a private torment, the sudden death of Sir Philip brought what little remained of Morton's former joy to an abrupt end. A final deathbed struggle to explain Stephen's nature to his wife and daughter was too late.

In town one day in her twenty-first year, Stephen encountered Angela, the discontented American wife of a humorless businessman. Friendship soon ripened into a passionate affair, although it was displayed with strictly "schoolgirl kisses." Stephen's conscience regarding Angela's happiness forced her to urge Angela to leave her husband and follow Stephen to Paris. Angela immediately refused, demanding, "Could you marry me, Stephen?" Month after month, the affair limped on, until one night Stephen spied Angela and Ralph in their garden tenderly embracing. Mortified, Stephen poured her soul into a long, explicit letter, but Angela, affronted by this indiscretion, showed it to Ralph, who in turn sent a copy to Lady Anna. Shocked and disgusted, Anna confronted Stephen and refused to share a home with her: One of them must leave. Stephen withdrew to her father's study and there discovered a hidden shelf of books about homosexuality by a German psychiatrist, annotated in her father's handwriting. Praying for a sign, she let a Bible fall open and read: "And the Lord set a mark upon Cain." The choice seemed clear; Puddle pledged to stand by Stephen in her exile.

Two years later, Stephen had achieved overnight success with her first novel, but her second novel had proven a disappointment even to its solitary and workaholic author. At a literary lunch, she renewed an acquaintance with Jonathan Brockett, a homosexual playwright who secretly recognized in Stephen a fellow "invert." Eventually, Brockett persuaded Stephen that she could only revive her creative energy, evidently flagging in the second novel, if she saw more of the world, starting with Paris. Stephen cut her remaining ties with her mother and Morton and moved to Paris with Puddle. There, Brockett introduced Stephen to a circle of sexually ambiguous writers surrounding Valérie Seymour, proving that Stephen's exile need not be utterly lonely.

World War I broke out, and during two years with the London Ambulance Column, Stephen noticed other homosexual women fitting comfortably into the new roles that war opened to them. Longing to serve her country near the front lines, she joined a unit of Englishwomen in a French Ambulance Corps, who drove wounded soldiers to the field hospital. There, Stephen fell in love with Mary Llewellyn, a young and equally brave volunteer. After the armistice, Stephen, scarred (an indication of the mark of Cain) and decorated, took Mary into her Parisian home. The young couple spent the winter in Orotava, Spain, but they became increasingly despondent and uneasy as Stephen tried to protect Mary from the consequences that Mary would suffer if she committed herself to Stephen. At a point of crisis, however, they declared a love that would withstand the world's judgment: "and that night they were not divided." Now utterly in love, they returned to Paris and established a household with Stephen as husband and Mary as wife. Their social isolation deepened, however, and while Stephen turned obsessively to writing, her only "weapon," Mary grew bored and unhappy. Brockett persuaded them to use Valérie Seymour's salon to extend their circle, and they found consolation in new friends, including courageous lesbians, however tormented and damaged. Stephen and Mary's glimpse of the seedy homosexual nightlife of Paris demoralized them, however, and after the sudden death of their friend Barbara and the suicide of her lover, Mary became too vulnerable for Stephen to confide in with the old frankness.

When Martin Hallam, living temporarily in Paris, reappeared, the three became fast friends. Stephen gradually realized that Martin and Mary were becoming romantically attached, and at last Martin challenged Stephen to let Mary go, insisting that Mary would prove unable to survive the trials of the taboo "marriage" with Stephen. A contest for Mary's heart ensued, although neither Martin nor Stephen revealed it to Mary, and at last Martin conceded defeat. Stephen, however, had already decided that Martin was right after all, that all her love was not enough to bring Mary true happiness. At last, Stephen's devotion made her lie to Mary, saying she had been unfaithful, and thus she drove Mary into Martin's arms. Together, Mary and Martin departed; alone, Stephen prayed for all inverts: "Give us also the right to our existence!"

Critical Evaluation:

The Well of Loneliness is the first novel in English to make an unabashed plea for an understanding of lesbians, or "female sexual inverts" to use the term used in Radclyffe Hall's time. In many respects it falls short of literary greatness—its heavy-handed moralizing, scenes of exaggerated melodrama, and frequently ponderous diction dull its effectiveness. It remains unique, however, in its era as a wholly sympathetic story of a lesbian's struggle to forge her identity. It stands first in a long succession of "coming out" novels, and continues to inform and inspire readers. If Hall's principal purpose was to persuade her readers that a lesbian minority not only exists but should be permitted to participate in society and contribute to its welfare, there can be little doubt that she has achieved considerable success through the years.

When *The Well of Loneliness* was published in 1928, the publisher of a novel that portrayed homosexuals could be charged with violation of laws against obscenity, and Hall's publisher was brought to trial. The judge, who refused either to read the book or to hear from the notable authors, including Virginia Woolf and E. M. Forster, who came to testify on its behalf, considered the work's literary merit irrelevant to the question of whether it was obscene, and banned it. It was not republished until 1949. Social and medical views of homosexuality have changed since Hall wrote.

The portrayal of the character of Stephen Gordon is colored by the psychological thinking of her day, particularly by the work of Havelock Ellis, who insisted that sexual inverts, far from being sociopaths who posed a danger to society, were capable of leading useful and honorable lives. Ellis' comments on *The Well of Loneliness* may be found as a preface to some editions.

The novel, however, does not propose that lesbians could lead happy, normal lives in the world as Hall knew it, but rather that inverts represent a distinct group who merit sympathy, perhaps even pity. Stephen Gordon is pictured as possessing the soul of a man in the body of a woman; in dress and manner she resembles a man, and Hall is less concerned to make her "normal" than sympathetic. This is only partly attributable to the assumptions of her time: Deeply traditional ideas of society and nature underpin the novel, and make Stephen's martyrdom heroic and, ironically, stigmatizing. Stephen is an aristocrat with a deep faith in the values of her class, but her journey is one of renunciation: She renounces Mary as she renounced Morton, but she rejects neither. The rootedness that Morton gave her becomes her gift for Mary when she delivers her to Martin and a conventional heterosexual future. Hall's portraits of homosexuals can be difficult to distinguish from ones meant to condemn: Other than Stephen, her inverts are casualties of the world's unkindness, and in the bar scenes their infirmity might be easy to mistake for depravity.

Stephen's virility is not merely the product of psychological theorizing, however, but rather the expression of the author's idealism and theological purpose. Religious conviction plays a crucial and frequently overlooked role in *The Well of Loneliness*; indeed, the novel amounts to a hagiography. Stephen's separation from Mary at the novel's end, although disappointing to some readers, expresses Stephen's commitment to an absolute good rather than to a personal one—to what is truly best rather than merely what she wants for herself. Hall, a Roman Catholic convert, saw a vast divide between the truth of the world and the truth of God. As Christ-figure and saint, Stephen makes the disapproval of mortals irrelevant. She acts out her homosexual desire while others (such as Puddle) remain hypocritically silent because she possesses inner strength to match her outer strength. Stephen possesses a strength that enables her to forge sanctity out of persecution, while other inverts must sooner or later crumble under the weight. This strength, moreover, enables her to become a war heroine, and so prove the value of lesbians to a nation in need. Her victimization is transformed by a moral idealism that, while fruitless in the eyes of this world, owes allegiance to God, who guides the chosen by an inner light along a path of righteousness.

Matthew Parfitt

Bibliography:

Baker, Michael. *Our Three Selves: The Life of Radclyffe Hall.* New York: William Morrow, 1985. The most authoritative biography of Radclyffe Hall. Contains an extensive reading of *The Well of Loneliness* that sheds light on its relation to Hall's life and beliefs.

Brittain, Vera. *Radclyffe Hall: A Case of Obscenity?* London: A. S. Barnes, 1969. A detailed account of the obscenity trial. Conveys valuable information regarding attitudes toward lesbianism in England in the 1920's.

McPike, Loralee. "A Geography of Radclyffe Hall's Lesbian Country." *Historical Reflections/ Reflexions Historiques* 20, no. 2 (1994): 217-242. Argues that lesbianism is only one focus of the novel. The novel also concerns the human condition.

Newton, Esther. "The 'Mythic Mannish Lesbian': Radclyffe Hall and the New Woman." *Signs* 9 (1984): 557-575. Argues that Stephen Gordon's masculinity was intended to offer an alternative to contemporary ideas of the new woman.

Ruehl, Sonja. "Inverts and Experts: Radclyffe Hall and the Lesbian Identity." In *Feminism, Culture and Politics*, edited by Rosalind Brunt and Caroline Rowan. London: Lawrence and Wishart, 1982. Discusses the influence of sexology of Hall's times on her attempt to define the lesbian.

WESTWARD HO!

Type of work: Novel
Author: Charles Kingsley (1819-1875)
Type of plot: Historical
Time of plot: Sixteenth century
Locale: England and South America
First published: 1855

Principal characters:
    AMYAS LEIGH, an adventurer
    FRANK LEIGH, his brother
    SIR RICHARD GRENVILE, Amyas' godfather
    EUSTACE LEIGH, Amyas' and Frank's cousin
    ROSE SALTERNE, the beloved of Amyas and Frank
    SALVATION YEO, Amyas' friend
    DON GUZMAN DE SOTO, a treacherous Spaniard
    AYACANORA, an Indian maiden
    MRS. LEIGH, the mother of Amyas and Frank

The Story:

Amyas Leigh had always had a secret longing to go to sea, but he had not spoken of it because he knew his parents thought him too young for such a rough, hard life. When he met John Oxenham and Salvation Yeo, who were recruiting a crew to sail to the New World after Spanish treasure, he begged to be allowed to join them, but his parents and Sir Richard Grenville, his godfather, persuaded him to wait a while. The next year, his father died of fever, and his brother Frank went to the court of Queen Elizabeth. Then Sir Richard Grenvile persuaded Amyas' mother to let the boy accompany Sir Francis Drake on the first English voyage around the world. Finally, Drake and his adventurers had returned, and Amyas, no longer a boy but a blond young giant, came back to his home at Bideford, in Devon.

He remembered one face in the village better than any: Rose Salterne, the mayor's daughter. All the young men loved and honored her, including Amyas and his brother Frank, who had returned from court. She was also loved by Eustace Leigh, the cousin of Amyas and Frank. Eustace was a Catholic. His cousins distrusted him because they suspected he was in league with the Jesuit priests. When Rose spurned his love, he vowed revenge. The other young men who loved Rose formed the Brotherhood of the Rose, and all swore to protect her always and to remain friends, no matter who should win her.

Shortly after Amyas had returned from his voyage with Drake, Salvation Yeo came to him and Sir Richard Grenville with a strange and horrible tale. The voyage that he had made with John Oxenham had been ill-fated, and Oxenham and most of the crew had been captured by the the Spanish Inquisition. Oxenham had had a child by a Spanish lady, and before they were separated, Yeo had vowed that he would protect the child. Yeo had done his best, but the child had been lost, and now Yeo begged that he might attach himself to Amyas and go wherever Amyas went. In his travels, he thought that he might someday find the little maid again. Amyas and Sir Richard Grenvile were touched by the story, and Amyas promised to keep Yeo with him. Before long, the two sailed with Sir Walter Raleigh for Ireland, where they would fight the Spaniards.

In Ireland, Raleigh defeated the Spaniards, and Amyas took Don Guzman de Soto, a Spanish nobleman, as hostage. Don Guzman accompanied him back to Bideford, to wait for his ransom from Spain. Don Guzman was a charming gentleman, and it was not long before he had caught the eye of Rose Salterne. After his ransom had been paid, he left England; then it was learned that Rose had also disappeared in the company of Lucy the witch. Her father, Amyas, Frank, and the other young men of the Brotherhood of the Rose were wild with grief. All vowed to sail to La Guayra in Caracas, where Don Guzman had gone to be governor and where they felt Rose had fled to join him.

Their voyage was an eventful one. When they neared La Guayra, they were seen by the Spaniards, and they had to fight many times before they reached the shore. Amyas and Frank went ashore with a few men to try to rescue Rose. There they learned that Eustace had known of their voyage and had beaten them to their destination to warn Don Guzman of their approach. Frank and Amyas heard Rose tell Eustace that she was happily married to Don Guzman, so they knew she would never leave with them. Nevertheless, they also heard Eustace beg her to run away with him, threatening to turn her over to the Inquisition if she refused. At that threat, Frank and Amyas attacked Eustace, but he escaped and was never to be heard of again. Rose fled into the fort. As they made their way back to their ship, Frank was captured by Don Guzman's men. Amyas was knocked unconscious, but his men carried him back to the ship.

When the ship was damaged in a later encounter with the Spaniards, the crew beached her and began a march toward the fabled city of Manoa. It was a long and hazardous journey over high mountains and through a land of hostile Indians. They found no El Dorado, but a young priestess of one of the tribes fell in love with Amyas and followed him the rest of the journey. She was called Ayacanora, and, although she was of an Indian tribe, she seemed to have the look of a white woman.

After more than three years, the little band reached the shore of New Granada. There, after a furious fight, they captured a Spanish galleon. After they had secured her and set sail, they went into the hold and released the prisoners the Spaniards had aboard. One of them was Lucy the witch, who told them of the horrible fate of Rose and Frank. Before Eustace disappeared from La Guayra, he had reported to the Inquisition that Rose had kept her Protestant faith. She and Lucy were taken before the terrible tribunal, where Frank had also been turned over to the torturers. Lucy confessed that she had accepted the Catholic faith, but Frank and Rose, refusing to yield to the Inquisitors, had been tortured for many days before they were burned at the stake. When Amyas heard this story, he was like a madman, vowing never to rest until he had killed every Spaniard he saw. Two Spanish dignitaries on the ship had witnessed the burning of Frank and Rose, and Amyas had them hanged immediately.

At last, the ship reached Devon, and Amyas took Ayacanora to his home, where his mother welcomed her and treated her as a daughter. During the voyage, Yeo had discovered that she was the little maid he had promised Oxenham to protect, and he became a father to her. Amyas treated her as he might a sister, but Ayacanora was not happy at this treatment.

After a time, Amyas fitted out a ship and prepared to go with Drake to Virginia, but before they sailed, the Spanish Armada arrived off English shores. Amyas, with his ship, joined the rest of the fleet in that famous battle. After twelve terrible days, the Armada was defeated, and almost every Spanish ship destroyed. Amyas, however, was not satisfied. Don Guzman was aboard one of the Spanish ships, and although Amyas pursued him relentlessly, he had to sit by and watch a storm tear the Spaniard's ship apart. Amyas cursed that he himself had not been able to kill Don Guzman and thus avenge his brother's death.

As Don Guzman's ship broke apart, a bolt of lightning struck Amyas' ship blinding him and killing Yeo. At first, Amyas was full of despair. One day, he had a vision. He saw Rose and Don Guzman together and knew that the Spaniard had really loved her and mourned her until his death. Then he saw himself with Don Guzman, acknowledging their sins to each other and asking forgiveness. After that, he felt at peace with himself.

Amyas returned to his mother's home, and there she and Ayacanora cared for him. Realizing how much the girl loved him, he was so grateful for the tenderness she showed him that he gave her his heart. In Bideford, the blind hero spent his remaining days dreaming of his past deeds and of the great glory to come for his country and his queen.

Critical Evaluation:

Charles Kingsley, the son of a clergyman of the Church of England, studied at Cambridge University and was the parish priest for the Anglican parish in Eversley, Hampshire, from 1842 until his death. Interested especially in historical subjects, his wide reading brought him the appointment of Regius Professor of Modern History at Cambridge University. He was known as a Christian Socialist because of his pamphlets in support of improving the social and economic life of the working classes. He also wrote poetry and novels.

Kingsley was perhaps best known for espousing what came to be called "Muscular Christianity." He believed that Christianity involved the warfare of the forces of good against the forces of evil and held up as role models figures such as Joshua and David from the Old Testament and Alfred the Great and Sir Philip Sidney from English history. He believed that the proper Christian life was one of action rather than contemplation, physical exertion rather than mental exertion, moral certitude rather than ambiguity, and bluster rather than meekness.

Kingsley wrote three other novels before *Westward Ho!* Two of them, *Yeast* (1848) and *Alton Locke* (1850), were problem novels that dealt with the political and social conditions of the Victorian working classes; the third, *Hypatia* (1853), was a historical romance set in the fifth century, which attacked indirectly the spread of rationalism and Catholicism in the nineteenth century. *Alton Locke* had been moderately successful, with sales stimulated by the book's reputation for socialism. The other two did not sell well. Always short of money, Kingsley wanted a story that would both be a good vehicle for his ideas and bring in some income. In February, 1854, just as Britain became involved in the Crimean War, a conflict to prevent Russian expansion in the eastern Mediterranean, he began thinking of a historical romance set during the days of the Elizabethan sea dogs. Kingsley paused to write a patriotic pamphlet, *Brave Words for Brave Soldiers*, which exhorted the British to believe that they were God's army fighting for God's cause, and then returned to his novel.

Westward Ho! reflects Kingsley's deep opposition to the growth of Catholicism in British society, a growth that took the forms of an invigorated Roman Catholic church and the appearance of a movement that emphasized a more Catholic style of worship in the Church of England, the Oxford Movement. A staunch Protestant, Kingsley had criticized Catholic practices in his earlier novels. The novel also reflects his belief that Britain's imperial expansion was God's way of spreading Protestantism throughout the world; he thus chose to dedicate *Westward Ho!* to Sir James Brooke, an adventurer who had carved out of the island of Borneo a territory that he ruled as "white rajah," and George Augustus Selwyn, Anglican missionary bishop of New Zealand. These men, he wrote in his dedication, exhibited the same "manful and godly, practical and enthusiastic, prudent and self-sacrificing" English virtues that had characterized the Elizabethan sea dogs. Finally, *Westward Ho!* is an example of war propaganda; reviewers and readers at the time knew that the novel's Spaniards stood for the Russians with whom their country was locked in combat.

The themes of *Westward Ho!* include patriotism to Great Britain, anti-Catholicism, violence, and Muscular Christianity. Patriotism and anti-Catholicism were linked in Kingsley's mind because he shared the common beliefs that Protestantism was the basis of the British constitu tion, that Protestant Britain was God's chosen country, and that Catholicism led to despotism. Thus, British institutions were superior to those of other countries because they were godly; they were godly because they were Protestant; and they were Protestant because they were British. Kingsley contrasted British manliness, good humor, simple Christian piety, and devo-tion to duty with Spanish effeminacy, deceit, semipagan worship of idols, and greed. The most clear-cut contrast was that between two female figures: the Virgin Queen Elizabeth I of England and the Spanish vision of the Virgin Mary. The English Virgin Queen possessed all the English virtues, while the Spaniards endowed the Virgin Mary with all their vices. Kingsley was strongly influenced in these views by the nationalist historian J. A. Froude.

Violence and Muscular Christianity were also linked in the novel. Kingsley presented violence as the appropriate response to dilemmas. Because one's enemies were evil, violence was the best, perhaps the only, godly response, whether it be Israelites smiting Canaanites and Philistines or Englishmen smiting Spaniards and Russians. On the personal level, Kingsley also saw violence as an appropriate way of solving problems. In the novel's opening, Amyas Leigh, tired of being intimidated by the priest-schoolmaster John Brimblecombe, broke his slate over the bumbling man's head. Muscular Christians thus dealt and received blows in the service of good against evil. The Elizabethan sea dog, who combined athletic and military prowess in the service of Protestant England, thus was the model Muscular Christian.

Kingsley allowed some ambiguity in his depiction of the ungodly enemy, an ambiguity that reflected his own uncertainty at Britain's incompetent conduct of the Crimean War. Yet, he remained certain that the English were good and that their enemies were bad. Hence, although he gave virtues to a few Spanish characters, such as Don Guzman, he made them virtuous in spite of their religion and nationality. At the end of the book, Kingsley wrote a powerful scene in which Don Guzman and his ship sink into the waves, denying Amyas Leigh his revenge; disappointed, Leigh hurled his sword into the sea and criticized God for having cheated him of vengeance. A bolt of lightning struck him blind. Kingsley's message was that Amyas' error lay in letting his revenge become personal rather than national and religious; it was for that that he was punished, not for seeking vengeance itself.

Westward Ho! was Kingsley's most successful novel. It sold well throughout the English-speaking world, securing the finances of the newly established Macmillan publishers. The book remained in print for more than a century and entered the canon of boys' literature. Its greatest cultural influence was on the generations of British and American boys who imbibed the novel's messages of ultra-nationalism, religious crusading, and lighthearted violence.

"Critical Evaluation" by D. G. Paz

Bibliography:
Chitty, Susan. *The Beast and the Monk: A Life of Charles Kingsley*. London: Hodder and Stoughton, 1974. Using confidential papers that had been closed to researchers for more than a century, Chitty attempts to link Kingsley's writings with his erotic sensibilities, especially his enjoyment of conjugal love. Chitty includes a chapter that discusses Kingsley's financial difficulties at the time of writing *Westward Ho!*, difficulties that influenced his choice of theme.
Collums, Brenda. *Charles Kingsley: The Lion of Eversley*. New York: Barnes & Noble, 1975.

This more conventional biographical approach is a useful introduction to Kingsley's public life. It includes substantial extracts from the novel as part of its investigation of the background to Kingsley's writing.

Houghton, Walter E. *The Victorian Frame of Mind, 1830-1870*. New Haven, Conn.: Yale University Press, 1957. This is a superb survey of the many currents of Victorian thought. Its section on the worship of force includes a good discussion of Kingsley.

Martin, Robert Bernard. *The Dust of Combat: A Life of Charles Kingsley*. New York: W. W. Norton, 1960. The most well-balanced biography of Kingsley. The author has an excellent analysis of Muscular Christianity.

Sutherland, J. A. *Victorian Novelists and Publishers*. Chicago: University of Chicago Press, 1976. This study of the relationship between writers and their publishers argues that financial considerations sometimes determined writers' choices of form, style, and subject matter. The chapter on *Westward Ho!* describes the artistic, financial, and personal factors that shaped the process of writing the book. Kingsley worked with his publishers to produce a spectacularly successful book that was distributed with a view to capitalizing on the Crimean War.

WHAT MAISIE KNEW

Type of work: Novel
Author: Henry James (1843-1916)
Type of plot: Psychological realism
Time of plot: 1890's
Locale: London, Folkestone, and Boulogne
First published: 1897

Principal characters:
>MAISIE FARANGE, the daughter of divorced parents
>IDA FARANGE, her mother
>BEALE FARANGE, her father
>MISS OVERMORE, a governess and, later, the second Mrs. Beale Farange
>MRS. WIX, a governess
>SIR CLAUDE, Ida Farange's second husband

The Story:

Beale and Ida Farange were divorced with much publicity. At first, each fought to keep their daughter Maisie, but at last it was arranged that the girl should spend six months with each. The first period was to be spent with her father. Maisie was confused by the divorce. At first, she truthfully reported to her parents what each said about the other, but finding that her candor led to furious outbursts and that she was being used as an innocent messenger, she soon became silent on the subject of the absent parent and appeared to absorb no knowledge during her visits.

Ida engaged Miss Overmore, a pretty governess, whom Maisie was unhappy to leave when it was time to return to her father. Soon, however, to Ida's fury, Miss Overmore was engaged to be Maisie's governess at Beale Farange's house. Upon her subsequent return to Ida, Maisie was placed in the care of Mrs. Wix. She learned no lessons from Mrs. Wix but adored her conversation and felt comfortable and secure with her.

During Maisie's next stay with Beale, he went to Brighton for a few days together with Miss Overmore. When the governess returned, she found Mrs. Wix waiting for her. Mrs. Wix alone was concerned for Maisie's welfare, and she was outraged by the child's environment. She announced that Ida was about to remarry, and she gave Maisie a photograph of Sir Claude, her future stepfather. Miss Overmore thereupon announced that she had just married Beale Farange.

Some time after his marriage, Sir Claude called and was received by the new Mrs. Beale Farange. Maisie was delighted by their apparent understanding and declared that she had brought them together. Sir Claude won Maisie's love by being gentle with her and by declaring that he intended to make her his responsibility. In spite of the pain of leaving the new Mrs. Farange, the girl was pleased to go home with him. Ida's love for her new husband, however, soon waned, and she had several lovers. When she accused Sir Claude of basely stealing Maisie's affections and threatened to drive Mrs. Wix out of the house for supporting him, Maisie felt that she belonged nowhere. Mrs. Wix was determined to meet her responsibility for Maisie, and she desired to "save" Sir Claude from Mrs. Beale Farange, whom he frequently visited. Fearing for the loss of her livelihood, she wished that Sir Claude would take a house for himself where she and Maisie would also live.

On one outing, Sir Claude took Maisie to her father's new house, which she was afraid to enter for fear of losing him if she remained there. Once in the house, however, she was again enthralled by Mrs. Farange's beauty and was interested to learn that Beale mattered no more to his wife than Sir Claude did to Ida. Maisie remained happily with her stepmother after Sir Claude assured her that he would provide for Mrs. Wix and visit her frequently.

After a long absence, Sir Claude visited Maisie again. While they were walking in the park, they met Ida with an unknown, military-looking man. Both Ida and Sir Claude became terribly angry, and Maisie was sent to talk with Ida's escort, whom her mother had called the Captain. Maisie, who was by that time thoroughly aware that neither parent loved her, wept when the Captain praised her mother highly and was eager to agree that she was "good." Sir Claude, unable to learn from Maisie what the Captain had said to her, sent her home alone in a cab.

Mrs. Farange told Maisie that she met Sir Claude away from her home but that he was reluctant to visit them and thus compromise Maisie. The three hoped to meet at a London exhibition; instead, they unexpectedly encountered Beale Farange. After a subdued but violent quarrel, Maisie was whisked away by her father to the house of his mistress. In a way that was intended to elicit Maisie's refusal, he offered to take her to America with him.

Encouraged by Mrs. Wix, Sir Claude took Maisie to Folkestone as the first step toward making a home for them in France. There Ida arrived suddenly and surrendered Maisie to Sir Claude's guardianship. The following day, they crossed to France, where Mrs. Wix joined them. Sir Claude intended to return to England and to Mrs. Beale Farange once Maisie's father had finally left. Sir Claude confessed that he feared Mrs. Farange as he had formerly feared Ida. Mrs. Wix, still strongly opposed to Mrs. Farange, asked to be sent to England to sever their relationship. Sir Claude refused this request and went off to England alone.

While he was away, Mrs. Wix explained to the bewildered Maisie that she refused to condone the immorality of Mrs. Farange and Sir Claude in living together with them. Also, she declared that she would never again leave Maisie. After several walks and much thought, the full implications of what this situation might mean became apparent to Maisie. She realized, too, that she had no moral "sense," and having rapidly absorbed the idea of such a sense from vague but emphatic conversations with Mrs. Wix, she decided to show in her future responses that she did indeed possess it.

When they returned to their hotel after a morning walk, Maisie was unexpectedly greeted by her stepmother. Mrs. Wix's own "moral sense" was nearly destroyed by Mrs. Farange's charm and determination to have the governess-companion as an ally. According to Mrs. Farange, now that the girl's father had left, Maisie was her own daughter. In this way, she intended to hold Sir Claude through his devotion to the girl. Mrs. Wix wavered, but Maisie declared that she would stay with Sir Claude only if he were alone.

The next morning, Mrs. Wix awakened Maisie with the news that Sir Claude had arrived. When Maisie breakfasted alone with him, he asked her if she would leave Mrs. Wix and live with him and Mrs. Farange. She asked to see Mrs. Wix before deciding. Later, while walking with Sir Claude, she said she would give up Mrs. Wix only if he would give up Mrs. Farange. Maisie made her decision when the four people confronted one another in a final struggle at the hotel. When she failed in her appeal that Mrs. Farange give up Sir Claude, Maisie decided to stay with Mrs. Wix.

Critical Evaluation:

Readers and critics alike at times feel frustrated with Henry James's *What Maisie Knew*, the careful, detailed record of the emergence of a young girl's consciousness. James scholars are still puzzled over why the artist turned a serious novel over to such an apparently unsophisticated protagonist, and some have wondered whether a complex, realistic social satire can be communicated through a medium who does not understand much of what she sees. Critics are equally perplexed at the moral ambiguity around which the plot of the novel revolves, an uncertainty the novel's disturbing conclusion does nothing to dispel. Such responses are probably inevitable, for *What Maisie Knew* seems to have escaped even the control of its author.

Written during a period of artistic transition for James, the novel is a strange mixture of the kind of masterful storytelling that characterizes such early works as *Washington Square* (1880) and the psychological complexity of later masterworks such as *The Golden Bowl* (1904). Perhaps the transitional aspect of the novel is best illustrated by the fact that James himself was not sure how long the manuscript should be. He originally conceived the work as a short story in which a young innocent is victimized by adults whose motives she cannot hope to fathom. The detailed notebooks James kept during the process of planning the story have shown that the idea grew steadily in James's imagination. Maisie's case became compelling for the writer, and he worked on the book with the kind of curiosity associated more with a reader than with an author. This sense of an outcome beyond anyone's control finds its way into the finished version of the novel in the form of the narrator's frequent admissions that, since what Maisie knows is so often more than she can put into thoughts or words, it is all one can do to follow the child's development, let alone interpret or control it. When even an author cannot make complete sense of a novel's events, a reader must expect some degree of uncertainty. Some aspects of the paradoxical nature of *What Maisie Knew* seem destined to remain unresolved.

From the outset, the novel is calculated to test the moral stance of its readers. James presents an abundance of low behavior but does not balance the text by providing high ground to which the heroine or the reader might escape. While the fact that the novel begins with a divorce was not enough to offend their sense of propriety, readers at the end of the nineteenth century were still unused to the practice. The hint of scandal surrounding Beale and Ida Farange's divorce would probably have been palpable even if James had not emphasized the "bespattered" and "damaged" condition in which Maisie's parents emerged from their ordeal. The undercurrent of dishonesty and adultery accompanying the divorce foreshadows not only the new lovers that both Beale and Ida take thereafter but also the irresponsible behavior of Maisie's estranged parents in communicating their hostilities through their daughter. The hateful words Beale and Ida send each other on the lips of their young daughter become "an epitaph for the tomb of Maisie's childhood." This mistreatment is compounded in the course of the novel in further examples of neglect and emotional cruelty suffered by the likable child, in whose confused thoughts it becomes increasingly uncomfortable to dwell.

The characters who might improve Maisie's lot, Miss Overmore, Sir Claude, and Mrs. Wix, each with whom Maisie falls in love, all fall short. They all use their bond with Maisie in attempts to forge or secure their relationships with each other or with Beale and Ida. The caretaking love of an adult that should surround and protect a child is invariably corrupted in the novel by the adults' sexual love for each other. By making sexual or romantic attachment the barrier to the nurturing that Maisie needs, James has transformed the traditional solution to Maisie's problems, a new mother and father, impossible to attain. Any pair that might emerge from the chaotic nexus of relations—Beale and Miss Overmore, Ida and Sir Claude, or Sir Claude and Mrs. Wix—would necessarily be lovers first and surrogate parents second. Because their relationships are based on sex, they are morally inappropriate guardians for Maisie. James's complex moral scheme weaves an insoluble paradox. In fact, he mocks the very possibility of a moral solution to the problems of the novel.

Mrs. Wix continually browbeats Maisie with the concept of moral correctness. She teaches the child disgust for the sexual relationships of the other adults (while secretly coveting just such a bond with Sir Claude). James makes Mrs. Wix the emblem of moral perspective by using the term "straighteners" for the woman's eyeglasses. As Mrs. Wix confronts the possibility of losing Maisie and Sir Claude forever, she becomes furious with moral outrage. The innocent Maisie watches as the governess' "straighteners . . . seemed to crack with the explosion of their wearer's honesty." Here it becomes clear that hypocrisy is the cause of the moral disintegration of the novel's perspective.

James seems to be declaring that it is precisely in those moments of ethical and emotional dilemma when good judgment is most urgently required that good judgment breaks down and solutions become impossible. Because none of the adults who are attracted to each other (Sir Claude does not desire Mrs. Wix) can pair off without continuing the cycle of scandal, Maisie's options eventually dwindle down to the hope that one of her caretakers will forsake sexual desires and commit exclusively to her. The novel's most poignant scene occurs in a provincial French train station, when Sir Claude appears to be considering the possibility of escaping to Paris with the little girl. The prose in this passage is full of pseudoromantic tension, and it may be that Sir Claude himself senses that, for he lets the train to Paris go and thus renounces both his claim on and responsibility for the pathetic little girl. Maisie's return trip across the Atlantic with Mrs. Wix is a typically Jamesian solution to an ethical muddle. In the works of Henry James, life's complexities do not yield to simple solutions, nor do misdeeds result in happy endings. This lesson is particularly painful in *What Maisie Knew* because an innocent child is the victim.

"Critical Evaluation" by Nick David Smart

Bibliography:
Cargill, Oscar. *The Novels of Henry James*. New York: Macmillan, 1961. A vigorous study of all of James's novels. Cargill draws on the observation of several prominent literary critics and discusses James in the light of English and American literary history. Evaluates moral and artistic aspects of James's work.
Kaplan, Fred. *Henry James: The Imagination of Genius*. New York: William Morrow, 1992. A thorough narrative account of the life of Henry James. Kaplan considers American and English political history, literary history, and the personal life of James while discussing the complete oeuvre.
Miller, J. Hillis. *Versions of Pygmalion*. Cambridge, Mass.: Harvard University Press, 1990. Miller's work on the ethics of narration is difficult, but his chapter on *What Maisie Knew* is valuable both for its background information on the social climate in which the novel was written and for its clearly written examination of the complexity of the ethical dilemma in which James places his characters and readers.
Mitchell, Juliet. "*What Maisie Knew*: Portrait of the Artist as a Young Girl." In *The Air of Reality: New Essays on Henry James*, edited by John Goode. London: Methuen, 1972. A complete examination of the pressures that shape Maisie's consciousness. Mitchell argues against reading a sexual undercurrent into the relationship between Maisie and Sir Claude.

WHAT THE BUTLER SAW

Type of work: Drama
Author: Joe Orton (1933-1967)
Type of plot: Farce
Time of plot: 1960's
Locale: A psychiatric clinic in England
First performed: 1969; first published, 1969

Principal characters:
 DR. PRENTICE, the head of a psychiatric clinic
 MRS. PRENTICE, his wife
 GERALDINE BARCLAY, a secretarial applicant
 NICHOLAS BECKETT, a hotel page
 DR. RANCE, an inspector of psychiatric clinics
 SERGEANT MATCH, a policeman

The Story:

Geraldine Barclay, an attractive young woman in search of her first job, appeared at Dr. Prentice's clinic one day to be interviewed for a secretarial position. Under interrogation from Prentice, she told him that her father had deserted her mother many years ago when the latter was a chambermaid at the Station Hotel. She herself had not seen her mother for a long time, and her stepmother, Mrs. Barclay, had died recently from having been penetrated with a certain part of a statue of Sir Winston Churchill that was destroyed in a gas-main explosion. Geraldine's legacy from her stepmother was that part of the Churchillian statue, which she carried with her in a box to the interview.

Prentice ordered Geraldine to undress for a physical examination and asked her to cooperate in the testing of a new contraceptive device. She agreed. His plan was foiled suddenly by the entrance of a disheveled Mrs. Prentice, who had spent the night at the Station Hotel with the hotel page after attending a lesbian meeting. With Geraldine naked behind a screen, Prentice made frantic attempts to hide Geraldine's clothes. His wife saw Geraldine's dress, however, and, having arrived wearing only a fur coat with a slip underneath, slipped on the dress.

Nicholas Beckett, the young hotel page, arrived to check Mrs. Prentice's bag for missing articles and to bribe her to let him sell pictures taken during their tryst at the hotel. Like Geraldine, Nick came from a broken family. He asked for the job in Prentice's office and left only when Prentice hurriedly gave him some money.

Yet a third intrusion into Prentice's plans occurred in the person of Dr. Rance, an inspector of psychiatric clinics. Discovering the naked Geraldine, he immediately proclaimed her insane, the first of many similar proclamations. His habit was to question patients only after he had issued insanity verdicts. He then interrogated Prentice about his background and followed with questions to Mrs. Prentice about her husband. He noted Prentice's apparent obsession with women's clothes. A fourth intruder, Inspector Match, arrived on a matter of national importance having to do with Sir Winston Churchill's statue.

Nick conveniently reappeared with Mrs. Prentice's freshly cleaned dress and wig. Prentice, desperate to find attire for Geraldine, ordered Nick to undress and Geraldine to put on his uniform. Nick was then asked to wear Mrs. Prentice's leopard-spotted dress and to impersonate Geraldine in a subsequent interrogation by Match. At the end of the first act, in the interest of professional correctness, it was agreed that Mrs. Prentice would examine Geraldine (actually Nick in disguise) and that Match would examine Nick (actually Geraldine in disguise).

At the start of the second act, the desperation of Geraldine and Nick to unravel what was so obvious that it needed no unraveling led Geraldine to insist on being arrested. Meanwhile, at the same time that Prentice rapidly lost control of events, Rance gained control by his obsessive insistence on giving Freudian interpretations of everything having the slightest appearance of a sexual nuance: bisexuality, transvestism, incest, nymphomania, sadomasochism, and the like. Even Match fell victim to Rance's freewheeling accusations, namely, that he, too, may have been a victim of a sexual assault by Prentice. When Rance insisted on examining Match and ordered him to undress, Nick was able to put on the policeman's uniform so as to arrest himself.

To ensure his ability to safely straitjacket Prentice, Rance asked Mrs. Prentice for a gun. She produced two, one for herself and another for Rance. As variously disguised persons fled out one door and in another, shots were fired that resulted in wounds to Match and Nick. By this time, Match found himself attired in Mrs. Prentice's leopard dress, and the confusion seemed total.

Geraldine was finally given a chance to tell her story, and when her lost brooch was produced Nick said he had one just like it. Mrs. Prentice then began her own story of having broken a brooch in two, pinning one half to the clothing of each of her twins, a boy and a girl. The Prentice family reunion was made complete with Mrs. Prentice's confession that the brooch had been given her in partial payment by an unknown man (who turned out to be Prentice) with whom she had enjoyed a liaison during a power outage at the Station Hotel, the result of which was the birth of twins. Mrs. Prentice's story concluded with an account of her tryst with Nick in the same room in which she had conceived him.

The revelations about the Prentice family, however, solved only one of the farce's two mysteries. Geraldine cleared up the mystery of Match's investigation when she opened the box she had brought with her to the interview, containing her stepmother's legacy to her, the lost part of Churchill's statue, a phallus.

In the final scene, all embraced. A skylight opened, a rope ladder was lowered, and a bloodied Match descended, announcing that the great man, Churchill, "can once more take up his place in the High Street as an example to us all of the spirit that won the Battle of Britain." Bedraggled, all picked up their clothes and followed Match back up the ladder.

Critical Evaluation:

Joe Orton's farcical world is diminished, at worst distorted, by a mere summary of the story. Although he followed the oldest of farce conventions—including the plot device of twins separated at birth, a situation that necessitates the use of disguises so as eventually to reveal true identities—he changed the very nature of farce by adapting those conventions in his own inimitable way. All farce depends on social satire as a main theme, and in this respect Orton is a traditional satirist. As farce conventions demand, Orton's characters are flat and represent the excesses of his age's vices. Tradition also dictates a happy ending in which families are reunited and social norms, purified of wrongdoings, restored.

It is in this restoration that Orton made a clean break with tradition. At the end of the play, nothing has changed. Mrs. Prentice's incest will not be punished. Dr. Rance will profit financially from the best-seller he envisions about sexual perversions. Dr. and Mrs. Prentice will continue in their customary sexual pursuits. Match will go on championing an England that is no more. Geraldine and Nick will look for jobs.

The basis for Orton's reputation is his probing of the difference between behavior and the language used to make that behavior appear respectable. The physical disguises are a mere structural underpinning for the characters' linguistic disguises, which they use to justify their actions. Orton's language is that of the accepted idioms of the time, understood by all, yet ingeniously alien to the context in which they are used.

The basic elements of a job interview rise to heights of absurdity when, in response to Geraldine's confession that she had no idea who her father was, Prentice replies that he cannot hire her if her birth was in any way miraculous; he adds "You did have a father?" He abuses professional ethics when he convinces Geraldine to test a new contraceptive device, at the same time asking her not to mention it to his nymphomaniacal wife, whom he confesses he married for her money and whose sexual pursuits he likens to the search for the Holy Grail. Two lies, then, begin a long procession of lies and disguises. All stem, as Prentice at one point tells Geraldine, from his misguided attempt to seduce her. Mrs. Prentice joins in the absurdity when she reminds Nick, who has told her that he had an offer for an option on the pictures, that her contract with him did not include "cinematic rights."

It is Rance, however, who raises Prentice's charade to the level of burlesque. Without any analysis, he immediately interprets Geraldine's nakedness as her attempt to "re-enact her initial experience with her parent." The result, he said, is madness. When Prentice attempts to convince Rance that Geraldine is no more mad than he (Prentice) is, Rance replies that "no madman accepts his madness. Only the sane do that." Rance, in fact, introduces himself to Prentice as the representative of "Her Majesty's government" and his "superior in madness." He fails to realize that he speaks of himself when he says that the sane seem as strange to the madmen as the madmen seem to the sane. Under questioning, Prentice confesses to Rance that his tutor, unable to reach madness, taught it to others, and that it is those students who now run the mental institutions. Orton considers the clinic a microcosm of modern England.

The farce is more than a satire on psychiatry, however. It enters new territory when Rance claims to be the representative of order while Prentice is the representative of chaos. The real Orton emerges in this line, which is at the center of his life and plays. Orton had a stultifyingly lower-middle-class upbringing in Leicester, after which he spent ten years in London unsuccessfully trying to act and write and six months in an English prison. Above all, Orton was a homosexual in a society in which homosexuality was illegal. His idea of chaos challenged existing sexual mores and, in a perverse way, liberated the characters temporarily to indulge in sexual identities that could exist only in fantasies or in the dreamworld.

The only characters who want to tell the truth but are denied the opportunity until the very end are Geraldine and Nick. By the time they can tell the truth, it is too late to have any influence. Geraldine and Nick, by being propelled from one disguise to another, also experience a kind of Alice-in-Wonderland adventure denied them in real life. In the end, both return to a world in which the job for which they search may continue to evade them.

Ronald Bryden's designation of Orton as the dramatist of welfare-state gentility is apt, for whether riding on a London bus listening to average people engaged in average conversation or while indulging in his own sexual proclivities, Orton experienced the life about which he wrote. He had already dealt with the shibboleths of small-town hypocrisies in *Entertaining Mr. Sloane* (1964), police dishonesty in *Loot* (1965), religious corruption in *Funeral Games* (1968), and corporate slavery in *The Erpingham Camp* (1966). In *What the Butler Saw*, he pulled out all stops in an uproarious farce in which the axioms of the new religion, psychiatry, are bared with ferocious hilarity. His insistence on truth, especially in his alteration of the traditional farce ending, freed him from the dishonesty that not only would have made him the kind of hypocrite he denounces in his farce but would have kept him imprisoned in a society whose antihomosexuality law was not repealed until 1968, a year after his death. Despite the fact that Orton wrote only three long stage plays and four short plays for radio and television, he has been accorded a place with Harold Pinter and Tom Stoppard, two other major dramatists known for their innovative language.

Susan Rusinko

Bibliography:
Bigsby, C. W. E. *Joe Orton*. London: Methuen, 1982. Deals with Orton's stylistic and thematic qualities in the context of contemporary European drama.
Charney, Maurice. *Joe Orton*. London: Macmillan, 1984. Places Orton's work in the farcical tradition that goes back to origins in Greece and Rome.
Innes, Christopher. "Joe Orton: Farce as Confrontation." In *Modern British Drama, 1890-1990*. Cambridge, England: Cambridge University Press, 1992. Introduces Orton as a playwright of his time.
Lahr, John. *Prick up Your Ears*. New York: Alfred A. Knopf, 1978. Traces influences on Orton's development as a dramatist.
Orton, Joe. *The Orton Diaries*. Edited by John Lahr. London: Methuen, 1986. An entertaining account by Orton about himself, written during the last year of his life.

WHEN WE DEAD AWAKEN

Type of work: Drama
Author: Henrik Ibsen (1828-1906)
Type of plot: Psychological symbolism
Time of plot: Nineteenth century
Locale: A coastal town of Norway
First published: Naar vi døde vaagner, 1899; first performed, 1900

Principal characters:
ARNOLD RUBEK, a sculptor
MAIA RUBEK, his wife
IRENE VON SATOW, his former model
ULFHEIM, a landed proprietor and hunter

The Story:

Professor Arnold Rubek, a noted sculptor, and his young wife Maia had returned to their home on the coast of Norway after four years abroad. At the baths and the hotel they admitted to being bored, and to break the summer tedium they planned to sail northward around the coast. Rubek had become world-renowned with the fashioning of his masterpiece, "The Resurrection Day," and success had brought him worldly riches. Other visitors at the baths were a sportsman named Ulfheim, called the bear-killer, and a strange pale woman, Madame von Satow, who, with a companion dressed in black, had taken the nearby pavilion for the summer. As Rubek and Ulfheim conversed, the dark Sister passed from the pavilion to the hotel, and Ulfheim said her passing was a portent of death. Maia accepted his invitation to see his sledge dogs fed, but Rubek remained seated on the lawn. The lady in white emerged from the pavilion. Rubek felt strangely drawn to her. Years before, he had wanted to create a sculpture which would represent Woman awakening from the dead on the Resurrection Day after the sleep of death. After he had found Irene, he saw in her the perfect model for his composition, and she became his great inspiration. Irene had wanted his human love but he had felt that if he touched her his soul would be profaned.

Now Rubek recognized the strange woman in white as Irene. When he questioned her about her life since she had left him, she declared that she had died then and was not really alive now, though she had married a South American diplomat who later committed suicide, and then a Russian who owned gold mines in the Urals. Rubek admitted that after she left him he had made no marble creations of lasting beauty but instead had begun doing portrait busts that were, literally, double-faced, because behind the visible face he hid the face of the animal that the artist maliciously considered the subject of the portrait to be. He told Irene that he and Maia were leaving the next day on a sea voyage. She suggested that he might prefer the mountains where she was going. At that moment Maia returned and announced that she would not make the sea voyage; instead, she wanted to go to the mountains with the bear-killer. To her surprise Rubek did not object. Maia ran out to inform Ulfheim. Meanwhile, unseen near the pavilion door, the Sister of Mercy watched intently.

The next day the bear-killer went off to hunt with his dog trainer Lars and his dogs, and Maia accompanied them. Before they left, Rubek told Maia that he could no longer live a life of indolent enjoyment with her.

Rubek found Irene near a brook. She said she had returned from the dead and had made the journey for the sake of the statue, which she called their child. She loved it and wanted to see it. When Rubek implored her not to, saying he had altered it since she had left, Irene covertly unsheathed a knife, but stayed her hand as he explained the changes he had made and told how he also was in the altered sculpture, a man eaten by remorse, imprisoned in a hell from which he could never rise. At this she sheathed her knife, rejoicing that he suffered. She bitterly reminded him that when he had finally finished the statue he had shrugged off their years together.

Together they stood and watched the sun go down. He then asked her to return and live with him in his villa, to help him find his real life again, but Irene said that for the life they had led there was no resurrection. Suddenly Irene challenged Rubek to dare the mountain heights and spend a summer night with her. Joyfully he agreed. As he did so a face stared down at Irene, the face of the Sister of Mercy. On the wild mountainside, cut by sheer precipices and overhung with snow-clad peaks, Maia and Ulfheim quarreled, but made up as they told each other of the disappointments of their youth. When the dangerous mountain mist began to close in, they decided to journey down together, but as they made ready to descend they saw Rubek and Irene climbing up. Ulfheim warned them of the impending storm and the dangers ahead and urged them to take shelter in a nearby hut. He said that he would send them help; he himself could assist only one person at a time down the precipice.

After Ulfheim and Maia had gone, Irene, terrified not by the approaching storm but that she might be taken away, that the woman in black might seize her, showed Rubek her knife ready for such an emergency. She added that the knife had been intended for him the previous evening. Startled, he asked why she had not used it; she told him she had then realized that he was already dead. Rubek passionately assured her that their love was not dead, for he realized with glaring certainty that she was the woman of his dreams. Irene said that such a love came too late, that desire for life was dead in her, and that she looked on him, too, as dead.

With his whole soul Rubek called on her, even if they both seemed dead, to awaken and live life to its fullest before they were forever put away in the grave. Exalted, they spurned the safety of the hut and joyously fought their way up to the peaks, through mist and storm, toward the sunrise. Far below the voice of Maia sang out free as a bird. The Sister of Mercy suddenly appeared. As Rubek and Irene were carried along and buried in the snow, she made the sign of the cross and wished that peace be with them.

Critical Evaluation:

When We Dead Awaken departs from the principles of art to which Henrik Ibsen's earlier social and later psychological dramas conform, and for this reason it is sometimes considered inferior to them. It delves into the realm of pathology, dealing with improbabilities rather than probabilities, with symbolic motive rather than actual motive. Solely as an artistic creation, however, the play has enduring merit. It is Ibsen's last production; the audience may read in it the intention of the dramatist to express some deeply felt final message, one that could be clothed only in poetically suggestive and symbolic language.

When Arnold Rubek, the aged sculptor hero of Ibsen's last work, describes the three stages of his masterpiece "Resurrection Day," he is actually presenting a thinly disguised outline of Ibsen's career as a playwright. After the early apprentice works came the idealized, poetic plays (*Brand*, 1866; *Peer Gynt*, 1867), then the great social and psychological plays of his middle period, from *The Pillars of Society* (1877) through *Hedda Gabler* (1890), and finally the late symbolic and highly personal—even autobiographical—dramas, beginning with *The Master Builder* (1892) and ending with *When We Dead Awaken*.

Two kinds of characters dominate the plays of this final phase: the aging but powerful artist, who, having been driven by his obsessive ambition to the top of his profession, finds that he has paid too high a spiritual price, and the mysterious female out of his past who, acting as a kind of nemesis figure, forces the hero to recognize and come to terms with his past failings, even though it destroys him. Although *When We Dead Awaken* may lack some of the dramatic intensity of *The Master Builder* or of *John Gabriel Borkman* (1896), the play is the most complete and final exploration of this process, and so it stands as Ibsen's final statement on the artist's relation to society and to his or her own soul.

Having achieved great personal success with his masterpiece, yet feeling unaccountably uneasy about it, Rubek attempts to satisfy his needs by taking a young wife and living in moderately luxurious indolence, satisfying his artistic and financial needs by turning out satirical portrait busts. He grows tired of Maia, and the ironical pleasure of making fun of his clients while taking their money wears off. So he tries to find out what it is that bothers him.

When he meets Irene, she reminds him of their life together many years before when, as an innocent young girl, she had modeled for the first version of "Resurrection Day." On the realistic level, Irene simply wants revenge on the man who cast her off and thereby turned her to a life of promiscuity, prostitution, and, finally, insanity. This is not a realistic play, however, and Irene's function is to probe Rubek's soul, not to get some mundane revenge. As he tells her about the evolution of the statue, Irene toys with her knife, but she declines to use it when Rubek confesses his own anguish and sense of failure. "I suddenly realized you are already dead," she tells him, "dead for years."

Rubek's crime in rejecting Irene's love in order to "create the one great work of my life" was the major reason for his failure not only as a human being, but also as an artist. By withholding his emotions from her, he stifled them, and, ironically, dissipated his own talent in the process. Without the knowledge and experience of love, Rubek was unable to respond to humanity's nobler aspects, and so his works could, at best, be inhuman, merely satirical portraits. When Irene understands the reason for his depression and sense of failure, her desire for revenge changes to a feeling of pity and rekindled love. Rubek cannot fully understand what is happening to him, but his feelings for her are awakened; he senses that his own vindication—salvation, perhaps—lies in her.

The Irene-Rubek affair is juxtaposed against that of Rubek's wife, Maia, and the bear hunter, Ulfheim. The young couple represents youth, vigor, and sensual experience of all kinds—eating, drinking, sex, physicality, and a joyous relationship to the immediate, natural environment. Rubek and Irene, on the other hand, stand for age, wisdom, and spiritual realization.

When We Dead Awaken ends on a note of reconciliation. Although he spurned her love in his youth, Rubek is ready to accept it in age. He and Irene go to seek a higher reality in the frozen mountains than Maia and Ulfheim will find in the lush valley. The living dead can awaken only into a spiritual reality beyond death. Ibsen suggests this idea at the play's conclusion, and it is exactly what happens to Irene and Rubek as they are swept up in an avalanche. With Maia's voice echoing "I am free as a bird" in the background, the nun in black, apparently a symbol for Irene's tainted past, emerges and blesses the couple with the sign of the cross and a *pax vobiscum.*

Bibliography:
Durbach, Errol. *"Ibsen the Romantic": Analogoues of Paradise in the Later Plays.* Athens: University of Georgia Press, 1982. An exploration of the lingering presence of romantic elements in Ibsen's later plays. Provides an interesting discussion of the relationship between man and woman in *When We Dead Awaken.*

Holtan, Orley I. *Mythic Patterns in Ibsen's Last Plays*. Minneapolis: University of Minnesota Press, 1970. A study of the mythic content in Ibsen's last seven plays, the book offers valuable insights to beginners and to more experienced readers. The chapter on *When We Dead Awaken* is focused on the resurrection myth.

Lyons, Charles R. *Henrik Ibsen: The Divided Consciousness*. Carbondale: Southern Illinois University Press, 1972. A study of how many of Ibsen's protagonists are simultaneously drawn to a life of thought and one of sensuous experience. Good chapter on *When We Dead Awaken*.

Meyer, Michael. *Ibsen: A Biography*. Garden City, N.Y.: Doubleday, 1971. A standard biography of Ibsen, it contains a chapter on *When We Dead Awaken* that is a good introduction to the play and a useful summary of various critical attitudes toward it.

Weigand, Hermann J. *The Modern Ibsen: A Reconsideration*. New York: Henry Holt, 1925. Long a standard in Ibsen criticism, this volume covers each of the twelve last plays and presents a careful reading of Ibsen's final drama.

WHERE ANGELS FEAR TO TREAD

Type of work: Novel
Author: E. M. Forster (1879-1970)
Type of plot: Social realism
Time of plot: Early twentieth century
Locale: England and Italy
First published: 1905

> *Principal characters:*
> LILIA HERRITON, a young English widow
> GINO CARELLA, an Italian
> PHILIP HERRITON, Lilia's brother-in-law
> HARRIET HERRITON, Lilia's sister-in-law
> MRS. HERRITON, Lilia's mother-in-law
> IRMA HERRITON, Lilia's daughter
> CAROLINE ABBOTT, a friend

The Story:

Lilia Herriton, a widow of several years who had been living with her husband's family since his death, cheerfully left Sawston, England, with her friend Caroline Abbott for an extended visit in Italy. The Herriton family had encouraged such a visit because of their concern over Lilia's growing relationship with a man they considered unsuitable for her and also because they welcomed a chance to train her daughter during the mother's absence. The trip, which had been Philip's idea, was quickly agreed to by everyone concerned. Fortunately, Caroline Abbott, a woman ten years younger but much more levelheaded than Lilia, was also planning such a trip and needed a companion.

The winter passed peacefully for everyone, and the tour seemed to be a success. Lilia was apparently gaining some degree of culture and taste under Miss Abbott's guidance, and back in England Lilia's daughter Irma was improving through the efforts of Mrs. Herriton. In the spring, however, Mrs. Herriton heard from Lilia's mother that Lilia was engaged to an Italian, supposedly someone she had met in a hotel. She immediately wired Miss Abbott for details but was answered only by the terse comment that Lilia was engaged to an Italian nobleman. Instinctively recognizing this to be a lie, she insisted that Philip go at once to Italy and stop the marriage.

Miss Abbott met Philip's train when he arrived at Monteriano, the village in which Lilia and Miss Abbott had been staying for a month. Nervously, she agreed to tell him everything. According to her story, Lilia and the man had fallen in love with each other, so she had rather offhandedly suggested marriage. Unfortunately, Signor Carella, who was about twelve years younger than Lilia, was the son of a dentist in that provincial village, and he had no money. His social position, therefore, was little better than that of a peasant. Philip was even more appalled when he saw the man, for everything about him except his physique was extremely vulgar. Philip was, however, too late to stop the marriage, for the couple had been married as soon as they heard he was coming. He could do nothing but return home, and he took Miss Abbott with him. The Herriton family refused to have anything more to do with Lilia, but they kept Irma with them to be brought up as one who bore the Herriton name.

It was some time before Lilia realized that she did not love her husband and could never be happy with him and that he had married her only for her money. She was never able to understand that as an Italian wife she could neither expect nor receive from her husband the things that English wives received from theirs as a matter of course. By the time she realized her unhappiness, she was cut off from everything in England and there was nothing she could do. Once, when she was particularly upset, she did write to her little daughter, telling of her unhappiness and the reasons for it, but the letter was intercepted by Mrs. Herriton and nothing ever came of it.

Lilia often thought that if she could present her husband with a son they might eventually regain some happiness. His one ambition was to be the father of a man like himself. Lilia did finally have a son, but she died in childbirth. The Herritons decided they must tell Irma about her mother's death but that it would be best if no one knew about the child who was, after all, no real relation of theirs.

Irma found out about the child when she began receiving postcards sent her by the father. Her childish pride prevented her from keeping such an event a secret, and soon all Sawston knew of it. Much to the chagrin of the Herritons, Miss Abbott, who still considered herself partly responsible for all that had happened, began to insist that something be done for the child, either by them or by herself. Mrs. Herriton, whose pride would not allow anyone else to do something that would in any way reflect on her family, immediately began negotiations that she hoped would enable her to adopt the boy.

When her letters elicited only polite refusals, she decided that Philip must again go to Monteriano and gain custody of the child at any cost; Harriet was to go along to see that he accomplished his mission. On their arrival, however, they found that Miss Abbott had preceded them and was also intent on seeing that the child be taken back to England. Philip and Miss Abbott soon began to be affected by the romantic and charming atmosphere. They still meant to carry out their mission, but they quickly lost all feeling of urgency in the matter.

On their second day in the village, they were to meet with Signor Carella. Miss Abbott went to the house early and alone; she was afraid that Philip would fail. While there, she was completely won over by the father's devotion to the son, and she found herself on the Italian's side and against the Herritons, although she knew she could do nothing to hinder their plans. When Philip saw Carella that day, although he would not openly admit that the Italian was right, he found that he was completely indifferent to the outcome of his mission, and he became friendly with his adversary. Success in the affair was left to Harriet, who, after apparently accepting Philip's failure, prepared to leave the village. Shortly before it was time for them to catch the train, she sent a note to Philip, telling him to pick her up just outside the gate to the village. When he got there, he found that she had also visited the Carella household and, not finding Carella at home, had simply picked up the baby and walked away.

On the way down the mountain to the train, their carriage was accidentally overturned, and the baby was killed. Philip had to tell Carella what had happened, and the Italian almost killed him. Miss Abbott, whom Carella had always revered, was the only person who could calm him and prevent the situation from resulting in yet more pain. By the time the English group had recuperated enough to leave Italy, the two men were good friends again.

On the way back to England, Philip received another disappointment. Because of the romantic atmosphere and their close association, he had fallen in love with Miss Abbott. He almost proposed to her when they were talking about love and the future, but she, thinking he had suspected it long before, told him of her passion for Carella. Philip had for years thought that he understood the world, but he now recognized that he really understood nothing.

Critical Evaluation:

E. M. Forster does more than mock English society. His comic novels perform the serious task of questioning the assumptions upon which identity is based. At the same time readers laugh at Forster's pompous or pathetic characters, they are being taught to recognize how much damage can result from human beings passing judgment on one another. *Where Angels Fear to Tread*, Forster's first novel, established his reputation as both artist and humanist.

More often than not, Forster's novels are set outside England. The irony of this strategy is that, while abroad, his characters satirize English social custom as acutely as do the homebound characters created by Forster's predecessor, Jane Austen. Forster incorporates many of her satiric impulses into his style. Social snobbery, religious hypocrisy, flighty liberalism, and ill-conceived romanticism are just a few of the aspects of the English character that Forster, like Austen, makes the target for his comic abuse.

In *Where Angels Fear to Tread*, Mrs. Herriton is the emblem of British arrogance. She fiercely guards a code of conduct that she would describe as "decency" but that really represents only a preference for English as opposed to Continental customs. The cruelly immoral consequences of Mrs. Herriton's brand of decency become gradually apparent as the plot unfolds. Mrs. Herriton's ferocity works as a baseline in the novel. Even though she is dislikable, the strength of her character is a foil against which the feebleness of the others is revealed.

Lilia, whose low breeding and high spirits make her the kind of ingenue who can be an agent of chaos in both Austen and Forster, threatens Mrs. Herriton's jealously guarded sense of order. Philip and Harriet, Mrs. Herriton's own children, help fill out the satiric register: Harriet, the woman who is warped by an embittered and ineffectual religiosity, and Philip, a snobbish worshiper of beauty. Through Philip, Forster carries out his trademark spoof of aesthetics, a school of literary criticism initiated by Walter Pater that dominated English letters in the period of transition between 1870 and 1930.

Perhaps Forster drops these stereotypical English characters into the provincial Italian setting of Monteriano (a fictional town modeled after San Gimignano near Florence) to draw attention to the fact that the novel is, at its core, a discussion of difference. English society, with its sometimes stuffy rules and expectations, becomes the source from which a series of divisions emerge. These divisions, all a form of the difference between the familiar and the strange and between self and other, form the intellectual substance of the novel. Forster thereby identifies and criticizes the often intolerant human instincts by which culture proceeds.

Indeed, the mistrust of cultures for one another, particularly England's low opinion of its European neighbors and colonial subjects, is the first opposition upon which Forster draws in *Where Angels Fear to Tread*. In his later *A Passage to India* (1924), the issue of cultural division found its fullest expression. Yet the tone of resentment—sometimes comic, then again verging upon the tragic—that flavors the relations in that novel between native Indians and so-called Anglo-Indians is already present in the Herritons' concerted attempt to run roughshod over Monteriano.

The arrogantly unyielding manner in which the English respond to other cultures is present throughout the novel. It is most comically concentrated in the theater scene, where Harriet tries to impose her reverential method of listening to music on the Italians, whose good-natured custom it is to respond with lustful exuberance. For a time, Harriet's sense of decorum prevails, but when the Italian audience mobs the heroine of that evening's opera (*Lucia di Lammermoor*), throwing flowers and playbills, Harriet pronounces the whole affair disrespectable and stomps out of the theater. In this comic scene, Forster does not allow the English sensibility to imperialize the Italian, but the tide tragically turns at the end of the novel when Harriet has her grim revenge. Tragedy is too often the result of intolerance. Forster issues this warning while testing his readership's tolerance of differences in class, gender, and even race.

Lilia's marriage to the dentist's son Gino repulses the Herritons because it introduces middle-class stock into their patrician family. Philip somehow understands this violation of class distinction as the death of romance. Always evenhanded in his satire, Forster also uses the Italian Gino as the representative of gender bias. After marrying Gino, Lilia is maddened by the dull, domestic life her new husband expects her to lead. Race is not an overt aspect of *Where Angels Fear to Tread*, but it is an underlying component in the power and menace of the swarthy Mediterranean Gino, who seduces both Lilia and the novel's true heroine, Caroline Abbott. Forster here introduces a hint of the kind of racial "contamination" that outrages the Anglo-Indians in *A Passage to India*.

The uneven ending of *Where Angels Fear to Tread* serves as an object lesson in the complex process of judging human behavior. Philip, Caroline Abbott, and Harriet all at various times attempt to persuade or coerce Gino into giving up his child. When Philip and Caroline gradually realize that Gino's right to the child is vindicated by his obvious love for him, they abandon the attempt to get the boy away from him. Forster champions this kind of learning, the gradual acquisition of wisdom, and Philip's and Caroline's spiritual growth earns for them at least partial redemption. Harriet, however, never loses her conviction that all that is English must triumph over all that is Italian. Harriet's inability to reform her prejudices results in the novel's tragic outcome. Forster shocked some of his readers by allowing the baby to die, but in doing so he hoped to nourish the spirit of tolerance not yet suffocated by the human inclination toward pettiness and spite.

"Critical Evaluation" by Nick David Smart

Bibliography:
Furbank, P. N. *E. M. Forster: A Life*. New York: Harcourt Brace Jovanovich, 1978. An exhaustive biography of Forster that also serves as a source of cultural information concerning Forster's settings in England, Italy, and India.
McConkey, James. *The Novels of E. M. Forster*. Ithaca, N.Y.: Cornell University Press, 1957. McConkey attempts to judge Forster's fiction in relation to the critical principles outlined in *Aspects of the Novel* (1927), Forster's book-length study of the genre.
Trilling, Lionel. *E. M. Forster*. 2d ed. New York: New Directions, 1964. Appreciative readings of Forster's works that are intended to elevate the novelist to the artistic status he deserves. Forster is seen as a practitioner of what Trilling termed the "liberal imagination."
Wilde, Alan. *Art and Order: A Study of E. M. Forster*. New York: New York University Press, 1964. Focuses on Forster's practice of and contribution to the aesthetic view of life. The value of beauty in human existence, and art's role in defining beauty, are the motivating issues in Wilde's first chapter, which begins with a discussion of *Where Angels Fear to Tread*.

WHERE I'M CALLING FROM

Type of work: Short fiction
Author: Raymond Carver (1938-1988)
First published: 1988

With Raymond Carver's death from lung cancer on August 2, 1988 (at the age of fifty), American letters lost a major voice. Carver is credited with beginning the renaissance of realism in the short story, countering the experimental fiction of the 1960's with a carefully observed, clean prose that inspired a generation of writers after him. Though he published his first story, "Pastoral," in 1963, his first short-story collection, *Will You Please Be Quiet, Please?* did not appear until 1976. One year later, the collection was nominated for the National Book Award, and that same year Carver suddenly stopped drinking, after having been hospitalized several times for alcoholism.

His second collection, *What We Talk About When We Talk About Love* (1981; written with the support of a Guggenheim Fellowship), is considered a minimalist masterpiece. Critic Michael Gorra defines minimalism as a kind of writing "in which the intentional poverty, the anorexia, of the writer's style [mirrors] the spiritual poverty of [the] characters' lives." In his essay "On Writing" (1981), Carver sketches his own views by citing the influence of three famous writers: Ezra Pound, from whom he took the quotation that "fundamental accuracy of statement is the one sole morality of writing"; Anton Chekhov, who showed him the importance of sudden awakenings, or epiphanies; and Geoffrey Wolff, from whose exhortation "No cheap tricks" he got his notion of no tricks at all. Carver's writer's creed is "Get in, get out. Don't linger. Go on." Reflecting this fear of wasted language, the stories of Carver's first two collections are lean and spare. Indeed, what is absent often matters as much as—or more than—as what is present. With *Cathedral* (1983; nominated for the National Book Critics Circle Award and runner-up for the 1984 Pulitzer Prize), Carver began to move away from the bleak pessimism of his first two collections toward a fuller and warmer vision of human nature.

Where I'm Calling From is Carver's tenth book and includes his selection of the best thirty stories from the earlier collections mentioned above, combined with seven new stories that had previously appeared only in *The New Yorker*. Maintaining his dedication to his craft, Carver revised or retitled a number of the stories for what he knew would be his last—and definitive— short-story collection. By organizing them in an essentially chronological sequence, Carver laid out a twenty-five-year writing career.

He begins *Where I'm Calling From* with "Nobody Said Anything," a story whose emphasis on fishing recalls the influence of Ernest Hemingway and his Nick Adams stories. In "Nobody Said Anything," a boy whose parents are quarreling bitterly feigns illness and cuts school. Once his parents are gone he heads for the creek, where he and another boy struggle together to catch a fish of near mythic proportions and color. When they catch their fish, they must decide how to apportion the single product of their shared labors and agree to divide the fish in half. The narrator takes the headed half home, where his parents are arguing so vigorously they do not notice the pan smoking on the stove. When he interrupts their quarrel to show them the fish, his mother screams and his father yells at him to get rid of it. The story closes with the narrator looking at the fish and saying, "I held him. I held that half of him." Of course he only has half the fish but, as critics have noted, things are not what they seem in Carver's fiction. Rather, they are much more than they seem. In "Nobody Said Anything" the dividing of the fish implies the imminent division of the family by divorce, while the half of the fish the boy holds suggests the one parent with whom he may soon be living.

"Neighbors" is the first story Carver published in *Esquire* (in 1971), where he published other stories under the guiding eye of the fiction editor, Gordon Lish, who moved Carver's writing from the careful work he had done with John Gardner at California State University at Chico to the pruned style that marked his most minimalist period. When the Stones go out of town, they ask their neighbors, the Millers, to care for their cat, plants, and apartment. The Millers take turns handling the responsibilities, each visit to the Stones' apartment becoming longer and more interesting as Bill and Arlene Miller, in turn, delve into the Stones' lives and belongings. Bill tries on both Jim and Harriet Stone's clothing, smokes her cigarettes, drinks their scotch, and returns to his own apartment with heightened desires. The Millers' sex life improves dramatically as a result of their visits across the hall. Finally, they decide to go into the Stones' apartment together, but Arlene discovers that she has locked the key inside. They are denied access to the apartment, to lives more interesting than theirs, and to the possibility of vicarious living.

"Are These Actual Miles?" (originally titled "What Is It?") is the last of twelve stories chosen from *Will You Please Be Quiet, Please?* Leo and Toni have fallen on hard times and are about to declare bankruptcy. Leo sends Toni out to sell their convertible before a creditor can "slap a lien on the car." The sale has to be that night and it has to be cash. Toni spends two hours on her hair and face, preparing to negotiate. Leo stays home, drinking Scotch. He relives their history while waiting, and the reader comes to know him and Toni: They are a blue-collar couple who, for a time, had more money than they could spend but then "sign up for it all" and get into credit-card debt. Hours pass; Toni should have been home by now. Leo "understands he is willing to be dead." His wife comes home the next morning with a check for "six and a quarter." The car dealer pulls into Leo's driveway in the convertible, leaves Toni's makeup bag on the porch, and Leo runs out to say "Monday." What is absent, but implied, is that Toni has been deliberately unfaithful to her husband to punish him for going bankrupt. Leo's enigmatic comment, "Monday," refers to the new beginning he hopes for Monday, but, typical of the stories of Carver's first collection, the ending seems pessimistic rather than hopeful.

Carver selected seven stories from *What We Talk About When We Talk About Love*, the collection that established his reputation as an important writer and a minimalist. In "So Much Water So Close to Home," Stuart Kane goes on a three-day fishing trip with his friends, returning home a day earlier than expected. The next morning, his wife Claire discovers that Stuart and his friends had found the nude body of a young woman but rather than report their discovery to the police had opted to stay on, only stopping their drinking and fishing long enough to secure the dead woman's body by tying a nylon cord around her wrist. Though nothing has changed for Stuart and nothing will change in their marriage, Claire perceives her husband differently as she identifies with the victim. Carver has said he likes it "when there is some feeling of threat or sense of menace in short stories," and in "So Much Water" the menace is Stuart's possible violence toward his wife. Susan Miller died at a man's hand, a victim of rape. When Claire refuses to have sex with Stuart after his first night home, he tries to force her and does not understand her behavior. He accepts no responsibility for his actions or inaction regarding Susan Miller and seems to feel that all his wife needs to make her happy is sex—the very thing she rejects because she now sees herself, like the dead woman, as an object and victim of men's desires.

Where I'm Calling From includes eight stories from *Cathedral*, including the story that gives his last collection its title. *Cathedral* manifests the definite shift in Carver's fiction from hopelessness and despair to the possibility of hope and redemption. Tragedies still occur, loss is a daily event, but characters cope better with the disasters of their lives and they do so in fuller narrative settings. In "A Small, Good Thing," for example, Scotty, a seven-year-old only son dies as a result of being hit by a car on his birthday. When his parents go to the bakery to berate the baker for repeatedly calling them to pick up a cake for their now-dead boy, the baker confesses that his difficult life has made him less humane. He apologizes, and the three adults break bread together in a communion of life's difficulties. In "Cathedral," a blind man comes to visit the narrator's wife, who had worked for him years ago and maintains their friendship. Bub, the narrator, belittles the blind man even before meeting him, and the early part of their evening together is awkward. After his wife is asleep, however, Bub finds himself "watching" television with Robert. He attempts to describe the cathedral on the screen but cannot, so he guides Robert's hand to sketch the structure. Robert has Bub close his eyes and complete the drawing. "It's really something," says Bub, whose attitude changes as a result of his sudden understanding.

The last seven stories Carver published differ substantially from his earlier works. They are longer and more detailed, they deal with family relationships rather than domestic situations between a husband and wife, their characters range beyond the blue-collar marginalized characters of earlier stories, and, as Carver commented, they are "somehow more affirmative." The collection closes with "Errand," a story of Chekhov's last days and of his death from tuberculosis. When the end is obvious and immutable, Chekhov's doctor brilliantly orders champagne. Chekhov, his wife, and his physician toast his life. He dies, but the wife waits with his body until morning, when a delivery boy comes to collect the glasses and bring her some flowers. She asks him quietly to find the best mortician in the city, without raising an alarm about the great writer's death. He nods in agreement, but before leaving on his errand he leans down and picks up the champagne cork that had fallen under the edge of the bed. The large event of Chekhov's death is paired with the small event of an anonymous errand boy's attention to detail. Carver brought the same attention to all of his stories, those of his minimalist period and those of his rich last days.

Linda Ledford-Miller

Bibliography:
Campbell, Ewing. *Raymond Carver: A Study of the Short Fiction.* New York: Twayne, 1992. A good overview of Carver's stories, with an analysis of twenty-seven stories from the four major collections. A section on "The Writer" includes an interview and Carver's own essay, "On Writing"; "The Critics" contains essays by three critics. Also includes a chronology and selected bibliography.
Meyer, Adam. *Raymond Carver.* New York: Twayne, 1995. An excellent overview of Carver's work. Contains a biographical sketch and situates Carver's influence on "minimalism," renewed realism, and the renaissance of the short story. Discusses each of his collections and comments briefly on his poetry. Includes an annotated bibliography of selected criticism.
Nisset, Kirk. *The Stories of Raymond Carver.* Athens: Ohio University Press, 1994. The first dissertation on Carver, which has been expanded into a useful introduction to his work.
Saltzman, Arthur M. *Understanding Raymond Carver.* Columbia: University of South Carolina Press, 1988. The first book-length study of Carver's work. Discusses three of the major collections. Does not include commentary on the seven new stories collected in the closing section of *Where I'm Calling From.* An empathetic reading that considers Carver a "Connoisseur of the Commonplace."

Stull, William L. "Raymond Carver." In *Dictionary of Literary Biography Yearbook: 1988*, edited by J. M. Brook. Detroit: Gale, 1989. The author updates his 1984 *Dictionary of Literary Biography Yearbook* entry with this obituary. Surveys Carver's life as it influenced his art. Includes an overview of the critical reception of Carver's work and discusses the Carver-Chekhov connection. Also includes two facsimile pages from Carver's last story, "Errand."

WHERE THE AIR IS CLEAR

Type of work: Novel
Author: Carlos Fuentes (1928-   )
Type of plot: Mythic
Time of plot: Early to mid-1950's
Locale: Mexico City
First published: La región más transparente, 1958 (English translation, 1960)

> *Principal characters:*
> FEDERICO ROBLES, a banker
> NORMA LARAGOITI, his wife
> HORTENSIA CHACÓN, Robles' mistress
> RODRIGO POLA, Norma's lover
> IXCA CIENFUEGOS, shadowy character symbolizing the spirit
>   of Mexico City
> MANUEL ZAMACONA, poet and friend of Ixca

The Story:

Rising from his peasant origins, Federico Robles subscribed to the myth of bourgeois stability and eventually made his way to the top of a powerful financial empire in Mexico City. He created this empire in the years immediately following the Mexican Revolution. In an act of rebellion against his mestizo heritage, Robles married a green-eyed woman named Norma Laragoiti, a self-absorbed materialist. During his marriage to Norma, Robles took as his mistress the blind mestizo woman Hortensia Chacón, who had abandoned her petty functionary husband. With Hortensia, Robles was able to find true love and happiness.

During one of the many intensely emotional battles between Norma and Federico, Norma accidentally burned to death in the Robles mansion. The fire began when Federico rushed downstairs from his wife's bedroom after she had refused to give him her jewels to sell. He needed the money because his financial empire was crumbling. Federico lost all his money and worldly possessions and returned to his peasant origins. He moved to a farm in the north of Mexico, where he lived with Hortensia and their son.

The writer Rodrigo Pola was on the opposite side of the social spectrum from Robles. Their sharing of Norma (whom Pola loved) underscored their parallel and contrasting movements in the novel. Pola was transformed from an aspiring poet to a successful screenwriter. Artistically, Pola experienced a rise in terms of worldly success that was a fall in terms of artistic accomplishment. Federico, in turn, experienced a financial fall that was a spiritual rise.

Moving among these lives, serving as a kind of adhesive, was Ixca Cienfuegos. Often described as a misty, insubstantial presence, he represented the spirit of the city. His mother, Teódula Moctezuma, was a genuine Aztec sorceress. Teódula kept dead family members under her floorboards and believed that for her ancestors to remain contented and for her life to continue, Ixca needed to sacrifice a human life for the gods. At dawn, after Norma burned to death, Teódula pointed to the sun, which she believed had risen again because of the rejuvenating sacrifice. Ixca searched for a victim in order to put his mother's beliefs into practice, but near the end of the novel he was exhausted by his attempts to conform to ancient rituals.

A number of briefer portraits surround the central figures of Carlos Fuentes' novel. These minor characters suffered in obscurity throughout the city. Gabriel, a migrant worker, whose brother occasionally served as a waiter at parties attended by the more affluent characters, returned from the United States with a blender for his mother, only to find that his family's shack had no electricity. They used the blender as a flower vase. Gabriel, one of the novel's many sacrificial victims, was senselessly killed by a local thug in a cheap dive on the poor side of town.

Critical Evaluation:

In *Where the Air Is Clear*, Carlos Fuentes offers a kaleidoscopic presentation, in numerous vignettes, of contemporary life in Mexico City. The title of the novel is a quotation from the work of the Mexican writer Alfonso Reyes and refers to Anahuac, the valley of Mexico, as a region where the air is clear. At least the region was so at one time, before the drying up of Lake Texcoco and modern industrialization brought dust and smog, changing what was once a high tableland with a relatively low population density into an overcrowded metropolis with air pollution.

Fuentes' novel is divided into three sections that are not equal in length or intent. Each section is in turn subdivided into parts, each with its title, generally the name of a character who provides the point of view for the section. Fuentes' great contribution to this modernist technique of fragmentation of point of view is largely the novel's use of setting, both philosophical and psychological. The novel presents a portrait of Mexico City.

In *Where the Air Is Clear*, myth occupies a significant place. Fuentes presents a mythical history of Mexico City and its inhabitants. The characters who represent the historical aspects of the novel are products of the Mexican Revolution and, at the same time, are representative of Mexican society during the 1950's. Robles is a revolutionary turned into a conservative banker. His wife Norma is a social climber who marries for money. Zamacona is a brooding intellectual.

Each one of the main characters is sacrificed for the sake of a myth. It is the myth of bourgeois stability in the case of Robles the banker. It is the myth of success in the poet Rodrigo Pola. It is the myth of narcissism in the case of Norma Laragoiti. It is the myth of the intellectual in the case of Manuel Zamacona (who dies by the pistol of a deadly drunk while trying to buy gas to escape from Acapulco). All myths, the author demonstrates, are false; all are deadly; all are projections of human desires.

Ancestral voices and indigenous mythologies are very powerful in the novel. For Fuentes, myth combines past, present, and future. As a creator and perpetuator of myths, Fuentes builds a modern version of ancient patterns, including rituals of sacrifice and battles between male and female principles. In the narrative, these ancestral voices link the reader not only with the past, present, and future but also with the universe. Fuentes works within the universal time of myth and within the limited, linear, and subjective time of individual history. In *Where the Air Is Clear*, the mythic mode predominates.

Ixca Cienfuegos (the name combines the Aztec and the Spanish; the surname means "hundred fires") moves through the novel as a unifying consciousness, a force for the elicitation of truth and a bearer of transcendence. He symbolizes Mexico's past, a mythical Mexico that still believes in ritual and in sacrifice as the only way to redemption. The Mexican people have been chosen by the gods to keep the sun moving so that humanity may survive. Without sacrifices this would be impossible. Norma and Zamacona are sacrificed.

This revelation of the mythical nature of Mexican history is accomplished by the use of image and metaphor. The characters, the description of the city, the action, and the plot are all expressed by uniting two worlds, that of the remote past and that of the present. The interactions among the characters representing both cultures become the central technique of mythmaking. History and myth balance each other to give the novel equilibrium.

Ixca Cienfuegos listens to the stories of many characters who are incarnations of Mexican history, constituting a landscape of moral, psychological, and social destiny. There are the revolutionary turned tycoon, the aristocratic woman frozen in nostalgia and sexlessness, the ambitious young woman from the provinces, the self-pitying unsuccessful poet, the aged avatar of Mexico's pagan past, and the lower-class youth yearning murderously for some way to feel alive.

All of these characters also function on another level within the novel's narrative. There is tension between their existence as specific examples of Mexican society and the deeper truth that Cienfuegos extracts from them. Interlocked, their destinies unfold in extreme violence. One by one, the shameful and false routes to social standing are blocked. On the other hand, the innocent, the ones who have remained true to themselves, suffer deaths of terrifying meaninglessness.

Fuentes presents many aspects of Mexican life in the novel, all, in one way or another, a reflection of the impact of the revolution on the city and its people. There is nostalgia for prerevolutionary Mexico City, the city of palaces that was orderly and reasonable, and for the times of Porfirio Díaz. There is the betrayal and fear in the death of Gervasio Pola, father of the poet Rodrigo, who leaves his wife and dies facing the firing squad with the three companions he has betrayed. There is the somewhat inhuman curiosity of Ixca Cienfuegos, who takes a sadistic delight in trying to make people face the truth about themselves. Through it all, there is the brutally frank presentation of a thoroughly tawdry society, mestizo and rootless. Finally, the question, posed by the author himself—What is the origin and identity of Mexico?—is unanswerable, and the reader is left only with questions.

In *Where the Air Is Clear*, an extraordinary and influential first novel, Fuentes attempts a "biography of a city" and a synthesis of Mexico. The novel contains insights into a country whose social revolution soon ceased to be truly revolutionary. Everyone—oppressed and oppressors—is represented in rapid, cinematic scenes. Through this spectrum of characters, the author seeks the essence of the modern Mexican among a collection of people and finds no shared philosophy or sense of purpose, nothing to prevent the strong from preying on the weak.

The novel is an attempt to extricate a living imagination from the entombed, self-devouring Mexican consciousness, forever mourning its divided past, incessantly projecting its possible future, and torn between its ill-defined cultural heritage and the influence of more advanced societies. Fuentes' wish is to understand and create images of the metamorphoses that the Mexican spirit has undergone, to work his way through old myths in search of a more viable new one, and finally to emerge at some point at which form and experience cooperate to raise an adequate philosophical and psychological structure.

Genevieve Slomski

Bibliography:

Brody, Robert, and Charles Rossman, eds. *Carlos Fuentes: A Critical View*. Austin: University of Texas Press, 1982. Good and varied collection of essays on the stories and novels.

Duran, Gloria. *The Archetypes of Carlos Fuentes*. Hamden, Conn.: Archon Books, 1980. Discusses female archetypes in Fuentes' major works of fiction.

Faris, Wendy B. *Carlos Fuentes*. New York: Frederick Ungar, 1983. Excellent introduction to

Fuentes' works. Focuses upon Fuentes' capacity to absorb, transform, and transmit multiple voices.

Foster, David W. "*La región más transparente* and the Limits of Prophetic Art." *Hispania* 56, no. 1 (March, 1973): 35-42. Insightful discussion of Fuentes' use of myth and archetype in the novel. Describes myth as a unifying principle between the present and the past in Mexican history.

Guzman, Daniel de. *Carlos Fuentes*. Boston: Twayne, 1972. Overview of Fuentes' work in a historical, social, psychological, economic, and cultural context. Bibliography.

THE WHITE DEVIL

Type of work: Drama
Author: John Webster (c. 1577-1580-before 1634)
Type of plot: Tragedy
Time of plot: Sixteenth century
Locale: Rome and Padua, Italy
First performed: c. 1609-1612; first published, 1612

Principal characters:

VITTORIA COROMBONA, a Venetian lady
PAULO GIORDANO URSINI, duke of Brachiano
FRANCISCO DE MEDICIS, duke of Florence
CARDINAL MONTICELSO, his brother
CAMILLO, Vittoria's husband
FLAMINEO, Vittoria's brother, secretary to Brachiano
MARCELLO, another brother, attendant on Francisco de Medicis
COUNT LODOVICO, a banished nobleman
ISABELLA, sister of Francisco de Medicis, Brachiano's wife
GIOVANNI, son of Isabella and Brachiano

The Story:

Antonelli and Gasparo, courtiers of Francisco de Medicis, duke of Florence, brought to Count Lodovico in Rome the news that he had been banished because of his notorious intrigues and bloody murders. Lodovico could not understand why he had been singled out for punishment when other noblemen, especially the duke of Brachiano, were guilty of crimes just as heinous.

Brachiano was trying to seduce Vittoria Corombona, wife of the aging Camillo. Helping Brachiano in his scheme was Vittoria's unscrupulous brother Flamineo, who convinced Camillo that the best way to keep Vittoria virtuous was to give her unlimited freedom. This privilege granted, Vittoria kept an assignation with Brachiano. Through the transparent symbolism of a dream which she had fabricated, Vittoria urged her lover to murder Isabella, his wife, and Camillo, her husband. Just as Brachiano was declaring his love for Vittoria and his understanding of her design, Vittoria's mother, Cornelia, disclosed herself to denounce the two and to announce the arrival of Brachiano's wife in Rome.

Isabella's brothers, Francisco and Cardinal Monticelso, summoned Brachiano to remonstrate against his philandering. When their appeal to Brachiano's sense of virtue resulted only in mutual recrimination, the brothers produced Giovanni, Brachiano's son, whose youthful innocence, they hoped, would inspire Brachiano with a sense of family duty. Confronted alone by Isabella, Brachiano proved the folly of such a hope by berating his wife and vowing never again to sleep with her. To forestall the war that would surely ensue if Francisco learned of this vow, Isabella pretended that she was unable to forgive her husband and declared that she was abandoning her husband's bed. Her ruse and Brachiano's acquiescence in it fooled Francisco so completely that he denounced Isabella for mad jealousy.

Disgusted by their sister's vow but convinced that she would soon retract it, Francisco and Monticelso turned their attention to Camillo and Marcello, another of Vittoria's brothers, whom they had decided to appoint joint commissioners in charge of combating the pirates reportedly led by the banished Lodovico. Camillo objected because he feared he would be cuckolded during his absence from home, but Monticelso's promise to keep an eye on Vittoria quieted him. Actually, Monticelso and Francisco were giving Camillo the commission to get him away from Rome so that Brachiano might have free access to Vittoria. By this scheme the two brothers hoped to plunge Brachiano into a shameful scandal.

Brachiano, however, had made his own plans, having arranged for Flamineo to murder Camillo, and for Julio, a physician, to kill Isabella. Through the magic of a conjurer, Brachiano was able to watch the murders, Isabella dying from kissing a poisoned portrait of her husband, and Camillo, from being pushed off a vaulting horse in a gymnasium.

Monticelso and Francisco immediately brought Vittoria to trial for the murder of her husband, although they knew they had no evidence other than her ill repute. At her trial before the ambassadors to Rome, a hearing presided over by Monticelso, Brachiano admitted that he had stayed at Vittoria's house the night of the murder. This testimony, along with other incriminating but circumstantial evidence of her adultery, was sufficient to convict Vittoria, although she protested her innocence and denounced the conduct of the trial. Monticelso sentenced her to confinement in a house of reformed prostitutes.

Immediately after the pronouncement of this sentence, Giovanni arrived to tell his uncles of his mother's death. Accompanying him was Lodovico, who secretly had been in love with Isabella and who, in fact, had witnessed her death. Francisco and Monticelso realized that Brachiano was responsible for the murder of their sister but disagreed on how to avenge it. Fearing that a war might result from an open attack on Brachiano, yet unwilling to defer vengeance, Francisco, inspired by a vision of Isabella's ghost, devised a trick. He wrote a letter to Vittoria, professing his love for her, and instructed his servant to deliver it when some of Brachiano's men were close by.

As Francisco hoped, Flamineo intercepted the letter and gave it to Brachiano, who was, as expected, enraged by Vittoria's apparent infidelity. A violent quarrel ensued between the two, refereed by the pandering Flamineo. It ended in a reconciliation so sweet that Brachiano resolved to have Vittoria stolen away from the home and then to marry her. To trick Brachiano into marrying a women of ill repute was exactly what Francisco had hoped for, but his lust for revenge was not yet satisfied. He engaged Lodovico, who had been pardoned, to murder Brachiano.

Monticelso, who had just been elected Pope, excommunicated Brachiano and his bride; then, learning of the plotted murder, he forbade Lodovico to commit it. Monticelso's command was ignored, however, when Francisco sent Lodovico a thousand crowns in Monticelso's name, a gift which convinced Lodovico that the Pope had been craftily insincere.

Francisco apparently decided to oversee the murder himself, for he disguised himself as Mulinasser, a Moor, and proceeded to Brachiano's palace in Padua, accompanied by Lodovico and Gasparo, who were disguised as Knights of Malta. Welcomed by Brachiano, the trio planned a horrible death for him.

Before they could carry out their scheme, another murder was committed. A quarrel between Marcello and Flamineo over the latter's amorous attentions paid to Zanche, Vittoria's Moorish maid, resulted in Flamineo's killing his brother. While Brachiano was passing judgment on the murderer, Lodovico sprinkled Brachiano's helmet with poison. The poison drove Brachiano mad. Soon thereafter, Lodovico and Gasparo, dressed as Capuchins, entered the room where the count lay raving; they revealed their true identity and strangled him.

After his lord's death, Flamineo sued to Vittoria for a reward in payment of his long, treacherous service. Rebuffed, he produced two pairs of pistols, claiming that he had promised

Brachiano to kill himself and Vittoria after Brachiano's death. Vittoria persuaded Flamineo to die first, but when she and Zanche fired the pistols at him they learned that Flamineo, to test Vittoria, had not loaded the weapons. Before he could murder the women, however, Lodovico and Gasparo rushed in and killed all three. Giovanni and a group of ambassadors discovered the murderers standing over the corpses. Wounded, Lodovico confessed and then disclosed the part Francisco had played in these bloody deeds. Giovanni swore vengeance on the duke of Florence.

Critical Evaluation:

The White Devil is one of John Webster's two exceptional revenge tragedies. The revenge tragedy is a subgenre that flourished during the Elizabethan and Jacobean periods. It is characterized by actions of lust, murder, and vengeance. The dark passions and questionable motives that govern the revengers distinguish these plays from more classically conceived tragedies, in which the hero who falls is noble, if flawed, and the fall arouses pity and awe. The high moral message is noticeably absent from revenge tragedies such as *The White Devil*.

To plot his play, Webster used real events that occurred some twenty-seven years before the play's first production. Conveniently, the scandalous affair between Vittoria Corombona and the duke of Brachiano took place in Italy, a country traditionally associated with corruption for the English. It is an appropriate setting for Vittoria, the white devil of the title. While some critics are unsure to whom the epithet is applied, only Vittoria Corombona combines satisfactorily its dual nature. Beautiful, intelligent, articulate, strong, Vittoria is also an unrepentant adulteress who is implicated in the murders of her husband Camillo and Brachiano's duchess Isabella. It is no accident, however, that in this drama of moral ambiguity, the extent of Vittoria's responsibility is left unclear; she may be guilty of no more than a wish, revealed in a dream, that Isabella and Camillo die.

In a world lacking nobility and goodness, Vittoria's stoicism and integrity emerge as admirable. By virtue of Webster's art, they contrast favorably with the pale pieties of her mother, Cornelia, and with the unfortunate Isabella. While one can sympathize with Cornelia's displeasure over her daughter's flagrant infidelity, the violence of her own language reveals her own viciousness. She curses Vittoria, wishing her life shortened if she should betray her husband—a dolt who is scorned by even his own faction. Later, her parading of her own sense of moral rectitude is revealed as a symptom of her madness in Act V, in which she appears onstage to strike Zanche, accusing her of being a whore. That she is, for the most part, correct, does not redeem her behavior; rather, it serves to set her up in opposition to Zanche. They are two extremes of the same failing.

Part of the equivocal moral atmosphere of this play is that Vittoria's adultery must demand censure, but it is impossible to imagine a life of contentment or fulfillment with Camillo. Modern readers might remind themselves that divorce was unavailable to Vittoria. Webster forces audiences to confront squarely the experience of joyless virtue. Isabella also faces this problem.

Isabella's situation is more complicated. Scorned by Brachiano, she nevertheless feigns repugnance to him in an effort to preserve his reputation. In this playacting, she rails against Vittoria in a manner that all critics see as revelatory of her real feelings. She dies kissing a poisoned picture of her unfaithful husband. All of this wifely devotion cries out for more pathos then it gets because Isabella's virtue is a barren thing. It brings her neither pleasure nor power, nor does it inspire or animate after her death. Even her dying is presented at a remove, in a dumb show, further distancing her from the audiences' compassion. In a better world, she would be a sympathetic figure, but ultimately, she comes across as unrealistic and slightly foolish, someone who knows no better than to cast her pearls before swine.

It is the hardheaded, luxurious Vittoria around whom the action revolves. Isabella expires in a dumb show, but Vittoria announces at her trial that all she can do is have a voice. She puts that voice to good use. The leaden-tongued lawyer bringing charges against her is no match for her poise and wit, forcing the judge, Cardinal Monticelso (Camillo's uncle) to take over for the prosecution. Even the judge is forced to a grudging admiration.

Webster steadily keeps the play's moral compass spinning. Vittoria is guilty of adultery, and perhaps complicity in the deaths of Camillo and Isabella, but her trial is manifestly corrupt, as she is quick to point out. The Cardinal is no better than she, only more powerful. He derives his power from his office, but Vittoria owes hers only to herself, to her own beauty and intelligence. The Cardinal, furthermore, abuses the power of his ecclesiastical office by participating in the mockery of justice that is the trial. Vittoria's is the fight of the underdog; her tragedy is that her aims are so impoverished.

The White Devil is a play in which reality and illusion are constantly shifting. The chaste women, Cornelia and Isabella, are exposed as self-deceived. Flamineo sets up the scene for his own death—with unloaded pistols—only to be actually slain moments later. Isabella dies kissing an image of her husband, instead of a real man. The real ecclesiastic, Cardinal Monticelso, presides over a compromised court, while Brachiano's assassins disguise themselves as Capuchins. It is a shimmering world of inconstancy and unreliability, but not an amoral one as some have claimed. In the play, morality and immorality are shifting and relative. What is most chilling in the play's landscape is the inefficacy of virtue. The innocent people such as Isabella and Marcello die just as the bad people do, and with rather less attention.

It is not surprising that when Count Lodovico tries to pass off the murders of Vittoria, Zanche, and Flamineo as a kind of pardonable vengeance for the deaths of Isabella and Camillo, he is rightly disabused of this idea. His refusal to confront his culpability is just as misplaced as Isabella's inability to confront the breakdown of her marriage. At the final moral tallying up, Vittoria proves to have been one of the better players. While the value of her successes is dubious, she accomplished what she set out to do, and she meets her death unsurprised and stoical. With the clarity of vision that has never deserted her, she confesses that her soul is embarked on a journey, but where, she knows not. Her worldly resourcefulness cannot help her in death.

The universe of *The White Devil* is one of moral collapse. In the hectic glamour of Vittoria's career, audiences see the final emptiness of a life defined only by pleasure. Her end is truly final, her lasting achievement is notoriety.

"Critical Evaluation" by Linda J. Turzynski

Bibliography:
Bliss, Lee. *The World's Perspective: John Webster and the Jacobean Drama*. New Brunswick, N.J.: Rutgers University Press, 1983. Discusses Webster in the context of his relation to his contemporaries and predecessors. Seeks to establish the existence of a social commentary of disillusionment in the play.
Forker, Charles R. *Skull Beneath the Skin: The Achievement of John Webster*. Carbondale: Southern Illinois University Press, 1986. A comprehensive study of Webster's life and work. Recounts the historical incidents upon which *The White Devil* is based and explores the nuances of the characters' relationships with one another by close reading.

Pearson, Jacqueline. *Tragedy and Tragicomedy in the Plays of John Webster*. New York: Barnes & Noble Books, 1980. Documents *The White Devil*'s pattern of repetitions—often ironic—which make for a tight, interconnected structure. Less convincing in the attempt to establish these patterns as tragicomic.

Waage, Frederick O. *The White Devil Discover'd: Backgrounds and Foregrounds to Webster's Tragedy*. New York: Peter Lang, 1984. A close reading of the play, with emphasis on how the structure reflects Webster's ethical stance. In the balance of action scenes with scenes of stasis, discovers a calculated attempt to capture more closely the rhythms and "irresolution" of life than traditional five act divisions do.

Wymer, Rowland. *Webster and Ford*. New York: St. Martin's Press, 1995. Discusses the relevance and appeal of Webster's work to twentieth century audiences. The chapter on *The White Devil* explores the dramatic potential of the play's symbolism of black and white—for example, having black actors take on some of the major roles—to highlight Webster's sense of moral ambiguity.

THE WHITE GODDESS
A Historical Grammar of Poetic Myth

Type of work: Literary theory
Author: Robert Graves (1895-1985)
First published: 1948

Begun in 1944, *The White Goddess* was to illuminate the path of Robert Graves's literary career for the next forty years, the larger part of his creative life. Beliefs it expressed concerning the obligations of poetry and poets, the rightful relationship of man to woman, and the priority of inspiration, would shape all of the novels, essays, and books of poetry that succeeded it. So central would it remain to his work that it is possible to claim that *The White Goddess* represented a way of life, or perhaps a religion, to Robert Graves. The book represents a way of life for Graves's scholars as well. Analyses of his work have stressed not merely the influence of *The White Goddess* upon poems written after it, but also poems that preceded it, examining them for the ideas and attitudes that *The White Goddess* crystallized.

The White Goddess is an indispensable tool for gaining fuller understanding of Graves's poetry. One may even suggest that this function is the book's saving grace. Although, as a work of prodigious learning, it leads readers to reevaluate their understanding of the Bronze Age, anthropologists have preferred to ignore *The White Goddess* or marginalize it as a poetical fancy or as an idiosyncratic embellishment upon the studies of James George Frazer, author of *The Golden Bough* (1890).

The blunt boldness and heterodoxy of Graves's assertions seem calculated to ward off conventional scholars. Indeed, assessing their anticipated reaction, Graves wrote: "They cannot refute it—they dare not accept it!" The richness of reference and the fluid intellectual arguments presented in *The White Goddess*, and the catlike balance it maintains between research, interpretation and pure imagination, make it one of the most idiosyncratic prose works of the twentieth century.

The White Goddess asserts that poetry embodies fundamental principles, and these may be traced back in time in Europe to a Neolithic faith that celebrated an inspirational figure linked with the moon, and known subsequently in a diversity of ancient and modern languages as the white goddess. "In Europe there were at first no male gods contemporary with the Goddess to challenge her prestige or power," Graves declares.

For evidence of this faith, Graves extends the anthropological and mythological studies of Jane Ellen Harrison and James George Frazer, weaving together an intricate system of natural, celestial, linguistic, and numerological relationships. Graves constructs what he terms a historical grammar of poetic myth. The figure at the center of his grammar is the theme, or the story of the birth, life, death, and resurrection of the god of the waxing year, and of his combat with his brother, the god of the waning year, for the love of the capricious threefold goddess. The goddess was, in her various incarnations, their mother, lover, and destroyer. "The male role was that of consort-lover, represented by a star-son, the Hercules type with which poets have traditionally identified themselves," Graves explains, "and a wise spotted serpent, Erechtheus, his hated rival. As summer succeeded winter, Star-son and Serpent superseded each other in the Moon-woman's favor."

This fundamental myth of Bronze Age matriarchal society also has served as inspiration for all poems capable of moving readers profoundly, according to Graves. He asserts that every poem succeeds only insofar as it recapitulates a part of the theme. Graves demonstrates the extraordinary precision of this statement in a succession of polarities, contrasting inspirational and classical poetry, poetic and prosaic modes of perception, proleptic and linear thought, intuitive and deductive reasoning, and so on. Graves argues that such dichotomies mirror the ancient struggle between the old matriarchal religion, and the patriarchal one that came later to vanquish and replace it.

Graves organizes his anthropological insights within a facile analysis of two Welsh poems preserved in the thirteenth century manuscript, *The Red Book of Hergest.* The two poems are "Câd Goddeu," or "The Battle of the Trees," and the *Hanes Taliesin,* or *The Tale of Taliesin.* Speculating that their lack of sustained clarity derives from their having been jumbled in order to conceal (and thus safeguard) heretical secrets they may contain, Graves seeks to decipher the poems by reordering their lines. He discovers that the *Hanes Taliesin* reflects a seasonal progression from winter solstice to winter solstice, in which is encoded the story of the year. The story of the year, in turn, is about the theme. The theme is the story of the birth, life, death, and resurrection of the god of the waxing year. "The Battle of the Trees" records a crucial intellectual conflict between rival bardic traditions, or a battle for religious mastery waged between the patriarchal worshipers associated with Dôn and the matriarchal worshipers associated with the gods Arawn and Bran. The patriarchal bards prevail by discovering and revealing the name of their adversaries' secret deity.

A great deal of readers' fascination with *The White Goddess* rests with Graves's wholly unorthodox assertions. Graves is able to persuasively argue that the secret name of the ancient Welsh deity revealed by the patrist bards (but not recorded in "The Battle of the Trees") is none other than Jehovah, the God of the Old Testament. Graves finds corroboration for this surprising conjecture in a number of interesting parallels between the Hebrews and ancient Britons, which include shared dietary restrictions against eating of pigs, rabbits, and certain seafood. Graves ascribes the Jewish suppression of vowels in written texts to their reverence for the secret name.

Graves's discovery of Jehovah's origin provides no less of a shock. Noting Plutarch's remark that the God of the Jews was actually Dionysus Sabazius, the Barley-god of Thrace and Phrygia, Graves documents various cultural similarities, such as comparable ritual celebrations in honor of Jehovah and of Dionysus. Pursuing the identification further, through African and Mediterranean religions, Graves establishes a basis in myth and in linguistics to associate Jehovah or Iahu with the worship of the moon goddess: Iahu, he asserts, stood for "the Moon goddess as ruler of the whole course of the solar year." Thus, the name of the God uncovered in "The Battle of the Trees" is, in reality, one name of the White Goddess, a name that endowed Bran with authority "to speak oracularly from her kingdom of Dis." Bran had earned this privilege by progressing through the five significant stages of the year, or "by being born to her, initiated by her, becoming her lover, being lulled to sleep by her, and finally killed by her."

The seasonal progression depicted in *Hanes Taliesin* represents an anthropomorphic view of nature; this view is central to matriarchal religion. The patriarchal victory of "The Battle of the Trees" symbolizes the fall of humanity into history and out of affinity with the natural world. Having established the beliefs and practices of the matriarchal age, Graves seeks to compare them with historical beliefs and practices. This comparison yields an understanding of all poetry.

In the matriarchal past, myth and ritual celebrated birth, life, death, and resurrection as indivisible elements of the sacred entirety of nature. This indivisibility was palpable in the seasonal round and in the process of human life. In the succeeding, Olympian, age, myth was turned toward recording "images of man's political will," as patriarchy sought to consolidate its triumph over woman by vanquishing nature. The Olympian age introduced the self-reliant

Thunder-child, Axe-child, or Hammer-child, superseding the Star-son and the serpent. This age divided the power of the goddess among a plurality of lesser female deities.

The purely patriarchal age, in which there are no goddesses at all (Mary is not a goddess), followed the transitional Olympian phase. This modern age is unfavorable to poetry. Not only has the theme been displaced from the center of culture, but also, concomitantly, an emphasis has been placed upon balance and stability, with an implicit warning to avoid extremes. The poet's quest for inspiration or poetic intoxication is denigrated. For Graves, the graceful classical verses of Horace, Vergil, and John Milton, for all their majesty and metrical beauty, never attain the immediacy of Catullus. Lacking inspiration, or a genesis in love—for Graves the sole surviving feature of the matriarchal world—the verse of patriarchs fall short of being poetry. Rather, it qualifies as Apollonian poetry, which, Graves suggests, is a type of musical prose, a poor substitute for the material it replaced.

Poetry and prose for Graves are not merely literary genres, but also radically divergent modes of thought. The difference between them is crucial in Graves's system. Prose, he asserts, originated with the classical Greeks and belongs to the patriarchal world. The prosaic mode of thought finds articulation through words carrying only a single sense at a time. The final effect of the prosaic mode is to produce specialists with stringently limited expertise. Of them Graves writes: "To know only one thing well is to have a barbaric mind."

The poetic mode, however, "resolves speech into its original images and rhythms and re-combines these on several simultaneous levels of thought into a multiple sense." The language of the poetic mode, Graves argues, must seem like nonsense to a mind trained in only comprehending prose. Words in poetry mean more than one thing at a time.

Appraising the modern development of poetic thought, Graves contrasts the ideas of originality held by Augustan and Victorian age poets with those of poets he accepts as true poets, such as William Shakespeare, Edmund Spenser, and John Keats. The Augustan Age discouraged originality because of its subversiveness. The mid-Victorian age, in which the monarchy and the social order it represented were unpopular, reevaluated originality. This age's yoking of originality to pedestrian themes, however, meant that originality became trivialized. By contrast, the true poet, addressing his poem to a real woman rather than to posterity, always has to be original, in the simple sense of telling the truth, in his own passionate and peculiar words, about himself and his beloved. Graves's sincere dedication to this romantic vision makes *The White Goddess* one of the most significant poetic treatises by an English poet.

Michael Scott Joseph

Bibliography:
Canary, Robert H. *Robert Graves.* Boston: Twayne, 1980. Combines an abstract of the book, a survey of critical perspectives, and a look at the book's relationship to the novels and poems that succeeded it.
Graves, Robert. *Five Pens in Hand.* Garden City, N.Y.: Doubleday, 1958. Contains "The White Goddess," a lecture given in New York in 1957, in which Graves tells how he came to write *The White Goddess.* Repeats some of the book's central themes, including Graves's idea of the poetic mode of thought.
Seymour-Smith, Martin. *Robert Graves: His Life and Work.* New York: Holt, Rinehart and Winston, 1982. Provides a chronology of the evolution of *The White Goddess.* Dismissive of Graves's notion of a prehistoric matriarchy. Emphasizes the book's indispensability as a tool for understanding Graves's poetry.

Snipes, Katherine. *Robert Graves*. New York: Frederick Ungar, 1979. A sound introduction to *The White Goddess*, comparable to Robert Canary's, although simpler.

Vickery, John B. *Robert Graves and the White Goddess*. Lincoln: University of Nebraska Press, 1972. The most thorough study of Graves's debt to James George Frazer's *The Golden Bough*. Vickery's impressive familiarity with Frazer at times verges on being disruptive, almost superimposing itself upon Graves's work.

WHITE-JACKET
Or, The World in a Man-of-War

Type of work: Novel
Author: Herman Melville (1819-1891)
Type of plot: Adventure
Time of plot: 1840's
Locale: A vessel of the United States Navy
First published: 1850

>*Principal characters:*
>WHITE-JACKET, a sailor on board the USS *Neversink*
>JACK CHASE, the captain of the maintop in the ship
>CAPTAIN CLARET, the commander of the vessel

The Story:

White-Jacket, as he was later nicknamed, was a common sailor, a member of the crew of the United States frigate *Neversink* on a cruise of the Pacific Ocean during the 1840's. After the ship left Callao, Peru, the sailor tried to purchase a heavy jacket that he would need as protection when the *Neversink* passed into the colder climate off Cape Horn. Because a heavy jacket was not available from the ship's purser, the vessel having been at sea for more than three years, the sailor had to make a canvas jacket for himself.

The jacket was full of pockets and quilted with odds and ends of rags and clothing for warmth. When the maker requested some paint to make it waterproof and to darken its color, he was told that no paint was available for the purpose.

As the ship moved southward toward the Antarctic, the sailor gradually came to be called White-Jacket by the crew because of the strange garment he wore. Some of the sailors, superstitious as old wives, disliked him because of the jacket; they said that White-Jacket was too much like a ghost when he went about his duties high in the rigging of the frigate.

The offensiveness of White-Jacket's strange apparel was revealed only a few days after the ship reached Callao. White-Jacket was forced to leave the mess group to which he had been assigned, because the sailors told him that anyone who wore such a weird garment was unwelcome. That White-Jacket had proved himself a very poor cook during his tour of duty for the group had not helped his cause.

White-Jacket was taken into the mess to which belonged the petty officer of the maintop under whom White-Jacket served. Jack Chase, a gentlemanly Britisher who shared White-Jacket's love of literature and who had returned to the *Neversink* after an absence of months, during which he had served as an officer on a Peruvian insurrectionist vessel, was admired by the rough sailors and respected by all the officers aboard the ship.

As the *Neversink* sailed southward along the western coast of South America the general ship's duties continued. White-Jacket and his fellows set sails and took them in, washed down the decks, stood their watches, and prepared for colder weather. To relieve the tedium of the long voyage, Captain Claret gave out word that the men would be permitted to stage a theatrical entertainment. The captain had permitted such entertainments in the earlier stages of the cruise but had discontinued them because one of the actors had behaved in an objectionable manner. White-Jacket noted that before the play, the captain perused and censored the script. Neither the captain nor the commodore who was aboard the *Neversink* dignified the men's entertainment by being present.

During the coastal voyage, a man fell overboard and was drowned. The incident demonstrated to White-Jacket how risky life aboard a ship was and how quickly a lost man was forgotten. The *Neversink* was becalmed in the waters off Cape Horn. After three days of cold and calm, the captain gave the unusual order for the crew to "skylark." The men gave themselves over to all kinds of activity and games of a rougher sort, all in an attempt to keep warm and to prevent frozen hands and feet. Shortly thereafter a wind came up. The ship rounded the cape and began to cruise steadily northward.

One day the lookout sighted a number of casks floating on the ocean. When they were hauled aboard, it was discovered that they contained very fine port wine. The discovery caused great joy among the crew. In the 1840's, the Navy still served spirits to the men twice a day, but the *Neversink*'s steward, for some unaccountable reason, had neglected to replenish the ship's supply of rum during the stop at Callao.

The most significant events during the run from Cape Horn to Rio de Janeiro, so far as White-Jacket was concerned, were a series of floggings, at that time still a punishment for offenses at sea. White-Jacket hated the cruel whippings, which all crew members and officers were forced to watch. White-Jacket reflected that even in Rome no citizen could be flogged as punishment and that the great naval officers of the nineteenth century were opposed to a practice so brutal and unnecessary.

The *Neversink* finally reached Rio de Janeiro. During many days in port, the men were not to be permitted ashore. At last, the petty officers appointed Jack Chase, the captain of the maintop, to request shore leave for the men. At first, the captain was unwilling to grant leave, but the commodore interceded and gave his approval. Once again, Chase was the hero of the men aboard the vessel.

One day, the emperor of Brazil was expected to visit the vessel. White-Jacket, amazed at preparations made by men and officers for the royal visit, wondered how men from a democratic nation could so easily fawn upon royalty. He decided the men would have made fewer preparations to receive the president of the United States.

On the voyage northward along the eastern coast of South America, one of White-Jacket's shipmates fell ill and died. White-Jacket watched the preparations for burial, including the traditional final stitch of the shroud through the nose, then stood by during the service. That event was as moving to him as an amputation demonstrated by the ship's doctor while the *Neversink* lay in the harbor at Rio de Janeiro. The operation was performed, White-Jacket believed, because the surgeon wished to show off to colleagues from other vessels anchored there at the same time. Convinced that the operation was unnecessary, White-Jacket was very bitter when the injured man died of shock.

White-Jacket himself had a close escape from death when the ship was off the Virginia capes. Sent aloft to reeve a line through some blocks, he lost his balance and fell from the rigging a hundred feet into the sea. He had to cut away his white jacket in order to keep afloat. He was barely out of his garment when a sailor, mistaking the jacket for a white shark, threw a harpoon into it. White-Jacket, rescued from the sea, was sent aloft ten minutes later to complete his task. White-Jacket was content to close his story of the voyage with the loss of his unlucky garment.

Critical Evaluation:

The fifth of Herman Melville's novels dealing with his travels around the world—on board a merchant ship, a whaler, and finally, a U.S. frigate—*White-Jacket* immediately precedes his greatest work, *Moby Dick* (1851). Critics usually group *Redburn* (1849), *White-Jacket*, and *Moby Dick* together because of their thematic similarities dealing with initiation, isolation, and communal relationships.

Herman Melville was not the first author to use an extended sailing experience as the setting for a novel, but he was the first to publish a poetic, philosophic, maritime novel. Only the later works of Joseph Conrad rival this accomplishment.

Several critics believe this work should not be identified as a novel. The many parts of the work—vivid characterizations, harsh depictions of punishment at sea, descriptions of scenes, information about the various divisions of labor, and the account of the daily experience aboard the closed world of a vessel at sea for many years—are insights and information about life at sea rather than incidents in a conventional plot. Although there is a protagonist, the author, by not giving this protagonist a Christian name or surname, seems to warn the reader not to expect conventional character development. Instead, Melville emphasizes his protagonist's symbolic significance by identifying the protagonist with his wearing apparel and calling both him and the work *White-Jacket*.

The title is significant because "white" identifies the fictional persona as a novice on board a man-of-war. It also calls attention to the fact that the protagonist, different in appearance from all the other men on board, who wear navy pea jackets, sees himself as different in character as well, a point he insists on as he relates his maritime experiences. White-Jacket believes he is not like the rough, uneducated, sometimes brutal common seamen who have no other professional alternatives, but he is also unlike the educated, overly genteel officers who seek this profession only because it is appropriate for someone in the upper social class. Out of the hundreds on board the *Neversink*, White-Jacket identifies only with a very select small group: the natural leader, Jack Chase; the poet Lemsford; the reclusive Nord; and his comrades of the maintop—in his estimation, the premier group in this very hierarchical world. Ironically, the narrator's personal bias toward his own superior value seems to compromise his reiterated criticism that a republican frigate should foster greater equality in its treatment of the crew.

The white jacket also underlines the injustice attendant on the protagonist's wearing it. The speaker should have received the same clothing as the other men, but he did not. When he improvised this jacket, he asked for dark paint to obliterate the glaring difference of his uniform but was denied the paint on the basis of its scarcity. This unfair, shortsighted decision becomes emblematic of the incompetent and unjust decisions made by the officers and of the suffering of the crew that results. White-Jacket almost loses his life twice because of the jacket: when the superstitious sailors suddenly lower the halyards and he nearly falls to his death from the main-royalyard, and later when the jacket becomes entangled about his head while he is working and causes him to fall from the yardarm into the sea.

The protagonist sheds his white jacket as he approaches the United States, an action emblematic of his departure from a deceptive, artificial life. The action of shedding his jacket provides the only suggestion that some change has taken place in the protagonist. Some critics call this change a maturing in a novel of initiation; however, shedding what has made him different and what is a symbol of injustice and superstition is perhaps only an external sign that the fictional persona leaving the frigate no longer has to protect his individuality nor fear the injustice experienced on board the frigate.

Melville chiefly uses the perceptions of White-Jacket to filter the extensive amount of information he supplies about every aspect of life on board this man-of-war, from the physical description of the various parts of the ship to the daily activities of the crew and officers. *White-Jacket* not only reports the complicated procedures of daily life but also contains several melodramatic scenes to support the narrator's criticism of the Navy: the use of flogging as a punishment for crimes ranging from the narrator's failure to know his battle station to an older seaman's refusal to shave his beard; the ship's surgeon's needless amputation of a seaman's leg; the illegal smuggling activities practiced by the ship's chief policeman, master-at-arms Bland; and the captain's inept command that almost costs the lives of hundreds of men who knew better than the captain how to handle the capricious storms haunting Cape Horn.

Because the chapters are much like informative essays, the philosophical perspective of the narrator is needed to provide unity. The order of the work, with its occasional melodramatic and stormy scenes, parallels the apparent order on a ship that masks the inefficiency, sadism, and brutality of its members. The subtitle, *The World in a Man-of-War*, explicitly identifies the author's theme. Life on board this ship is a microcosm of the real world. The close quarters and enforced confinement highlight and intensify human characteristics of good and evil that are more easily hidden in the constantly changing variables of urban or rural life. Melville's attacks on the inhumane and unjust conditions existing in the U.S. Navy also express his criticism of humanity itself.

"Critical Evaluation" by Agnes A. Shields

Bibliography:

Anderson, Charles Roberts. *Melville in the South Seas.* New York: Columbia University Press, 1939. Deals with Melville's life on board the frigate *United States*, a source for *White-Jacket*. Notes that despite the obvious biographical relevance of his maritime experiences to his sailing novels, Melville's intention was to write fiction.

Arvin, Newton. *"Mardi, Redburn, White-Jacket."* In *Melville: A Collection of Critical Essays*, edited by Richard Chase. Englewood Cliffs, N.J.: Prentice-Hall, 1962. Unlike many other critics, Arvin believes that *White-Jacket* is inferior to the novel written prior to it, *Redburn*. The title, *White-Jacket*, symbolizes the wearer's isolation from the majority of the crew.

Branch, Watson G., ed. *Melville: The Critical Heritage.* London: Routledge & Kegan Paul, 1974. Eleven rather favorable reviews published when *White-Jacket* was released in 1850 attest to early appreciation of Melville's talent as a writer re-creating life at sea.

Justus, James H. *"Redburn and White-Jacket*: Society and Sexuality in the Narrators of 1849." In *Herman Melville: Reassessments*, edited by A. Robert Lee. New York: Barnes & Noble Books, 1984. Discusses the fact that in *White-Jacket* the unnamed protagonist identifies himself with a highly select group of friends while criticizing both the grog-swigging members of the crew and the silk-stockinged officers on a U.S. man-of-war.

Seelye, John. *Melville: The Ironic Diagram.* Evanston, Ill.: Northwestern University Press, 1970. Using Homeric and domestic similes, Melville contrasts the natural leader, Jack Chase, with the politically appointed, incompetent Captain Claret to exemplify the undemocratic, irrational conditions aboard U.S. naval ships.

THE WHITSUN WEDDINGS

Type of work: Poetry
Author: Philip Larkin (1922-1985)
First published: 1964

Philip Larkin's *The Whitsun Weddings* is his first collection of poems fully to embody his mature style. His early work, collected in *The North Ship* (1945), shows strongly the influence of Romanticism, especially that of William Butler Yeats and Dylan Thomas. In his second collection, *The Less Deceived* (1955), there is a move toward ironic, measured, occasionally bitter poetry. That shift in tone and style reflects his involvement with the group of poets known as the Movement, whose practice generally adhered much more closely to Thomas Hardy than to Dylan Thomas. Indeed, much of the Movement's program centered on a rejection of both the mytho-experimentalism of modernist poetry and the "sloppy excess" of late-phase Romanticism. Instead, these poets—Thom Gunn, Elizabeth Jennings, Donald Davie, John Wain, and Kingsley Amis—sought a more traditional versification and a more accessible message, and they exerted a tremendous influence over poetic practice in the 1950's, 1960's, and beyond. Their irony, skepticism, empiricism, and anti-modernism pushed British poetry in a radically different direction from the freewheeling American poetry of the same period. What the Movement poets shared was an experience of wartime and postwar privation and disappointment. Indeed, Larkin has suggested that the severe limitations placed on wartime Oxford University, where he was an undergraduate, did much to shape both his worldview and his poetry.

That sense of limitation is at work from the first page of *The Whitsun Weddings*. In "Here," the opening poem, the speaker describes his northern English city (presumably Hull, where he was for many years head librarian at the University of Hull), in terms of its modern squalor and meanness. The image of contemporary wretchedness recurs throughout the book, notably in "Sunny Prestatyn" (the kind of oxymoron that delights Larkin), in which a travel poster of a bathing beauty is disfigured by obscene graffiti before finally being ripped down and replaced by a Cancer Society poster. In "Here," he contrasts that urban blight first with isolated villages out in the countryside, where life is less demeaned, and finally with the "bluish neutral distance" of the ocean, where existence is "unfenced." The openness contrasts with the hemmed-in quality of city life and the constant reminders of the lack of horizon, yet the openness is ultimately "out of reach." The image anticipates the infinite nothingness of the title poem of *High Windows* (1974) in suggesting the impossibility of attaining freedom and limitless horizons in this life.

The horizon becomes even more delimited in "Mr. Bleaney," where the speaker meditates on the previous occupant of his tiny boardinghouse room. The speaker knows many of the mundane details of Mr. Bleaney's existence: where he summered, that he spent Christmas with his sister in Stoke-on-Trent, even his eating preferences. What he does not know, and what he wonders about, is whether Bleaney shared his own sense of loneliness and failure, whether having only this pathetically small room convinced him that it was all he deserved. The room is a kind of coffin, a place that reminds the speaker of his final end, and as such it becomes an instance of death encroaching on life. That sensation is reinforced in the next poem, "Nothing to be Said," which notes that all human activities lead equally to death. It concludes that such information to some people "Means nothing; others it leaves/ nothing to be said." Delineating a divide between people for whom an awareness of mortality is meaningless and those for whom it means everything is characteristic of Larkin, who sees himself as one whose eyes are wide open to harsh reality.

Also characteristic is the play on the word "nothing." That such knowledge "means nothing" suggests that it lacks meaning but also that it hints at nothingness. For Larkin, nothing indicates not merely an absence but an entity in its own right. Larkin consistently embraces that paradoxical understanding, so that leaving "Nothing to be said" can be interpreted not only in the literal sense but also to mean that a knowledge of the void must be explored and articulated. Otherwise, there would be no point in writing poetry in the face of nullity.

Emptiness and disappointment are the hallmarks of the twentieth century for Larkin, who indicates the starting date in "MCMXIV." The great shock to the English nervous system, he contends, was World War I, in which a summer idyll turned into four years of horror. The achievement of "MCMXIV," however, is that the horrors are present without ever being mentioned; the reader is made to see that the Great War ripped out the country's heart by focusing entirely on the idyllic illusion. As if looking at a photograph of the country, the speaker remarks on the long lines at recruiting offices, the men in their now-archaic attire, the outmoded currency, the country still trapped in the previous century, blissfully unaware of the modern warfare to come. Men waited patiently, Larkin recalls, to subdue what they were calling the Hun, and they expected to be home for Christmas, as if they were merely going off for a long weekend. In two mild images he captures the innocence and that lack of understanding that allowed them to leave so blithely. The first image is of the way the men left their gardens neat and orderly, as if they would shortly return to them. The very brevity of the statement points up the error of their thinking, and it recalls, if dimly, the lines in T. S. Eliot's great postwar poem *The Waste Land* about the corpse planted in the garden. The second image is of "thousands of marriages/ Lasting a little while longer." The couples in these marriages have no idea, of course, that their marriages will last only a little while more; in that naïveté, so soon to be exploded, and in the repeated phrase "Never such innocence," he conjures up all the horrors for which those English men and women of 1914 were so manifestly ill-prepared.

The poem stands as a postlapsarian look at life before the Fall, in this case a very recent one. Stories of the Fall inevitably deal with being cast out, and the status of the outcast, the outsider, the person peripheral even to his or her own life runs through the book. In "Afternoons," Larkin looks at young women taking their children to the playground and sees that the demands of marriage and motherhood are "pushing them/ To the side of their own lives." In "Ignorance," he notes that it is "strange" to understand virtually nothing of how the world works, of how people live or why they die. "Ambulances" recognizes the isolating nature of that conveyance, a self-contained room making its way through parted traffic, toward the inevitable (and reminding the reader of the "emptiness" that underlies all human activity). In "The Importance of Elsewhere," he argues that in Ireland his loneliness was reasonable, since the places and rituals were alien to him, while the same loneliness in England, where he is an outsider in his own place, is harder to understand. Throughout the volume, the sense of marginalized existence weighs oppressively on the speaker.

Occasionally, Larkin rises above the bleakness to achieve tenderness toward his fellow humans. The title poem recounts a train ride on Whitsun Saturday (the seventh weekend after Easter), on which he is accompanied by many honeymooning couples. His position remains marginal to their self-involved, unreflective scenes. When the speaker leaves the station, his train is only one-quarter full. At first during the sleepy trip, he notices only the countryside, both in its pure and adulterated aspects that include farms, hedges, villages, junkyards, and canals filled with industrial waste. All the while, he creates the impression of passivity and displacement that the rail traveler experiences, of sitting in a stationary enclosure and watching through a frame while the world flashes past. The stance as marginalized voyeur leads him to his observation of the wedding parties, which at first did not even register on him but then become a repeating part of the landscape. Indeed, it is the repetition that he emphasizes. It is the generic quality of the experience rather than its uniqueness that catches his attention—the bridesmaids in their "parodies of fashion," the ill-dressed fathers, the foul-mouthed uncles attempting to be clever, the cheap costume jewelry. By the time the train approaches London, newlyweds have filled the carriages and the speaker watches them as they settle into their own watching of the now-suburban landscape of movie houses, power plants, and cricket matches.

The poet himself is cut off from direct understanding of their moment, since he never married, and his speaker seems similarly isolated; he can only envision the scene from the outside. His alienation from the event of these new marriages shows in his glibly dismissive descriptions. At the same time, however, he recognizes something that eludes the young couples, wrapped up as they are in their private excitement: All their lives, his as well as theirs, will contain this shared experience. That wholly unintended sharing leads him to reflect on the communal necessity of marriage through the image of the cycle of fertility resuming. In an astonishing moment, he envisions the London postal zones resembling fields of wheat, and the sudden braking creating a falling sensation "like an arrow shower/ Sent out of sight, somewhere becoming rain." Although the results, as seen on the rail platforms, are not encouraging, these couples, bringing new life like rain on wheat fields, are the hope for the future, the promise of fertility.

He is brought to a similar consideration in "Dockery and Son" when he discovers that a schoolmate now has a son at university. He decides that "innate assumptions" lead Dockery to have a son, the speaker to have "nothing," while all roads lead to the same end. His brooding on mortality leads him to the ironic notion that all efforts are ultimately futile but that we persist in them anyhow.

The negating quality of death is seen in the final poem, "An Arundel Tomb." The earl and countess have long since ceased to be themselves, having become their effigies. Seasons have swept over them, and, with time, innumerable people have like a tide eroded their identity. The intended message of the tomb, in Latin, is lost on the modern observer, and what remains is the image of a couple joined by the carver's art, nearly proving, the speaker says, what we hope to be true, "What will survive of us is love." While he ironically undercuts that final statement, it nevertheless stands as the gem at the bottom of this Pandora's box of a book: Through all the bleakness and irony, the hope remains that love might be able to provide meaning, to make life worth living, to save humankind.

Thomas C. Foster

Bibliography:

Hassan, Salem K. *Philip Larkin and His Contemporaries: An Air of Authenticity.* Basingstoke, England: Macmillan, 1988. A survey of Larkin's poetry that focuses on the role of time and attempts to place the poet among his important contemporaries John Wain, Kingsley Amis, Thom Gunn, and D. J. Enright. Contains a separate chapter on *The Whitsun Weddings* and helpful discussions of Larkin's prosody.

Martin, Bruce K. *Philip Larkin.* Boston: Twayne, 1978. A significant early overview of Larkin's poetry and fiction. Makes use of the then-limited biographical information and the social contexts of the poetry.

Motion, Andrew. *Philip Larkin.* London: Methuen, 1982. Places Larkin initially within the tradition of Thomas Hardy and William Butler Yeats, then in that of his Movement contemporaries. Ably captures the poet's wide range of subject matter and treatment, and discusses his symbolist tendencies. Anticipates, in many ways, the author's subsequent biography of the poet.

Petch, Simon. *The Art of Philip Larkin.* Sydney: University of Sydney Press, 1981. A helpful, brief introduction to the Larkin's verse, organized by volume. Emphasizes Larkin's status as humane poet who closely, if critically, examines important aspects of human experience.

Rossen, Janice. *Philip Larkin: His Life's Work.* New York: Simon & Schuster, 1989. An accessible and intelligent discussion of Larkin's poetry, organized thematically. Particularly useful on the subject of Larkin's "Englishness" and on the use of direct and even obscene language in his otherwise conservative and formal poetry.

WHO'S AFRAID OF VIRGINIA WOOLF?

Type of work: Drama
Author: Edward Albee (1928-   )
Type of plot: Absurdist
Time of plot: Mid-twentieth century
Locale: New Carthage, a small New England college town
First performed: 1962; first published, 1962

> *Principal characters:*
> MARTHA, a large, boisterous, fifty-two-year-old woman
> GEORGE, her thin, graying, forty-six-year-old husband, a history
>   professor
> HONEY, a young, rather plain blonde woman
> NICK, her blond, good-looking husband, a biology professor

The Story:

Having returned home at 2 A.M. from a party welcoming faculty, Martha, the college president's daughter, and her husband, George, were squabbling. Martha echoed Bette Davis and called the place a dump but could not recall from which film the line had originated. George suggested *Chicago*, but Martha rejected that title. George had disappointed her, failing to mix at the party. Despite the hour, Martha had invited another couple home. She demanded liquor and recalled her delight when "Who's afraid of Virginia Woolf?" was sung instead of "Who's afraid of the Big Bad Wolf?" George was not amused.

When she asked for a kiss, he demurred, pleading that their guests might surprise them. As the chimes rang, he warned Martha not to mention a certain child, and she cursed him. The guests, Honey and Nick, overheard and felt awkward.

After serving brandy to Honey and bourbon to Nick, Martha and George continued skirmishing. The guests agreed that "Virginia Woolf" was funny, and they praised the president's party, which served new faculty. George wondered how he had grown rich. He regretted having married Martha, who had pushed him to become her father's successor. She claimed other men would sacrifice an arm to marry a college president's daughter, but George felt more private parts were forfeited.

Responding to Honey's need for the bathroom, Martha showed her the house. While the women were gone, George confessed that he mistrusted biology. Slim-hipped Honey did not appear suited to having children, he observed. On returning, Honey unknowingly retaliated, expressing surprise that he had fathered a son. Martha, provocatively dressed, remembered flooring George in a boxing match. Embarrassed, he found a shotgun, aimed, and pulled the trigger. An umbrella popped out. Terrified and stimulated, Martha asked for a kiss, but George refused, ceding the palm of terror to Nick, since genetic engineers would alter humanity.

George doubted his paternity, Martha said, but he refuted this. When he left for more liquor, she confessed that, like Lady Chatterley, she had once eloped with a gardener. "Revirginized" by annulment, she was graduated from Miss Muff's Academy, returned to her father, and married George, who showed promise. When George returned, she detailed his failures until he drowned her out with "Virginia Woolf." Honey, nauseated, rushed off, followed by Nick and Martha.

Nick returned, and, though hostile, he exchanged intimate personal details with George such as the fact that Martha spent time in a rest home; that Honey vomited often; and that Nick had married her when she "puffed up" and seemed pregnant (the condition had passed). George remembered a classmate who accidentally killed his mother. When his prep-school pals had visited a speakeasy, he had delighted customers by ordering "bergin," and the delighted management had treated the boys to champagne. The lad felt lionized, but the following summer, while taking driving lessons, the boy had swerved to avoid a porcupine and his father had died in the crash. The boy had been institutionalized—and remained so, George concluded. As for George's child, he dismissed him as a beanbag. Nick wanted an explanation, but Martha returned to announce that she and Honey were drinking coffee.

Alone again, the men talked of marriage. A false pregnancy had led to Nick's, but he and Honey, childhood friends, had been expected to wed. The money of her preacher father, who built hospitals, churches, and his own wealth, also helped. Martha was wealthy, too, George observed, because her father's second wife was rich.

Nick, coveting power, spoke of wanting to replace colleagues in courses, start his own, and provide sex to important wives. George warned him of quicksand, saying that college wives hissed like geese, like South American whores, but Nick dismissed him.

Martha blamed Honey's nausea on George, but Honey said she often threw up and that she suffered symptoms of disease without actually having the disease. Martha said George had been to blame for their son's vomiting, but he countered that it was the result of her overzealous mothering; she had smelled of alcohol and had always been pawing the boy.

When Honey asked for brandy, George remembered that he loved brandy, but Martha recalled his taste for "bergin." She mentioned a novel George had written but was unable to publish because of her father's objections.

Honey, tipsy, wanted to dance and urged Martha to dance with her, but George insisted on playing Beethoven. Honey was undeterred, but Martha objected and, rejecting George's suggestion that Stravinsky's *Le Sacre du printemps* would suit, chose jazz. George offered to dance with Honey, alluding to her breasts as angelic, and Martha deflected Nick from confronting George by getting Nick to dance with her. When Honey noticed their familiarity, George called it a ritual, this time referring to Honey's breasts as monkeylike.

Martha now launched into the game Humiliate the Host: George's unpublished novel was autobiographical, she claimed. As a boy, he had accidentally killed his mother and father. When her father vetoed publication of the book, George argued that it was true.

Chagrined, George suggested that the next game involve sex with the hostess. Martha and Nick seemed reluctant, so George substituted one he called Get the Guest. When he revealed his knowledge of the hysterical pregnancy, Honey, betrayed, rushed out. Nick followed, promising revenge. Martha upbraided George, but he said that she had attacked first. Seething, she claimed he had married her to be humiliated. George threatened her for mentioning their son.

Nick returned for ice to relieve Honey's headache, and Martha sent George to get it. She turned seductive, and Nick soon proved susceptible. George discreetly sang "Virginia Woolf" before he returned and announced that Honey was asleep. He resolved to read a book. Martha threatened to entertain herself with Nick if George ignored them, but the threat failed. When she and Nick left together, George read a few sentences about the decline of the West, then, furious, hurled the book at the chimes.

The noise woke Honey, who had dreamt that her covers were falling away. George deduced that she was pregnant and had been intentionally aborting to avoid having children. He confessed that his son, too, was dead; Martha did not know, but he would tell her. Honey responded by getting sick again.

Alone, Martha felt abandoned and, while mixing a drink, invented cordial but improbable exchanges between herself and George. Reminded of "The Poker Night" from Tennessee Williams' *A Streetcar Named Desire* (1947), she confessed to herself that they were miserable.

Nick believed himself the only sane person in the house. As she was entering the bathroom with a liquor bottle from which she was peeling the label, Honey had winked at him. Madness is refuge from the world's lack of reality, Martha observed, reminding Nick that he had failed her sexually. She saw herself as Earth Mother and men as impotent fools. The only one who satisfied her was George.

The chimes rang, and she ordered Nick to the door; having failed as a sexual partner, he could play houseboy now. George entered with snapdragons, offering flowers for the dead, another allusion to Williams that delighted Martha. George pretended Nick was his son, but Martha preferred houseboy, misidentifying the snapdragons as her wedding bouquet—pansies, rosemary, and "Violence."

George claimed the moon had lighted his flower gathering. If it had gone down as Martha asserted, it must have come up again. It had happened to him before, on his family's trip past Majorca after his graduation. Nick reminded George that he had killed his parents earlier, but George declared that truth and illusion are intermixed. Even the question whether Nick was lover or houseboy was hard to resolve. George said they were all, like Honey, label peelers, except that they peeled skin and muscle. They separated organs and bones to the marrow. Martha, he asserted, tried to bathe their son when he was sixteen, violating him.

When Martha accused George of bungling, he countered that their son crashed into a tree while trying to avoid a porcupine. Martha denied the death, demanding to see a telegram, but Honey confirmed that George had eaten it. When Nick asserted that the child was fiction, Martha acknowledged that the boy was dead, but she said, weeping, that George should not have killed him. After Nick and Honey left, George concluded that the death was necessary. He sang "Virginia Woolf" and coaxed Martha into accepting their loss. Tentatively, she resolved to live without the fiction of a son.

Critical Evaluation:

Edward Albee, one of the most distinguished American playwrights, wrote *Who's Afraid of Virginia Woolf?* when he was in his early thirties. The title highlights his concern with fictions and with the way they allay fears and become actual events in people's lives. By substituting a bisexual feminist writer for a more generally threatening enemy, Albee confronts his audience with more pointed fears: Animal death still lurks behind the title, augmented by the bold and frightening challenges represented by Virginia Woolf's honesty, experimentation, and suicide.

Albee's great European predecessors, Luigi Pirandello, Samuel Beckett, and Eugène Ionesco, saw the fundamental absurdity of life. They destroyed surface presumptions by presenting as surface the underlying truths that people are characters searching for roles in an unwritten play (Pirandello's *Six Characters in Search of an Author*, 1921), that they await deliverers who never come (Beckett's *Waiting for Godot*, 1951), that husbands and wives do not know each other (Ionesco's *The Bald Soprano*, 1950). Albee's major American predecessors, Eugene O'Neill, Tennessee Williams, and Arthur Miller, were engaged in capturing human experience more realistically, using surreal techniques to help convey the deep psychology of their characters. In *Who's Afraid of Virginia Woolf?* Albee adapts elements from both traditions.

Like his European counterparts, he exposes absurdity with biting comedy in which viewers laugh as much at themselves as at the characters. Like his American counterparts, he deals with problems that can be seen on the surface as "real." He explores the daily absurdity that life imitates art—both the art that declares itself and the fictions by which people guide themselves. People live in a world of allusions, he declares, their actions determined by lines in their heads as well as by unmediated responses to stimuli. Albee regards the composition of his plays as analogous to music, and through his instruments, the actors, sounds sometimes dissonant themes. His characters range temporally through history and spatially across the eclectic spectrum of modern life, creating chords of allusion—to film, literature, and chronicle, as much as to their own pasts—that govern their lives.

Martha and George share a fictional child. They accuse each other of having abused him in ways that became discussed in the twentieth century. Their conversation is a patchwork of quotations, and they fall into prearranged games of assault that differ in specifics but whose results are predictable. Love oddly undergirds the relationship between the would-be adulterous Martha and her inadequate historian husband, who cannot abide the present and takes refuge in the past. Endearing innocence colors the vapid Honey, and touching insecurities drive her seemingly confident husband Nick, who, if George is right, wishes to change the future because he, too, cannot abide the present.

In the end, the frustrating night the audience shares with them may usher in change. Martha goads George into killing their imaginary child, who dies in an imaginary accident that simulates George's unpublished autobiography, which is disguised as a novel. The fictional reality of the play thus mirrors its realized fiction. It replicates the patterning of human lives, forcing the audience to consider what real means in a world interpenetrated by fantasy. When actions and their interpretations are tied to scenarios that enter the mind from outside, only the murder of false offspring can usher in hope.

Albert Wachtel

Bibliography:
Bigsby, C. W. E., ed. *Edward Albee: A Collection of Critical Essays*. Englewood Cliffs, N.J.: Prentice-Hall, 1975. Five challenging essays on the play give this general survey shape.
Cohn, Ruby. *Edward Albee*. Minneapolis: University of Minnesota Press, 1969. An invaluable introduction to the playwright that offers sensitive scholarship and understanding. Includes a bibliography.
Kolin, Philip C., ed. *Conversations with Edward Albee*. Jackson: University Press of Mississippi, 1988. Valuable interviews containing Albee's assessments of the creative process, critics, theater, drama, and life.
Paolucci, Anne. *From Tension to Tonic: The Plays of Edward Albee*. Carbondale: Southern Illinois University Press, 1972. A thoughtful assessment of Albee's genius and use of language in relation to European absurdist and existentialist traditions.
Roudane, Matthew Charles. *"Who's Afraid of Virginia Woolf?" Necessary Fictions, Terrifying Realities*. Boston: Twayne, 1990. A book-length historical and critical study of the play. Useful and well written.

WIDE SARGASSO SEA

Type of work: Novel
Author: Jean Rhys (Ella Gwendolen Rees Williams, 1894-1979)
Type of plot: Domestic realism
Time of plot: Late 1830's
Locale: Jamaica, Dominica, and England
First published: 1966

> *Principal characters:*
> ANTOINETTE (BERTHA) COSWAY, a young Creole woman
> THE YOUNG ENGLISHMAN, a man who marries Antoinette
> CHRISTOPHINE, a servant woman, practitioner of obeah, or voodoo

The Story:

Antoinette's immediate family consisted only of her impoverished, widowed mother and her idiot brother; a small number of black servants remained at the dilapidated Coulibri estate. Rejected by blacks and whites because of her mixed heritage and her family's poverty, Antoinette drifted through a troubled and lonely childhood. Her mother ignored her, pushed her away without emotion of any kind, and only Christophine, the servant from Martinique, was kind and nurturing.

Annette Cosway, Antoinette's mother, still young and beautiful, fought for survival by using her beauty, her only resource, marrying Mr. Mason, a wealthy Englishman. This rescue did not last long, however; one night an angry mob of newly freed slaves burned down Coulibri. Antoinette's brother died. Antoinette was physically attacked. The terror of the night drove Antoinette's mother completely insane.

For six weeks Antoinette lay ill at her Aunt Cora's. After having regained her strength, Antoinette attended convent school. Mount Calvary convent provided a refuge of sorts. Antoinette first prayed there for the freedom of death, then stopped praying and felt "bolder, happier, more free. But not so safe."

Antoinette's stepfather visited her and finally told her she would soon be leaving. Just prior to her departure from the convent, she dreamed of herself dressed in white following a man with eyes of hatred into the dark of the jungle. She awoke and recalled the dream as one of "Hell," and the hot chocolate she was given to calm her recalled her mother's funeral, one year prior.

The Englishman proceeded on horseback with his new bride, Antoinette, to their honeymoon house, Grandbois. The rain, the colors, the mountains, and even the servants all seemed "too much" to him, too bright, too vibrant. All of this world seemed uncivilized, including his recent wife, and already he regretted this marriage. When Antoinette had refused at the last minute to marry, the Englishman persuasively reassured her, most concerned with having to return to England "in the role of the rejected suitor jilted by this Creole girl." After he settled into the house, he wrote to his father but left out any anxiety regarding his marriage. The Englishman had married for money: Antoinette owned property.

At Gambois, their differences were inescapable, although initially Antoinette enchanted him. He desired the alien nature of the island passionately. He desired Antoinette, yet he was bewildered at the numerous differences between them and was mystified at Antoinette's dependence on him for both her happiness and her very will to live. He "was thirsty for her, but that was not love."

One morning, the Englishman received a letter from Daniel Cosway that detailed the wickedness and history of madness in the slave-owning family into which the Englishman had just married. Antoinette, still unaware of her husband's new knowledge, cried out to him that she did not know who she was, where she belonged, and why she existed. That night, the Englishman wandered into the dark forest and wondered how he could know the truth of anything.

Antoinette soon realized the truth that her husband did not love her, perhaps even hated her, and, in desperation, she rode to Christophine's in search of obeah, or voodoo. Christophine advised Antoinette to leave him, and warned that the obeah could only make him come to Antoinette's bed, not make him love her. Antoinette and the Englishman fought after he told her that he had spoken with Daniel Cosway and learned about her mother. She told her husband her side of the story, and he heard her reluctantly. She also gave him a potion supplied by Christophine. After their battle, he slept with her and woke to realize he had been drugged by his wife. Angered and still influenced by the obeah potion, the Englishman committed adultery with Amélie, a black servant who hated Antoinette, in the room adjacent to his wife's bedroom.

Antoinette, traumatized by this final act of hatred, turned to alcohol. Husband and wife fought again, physically this time. Christophine argued with the Englishman and pleaded for him to try again to love Antoinette. Filled with bitterness, the Englishman refused Christophine's offer to return to England and leave Antoinette behind in Christophine's care. Christophine left in anger.

He prepared for the two of them to move to Jamaica and then indulged himself in rum and self-pity, all the while damning the "drunken lying lunatic" to whom he was married. As they began their departure, the Englishman momentarily wavered in his feelings toward Antoinette only to be finally overcome by his own hatred; the island world was detestable to him, and he hated it most because Antoinette belonged to its "magic and . . . loveliness."

Grace Poole spoke of her acceptance, after careful consideration, of the position as caretaker for Antoinette. Antoinette, herself, questioned the reality of the English prison to which she had been brought, amazed that she had been captive for so long. She wondered over her lost identity, her name changed from Antoinette to Bertha, her inability to see her own visage in a mirror. She was smarter than her keeper and easily and frequently stole the keys from the sleeping Grace Poole. Antoinette, renamed Bertha, roamed freely through the "cardboard world" of a house which she would not believe was in England.

Antoinette, dwelling on the loss of her dreams and her self, grasped for anything tangible, like her red dress, which she was convinced would reestablish her identity. In a dream state, Antoinette wandered through the halls of the house, searching. She passed a gilt frame mirror, saw her reflection, and was startled by the familiarity and the strangeness of her own image. Her candle, which she dropped when startled by the image, caused a fire. She felt a rush of memories descend upon her; the fire returned her to horrible images of burning Coulibri. She knew what she should do. Ultimately, she was successful in burning down the Englishman's house and destroying herself with it.

Critical Evaluation:

Published twenty-five years after Jean Rhys's previous book, *Wide Sargasso Sea* was Rhys's last novel. Different in some respects from the rest of Rhys's work (*Wide Sargasso Sea* is set in the Caribbean, not in London or Paris, and occurs in the nineteenth rather than twentieth century), Rhys's last novel continues her passionate explorations into the lives of tragic heroines who are alone, outsiders, and underdogs. Continuing in a long tradition of women's writing, Rhys explores the cultural alienation that results from imperialism and gender roles. *Wide Sargasso Sea* is Rhys's revision of Charlotte Brontë's 1847 novel *Jane Eyre*. The novel's position within the literary canon is thus significant both as a continuation in the tradition of women's writings and as a rebellion to a woman's text within that tradition. Voicing approval and contempt, Rhys creates a dialogue with her literary predecessor.

Rhys grants Antoinette what Brontë denied Bertha, a voice. Rhys does the same for *Jane Eyre*'s Rochester. The two main characters in *Wide Sargasso Sea*, Antoinette Cosway Mason and the unnamed Englishman, tell their versions of the tale in their own voices. *Wide Sargasso Sea* is in three parts: Antoinette's childhood, the newlywed period, and Antoinette's period of imprisonment in the attic of her husband's English home. Of the three parts, the first and third are told in Antoinette's voice. The second is told primarily in the Englishman's voice but is interrupted by a brief section in Antoinette's voice at a point of crisis. This intermingling, modern in technique, symbolizes the attempt at dialogue. The intermixed voices of Antoinette and the Rochester character reveal two sides of the same story, but the characters neither hear nor understand the other person or the other culture.

The dialogue between authors is effected by Rhys's choice not simply to vindicate the West Indian woman that Brontë depicts, but also to write that particular woman's story. Writing within the framework of the earlier novel, Rhys responds to the stereotypes informed by Brontë's nineteenth century English culture and social status. Rhys develops sympathetically the complex character of the woman who in *Jane Eyre* is merely a lunatic. Antoinette's story, as told in *Wide Sargasso Sea*, predates the story in *Jane Eyre*. It explains the Englishman's inability to understand or love his wife, and it shows what lies behind Antoinette's suicide. Rhys speaks back to Brontë, but by placing her story within the narrative of Brontë's work, allows Brontë to have her say. Rhys juxtaposes the English heroine of *Jane Eyre*, who fights for and acquires selfhood, equality, independence, and happiness, with the alienated Antoinette, who not only loses all that the English heroine gains, but also loses her freedom and her life.

Still, as obviously as *Wide Sargasso Sea* rejects the optimism of *Jane Eyre*, a kinship exists between the two women characters. Rhys locates her story in five places—Coulibri, Mount Calvary, Grandbois, Jamaica, and Thornfield—closely paralleling the five physical locations of *Jane Eyre*. Additionally, Rhys's novel shifts smoothly between reality and an otherworldly, dreamlike state, echoing the gothic and romantic elements of the earlier work. Rhys begins and ends *Wide Sargasso Sea* in the voice of Antoinette, the character Brontë leaves utterly voiceless. Rhys also leaves Brontë's main character, and narrator, not merely voiceless but completely unconsidered. These techniques provide the opportunity to compare the intimacies of both characters and unites them. They are both isolated women struggling for survival in a world dominated by men. Connecting these women and contrasting their fates, Rhys voices the conflict between her theory and that of Brontë on the available opportunities for women, yet ultimately reaffirms Brontë's essential argument in *Jane Eyre*. As Christophine declares: "Women must have spunks to live in this wicked world."

Tiffany Elizabeth Stiffler

Bibliography:
Hite, Molly. *The Other Side of the Story: Structures and Strategies of Contemporary Feminist Narrative*. Ithaca, N.Y.: Cornell University Press, 1989. Hite maintains Rhys's assertion that the advancement of some groups of women necessitates the deprivation of other women.
Howells, Coral Ann. *Jean Rhys*. New York: St. Martin's Press, 1991. Howells calls *Wide*

Sargasso Sea Rhys's "most rebellious text." In discussing Rhys's revolt against, yet ambivalence toward, Brontë's Victorian novel, Howells contends Rhys's novel is not easily classified.

James, Louis. *Jean Rhys*. New York: Longman, 1978. A well-detailed account of Rhys's great-grandfather provides insight to Rhys's "fidelity to experience."

Nasta, Susheila, ed. *Black Women's Writing from Africa, the Caribbean, and South Asia*. London: Women's Press, 1991. One chapter in this anthology explores the "devastating results when the mother-bond is denied" and another establishes Rhys as the literary foremother of following generations of Caribbean women writers.

Thurman, Judith. "The Mistress and the Mask: Jean Rhys's Fiction." *Ms*. 4, no. 7 (January, 1976): 50-53. Analyzes Rhys's depiction of women as underdogs.

Wolfe, Peter. *Jean Rhys*. Boston: Twayne, 1980. Approaches *Wide Sargasso Sea* both autobiographically and historically, examining the artistry of Rhys's content and form.

WIELAND
Or, The Transformation, an American Tale

Type of work: Novel
Author: Charles Brockden Brown (1771-1810)
Type of plot: Gothic
Time of plot: Eighteenth century
Locale: Pennsylvania
First published: 1798

>   *Principal characters:*
>   THEODORE WIELAND, a madman
>   CLARA, his sister
>   CATHARINE PLEYEL, his wife
>   HENRY PLEYEL, Catharine's brother
>   CARWIN, a ventriloquist

The Story:

In a long letter to a friend, Clara Wieland told the story of the tragedy of her family. Her father had been something of a religious fanatic, a strange man who feared some dreadful punishment because he had not answered a call to the mission field. He became more and more depressed and withdrawn until his life ended in a horrible fashion. One night, he visited a temple he had built for solitary meditation. His wife, fearing the appearance and manner of her husband, followed him and saw his clothing suddenly go up in flames. She found him insensible, muttering incoherently about having been struck down by an unseen hand. Soon afterward, he died. Within a few months, the mother followed her husband to the grave, leaving Clara and her brother orphaned but wealthy. They were happily reared by an aunt who gave them love and comfort and a good education.

One of their companions was Catharine Pleyel, a rich and beautiful girl with whom Wieland fell in love when he reached young manhood. Catharine returned his love, and when Wieland came of age they were married. Wieland took possession of the family house and half of the fortune, Clara the other half of their inheritance. Since she and Catharine and Wieland were beloved friends as well as relatives, Clara took a house only a short distance from her brother and sister-in-law. The three spent much time together. Clara and Catharine were frank and cheerful, but Wieland was more somber and thoughtful in disposition. He was, however, always considerate of their happiness and nobly devoted his life to it. His melancholy was not morbid, only sober. The temple in which their father had met his strange fate was used by the three as a setting for long and delightful conversations, although Wieland's talk dwelt too often on death to suit Clara and Catharine. Their circle was soon augmented by the addition of Catharine's beloved brother Henry, who had been for some time in Europe. His boisterous mirth enlivened the little group. Henry and Wieland found one great difference in their beliefs: Wieland built his life on religious necessity, Henry, on intellectual liberty. Their fondness for each other, however, allowed them to differ without altering their mutual affection.

Wieland's family was enlarged during the next six years by four natural children and a foster child whose mother had died. About that time, another strange occurrence took place in the Wieland family. One day, Wieland went to the temple to pick up a letter which would settle a minor dispute. Before he reached the temple, he was stopped by his wife's voice, telling him that danger lay in his path. Returning quickly to the house, he found his wife there. Clara and Henry verified her statement that she had not left the room. Although the others soon dismissed the incident from their minds, it preyed on the already melancholy Wieland to the exclusion of everything else.

Not long after that incident, Henry Pleyel learned that Wieland had inherited some large estates in Europe, and he wanted Wieland to go abroad to claim them. Henry would accompany his friend because he had left his heart with a baroness, now widowed and willing to accept his suit. When Wieland seemed reluctant to make the journey, Henry, in an effort to persuade him, asked him one night to go for a walk. Their walk was interrupted by a voice telling them that the baroness was dead. Again, the voice was Catharine's, but again Catharine had been nowhere near the men when the voice was heard. More frightening was the verification of the baroness' death given to Henry a few days later. Some dread supernatural power, Wieland believed, had spoken to them.

Shortly after these two mysterious occurrences, a stranger appeared in the neighborhood. He was dressed like a clown or a pathetically humorous beggar, but his voice had the musical ring of an actor. Clara, who saw him before the others knew of his existence, was strangely drawn to him. She forgot him, however, because of another frightening incident. One night, alone in her room, she heard two voices in the closet planning her murder. One voice advised shooting; the other, choking. She fled to her brother's house and fell at his door in a faint. Wieland and Henry came to her rescue in answer to a summons from an unknown source, a voice calling that a loved one lay dying at the door.

Henry insisted upon occupying a vacant apartment in Clara's home in order to protect her from her unknown enemies. Clara was beset with nightmares, the mystifying voice having warned her of danger from her brother. Soon after the affair of the voices in the closet, she met the stranger she had seen and to whom she had been unaccountably drawn. His name was Carwin, and he had known Henry in Spain. His intelligent conversation and his wide travels made him welcome in the little group, and he joined them frequently. When they discussed the supernatural voices they had all heard, Carwin dismissed the voices as fancy or pranks.

Clara, beginning to feel herself in love with Henry, believed that he returned her love but feared to tell her of it because he did not know her feelings. Then he confronted her with the accusation that she was a wanton. He said that he had heard her and a lover, Carwin, talking and that her words made her a sinner and a fallen woman. Henry had also learned that Carwin was wanted for murder, and he heaped abuses on the innocent Clara for consorting with such a man. All of her pleas of innocence went unheeded, and she was thrown into despair. Thinking that Carwin had set out to ruin her, she was enraged when she received a note in which he asked for an interview. Reluctantly, she agreed to meet him and hear his story. He was to come to her home, but when she arrived there she found only a note warning her of a horrible sight awaiting her. In her room, she found Catharine on the bed. She had been murdered.

Wieland entered her room, his manner strange and exulted, and begged that this sacrifice not be demanded of him. Before he reached Clara, however, others came into the house. From them she learned that her brother's children were also dead, killed by the same hand that had murdered their mother.

Clara was taken by friends to the city. There, after a time, she learned the tragic story. The murderer had been Wieland, his hand guided, he said, by a voice from heaven demanding that he sacrifice his loved ones to God. He felt no guilt, only glory at having been the instrument through whom God worked. Twice Wieland had broken out of prison, his belief being that he must also kill Clara and Henry. Clara suspected that Carwin had somehow influenced Wieland to kill.

Carwin went to Clara and protested his innocence. He admitted that his had been the other voices heard. He was a ventriloquist who had used his tricks either to play some prank or to escape detection while prying into other people's affairs. Clara refused to believe him. While they talked, Wieland entered the apartment. Prepared to kill Clara, he had again broken out of prison to fulfill his bloody destiny. This time Carwin, using his skill to save Clara, called out to Wieland that no voice had told him to kill, that only his own lunatic brain had guided him. At his words, Wieland regained his sanity and seemed to understand for the first time what he had done. Picking up a knife, he plunged it into his throat.

Three years passed before Clara knew peace. Her uncle cared for her and arranged a meeting between Carwin and Henry so that Carwin might confess his part in the defamation of Clara's character. Carwin had been jealous and thus tried to destroy Henry's affection for her. Henry also learned that his baroness was not dead; the report had been another of Carwin's tricks. Henry married the baroness and settled down near Boston. Carwin, not a murderer but the victim of a plot, escaped to the country and became a farmer. Henry's wife died soon after their marriage, and he and Clara renewed their love. Their later happiness was marred only by sad and tragic memories.

Critical Evaluation:

Wieland was the first gothic novel written and published in America. Gothic fiction, a genre popular in Europe (especially England and Germany), had its inception in Horace Walpole's *The Castle of Otranto* (1764). In the tradition of the romance, the gothic novel offers an outlet for its readers' emotions—particularly fear. Characterized by ghosts, goblins, and supernatural occurrences, gothic tales take place in such places as ruined cathedrals and crumbling mansions. Their usual theme is the restoration of a usurped inheritance to its rightful heir. Although the earlier gothic authors presented supernatural phenomena as objective realities, later writers tended to present the supernatural as perhaps the result of imagination or sensory delusion.

In *Wieland*, Charles Brown develops and Americanizes the gothic novel by adapting its theme, setting, and purpose. Unlike its predecessors, the work does not center on acquiring a European patrimony. Although Theodore Wieland, Jr., has fallen heir to lands in Lusatia, he has no desire to claim his holdings in the old country. He prefers to stay in America, where life is stable and familiar.

Rather than setting his novel in an archaic building, Brown has the story take place in a rural region in eastern Pennsylvania. Clara's house is situated on a rugged river bank; the temple sits atop a cliff; and the summer house rests in a rocky crevice near a waterfall. These places are beautiful, and their wild isolation lends them an eeriness suggesting the presence of sprites. In selecting a natural site, Brown began a trend for other American writers, such as Washington Irving and William Cullen Bryant, who emphasized the appeal of nature.

Earlier gothic writers supplied rational explanations for mysterious phenomena, but Brown went a step further in *Wieland* by suggesting that the degree of one's belief in the supernatural derives from one's psychological makeup. That is, some people are predisposed toward the paranormal as a result of childhood memories, their innate psychic status, and their religion. When the elder Wieland undergoes his horrendous experience in the temple, Clara is six. Clara later admits that her father's tragedy left an indelible impression, causing her to ponder the existence of divine intervention. Consequently, she is open to the possibility of supernatural machination when she hears the mysterious voices.

In addition to early experience, one's inherent mental and emotional balance may account for one's receptivity to the supernatural. Clara describes her brother as a brilliant but somber man who never laughs. This signals the reader that he is imbalanced and on the verge of disaster. Since Wieland's temperament is so dark and attuned to gloom, it is not surprising that he should hear a voice telling him to destroy his family, the source of his joy. Clara, on the other hand, is more carefree. It seems significant that although both brother and sister hear voices, Clara's injunctions ("Hold, hold!") are protective while Theodore's voice is destructive.

Brown begins his story with Clara's account of her father's fanaticism. The author thus foreshadows the younger Wieland's insanity.

It is possible that the younger Wieland's madness has been augmented by religion as well as heredity. Although he and Clara are raised without religion, they seem not to have escaped the traces of Puritanism and Calvinism permeating their culture. The emphasis that these faiths place on the sinfulness of earthly happiness may have convinced Theodore—already predisposed to gloom and tragedy—that his family afforded him too much joy and must therefore be annihilated.

As well as presenting the issue of psychological predisposition, Brown treats the issue of moral responsibility. In *Wieland*, responsibility for the most part is assigned to the individual level. For example, Carwin uses his ventriloquism only to remove himself from embarrassing situations. Nevertheless, he is indirectly and partially responsible for Wieland's tragic act. Had Wieland not been accustomed to hearing inexplicable voices, he might not have heard the command to sacrifice his family.

Brown also uses his novel to portray eccentricities of human nature. Unlike earlier gothic characters—simplistic figures representing shades of vice and virtue—Clara and Carwin are complex and real. Although Clara is a learned and independent woman, she seems to have no life of her own. She centers her activities entirely on her brother and his wife. Her fascination with Carwin appears to be her first attraction to the opposite sex. Despite her outward contentment, it seems possible that inwardly she aches for a love of her own, and easily mistakes Henry's friendship for romantic attachment. Her lonely life has removed her from reality.

Carwin exemplifies those persons who set out to test and undo one whose integrity they envy. In counterfeiting a dialogue between two murderers, for example, he intends to test Clara's alleged courage, to see whether she will run or stay to protect her servant. Carwin also simulates Clara's voice in order to delude Henry regarding her virtue. Confounding Henry, in Carwin's words, is the "sweetest triumph" over this man of "cold reserves and exquisite sagacity."

Brown's style is erudite and his dialogue stilted. Nevertheless, his story sustains readers' curiosity. Creating a gothic thriller, however, does not seem to have been Brown's sole purpose. In addition to presenting the intrigue of the voices, he subtly introduces themes of psychology, morality, and society.

"Critical Evaluation" by Rebecca Stingley Hinton

Bibliography:

Jones, Howard Mumford. *Belief and Disbelief in American Literature*. Chicago: University of Chicago Press, 1967. Discusses the religious ideologies characterizing American thought from the colonial era to the twentieth century. Cites specific writers. Explains eighteenth century rationalism and its coexistence with Calvinistic guilt.

MacAndrew, Elizabeth. *The Gothic Tradition in Fiction*. New York: Columbia University Press, 1979. Maintains that from the inception of the gothic novel, authors consciously employed symbolic elements and sought to educate their readers in the workings of the mind. Claims that the infusion of psychology into literature derived from the interest generated by the studies of eighteenth century thinker John Locke.

Punter, David. *The Literature of Terror*. New York: Longman, 1980. Treats the relationship between the eighteenth century novel and the philosophy of rationalism. The chapter on early American Gothic fiction discusses Brown's contribution regarding the effects of heredity and Puritanism on one's psychological composition.

Ringe, Donald A. *American Gothic: Imagination and Reason in Nineteenth Century Fiction*. Lexington: University Press of Kentucky, 1982. Recounts the characteristics of Gothic fiction, and discusses the psychological and moral insight Brown brings to his writing.

Thompson, G. R., ed. *The Gothic Imagination: Essays in Dark Romanticism*. Pullman: Washington State University Press, 1974. Argues that gothic literature is directly descended from the Gothic architecture of the Middle Ages. A chapter on religious terror in the gothic novel offers enlightenment regarding Wieland's perception of grace.

would make him the victor. After shooting his opponent in the heart, he fled back to Paris with his magic skin. It was now no larger than an oak leaf.

Although he consulted the best doctors available, they gave him no comfort or help. They could scarcely believe his story of the skin, yet they could find no cause for his grave illness. At last he lay dying. Wishing to have Pauline near him but knowing that his desire would consume the last shred of the magic skin, he asked her to leave him. As he called her name, she saw the skin growing smaller. In despair she rushed into the next room and tried to kill herself by knotting a scarf around her neck. The dying man tottered after her, and as he tore away the cloth, he tried vainly to utter a final wish. No words would come. He died while holding her in that last, desperate embrace.

Critical Evaluation:

The Wild Ass's Skin is the first volume of the sprawling sequence of novels which occupied Honoré de Balzac between 1829 and 1850. The French title, *La Peau de chagrin*, embodies an untranslatable pun, in that the name of the fabric of which the magical object is made (equivalent to the English shagreen) also carries the meaning which crosses directly into English in the word "chagrin": a kind of vexation which grates continually and tortuously upon the mind. When Raphael has acquired his talisman, he invites his friend Émile to bear witness to "how my chagrin will shrink"—and so it does, in both senses of the word. Unfortunately for Raphael, the shrinkage of the skin quickly reaches the point at which his own state of mind acquires a new and much sharper desperation, the temporary banishment of his chagrin merely serves to clear the way for a more profound and inescapable regret.

Balzac is famous as one of the boldest pioneers of narrative realism, and there are descriptive passages in *The Wild Ass's Skin* which are closely observed studies of life in contemporary Paris, foreshadowing the naturalistic triumphs to come in literature. Before this, however, Balzac had written a number of pseudonymous thrillers heavily influenced by gothic tales of terror, and he understood well enough the imaginative power exerted by such motifs as the diabolical bargain. In bringing such a motif out of the quasi-medieval settings favored by the gothic novelists and planting it firmly in contemporary Paris, he was helping to pave the way for a distinctly modern kind of horror story as well as recruiting a useful allegorical device.

Like any modern hero would, Raphael looks to science for assistance when the power of his magic is exhausted, but science cannot help him; he has surrendered his soul to the judgment of superstition and must accept its cruel verdict. This is the fear which haunts all modern tales of unease: that knowing the truth might not be enough if there is some deeper and darker region of the mind which cannot and will not admit it. The juxtaposition of the gothic and the realistic in Balzac's allegory thus anticipates later ideas regarding the uneasy relationship between the conscious and unconscious minds, the one being unsafely held by reason and the other, unconquerably, by desire.

The final section of the book is called "The Agony" not so much because of the depth of Raphael's anguish—*agonie* in French signifies a struggle against death rather than excruciating pain—as because of the way in which he is fatally divided against himself. No matter how anxious he becomes to preserve the skin by conserving his demands, he is helpless to prevent it from wasting away; he is not the master of his own desires and his uncontrollable appetites destroy him by degrees. Such, Balzac implies, is the fate of everyone who cannot control his lusts. Pauline's attempts to help him only serve to prove to him that had he adopted a realistic view of his own potential and made a life with her much sooner, instead of chasing after the deceptive Foedora, he would have done far better in the long run.

To some extent, this message must be construed as an attack on the bourgeois materialism which Balzac affected to hate and despise (in himself as well as in others), but the allegory is not simply political. It cuts much deeper than that, to the root causes of human envy and human unhappiness. When Balzac wrote it, he had only just begun to accumulate the debts whose burden was to weigh on him for the rest of his life, and he had not long introduced the fanciful "de" into his name which laid false claim to an aristocratic heritage; even so, he clearly had an anxious understanding of where such pretentious follies might eventually lead him.

The motif of wish fulfillment in *The Wild Ass's Skin* is obvious. Raphael is an ambitious writer who divides his time between a comedy and a study of the will; his tempter, Rastignac, initially bribes him away from these endeavours with commissions for vulgar hackwork, then seduces him into reckless gambling. Had he been left to his own devices Raphael might still have been inclined to make a Faustian bargain with the devil, offering his soul for an enlightenment that might have made his work brilliant, but under Rastignac's influence the treasures he claims are far more transitory. In real life, Balzac had it both ways; he obtained the transitory delights and a reputation as a man of considerable insight and ability, one of the great chroniclers of his age. Raphael de Valentin would doubtless have envied him, but the author of *The Wild Ass's Skin* might well have felt fully entitled to say "I told you so" to his later self.

"Critical Evaluation" by Brian Stableford

Bibliography:

Kanes, Martin. *Balzac's Comedy of Words*. Princeton, N.J.: Princeton University Press, 1975. Chapter 3 deals with *The Wild Ass's Skin*, exploring the problem of creativity.

Pritchett, V. S. *Balzac*. London: Chatto & Windus, 1973. A chapter on *The Wild Ass's Skin* puts the novel into its biographical context.

Robb, Graham. *Balzac*. London: Picador, 1994. A comprehensive biographical and critical study. *The Wild Ass's Skin* is discussed in chapter 8, "Absolute Power."

Testa, Carlo. *Desire and the Devil: Demonic Contracts in French and European Literature*. New York: Peter Lang, 1991. Part one of the study deals with "Balzac's Laicized Demonism," including a detailed analysis of *The Wild Ass's Skin*.

Weber, Samuel. *Unwrapping Balzac: A Reading of "La Peau de chagrin."* Toronto: University of Toronto Press, 1979. The only full-length study of the work.

THE WILD DUCK

Type of work: Drama
Author: Henrik Ibsen (1828-1906)
Type of plot: Social realism
Time of plot: Nineteenth century
Locale: Norway
First published: Vildanden, 1884 (English translation, 1891); first performed, 1885

> *Principal characters:*
> WERLE, a wealthy industrialist
> GREGERS WERLE, his son
> OLD EKDAL, Werle's former partner
> HJALMAR EKDAL, his son
> GINA EKDAL, Hjalmar's wife
> HEDVIG, their daughter
> RELLING, a doctor

The Story:

Gregers Werle, the son of a rich industrialist and a sensitive, high-minded mother, had early in life developed a loathing for the unscrupulous means his father had used to amass his fortune. After his mother's death, young Werle left his father's house for a time, but he eventually returned. His father, hoping to persuade his son to accept a partnership in the business, gave a large dinner party to which Gregers invited a thirteenth guest, his old school friend, Hjalmar Ekdal. This act displeased his father very much because Hjalmar did not belong in the Werles' social set and because he was the son of a former business partner old Werle had wronged. The older Ekdal now held a menial position in Werle's employ, to which he had been reduced after a term in prison had broken his mind and spirit.

Gregers was aware that his father's machinations had sent Ekdal to prison after a scandal in which both had been involved, and he hated his father for this injury to his friend's father. He discovered also that the older Werle had arranged a marriage between Hjalmar Ekdal and Gina Hansen, a former maid in the Werle household and, Gregers suspected, his father's mistress. Gregers was therefore displeased both at his father's offer of a partnership and at his father's forthcoming marriage to Mrs. Sorby, his housekeeper. Gregers announced that his future mission in life was to open Hjalmar Ekdal's eyes to the lie he had been living for the past fifteen years.

The Ekdal home was shabby. Werle had set Hjalmar up as a photographer after marrying him to Gina, but it was really Gina who ran the business while her husband worked on an invention he hoped would enable his aged father to recoup some of his fortune. Old Ekdal himself, now practically out of his mind, spent most of his time in a garret where he kept a curious assortment of animals. Ekdal believed that the garret was a forest like the one in which he had hunted as a young man. He occasionally shot a rabbit up there, and on holidays and special occasions he appeared before the family dressed in his old military uniform.

Although based almost entirely on self-deception and illusion, the Ekdal home was a happy one. Gina took good care of her husband, Hedvig, their fourteen-year-old daughter, and Hjalmar's father. Hedvig was very dear to both Hjalmar and Gina, who kept from her the fact that she was rapidly losing her eyesight. Gregers Werle was shocked when he saw the Ekdals' home. Old Ekdal showed him Hedvig's prize possession, a wild duck that Werle's father had once shot and wounded; the duck had dived to the bottom of the water, but Werle's dog had retrieved it. Gregers saw himself as the clever dog destined to bring the Ekdal family out of their straitened circumstances.

To accomplish his end, he rented a room from the Ekdals, though Gina was unwilling to let him have it. She was not the only one to resent his presence in the house. Dr. Relling, another roomer, knew Gregers Werle, and was aware of his reputation for meddling in the affairs of others. He agreed that Gregers was the victim of a morbid conscience, probably derived from his hysterical mother. Hjalmar, in his innocence, saw nothing amiss in his friend's behavior and allowed him to stay.

Gregers set about the task of rehabilitating his friend in a systematic way. He discovered that the family was supported by the older Werle and not, as Hjalmar supposed, by the photographic studio. More important, the coincidence of Hedvig's progressive blindness and Werle's father's weak eyesight made Werle suspect that Hjalmar was not the child's natural father. During a long walk he took with Hjalmar, Gregers tried to open his friend's eyes to his true position in his own house; he told him everything he had discovered except his suspicion of Hedvig's illegitimacy.

Having no real integrity or resources within himself, Hjalmar fell into all the clichés of stories he had read about the behavior of wronged husbands. He demanded an accounting from Gina of all the money Werle had paid into the household, and he asserted that every cent should be paid back out of the proceeds from his hypothetical invention. His outburst did nothing but disturb Gina and frighten Hedvig. Hjalmar's pride might have been placated and the whole matter straightened out had not a letter arrived from old Werle, who was giving Hedvig a small annuity. Hjalmar announced that Hedvig was no child of his and that he wanted nothing more to do with her. Hedvig was heartbroken at her father's behavior, and Gregers Werle, beginning to realize the consequences of his meddling, persuaded the girl that her one hope of winning back her father's love was to sacrifice for his sake the thing she loved most. He urged her to have her grandfather kill the wild duck.

Gina had succeeded in convincing Hjalmar that he was quite helpless without her. They were discussing their plans for the future, when they heard a shot. At first they thought old Ekdal was firing at his rabbits, but it was Hedvig, who, in her despair, had put a bullet through her breast.

Critical Evaluation:

The Wild Duck is one of Henrik Ibsen's most important problem plays. From the time of its first appearance, it captured audiences and readers with its vitality and universality. Ibsen, known as "the father of modern drama," achieved this recognition over tremendous obstacles, not the least of which was that he wrote in a little-known language. Born into a provincial milieu in Norway, Ibsen suffered early poverty and hardships, including poor education. In 1851, he became the assistant manager of the Bergen Theater, studied stage production abroad, and in the next six years gained invaluable practical theatrical experience by putting into production 145 plays. By the time he started writing his own plays, he had a knowledge of the theater and its literature matched by very few playwrights.

In *A Doll's House* (1879), *Ghosts* (1881), *An Enemy of the People* (1882), *The Wild Duck*, and *Hedda Gabler* (1890), Ibsen introduced realism to the stage and established it so overwhelmingly that it remained the dominant approach to the stage throughout the twentieth century. Ibsen substituted middle-class protagonists for kings and queens and wrote prose dialogue rather than poetry, stating that "My plays . . . are not tragedies in the old meaning of the word; what I have wanted to portray is human beings and that is just why I did not want them to speak the language of the gods." He introduced detailed stage directions to authenticate the background scene, and he approached his characterizations with a desire to reveal them to the audience almost scientifically, thus incorporating his age's new discoveries of the importance of instincts, biology, heredity, and environment. In his plot innovation, he dispensed with the intrigue and trickery of then popular "well-made plays." While maintaining his skillful manipulation of plot, he ended each act with strong, theatrical curtain scenes. Some of his innovations—as in his extensive use of light-dark imagery; his pervasive irony; his elimination of all events antecedent to the critical situation; and his use of the unities of time, place, and action—reveal his study of Greek tragedy.

The Wild Duck marked Ibsen's turning away from realistic problem plays. From that time on his plays were complex, enigmatic studies of the human condition, and they employed expressionistic and symbolic techniques. *The Wild Duck* reflects some of his most important preoccupations. These include the presentness of the past; man's search for his true identity and place in life; the effects of idealism as a social force; the conflict of reality and illusion; and the problem of man's ultimate freedom. Ibsen himself said that the critics would "find plenty to quarrel about, plenty to interpret" in this play.

The key to the universality of the play lies in the complexity of the strong, well-rounded characters. A lesser playwright would have settled, for example, for making old Werle the villain of a melodrama. Ibsen, instead, presents his human complexity. Gregers, the son, sees the elder Werle as an unredeemable villain who has ruined old Ekdal, made his housemaid pregnant, and then foisted her off on the unsuspecting son of Ekdal. Hjalmar Ekdal, however, describing what old Werle has done for him and his family, sees him as a fairy godfather. The truth in Ibsen, as in life, lies somewhere in between—perhaps in old Werle's espousal of "the attainable ideal." Gina Ekdal, too, moves far beyond the stereotype of the fallen woman redeemed by marriage. It is Gina's work on the photographs and her sewing, her concern for practicalities and the welfare of Hedvig and her husband, that keep the family going and enable Hjalmar to indulge in his dreams.

The two major characters, Gregers Werle and Hjalmar Ekdal, are even more complex. Both men see themselves as intellectually and morally superior to all around them; both are judged by the audience as self-indulgent, egocentric men with no true sympathy or love for others, not even their own family. Both wish to attain truth, but both harbor illusions about the nobility and goodness of their actions. Gregers admired Hjalmar as the most gifted and intelligent of his schoolmates, yet Ibsen characterizes his intelligence as that of a photographer and speech writer, not of an artistic creator. Gregers lacks the moral strength to stop his father from trapping Ekdal; Hjalmar lacks the courage to commit suicide as he claims to wish to do; both men fail to face their responsibility in the death of Hedvig. Yet Ibsen does not dismiss the quest for truth out of hand but shows instead the ambiguity and complexity of the undertaking.

Dramatic irony is an important device throughout the play. Gregers, who ends up destroying a home and contributes to the suicide of a young girl, had earlier accused his father of leaving things like "a battlefield strewn with broken lives." Hjalmar remarks that happiness is home, just as Gregers knocks on his door to bring the information that will help destroy that happiness and that home. Many of the ironic reverberations are connected with the sense of sight. Those who are blind—old Werle and Hedvig—often see more clearly than those who have good physical vision. Like Oedipus, Gregers and Hjalmar are metaphorically blind to the real truth of their human condition. Unlike Oedipus, however, they never face the truth and thus remain in darkness at the end of the play. Ibsen also employs light and dark imagery in the set and dialogue: Act I begins in brightness and candle glow, but the other acts grow ever darker and Act V ends cold and gray.

The title of the play carries the complexity of meanings with it. The duck, wounded by old Werle, is saved and trapped. Relling sees it as a symbol of all the world's people who are wounded while attempting to live in this world. Hedvig associates the duck with herself, wounded and unable to fly yet happy to stay at home in that created world. Old Werle connects the duck with old Ekdal, who is unable to live in reality. Gregers at one time sees himself as the dog who rescues the duck from drowning in the sea of lies and illusions; later he identifies with the duck; still later, he suggests the identification of Hedvig with the duck. The duck's world is a surrogate for the real forest in which, with its clipped wings, it could no longer live. The family questions whether the duck can adapt; they decide that as long as it cannot see the real sky, it can survive unconscious of its trapped condition. The sky, associated with light and freedom and the natural state of bird and man, is thus juxtaposed with the darkness of Ekdal's attic, the unnatural state that humans create for themselves. Old and young Ekdal are capable only of hunting tamed or disabled animals in their artificial forest and are as unable as the duck to survive in the real world.

"Critical Evaluation" by Ann E. Reynolds

Bibliography:
Caputi, Anthony, ed. *Eight Modern Plays.* 2d ed. New York: W. W. Norton, 1991. Dounia B. Christiani's translation of *The Wild Duck* is supplemented with excerpts from Ibsen's letters and speeches and two chapters from books by M. C. Bradbrook and Dorothea Krook. Bradbook's contribution explains how the play works on different levels simultaneously, and Krook remarks on the subtlety of Ibsen's theme of self-deception. Caputi's foreword provides an excellent introduction to Ibsen and twentieth century drama.
Clurman, Harold. *Ibsen.* New York: Macmillan, 1977. An introductory study that provides the general reader with a good starting place for reading about Ibsen. Clurman, a renowned stage director, comments with sensitivity on the plays as both theater and literature. Includes an instructive discussion of *The Wild Duck*, which concludes that Gregers' zealotry leads him to misjudge Hjalmar's essentially mundane nature.
Fjelde, Rolf, ed. *Ibsen: A Collection of Critical Essays.* Englewood Cliffs, N.J.: Prentice-Hall, 1965. Sixteen essays cover, among other topics, Ibsen's conception of truth, realism, and stage craftsmanship. Robert Raphael discusses the theme of self-deception in *The Wild Duck* and two other Ibsen plays.
Lyons, Charles R., ed. *Critical Essays on Henrik Ibsen.* Boston: G. K. Hall, 1987. A thorough and useful volume of essays that collects discussions addressing the ideology, realism, and dramatic form of Ibsen's plays. The remarks on *The Wild Duck* explore the play's structure, language, and exposition.
McFarlane, James, ed. *The Cambridge Companion to Ibsen.* Cambridge, England: Cambridge University Press, 1994. A collection of sixteen newly written essays on Ibsen's life and work, which include discussions of Ibsen's working methods and the stage history of the plays. A helpful source.

THE WILD GEESE

Type of work: Novel
Author: Mori Ōgai (Mori Rintarō, 1862-1922)
Type of plot: Psychological realism
Time of plot: 1880
Locale: Tokyo, Japan
First published: Gan, 1911-1913 (English translation, 1959)

> *Principal characters:*
> OKADA, a medical student
> OTAMA, a beautiful and innocent girl
> OTAMA'S FATHER
> SUEZO, a moneylender
> OTSUNE, Suezo's wife

The Story:

Okada, a medical student at Tokyo University, was viewed by his fellow students as an exceptionally balanced young man. A good student, an athlete, and a man who knew how to relax in his free time, he lived a well-ordered life free from any kind of obsession. When he was not studying, he liked to go for walks, and he often stopped to browse in the local bookshops, looking for the historical romances that were his preferred reading.

Once, during his evening walk, Okada noticed an attractive young woman entering a small house that seemed to be an oasis of calm in a generally noisy neighborhood. He thought little about it at the time, but when he passed the house two days later, he saw the woman in the window, and she smiled at him. After that, he always looked for her when he passed by and began to feel that in some way he and she were friends. One evening, he spontaneously took off his cap and bowed to the woman, who smiled warmly in return. From then on, Okada bowed to the woman whenever he passed her house.

The woman's name was Otama, and she was the daughter of a candy dealer who sold his wares from a stall. Otama's mother had died giving birth to Otama, and the girl had been reared by her father, who adored her. She had grown to be a beautiful, charming, and obedient young woman in whom it was difficult to find fault. Otama's father refused various proposed matches for Otama because he did not want to lose his daughter, but ultimately he permitted her to marry a policeman. The policeman forced the issue because he desired Otama, and the father was afraid to refuse the somewhat frightening prospective son-in-law. As it turned out, the policeman already had a wife and children, and Otama's marriage broke up when that information came to light. Although it was obvious to everyone that Otama had done nothing wrong, the incident made it almost a certainty that she would never receive a decent proposal of marriage.

A local man named Suezo learned of the disaster that had befallen Otama and her father. Suezo had begun his career as a servant working for medical students at Tokyo University. Most of his time had been spent running errands for the students. Suezo, however, had had no intention of remaining a servant all of his life, and he had begun to lend small amounts of money to students who were in need, making a small profit on each transaction. Over a long period of time, he had become wealthy. He dressed in fine clothes and dreamed of living in even greater comfort. As his financial status improved, Suezo became dissatisfied with his wife. Although she did a good job of caring for the children, Otsune was undeniably ugly and argumentative.

Suezo began to believe that he deserved the companionship of a better kind of woman. He told himself that, since he never frequented geisha houses or wasted his money gambling, he had every right to indulge himself by having a mistress.

Remembering how beautiful Otama was and her skill in playing the samisen, Suezo decided that he would use a go-between to propose that Otama become his mistress. He knew that her prospects were limited, but he decided to improve his chances of success by concealing the fact that he was a usurer, since that means of livelihood was despised in Japan. He courted Otama and finally won her by offering to provide generously for her father. The girl accepted his proposal primarily because she believed that it was her duty to see that her father would be cared for.

Suezo installed Otama, along with a maid, in the small house in which she lived when Okada first saw her. He also rented a house nearby for her father. All went fairly well until Otama learned from a fish seller that Suezo was a usurer. She was upset that he had tricked her, and she decided that she would never again be so trusting and naïve.

After Otama first saw Okada, she began to fantasize about him, viewing him as a romantic savior. She tried to think of ways in which she could meet him. As she thought more and more about Okada, Otama began to be less attentive to Suezo, and even her father noticed that she had changed. One day, Okada walked toward Otama's house and found the place in an uproar. A snake had crawled up the eaves of the house and into a cage that held two linnets that Suezo had given Otama. The snake had killed one of the birds. A crowd of women and children had gathered, and one of the women asked Okada to help. With the help of a young boy, Okada killed the snake before it could kill the other bird. Otama helped Okada wash the snake's blood from his hands, but, in spite of her desire to do so, she could not bring herself to speak to him at length. After that, however, she began to think about Okada even more.

Otama finally decided that she would speak to Okada when he passed by. For the occasion, she had her hair done and wore makeup, which was something she usually did not do. That evening, however, Okada was walking with a friend (the novel's narrator), and Otama was unable to speak to Okada. The friend noticed that Okada was visibly disturbed at the sight of Otama, who looked even more beautiful than usual. Later, Okada and the narrator met a friend, Ishihara, who pointed out some wild geese at the far end of a pond. Ishihara urged Okada to try to hit one of the geese with a stone, but Okada was reluctant to hurt the geese. Okada finally agreed to throw a stone because he knew that if he did not, Ishihara would attempt to kill one of the geese. Okada intended only to make the geese fly away, but his stone struck and killed one of the birds. Ishihara later retrieved the goose, intending to cook and eat it. The three students walked back to their boardinghouse, and Okada carried the dead goose under his cloak. When the trio came near Otama's house, they saw her there waiting for Okada, but because Okada was with his friends, Otama was again unable to speak to him. She never had another opportunity to meet Okada. The next day, he traveled to Germany, where he went to work translating Chinese medical texts into German.

Critical Evaluation:

Mori Ōgai, one of Japan's most highly respected writers, is a member of the samurai class who studied Dutch and German and went to Germany to study medicine. In Germany, he was deeply influenced by the concern for the individual that is so much a part of Western culture. He became a lifelong advocate of logic and the scientific method, as well as a champion of Westernization in those areas—particularly those of scholarship and science—in which he believed the West to be superior to the East. At the same time, however, he believed that Japan had to retain what was unique and valuable in its own culture. He never proposed breaking with tradition unless he was convinced that tradition could be improved in some way.

Ōgai became known for the quality of his prose. He was thoroughly versed in literary Chinese as well as Dutch and German, and his writing is that of the quintessential classicist. His work is clear and precise as well as graceful, and it reflects the various traditions with which he was familiar. Although Ōgai never hesitated to deal with emotions, passions, and controversial subjects (in fact, his novel *Vita Sexualis*, 1909, was banned because of its frank treatment of sexuality), he always believed that logic was more important than emotion. He was an Apollonian, rather than a Dionysian, artist.

One of the primary characteristics of Ōgai's work is its examination of the problems that arise in people's lives when their desires conflict with the demands made upon them by society. This is certainly true of Otama in *The Wild Geese*, who, as a woman in Meiji-era Japan, has little freedom to make choices in her life. She understands all too well that she is being badly treated through no fault of her own, but she continues to be bound by duty. She accedes to Suezo's wishes out of filial piety, so that her father can live out his remaining years in comfort. When she finally decides to rebel by making contact with Okada, she is thwarted because she is unable to overcome her fear of speaking to him when he is not alone. Societal constraints win out against the desires of the individual.

In the same way that Otama is hemmed in by society, so are Okada, Suezo, Otsune, and Otama's father. Okada makes no real move to meet Otama; instead, he simply bows to her so that he can continue to indulge in his own fantasies while keeping his distance. Perhaps he is afraid of the consequences of becoming involved with her; perhaps he is simply afraid of intimacy. It is certainly easier to deal with idealized female characters in Chinese romantic novels than it is to relate to a real woman with real desires and problems. Suezo, who is perhaps the most realistic character in the novel—he is certainly the most effective manipulator—is also bound by convention. His relatively uncomplicated life becomes problematic when he tries to keep a mistress while keeping his wife in the dark. His wife, Otsune, knows on some level that he is unfaithful, although he is able to confuse her with clever explanations whenever her accusations become too strident. She finally retreats into sullenness and passive aggression, which Suezo finds difficult to control. Otama's father is probably the weakest character in the novel. He turns down various marriage proposals in an attempt to keep his daughter to himself, only to have a strong, threatening man force himself upon Otama, thereby ruining her chances of having a good, socially acceptable marriage. (In fact, the only character in the novel who gets what he wants, if only temporarily, is the policeman, although there is no question that the author disapproves of his behavior.) Otama is finally destroyed by her situation and her powerlessness, just as the innocent goose is destroyed by Okada's unintentional act of violence.

It is clear that no one in the novel is free from the shackles of social demands and expectations, and Ōgai shows no way out for anyone. In fact, the author believed that people have to resign themselves to their positions in society. He himself gave in to societal pressure when he rejected the lover whom he had met in Germany. She followed him to Japan when he returned home, but he sent her away when his family and peers insisted that he marry within his class. Ōgai believed that society should be changed from within to accommodate more effectively the needs and desires of individuals, but he was unwilling to flout conventions that were still firmly in place.

In spite of its brevity and outward simplicity, *The Wild Geese* is a rich and complex work. Although it is a novel, it has the flavor of a fairy tale. Its symbolism is powerful and evocative, and it does not lend itself to clear-cut interpretation. There is, for example, no consensus regarding the symbolism of the linnets and the snake. Many widely divergent interpretations have been put forward. Ultimately, the power of the novel lies in its use of believable and sympathetic characters to portray the inherent sadness of the human condition.

Shawn Woodyard

Bibliography:

Johnson, Eric W. "Ōgai's *The Wild Goose*." In *Approaches to the Modern Japanese Novel*, edited by Kinya Tsuruta and Thomas E. Swann. Tokyo: Sophia University, 1976. An excellent examination of the novel. Particularly good regarding the problem of the narrator and the difficulties of interpreting the novel's symbolism.

Kato, Shuichi. "The Age of Meiji." In *The Modern Years*, translated by Don Sanderson. Vol. 3 in *A History of Japanese Literature*. Tokyo: Kodansha International, 1979-1983. Contains a section that examines Ōgai's life and works. Provides interesting historical background.

Keene, Donald. "Mori Ōgai." In *Fiction*. Vol. 2 in *Dawn to the West: Japanese Literature in the Modern Era*. New York: Holt, Rinehart, and Winston, 1984. A fine study of Ōgai by the foremost American expert on Japan. Includes a brief examination of *The Wild Geese*.

Powell, Irena. "In Search of Logic and Social Harmony." In *Writers and Society in Modern Japan*. Tokyo: Kodansha International, 1983. Contains a brief but informative section on Ōgai and his work. Especially useful for placing the author and his work in a societal perspective.

Rimer, J. Thomas. *Mori Ōgai*. New York: Twayne, 1975. A thorough study of Ōgai's life and work that includes much information about *The Wild Geese*.

THE WILD PALMS

Type of work: Novel
Author: William Faulkner (1897-1962)
Type of plot: Tragicomedy
Time of plot: 1927 and 1937
Locale: United States
First published: 1939

> *Principal characters:*
> HARRY WILBOURNE, a twenty-seven-year-old intern
> CHARLOTTE RITTENMEYER, a young married woman
> FRANCIS "RAT" RITTENMEYER, her husband
> THE TALL CONVICT, a man serving a ten-year term for train robbery
> THE PALE CONVICT, his work partner in the flood
> THE WOMAN, pregnant and stranded in the flood

The Story:

Old Man. There were two convicts. One was tall, lean, about twenty-five, with long Indian-black hair, who was serving fifteen years for a botched train robbery. The second convict was short and plump, and almost hairless, like something exposed when one turned over a rock or a log. The second convict was serving 139 years for his participation in a gas station robbery in which the attendant was killed, although probably not by the second convict. Both convicts were doing time at the Mississippi State penal farm, which ran along the Mississippi. The river was flooding over its banks, forcing the evacuation of the prisoners.

The convicts were moved by truck, train, and boat, and everywhere they were surrounded by National Guard troops and by the muddy water of the rising river. The two convicts were provided with a skiff and told to pick up stranded farmers and their families. The short convict returned to the staging area alone and reported to the authorities that the boat had overturned and that the tall convict had disappeared beneath the water. The warden decided to list the tall convict as missing and presumed dead while trying to save lives; the tall convict had served his time.

The tall convict had in fact resurfaced. He managed to scramble back into the skiff but was unable to control it. He drifted for some time before he encountered a pregnant woman sitting in a tree. He tried to paddle upstream with her but at night they were swept downstream. They met others who were stranded by the flood; the others refused to give food and shelter to the convict and the woman. The convict also encountered some National Guard troops and tried to surrender, but they misunderstood and shot at him. He fled. Finally, the two found higher ground and struggled ashore. The convict passed out.

By the time he revived, the woman had delivered her baby. They got back on the water and were picked up by a riverboat and taken farther south. They were left beside a levee. Taking to the water again, they were befriended by a Cajun, and the convict helped him hunt for alligators. The convict fled again, however, unable to tell the Cajun and the woman that the area was about to be flooded. All three were rescued again and evacuated to safety with other refugees. The convict surrendered himself, dressed in his cleaned prison uniform, to a sheriff's deputy.

A state official and the warden discussed the prisoner's case. Officially he was dead and therefore free; the young state official was afraid that the administrative mistake would be discovered. The warden pointed out that the prisoner had turned himself in and that he had even returned the skiff. To avoid declaring a mistake had been made, the prisoner was nevertheless declared to have attempted escape and was given ten additional years to his sentence. The tall prisoner reunited with the short one and the novel concluded with them talking about women and prison life, especially the tall one's extra ten years.

The Wild Palms. A young man called on a local doctor to help an ailing woman. The doctor and his wife lived next door, and they had already been intrigued by the couple but knew nothing about them. The doctor had been speculating for days about the woman's condition, which he diagnosed in various ways. Before he was admitted to see her, he had overheard the delirious ravings of the woman; during these ravings, she called the young man a "bloody bungling bastard."

The young man and the woman were Harry Wilbourne and Charlotte Rittenmeyer. Harry was an intern at New Orleans Hospital. He was an orphan who had struggled through medical school on a $2,000 legacy left him by his doctor father. On the day he met Charlotte, he had just turned twenty-seven, and his roommate had lent him a suit and dragged him to a party in the artist's quarter. Charlotte was a little older; she was married to Francis "Rat" Rittenmeyer and had two daughters. She immediately adopted Harry at the party and insisted that he see her home. Harry and Charlotte began to have lunch together; eventually, they sought out a hotel—but nothing happened. Soon they talked of escaping New Orleans together; the lack of money, however, prevented them from doing so. Then Harry found a wallet containing more than a thousand dollars. He debated whether to turn it in, but, instead, they used the money to run away to Chicago. In a strange scene at the train station, Rat gave Harry a Pullman check for $300 to cover the costs of Charlotte's return ticket if she decided to come back to him. He also exacted a promise from Charlotte to write on the tenth of every month to let him know that she was all right; otherwise, he would send a detective after her. Finally, in a drawing room on the train, they consummated their love.

In Chicago, Charlotte found an inexpensive apartment with a skylight; she could work at her art while Harry was working. At first, Harry had difficulty finding a job, since he had not completed his internship, but he was eventually hired to do syphilis testing at a charity hospital in the Negro tenement district. Charlotte made figurines which, initially, sold well in local department stores. Harry was fired, however, because Charlotte forgot to write Francis one month, and the detective contacted the hospital. Soon, Charlotte could not sell her creations; in order to save money, the couple retreated to a cabin overlooking the lake in Wisconsin.

Here they lived an idyllic life, swimming, sketching, and making love, until winter arrived, and their food ran out. They moved back to the city; they lived in a dreary, one-room efficiency apartment; and Charlotte took a temporary holiday job dressing windows for a local store. When the job became permanent, Harry decided that they were becoming too much like a conventional, married couple, the very condition they had once escaped. He took a job as company doctor for a mining operation in the mountains of Utah; in February they left Chicago.

In Utah, it was mid-winter, and they were unprepared for the bitter cold and the isolation of the mountains. They met the mine foreman and his wife, Buck and Billie Buckner, and learned that the operation was about to collapse, that the men had not been paid for months, and that they would not be paid either. Forced to live with the foreman and his wife, even sleeping in the same room with them to keep warm, Charlotte and Harry ceased having sex. Buck confided to Harry that Billie was pregnant; Buck asked him to abort the fetus. At first, Harry refused, but he finally did perform the operation. Soon after, the Buckners left, and Harry assumed the role of overseerer of the mine. He then realized that the situation was futile, and he informed the miners, sending them off with the contents of the company store. Charlotte and Harry took the mining train out of the mountains; they went to San Antonio, Texas. Charlotte confided in Harry that she was pregnant, too, the result of a period of passion following the weeks of abstinence. At first, Harry tried to find medicine to induce the abortion, but when that proved ineffective, he reluctantly performed it himself. Charlotte was rejected by her daughters during an attempted meeting with them back in New Orleans. Charlotte, who knew that she was ill from the abortion, made Francis promise not to prosecute Harry if she should die.

Back on the Mississippi Gulf coast, Charlotte was dying of a botched abortion. The doctor agreed to call an ambulance in order to take Charlotte to the hospital, but he admitted that she was going to die. He also insisted on calling the police to arrest Harry, and they took Harry to the hospital where Charlotte died. Harry was then taken to jail to await the legal proceedings. He was tried and convicted of manslaughter and sentenced to fifty years at hard labor. True to his promise, Rat tried to help Harry, but the judge refused to be lenient. Rat made one last attempt to help Harry by smuggling him a cyanide capsule to save himself the fifty years at hard labor. Harry refused.

The end of the novel focused on Harry's musings about his life as he gazed out his cell window. He noticed a woman hanging out her washing on the deck of an abandoned ship in the harbor. That domestic scene reminded him of the time he and Charlotte had spent together. A palm tree rustling in the wind made a dry, wild sound which filled Harry's cell. Harry decided to remain alive in order to keep the memory of Charlotte and their time together also alive; this thought gave him the courage to face his long hard time. Between grief and nothing, Harry mused, I will take grief.

"The Story" by Charles L. P. Silet

Critical Evaluation:

The Wild Palms has had a curious history, for it has most often been reprinted as two short novels, *The Wild Palms* and *Old Man* (which is part of *The Wild Palms*), sometimes in the same volume and more often as two separate books. That it has been so casually treated is unfortunate, because structurally it is perhaps the subtlest and most demanding of William Faulkner's novels, and it is also his best approach to the comically absurd world of male-female relationships.

Most of the misunderstanding of the novel grows from its unique structure. The two short novels, either of which appears to be able to stand alone, are presented in alternating chapters. Their plots never cross or relate directly to each other; but they are so deeply involved in theme and symbolic and imagistic texture that apart each seems almost a thematic contradiction of the other. Together, however, they form an organic unit in which contrasts form parallels and contradiction becomes paradox. The novel demands of its readers an imaginative commitment beyond that of a more conventionally constructed novel, for its paradox, of both meaning and structure, must be solved by readers willing to read the book with the attention to rhythm and form that they would normally give to a piece of music and the attention to images and words that they would normally give to a poem.

The pattern of events of the two parts of the novel are relatively simple. "The Wild Palms" takes place in 1937, in the heart of the Depression, and is the love story of Harry Wilbourne and Charlotte Rittenmeyer. Charlotte leaves her husband for Harry who, not having finished his internship, is incapable of gaining any steady work. They wander from New Orleans to Chicago to Wisconsin and even to a remote mining camp in Utah until Charlotte accidentally becomes pregnant; their journeys, too, have carried them deeper into squalor and their love from romance into the physically sordid. Urged by Charlotte, Harry performs an unsuccessful abortion which results in her death. In prison for her death, he refuses suicide, choosing grief over nothing.

The events in "Old Man" take place ten years earlier, during the great Mississippi River flood of 1927. They are the chronicle of a comic hero in a physical world gone quite as mad as the social world of the Depression has in "The Wild Palms." A young convict is sent out onto the flooded Mississippi in a skiff with another convict to rescue a woman stranded in a tree and a man on a cotton house. He loses the other convict, rescues the woman, who proves to be very pregnant, and is carried downstream by the flood. Battered by gigantic waves, he is offered three temptations for escape. After a time killing alligators with a group of Cajuns, he returns the boat and the woman with her safely born child and is given an additional ten-year sentence for attempted escape.

Neither of these brief descriptions approaches the complexities of the two stories, separately or as a unit, for theirs is an artistic value of reflection and texture in which event is a matter of form, and form a vehicle for imaginative idea. "The Wild Palms" is a tragicomedy, a parody of Ernest Hemingway's romantically anti-Romantic ideas (particularly those in *A Farewell to Arms*, 1929), a parable of a fallen world. "Old Man" is also a bitter comedy, but one in which the comic hero, God's fool, bears the burdens of the world and finds his victory in seeming defeat, his reward in the last ironic slap of "risible nature." "The Wild Palms" resolves itself in onanistic frustration, and "Old Man" discovers the spiritual rewards of struggle. The novel's comic sense makes it more than an existential lament for a meaningless world. The novel transforms the world's madness and ugliness into a Christian comedy of human folly which shows people at their worst, only to remind readers of the necessity of striving toward their best. The novel is not simply a moral allegory, although "Old Man" often verges on Christian parable. It is a compendium on the vanity of human wishes and on the follies of this earth.

The primary themes of both parts of the novel are those of human folly: the tragic consequences of romantic but earthly ideals and the failure of sex as the essential element of human fulfillment. Harry and the convict are victims of romantic ideals: The convict was sent to prison for an attempted train robbery inspired by reading dime novels and intended to impress a young woman; Harry was led into his affair with Charlotte by an impulse away from his ascetic student's life and his belief (fostered by Charlotte) in physical love and the value of the physical in a spiritless world.

The heroes of both stories are innocents in a confusing world, and women offer them little aid or solace. The women in the novel represent the two emasculating extremes of the female character. Charlotte is the defeminized female artist of masculine mind and manner, the aggressor in the sexual act and in life. The woman in "Old Man" is simple nearly to mindlessness; she is the mother, the primitive force of life to be borne by man as the weight of his duty. Charlotte is destroyed by the sex that she attempts to use as a man would. She cannot do so, however, because she is what she wishes to deny—a woman, a vessel, and bearer of man's seed and progeny. The woman in "Old Man" realizes and fulfills her role as mother, but in this comic world fails as a romantic sexual figure. She lives on but without her man, the convict who had complained that she, of all the women in the world, is the one with whom he has been thrown by chance.

The men are innocents; the women are failures with them. "Old Man" ends with the convict's brief, violent summation of his feelings about the world of sex and women. "The Wild Palms" ends with Harry's refusal to kill himself only because in his grief he can find the onanistic solace of the memory of Charlotte's flesh. Both stories end in hollowness and ugliness. Each, taken by itself, presents a vision of frustration and despair, yet the novel itself has no such effect.

The two stories present opposing accounts of the nature of failure and success. The novel's dualistic, contradictory vision causes readers to apply their own norms to the events and to see the exact nature of the folly of both extremes, of sex and sexlessness, of romantic and anti-romantic ideals. The world of *The Wild Palms* is a mad world, but its madness resembles this world, mad in its own right but held in the balance of equal and opposing forces.

Faulkner does not explicitly offer his reader the moral of his novel, but it is there to be drawn. That readers find it by an imaginative and creative act of synthesis is the true power of the novel. When one can laugh for joy even as one weeps in sorrow, one can survive and prevail. Such is the message of this novel, which, for all of its difficulty, is an extraordinary example of Faulkner's artistic genius.

Bibliography:

Howe, Irving. "*The Wild Palms.*" In *William Faulkner: A Critical Study*. 3d ed., rev. and expanded. Chicago: University of Chicago Press, 1975. Provides a valuable, but dated, introduction to Faulkner's life and work.

Mchaney, Thomas L. *William Faulkner's "The Wild Palms": A Study*. Jackson: University Press of Mississippi, 1975. Traces the origins of *The Wild Palms* and provides analyses of the themes and characters. Includes a chronology of the story.

Mortimer, Gail L. "The Ironies of Transcendent Love in Faulkner's *The Wild Palms.*" *The Faulkner Journal* 1, no. 2 (Spring, 1986): 30-42. In spite of the fact that this novel contains a love story, Faulkner's use of language and imagery denies transcendent love as being anything but illusory.

Privratsky, Kenneth L., ed. "*The Wild Palms": A Concordance to the Novel*. Ann Arbor, Mich.: Faulkner Concordance Advisory Board, 1983. The concordance lists all the words used in the novel. Examines Faulkner's patterns of word choice and usage.

Zender, Karl F. "Money and Matter in *Pylon* and *The Wild Palms.*" *The Faulkner Journal* 1, no. 2 (Spring, 1986): 17-29. Projects Faulkner's Hollywood experience onto *The Wild Palms* as a meditation on the theme of money. Reads the novel as a reflection on the plight of the artist in the world of wage labor and commercial art.

WILHELM MEISTER'S APPRENTICESHIP

Type of work: Novel
Author: Johann Wolfgang von Goethe (1749-1832)
Type of plot: Bildungsroman
Time of plot: Late eighteenth century
Locale: Germany
First published: Wilhelm Meisters Lehrjahre, 1795-1796 (English translation, 1824)

> *Principal characters:*
> WILHELM, a young poet and actor
> MARIANNE, an actress and Wilhelm's lover
> OLD BARBARA, Marianne's maid
> WERNER, Wilhelm's best friend
> PHILINE, an actress
> LAERTES, an actor and Philine's companion
> MIGNON, Wilhelm's adopted daughter
> LOTHARIO, a nobleman
> NATALIE, Wilhelm's wife
> FELIX, Wilhelm's son
> JARNO, an actor and teacher

The Story:

A naïve young man from a prosperous family, Wilhelm Meister was allowed to choose between a bourgeois, middle-class life in business and a bohemian, independent life as an artist. Rejecting his father's advice that he settle down and study business, Wilhelm decided to pursue a career in the theater as both an actor and a playwright. Wilhelm was distracted, though, by his love for Marianne, an actress, who, with her maid Old Barbara, conspired to keep Wilhelm in addition to a rich, older lover. One evening, Wilhelm observed his rival leaving Marianne's room. Heartbroken, Wilhelm finally took his father's advice and began a business trip that his father and Wilhelm's best friend, Werner, hoped would teach him about the world.

Before leaving, Wilhelm broke down weeping in front of Werner. He declared that he had no artistic talent and, parting with his Muses, he threw the bundles of his poetry into a fire. He then set off on his journey to collect the debts his father held on account. In his heart, however, Wilhelm remained "a restless, disorganized youth who wanted to live apart from the humdrum circumstances of middle-class life." In a small town not far from his father's estate, Wilhelm found himself drawn to an amateur theater production. Observing the director beat a young girl for refusing to play her part, Wilhelm rescued her, ousted the director, and began his association with the troupe. As the company's new director, Wilhelm took on the girl, Mignon, as his adopted daughter, and together they traveled the countryside staging plays and amusements for the local nobility.

Laertes and Philine, two of the best actors in the troupe, took Wilhelm and Mignon on sunny picnics where they flirted and joked. One afternoon, they were attacked by bandits in the forest. Wilhelm fought valiantly, drawing a pistol and shooting a bandit from his horse. Laertes joined him in the battle, but the other actors fled, and Wilhelm was badly wounded. Near death, he was saved by Mignon, who gathered up her long hair and used it to staunch the flow of blood from a bullet wound in his chest.

Taken to recuperate at the house of a nobleman, Wilhelm slowly regained his health. During his convalescence he engaged in many debates on the nature of art and poetry, especially on the topic of William Shakespeare. In the company of educated people, Wilhelm realized that the actors had taken advantage of him, that they had spent his money freely and failed to thank him, and that worst of all they had abandoned him and left him for dead.

Forced to see that his own talent was mediocre, Wilhelm again felt compelled to choose a life in business. His new friend, the nobleman Lothario, encouraged him to develop all of his talents, without focusing on any one in particular. To inform himself further, Wilhelm read the diary of a saintly woman and concluded that there were two sources of truth, internal and external. He had just come to this realization when Mignon, who had long endured poor health, suffered a heart attack and died in his arms. Wilhelm then encountered Old Barbara, who told him that his former lover Marianne had died, swearing her love for him.

At his host's castle, Wilhelm was surprised to meet his old friend Werner, who had traveled inot the countryside on business. Each quickly saw that the other had changed. Werner had become rich, but also sickly, stoop-shouldered, and bald, whereas Wilhelm, who had become relatively poor, had grown into a handsome, fine figure of a man.

Parting from Werner, Wilhelm continued his journey and discovered that he had a son by Marianne. The boy, Felix, came into Wilhelm's care and changed his father's outlook on life. Wilhelm realized that he lacked the talent to succeed in the theater. When he faced the truth about himself he discarded his illusions and ended his apprenticeship, realizing that "art is long, life is short." Having matured, he proposed to Natalie, a young woman his friends had selected as the perfect mate. She refused to give him an answer, but Wilhelm was distracted from his hopes and fears when Felix accidentally drank opium. Fearing for the child's life, Wilhelm summoned a doctor. Natalie swore that if Felix survived, she would accept Wilhelm's hand in marriage. Felix recovered, and Wilhelm joyfully accepted his new responsibilities as father and husband. Renouncing the artistic life, he took his friend Jarno's advice and began a happy domestic life, while Jarno set sail for the new world in America.

Critical Evaluation:

Considered the prototype of the *Bildungsroman*, a novel focusing on a character's coming of age, *Wilhelm Meister's Apprenticeship* is both a chronicle of the German theater and a sort of handbook for innocents. Wilhelm's many adventures and mishaps create the obstacles that force him to learn about the world around him. Johann Wolfgang von Goethe shows the reader that, even in the face of temptation and greed, and despite his naïveté, Wilhelm remains true to his principles and morals. When he is surrounded by scoundrels and abused and taken advantage of, Wilhelm never repays these injustices in kind. Instead, he simply accepts the foolishness and selfishness of others and moves on, hoping steadfastly to encounter not only his one true love but also a friend to whom he can entrust his heart.

The plot of the novel is episodic, without being tightly connected. Characters often engage in long philosophical debates, acting more as mouthpieces for the author than as independent personalities. The narrative is therefore uneven, especially during breaks in the action when characters function primarily as pawns or ciphers. Nevertheless, Goethe executes one rhetorical flourish after another and creates a lyrical prose that is symphonic in its scope and fluidity. Nor is this musicality lacking in content. The author sows the dialogue with so many epigrammatic seeds and nuggets of wisdom that he creates the impression that he might yet create a dazzling whole from the revealing bits of a cosmic puzzle. Instead, however, it becomes clear that the author considers it his task to deepen the mystery of life, not to explain it. Wilhelm learns that "the sum of our existence divided by reason never comes out exactly and there is always a wondrous remainder."

Goethe celebrates the end of Wilhelm's apprenticeship with an epiphany, a sudden burst of inner knowledge, for having passed through the gates of initiation Wilhelm witnesses the death of his adolescent self and the birth of his adult identity. In embracing his son Felix, Wilhelm continues the cycle of life. The irony is that in the acceptance of responsibility and parenthood Wilhelm finds freedom. Goethe's thesis is that people must accept the natural evolution of the self, and that they must not seek to retard their growth by indulging in nostalgia or by clinging to youthful dreams and illusions. On the contrary, individuals must embrace their lost innocence in order to grasp something new, in a process of accepting and letting go at the same time. Change must be cultivated, as it is the agent that propels the individual through a happy and productive life.

Goethe considered the movement forward more important than the success of the venture. The author thus poses a moral question, whether it is better to exist in a state of being or in one of becoming. Existence in a state of being may imply inertia and stagnation, whereas existence in a state of becoming may degenerate into counterproductive restlessness. The central theme of *Wilhelm Meister's Apprenticeship* lies in the search for a compromise not only between being and becoming but also between thought and action and, with regard to the influences that cause an individual to act, between the external—which is the world—and the internal, which is the heart. Life is thus seen as a series of judgment calls. Yet it is precisely this free will that Goethe celebrates, for the human ability to raise and improve its own consciousness reveals its connection to the divine. The ability to imagine God, and to reveal that conception with good works—that is to say through loyalty, devotion, and steadfastness—is to confirm God's existence. Particularly in the section entitled "Confessions of a Beautiful Soul," Goethe illustrates the distance between the mind of God and the human mind, while also suggesting that this gap may be bridged by faith and courage. Again, however, Goethe implies that the source of this faith must not come from outside the individual but must be the product of that individual's heart. The alternative is to accept "the monster that grows and feeds in every human breast, if some higher power does not preserve us."

Despite the strength of this section, it might be critically faulted for its form. The transition from a third-person, omniscient point of view, centered in Wilhelm, to the first-person confession is abrupt and jarring. This threatens the book's unity and raises the question whether the novel is about theatrical life or about a young man finding himself. As it happens, the author composed the novel during two different time periods separated by eight years—1786 and 1794—which may account for the shift in focus and for the feeling that the work is comprised of two halves that do not necessarily make a whole.

Wilhelm Meister's Apprenticeship remains an important novel about initiation. When Wilhelm accepts Felix as his son, he reaches the end of his quest for identity. He acknowledges what he has created and claims it for his own, rejecting the illusions foisted on him by his society and by his own idealism. Intellectually he has learned to separate the wheat from the chaff. He sees what he can and cannot do, and he accepts the difference. The ultimately pragmatic philosophy that emerges from the novel is that people should play to their strengths and avoid their weaknesses. Such intellectual honesty, however, can only be achieved through a brutal though not despairing candor with the self and with trusted friends. *Wilhelm Meister's Apprenticeship* is about the ongoing discovery of self and the continuing process of maturation and development—universal themes that secure Goethe's place and that of this novel.

David Johansson

Bibliography:

Brown, Jane K. *Goethe's Cyclical Narratives: "Die Unterhaltungen deutscher Ausgewander-ten" and "Wilhelm Meisters Wanderjahre."* Chapel Hill: University of North Carolina Press, 1975. Examines Goethe's use of episodic technique and cyclical narrative. Also presents a methodology that allows the reader to appreciate the contradictions and parody in Goethe's work.

Fairley, Barker. *A Study of Goethe.* Oxford, England: Clarendon Press, 1947. A noted Goethe scholar explores the life of the writer. Includes a discussion of the effect of German theater on *Wilhelm Meister's Apprenticeship.*

Leppmann, Wolfgang. *The German Image of Goethe.* Oxford, England: Clarendon Press, 1961. Explores Goethe's changing reputation within his own country, noting a gradual decline in popularity.

Maugham, W. Somerset. "The Three Novels of a Poet." In *Points of View.* London: Heinemann, 1958. Maugham argues that Goethe was a better poet than novelist. Maugham, who brings a creative as well as a critical faculty to bear on Goethe's work, examines poetic technique, including imagery and meter.

Pascal, Roy. "The Bildungsroman: Johann Wolfgang von Goethe." In *The German Novel: Studies.* Manchester, England: Manchester University Press, 1956. Considers the formal and stylistic features of *Wilhelm Meister's Apprenticeship.* Briefly discusses Goethe's career as a theater director in Weimar and its influence on his novels.

Reiss, Hans. *Goethe's Novels.* New York: St. Martin's Press, 1969. Critical discussion of *The Sorrows of Young Werther* (1774), *Wilhem Meister's Apprenticeship*, and *Elective Affinities* (1809). Examines Goethe's natural philosophy, the sociological aspects of his writings, and his influence on German theater.

WILHELM MEISTER'S TRAVELS

Type of work: Novel
Author: Johann Wolfgang von Goethe (1749-1832)
Type of plot: Philosophical
Time of plot: Early nineteenth century
Locale: Germany
First published: Wilhelm Meisters Wanderjahre: Oder, Die Entsagenden, 1821, 1829
  (English translation, 1882)

> *Principal characters:*
> WILHELM MEISTER, a Renunciant
> FELIX, his son
> HERSILIA, a girl admired by Felix
> HILARIA, a young girl
> LENARDO, Wilhelm's friend

The Story:

Wilhelm Meister was traveling on foot with his young son, Felix. As a consequence of his liberation from ordinary desire through the noble Lothario and the abbot, the once troubled Wilhelm had become a Renunciant. Under the terms of his pledge, he was to wander for years, never stopping in one place more than three days. His travels were intended to give him a final philosophical polish. Gone were the countinghouse and the stage; he was now undertaking a last purifying sacrifice.

While Felix played merrily on the mountainside, Wilhelm mused beside a steep path. Hearing voices, he turned to see his son with a group of children running downhill before a donkey driven by a holy-looking man. The beast carried a sweet-faced woman with a small baby. The adults smiled at Wilhelm, but the path was too steep for them to stop. When Wilhelm caught up with the party, the man invited him to visit his household, and his wife amiably seconded the invitation. It was decided that Felix should go on ahead with the family and Wilhelm would follow the next day, after he had retrieved his wallet, left high on the mountain.

When he arrived, Wilhelm was charmed to find the family living in a restored chapel. He was struck by the fact that the man's name was Joseph and his wife's was Mary; they did indeed seem a holy family. When he learned their story, Wilhelm was reverent.

Joseph's father had been a rent collector for an absentee landlord. Joseph had been promised that if he grew to be a steady man and a competent craftsman, he would succeed his father, but instead, he decided to be a woodworker. When he was sufficiently skilled, he began to restore the paneling in the old chapel. His best work was the reworking of an elaborate wood panel depicting the flight of the Holy Family into Egypt.

One day, as Joseph was wandering on the trail, he found a beautiful woman weeping beside the path. Her husband had been killed by robbers. Joseph, alarmed by the woman's distress and condition, took her to his home and summoned his mother. Soon the widow delivered a child. After a patient courtship, Joseph married the widow, Mary, and took her to live in the old chapel. Now he was the rent collector in his father's place and possessed a loving family.

While playing, Felix came upon a box of stones that had been given to Joseph by a scientist who was searching for minerals in that region. He learned that the geologist's name was

Montan, a name frequently used by his old friend Jarno. Wilhelm hoped to overtake the scientist in the course of his own wanderings. He and Felix started out, led by Fitz, a beggar boy who had been a playmate for Felix during the stay with the collector and his wife. On the way, they came to a barrier of fallen trees. While their guide was looking for another path, Felix wandered into a nearby cave and there found a small box, no larger than an octavo volume, rich-looking and decorated with gold. Wilhelm and his son decided to conceal the box among their belongings and to tell no one of its discovery for the time being.

A short time later, Fitz led them to the place where Montan was prospecting. As Wilhelm had expected, the scientist was Jarno, whom Wilhelm had known in his acting days, now a Renunciant geologist. They stayed with Jarno for three days, while the scientist tried to satisfy Felix's great curiosity about minerals and their properties.

The party left Jarno and started off to survey a natural phenomenon known as the Giant's Castle. Sending the pack animals around by road, the travelers followed a rugged path until they came in sight of a beautiful garden, separated from them by a yawning chasm. Fitz led them into an aqueduct which gave entrance to the garden. Suddenly they heard a shot. At the same time, two iron-grated doors began to close behind them. Fitz sprang backward and escaped, but Wilhelm and his son were trapped. Several armed men with torches appeared, and to them Wilhelm surrendered his only weapon, a knife. He told his son to have no fear, for there were pious mottoes carved on the walls leading to the castle to which their captors conducted them.

After spending the night in a well-appointed room, father and son breakfasted with the lively Hersilia and her older, more sedate sister Julietta. Felix was charmed with Hersilia, as was his father. Hersilia gave Wilhelm a romantic manuscript to read. The next day the eccentric uncle of the girls appeared and took them to lunch in a shooting lodge.

Finding himself in such agreeable and learned company, Wilhelm exerted himself to please. Hersilia accepted him as one of the family; to show her trust, she gave him a packet of letters to read, which told of her cousin Lenardo. Some years ago Lenardo had determined to set out on his travels. In order to get the necessary funds, his uncle had to collect all outstanding debts. While arranging his affairs, he dispossessed a tenant farmer with a beautiful daughter called the Nut-Brown Maid. Although the girl pleaded with Lenardo for mercy, she and her father were evicted. Now Lenardo wrote his aunt that he would not come home until he learned what had happened to the girl.

After reading the letters, Wilhelm took his son to visit the aunt, a wise woman called Makaria. In her castle Wilhelm met an astronomer who revealed to him many of the secrets of the stars. Advised by the savant, Wilhelm deposited the box Felix had found with an antiquarian until the key could be located.

At a distant castle, a major came to visit his sister. His intention was to consolidate the family fortunes by marrying his son Flavio to his sister's daughter Hilaria. To his surprise, Hilaria claimed to love him. So the major, after getting a valet to make him look younger, went to tell Flavio the news. He was heartened to learn that Flavio was in love with a widow.

One night, Flavio burst hysterically into his aunt's castle. The widow had repulsed him when he became too eager in his lovemaking. Flavio soon found solace in Hilaria's company. When the major returned, the atmosphere grew tense. The gloom lifted only after Hilaria's mother wrote for advice to Makaria, who advised the widow to tell the major that young Flavio and Hilaria had fallen in love. Then Hilaria and the pretty widow set out to travel to Italy.

In his wanderings, Wilhelm had come upon Lenardo, who begged his aid in learning what had become of the Nut-Brown Maid. When Wilhelm agreed to the quest, Felix was put in a school run by wise men who taught the dignity of labor and the beauty of art. Shortly after

Wilhelm left the school, he was able to send Lenardo word that the girl was now well-off and happy. The wandering nephew then returned to Makaria.

With an artist friend, Wilhelm traveled among the beautiful Italian lakes. This neighborhood was especially dear to him, for it was the home of his beloved Mignon, his foster daughter. The two men were lucky enough to meet Hilaria and the widow, but the ladies disappeared before any serious interests could develop.

Hersilia wrote to Wilhelm that she was keeping Felix's box, as the antiquarian had gone away, and that she also had a key to the chest. Returning to Germany, Wilhelm went to the school to get Felix. He was pleased to find him a well-grown young man with considerable artistic ability. Father and son, once more together after their long separation, began to visit their old friends.

They discovered that Hilaria and Flavio had married and that Flavio had become a prosperous merchant. Felix was greatly attracted to Hersilia. When he learned that she had both key and box, he persuaded her to let him try to open it. The key, however, was magnetic, and the halves came apart when he tried to turn the lock.

Felix tried to embrace Hersilia, and the girl pushed him away much harder than she had intended. Fearing she did not love him, Felix impetuously dashed away and was injured when he fell on the shore beside a stream. There Wilhelm found him unconscious. His old training in medicine proved valuable, however, and Wilhelm was able to bleed his son and restore him to consciousness.

Critical Evaluation:

Johann Wolfgang von Goethe was considered by many critics to be the greatest writer of his time. His output included works of poetry and plays, as well as works in the novel form. An innovator in each of the genres he mastered, Goethe experimented freely and dynamically with the novel. Indeed, in *Wilhelm Meister's Travels*—also known as *The Renunciants*—Goethe expanded the novel form to reach beyond the story of the individual to the story of society itself. At the onset of *Wilhelm Meister's Travels*, in a continuation of the story in *Wilhelm Meister's Apprenticeship*, a letter written by the protagonist sets the stage for the rest of the work. Wilhelm Meister writes, "My life is to become a restless wandering. Strange duties of the wanderer have I to fulfill, and peculiar trials to undergo." The novel concerns the main character's continuing pilgrimage toward an understanding of himself and the world.

Goethe was a master of the mosaic. Throughout *Wilhelm Meister's Travels*, Goethe successfully weaves several different narrative strands and thereby expanded the structure of the novel as it was then known. The early part of the nineteenth century was generally a time of growth and experimentation in the novel form, but Goethe reached far beyond anything then being done to create a highly complex narrative structure.

Throughout the work, Goethe interweaves soliloquies and dialogue, letters and observations, all of which demonstrate varying points of view on the nature of reality and knowledge, geology and art, and the practice of learning one's place in the world. Within this complex structure a narrator describes Wilhelm's travels. The letters that are inserted into the narrative structure— letters from Wilhelm to Natalia; from Lenardo to his aunt, from his aunt to Julietta; and from Julietta back to the aunt—show different temperaments and responses to stated events. Each letter works without a narrator or the interpretation the narrator provides. Through these shifting points of view on the same event it may be said that Goethe questions the validity of a singular point of view. In addition, the letters demonstrate the intimate connection between human lives.

Some of the letters in the narrative contain stories that could stand on their own as separate tales. Such is the case in one letter sent to Wilhelm, in which Hersilia, an admirer of Felix, relates a story that explores the context of Wilhelm's travels and thus weaves the story of Wilhelm Meister the individual into a larger social and cultural framework.

Interestingly, Hersilia orders Wilhelm to deduce whether the story she relates to him in her letter is true or fictitious. By doing so, she sets the whole act of storytelling on its head. Not only must Wilhelm Meister decide for himself the veracity of what he is told, but the reader, too, must question the validity of the plot. In this sense, Goethe transforms the reader into a pilgrim as well, who must sort through the available evidence of the journey to determine fact from fiction and perhaps eventually understand the present and the past.

To further complicate matters, the reader is also addressed by an "Editor," who comments on the difficulty of selecting and arranging the anecdotes, "more complex narratives," and poems that make up *Wilhelm Meister's Travels*. In his comment on the arduous process of selection, the Editor laments: "We still find ourselves in more than one way impeded, at this or that place threatened with one obstruction or another." Goethe has constructed *Wilhelm Meister's Travels* so that the reader experiences the sense of obstruction and diversion created by the complex narrative. The reader's reaction may parallel that of Wilhelm Meister when he encounters obstacles and diversions on his spiritual, moral, and psychological journey toward wisdom and understanding. Among other things, the protagonist journeys through castles, jostles with armed men, weaves his way through the lakes region, and wrestles with locked boxes to which he cannot find the key. Goethe has set up his novel in such a way that the reader takes a parallel journey of questions and discovery.

Beyond the experiment with form, *Wilhelm Meister's Travels* also provides a glimpse into the interrelation between human beings and their environment. The obstacles that Wilhelm Meister confronted during his pilgrimage had a profound effect on him, yet it was Goethe's belief that individuals, too, shape the society in which they live. Speculations on mathematics, astronomy, and geology are interspersed throughout the story, reflecting the importance of constantly questioning one's world. It can be said that part of the purpose behind the pilgrimage carried out by Goethe's protagonist is to determine his relationship to his age.

Wilhelm Meister's Travels was created during a time of great social, economic, and religious flux in Europe. Napoleon had instigated great political strife, which was followed by the restoration of the monarchy. Goethe, grown older, used *Wilhelm Meister's Travels* to look back at the ways in which the individual moves through society and at the eternal reshaping and changing of society itself.

"Critical Evaluation" by R. C. S.

Bibliography:

Boyle, Nicholas. *Goethe, the Poet and the Age*. Oxford, England: Clarendon Press, 1991. An exceptionally detailed study of Goethe's development as an artist. Discusses Goethe's novels and includes an extended analysis of the culture and times in which he lived and worked.

Dieckmann, Liselotte. *Johann Wolfgang von Goethe*. New York: Twayne, 1974. A lucid overview of Goethe's novels, plays, and poetry. An excellent introductory source. Contains interesting chapters on biography and autobiography and chapters focused on the novels, including *Wilhelm Meister's Travels*.

Emerson, Ralph Waldo. "Goethe: Or, The Writer." In *Representative Men: Seven Lectures*. Boston: Houghton Mifflin, 1876. A vivid, extremely keen assessment of Goethe's role as one of the legendary writers of his century. Of continuing relevance to later times. Discusses

Goethe in the context of American and European writers. Also discusses the merits of *Wilhelm Meister's Travels*.

Goethe, Johann Wolfgang von. *Goethe's Literary Essays*. Arranged by J. E. Spingarn. 1921. Reprint. New York: Frederick Ungar, 1964. Several essays place *Wilhelm Meister's Travels* in the context of Goethe's theories on the art of world literature. Contains Goethe's own thoughts on the development of fiction and art.

Lange, Victor, ed. *Goethe: A Collection of Critical Essays*. Englewood Cliffs, N.J.: Prentice-Hall, 1968. A representative selection of essays. Important essays on Goethe's craft of fiction shed light of the construction of *Wilhelm Meister's Travels* for the beginning reader. Includes a selected bibliography.

WILLIAM TELL

Type of work: Drama
Author: Friedrich Schiller (1759-1805)
Type of plot: Historical
Time of plot: Fifteenth century
Locale: Switzerland
First performed: 1804; first published, 1804 as *Wilhelm Tell* (English translation, 1841)

Principal characters:
WILLIAM TELL, a forester
WALTER, his son
WALTER FÜRST, William Tell's father-in-law
GESSLER, the governor of the Swiss Forest Cantons
WERNER, a nobleman
ULRICH, his nephew
BERTHA VON BRUNECK, a wealthy heiress

The Story:

A storm was rising on Lake Lucerne, and the ferryman was making his boat fast to the shore as Baumgarten rushed up, pursued by the soldiers of the tyrannous governor, Gessler. He implored the ferryman to take him across the lake to safety. First, however, the crowd asked why he was being pursued. Baumgarten told them that the Wolfshot, a nobleman who had been appointed seneschal of the castle, had come into his house and started taking liberties with his wife. She had escaped and run to her husband in the forest, whereupon Baumgarten had returned home and split the Wolfshot's skull with his ax. Now he had to flee the country.

The sympathies of the common people were with Baumgarten, and they begged the ferryman to take him across. The storm was almost upon them, however, and the ferryman was afraid. Then the hunter William Tell came up, the only man in the crowd with the courage to steer the boat in a tempest. When he heard Baumgarten's story, Tell unhesitatingly made preparations to take the fugitive across the lake. As they cast off, soldiers thundered up. When they saw their prey escaping, they took their revenge on the peasants, killing their sheep and burning their cottages.

The free Switzers were greatly troubled because the emperor of Austria had sent Gessler to rule as viceroy over the Forest Cantons. Gessler, a younger son of no fortune, was envious of the prosperity of these thrifty people and enraged by their calm and independent bearing. The Switzers held their lands directly in fief to the emperor, and the rights and duties of the viceroy were carefully limited. Hoping to break the proud spirit of the free people, Gessler placed a cap on a pole in a public place and required that each man bow to the cap.

Gessler's soldiers came to Henry of Halden, an upright farmer, and attempted to take from him his best team of oxen. Only when Arnold, his son, sprang on the men and struck them with his staff, did they release the oxen and leave. Arnold thought it best to go into hiding, but while he was away, the soldiers returned and tortured old Henry and put out his eyes. Arnold thereupon joined the malcontent Switzers against Gessler. Fürst became their leader, and it was agreed that ten men from the three cantons would meet and plan to overthrow the viceroy.

At the mansion of the nobleman Werner, the common people and their lord gathered for a morning cup of friendship. Old Werner was happy to drink with his men, but his nephew Ulrich refused, for he was drawn to the Austrian rulers and felt no bond with free Switzerland. Werner upbraided him for being a turncoat and accused him of turning to Austria because he was in love with the wealthy heiress Bertha von Bruneck.

The representatives of the people met at night in great secrecy. Some of the more fiery members were in favor of an immediate uprising, but the cooler heads followed Fürst and voted to wait until Christmas, when by tradition all the peasants would be present in the castle.

Ulrich at last approached Bertha and told her that he loved her. She, a true Switzer at heart, spurned him for his loyalty to Austria.

Tell and his sons happened to come near the hated cap. When Tell, more by accident than by design, paid no attention to the symbol of authority, he was arrested by two guards, who tried to bind him and lead him to prison. Although Fürst came and offered bail for his son-in-law, the law-abiding Tell submitted to his captors. He was being led away when Gessler himself rode by.

Gessler ordered an apple placed on Walter Tell's head and commanded William Tell to shoot it from his son's head. Tell protested in vain. Ulrich courageously defied Gessler and hotly opposed the tyrant's order, but Gessler was unmoved. In the confusion, Tell took out two arrows, fitted one to his crossbow, and neatly pierced the apple.

While the crowd rejoiced, Gessler asked Tell why he had taken out two arrows. Tell refused to answer until Gessler promised not to punish him no matter what the reply might be. Then Tell boldly declared that if he had missed the apple and hurt his son, he would have killed Gessler with the second arrow. Infuriated, Gessler ordered Tell led away to life imprisonment.

Tell was chained and put on a boat to take him to Gessler's castle; Gessler himself went along to gloat over his victim. Once again a terrible storm arose. Fearing for his own life, Gessler had Tell unbound and made him helmsman. Tell watched for his chance and steered the boat close to shore, then sprang to safety on a rocky ledge.

He came with his crossbow to a pass through which Gessler must travel if he escaped the fury of the storm. Under Tell's hiding place a poor woman and her children waited for Gessler. Her husband was in prison for a minor offense, and she intended to appeal to Gessler for clemency. At last, Gessler approached with his entourage. The woman blocked his way and appealed for mercy on behalf of her husband. Tell waited long enough to hear her plea denied, then he pierced the breast of the tyrant with a bolt from his crossbow. Dropping down on the road, Tell announced to the gathered people that he had killed Gessler; then he disappeared into the forest. Gessler lay in the road, with no friendly hand to pull the arrow from his bleeding heart. So died Switzerland's oppressor.

The people had hoped that Werner would lead them in their revolt, but he was on his deathbed. He died before he could pass on the leadership to Ulrich, but when his nephew arrived, the assembled peasants acknowledged him as their leader and found him to be a loyal Switzer after all, the more so as the Austrians had abducted Bertha. At last, the three cantons rose up against harsh Austrian rule.

At the height of the revolt, news came that the emperor himself had been assassinated. Duke John of Austria, his nephew, had struck down the emperor after being robbed of his estates. The Switzers despised the duke for the crime because they considered assassination for robbery unjust. When Duke John sought refuge with Tell, the forester was indignant, for he was a soldier for freedom, not a murderer. His natural humanity kept him from exposing John, however, and the duke left unharmed to seek a safer sanctuary in Italy.

Tell put away his crossbow for good when the announcement came that the count of Luxembourg had been elected emperor. The cantons settled down to peaceful days once more. Bertha gave her hand freely to Ulrich, as one proud Switzer to another.

Critical Evaluation:

Friedrich Schiller reports of his *William Tell* that he never planned to write it until after reading rumors that he was working on a drama on the subject of Tell, at which point he decided to look into the Swiss chronicles. There he found material that, he said, brought him to desperation: many plot threads, no cohesion of time or location, masses of characters, and nothing, aside from the apple shooting, that lent itself to dramatic presentation. Yet he sensed something classical, almost Homeric in the story. His imagination was captivated by the popular movement of the Swiss cantons, as well as by the paradoxical relationship between the group and the individual.

In his play, he wove together two separate events: the Rutli Oath, a community decision to act against their tyrant, and the Tell sequence, an individual's personal act. Schiller deliberately kept Tell out of the Rutli scene, allowing him no part in the plans of the community. These plans were in any case quite conservative, despite all the talk about freedom. The uprising the people sought was to be strictly regulated, coordinated, and free of personal, private acts. Tell, on the other hand, is a loner, a hunter, and an essentially unpolitical man. He has a deep sense of humanity, as exhibited in the first episode, but he keeps his distance from the community action. It is by Gessler's own provocation that he is drawn into the communal fight against tyranny. Yet his subsequent murder of Gessler is a private action, retribution for the insult and outrage he himself had suffered. That his act becomes the high point of the liberation of the Swiss cantons is ironic, and Tell's discomfort is evident. He renounces his crossbow, the means of his livelihood but also now a murder weapon. In the enigmatic scene with Duke John, who has just murdered the emperor, Tell is at first horrified; then, in a recognition of their common humanity and sinfulness, he aids John on his way to Rome to seek absolution from the pope. Tell remains behind, a hero to his people, but silent amid the jubilation.

Bibliography:

Garland, H. B. *Schiller*. Westport, Conn.: Greenwood Press, 1976. A well-written biography that includes interpretation of the major plays. Compares *William Tell* to the earlier works with regard to stage direction and setting. Discussion extends to criticism of the characters and plot.

Graham, Ilse. *Schiller's Drama: Talent and Integrity*. New York: Barnes & Noble Books, 1974. A serious study of Schiller. Gives a reading and explanation of *William Tell* with many quotes in German. Concentrates on symbolism and the character of William Tell as archetypal hero.

Sharpe, Lesley. *Friedrich Schiller: Drama, Thought and Politics*. Cambridge, England: Cambridge University Press, 1991. Extensive chronology, bibliography, notes, and index to Schiller's works. Studies the story from which Schiller borrowed and reinvented the dialogue for *William Tell*. Compares Schiller with Johann Wolfgang von Goethe.

Simons, John D. *Friedrich Schiller*. Boston: Twayne, 1981. Includes a discussion of Schiller's aesthetics and examinations of his poetry and dramatic works. Notes Schiller's research into the Swiss legend of William Tell and analyzes elements of the plot of his subsequent drama and its success as a monomyth.

Thomas, Calvin. *The Life and Works of Friedrich Schiller*. 1901. Reprint. New York: Ams Press, 1970. Discusses the works of Schiller in chronological order and in great detail. Explains Schiller's attention to local color and describes the public reception of *William Tell*. Analyzes the plot as well as several scenes and characters.

THE WIND IN THE WILLOWS

Type of work: Novel
Author: Kenneth Grahame (1859-1932)
Type of plot: Allegory
Time of plot: Early twentieth century
Locale: England
First published: 1908

> *Principal characters:*
> MOLE, an introvert
> WATER RAT, an extrovert
> TOAD, a playboy
> BADGER, a philosophical recluse

The Story:

Mole had spring fever, for he had been busy with his cleaning and repairing for too long. Because the new spring smells and the sight of budding green were everywhere about him, he could not resist them. Throwing aside his tools and mops, together with his ambition for cleaning, he left his little home under the ground and traveled up a lovely meadow. There he wandered through the grass and along the river. He had never seen a river before, and he was bewitched by its chuckling and glimmering in the sunlight.

As he watched, Mole saw a dark hole in the bank. From it protruded the bewhiskered face of Water Rat, who promptly invited Mole to visit him. Mole, of course, could not swim, and so Rat took his little boat and rowed across to get him. Such enchantment was almost too much for quiet Mole. As they glided across the gurgling water, he thought this the best day of his entire life. After a little accident, they reached Rat's house. There they packed a picnic basket and set out on a real excursion. They stayed carefully away from the Wild Wood, for fierce animals lived there. Badger kept his home there, but nobody would dare bother Badger.

As they floated down the river, Rat told Mole about other animals and about the Wide World. Rat had never seen the Wide World and never wanted to see it, and he warned Mole against it. It was no place for respectable animals. When they stopped for their picnic lunch, they were joined by Otter. Badger looked in on them but would not join them. Badger hated society. He liked people all right, but he hated society. Rat promised that they would meet Badger later, for Mole could learn much valuable knowledge from Badger.

After another accident, which was Mole's fault, the two new friends went to Rat's home and ate supper. Following the meal, Rat entertained Mole with many wonderful tales. It was a sleepy but happy Mole who was helped into bed by the kind Rat that night. From then on, the two remained friends. Rat taught Mole to swim and to row, to listen to the music of the running water, and to catch a little of the meaning of the song the wind sang as it whispered in the willows.

One day, the two went to visit Toad at Toad Hall. It was the most beautiful residence in animal land, for Toad was wealthy. He was also a playboy. Every new fad that came along attracted him. When Rat and Mole arrived, Toad was busy getting together a gypsy caravan. He persuaded the others to join him on the open road. Although the venture was against Rat's better judgment, poor Mole was so desirous of joining Toad that Rat finally submitted.

Their adventure was short-lived. When the wagon was upset by a racing motorcar, Rat was so furious that he wanted to prosecute the owners of the car to the limit. Toad had other ideas;

he must have the biggest, fastest, gaudiest car that money could buy.

Spring, summer, and fall passed—days filled with pleasure for Mole and Rat. Then, one cold winter day, Mole went out alone and got lost. He found himself in the Wild Wood and was terrified by the strange noises and evil faces he saw around him. Rat finally found him, but before they could reach Rat's home, snow began to fall. By luck, they stumbled upon Badger's home, where the old philosopher welcomed them, although he hated being disturbed from his winter's sleep. Badger asked for news of the other animals, particularly of Toad. He was not surprised to learn that Toad had been in trouble constantly because of his motorcars. There had been seven crashes and seven new cars. He had been hospitalized three times and had paid innumerable fines. Badger promised that when the proper time came, he would attend to Toad.

When their visit was over, Badger led Rat and Mole through a labyrinth of tunnels and underground passages until they reached the far edge of the Wild Wood. There he said good-bye, and the two animals scampered for home. Not long afterward, in December, Mole felt a great desire to return to his own house that he had left on that spring day so long ago. Rat understood the feeling and gladly went with Mole to find his old home. It was a shabby place, not at all as fine as Toad Hall or Rat's house, but Rat was polite about it and praised it to Mole. On their first night there, they gave a party for the field mice; Mole then rolled into bed and slept the sleep of weary travelers.

Early the next summer, Badger turned up and said that now he was ready to deal with Toad. Taking Mole and Rat with him, he went to Toad Hall and tried to persuade Toad to give up his cars and his reckless ways. Since only force could accomplish that end, they locked Toad in his room until he should come to his senses. Toad, however, slipped out of the window and stole a car. He was arrested, tried, and sentenced to prison for twenty years. There Toad had ample time to think about his foolish ways, but he could not be restrained for long. Bribing the jailer's daughter, he escaped in the disguise of a washerwoman.

Finally, Mole learned the true meaning of the wind's song in the trees. One evening, when birds and insects were still, Mole suddenly felt the awe that brought peace and contentment. He felt himself in the presence of him who brought life and death. There was not terror, only peace. Then Mole and Rat really saw him, his horns gleaming and his eyes smiling. The mood was over soon, and with its passing came complete forgetfulness. While the wind sang gently on through the willows, Mole and Rat felt only as if they had had an unremembered dream.

That fall Rat, while out walking, met Sea Rat, a seafarer who told wonderful tales of adventure throughout the Wide World. Rat had a dreamy look in his eyes as Sea Rat painted his pictures. It was all Mole could do to remind Rat of the fearsome things he had said about the Wide World. The spell, however, was broken at last, and Rat settled down again, contented with his narrow world.

Meanwhile, Toad's escape was almost ruined by his conceit and his carelessness. As he was about to be caught again, Rat rescued him and took him home. There Rat told Toad that the weasels and stoats had taken over Toad Hall while Toad was in prison. Badger had a plan to recover Toad Hall. Through a tunnel known only to Badger, the four friends sneaked up on the intruders and captured Toad Hall again for its rightful owner. Toad, of course, took all the credit.

The four continued to live in joy and contentment. Unafraid, they walked in the Wild Wood, for the weasels had learned their lesson, and they heard the wind whispering its gentle song.

Critical Evaluation:

Kenneth Grahame wrote his fantasy-allegories, including *The Wind in the Willows*, while employed as Secretary of the Bank of England. His animal characters belong to the same world in which human beings live; the same foibles and excesses, the same motives and loyalties possess them. Nevertheless, it is an optimist's world as well, where hope exists and where the visionary experience reveals "The Friend and the Helper."

Whether or not *The Wind in the Willows* is a children's book is a moot question. Mole's discoveries parallel a child's explorations in the world. The story, however, has wider appeal, for Mole learns, as all human beings must, to live in the larger world outside his home. When he returns to the familiar scents and the simple welcome of his home, Mole realizes that, although it is an important part of his life, home is no longer his entire life. He returns to the world of sunlight and further discoveries. Together with his friends—Rat, Badger, and Toad— he learns to live in the world they call the "Wild Wood."

The theme of escape, therefore, is quite important in the novel. Mole desires to escape from the boredom of maintaining his home and his everyday existence; Badger's escape is from Society. Although he does not succumb, Rat is strongly intrigued by the stories of the Wide World told by Sea Rat, and Toad desires to elude every trace of responsibility to the rest of the world. Children's story or not, Grahame's book contains a certain amount of didacticism. Animals in the story, especially Rat, live according to a codified standard of existence. In this standard, the reader finds an implied but not explicit correspondence between the codes of conduct in the story and those normally taught to children. The reader is encouraged to reach for one's potential but not to exceed it—a difficult concept to explain to adults, let alone children. Nevertheless, maturity emerges here as the ability to recognize oneself realistically.

Grahame combines gentle satire with a keen understanding of the psychological realities that lie behind his characters' actions. Rat is the cautious judgmental teacher; Badger, the philosopher who hates society but likes people; and Toad, the incorrigible playboy, conceited, careless, and always in trouble. Along with Mole, the four represent an example of true friendship. By banding together, they retake Toad Hall from the weasels and restore the place to order with clean bed linens and fresh bars of soap.

The meaning of the song of the wind in the willows is revealed only to Rat and Mole. Badger survives through his philosophical stance, Toad with his indomitable will to have fun. Rat and Mole, however, need a vision. Like modern-day Everymen, Rat and Mole are allowed to see the pantheistic "Friend and the Helper," the horned, hook-nosed creature who plays panpipes at dawn and smiles benevolently through his beard. The vision is a moment when Rat and Mole fear neither death nor life, and, as they drop into the sleep of forgetfulness, their faces keep a blissful smile of peace.

Bibliography:
Carpenter, Humphrey. "The Wind in the Willows." In *Secret Gardens: A Study of the Golden Age of Children's Literature*. Boston: Houghton Mifflin, 1985. Carpenter, coauthor of *The Oxford Companion to Children's Literature*, concludes that, of all the subjects in his study, only Grahame managed to create a utopian world. For Carpenter, it is the level at which *The Wind in the Willows* explores the artistic imagination that gives it coherence.
Chalmers, Patrick R. *Kenneth Grahame: Life, Letters, and Unpublished Work*. London: Methuen, 1933. This biography, appearing a year after Grahame's death, sentimentalizes the genesis of *The Wind in the Willows*. Valuable in its extracts from Grahame's letters to his son documenting the development of the story, and from correspondence between Grahame and his readers and publishers.
Green, Peter. *Kenneth Grahame 1859-1932: A Study of His Life, Work, and Times*. London: John Murray, 1959. Considered a groundbreaking study. Presents as in-depth analysis of the

psychological undercurrents, social context, literary sources, and creative method that produced *The Wind in the Willows*.

Kuznets, Lois R. *Kenneth Grahame*. Boston: Twayne, 1987. Cogently discusses the work's thematic and formal complexity, from its mock-epic structure and density of style to its archetypal associations. Surveys modern evaluations and adaptations.

Sale, Roger. "Kenneth Grahame." In *Fairy Tales and After: From Snow White to E. B. White*. Cambridge, Mass.: Harvard University Press, 1978. Examines *The Wind in the Willows* as a classic of children's literature. Sale argues that the book, reflecting Grahame's own anxieties, offers reassurance in the face of the demands of adult life.

WIND, SAND AND STARS

Type of work: Novel
Author: Antoine de Saint-Exupéry (1900-1944)
Type of plot: Autobiographical
Time of plot: 1920's and 1930's
Locale: North Africa, South America, and Spain
First published: Terre des hommes, 1939 (English translation, 1939)

> *Principal characters:*
> ANTOINE DE SAINT-EXUPÉRY
> PRÉVOT, a navigator
> HENRI GUILLAUMET, a friend, and
> MERMOZ,
> NÉRI,
> DELY,
> RIGUELLE, fellow pilots
> EL MAMMOUN, a Moor at the Dakar-Juby division base
> LEFEBVRE and
> ABRI, mechanics

In 1926, Antoine de Saint-Exupéry embarked on a career as an airline pilot for the aviation company that eventually became Air France. His memories of adventurous and fulfilling years as a pilot and, to a lesser degree, his experiences as a newspaper reporter at the front during the Spanish Civil War constitute the raw material for the varied and isolated episodes of this work. It is a book that barely qualifies as a novel, for there is no continuity of action and no real attempt to disguise the autobiographical orientation of the book. Yet the brilliance of the imagery, the epic proportions that the narration assumes at times, and, above all, the unity of meaning that fuses together the episodes transform the work beyond pure autobiography.

Despite the legendary aspect of the pilot's exploits, the tone of the novel is one of sobriety and modesty. For Saint-Exupéry, courage in its highest conception is born out of a sense of responsibility. When courage becomes temerity, tempting death for the sake of vanity and excitement, it serves no moral purpose and therefore should be condemned. For this reason, toreadors do not elicit the admiration of the narrator of *Wind, Sand and Stars.* Toreadors seek primarily the glory of one Sunday afternoon, whereas the sacrifices of the pilots who carry the mail are performed out of a feeling of chosen and accepted duty. Those who carry out a dangerous mission conscientiously, quietly, and to its final conclusion discover a kind of spiritual truth; they free themselves of earthly and selfish concerns and discover that what really animates them are the bonds that connect them to other human beings.

Lucid gravity in the face of imminent death and a profound sense of duty are vividly illustrated by the harrowing experience of Henri Guillaumet, the narrator's close friend and fellow pilot. When he crashed in the Chilean Andes in mid-winter of 1930, he took shelter from a blinding snowstorm and remained under his cockpit for two days and two nights. On the third day, he set out in temperatures far below zero. He was obliged to hack out steps in steep ice walls with his boots, and his feet soon became swollen and bleeding from frostbite. On the third day he fell from exhaustion many times. At last, he no longer tried to get up. Then he remembered that when a man disappears without a trace, his death is not declared legal for four years and his wife cannot receive the pension. He decided to prop his body up against a rock so that it would be found when the snows melted. Once on his feet again, however, he continued on for three more days, and was eventually rescued by a peasant woman. For Saint-Exupéry, Guillaumet's grandeur resided in his refusal to discuss his act in terms of courage; his determination was born of the realization that he held in his hands the fate of his wife and comrades and that he was still responsible for the mail that had gone down in the plane. The greatness of the man was in his disinterestedness.

Through the act of flying, Saint-Exupéry was able to perceive another basic verity that he illustrates concretely in his work: The obstacles that natural elements place in the way of human beings offer them the means to discover themselves. In measuring himself against the forces of nature—the mountains, the snowstorm, the cyclone, the desert—Saint-Exupéry the pilot finds himself face-to-face with the fundamental problems of his relationship to the earth and to death. Like farmers who use their plow to struggle against the soil, aviators had a tool that put them in contact with the natural elements: their airplane.

In 1936, the author's plane took him on an adventure that led to certain self-discoveries. It is these that he recounts vividly in *Wind, Sand and Stars*. On the flight from Paris to Saigon, he and his navigator crashed in the Egyptian desert. They made a march of three days in the torrid heat, covering about one hundred twenty-five miles, and had only a little more than a pint of liquid between them. Yet the sterility of the desert and the proximity of death were spiritually rewarding. The smallest signs of life—the tracks of a desert fox, for example—prompted feelings of appreciation and gratitude for the pleasures that existence offers. The imminence of death led not to panic but to a detached sense of self-fulfillment. Because of his tool, the plane, and his combat with nature, the pilot felt himself rich with treasures that cannot be judged by material standards.

The plane becomes for this "poet of the air" a way of annihilating time and space in order to link human beings of all nations and races. Pilots themselves profit enormously from the opportunity to deepen their knowledge of humanness. Writing at a time when people were obsessed with the performance of machines, Saint-Exupéry stressed above all the plane's capacity for surmounting the natural barriers that separate human beings. At the beginning of his career, the author spent a great deal of time among the refractory Moorish tribes in the western Sahara. In charge of a refueling station in this almost uninhabited part of the world, he succeeded in gaining the esteem of these nomads and was eventually regarded by them as a kind of sage. They were struggling to preserve their freedom, and in this book, Saint-Exupéry evokes the memory of one of his friends, el Mammoun, who could not bear the degradation of being a vassal of another people. Honored and trusted by white officers, he revolted against them one day during an excursion into the desert, massacred them, and fled into free territory. This Moor had suddenly realized that he was betraying his tribe, his religion, and his past as a famous warrior by submitting to Christians who had encroached on his people. Contact with this desert chieftain permitted Saint-Exupéry to develop one of the most important tenets of his code of ethics: All people seek a climate and terrain favorable to their self-fulfillment, and each individual must acquire tolerance and sympathy for each other individual's particular truth.

In Argentina, the narrator's plane took him for a brief moment into the mysterious domain of the human soul. After landing in a field near Concordia, the pilot was taken into a strange house that, like a massive citadel, seemed to want to keep all of its secrets. The two girls who lived there assessed the stranger to determine whether he merited acceptance into their intimate world. At dinner, the aviator heard a noise under the table and was informed that snakes had made a nest there. The girls awaited his reaction. He smiled, and was admitted. As he notes, these two young girls seemed to possess a universal quality. The plane opens new horizons to the pilots and raises the veil of mystery that surrounds people who differ from them.

The first step on the road to this humanism is the willingness to give of the self. In the closing pages of *Wind, Sand and Stars*, a Spanish soldier who is about to take part in a suicidal attack is presented as another living incarnation of the quintessence of Saint-Exupéry's thought. This soldier who smiles on the eve of battle has consented to sacrifice his life for a goal situated completely outside his own selfish interests. He has given up a comfortable existence in Barcelona because he sensed intuitively that a struggle accepted in common with other men—the esprit de corps that motivated the pilots of the airmail service—is a condition of inner liberation. The ideologies in conflict in the Spanish Civil War hold no interest for this soldier; selfless action and duty inspire in him a love infinitely more elevated and satisfying than he had ever known before.

Bibliography:
Cate, Curtis. *Antoine de Saint-Exupéry*. New York: Putnam, 1970. Contains many informative details and is well written. Portrays Saint-Exupéry as an eccentric figure. This voluminous work serves as an excellent starting place.
Galantière, Lewis. "Antoine de Saint-Exupéry." *Atlantic Monthly* 179, no. 4 (April, 1947): 133-141. Galantière, who translated *Wind, Sand and Stars*, discusses such aesthetic aspects of Saint-Exupéry's writing as his philosophy of art and the influences on his development.
Migeo, Marcel. *Saint-Exupéry*. Paris: Flammarion, 1958. An interesting, reliable account of Saint-Exupéry's life by someone who knew Saint-Exupéry during his military service. Migeo is mainly concerned with Saint-Exupéry's personal life, but he also examines the role the author's experiences as a pilot in the French military played in forming his theories of art.
Peyre, Henre. "The French Novel at Mid-century." *New Republic* 129, no. 6 (September 7, 1953): 16-17. Useful for a literary analysis of Saint-Exupéry's work. Provides a critical evaluation of Saint-Exupéry's novels and places the author in the tradition of contemporary French novels.
Robinson, Joy D. Marie. *Antoine de Saint-Exupéry*. Boston: Twayne, 1984. Explores the philosophies and themes that underlie all Saint-Exupéry's works. The study is enriched by the extensive use of biographical material. Includes a chronology and a selected bibliography of English and French sources. Essential for any literary discussion of Saint-Exupéry.

WINESBURG, OHIO
A Group of Tales of Ohio Small Town Life

Type of work: Novel
Author: Sherwood Anderson (1876-1941)
Type of plot: Psychological realism
Time of plot: Late nineteenth century
Locale: Winesburg, Ohio
First published: 1919

Principal characters:
> GEORGE WILLARD, a young reporter
> ELIZABETH WILLARD, his mother
> DR. REEFY, Elizabeth's confidant
> HELEN WHITE, George's friend
> KATE SWIFT, George's former teacher
> THE REVEREND CURTIS HARTMAN, Kate's unknown admirer
> WING BIDDLEBAUM, a berry picker

The Story:

Young George Willard was the only child of Elizabeth and Tom Willard. His father, a dull, conventional, insensitive man, owned the local hotel. His mother had once been a popular young belle. She had never loved Tom Willard, but the young married women of the town seemed to her so happy, so satisfied, that she had married him in the hope that marriage would somehow change her own life for the better. Before long, she realized that she was caught in the dull life of Winesburg, her dreams turned to drab realities by her life with Tom Willard.

The only person who ever understood her was Dr. Reefy. Only in his small, untidy office did she feel free; only there did she achieve some measure of self-expression. Their relationship, doomed from the start, was nevertheless beautiful, a meeting of two lonely and sensitive people. Dr. Reefy, too, had his sorrows. Once, years ago, a young girl, pregnant and unmarried, had come to his office, and shortly afterward, he had married her. The following spring she had died, and from then on, Dr. Reefy went around making little paper pills and stuffing his pockets with them. On the pieces of paper he had scribbled his thoughts about the beauty and strangeness of life.

Through her son George, Elizabeth Willard hoped to express herself; she saw in him the fulfillment of her own hopes and desires. More than anything, she feared that George would settle down in Winesburg. When she learned that he wanted to be a writer, she was glad. Unknown to her husband, she had put away money enough to give her son a start; but before she could realize her ambition, Elizabeth Willard died. Lying on her bed, she did not seem dead to either George or Dr. Reefy. To both, she was extremely beautiful. To George, she did not seem like his mother at all. To Dr. Reefy, she was the woman he had loved, now the symbol of another lost illusion.

Many people of the town sought out George Willard; they told him of their lives, of their compulsions, of their failures. Old Wing Biddlebaum, the berry picker, had been a schoolteacher years before. He had loved the boys in his charge, and he had been, in fact, one of those few teachers who understood young people. One of his pupils, however, having conceived a strong affection for his teacher, had accused him of homosexuality. Wing Biddlebaum, although innocent, had been driven out of town. In Winesburg, he became the best berry picker in the region, but always the same hands that earned his livelihood were a source of wonder and fear to him. When George Willard encountered him in the berry field, Wing's hands went forward as if to caress the youth; but a wave of horror swept over him, and he hurriedly thrust them into his pockets. To George, also, Wing's hands seemed odd, mysterious.

Kate Swift, once George's teacher, saw in him a future writer. She tried to tell him what writing was, what it meant. George did not understand exactly, but he understood that Kate was speaking, not as his teacher, but as a woman. One night, in her house, she embraced him, for George was now a young man with whom she had fallen in love. On another night, when all of Winesburg seemed asleep, she went to his room, but just as she was on the point of yielding to him, she struck him and ran away, leaving George lonely and frustrated.

Kate lived across the street from the Presbyterian church. The pastor, Reverend Curtis Hartman, accidentally had learned that he could see into Kate's room from his study in the bell tower of the church. Night after night, he looked through the window at Kate in her bed. He wanted at first to prove his faith, but his flesh was weak. One night, the same night Kate had fled from George Willard, he saw her come into her room. He watched her. Naked, she threw herself on the bed and furiously pounded the pillows. Then she arose, knelt, and began to pray. With a cry, the minister got up from his chair, swept the Bible to the floor, smashed the glass in the window, and dashed out into the darkness. Running to the newspaper office, he burst in upon George. Wild-eyed, his fist dripping blood, he told the astonished young man that God had appeared to him in the person of a naked woman, that Kate Swift was the instrument of the Almighty, and that he was saved.

Besides Kate Swift, there were other women in George's life. There was Helen White, the banker's daughter. One night, George and Helen went out together. At first, they laughed and kissed, but then a strange new maturity overcame them and kept them apart. Louise Trunnion, a farm girl, wrote to George, saying that she was his if he wanted her. After dark, he went out to the farm, and they went for a walk. There, in a berry field, George Willard enjoyed the love that Helen White had refused him.

Like Louise Trunnion, Louise Bentley also wanted love. Before going to live in Winesburg, Louise had lived on a farm, forgotten and unloved by a greedy, fanatical father who had desired a son instead of a daughter. In Winesburg, she lived with the Hardy family while she went to school. She was a good student, praised by her teachers, but she was resented by the two Hardy girls, who believed that Louise was always showing off. More than ever, she wanted someone to love. One day, she sent young John Hardy a note, and a few weeks later, she gave herself to him. When it became clear that she was pregnant, Louise and John were married.

John reproached her for cruelty toward her son David. She would not nurse her child, and for long periods of time, she would ignore him. Since she had never really loved her husband, nor had he loved her, the marriage was not a happy one. At last, she and John separated, and shortly afterward, her father took young David to live with him on the farm.

Old Jesse Bentley was convinced that God had manifested himself in his grandchild, that the young David, like the biblical hero, would be a savior, the conqueror of the Philistines who owned the land Jesse Bentley wanted for himself. One day the old man took the boy into the fields with him. Young David had brought along a little lamb, and the grandfather prepared to offer the animal as a sacrifice to the Almighty. The youngster, terrified, struck his grandfather and ran away, never to return to Winesburg.

The time came when George Willard had to choose between staying in Winesburg and starting out on his career as a writer. Shortly after his mother's death, George got up early one morning and walked to the railroad station. There, with the postmistress' expression of good luck in his ears, he boarded the train and left Winesburg behind him.

Critical Evaluation:

Winesburg, Ohio has the stature of a modern classic. It is at once beautiful and tragic, realistic and poetic. Without being a novel in the usual sense of the word, the connected stories have the full range and emotional impact of a novel. In simple, though highly skillful and powerful language, Sherwood Anderson tells the story of a small town and the lonely, frustrated people who live there. Although regional in its setting and characters, the book is also intensely American. No one since Anderson has succeeded in interpreting the inner compulsions and loneliness of the national psyche with the same degree of accuracy and emotional impact.

Using young George Willard as protagonist and observer, Anderson creates his probing psychological portrait of small-town America. Although his characters outwardly seem dull and commonplace, Anderson is acutely tuned to the tensions between their psychological and emotional needs and the restrictions placed upon their lives by the small-town atmosphere of Winesburg. Although not methodically psychoanalytical, Anderson's work probes deeply into the psychological lives of the characters to discover the emotional wounds that have been inflicted by the Puritan attitudes of the midwestern village. Anderson may not have been directly influenced by Sigmund Freud or Carl Jung, but his interests clearly parallel the interest in psychology among American intellectuals during the first quarter of the twentieth century. In this respect, Anderson can legitimately be called America's first psychological novelist.

Anderson believed the traditional forms of the novel were too restrictive and formal to adapt well to his American subject matter, so *Winesburg, Ohio* represents in part an experiment in form. Rather than unifying his work through a plot in the usual sense, Anderson uses patterns of imagery, tone, character, and theme to achieve a sense of wholeness. It is, however, George Willard's narrative voice and presence as either observer or protagonist in the stories that ultimately unify them. As a small-town reporter, Willard can credibly serve as a confidant for his townspeople. Also, he is a kind of professional observer recording the surface lives of his people for the newspaper. At the same time, readers see him as the budding artist who is interested in discovering the deeper and more meaningful truths of peoples' lives than those seen at the surface. Eventually, George must make his choice as to which of these roles he will elect, and his function as the central consciousness of the book is vital to its aesthetic success.

Winesburg, Ohio also follows the classic pattern of the *Bildungsroman*, or novel about reaching maturity, as it traces George Willard's growth from adolescence to maturity. Central to this aspect of the novel is George's relationship with his mother, whose death eventually frees him to escape from Winesburg. Mrs. Willard is the first person to see, in George's ambition to write, a potential release for her own inarticulate suffering, so she encourages his ambition partly to fill her own needs. As George comes into contact with other characters in the novel, they too see in him a way to make their voices heard, so they tell him their stories so he might write them down.

Part of George's growing maturity results from the understanding he finds as a result of his willingness to listen, but this passive development is paralleled by more overt experience. In particular, sexual initiation is an essential part of George's learning and growth, as is his coming to understand something of the nature of love in its various aspects. Through this combination of active and passive experiences, George eventually comes to the realization that isolation is an essential part of the human condition. People, George realizes in the sketch called "Sophistication," must learn to live with the limited relationships possible in a world that isolates them, and they must develop the strength not to be destroyed by loneliness. This knowledge gives George the maturity he needs to break with Winesburg and face the future as an adult and an artist. In "Departure," the final sketch, he goes toward that responsibility.

Anderson's introduction to *Winesburg, Ohio*, called "The Book of the Grotesques," suggests yet another way in which this work is unified. Conceived as a whole within which the sketches and stories are pulled together by the idea of the grotesques, the work can be seen as a group of stories connected by a central thematic concern. Anderson defined his grotesques as people who had seized upon some aspect of the truth which so dominates their lives as to distort their entire beings. This definition, however, only loosely fits the characters actually encountered in the novel. Rather, the failure in some way of emotional life seems to account for the twists of character which lead Winesburg's citizens to their universal sense of failure and isolation. In spite of apparent differences, virtually all of Anderson's figures suffer from a deep sense of failure—frequently of material failure as well as emotional—and from a frustrating inability to express their pain and rage in a meaningful way. Essentially, they are emotional cripples who must turn to George Willard in search of a voice to articulate their suffering.

Paralleling that level of *Winesburg, Ohio* which is concerned with individual psychology is a general reaction against the American small town and its atmosphere of Puritanical repression. Although Anderson is not without some nostalgia for the village life that was already passing from the American scene when *Winesburg, Ohio* was published in 1919, he does not allow his sentiment to stand in the way of a powerful condemnation of the cultural and spiritual sterility characteristic of American village life. While other writers were mourning the passing of the nation's innocent youth by sentimentalizing the small agrarian community, Anderson reveals its dark underside of destroyed lives, thwarted ambitions, and crippled souls—all of which resulted in part from the repressive atmosphere of towns like Winesburg. Thus, while *Winesburg, Ohio* marks the end of an era of agrarian order in America, it raises the possibility that an innocent past was less of a paradise than the sentimentalist would have one believe.

Studies of the modern American novel tradition often begin with *Winesburg, Ohio* which, by its pioneering of new techniques, introduction of new subject matter, and development of new attitudes and ideas as well as a new frankness, changed the course of American literary history. In addition, Anderson's generous help to such younger writers as Ernest Hemingway and William Faulkner, who would continue to shape the course of the American novel, justifies his position as the father of the modern American novel.

"Critical Evaluation" by William E. Grant

Bibliography:
Burbank, Rex. *Sherwood Anderson*. Boston: Twayne, 1964. This accessible study of Anderson's life and work provides a fine introduction to his first novel.
Crowley, John W., ed. *New Essays on Winesburg, Ohio*. New York: Cambridge University Press, 1990. Presents a variety of critical points of view and provides a forum of interpretative methods about *Winesburg, Ohio*.
Dewey, Joseph. "No God in the Sky and No God in Myself: 'Godliness' and Anderson's *Winesburg*." *Modern Fiction Studies* 35, no. 2 (Summer, 1989): 251-259. Dewey's essay searches the novel for its religious implications by focusing on the character of Jessie Bentley and shows how George Willard, as an artist, reshapes her search for spiritual communion.
Reist, John S., Jr. "An Ellipse Becomes a Circle: The Developing Unity of *Winesburg, Ohio*." *CEA Critic* 55, No. 3 (Spring-Summer, 1993): 26-38. This general study highlights the way

the reader's experience can grow through a close examination of the text.

Rigsbee, Sally Adair. "The Feminine in *Winesburg, Ohio.*" *Studies in American Fiction* 9, no. 2 (Autumn, 1981): 233-244. Argues that the meaning given to the women characters in *Winesburg, Ohio* provides the novel with an important source of its artistic unity.

White, Ray Lewis. *Winesburg, Ohio: An Exploration.* Boston: Twayne, 1990. This book-length study examines the novel's historical context, the general importance of the work, and its critical reception. Provides a close reading of the text and a selected bibliography.

THE WINGS OF THE DOVE

Type of work: Novel
Author: Henry James (1843-1916)
Type of plot: Psychological realism
Time of plot: c. 1900
Locale: London and Venice
First published: 1902

Principal characters:
>MILLY THEALE, a wealthy American girl
>MRS. SUSAN SHEPHERD STRINGHAM, an American friend of Milly Theale
>MRS. MAUD LOWDER, an English friend of Mrs. Stringham
>KATE CROY, Mrs. Lowder's niece
>MERTON DENSHER, Kate Croy's fiancé
>LORD MARK, another suitor for Kate Croy's hand
>SIR LUKE STRETT, an eminent British doctor

The Story:

Kate Croy was dependent on her aunt, Mrs. Lowder, because Kate's own father was a ne'er-do-well. Mrs. Lowder had great plans for her niece and encouraged Lord Mark as a suitor for Kate's hand. Kate's own mind was set on a young reporter, Merton Densher, who worked for one of the London papers. Mrs. Lowder liked Densher and even invited him to her home, but she did not want him to marry her niece, for he had no apparent prospects of money or a place in society. Mrs. Lowder breathed more easily when she learned that the young man was being sent by his newspaper to the United States to write a series of articles on life there.

While he was in New York, Densher made the acquaintance of a pretty young American, Milly Theale, who had recently inherited a large fortune through the death of her parents. A few weeks later, Milly Theale asked a Boston friend, Mrs. Susan Stringham, who was a widow and a writer, to go with her to Europe. They took passage on a liner and arrived in Italy, from where they traveled up the Italian peninsula and into Switzerland. Milly was restless, though, and soon decided that she would like to go to London.

Once they had arrived in England, Mrs. Stringham sent word to Mrs. Lowder, the only acquaintance she had in that country from her school days many years before. Mrs. Stringham and Milly Theale immediately became familiar callers at Mrs. Lowder's home. Because of her beauty, money, and attractive personality, Milly was a great success in London society. Lord Mark became infatuated with her, and Milly and Kate Croy became fast friends.

Aware that she was ill, Milly went to see Sir Luke Strett, an eminent surgeon, who informed her that there was nothing surgery or medicine could do to save her; he advised her to make the best of the time she had left. Although Kate Croy, Mrs. Lowder, and Mrs. Stringham knew that she had only a few months to live, Milly requested them not to mention it to others. She intended to enjoy herself as much as possible.

Great friends as Kate Croy and Milly Theale were, they had never discussed their mutual acquaintance, Merton Densher. One day, while walking in the National Art Galleries, Milly saw him and Kate together. Kate and Densher enlisted the aid of Mrs. Stringham and Milly to further their courtship. Milly, herself a little in love with Densher, was only too glad to help.

Eventually Kate devised a way to bring her affair with Densher to a happy conclusion.

Having noticed that Milly was falling in love with Densher, Kate suggested that Densher marry Milly and make her happy for the few remaining months of her life. After her death, Milly's fortune would go to Densher, who would then be free to marry Kate and be in a financial position to allay any objections Mrs. Lowder might have to the match. Kate was sure that neither Mrs. Lowder nor Mrs. Stringham would try to prevent a marriage between Milly and Merton Densher, for both of them loved Milly and would have gone to any lengths to make her final days happy.

On the advice of Sir Luke Strett, the three women and Densher accompanied Milly to Venice for the winter months. Densher made little effort to bring about Kate's plan and marry Milly until after Mrs. Lowder and Kate returned to England for a few weeks. Before they left, Kate made Densher promise to follow her plan. Densher's conscience rebelled at the duplicity of the scheme, however, and he was not sure that when the plan was worked out to its finish Kate would still want him. As a sign that there was mutual trust between them, he asked Kate to come to his rooms with him. She did so the day before she left Venice.

One day, as Densher approached the house Milly had taken for the winter, he saw Lord Mark leaving. He soon found out from Mrs. Stringham that Lord Mark had proposed to Milly and had been rejected because the girl had detected unwanted sympathy in his proposal and had suspected that he was after her money rather than her love. Densher believed, rightly, that Lord Mark's rejection gave him some reason to be hopeful. He informed Milly that she was the only reason he was neglecting his work. She was pleased and hoped that he would propose.

Lord Mark disappeared from Venice for almost a month. Then, shortly after he had been refused admittance to Milly's house, Densher saw Lord Mark in a café. Densher knew immediately that Lord Mark had somehow discovered and told Milly about the engagement between Densher and Kate. Densher tried to think of a way to right the situation. Three days later, Mrs. Stringham came to him and told him that it was as he had guessed. What he had not guessed, however, was that Milly no longer took any interest in living and was refusing to eat or talk to anyone. Mrs. Stringham was in despair and had sent for Sir Luke Strett.

Densher returned to London but did not, at first, go to see Kate. He could not face her after the turn which their plans had taken, and he could not bear the idea of having hurt Milly as he had done. Finally, on Christmas Day, he had a premonition. He hurried to Sir Luke Strett's residence. There he found Mrs. Lowder, who told him that she had received a telegram the previous day with news of Milly's death. A few days later, a letter arrived from Venice. Without opening it, Densher knew what the message was, for it was addressed in Milly's handwriting. He immediately went to see Kate, who also guessed that it was a letter to tell Densher that Milly had left him part of her fortune so that he and Kate might marry. Neither of them dared open the letter because they were ashamed of their conduct, and they burned the letter in the fireplace.

Ten days later, a letter came from a New York law firm. Densher sent it to Kate unopened, whereupon she came to his rooms, wanting to know why he had sent it to her. He replied that it was up to her whether he should take the money that was offered, but that he could never marry her with the money Milly had left him.

Kate refused to answer him or to open the letter, lest the large amount of the fortune tempt either of them into accepting it. Finally Densher said he wanted to marry her, but only as they had been before the arrival of Milly Theale. Kate left, after reminding him that they could never be the same.

Critical Evaluation:

Henry James came of a family whose members considered themselves viewers of, rather than participants in, society. Henry and his father both suffered from physical disabilities that to some degree enforced this detachment, which was emotional as well as physical. The family traveled continually during the author's youth. As an adult, James lived chiefly in Europe, and though he maintained close relations with his parents and siblings he considered himself a citizen of the world. He regarded the life of his countrymen with the same objective, albeit curious and sympathetic view he accorded society in general. Coming as he did of parents whose chief business in life was the cultivation of their own and their children's sensibilities, and sharing the family's strong if eccentric religious bent, he took it as his artistic mission to examine the condition of human society at large as that condition manifested itself in the most subdued and civilized of human milieus.

The outline of the plot of *The Wings of the Dove* was suggested to the author by the premature death of his cousin Mary Temple, called Minny. The girl had charm, beauty, money, and love. She had, as it is said, everything for which to live and she resisted her fate to the end. After her death from tuberculosis in 1870, James was, as he later wrote, "haunted" by the tragedy of her situation. Two of his most appealing heroines take their essential lines from her, Isabel Archer of *The Portrait of a Lady* (1880-1881), and Milly Theale.

James wrote three of his best novels in quick succession shortly after 1900. As the new century began, he produced *The Wings of the Dove* (1902), *The Ambassadors* (1903), and *The Golden Bowl* (1904). According to one critic, the three themes that impel these novels, as well as most of James' previous works, are "the contrast of American sincerity and crudity with European deceit and culture, the conflicting realities of life and art, and the substitution of psychological for ethical measurements of good and evil."

The first is most neatly illustrated by the characters Mrs. Lowder and Mrs. Stringham. Mrs. Lowder's wardship of Kate has a monetary quality to it that is made explicit in her remark to Merton Densher: "I've been saving [Kate's presence] up and letting it, as you say of investments, appreciate, and you may judge whether, now it has begun to pay so, I'm likely to consent to treat for it with any but a high bidder." Mrs. Stringham's attachment to Milly, on the other hand, has the quality of a holy mission to shepherd through the hazards of the world a being so exalted that the heroines of literature pale beside her. Her view of Milly is essentially romantic; she calls her "an angel," "a princess in a palace," and, ironically, "the real thing." The differences between Kate and Milly enlarges on this theme; Kate accepts her aunt's definition of herself and uses it but succumbs to its corrupting influence, thus losing both love and honor. Milly, resisting the dehumanizing effects both of hero-worship and of pity, works her own salvation as well as Densher's.

The life that Milly makes for herself, knowing her days are numbered, comprehends abysses both sublime and terrible. She recognizes from the first the effects of her money on the company into which she is betrayed by her shepherd, so graphically if unintentionally particularized for her by kind, corrupt Lord Mark, who takes her to see the Bronzino portrait, which is so like her but, most poignantly to Milly's sense, "dead, dead, dead." She has, even before she hears her sentence pronounced by Sir Luke Strett, a trick of deferring judgment, of not permitting the baseness of others to circumscribe or debase her experience. Afterward, this tendency flowers into a kind of divine duplicity, a double reverse, which consists of her keeping from everyone but Mrs. Stringham the fact that she is dying. After a certain point, she inevitably sees everyone else acting in the knowledge of her limited future, yet she makes no move to defend herself but simply, profoundly, trusts. In short, she offers herself as a dove for sacrifice, a gesture that parallels the willingness of others to sacrifice her to their own designs. All her putative friends deceive themselves in regard to her, acting in the name of her happiness but actually for their own good. Milly does not deceive herself. Her surrender is deliberate. In this she is a supreme artist; she makes of her life an instrument for Mrs. Stringham's gratification, for Kate's enlightenment, and for Densher's redemption, a creative act of the highest kind.

James captures these characters, as well as diverse strokes of their wickedness, in a few murmured words, a nod or a look, an invitation accepted or declined, gestures always within the bounds of propriety. Such an exposition of the instincts of the jungle expressed in the manners of the salon generates, in the end, more force than many a less subdued narrative. For the reader is treated not only to the powerful spectacle of Kate Croy prowling within her situation with the disciplined rage of a caged tigress but also to the vision of Milly Theale triumphant over betrayal and death and fulfilling her extraordinary nature.

"Critical Evaluation" by Jan Kennedy Foster

Bibliography:

Cargill, Oscar. *The Novels of Henry James.* New York: Macmillan, 1961. In a substantial chapter on *The Wings of the Dove,* the author analyzes the novel's plot, central characters, and main themes. Also reviews and critiques previous scholarship.

Fowler, Virginia. "The Later Fiction." In *A Companion to Henry James Studies,* edited by Daniel Mark Fogel. Westport, Conn.: Greenwood Press, 1993. Discusses the structure, international theme, possible redemption motif, and psychodynamics of the main characters in *The Wings of the Dove.* Emphasizes the constraints placed by society on the female characters, especially Kate Croy and Milly Theale, and analyzes Merton Densher's threatened masculinity.

Gale, Robert L. *A Henry James Encyclopedia.* Westport, Conn.: Greenwood Press, 1989. Contains a critical summary of the plot of *The Wings of the Dove* and descriptive identifications of its twenty-five characters. Discusses James's preface to the novel and entries in James's *Notebooks* that are relevant to the novel.

Tintner, Adeline R. *The Museum World of Henry James.* Ann Arbor, Mich.: UMI Research Press, 1986. Shows how art objects, especially paintings (mostly from the Italian Renaissance) but also architectural details, costumes, and furniture, provide James with sources and analogues for his fiction, notably including *The Wings of the Dove.*

Wagenknecht, Edward. *The Novels of Henry James.* New York: Frederick Ungar, 1983. Includes a conservative discussion of *The Wings of the Dove* that touches on composition and publication data, the inspiration that led to the work, an analysis of the plot (referring also to the two-part structure and stressing the closure), and an evaluation of the central characters.

THE WINTER OF OUR DISCONTENT

Type of work: Novel
Author: John Steinbeck (1902-1968)
Type of plot: Social realism
Time of plot: 1960
Locale: New Baytown, Long Island
First published: 1961

> *Principal characters:*
> ETHAN ALLEN HAWLEY, a storekeeper
> MARY HAWLEY, his wife
> JOE MORPHY, a bank teller
> MARULLO, a storeowner and Ethan's boss
> MARGIE YOUNG-HUNT, a divorced woman
> MR. BAKER, the town banker
> DANNY TAYLOR, the town drunk

The Story:

Ethan Allen Hawley awoke on a Good Friday morning in April, 1960, and greeted his wife, Mary, in his usual manner by making funny faces at her. Mary was amused but a bit unnerved; she disapproved of his constant teasing and flippancy, especially on "serious" holidays. At breakfast she asked him if he was going to close the store early for Good Friday. Ethan worked as a grocery clerk in Marullo's store, a position he resented when he remembered that his Puritan forebears had once been influential in the village. His grandfather, in fact, had owned a ship, which was mysteriously burned, and his father had failed in business.

On his way to work, Ethan chatted with Joe Morphy, the teller at Mr. Baker's bank. "The Morph," as he was called, was the village "newspaper" and knew the local gossip and everyone in town. This morning, he told Ethan, purely as small talk between friends, his "philosophy" on how to rob a bank. At the store, Ethan plunged into his daily routine, beginning with his ritual of addressing the shelves of canned goods. It was a ritual he performed half in celebration of life, half in self-deprecation, sensing how far he, a Harvard graduate and veteran of World War II, had fallen. As he was sweeping, Ethan was greeted by Mr. Baker, president of the bank. A leading citizen of New Baytown and respectable, monied, and secure, Baker reminded Ethan of the money Mary had inherited and urged him to invest it wisely. He assured Ethan that in spite of the Hawleys' setback, he wanted to see Ethan and his family succeed for the sake of the Hawley "tradition."

Later that day Margie Young-Hunt entered the store. An attractive divorcée, flirtatious and sexually predatory, she had on occasion slept with Joe Morphy and had shared her evenings with other men like Biggers, the traveling salesman. She was attracted to Ethan. On this morning, she announced to him that she was going to read her cards for Mary that night, and she predicted good fortune for Ethan.

After Margie left, Marullo came in. Half bully, half father figure, Marullo offered Ethan, whom he called "kid," advice on how to run the store better by thinking more of making money than of friends. At Marullo's departure, Ethan was approached by an agent for a grocery distributor who offered Ethan a bribe to stock his product; Ethan refused.

At home, Ethan learned that his children were entering the I Love America essay contest.

Disappointed at his son's attempt to find an easy way to write the essay, Ethan told him to read the books in the attic, books of the great American orators and statesmen. That night, before going to bed, Ethan walked to his place by the water, where he meditated on the day's events and gave Danny Taylor, his boyhood friend and now the town drunk, a dollar so that Danny could buy a "skull buster" and sink into drunken oblivion.

On Saturday, Margie held a card reading and predicted that Ethan's fortunes would turn. Ethan himself was cynical, but he began to feel the pressure of Margie's prediction, Mr. Baker's advice, Marullo's admonitions, and Joey Morphy's playful remarks on how to rob a bank. He began to formulate his own plan for making money. His meditations that night were filled with images of Danny Taylor, whose personal failure was to be connected with Ethan's success.

Easter Sunday saw the Hawleys invited to tea at the Bakers. Ethan was suspicious and resentful, convinced that Baker would try somehow to further his own ends under the pretext of helping Ethan, The conversation between them that afternoon centered on Baker's conviction that New Baytown was the perfect place for an airport and that with the right money buying the right land fortunes would be made. That night Ethan went to Danny's shack by the edge of the meadow. Danny was drunk, as usual, and Ethan learned that Baker had given Danny the bottle and had tried to get him to sign over the property, but Danny had refused. Ethan pleaded with Danny never to sell the land, telling him that his meadow was coveted by Baker and others for an airport. Danny accepted Ethan's offer of a thousand dollars for a "cure," though Danny cynically—and rightly—accused Ethan of harboring his own designs on Taylor Meadow.

The next day, when Ethan and Joey Murphy talked about Marullo, Morph suggested that the old man probably came to America illegally after the immigration laws changed. Back at the store, Ethan began to plot the bank robbery. After learning that Danny Taylor had made him a beneficiary in his will, Ethan at first felt bad, realizing that he had tricked Danny into trusting him. Later, when Marullo offered Ethan fatherly advice, Ethan called the Department of Immigration and turned him in.

Now deeply involved in treachery, Ethan once again contemplated his actions, judging personal success as a form of immorality. Baker told him of a scandal that was about to break—the town leaders were involved in bribery and payola. Meanwhile, Marullo had ostensibly left the country and, as a father would have done, left Ethan the store. Danny Taylor was found dead, which put Ethan in possession of Taylor Meadow and gave him an advantage over Mr. Baker, who now had to deal with Ethan in his airport plans.

Ethan's own scheme to rob the bank was almost concluded, but he was frustrated at the last minute by the arrival of the Immigration official inquiring about Marullo. Ethan dropped the plan. On returning home he learned that his son had won honorable mention in the national essay contest but that he had cheated, having plagiarized whole passages from the great orators to whose works Ethan had directed him.

Ethan now had Taylor Meadow, Marullo's store, and, given the town scandal, a favored position to become town mayor. Yet his personal life was in ruin: His son was a cheat, he himself was as dishonest as those earlier "pirates" who had brought down his family, and he had become a stranger even to his wife.

In a final confrontation with Baker, Ethan demanded a controlling interest in the corporation formed to build the airport in exchange for his turning over Taylor Meadow. Later, sensing Ethan's essential loneliness, Margie attempted to seduce him, but Ethan declined. That night, he went back to his private place by the sea and attempted to kill himself. At the last minute, however, he resisted, preferring instead to go on, hoping for self-renewal.

Critical Evaluation:

John Steinbeck's last novel, *The Winter of Our Discontent*, had its origins in a short story Steinbeck first published in *The Atlantic Monthly* in 1956, entitled "How Mr. Hogan Robbed a Bank." More than one critic has noted the story's clarity and narrative drive. The basic plot is meshed, though somewhat awkwardly, with the broader events surrounding Ethan Allen Hawley's "temptation" and "fall." The novel centers on Ethan as a basically honest man whose fall into corruption is paradigmatic of the moral disease of society as a whole. The time of the novel, 1960, was a time of public scandals in America, including a quiz show fraud and cases of payola and other forms of venality. Steinbeck obviously believed that the materialism of American society had weakened the moral fiber of even basically good men like Ethan Hawley. During the late 1950's, in fact, Steinbeck had written letters to Adlai Stevenson, then a senator and presidential candidate, and United Nations Secretary General Dag Hammarskjold, among others, in which he lamented America's pursuit of "Things." He was fearful, he wrote, that his sons would not understand the ways of virtue and courage in an age of treachery and deceit.

Such basic pessimism, first notable in Steinbeck's work after 1945, is the formative principle of the novel. The corruption is so pervasive as even to reach Ethan's son Allen, who seeks the easy way to success because "everybody does it." Characters like Mr. Baker talk of nothing but money; decent people like Joey Morphy are discontented with their present but uncertain of their future; Margie is unable to keep a husband and is dependent on alimony to survive; Marullo is hardened by the ethos of making money and continually preaches his ethic to Ethan; Danny Taylor keeps the pressure of life at bay with alcohol.

The time of the main action corresponds with the mystery of Easter. The "passion" of Ethan begins on Good Friday, and the first stages of his lapse into corruption as a kind of moral death occur ironically on Easter Sunday at Baker's tea and later in Danny's shack. Ethan's total collapse occurs over the Fourth of July holiday, America's birthday. The connection between the holiest of Christian holidays and the most patriotic of American holidays is clear—moral corruption is all-pervasive. The novel is thus a kind of domestic allegory. The characters, as if in a medieval play, appear in procession, approach Ethan, tell their "story" of greed or disaffection, and then recede, forcing Ethan to contemplate his role and make his next decision.

Steinbeck's last novel is, in some ways, a disappointment. The plot involves incidents of domestic life hardly distinguishable from those portrayed on television sitcoms of the period, and the action is static, lacking the force and clarity of Steinbeck's best work. Much of the action is stalled by Ethan's "philosophizing" and his wry observations, and the story's direction is further slowed by the rather awkward, if interesting, narrative structure. The first two chapters of each of the two parts use the conventional third- person narrator, but the remaining chapters in each section are told from Ethan's first-person point of view.

Steinbeck had used a similar method in earlier works. *The Grapes of Wrath* (1939), for example, unfolds the action by a series of intercalary chapters that shift the point of view from the Joads and their personal experiences to that of the country at large. Such a technique had the effect of universalizing the Joads' experience, as one world and one chapter commented on the other. In *The Winter of Our Discontent*, however, the third-person narration neither comments on nor illuminates Ethan's thoughts and actions.

The characters, too, lack the sense of commitment or mystical brotherhood of many of Steinbeck's people. Ethan is vaguely reminiscent of Doc in *Cannery Row* (1945). Like Doc, Ethan often ponders great questions of ethics and laments the loss of honesty and courage in himself and others. Doc's philosophy was largely based on a kind of biological determinism, but it was infused with a deeper belief in the ultimate triumph of the group, in humankind as a force in itself. Doc had a zest for living. Ethan's philosophy, on the other hand, is more cynical and hopeless. His near suicide at the end is testament to his personal pessimism and despair.

It is this aspect of the book, finally, that separates *The Winter of Our Discontent* from Steinbeck's previous work. Though Ethan pulls back from the brink of suicide and decides to try living the honorable life, his act is almost like an afterthought. Though he may be saved from a physical death, his spiritual death has already come to pass, a death brought on by disillusionment, failure, and discontent.

Edward Fiorelli

Bibliography.

Fontenrose, Joseph. *John Steinbeck: An Introduction and Interpretation*. New York: Barnes & Noble Books, 1963. A very readable study that discusses Steinbeck's use of myths and legendary material as structural elements in his plots. An influential work.

French, Warren. *John Steinbeck*. Boston: Twayne, 1961. Probably the best general treatment of Steinbeck's work, and an example of the approach called New Criticism, which was prevalent in the 1960's. Each major work is closely analyzed, with discussions centered around the meaning of the text.

Hughes, R. S. *Beyond "The Red Pony": A Reader's Companion to Steinbeck's Complete Short Stories*. Metuchen, N.J.: Scarecrow Press, 1987. The first study dealing exclusively with the more than fifty works of Steinbeck's short fiction. Particularly interesting discussions of Steinbeck's uncollected works, stories he published in magazines during the 1940's and 1950's. Discusses the source of *The Winter of Our Discontent*.

Levant, Howard, *The Novels of John Steinbeck: A Critical Study*. Columbia: University of Missouri Press, 1974. A constructionist approach, this study discusses the structural patterns of the novels. Suggests that Steinbeck's intentions, his "blueprints," were often at odds with the finished products and that his works reveal his inability effectively to fuse material with structure and theme with pattern. Interesting discussion of similarities between Steinbeck's first novel, *Cup of Gold* (1929) with his last, *The Winter of Our Discontent*.

Lisca, Peter. *The Wide World of John Steinbeck*. New Brunswick, N.J.: Rutgers University Press, 1958. First comprehensive study of Steinbeck; emphasizes his versatility.

THE WINTER'S TALE

Type of work: Drama
Author: William Shakespeare (1564-1616)
Type of plot: Tragicomedy
Time of plot: The legendary past
Locale: Sicilia and Bohemia
First performed: 1610-1611; first published, 1623

> *Principal characters:*
> LEONTES, the king of Sicilia
> HERMIONE, his queen
> POLIXENES, the king of Bohemia
> CAMILLO, Leontes' counselor
> PERDITA, Leontes' daughter
> FLORIZEL, Polixenes' son
> PAULINA, Hermione's maid
> AUTOLYCUS, a rogue

The Story:

Polixenes, the king of Bohemia, was the guest of Leontes, the king of Sicilia. The two men had been friends since boyhood, and there was much celebrating and joyousness during the visit. At last Polixenes decided that he must return to his home country. Leontes urged him to extend his visit, but Polixenes refused, saying that he had not seen his young son for a long time. Then Leontes asked Hermione, his wife, to try to persuade Polixenes to remain. When Polixenes finally yielded to her pleas, Leontes became suspicious and concluded that Hermione and Polixenes must be lovers and that he had been cuckolded.

Leontes was generally of a jealous disposition, and he sought constant reassurance that his son Mamillius was his own offspring. Having now, out of jealousy, misjudged his wife and his old friend, Leontes became so angry that he ordered Camillo, his chief counselor, to poison Polixenes. All Camillo's attempts to dissuade Leontes from his scheme only strengthened the jealous man's feelings of hate. Nothing could persuade the king that Hermione was true to him. Eventually Camillo agreed to poison Polixenes, but only on condition that Leontes return to Hermione with no more distrust.

Polixenes had noticed a change in Leontes' attitude toward him. When he questioned Camillo, the sympathetic lord revealed the plot to poison him. Together, they hastily embarked for Bohemia.

Upon learning that Polixenes and Camillo had fled, Leontes was more than ever convinced that his guest and his wife had been guilty of carrying on an affair. He conjectured that Polixenes and Camillo had been plotting together all the while and planning his murder. Moreover, he decided that Hermione, who was pregnant, was in all likelihood bearing Polixenes' child and not his. Publicly he accused Hermione of adultery and commanded that her son be taken from her. She herself was imprisoned. Although his servants protested the order, Leontes was adamant.

In prison, Hermione gave birth to a baby girl. Paulina, her attendant, thought that the sight of the baby girl might cause Leontes to relent, so she carried the child to the palace. Instead of forgiving his wife, Leontes became more incensed and demanded that the child be put to death.

He instructed Antigonus, Paulina's husband, to take the baby to a far-off desert shore and there abandon it. Although the lord pleaded to be released from this cruel command, he was forced to put out to sea for the purpose of leaving the child to perish on some lonely coast.

Leontes had sent two messengers to consult the Oracle of Delphi to determine Hermione's guilt. When the men returned, Leontes summoned his wife and the whole court to hear the verdict. The messengers read a scroll that stated that Hermione was innocent, as were Polixenes and Camillo, that Leontes was a tyrant, and that he would live without an heir until that which was lost was found.

The king, refusing to believe the oracle, declared its findings false, and again accused Hermione of infidelity. In the midst of his tirade a servant rushed in to say that young Mamillius had died because of sorrow and anxiety over his mother's plight. On hearing this, Hermione fell into a swoon and was carried to her chambers. Soon afterward, Paulina returned to announce that her mistress was dead. At this news Leontes, who had already begun to believe the oracle after news of his son's death, beat his breast with rage at himself. He reproached himself bitterly for the insane jealousy that had led to these unhappy events. In repentance, the king swore that he would have the legend of the deaths of his son and wife engraved on their tombstones and that he himself would do penance thereafter.

Meanwhile, Antigonus had taken the baby girl to a desert country near the sea. Heartsick at having to abandon her, the old courtier laid a bag of gold and jewels by her with instructions that she should be called Perdita, a name revealed to him in a dream. After he had done this, he was attacked and killed by a bear. Later, his ship was wrecked in a storm and all hands were lost. Although no news of the expedition reached Sicilia, the kind shepherd who found Perdita also saw the deaths of Antigonus and his men.

Sixteen years passed, bringing with them many changes. Leontes was a broken man, grieving alone in his palace. Perdita had grown into a beautiful and charming young woman under the care of the shepherd. So lovely was she that Prince Florizel, the son of Polixenes and heir to the throne of Bohemia, had fallen madly in love with her.

Unaware of the girl's background, and knowing only that his son was in love with a young shepherdess, Polixenes and Camillo, now his most trusted servant, disguised themselves and visited a sheep-shearing festival, where they saw Florizel, dressed as a shepherd, dancing with a lovely young woman. Although he realized that the shepherdess was of noble bearing, Polixenes in great rage forbade his son to marry her. Florizel thereupon made secret plans to elope with Perdita to a foreign country. Camillo, pitying the young couple, advised Florizel to embark for Sicilia and to pretend that he was a messenger of goodwill from the king of Bohemia. Camillo supplied the young man with letters of introduction to Leontes. It was part of Camillo's plan to inform Polixenes of the lovers' escape and travel to Sicilia to find them, thus taking advantage of the situation to return home once more.

The poor shepherd, frightened by the king's wrath, decided to tell Polixenes how, years before, he had found the baby and a bag of gold and jewels by her side. Fate intervened, however, and the shepherd was intercepted by the rogue Autolycus and put aboard the ship sailing to Sicilia.

Soon Florizel and Perdita arrived in Sicilia, followed by Polixenes and Camillo. When the old shepherd heard how Leontes had lost a daughter, he described the finding of Perdita. Leontes, convinced that Perdita was his own abandoned infant, was joyfully reunited with his daughter. When he heard this, Polixenes immediately gave his consent to the marriage of Florizel and Perdita. The only sorrowful circumstance to mar the happiness of all concerned was the earlier tragic death of Hermione.

One day, Paulina asked Leontes to visit a newly erected statue of the dead woman in Hermione's chapel. Leontes, ever faithful to the memory of his dead wife—even to the point of promising Paulina never to marry again—gathered his guests and took them to view the statue. Standing in the chapel, amazed at the wonderful lifelike quality of the work, they heard strains of soft music. Suddenly the statue descended from its pedestal and was revealed as the living Hermione. She had spent the sixteen years in seclusion while awaiting some word of her daughter. The happy family was reunited, and Hermione completely forgave her repentant husband. He and Polixenes were again the best of friends, rejoicing in the happiness of Perdita and Florizel.

Critical Evaluation:

Written after *Cymbeline* (1609-1610) and before *The Tempest* (1611), *The Winter's Tale* is as hard to classify generically as is the fully mature dramatic genius of its author. Partaking of the elements of tragedy, the play yet ends in sheer comedy, just as it mingles elements of realism and romance. William Shakespeare took his usual freedom with his source, Robert Greene's euphuistic romance *Pandosto: The Triumph of Time* (1588). Yet time remains the most crucial element in the play's structure, its clearest break with the pseudo-Aristotelian unities. The effect of time on Hermione, moreover, when the statue is revealed to be wrinkled and aged, heightens the pathos and credibility of the triumphant discovery and recognition scene. In order to allow that final scene its full effect, Shakespeare wisely has Perdita's discovery and recognition reported to the audience second-hand in Act V, scene ii. In keeping with the maturity of Shakespeare's dramatic talent, the poetic style of this play is clear, unrhetorical, sparse in its imagery, as well as metaphorically sharp. Verse alternates with prose as court characters alternate with country personages.

Mamillius tells his mother, who asks him for a story, that "a sad tale's best for winter." Ironically the little boy's story is never told; the entrance of Leontes interrupts it, and Hermione's son, his role as storyteller once defined, strangely disappears. In his place, the play itself takes over, invigorated by Mamillius' uncanny innocent wisdom, which reflects a Platonic view of childhood. The story that unfolds winds a multitude of themes without losing sight of any of them. It presents two views of honor, a wholesome one represented by Hermione and a demented one represented by Leontes. Like many of Shakespeare's plays, the narrative concerns the unholy power of kings who can be mistaken but whose power, however mistaken, is final. Yet the finality, here, is spared, the tragic ending avoided. For the absolute goodness of Hermione, Paulina, Camillo, the shepherd, and Florizel proves to be enough to overcome the evil of Leontes. Moving from the older generation's inability to love to the reflowering of love in the younger, the play spins out into a truly comic ending, with the reestablishment of community, royal authority, and general happiness in a triple *gamos*. The balance of tension between youth and age, guilt and innocence, death and rebirth is decided in favor of life, and the play escapes the clutches of remorseless tragedy in a kind of ultimate mystical vision of human life made ideal through suffering.

Leontes is a most puzzling character. His antifeminism, as expressed in his cynical speech on cuckoldry, seems more fashionable than felt. In his determined jealousy, he resembles Othello, and in his self-inflicted insanity, Lear. In fact, the words of Lear to Cordelia resound in Leontes' great speech, beginning, "Is whispering nothing?" and concluding, "My wife is nothing; nor nothing have these nothings,/ If this be nothing." It is almost impossible to sympathize with him further when he condemns even his helpless child in the face of Paulina's gentle pleas; and it is not surprising that he at first even denies the oracle itself. Yet his sudden recognition of culpability is no more convincing than his earlier, unmotivated jealousy. It is as if he changes too quickly for belief; perhaps this is the reason for Hermione's decision to test his penitence with time, until it ripens into sincerity. Certainly his reaction to his wife's swoon shows only a superficial emotion. Leontes is still self-centered, still regally assured that all can be put right with the proper words. Only after the years have passed in loneliness does he realize it takes more than orderly words to undo the damage wrought by disorderly royal commands. His admission to Paulina that his words killed Hermione paves the way for the happy ending.

Even the minor characters are drawn well and vividly. Camillo is the ideal courtier who chooses virtue over favor. Paulina, like the nurse Anna in Euripides' *Hippolytus* (428 B.C.E.), is the staunch helpmate of her mistress, especially in adversity, aided by magical powers that seem to spring from her own determined character. Her philosophy is also that of the classical Greeks: "What's gone and what's past help/ Should be past grief." This play does not have the tragic Greek ending, because Paulina preserves her mistress rather than assisting her to destroy herself. Even the rogue Autolycus is beguiling, with his verbal witticisms, his frank pursuit of self-betterment, and his lusty and delightful songs. His sign is Mercury, the thief of the gods, and he follows his sign like the best rascals in Renaissance tradition, Boccaccio's Friar Onion, Rabelais' Panurge, and Shakespeare's own Falstaff.

In Hermione and Perdita, Shakespeare achieves two of his greatest portraits of women. Hermione's speech reflects her personality, straightforward, without embroidery, as pure as virtue itself. Her reaction to Leontes' suspicion and condemnation is brief, but telling. "Adieu, my lord," she says, "I never wish'd to see you sorry; now/ I trust I shall." She combines the hardness of Portia with the gentleness of Desdemona; in fact, Antigonus' oath in her defense recalls the character of Othello's wife. Like Geoffrey Chaucer's patient Griselda, Hermione loses everything, but she strikes back with the most devastating weapon of all: time. Yet in the final scene of the play it is clear that her punishment of Leontes has made Hermione suffer no less. Perdita personifies, though never in a stereotyped way, gentle innocence: "Nothing she does or seems/ But smacks of something greater than herself/ Too noble for this place." Indeed, when Polixenes' wrath, paralleling Leontes' previous folly, threatens Perdita's life for a second time, the audience holds its breath because she is too good to be safe. When Shakespeare saves her, the play, sensing the audience's joy, abruptly ends on its highest note.

In its theme and structure, *The Winter's Tale* bears a striking resemblance to Euripides' *Alcestis* (438 B.C.E.). In both plays, the "death" of the queen threatens the stability and happiness of society and, in both, her restoration, which is miraculous and ambiguous, restores order to the world of the court. Shakespeare, however, widens the comic theme by adding the love of the younger generation. So *The Winter's Tale* defies the forces of death and hatred romantically as well as realistically. The sad tale becomes happy, as winter becomes spring.

"Critical Evaluation" by Kenneth John Atchity

Bibliography:
Lloyd Evans, Gareth. *The Upstart Crow: An Introduction to Shakespeare's Plays.* London: J. M. Dent and Sons, 1982. A comprehensive treatment of the dramatic works of William Shakespeare, with major emphasis on critical reviews of the plays. Also discusses the sources from which Shakespeare drew and circumstances surrounding the writing of the plays.
Muir, Kenneth, ed. *Shakespeare—The Comedies: A Collection of Critical Essays.* Englewood Cliffs, N.J.: Prentice-Hall, 1965. An anthology of essays by a variety of authors, discussing Shakespeare's comedies from various points of view. Derek Traversi's treatment of *The*

Winter's Tale is mainly concerned with the later scenes of the play and includes an intensive discussion of the characters' motivations.

Overton, Bill. *The Winter's Tale*. Atlantic Highlands, N.J.: Humanities Press International, 1989. A critical evaluation of Shakespeare's play from a wide variety of points of view, including Marxism, feminism, and psychoanalysis. Also discusses previous critical studies of the play.

Sanders, Wilbur. *The Winter's Tale*. Boston: Twayne, 1987. A thorough critical evaluation of the play. Also includes information on the work's stage history and original reception by critics. Sanders also discusses the psychological factors of the play and the use of language.

Shakespeare, William. *The Winter's Tale*. Edited by J. H. P. Pafford. Cambridge, Mass.: Harvard University Press, 1963. A new edition of the play, containing more than eighty pages of introductory notes and twenty pages of appendices. Discusses the sources, the text itself, and the music and songs. Also includes an extensive critical evaluation of the play.

WINTERSET

Type of work: Drama
Author: Maxwell Anderson (1888-1959)
Type of plot: Tragedy
Time of plot: Twentieth century
Locale: New York
First performed: 1935; first published, 1935

> *Principal characters:*
> ESDRAS, an old man
> GARTH, his son
> MIRIAMNE, his daughter
> TROCK, a murderer
> SHADOW, his henchman
> JUDGE GAUNT
> MIO, Romagna's son

The Story:

Trock and Shadow walked warily under the bridge by the tenement where Garth lived with his old father, Esdras, and his fifteen-year-old sister, Miriamne. Trock had just been released from prison, where he had served a sentence for his part in a murder for which Romagna had been electrocuted. Judge Gaunt, who had presided over the trial when Romagna had been convicted, was said to be mad and to be roaming the country telling people that the trial had been unfair. A college professor had also begun an investigation of the old murder trial. Trock had come to the tenement district to see Garth, who had witnessed the murder that Trock had really committed. Garth had not testified at the trial, and Trock wanted to warn him never to tell what he had seen.

Trock threatened to kill Garth if he talked. Miriamne knew nothing about her brother's part in this crime, but after she heard Trock threaten her brother, she questioned him and learned a little about the killing. Miriamne loved Garth, but she knew that his silence about the murder was wrong. Old Esdras watched and comforted his two children.

To the same tenement district came Mio and his friend, Carr. Mio was seventeen, and he had learned that somewhere in the tenements lived a man who knew that Romagna was innocent. Mio and Miriamne saw each other on the street and fell in love. Knowing that he had to speak to Miriamne, Mio sent Carr away. When Miriamne heard Mio's full name, Bartolemeo Romagna, she told him that he must go away and never see her again, for Miriamne knew then that Mio was the son of the man who had died for the murder Trock had committed. Mio told Miriamne that he had been four years old when his father had been electrocuted and that he lived only to prove his father's innocence.

While the lovers were talking, Shadow and Trock appeared on the street, and Miriamne hid Mio in the shadow so that the two men could not see him. The gangsters were looking for Judge Gaunt in order to silence him. The judge had also come to the tenement, and Garth, meeting him, had made the crazed man go to Esdras' apartment for safety. Shadow, however, wanted no part in killing the judge. As he left, Trock sent two henchmen after Shadow to kill him. Mio saw the shooting. Feeling that he had come to the right place to learn the truth of the old killing, he waited.

In Esdras' room the judge awoke, refreshed and normal once more. Realizing where he was

7215

and what he had done, the judge asked Garth and Esdras to say nothing of his mad claims that Romagna's trial had been unfair. The judge did not want the case to be reopened any more than did Trock. Esdras offered to guide Judge Gaunt part way back to his home.

After the two old men had left, Mio knocked on the door. He had been directed to Garth's home by neighbors. He was bewildered at the sight of Miriamne until she explained that Garth was her brother. She asked Mio to leave, but first she wanted him to tell her that he loved her. Garth angrily interrupted the lovers and ordered Mio to leave. As Mio was preparing to go, Judge Gaunt and Esdras returned, forced to turn back by driving sleet. Mio recognized the judge and began questioning him and Garth about the trial. Garth's story was that he had not witnessed the murder for which Mio's father had died. Judge Gaunt insisted that Romagna was guilty. Mio pointed out that evidence at the trial was biased because his father had been an anarchist. The judge said that if he had thought the trial unjust, he would have allowed a retrial.

The steady denials of Garth and Judge Gaunt nearly broke Mio's spirit. Suddenly Trock entered the apartment. Mio grew more suspicious. Then Shadow came to the door. The sight of the henchman he had thought dead terrified Trock. Shadow had been shot, but he lived long enough to accuse Trock of his murder. After Shadow died, Judge Gaunt again became deranged. He thought he was in court, and Mio tricked him into admitting that Romagna had been an anarchist and as such should have been put to death. When Trock threatened to kill them all, Mio knew that he was near the end of his search.

In the midst of Mio's discoveries the police came looking for Judge Gaunt, who had been missing from his home for many days. Mio accused Trock of murdering Shadow, but when he sent the police into an inner room where Garth had dragged the body, the corpse was not there. When Miriamne also denied his charges, Mio admitted that he must have been dreaming, for he had seen a pleading message in Miriamne's eyes that directed his decision.

As the police took Judge Gaunt away, Trock went also, leaving Garth to face Mio's accusations. Mio was helpless, however, because he loved Miriamne. Free at last to vindicate his father's name, he was tied by Miriamne's love for her brother. In spite of Miriamne's fears that his life was in danger, Mio left Esdras' home.

Mio felt that there was nothing left for him but to die, for he could not live and remain silent about his father's death. While he hesitated outside the tenement, Miriamne came to join him, and they saw Garth carrying the body of Shadow from the alley. Esdras joined Mio outside. The boy's search for justice and his courage had made the old man see that Garth's silence had been wrong. Esdras told Mio that he was going to the police to report Shadow's murder. Mio cautioned Esdras that he would not try to save Garth by remaining silent about the Romagna case, but Esdras said that Mio owed them nothing. He went to inform the police.

Alone with Mio, Miriamne tried to find hope of happiness for him. At last she reminded him that his father would have forgiven his killers, and Mio realized that she was right. Still, he was determined to reveal the truth. Then Esdras returned and told him that Trock's henchmen were guarding the streets and that there was no way of escape.

As Mio dashed down a passage toward the river, Miriamne heard the sound of shooting. She ran to her lover and found him dying. Then she ran toward the same passage, into the fire of Trock's machine gun. Dying, she crawled back to Mio. Esdras and Garth, still alive, carried the dead lovers out of the cold, wet winter night.

Critical Evaluation:

Throughout his career, Maxwell Anderson boldly attempted to bring poetic drama to the American commercial theater. Always convinced that drama should provide a spiritual experience for the audience and committed to tragedy, Anderson also believed that poetry was the most appropriate medium for the expression of the emotions inherent in humanity's tragic condition. He revered the Greek and Roman tragedies and was devoted to William Shakespeare. He followed these models in most of his commercial successes, choosing historical plots and characters to speak to ageless human concerns. Plays such as *Elizabeth the Queen* (1930) and *Anne of the Thousand Days* (1948) found receptive audiences who appreciated the Shakespearean echoes and accepted the poetic lines with enthusiasm. In *Winterset*, however, Anderson rejected the tragic stories of the distant past when he decided to write a poetic tragedy about contemporary events. That the play, in spite of unevenness, was a popular success and continues to be Anderson's best-known effort suggests the skill of the author and his creative ability at draping contemporary events with an aura of timelessness.

The notorious case of Nicola Sacco and Bartolomeo Vanzetti provides the background for *Winterset*. Anderson, like many other artists and intellectuals of the time, believed that the two radical Italian aliens had been wrongly accused and convicted of murder. Several years after their executions, a friend of Anderson's told him that the judge in the case was now nearly out of his mind and was continuously attempting to justify his decisions during the trial to any who would listen. From this kernel, Anderson built the drama.

The surface structure of the play parallels Renaissance revenge tragedy with Mio, the son of the wronged father, setting out to avenge the injustice of the court system to his father by finding the real murderer and punishing him. In its revenge pattern and in the characterization of Mio, the Anderson play seems consciously patterned on *Hamlet* (1600-1601). Mio, like Hamlet, is the wronged son in search of vengeance. Like Hamlet, Mio has recently been a student, is given to cynicism, and seems indecisive and inconsistent in his speeches and actions.

It is not only *Hamlet* that the play parallels. There are similarities to *Macbeth* (1604-1606) in the characterization of Trock, a murderer who blames others for his act and who wants to destroy those who know the reality of his guilt. His sidekick, Shadow, seems equivalent to Banquo, when he mysteriously reappears after his "death." The character of Judge Gaunt mirrors the central figure of *King Lear* (1605-1606). Lear and Gaunt both misjudge on emotional, not rational, grounds; both go mad; both abdicate official positions, but want to hold on to the trappings of their offices; both become insanely eloquent in the middle of storms; both neglect their clothes; and both have a fool (in Gaunt's case, the hobo).

Unlike the typical revenge tragedy, however, *Winterset* does not end with the punishment of the villains. Anderson was convinced that the best tragedies involved recognition scenes. In *Winterset*, Anderson attempts to show that revenge is evil and that love and forgiveness are good. Rather, therefore, than have Mio be successful in his punishment of the murderer, Anderson instead has Mio transformed by love for Miriamne. In its love plot, *Winterset* is imitative of yet another Shakespeare play: *Romeo and Juliet* (1594-1595). Like the two famous Shakespearian star-crossed lovers, Mio and Miriamne are from alienated families, they fall in love at first sight, and they are transformed by their love. When Mio finds out the truth about his father's innocence in Act II, his love outweighs his desire for vengeance, and he refuses to take action because he does not want to place Miriamne's brother in jeopardy. In Act III, Miriamne convinces Mio that his father also would forgive, had he been alive. This recognition of the importance of love and forgiveness prepares the way for the Romeo-and-Juliet-like deaths of the two lovers, in each other's arms, as the play ends. *Winterset*, like *Romeo and Juliet*, includes an abundance of light and dark imagery. Mio's final speech links light to love and forgiveness: "I came here seeking/ light in darkness, running from the dawn,/ and stumbled on a morning."

The stage-setting underscores the starkly contemporary events traced in the drama. The backdrop—a huge representation of a bridge—emphasizes the mechanistic elements of twentieth century life as well as the contrast between wealth and poverty, a particularly important statement for the Depression-era audience who first viewed the production. Huddled at the foot of the bridge are the lower-class masses, at least as isolated as they are connected by the bridge.

As noble as Anderson's attempt was in linking contemporary events to poetic tragedy, most critics have recognized some of the weaknesses of the effort. The play has been criticized as being a disunified mishmash of Shakespeare, and as being overly melodramatic and implausible. The reliance on love and forgiveness has been thought to be unduly simplistic as means of dealing with the dilemma of twentieth century social injustice. Similarly, critics have harshly judged the poetry in the play. Anderson's irregular blank verse has seemed inadequate to the task, both in its occasional inclusion of overly purple passages as well as in its long sections of relatively mundane language.

In spite of such criticism, however, the play remains as the most successful and challenging American commercial artistic attempt at verse tragedy in the twentieth century.

"Critical Evaluation" by Delmer Davis

Bibliography:

Abernathy, Frances E. *"Winterset:* A Modern Revenge Tragedy." *Modern Drama* 7 (September, 1964): 185-189. Provides a careful comparison of the play to Renaissance revenge tragedies, with special emphasis on *Hamlet.* Contrasts the Hebraic code of eye for an eye in *Hamlet* with the Christian gospel of love and forgiveness in *Winterset.*

Hazelton, Nancy J. Doran, and Kenneth Krauss, eds. *Maxwell Anderson and the New York Stage.* Monroe, N.Y.: Library Research Association, 1991. A collection of essays in honor of Anderson's centennial in 1988. Contains an insightful interview with George Schaefer regarding a production of *Winterset.*

Shivers, Alfred S. *The Life of Maxwell Anderson.* Briarcliff Manor, N.Y.: Stein & Day, 1983. Provides numerous details about the writing and staging of *Winterset.*

_____. *Maxwell Anderson.* Boston: Twayne, 1976. The best brief critical introduction to Anderson and his works. Sees *Winterset* as a continuation of Anderson's compulsion to portray an idealistic central character "marked for some kind of self-willed defeat for the sake, usually, of a worthwhile cause."

_____. *Maxwell Anderson: An Annotated Bibliography of Primary and Secondary Works.* Metuchen, N.J.: Scarecrow Press, 1985. A very complete listing, often with annotations, of works by and about Anderson, including numerous citations about *Winterset.*

WISE BLOOD

Type of work: Novel
Author: Flannery O'Connor (1925-1964)
Type of plot: Psychological realism
Time of plot: Early twentieth century
Locale: Taulkinham, a city in the American South
First published: 1952

Principal characters:
    HAZEL MOTES, a preacher despite himself
    ENOCH EMERY, Hazel's disciple
    ASA HAWKS, charlatan preacher, rival to Hazel
    SABBATH LILY, Hawks's daughter
    HOOVER SHOATS, Hazel Motes's rival
    MRS. FLOOD, Hazel's landlady

The Story:
    When Hazel Motes was released from the army, he found his old home place deserted. Eastrod had been the home of his grandfather, a backwoods preacher who had assured Hazel that Jesus was hungry for his soul. Hazel had packed up his mother's Bible and reading glasses and caught the train for Taulkinham. He rode uneasily in his $11.98 suit, startling one middle-class lady by suddenly telling her, "If you've been redeemed . . . I wouldn't want to be."
    In the army, Hazel had decided that his grandfather's preaching had been false, that sin did not exist. In Taulkinham, Hazel intended to prove this to himself, but even the cab driver who took him to his first room identified him as a preacher.
    On his second night in the city, Hazel met Enoch Emery as they watched a sidewalk potato-peeler salesman. Enoch had come to Taulkinham from the country and had found a job working for the city zoo. He was desperately lonely, and despite Hazel's surliness, Enoch immediately attached himself to Hazel as a potential friend. Hazel's attention, however, was focused on a blind man whose face was scarred. The blind man's daughter, Sabbath Lily, accompanied him, handing out religious pamphlets. Hazel and Enoch followed the pair until the blind man, Asa Hawks, insisted that he could smell sin on Hazel and that he had been marked by some past preacher. Hazel denied it, saying that the only thing that mattered to him was that Jesus did not exist.
    The next day Hazel bought a car. Even at $40 it was no bargain, an ancient Essex that barely ran, but it pleased Hazel. Later that day he met Enoch Emery at the zoo so that Enoch could show Hazel something at the museum. Enoch led Hazel to a case which contained a tiny mummified man. Enoch found the mummy very compelling and believed that he had received a sign to show it to Hazel, whose only response was to demand Asa Hawks's address.
    That evening Hazel began his career as a street preacher; he called his church "the Church Without Christ" and denied the existence of sin, judgment, and redemption. Later that evening he rented a room in the rooming house where Hawks and his daughter lived, planning to seduce Sabbath Lily and thus to make the blind preacher take his denial of Christ seriously. Hazel had no idea that Hawks's blindness was fake; he had believed a news clipping Hawks had shown him that described Hawks's promise to blind himself by way of dramatizing his conviction that

Jesus' death had redeemed him. Hawks had not shown Hazel the second clipping: "Evangelist's Nerve Fails." At the moment when he had planned to rub lime into his eyes, Hawks believed that he had seen Jesus expel the devils that had drawn him to this testing of God, and the sight had made him flee.

The next afternoon, Sabbath Lily tricked Hazel into taking her for a ride in the country. As they lay in a field, Hazel was beginning to formulate his plan for seducing her without realizing that she had already planned the same thing. When she looked into his eyes and playfully said "I see you" to Hazel, however, he suddenly bolted.

Meanwhile, Enoch Emery had been going through an elaborate cleansing ritual in preparation for his theft of the mummy from the museum. He called it the "new jesus" and felt that Hazel needed it for his church. At the same time, Hazel was coping with unwanted help from a volunteer preacher, Onnie Jay Holy, who confided to Hazel that they could make a lot of money from his church with the right promotion. Outraged, Hazel refused. The same night, Hazel learned that Hawks was not blind. His deception revealed, Hawks skipped town, leaving Sabbath Lily behind.

When Enoch Emery delivered the "new jesus" to Hazel, he was obliged to leave the mummy with Sabbath Lily instead. When Hazel found her holding the mummy like an infant, he became furious and slammed the thing against a wall, releasing its sawdust stuffing. Then he went out to preach, only to find that Onnie Jay Holy (his real name was Hoover Shoats) had hired a double, Solace Layfield, to preach a distorted version of Hazel's "Church Without Christ." Furious, Hazel lured the man into the country and killed him by running over him with the Essex. Enoch Emery had also disappeared into the country, wearing a gorilla suit stolen from a movie promotion.

After he had killed his rival preacher, Hazel Motes returned to town and blinded himself in just the way Hawks had failed to. The last months of Hazel's life were marked by his increasing need to scourge himself until at last, blind and wearing barbed wire under his clothes, Hazel was dead in a ditch in a wintery rain.

Critical Evaluation:

Wise Blood was the first of Flannery O'Connor's novels to be published. It bears some marks of the writer's learning her way, but it also contains many of the elements that mark O'Connor's mature fiction—her strong sense of character and voice, her comic vision, and her concern with religious themes.

It is in the novel's structure that some scholars have seen *Wise Blood* as suffering from O'Connor's apprenticeship. Although the early scenes of Hazel Motes on the train, his confrontations with the passengers, and his first day in Taulkinham begin to establish Hazel's character, they seem not to be tied securely to the novel's main narrative. The same might be said for O'Connor's disposal of Enoch Emery and his retreat into the world of beasts. It may be an appropriate conclusion for a character like Enoch, but it seems detached from the novel's central concerns. Concerns about minor failures of structure seem insignificant, however, in the light of the novel's successes, particularly in its characters and their language. Hazel Motes is one of many of O'Connor's Christ-haunted characters. Inarticulate, uneducated, unsophisticated, and distrustful of sophistication (and rightly so, O'Connor implies), he nevertheless is able to focus on life's most important concern—the gospel's message of salvation. Hazel's attempt to reject that message is the central action of the novel, and the fact that it cannot be rejected is O'Connor's chief theme. Even after he tries to create an antichurch, after he has distracted himself with the world in the form of his car and Sabbath Lily, Hazel is still left with his sense that Jesus is hunting him down. Hazel's murder of the person he calls the false prophet, Solace Layfield, is in some ways the crisis of the novel. Layfield is hired to mimic Hazel's preaching; he even dresses like Hazel. In killing him, Hazel seemed to be killing himself. Only after the murder does Hazel take on the penances he acts out at the end of his life.

The voices of O'Connor's characters often reveal their author's skill at re-creating Southern speech. Hazel says, for example, "Nobody with a good car needs to be justified." Enoch Emery relates how he escaped the head teacher at Rodemill Boys Bible Academy when he "giver a heart attack." Sabbath Lily describes a woman whose allergies made her break out in "welps." The inflections of the rural South become a point of entry to O'Connor's comic vision of the world.

O'Connor's is a dark world and her humor is often satiric, portraying a secular society in which God is essentially irrelevant. Sabbath Lily, for example, once writes to an advice columnist, Mary Brittle, in an attempt to reconcile her belief that her illegitimacy condemns her with her interest in men. The heart of the columnist's answer lies in her last sentence: "A religious experience can be a beautiful addition to living if you put it in the proper perspective and do not let it warf you." Toward the end of the novel, when the blind Hazel Motes has moved into Mrs. Flood's house, she questions him about the barbed wire he wears under his shirt. When he says it is natural, she retorts: "Well, it's not normal . . . it's something that people have quit doing—like boiling in oil or being a saint or walling up cats."

O'Connor prods the reader to recognize and laugh at the ugly and vulgar in her characters' worlds. Enoch Emery's rented room contains a picture of a moose whose gaze intimidated him. He lost his front teeth to the spring in a can of gag gift candy. The movies Enoch attends are either violent or sentimental.

The sense that the world is fraudulent is tied directly to O'Connor's central theme: In a world of falsities, the only reality is the grace that leads to salvation. This is the reality that Hazel Motes tries to deny throughout the novel. At the end, however, his ruined eyes looking like the star at Bethlehem, he seems to have submitted to the inexorable call of the Jesus who haunts him. As a character, Hazel is so inarticulate that by the end of his tortured life he is quite incapable of talking to anyone about his spiritual state. Readers draw their conclusions about the significance of the ending through the viewpoint of Mrs. Flood, a woman who is little given to insights about others. It is she who thinks of Bethlehem when she looks at Hazel's eyes. At the very end of the novel, she believes that in Hazel's empty eye sockets she can see him retreating away from her into tiny pinpoints of light, and she suspects that somehow she has been cheated of something. O'Connor implies that she has lost what she has refused to be found by—the Christ who insists on finding Hazel.

Ann Davison Garbett

Bibliography:
Brinkmeyer, Robert H., Jr. *The Art and Vision of Flannery O'Connor*. Baton Rouge: Louisiana State University Press, 1989. Devotes a chapter to O'Connor's two novels, arguing that, unlike the stories, they portray characters who are intent on denying Christ.
Browning, Preston M., Jr. *Flannery O'Connor*. Carbondale: Southern Illinois University Press, 1974. The chapter on *Wise Blood* offers a good general explication of the novel. Other chapters cover *The Violent Bear It Away* and O'Connor's major short stories.
Giannone, Richard. *Flannery O'Connor and the Mystery of Love*. Champaign: University of Illinois Press, 1989. Giannone's main concern is an examination of the relationship between

love and guilt in O'Connor's work. His detailed reading of *Wise Blood* establishes the theme of guilt in the novel.

Kessler, Edward. *Flannery O'Connor and the Language of Apocalypse.* Princeton, N.J.: Princeton University Press, 1986. Shows how metaphor transforms O'Connor's prose. Her use of metaphor allows her to address the mystery of grace, her central fictional concern. References to *Wise Blood* are frequent throughout this short book.

O'Connor, Flannery. *Mystery and Manners: Occasional Prose.* Edited by Sally and Robert Fitzgerald. New York: Farrar, Straus & Giroux, 1969. Essays selected and edited by friends of O'Connor offer the reader an introduction to O'Connor's ideas about her work and what she intended it to accomplish. She discusses the relationship between religion and fiction and the treatment of her work in the classroom.

Walters, Dorothy. *Flannery O'Connor.* Boston: Twayne, 1973. Good introduction to the novelist; it places *Wise Blood* in the context of her other work and gives it an explication.

WIVES AND DAUGHTERS

Type of work: Novel
Author: Elizabeth Gaskell (1810-1865)
Type of plot: Domestic realism
Time of plot: Mid-nineteenth century
Locale: Hollingford, a country town in England
First published: serial, 1864-1866; book, 1866

Principal characters:
MOLLY GIBSON, the only child of a widower
MR. GIBSON, the town physician, Molly's father
CLARE HYACINTH KIRKPATRICK, Gibson's second wife
CYNTHIA KIRKPATRICK, Molly's stepsister
OSBORNE and ROGER, the sons of Squire and Mrs. Hamley

The Story:

When Molly Gibson's widower father, the town doctor, married the widow Clare Hyacinth Kirkpatrick, Molly lost her preeminent position in her father's household and acquired a frivolous, silly stepmother as well as a stepsister with whom she had little in common. The marriage was undertaken for practical reasons on both sides; the father thought that his motherless young daughter needed the protection and tutelage of a mature woman, and the widow was grateful for a rise in social status and material comfort in place of the struggle to make a living as a governess. The marriage was not a happy one because of differences in temperament and intellect.

Molly and Cynthia, the two young girls, did become fast friends, however, although they were very different in character and personality. Each girl admired the other for qualities she herself lacked. Cynthia captivated Roger Hamley, the younger son of Squire Hamley, and they became unofficially engaged just before Roger left England to do two years of scientific research in Africa. Molly never spoke of her own love for Roger.

While Roger was gone, Cynthia wrote to him to break off the relationship because she realized that she did not love the young scientist; moreover, she had received a more advantageous proposal from Walter Henderson, a young lawyer whom she had met while visiting relatives in London.

Squire Hamley counted on his son Osborne, Roger's older brother and the heir to the Hamley estate, to save the family's declining fortunes by marrying into a wealthy family. Osborne was, however, secretly married to a penniless Frenchwoman whom he had met in France. When he developed a heart ailment, Osborne returned home ill and depressed. He died before he had revealed to his father that a son had been born, but his wife, Aimée, came to Hollingford when she heard of Osborne's illness.

The squire immediately doted upon his young heir, but he was unable to accept Aimée. Molly tried hard to reconcile the two; when Roger returned to England upon learning of his brother's death, the squire acknowledged his daughter-in-law and agreed that she should live nearby where she could care for her son.

Roger had hoped to persuade Cynthia to marry him, but when he saw her with Walter Henderson, he himself realized that he had merely been infatuated with her and that he really loved Molly, who had loved him steadfastly so long. They reached an understanding before

Roger left to complete his contractual obligation to his research sponsors. They looked forward confidently to the future, when they planned to marry, leave Hollingford, and live in London.

Critical Evaluation:

Although *Cranford* (1851-1853), Elizabeth Gaskell's idyll of village life, was probably her most popular work, scholars and critics as well as many serious readers of fiction consider *Wives and Daughters* her greatest novel. This work, too, concerns provincial life in the first half of nineteenth century England, but it is more complex in scope and deals with broader social and moral issues. It was Gaskell's last novel, and it was not quite complete at the time of her death. The romantic, satisfying conclusion toward which she was working, however, was clear.

Born on September 29, 1810, in London, Elizabeth Gaskell was the daughter of a Unitarian minister, and she grew up in her aunt's household after the death of her mother in 1811. She was educated in a school for young ladies and was well read in literature and philosophy. She married a Unitarian minister and was active in working with the poor and the sick, but after her only son died, she fell into a depression. With the encouragement of her husband, she became a professional writer and eventually attained an international reputation, a distinction earned by only a handful of other female writers of her time. She was the author of five novels, a biography of Charlotte Brontë, and numerous short stories.

The title *Wives and Daughters* indicates the only two recognized roles for women in the society that Gaskell describes. She presents a cross section of provincial society, in which Lord and Lady Cumnor and their family represent the aristocracy, Squire Hamley, his wife, and their two sons represent the landed but not wealthy gentry, and the physician, known as Mr. Gibson, and his young daughter, Molly, represent the professional middle class. Many other characters—including servants, townspeople, and laborers—round out the picture of this society.

Gaskell depicts the changes that take place in the lives of the principal family groups as well as the changes in their relations with each other. The principle upon which all the members of these groups base their lives is the sanctity of the family, and the novel focuses on the duties and obligations of family members. All the action and the shortcomings, as well as the successes, of the characters are related to the overriding importance of the basic social unit, the family.

The story is told primarily through the thoughts and actions of the main character, Molly Gibson. Most of the characters reach an understanding of the truth about themselves during the course of the novel, but it is primarily Molly who facilitates this, though without intending to do so. She exercises influence over others because, although she is a simple, uneducated country girl, she is able to see things as they are and has a strong sense of how they ought to be. She represents the moral conscience of her world and acts as a mediator and source of moral strength, especially for her father, her stepmother, her stepsister Cynthia, and her friend, Osborne Hamley.

The author of *Wives and Daughters* makes very few authorial comments; instead, she allows her characters to reveal themselves in their conversations, their inner reflections, and their behavior toward each other. With gentle, good-humored satire, Gaskell creates a picture of rural society that can easily be seen to represent the larger human condition, regardless of time or setting. One of the many critics who have lauded the author's works commented that Gaskell's vision and tone provided a link between the Romantics of the nineteenth century and the psychological realists of its waning years.

Natalie Harper

Bibliography:

Cecil, David. *Early Victorian Novelists: Essays in Reevaluation.* London: Constable, 1934. Establishes Gaskell's importance in comparison with the other great Victorian novelists. Contains a lengthy essay on Gaskell, including critical discussion of *Wives and Daughters.*

Gérin, Winifred. *Elizabeth Gaskell: A Biography.* Oxford, England: Clarendon Press, 1976. A highly personal rather than scholarly discussion of Gaskell's work. Includes a chapter on *Wives and Daughters.*

Horsman, Alan. *The Victorian Novel.* Oxford, England: Clarendon Press, 1990. Includes a chapter on Gaskell, in which Horsman analyzes the way she discussed the problems of a changing society in her work. Analysis of *Wives and Daughters* emphasizes the effect of outsiders in a self-contained society.

Lansbury, Coral. *Elizabeth Gaskell.* Boston: Twayne, 1984. A chapter considers *Wives and Daughters* in detail.

_____. *Elizabeth Gaskell: The Novel of Social Crisis.* London: Elek, 1975. Evaluation of Gaskell's work. Emphasizes the economic and social aspects of *Wives and Daughters.*

Rathburn, Robert C., and Martin Steinmann, eds. *From Jane Austen to Joseph Conrad.* Minneapolis: University of Minnesota Press, 1958. A collection of essays. Includes a chapter on Gaskell by Yvonne French, who presents an overview of Gaskell's life and work and gives a balanced analysis of *Wives and Daughters.*

Rubenius, Aina. *The Woman Question in Mrs. Gaskell's Life and Works.* 1950. Reprint. New York: Russell & Russell, 1973. Discusses women's issues and focuses on the treatment of these matters in *Wives and Daughters.*

THE WOMAN IN THE DUNES

Type of work: Novel
Author: Kōbō Abe (1924-1993)
Type of plot: Allegory
Time of plot: 1962
Locale: A Japanese seaside village
First published: Suna no onna, 1962 (English translation, 1964)

Principal characters:
NIKI JUMPEI, a teacher on vacation
THE WOMAN, a widow, resident of a small village

The Story:

A teacher and an amateur entomologist, Niki Jumpei decided to take a vacation to gather specimens for his collection of insects. He took a train to a location near the ocean and, carrying a canteen and a large wooden box, disappeared from the sight of the urban life he had known. Eventually, he was missed by his mother and by his lover. The mother filed a report with the missing persons bureau, but no trace of him was ever found by the authorities.

Jumpei had taken a train to a small town and had walked from the town where the railroad station was located to an area of dunes near the ocean. He came upon a strange village, where many of the houses were located in pits created by huge sand dunes. As night approached, he began to look for a place to sleep; villagers directed him to a building that was little more than a shack, located in one of the depressions in the dunes. It turned out to be the home of a youngish woman, who offered to accommodate Jumpei. Unenthusiastically, Jumpei accepted the unnamed woman's hospitality.

Jumpei was horrified by the woman's story. He learned, soon after his stay began, that she was a widow whose husband and small daughter were both victims of the ever-encroaching sand. Her life consisted of a constant struggle against the sand, shoveling it to a place from which it could be hauled up for shipment to shoddy contractors for use in making cheap concrete. This industry was the sole economic support of the entire village. The woman made it clear that Jumpei was expected to help with the work of shoveling sand in exchange for his room and board. Their shoveling was essential; without constant efforts to remove sand and send it to the top, the little house would be overwhelmed by sand-slides.

Jumpei soon discovered that he could not escape from the depression in the dunes in which the house was placed. He attempted a variety of ways to evade the fate to which he had been condemned. He tried to bully and threaten the woman to force her to help him leave, but he failed. He tried to bargain with and to threaten the only other villagers he saw, the men who came to the top of the dune, lowered buckets to the pit below to be filled with sand, and raised the buckets on ropes; they did not respond to any of his overtures. Finally and reluctantly, he gave in and helped the woman with her unceasing labor, but he could not get used to the constant presence of sand. It was in his clothes, in his eyes, on his skin, in his mouth; when he slept, it coated his entire body.

When he was not shoveling sand, sleeping, or eating his meals, Jumpei continued to spend his time plotting ways of escaping from his prison. He tried to climb out, only to be half-buried by a slide. He threatened the villagers with criminal prosecution if they failed to provide him with a ladder, but they had no reason to fear him; the police did not interfere with the villagers.

Even if someone had reported his absence, there was little likelihood that an investigation would reach the village, and, if it should, they would simply deny knowledge of Jumpei's existence.

Jumpei and the woman formed a strange kind of relationship. As the days passed, she became more attractive to him, and they finally became sexual partners, although their other interactions remained tense and intermittent. She nursed him when he was sick and began to treat him with some tenderness. She pointed out that her life was easier with him to help shovel the sand, and Jumpei showed at least some affection in helping her with the chores. Still, there was no escaping the relentless sand.

Finally, Jumpei was able to find a way out, using a rope ladder which caught on something on the surface, enabling him to hoist himself out of the pit. He was free for a while, passing through the village and finding his way to the sea, but this freedom was an illusion. In a very long passage describing his attempted escape, he carried on internal dialogues with the woman, with a friend from his earlier life, and with himself. He was chased by dogs and lost his way several times, never finding his way out of the village area. He found the ocean, but he strayed into quicksand and survived only because the villagers, who were aware of his attempts to escape, had followed him. They saved him from the quicksand and returned him to the woman's care.

Jumpei made one final attempt to flee. When the workers came to take away the accumulated sand, he pleaded with them to help him leave. They laughed at him, but finally an old man offered him escape if he and the woman would have sexual intercourse in front of the crowd that had gathered. He tried to persuade the woman and, when she refused, he tried to force her, finally pleading with her to pretend to submit, since he was unable to perform anyway. She beat him, hurting his stomach and bloodying his nose, and the watching villagers lost interest in the proceedings. Finally, he realized that they had no intention of letting him go.

In the end, Jumpei accepted the struggle against the sand as a way of life. He did not give up planning to escape, but it became an abstraction for him, with no real effect on the way he lived. The woman became pregnant, but this seemed to affect him very little. When she suffered great pain and a villager (who was related to a veterinarian) diagnosed her condition as an extrauterine pregnancy, Jumpei hardly paid any attention when she was taken away to a hospital in the city. The rope ladder used to lift her from the pit remained in place, and Jumpei climbed it, getting a view of the sea. He was tempted to try to escape once again, since the attention of the villagers was on the woman. Rather than try to leave, however, he went back down to continue an experiment he had begun. Escape could wait for another day.

Critical Evaluation:

The Woman in the Dunes is the best known of Kōbō Abe's works, at least in the Western world, perhaps in part because it was made into a memorable motion picture. More important, however, is the fact that this grim, almost allegorical picture of the state of humanity echoes a Greek myth which has resonated in the twentieth century: the myth of Sisyphus, who was condemned to spend his days pushing a heavy rock up a steep slope, only to have the rock slide back down every time. Albert Camus, one of the major writers influenced by French existentialism— a philosophy that dominated much of Western thought and literature after World War II—used Sisyphus as a symbol of human fate in one of his major essays. Very simply stated, the existentialists held that life was similar to the experience of Sisyphus: Human hopes and dreams (particularly that of the Christian afterlife) were doomed never to be realized, but human nobility was nevertheless confirmed in accepting this fact and carrying on with the struggle.

The Woman in the Dunes has a distinctly Japanese style. The setting for almost all the action is an isolated village whose inhabitants have no interest in and little connection with the larger world outside their immediate area. They are primitives who accept their harsh fate, condemned to an eternal struggle with the encroaching sand, because they can conceive of no other way of life. Their sense of humor is crude and cruel, their imaginations limited. The simple experiment with water that Jumpei is conducting at the end of the novel would never have occurred to any of them, and yet it could lead to a major easing of one of the harsh conditions of their existence. Still, even should the experiment turn out to be a success, there is no reason to believe that the villagers will use Jumpei's results to their benefit.

The allegorical nature of *The Woman in the Dunes* is underlined by the relatively small amount of interest Abe shows in making his characters into individuals; the fact that the second of the novel's two major characters, the woman in the dunes herself, is never given a name is evidence of this. Even Jumpei is almost always referred to as "he" or "him" in the narrative. He is a most ordinary man, with the single unusual character trait of an interest in collecting insects. The reader knows only that he has had a mother and a lover, as well as a single friend, and that he is a teacher. Otherwise he is simply Everyman, and he is lost.

The central symbol in this allegory is the sand. Its presence in the novel is relentless, representing not only the dreariness and inevitability of everyday life but also the material out of which people make their living and the capriciousness of the natural world in which they are fated to try to survive. It is sand that killed the woman's husband and daughter and that almost kills Jumpei in his attempt to escape. More than anything, however, the sand is the symbol of a reality which is so continuously present, forming a kind of film over everything in the lives of these characters, that it becomes an integral part of every moment of their lives. They nearly come to a point at which they are no longer aware of the unpleasantness of its continual presence.

Abe, with Yukio Mishima and Nobel Prize winner Kenzaburō Ōe, was a leader of a post-World War II generation of Japanese writers who took a major interest in politics, a subject not traditionally important in Japanese literature. There is evidence of this interest in *The Woman in the Dunes:* The villagers are exploited to haul sand that is then sold by a corrupt business society to make shoddy concrete. There is also a political dimension in the helplessness of the characters. They continue providing this sand for corrupt businesses without questioning or attempting to change their situation.

More important, however, many critics have seen in *The Woman in the Dunes* a distinct similarity to the work of the Czech writer Franz Kafka, in such works as *The Trial* (1925) and *The Castle* (1926). Both writers use the same kind of nearly anonymous characters, both place their characters in hopeless situations they did little or nothing to create, and both depict people at the mercy of forces they have no means of understanding. Abe once said that he intended to provide hope for his characters, and perhaps Jumpei's experiment can be seen as a small ray of light, but the tone of *The Woman in the Dunes* and the fate of its characters leave little room for this possibility. Abe, like Kafka, has created in his works situations that mirror humanity's helplessness in the face of incomprehensible and overwhelming forces.

John M. Muste

Bibliography:
Dissanyake, Wimal. "Kōbō Abe: Self, Place, and Body in *Woman in the Dunes:* A Comparative Study of the Novel and the Film." In *Literary Studies and West*, edited by Jean Toyama and

Nobuko Ochner. Honolulu: University of Hawaii Press, 1990. Pays special attention to the theme of alienation and identity and to the importance of the sense of place in *The Woman in the Dunes*.

Hardin, Nancy. "Interview with Kōbō Abe." *Contemporary Literature* 15, no. 4 (Autumn, 1974): 439-456. The major published interview with Abe. Includes important information about his life and his literary influences.

Leithauser, Brad. "Severed Futures." *The New Yorker* 44, no. 12 (May 9, 1988): 122-126. This essay discusses the recurrent theme of the uncertainty of human life in Abe's fiction.

Remnick, David. "Kōbō Abe: A Figure Apart." *The Washington Post*, January 20, 1986, C1. Provides a wealth of information about Abe's life and the experiences underlying his fiction.

Van Wert, William F. "Levels of Sexuality in the Novels of Kōbō Abe." *International Fiction Review* 6, no. 2 (Summer, 1979): 129-132. Discusses Abe's affinities with Fyodor Dostoevski, Franz Kafka, and Alain Robbe-Grillet.

THE WOMAN IN WHITE

Type of work: Novel
Author: Wilkie Collins (1824-1889)
Type of plot: Detective and mystery
Time of plot: 1850's
Locale: England
First published: 1860

>*Principal characters:*
>WALTER HARTRIGHT, a young artist
>FREDERICK FAIRLIE, the owner of Limmeridge House
>LAURA FAIRLIE, his niece and ward
>MARIAN HALCOMBE, her half sister
>SIR PERCIVAL GLYDE, Laura Fairlie's suitor
>COUNT FOSCO, a scheming nobleman
>ANNE CATHERICK, the woman in white

The Story:

Through the help of his Italian friend Professor Pesca, Walter Hartright was engaged as drawing master to the nieces of Frederick Fairlie, of Limmeridge House in Cumberland. On the day before he left to take up his new position, he met a young woman dressed in white wandering about the outskirts of London. Walter discovered that she knew Limmeridge and had once gone to school there with Laura Fairlie. The young woman left him very suddenly, and soon after a coach came by whose passenger leaned from the window to ask a policeman if he had seen a girl in white. The policeman had not, and Walter hesitated to intrude. As the coach left, he heard the man say the girl had escaped from an asylum.

Upon his arrival at Limmeridge, Walter met the first of his two pupils, Marian Halcombe. Marian was homely but intelligent and charming in manner. Her half sister, Laura, was the beauty of the family and heiress of Limmeridge House. The two girls were living under the protection of Laura's uncle, Frederick Fairlie, a selfish and fastidious hypochondriac. Walter fell in love with Laura almost at once. After hearing his story about the mysterious woman in white, Marian searched her mother's letters and discovered that she must have been Anne Catherick, a young woman in whom Mrs. Fairlie had taken great interest because she so greatly resembled Laura.

After several months, Marian realized that Walter was deeply in love with Laura. She advised him to leave, as Laura's father had asked her on his deathbed to marry Sir Percival Glyde. One day, Walter met the woman in white again. She was in the graveyard cleaning the stone that bore Mrs. Fairlie's name, and she admitted that she hoped to thwart Laura's coming marriage to Sir Percival. Told of this incident, Marian promised to ask Sir Percival for a full explanation.

Walter left Limmeridge. When Sir Percival arrived, he explained to Marian that Anne Catherick was the daughter of a woman who had been in his family's service in the past and that she was in need of hospital treatment. He said he had kept her in an asylum at her mother's request, and he proved the statement with a letter from Mrs. Catherick. His explanation was accepted, and his marriage to Laura took place. Walter, heartbroken, went to Central America as a painter for an archaeological expedition.

When Sir Percival and Laura came home from their wedding trip some months later, Marian found them much changed. Laura was extremely unhappy, and Sir Percival showed his displeasure at having Marian living with them in his house at Blackwater Park. Count Fosco, a huge and self-assured Italian, arrived with his wife, Laura's aunt, for a visit. Marian soon learned that the count was involved in money matters with Sir Percival. When Laura was asked to sign a document without looking at it, both she and Marian knew Sir Percival and Count Fosco were trying to obtain money from her by fraudulent means. Over Sir Percival's loud protests, Laura refused to sign the paper unless he would let her read it. The count interfered and made Sir Percival give up the matter for a time. Marian overheard a conversation between the two men, in which they decided to get loans and wait three months before trying again to persuade Laura to sign away her money. The household became one of suspicion and fear.

By chance one day, Laura met the woman in white and learned that there was a secret in Sir Percival's life involving both Anne Catherick and her mother. Before Anne could tell her the secret, Count Fosco appeared and frightened the woman away. Sir Percival became alarmed when he learned that Anne was in the neighborhood. He locked both Marian and Laura in their rooms, but Marian spied on the two men by climbing to the roof during a pouring rain and overheard a plot to get Laura's money by killing her. Before she could act on this information, however, Marian caught a fever from the chill of her rain-soaked clothing. She was put to bed, and Laura, too, became mysteriously ill.

When Laura was better, she was told that Marian had gone to London. She could not believe her sister had left her without saying good-bye and insisted on going to London herself. Actually, Marian had been moved to another room in the house. When Laura arrived in London, she was met by Count Fosco. She was given drugs, falsely declared insane, dressed in Anne Catherick's old clothes, and taken to the asylum from which Anne had escaped. Sir Percival had found Anne in the meantime. Because of her resemblance to Laura, he planned to kill her and bury her as Laura. Anne was already very ill, and when she died suddenly in London of natural causes, Sir Percival announced that Laura, Lady Glyde, had died.

After Marian recovered, she was told that her sister was dead. She refused to believe either the count or Sir Percival. Determined to find Anne, she discovered that the woman in the asylum was really Laura. She arranged Laura's escape and took her back to Limmeridge. At Limmeridge, however, Frederick Fairlie refused to recognize the sickly Laura as anyone but Anne Catherick. Laura's memory had been so impaired by the experience that she could not prove her identity. Marian and Laura went to look at the false tomb bearing the name of Lady Glyde. There they met Walter Hartright, who had recently returned from Central America. He had come to pay his respects at Laura's grave.

There was no possibility of returning Laura to her rightful estate as long as her mind was impaired by her terrible experience. While she was recovering, Walter Hartright attempted to learn Sir Percival's secret. He finally discovered that Sir Percival's father and mother had never been legally married. Hoping to destroy the evidence of his birth, Sir Percival attempted to burn an old church record that Walter needed. In the fire he set, Sir Percival burned up the church and himself as well. After his death, Mrs. Catherick hinted that Laura's father had been the father of illegitimate Anne as well. After searching, Walter found that this must be true.

Walter returned to London. Together, the three planned to clear Laura by forcing the count to confess. Walter's old friend Professor Pesca revealed that Count Fosco was a traitor to the secret society to which both Pesca and the count had belonged. Through Pesca's help, Walter was able to frighten the count into giving him a confession and written proof in Sir Percival's handwriting that Laura was still alive when Anne had been buried under the name of Lady Glyde. The count fled England and was killed soon afterward by the secret society he had betrayed.

Walter, Marian, and a much improved Laura were happy to have proof of the substitution that had been made. Walter and Laura married and went to Limmeridge to confront Frederick Fairlie with the evidence. He was forced to admit Laura's identity. The friends then left and did not return until after Fairlie's death, when the son of Laura and Walter took over the estate. Marian lived with the family until she died.

Critical Evaluation:

Throughout his career, Wilkie Collins, like many other writers, was torn between a need to satisfy the demands of the popular reading public and a personal desire to create works of lasting artistic merit. He achieved the desired synthesis only twice, initially with *The Woman in White* and, six years later, with *The Moonstone*. *The Woman in White* was both his most popular work and his most important serious book.

Although the plot of *The Woman in White* is fantastic, it was based, as were many of Collins' crime stories, on an actual case history he discovered in Maurice Méjan's *Recueil des causes célèbres*. In 1787, Madame de Douhault was cheated out of a portion of her father's estate by a brother. On her way to Paris to launch proceedings against her brother, she stopped at a relative's home, where she was drugged, confined to a mental hospital, and declared dead. The unscrupulous relatives collected all that remained of the father's estate. Like her fictional counterpart, Madame de Douhault—wearing a white dress—finally escaped, but, unlike Laura Fairlie, she was never able legally to reestablish her identity, despite positive identifications from friends and associates. She died a pauper in 1817.

The crime becomes more elaborate and complicated in Collins' hands. Not only is the heroine drugged and secreted in an asylum, but a deceased double is buried in her place. "The first part of the story," Collins commented in a newspaper interview, "will deal with the destruction of the victim's identity. The second with its recovery." Collins added a number of secondary lines to this basic plot movement: the question of Laura Fairlie's marriage to Percival Glyde; the identity and story of Anne Catherick, the mysterious "woman in white"; the love affair between Laura and Walter Hartright; Laura's supposed death and the events surrounding it; Percival Glyde's relationship with Anne's mother, Mrs. Catherick, and his mysterious secret; and, finally, Count Fosco's mysterious background.

Complex as the plot is, Collins handles the threads of the narrative in such a way that they support and complement one another without obscuring the central thrust of the book. While answering one question, Collins uses that answer to introduce new, more provocative questions. As the puzzles are gradually unraveled, the pressures on the hero and heroines become more extreme. Throughout much of the book, the victims seem nearly helpless before the villains' power. The reversal does not come until late in the novel and, when it does, the shift is sudden. Yet even in the last important scene, Hartright's confrontation with Fosco, when the initiative is clearly the hero's, the sense of danger remains intense. Nowhere does Collins demonstrate his mastery of intricate plotting more effectively than in *The Woman in White*, and it remains, with the possible exception of *The Moonstone*, the most perfectly structured example of the sensation novel.

The gradual revelation of the intricate conspiracy is made doubly effective by Collins' narrative method. The story is told in bits and pieces by a number of characters who reveal only as much as they know. Some of the narrators, among them Walter Hartright, Marian Halcombe, and Count Fosco, are major participants who explain and interpret events as they occur or after the fact. Others, such as Laura's uncle, Frederick Fairlie, Glyde's housekeeper, Eliza Michelson, and Laura's tombstone, are minor personages who can only provide fragments of information that reflect their brief connection to the story. This technique, in which he reveals only so much information at any one time as convenient, gives Collins a great deal of flexibility and control over the suspense, ensures variety in the narrative style, mood, and tone, and sharpens the characterizations. As the speakers offer their information, they characterize themselves through their diction, prose style, habits, and attitudes. Most important, Collins' narrative method offers readers a gigantic prose jigsaw puzzle. A few years later, Collins used this same method in writing what many have called the first English detective novel, *The Moonstone*.

The object of the conspiracy, Laura Fairlie, is a passive creature with little color or character. The real conflict is between Marian Halcombe and Walter Hartright on the one hand and Percival Glyde and Count Fosco on the other. In the first half of the book leading up to Laura's falsified death, Marian acts as a foil to the villains. After Laura's escape, Walter Hartright becomes the principal hero. Glyde enters the novel before Fosco but quickly retreats in the reader's mind to a subordinate position. Fosco, the most impressive character, dominates all the other characters.

As Walter Hartright describes her, Marian Halcombe is a physically unattractive woman: "the lady's complexion was almost swarthy, and the dark down on her upper lip was almost a mustache. She had a large, firm, masculine mouth and jaw; prominent piercing resolute brown eyes and thick coal-black hair, growing unusually low on her forehead." Morally and intellectually, she is nevertheless a very strong character. Her qualities, when summed up—loyalty, steadfastness, courage, propriety, intelligence, sensitivity—sound like a list of stock Victorian virtues, but as Collins presents her she seems real.

It is Marian who first senses a conspiracy. It has gone too far to stop, but she manages to hamper the villains for a time. The irony of her situation is that when, having courageously risked her life and gained the information she needs to expose the plot, she catches pneumonia in the act—thus exposing herself and becoming helpless at the critical point. Her illness gives Fosco an opportunity to read her journal and learn everything about her counterstrategy. Having read Marian's comments, however, Fosco is so impressed by her character and resourcefulness that, for the first time, he allows sentiment to mitigate his treatment of an adversary. This slight moral hesitation is ultimately a significant factor in his downfall.

Fosco is one of the most memorable literary criminals of all time. By contrast, Glyde, in Collins' own words, is "a weak shabby villain." Glyde is clearly dominated by Fosco and does very badly when he operates alone. He reacts to situations emotionally and physically, with little planning and crude execution; the most obvious example is the vicarage fire that costs him his life. Because Collins thought "the crime too ingenious for an English villain," he felt it necessary to create Isidor Ottavio Baldassare Fosco.

Collins wisely never introduces or describes Fosco directly but allows his presence to grow by means of the reactions and impressions experienced by the other characters. The count's most obvious physical feature is his size; he is the first of the great fat criminals, a common type in later crime fiction but still unusual in Collins' time. "I had begun my story when it struck me that my villain would be commonplace, and I made him fat in opposition to the recognized type of villain." Fosco's physical size is matched by his appetites for food, culture, money, and intrigue: he is, in short, a demonic Falstaff.

Fosco's intellectual powers are likewise impressive. His conspiracy has style as well as intelligence, and he is witty, extremely articulate, and suavely ironical. Furthermore, he is no ordinary criminal; he justifies his amoral actions philosophically: "Crime," he tells Marian, "is a good friend to man and to those about him as often as it is an enemy."

Despite the evil he does, Fosco is an attractive man. In addition to his intelligence, style, courage, and strong, if distorted, sense of honor, he also possesses a number of vivid humanizing traits: his fondness for animals, especially his birds and mice, his feelings for his wife, and his honest admiration, even devotion, toward Marian Halcombe. Perhaps Collins assigned Fosco's punishment to a mysterious Italian political group rather than to Walter Hartright because he realized that his readers' ambiguous feelings about Fosco would place some onus on the man who brought him to justice.

Although critics have long lauded the characterizations of Marian and Fosco, they have tended to ignore Walter Hartright, though he is too important to the novel to be so easily dismissed. He lacks some of the color and sympathy of Marian but is, nevertheless, her equal in courage and intelligence. More important, looking at the novel from the standpoint of a nineteenth century reader, it is Hartright that one would most likely identify with, and it is he who upholds the English national character and middle-class morality in the face of Fosco's threat.

Hartright, the hardworking son of a thrifty drawing master, confronts a nobleman, a baronet, and a decadent member of the gentry (Fairlie), all vestiges of aristocracy. Walter takes his work seriously; he is industrious, loyal, rational, courageous, and tenacious—in short, he possesses all the Victorian middle-class virtues. In contrast to the amoral Fosco, Hartright believes that virtue, truth, and justice must ultimately triumph, and he is given the job of demonstrating that assumption in the action. Because he does it so efficiently, the novel answers the intellectual and moral expectations of the Victorian reading public. Despite Fosco's style and charm, even twentieth century readers find Hartright's final victory inevitable and satisfying.

"Critical Evaluation" by Keith Neilson

Bibliography:
Caracciolo, Peter. "Wilkie Collins' Divine Comedy: The Use of Dante in *The Woman in White*." *Nineteenth-Century Fiction* 25, no. 4 (March, 1971): 383-404. Detailed and excellent analysis of the use of imagery in the novel, which offers a different view of the novelist.
Collins, Wilkie. *The Woman in White*. Edited by Harvey Peter Sucksmith. Oxford, England: Oxford University Press, 1980. A most accessible edition with a valuable bibliography and notes explaining vocabulary and the legal statutes of the era. Sucksmith's introduction contains a good discussion of the Dauhault case that served as the probable source of inspiration for Collins.
Hyder, Clyde K. "Wilkie Collins and *The Woman in White*." *PMLA* 54 (1939): 297-303. Discusses the stories about the real identity of the woman in white and debunks the myth that Wilkie Collins' mistress served as the prototype.
Peters, Catherine. *The King of Inventors: A Life of Wilkie Collins*. Princeton, N.J.: Princeton University Press, 1993. Contains an extensive bibliography especially pertaining to the Collins family's personal documents. Also provides an interesting discussion of the theme of identity in *The Woman in White*.
Symons, Julian. *Mortal Consequences: A History from the Detective Story to the Crime Novel*. New York: Harper & Row, 1972. Analyzes *The Woman in White* and discusses Collins' role as one of the earliest masters of the suspense novel.

A WOMAN KILLED WITH KINDNESS

Type of work: Drama
Author: Thomas Heywood (c. 1573-1641)
Type of plot: Tragedy
Time of plot: Early seventeenth century
Locale: Yorkshire, England
First performed: 1603; first published, 1607

> *Principal characters:*
> JOHN FRANKFORD, a provincial gentleman
> ANNE, his wife
> WENDOLL, her paramour
> SIR FRANCIS ACTON, her brother
> SIR CHARLES MOUNTFORD, a provincial nobleman
> SUSAN, his sister
> NICHOLAS, servant of the Frankfords
> SHAFTON, a schemer

The Story:

John and Anne Frankford celebrated their marriage feast in the company of a group of relatives and friends. Everyone joined in complimenting the bride on her beauty and on her charming submission to her husband. As the group joined the crowd dancing in the great hall of the house, Sir Francis Acton and Sir Charles Mountford arranged a wager on hawking for the next day. Out in the courtyard, tenants of the Frankford estate celebrated their master's wedding.

Early the next morning Acton and Mountford and their companions went into the field to match their falcons. Acton lost the wager, but declared that Mountford's falcon had broken the rules of the hunt. Following an exchange of hot words, the hunting party divided into two sides. In the fighting Mountford killed two of Acton's men. Susan, Mountford's sister, went to him in the field and advised him to flee, but he declared that he could never leave her. The sheriff arrived and apprehended Mountford.

Frankford, at his home, felt himself supremely happy; he was affluent, well-educated, and blessed with a lovely and virtuous wife. As he reflected upon his felicity, Wendoll, who had been in the hunting party, excitedly arrived to report the details of the fatal fight. Frankford, already impressed by Wendoll's manner, invited the young gentleman to live in his house and to be his companion. Nicholas, Frankford's faithful servant, observed to himself that there was something about Wendoll that he did not like; he and the other servants expressed distaste that Wendoll should become a guest in the house.

Mountford, meanwhile, had been forced to spend almost his entire patrimony in order to gain his liberty. As he left the jail, he encountered Shafton, an unprincipled man who forced a large sum of money upon him. It was Shafton's purpose eventually to cheat Mountford out of a small ancestral house he still possessed and somehow to win the hand of Mountford's sister Susan.

Wendoll fell passionately in love with Anne Frankford. Conscience-stricken, he was distracted by the dreadful thoughts that went through his mind. When Frankford rode away on business, Anne innocently told Wendoll that Frankford wished him to take his place in the household during his absence. Torn between reason and passion, Wendoll succumbed to passion and disclosed to Anne his great love for her. Anne at first resisted his blandishments, but she was soon overcome by his insistence that his love for her in no way reduced his great affection for and obligation to Frankford. Nicholas, undetected, overheard the conversation and vowed to bring the affair to light.

The term of Mountford's debt to Shafton having come due, the lender offered to buy Mountford's house, his last worldly possession. When Mountford refused to sell at any price, Shafton ordered a sergeant to handcuff Mountford and clap him in jail for debt. Hearing what had happened, Acton, who was filled with hatred for Mountford because of the violent dispute over the hawks, declared that he would seduce Susan Mountford. When Acton actually saw Susan, he immediately fell in love with her.

On his return Frankford learned from Nicholas that Anne and Wendoll were unfaithful, she to her marriage vows, Wendoll to the bonds of friendship. When Frankford, Anne, Wendoll, and a guest, Cranwell, played cards after dinner, it seemed all too clear from the irony revealed in the conversation that Nicholas had indeed told the truth. Frankford planned to make certain that Anne was untrue to him.

Susan, meanwhile, asked her uncle, Old Mountford, to help her brother. The old man refused, as did other men to whom Mountford had been generous in former days. When Acton offered Susan a bag of gold, she spurned help from her brother's enemy. Acton cleared Mountford's debts anonymously. Mountford, released again from jail and from all of his debts, encountered Susan and, to her bewilderment, thanked her for her good work. When the jailer informed the pair that it was Acton who had aided them, Mountford, unable to accept the generosity of an enemy, proposed to return to jail. The jailer, having been paid, refused to admit him. At last Susan confessed that Acton had paid the debts because of his love for her. Knowing that fact, and shamed by his debt to Acton, Mountford felt that there was only one thing to do.

During supper at the Frankfords, Nicholas, by prearrangement, brought a letter to his master at the table. Frankford announced that he was called away immediately on legal business. After he had gone, Wendoll thanked fortune that matters worked out so well for him and Anne. Anne, however, was not happy in her affair with Wendoll; her conscience told her that she was lost in sin. Although she had succumbed to Wendoll because of his clever rhetoric, she suffered remorse. After dining with Wendoll in her chamber, she directed the servants to lock up the house and to bring her the keys.

Frankford, meanwhile, tied his horse to a tree near the house and with keys that he had made for the purpose he and Nicholas crept into the darkened house at midnight. Discovering Wendoll and his wife asleep in each other's arms, Frankford expressed a desire to turn back the clock so that the shame to his honor might have been prevented. Awaking the couple, he chased Wendoll with drawn sword, but a housemaid caught his arm and kept him from taking Wendoll's life. Anne, conscience-stricken, asked Frankford to end her life. He decided, however, that death was too good for her; he condemned her to live the rest of her life comfortably but in seclusion in a house on the estate. She was never to set eyes on him again.

In the meantime Mountford suggested to Susan that she give herself to Acton in return for his deed. When Susan objected on grounds of honor, Mountford declared that his soul would not rest until Acton had been repaid, and Susan finally agreed to this proposal. When Acton went to their house, Mountford bitterly offered his sister as payment. Acton was overcome by the magnanimous gesture. At one time he had not dreamed of marrying poverty-stricken Susan; now he declared that he would proudly take her as his wife.

As Anne, accompanied by her servants, prepared to start on her exile, Nicholas rode up and handed her a lute, the only one of her possessions she had left behind her. Tearfully, she declared that the lute, untuned as it was, was a symbol of her marriage. Wendoll, now repentant, met Anne on the road. When he began to express his remorse, she, fearful lest he tempt her again before she died, commanded the coachman to drive on to the house where she would end her days.

Later, learning that Anne was near death from a broken heart, Frankford went to her and forgave her sins. After her death Frankford declared that her epitaph would recall her as a woman killed by her husband's kindness.

Critical Evaluation:

A Woman Killed with Kindness is commonly regarded as the best of the domestic tragedies of its time. Domestic tragedies are so called because of their treatment of the lives of ordinary people rather than of royalty. The conflicts in a domestic tragedy may bring down the head of a household but never a head of state. The family struggle in *King Lear* (c. 1605-1606) with its ensuing horrors, may suggest some great breach in nature, but the ordinariness of life in the domestic tragedies works against grand cosmic interpretations. The simple, direct language of the domestic tragedy contrasts with the grandiloquent rhetoric of Renaissance tragedies involving royalty or other larger-than-life figures.

Thomas Heywood did not invent the plots of *A Woman Killed with Kindness*. The subplot featuring Sir Francis Acton and Sir Charles Mountford has been traced to an Italian source that evolved through several versions and appeared in William Painter's popular collection of stories *The Palace of Pleasure*, the first edition of which appeared in 1566. Painter summarized the story this way: "A gentleman of Siena, called Anselmo Salimbene, curteously and gently delivereth his enemy from death. The condemned party seeing the kinde parte of Salimbene, rendreth into his hands his sister Angelica, with whom he was in love, which gratitude and curtesie, Salimbene well markinge, moved in conscience, would not abuse her, but for recompence tooke her to his Wife." As for the main plot, several sources have been suggested, especially several other stories from Painter's collection.

Critical judgments on *A Woman Killed with Kindness* vary widely. Some critics charge that the two plots fail to come together in any unity and that both plots are improbable and sentimental. Frankford, moreover, is a despicable man among a cast of unconvincing characters. These are major criticisms, but the play's supporters argue passionately for it as a tragic masterpiece. They assert that both plots are set in motion in the first scene and run parallel, and that Wendoll joins the two plots by playing a crucial role in each.

Furthermore, structural parallels appear in the scenes that counterpoint masters and servants. The servants' dancing party in the second scene follows the opening wedding feast, and the two lighthearted celebrations set a mood that contrasts with the events that follow, serving as an emotional foil to the tragedy. The masters debate intensely the virtues of their hawks and hounds and the country people quarrel amiably over the dances they will perform. Supporters of Heywood's dramatic techniques cite more instances of contrasts and parallels. In the seventeenth and final scene, for instance, Frankford and Anne's reunion parallels the reunion scene of the subplot and differs from it in being a reunion only in death. In this final scene, only one figure from the wedding party is absent: Wendoll, the villain. Only one person, Susan, appears who was not at the wedding, and she represents the virtue that the weak Anne had lacked. Admirers of the play point also to the contrasts between paired characters as a unifying device: Susan and Anne, Frankford and Acton, and Acton and Wendoll. All of these patterns provide evidence of Heywood's careful craftsmanship.

Sentimentality is the most difficult charge against which to defend *A Woman Killed with*

Kindness. Even the play's admirers generally concede the weaknesses of the subplot, in which the characters lack the complexity that would generate the audience's sympathy for their plights. Attacks on the main plot center on Anne. Her qualities as the perfect wife are never demonstrated, only stated; she never earns, in the audience's eyes, the virtue attributed to her that makes her fall into sin pathetic. Her death is sentimental rather than tragic.

Domestic tragedies such as *A Woman Killed with Kindness* avoid affairs of court and focus on the lives of ordinary people. Heywood stresses this feature when he opens his prologue with the remark, "Look for no glorious state, our Muse is bent/ Upon a barren subject, a bare scene." This strain in domestic tragedy reflects the influence of fifteenth century morality plays, which introduced ordinary people as suitable subjects for serious theater. The best-known morality play, *Everyman,* an anonymous play whose earliest extant version dates from 1508, is no more than a parade of allegorical figures. *Everyman,* however, represents all humanity rather than a courtly elite, and the gritty realism that pervades his story agrees with the settings in domestic tragedy.

The strong didactic strain of the morality plays also appears in the domestic dramas. In both types of plays, there are lessons for all to learn about good and evil. *A Woman Killed with Kindness* dramatizes Christian teachings about sin, repentance, and forgiveness, and Frankford alludes several times to the biblical story of Judas. For instance, Frankford's reference to "that Judas that hath borne my purse,/ And sold me for a sin . . ." refers to John 13:29 and to Matthew 27:3-4. Later, when Frankford discovers the sinners, he says, "Go, to thy friend/ A Judas; pray, pray, lest I live to see/ Thee Judas-like, hang'd on an elder tree," a passage alluding to Matthew 27:5.

Other biblical references include Frankford's remark about the book of life (the record of those who shall live eternally) with sources in Philippians 9:3 and Revelation 20:12. Sir Charles also refers to "a huge beam/ In the world's eye," which is drawn from the Sermon on the Mount in Matthew 7:3. These biblical references, along with the many proverbial expressions (the title, for example) all contribute to making the play a text of moral instruction.

"Critical Evaluation" by Frank Day

Bibliography:
Adams, Henry Hitch. *English Domestic: Or, Homiletic Tragedy 1575 to 1642.* New York: Columbia University Press, 1943. *A Woman Killed with Kindness* gets a chapter in this comprehensive study. Stresses that it is not Elizabethan psychology but religious didacticism that drives the plot.
Baines, Barbara J. *Thomas Heywood.* Boston: Twayne, 1984. An excellent overview of Heywood's life and works, with a list of primary sources and an annotated secondary bibliography. Analyzes in detail the themes and structure of *A Woman Killed with Kindness* and responds to criticisms of the play's characterizations and moral vision.
Clark, Arthur Melville. *Thomas Heywood: Playwright and Miscellanist.* New York: Russell & Russell, 1967. A detailed account of Heywood's life and career. A chapter praises *A Woman Killed with Kindness* as preeminent among domestic tragedies and says it "anticipates the bloodless tragedies of Ibsen."
Heywood, Thomas. *A Woman Killed with Kindness.* Edited by R. W. Van Fossen. Cambridge, Mass.: Harvard University Press, 1961. A superb modern edition with full notes, an appendix on the source of the subplot, and analyses of sources, theme, structure, characters, style, stage history, and the text.

Velte, Mowbray. *The Bourgeois Elements in the Dramas of Thomas Heywood*. New York: Haskell House, 1966. Finds the main plot much superior to the subplot and discusses their parallels to their sources. Praises *A Woman Killed with Kindness* for its realism and points out that the play does not resort to a depiction of a murder or a sensational local event.

THE WOMAN OF ROME

Type of work: Novel
Author: Alberto Moravia (1907-1990)
Type of plot: Naturalism
Time of plot: 1930's
Locale: Rome
First published: La romana, 1947 (English translation, 1949)

Principal characters:
ADRIANA, a prostitute
HER MOTHER
GINO, a chauffeur
MINO, a student
SONZOGNO, a thug
ASTARITA, a police official
GISELLA, Adriana's friend

The Story:

Sixteen-year-old Adriana was beautiful in face and body. Her lips were red and full, her breasts high and firm. Her mother, a poor sewing woman, thought of Adriana as her only capital; the family had been poverty-stricken since the illness and death of the father. Adriana's mother did not conceal her opinion that their poverty could be traced to her marriage and Adriana's unwanted birth.

Thinking her daughter mature enough, the mother took her to an artist to arrange for her career as a model. Adriana was not embarrassed by undressing before a strange man, nor was she much embarrassed when her mother punched and patted her naked body as she stressed her good points. Nevertheless, her mother's shrill arguing about the pay was quite rude. She was especially violent with polite people, such as the artist, because they usually gave in before her temper displays.

The artist agreed to pay a higher fee with good grace. As he talked with Adriana afterward, he tried to tell her that her mother loved money above all else. Adriana was unconvinced. The artist was about forty years old and always correct in his behavior. When his pictures did not sell, he had no more work for Adriana. She had little difficulty in obtaining other jobs, because her figure was so fine, even heroic in proportions.

When modeling did not pay well enough, her mother tried to get Adriana a job as a dancer, and she secured an interview with a vaudeville manager. Adriana did her best, but she was miserably conscious of her clumsy feet. Even her mother's shrewish scolding could not win Adriana a job on the stage.

Adriana dutifully took as many modeling jobs as she could, built up a reputation for virtue among the artists, and sewed shirts in the afternoons and evenings. A turning point came when she met Gino.

Gino was soft-spoken and gentle despite his rough workman's hands. He was a chauffeur for a wealthy family, and when he could, he took Adriana for long rides. Her mother objected to the friendship, for she thought Adriana's beauty could win her a gentleman.

Adriana did not object when Gino invited her to his employer's villa while the family was away. She willingly went to his room, and afterward they slept until past midnight. Adriana had never been out so late before, and her suspicious mother was furious. She set on her daughter with her fists and beat her as long as she had strength. Then she took Adriana to an all-night clinic and had her examined by a doctor. When the doctor confirmed her fears, she was glum but calm.

It was understood that Gino and Adriana would be married, but Gino found excuses for delaying the wedding. The mother was pessimistic about the marriage. Gisella, Adriana's friend, was also doubtful of Gino's intentions and urged her to accept a rich lover while she could. She finally induced Adriana to go out to dinner with Astarita, a rich police official who was anxious to meet her. At the dinner in a hotel Gisella almost forced Adriana to go into a bedroom with Astarita. On the way home Astarita gave Adriana money.

So Adriana was launched on a new career. She did not dissolve her relationship with Gino, for she still thought that perhaps they would be married. That hope vanished, however, when Astarita produced evidence that Gino was married and had a daughter. For revenge, Adriana let Gino take her to the villa again, but she insisted on making love in the mistress' bed. After she told Gino that she knew the truth about his wife, she stole a compact from the dresser.

Adriana became a prostitute. She usually brought her clients home, and her mother accepted the state of affairs with good grace because there was more money in the house. Adriana usually slept late and led an indolent, satisfied existence. She really liked men. Her mother became fat and much less attractive.

One night she met Gino again. He wondered about the compact. On their return home, the wealthy family had missed it, and Gino suspected Adriana. Gino arranged to have suspicion fall on a maid, who was arrested and sent to jail. After getting the compact from Adriana, Gino planned to sell it to a fence. When he said he would divide the money with her, Adriana, filled with pity for the falsely arrested maid, refused.

She found Gino one night in company with Sonzogno, a strong man and a thug. When Gino and Adriana left a café together, she felt repelled by her former fiancé and on an impulse called to Sonzogno for help. He promptly knocked Gino down and went home with Adriana. Adriana was both attracted to Sonzogno and in terror of him. He had the stolen compact in his possession. Gino had given it to Sonzogno to sell, and Sonzogno had murdered an old jeweler to whom he had taken it for that purpose. After listening to callous boasts of his crime, Adriana succeeded in getting the compact away from him. She experienced a horrible evening, for Sonzogno beat her. Later she had her confessor give the compact to the police, and the maid was released.

Gisella and Adriana went out for the evening and were picked up by two men. The four went to Adriana's house. Soon afterward, Gisella became the mistress of her pickup and was promptly installed in her own apartment. Adriana's pickup was Mino, a nineteen-year-old student. Thin and withdrawn, he was not much interested in lovemaking. His attitude attracted Adriana and thereafter she pursued him, even to his respectable rooming house.

Adriana's affairs became more complicated. The friendly clinic doctor confirmed her fears; she was pregnant. As she thought back, she knew that Sonzogno was the father. She was rather pleased to have a child, but her baby would be born of a murderer and a prostitute. When Mino came to live at her house, she told him that he was the father of her expected baby.

Mino was an anti-Fascist engaged in subversive work. When he was arrested, he promptly betrayed his fellow conspirators under the sympathetic questioning of Astarita. As soon as he learned that Astarita was an admirer of Adriana, he proposed that she should invite him to her house, and there Mino would shoot him.

Sonzogno, sure that Adriana had betrayed him to the police, arrived just before Astarita was expected. When Astarita appeared, he slapped the submissive Sonzogno's face and sent him away. Then he told Adriana that Mino's confession had not been written down and the police had taken no action against his friends.

Adriana was nevertheless apprehensive. It was not like Sonzogno to be meek. When she went to the ministry, her fears were justified. Astarita was dead in the courtyard; Sonzogno had followed him to his office and had thrown him off a balcony. Adriana went home to find Mino gone. He had left a note saying that his parents would look after her and his son; he was going to kill himself. His body was found in a hotel near the station.

Critical Evaluation:

Alberto Moravia self-published his first novel, *The Time of Indifference* (1929), at the age of twenty-two, and it became an overnight scandal in Italy. Controversy swirled about Moravia, who was called immoral by some, while others pointed out that he was simply the messenger who was bringing the bad news about the collapse of Italian society. Six more novels consolidated his reputation in Italy, but it was not until *The Woman of Rome* was published in English in 1949 that he achieved an international reputation.

Moravia was a thinker who wrote novels to embody his ideas, which often concerned the present and the ways in which it differed from the past in European civilization. People were losing touch with their humanity, he said, and they were becoming caught up in a life of action, rather than a life of contemplation. Humanity was no longer its own goal; human beings were being turned into a means to another end. Moravia believed that the mindless, uncontemplative activity of modern people, whether acquiring money or squandering it, amounts to nothing, and that, he added, is what modern art embodies: nothingness.

The bustle of Euro-American civilization in the twentieth century is inauthentic, he declares, and he even goes so far as to maintain that, given the present state of affairs, authenticity exists solely in thought and fantasy. *The Woman of Rome* can be read as part-demonstration, part-embodiment of Moravia's beliefs. Adriana's first step on the road to prostitution is taken when she allows herself to be date-raped by Giacinta, a man she does not desire, because he threatens to tell her fiancé, Gino, that he, Giacinta, has already had sex with her. Adriana, instead of holding firm to her feelings, is betrayed by the end she has in mind: her forthcoming happy marriage with Gino. She permits herself to be blackmailed into having sex with an unappealing stranger because she doesn't want to risk losing her marriage. For that afternoon, Adriana turns herself into the means to an end, instead of preserving her authentic being as an end in itself.

Under the circumstances, it would not have been easy to have behaved in an authentic manner. Moravia's skill as a novelist enables him to show just how compromised Adriana finds herself on this day in Viterbo, pressured not only by Giacinta, but also by her best friend, Gisella, and her boyfriend, Riccardo, as well as by the wine she has drunk. Her naïveté and inexperience are also handicaps. Then, after the deed is done, the unexpected thrill she feels when Giacinta pays her with a large sum of money virtually seals her fate. Given the poverty of her background, given her considerable physical charms, given her mother's constant sermonizing on the need for Adriana to marry a rich man in order to get the proper cash value for her beauty, Adriana has already had a lot of things pushing her in this direction.

Although sex becomes her job, refreshingly, Adriana continues to enjoy the act, and, although for some months she takes care not to fall in love, she appreciates—and can be stirred by—the physical qualities of her clients, as well as by their personalities. She takes society's judgment of her as a criminal, however, seriously enough to think, "Might as well be hung for [stealing] a sheep as a lamb," and to become a thief into the bargain. Her confusions seem similar to those confusions of anyone living in such a society: Do people work for pleasure, or for survival, and do people resent or relish their work?

Moravia, in other books as well, suggests that in a society as empty of meaning as the one he writes about and for, even sex without love can be a good, kindling feeling between creatures otherwise empty and numb. Some critics assert that Moravia is imposing a male-centered view upon his female mouthpiece, just as he is accused of giving her powers of intellectual reflection that would not belong to a woman of her class. The first charge must remain controversial: Might there not be a woman, and more than one, whose self is substantially composed of male-introjected elements? The second charge is more telling: Adriana's powers of intellectual reflection—indeed, her very vocabulary—are those of Moravia, rather than of a poor woman from the slums of Rome. Although this discrepancy violates the realism of the novel, it also paints a marvelous psychological portrait—it is as if Moravia is an analyst providing commentary behind her every move.

The strongest passages of the novel are those in which Adriana learns something new about herself and about life. She is forever saying that she knows how and who she is, and then she discovers through some new experience that, in fact, she is not that way, or not only that way. The plot is second-rate, and its climax is a near-farcical concatenation of coincidence, but the novel is always readable, because readers want to learn about love and sex—and the entire life of the feelings—along with the young heroine.

"Critical Evaluation" by David Bromige

Bibliography:

Heiney, Donald. *Three Italian Novelists.* Ann Arbor: University of Michigan Press, 1968. Discusses Moravia's change in technique in this novel, to a first-person, female, lower-class narrator. Also examines Moravia's impatience with omniscient narration.

Lewis, R. W. B. "Eros and Existence." In *The Picaresque Saint.* New York: Lippincott, 1959. Worth looking at for Lewis' analysis of Moravia's use of sexual encounters as proving-grounds of the existential.

Moravia, Alberto. "Interview with Alberto Moravia." Interview by Ben Johnson and Maria de Dominiciis. *The Paris Review,* no. 6 (1955). Contains useful information regarding *The Woman of Rome.*

_____. *Man as End.* New York: Farrar, Straus & Giroux, 1966. Eighteen essays that provide invaluable information about the author's philosophy and his approach to the novel as a literary form.

Ross, Joan, and Donald Freed. *The Existentialism of Alberto Moravia.* Carbondale: Southern Illinois University Press, 1972. Good attempt to place Moravia's writings in relation to his philosophical and literary tendency.

THE WOMAN WARRIOR
Memoirs of a Girlhood Among Ghosts

Type of work: Memoir
Author: Maxine Hong Kingston (1940-   )
First published: 1976

Maxine Hong Kingston's *The Woman Warrior: Memoirs of a Girlhood Among Ghosts* focuses on Chinese and American female identities by blending mythology, history, and poetry. She explores these identities by reconstructing her mother's (Brave Orchid's) life for fifteen years in China during the 1920's and 1930's and through her own experiences growing up in Stockton, California, in the 1940's and 1950's. A second book, *China Men* (1980), a companion piece to *The Woman Warrior*, tells the story of the Chinese men in Kingston's family. Both books span continents and generations, the first focusing on the women, the second on the men, although *China Men* has a female storyteller.

Kingston, a writer of both fiction and nonfiction, received her first great acclaim after the publication of *The Woman Warrior*. Although her work continued to be well received, her later books have moved in other directions. Kingston published *Hawaii One Summer* in 1987, exploring the Chinese American history of Hawaii. The novel *Tripmaster Monkey: His Fake Book* (1989) tells the story of twenty-three-year-old Berkeley graduate Wittman Ah Sing. In the early 1990's, Kingston's only copy of her recent novel was destroyed by fire, and she had to start over from scratch.

The Woman Warrior is divided into five sections, each of which can be easily anthologized. "No Name Woman" and "Tongue-Tied," for example, may be read alone. Despite the stories' ability to be separate and remain powerful, they tie together into a coherent whole. The second and fifth sections focus on Kingston, who identifies herself as a "legendary warrior woman." The other three sections focus on Kingston's mother's stories and Kingston's retelling of them. The complex narrative patterns of *The Woman Warrior* are intertwined; the first three stories are about the mother, and the final two stories are about the daughter.

"No Name Woman," the first and shortest section, begins with the voice of Kingston's mother warning the young Kingston, "You must not tell anyone . . . what I am about to tell you." In telling the story of her father's nameless sister, Kingston, as narrator, breaks the taboos and the silence of tradition. The breaking of the silence begins Kingston's war on traditions that have destroyed people, women in particular. Once Kingston has broken the silence by repeating her mother's story, she tries to fill in the gaps.

Her mother has told her only what Kingston calls a "story to grow up on," the parts necessary to guide a growing adolescent, so that she will not humiliate her parents. The nameless aunt bore a child two years after her husband's departure for America. The villagers, to punish the family for their daughter's impropriety, came to the home when the child was due. Disguised, they killed livestock, stoned the house, and destroyed the inside of the home. The disgraced family stood together in the middle of the room and looked straight ahead. They neither locked their doors against the attack nor resisted it. During the night, the aunt gave birth, unattended, in the pigsty. Kingston's mother concludes, "The next morning when I went for the water, I found her and the baby plugging up the family well." The story is meant to introduce Kingston to the dangers that accompany the beginning of menstruation. Kingston, however, hungers for the details of the aunt's story, details that she cannot get from her mother because the details are not necessary to make her point: "Adultery is extravagance."

Kingston fills in the gaps in the story through various retellings of it. In these retellings, she explores gender inequality in her speculations about the lives of the men who have left their wives behind and the life of the man who fathered her aunt's child. Kingston acknowledges her guilt for participating in the punishment of the aunt for twenty years. She says that she still does not know her aunt's name, but at least she has broken the silence, an act that ends her participation.

"White Tigers," the second section, retells Kingston's mother's story of Fa Mu Lan, the woman warrior who took her father's place in battle. Kingston becomes the woman warrior, doing battle against the devaluation of girl children, especially in Chinese culture. Fa Mu Lan is led away from her family by a white crane who teaches her boxing and then delivers her to an "old brown man" and an "old gray woman." They give her a choice of returning home to the life of a traditional girl—a wife and slave—or staying with them for fifteen years of hard training to become a woman warrior. She chooses the hardships of the rigorous training over the devaluation of tradition.

In the seventh year of her training, at age fourteen, she is taken blindfolded to the mountains of the white tigers, where she must learn to survive on her own. In the mountains, she learns many lessons about survival, both physical and spiritual. For example, she realizes that hunger "changes the world—when eating can't be a habit, then neither can seeing," and she learns to make her "mind large, as the universe is large, so that there is room for paradoxes." Fa Mu Lan, when she eventually returns home, is valued like a son by her family.

Kingston deals squarely with gender issues in this section. As Fa Mu Lan, she liberates a group of abandoned women, who become a mercenary army that takes in unwanted girls and that kills men and boys. When she returns to her modern narrative, she explores her devaluation as a Chinese American girl, one who earns high grades in school but must listen to Chinese sayings about the worthlessness of girl children. "Even now," Kingston says, "China wraps double binds around my feet." She realizes that, unlike Fa Mu Lan, she dislikes armies and she cannot save her relatives from the horrors they experience in China. She can, nonetheless, use words—both Chinese and English—to fight the devaluation of females.

"Shaman," the third section, begins as Brave Orchid shows Kingston the metal tube that holds the medical diploma from China. Through the mother's recollections and Kingston's imagination, Brave Orchid's years in China as a married woman are reconstructed. Her two children die; her husband is in the United States. When Brave Orchid finds herself alone, she decides to attend medical school. Among Brave Orchid's stories from these times are accounts of facing ghosts, of buying a slave girl, and of trying to stop people from stoning a crazy woman. Six months after the stoning, in the winter of 1939, Brave Orchid leaves China and arrives, almost a year later, in New York Harbor.

As Brave Orchid ages, she laments the loss of her medical practice in China, her inability to return to her homeland, and finally, her powerlessness in keeping her six children and their families close to her. The section ends with her urging Kingston, a mature woman, to remain with her. Ultimately, however, Brave Orchid realizes that her daughter must go out into the world.

"At the Western Palace," the fourth section, begins as Brave Orchid awaits the arrival of her sister, Moon Orchid, from China. After her arrival, Moon Orchid, clearly disoriented, stays for several weeks with Brave Orchid's family and with her own daughter, who is visiting from Los Angeles. The suspense builds throughout the story as the sisters debate if, how, and when Moon Orchid will reunite with the husband who left her behind in China thirty years earlier. When Moon Orchid's daughter announces that it is time for her to return to her husband and children, Brave Orchid's oldest son drives her and the two elderly sisters to Los Angeles, where Moon Orchid's husband also lives with his younger wife. When the sisters go to the husband's place of business, he becomes angry and distraught. He sends them away and agrees that he will continue to send money to Moon Orchid. She never sees him again and ends up in a California state mental asylum, where she dies.

Moon Orchid's unhappy fate greatly alters Brave Orchid's family. Brave Orchid fears that her elderly husband may take a younger wife—although he promises he will not. Her daughters decide "fiercely" that they will "never let men be unfaithful to them." All of Brave Orchid's children decide to "major in science or mathematics." The family's faith in family and tradition is shaken.

"A Song for a Barbarian Reed Pipe," the final section, relates several events from Kingston's childhood. Among the most jarring of these stories is that of her attack on a schoolmate, a Chinese American girl a year older than Kingston. Kingston corners the odd schoolmate after school and tries to force her to speak. Kingston realizes, even as she repeatedly hurts the girl, that this is "the worst thing [she] had yet done to another person." When the girl refuses to make any sound, Kingston becomes unnerved and cries. Immediately following this event, Kingston becomes ill and spends the next eighteen months "sick in bed with a mysterious illness." Upon her return to school, she learns that the odd classmate will not need to speak, that she comes from a well-to-do family that can take care of her. Through these experiences, Kingston explores the ideas of justice and necessity in women's lives. As Kingston contemplates variations of oddness and insanity in Chinese women, she worries that she, too, may be destined for insanity.

Ultimately, she and her mother end up in a noisy scene in which both are talking, refuting each others' misunderstandings. The scene shows both the separation and the unity of Kingston and her mother. Kingston, the adult, wants to go to China to learn the truth about her relatives and about communism. She needs to distinguish between what is fiction and what is true, yet she recognizes the irony of her need. The final story of the section is a synthesis, a story begun by Kingston's mother and finished by Kingston. It is the story of Ts'ai Yen, a poet born in 175 C.E. During Ts'ai Yen's twelve years as a captive of the barbarians, she composes "Eighteen Stanzas for a Barbarian Reed Pipe." When Ts'ai Yen returns from her captivity, she brings the music with her. Kingston concludes, "It translated well."

The Woman Warrior has earned its place in literary studies. In 1976, it won the National Book Critics Circle Award for nonfiction. In 1979, it was named one of the top ten nonfiction works of the decade by *Time* magazine. It is a staple in classrooms in American colleges and has been translated into other languages. It is a book with international appeal. Through *The Woman Warrior*, Kingston explores not only gender identity and national identity but also human identity. The five narrative sections of her memoir become the vehicle for this exploration. The locations, China and the United States, are as much psychological states for Kingston, for her parents, and for her readers as they are places on a map. The human and global qualities of *The Woman Warrior* no doubt account for its continuing success.

Carol Franks

Bibliography:
Kingston, Maxine Hong. *China Men*. New York: Alfred A. Knopf, 1980. A companion piece to *The Woman Warrior*. The two works illuminate each other.
Perry, Donna, ed. *Backtalk: Women Writers Speak Out*. New Brunswick, N.J.: Rutgers Univer-

sity Press, 1993. Perry's collection of interviews contains a brief introduction, photographs of the writers, and an interview with Kingston on her work, including *The Woman Warrior*.

Rainwater, Catherine, and William J. Scheick, eds. *Contemporary American Women Writers: Narrative Strategies*. Lexington: University Press of Kentucky, 1985. Of particular interest is Suzanne Juhasz's essay "Maxine Hong Kingston: Narrative Technique and Female Identity."

Smith, Sidonie, and Julia Watson, eds. *De/Colonizing the Subject: The Politics of Gender in Women's Autobiography*. Minneapolis: University of Minnesota Press, 1992. Chapter 14, written by Lee Quinby, explores *The Woman Warrior* as a memoir that shows the "technology of ideographic selfhood."

A WOMAN'S LIFE

Type of work: Novel
Author: Guy de Maupassant (1850-1893)
Type of plot: Naturalism
Time of plot: Early nineteenth century
Locale: Normandy and the island of Corsica
First published: Une Vie, 1883 (English translation, 1888)

> *Principal characters:*
> JEANNE DE LAMARE
> JULIEN DE LAMARE, her husband
> PAUL DE LAMARE, her son
> BARON SIMON-JACQUES LE PERTHUIS DES VAUDS, her father
> ROSALIE, her foster sister

The Story:

In the spring of 1819, Jeanne Le Perthuis des Vauds and her parents went to live in an old chateau, The Poplars, on the Normandy coast. Baron Simon-Jacques Le Perthuis des Vauds had been left a large inheritance, but he had so reduced it by his freehandedness that he was eventually forced to reconcile himself for the remainder of his days to a simple country life.

Jeanne, who had spent the preceding five years in a convent, looked forward happily to her new life and dreamed of the day when she would find the man who loved her. All her expectations were fulfilled. She found a beautiful countryside to wander over and the sea to bathe in and to sail on. She met a neighbor, the handsome young Viscount Julien de Lamare, who came to call, and they quickly became good friends. When the baron presented his daughter with a boat, he invited the village priest and his acolytes to christen it. To Jeanne, the ceremony seemed like a wedding, and under the spell of her illusion, she accepted his proposal when Julien asked her to marry him. The wedding took place that summer, six weeks after they had become engaged.

At Jeanne's wish, the couple journeyed to Corsica on their honeymoon. She had been romantically in love with her husband before her marriage, but during the two months she was away from home with him her emotion grew into a passion. Thus she was amazed, when they stopped in Paris on their way home, to find that Julien was not perfect. She had given him her filled purse, her mother's present, to look after, and when she requested it back to buy some gifts for her family, he gruffly refused to dole out more than a hundred francs. Jeanne was afraid to ask for more.

When Jeanne and Julien returned to The Poplars, Julien took over the management of the estate. During the long, monotonous days of winter, he began to wear old clothes and he no longer bothered to shave. He paid little attention to his wife. Having sold the carriage horses to save the cost of their feed, he used the tenants' nags and became furious when Jeanne and her parents laughed at the ugly team.

In January, Jeanne's parents went to Rouen and left the young couple alone. It was then that Jeanne became completely disillusioned with her husband. One day, the maid, her foster sister Rosalie, bore a child. Julien insisted that the mother and her illegitimate infant should be sent off immediately, but Jeanne, who was fond of Rosalie, opposed him. A few weeks later, she found the pair in bed together.

The shock was so great that Jeanne could only think of getting away from her husband. Still in her nightclothes, she ran out of the house to the edge of the cliffs that hung over the sea. There Julien found her and brought her back to the house before she could jump. For several weeks, the young wife was ill as the result of her exposure. When she began to recover and had an opportunity to convince her parents of her discovery, Rosalie confessed that Julien had seduced her on the first day he had come to call at the house.

The maid and her baby were sent away. Jeanne would have preferred separation from her husband, but the knowledge that she herself was pregnant and the priest's intercession on Julien's behalf made her agree to a reconciliation.

Jeanne's baby was born in July, nearly a year after her marriage. She lavished all the love that Julien had not accepted on the infant Paul. After the baby's birth, the de Lamares became friendly with their neighbors, the Count and Countess de Fourville. The count was passionately in love with his wife, Gilberte de Fourville, but she rode alone with Julien almost every day. One morning, as Jeanne was walking her horse through the woods where Julien had proposed, she found her husband's and Gilberte's horses tied together.

Shortly afterward, the baroness died after an illness that had kept her partly crippled for many years. To Jeanne, who had been deeply attached to her mother, it came as a great shock to find that she, too, had not been above an affair, documented in the letters she had saved.

Jeanne had kept the secret of Julien's latest affair to herself, fearful of the steps the count might take if he ever discovered his wife's unfaithfulness. The old village priest, Abbé Picot, also held his peace. Unfortunately, Abbé Picot was called elsewhere. His successor was not so liberal in his views. Abbé Tolbiac was conscious of his parishioners' morals and was determined to guard them. By chance he discovered the affair between Julien and Gilberte de Fourville. He had no hesitation about discussing the subject with Jeanne, and when she refused to desert her husband or to inform the count, he took the story to Gilberte's husband. One day, while the couple were in a shepherd's hut, the count, a powerful giant, pushed the building down an incline and into a ravine. He then dashed home without being seen. Under the wreckage of the hut lay the two mangled bodies.

That night, after Julien's body had been carried home, Jeanne bore her second child, a stillborn girl. Although she suspected that Julien's death had not been an accident, she remained silent. The memories of her husband's infidelities faded quickly, leaving her at peace with her recollections of their early life together, as it had been on Corsica. Soon even these memories began to dim, and she turned all of her attention to her son. Paul de Lamare did not go to school until he was fifteen years old. At home, he was petted and indulged by his mother, grandfather, and a maiden aunt who had come to live at The Poplars after the death of the baroness. When he was finally sent off to Le Havre to school, Jeanne visited him so frequently that the principal had to beg her to restrict her visit.

In Paul's third year away from home, he stopped spending his Sundays with his mother. When a usurer called on her to collect money for the young man's debts, Jeanne visited his school and learned that he had not been there for a month. He had been living with a mistress and he had signed his mother's name to letters stating that he was ill.

After this escapade, Paul was taken home to The Poplars and closely watched. He managed to escape, however, and two days later Jeanne received a letter from him from London. It was the first of many begging notes he was to send her. In addition to asking for money, he announced that the woman he had known in Le Havre was living with him.

For more than a year, Paul sent a series of requests for financial help that were never ignored, even though they meant the mortgaging of The Poplars and the two farms that went with the estate. Anxiety over his grandson and his property caused the baron's death from apoplexy.

Soon after the baron's death, Jeanne's aunt followed him to the grave. Jeanne would have been alone then if Rosalie, who had since been married and widowed, had not returned to look after her. Her foster sister insisted on working without pay and on putting a much-needed check on Jeanne's expenditures. It was necessary to sell The Poplars, however, and the two women settled down in a small farmhouse.

Although Jeanne was forced to limit the sums she sent Paul, her affection for him did not decrease. When he had been away from home for seven years, she wrote begging him to come home. Paul's reply was that before he would return he wanted her consent to marry his mistress, with whom he was living in Paris. Jeanne, who was not without a strain of jealousy, decided that she would persuade him to come without the woman. As quickly as possible she set out for Paris. Although she had written to announce her visit, Paul did not meet her. To avoid his creditors, he had moved without leaving a forwarding address. His disconsolate mother returned to Normandy.

Some months later, Jeanne heard from her son once more. His wife, whom he had married without his mother's blessing, was dying, and he entreated Jeanne to come for their little daughter. This time, it was Rosalie who went to Paris. When she returned, she had the infant with her, and she brought the news that Paul would follow her the next day.

Critical Evaluation:

The first of Guy de Maupassant's six novels, *A Woman's Life* was published in 1883, three years after the death of his teacher, Gustave Flaubert. Maupassant had tried and mostly failed to please Flaubert by aspiring to the highest distinction as an artist in poetry and the theater. With the publication of "Madame Tellier's Excursion" in 1881, he found a ready market for short stories that were admirably crafted but—judged by Flaubert's exacting standards—needlessly cynical, inelegant, and often mechanically contrived. Nevertheless, their pungency, realism, and shrewd observation of character attracted many readers who had ignored *Des Vers* (1880), Maupassant's only volume of poetry. Many of the qualities of the stories also appear in *A Woman's Life*, a sustained, psychologically honest study of Jeanne de Lamare from the time she completes her idealistic education at a Rouen convent in 1819 until about 1855, when she is middle-aged, disillusioned, and worn with many sorrows.

Maupassant's novel has frequently been compared, usually to its disadvantage, with two other novels that examine the fate of disappointed women, Flaubert's *Madame Bovary* (1857) and Arnold Bennett's *The Old Wives' Tale* (1908). For subtlety, richness of characterization, and harmonious prose style, *Madame Bovary* is assuredly a more profound work of art. Bennett's novel, which was inspired by *A Woman's Life*, is more detailed than its model and has a surer grasp of social history and specific place and a deeper sense of the poignancy of time passing. Yet Maupassant's short novel—half as long as *Madame Bovary* and less than a third the length of *The Old Wives' Tale*—is remarkable in its own right. Compact, unsentimental, and stark, this work is a disturbing but affectionate study taken from human experience. The portrayal of Jeanne is thought to have been drawn, emotionally if not exactly, from Maupassant's memories of his mother, and his description of The Poplars recalls the setting of the Chateau de Miromesnil in Normandy, where the author spent his early childhood. The book, which was Maupassant's favorite among his novels, is memorable for its tender appreciation for the sufferings of women who are dominated by insensitive men.

Indeed, although Jeanne's story is central to the narrative, she is not the only woman whose life is one of disillusionment and quiet despair. Her mother, the Baroness Adelaide, lives a protected yet narrow life, she dissembles her knowledge of her husband's philandering with house servants and secretly revenges herself on the baron with her own infidelity. Rosalie, Jeanne's foster sister, is seduced and betrayed by her brother-in-law. Aunt Lison, neglected and pathetic, voices the lonely agony of a woman who has never been attractive to men. When Julien, courting pretty Jeanne early in the novel, solicitously asks whether her "darling little feet" are cold, Lison exclaims that "No one has ever asked me a question like that . . . never . . . never." Even when women give themselves to their lovers out of passion, Maupassant sees them as frail, unequal partners in romance. Rosalie confesses to Jeanne that she had submitted to Julien's lust, despite knowing the consequences and her delicate position in the household, because he pleased her sexually. The Countess de Fourville imprudently hazards a liaison with Julien out of a similar weakness. Paul's mistress submits to her lover, excusing his spendthrift ways and casual neglect of her, because she is without resources of her own. While *A Woman's Life* focuses on the history of Jeanne, her experiences are shown to represent those of her sex.

It is important to note that the story begins during the spring of 1819 and concludes about thirty-five years later. Hence Maupassant's view is retrospective, looking backward to a time of relative calm and a settled, conservative society. Most of his short stories, however, concern his own time, the Third Republic, from 1870 to 1890. Reviewing the sources of his own turbulent age, Maupassant shows that the calm of Jeanne's provincial society is illusionary, fixed in complacency rather than real tranquillity. It is founded on hypocrisy and outworn traditions. The Abbé Picot, Jeanne's casuistic parish priest, is more a diplomat than a religious man, who smoothes over problems of moral turpitude for the sake of expediency. His successor, the Abbé Tolbiac, is a fanatic, inflexible in his doctrine of sin. In the narrow society in which she moves, Jeanne has not the freedom to change or to reconstruct her life, guided as she is by the dead hand of tradition.

In spite of her limited opportunities, Jeanne never surrenders to self-pity. Instead, she develops strength of character. Although she does not master her fate, she learns to endure its vicissitudes. She is brutally mistreated (if not, indeed, raped) on her bridal night; denied the affection and even attention of her husband; humiliated, almost maddened, by his infidelities; and finally neglected by her wastrel son Paul. Yet she maintains a sense of personal dignity and courage in the face of defeat. Like Rosalie, who has also suffered much and matured in worldly competence, she sustains life. At the end of the book, Jeanne accepts the infant daughter of Paul and his dead wife, probably only to repeat with this child the pattern of indulgence that began with her worthless son. Although she is life's victim, she is willing to take further risks for the sake of advancing life. Rosalie's final words, which express Maupassant's stoic philosophy, allow the reader to understand the ambiguities of her choice: "You see, life is never as good or as bad as one thinks."

"Critical Evaluation" by Leslie B. Mittleman

Bibliography:
Donaldson-Evans, Mary. *A Woman's Revenge: The Chronology of Dispossession in Maupassant's Fiction.* Lexington: French Forum, 1986. A structural analysis of the chronological development in the way Maupassant depicts the relations between men and women.
Harris, Trevor A. Le V. *Maupassant in the Hall of Mirrors.* New York: St. Martin's Press, 1990. Posits that Maupassant's use of irony is an attempt to separate himself from and to criticize the excesses of French society. Examines Maupassant's narratives and journalism and focuses on his narrative technique, syntax, characterization, structure, and imagery.

Lerner, Michael G. *Maupassant*. New York: George Braziller, 1975. Reviews Maupassant's early life, his tutelage under Gustave Flaubert, the influence of Émile Zola, and the use of naturalistic techniques in Maupassant's work. Includes photographs.

Sullivan, Edward D. *Maupassant the Novelist*. Princeton, N.J.: Princeton University, 1954. Reviews aesthetics and theme in Maupassant's novels. Addresses the function of a critic, the opposition between realism and idealism, style, and Maupassant's objective point of view. The author traces a subtle but growing element of the psychological in Maupassant's last three novels. Presents *A Woman's Life* as a collection of short stories about a central, passive character.

Wallace, A. H. *Guy de Maupassant*. New York: Twayne, 1973. Depicts Maupassant's fiction as reflections of the life of a "doer" rather than an observer. Offers analysis of specific themes in the author's work, including infidelity, female servitude in marriage, and naturalism.

WOMEN BEWARE WOMEN

Type of work: Drama
Author: Thomas Middleton (1580-1627)
Type of plot: Tragedy
Time of plot: Early seventeenth century
Locale: Florence, Italy
First performed: c. 1621-1627; first published, 1657

Principal characters:
> LEANTIO, a Florentine clerk
> BIANCA, his wife
> FABRICIO, a Florentine gentleman
> ISABELLA, his daughter
> LIVIA, Fabricio's sister
> HIPPOLITO, brother of Livia and Fabricio
> THE DUKE OF FLORENCE
> A CARDINAL, the duke's brother
> THE WARD
> GUARDIANO, his uncle and guardian

The Story:

Leantio, a Florentine merchant's clerk, married Bianca, a beautiful and well-born Venetian, and brought her to his mother's house. On her arrival there, she responded graciously to his mother's words of welcome and spoke of her love for Leantio. He, in turn, informed his mother of Bianca's luxurious background and of his inability to equal it. He explained also that Bianca was a great prize who must be kept hidden from other men's eyes. His mother feared that Bianca would be discontented with her new and poorer home.

In a richer house, Livia was entertaining her brother Fabricio, the father of Isabella, and Guardiano, the uncle of a rich and foolish boy called "the Ward." They discussed the proposed marriage between the Ward and Isabella. Livia, protesting against loveless marriages, lectured Fabricio on man's unfaithfulness and woman's obedience, and declared that she would never remarry. When Isabella was sent for, Fabricio declared that her uncle Hippolito would surely follow her in her married state because they were as inseparable as links in a chain. Isabella's ideals, especially her ideas on marriage, were in marked contrast to the Ward's foolishness and vulgarity. She dreaded marriage to him and regarded it as slavery. This was her explanation to Livia, who sent Hippolito to comfort her. At that time, Isabella's conscious feelings toward her uncle were those of deep friendship. Unaware at the time of any sexual attraction toward him, she was horrified and sadly left him when he told her he loved her as a man loves his wife.

When Leantio finally left Bianca at his mother's house and returned to his work, Bianca wept bitterly. She was distracted from her grief by the noise and excitement of the annual religious procession to the cathedral. Deeply impressed by the noble bearing of the duke of Florence, Bianca was sure that he noticed her as she watched him passing by.

Meanwhile, Hippolito had told Livia of his love for Isabella and of her reaction, and Livia promised to procure Isabella as his mistress. When Isabella confided her unhappiness to Livia, her aunt took the opportunity to tell her that Hippolito was not her uncle, that she was in fact the child of Fabricio's wife by a Spanish nobleman. She insisted, however, that Isabella keep this matter a secret, because Fabricio and Hippolito were ignorant of it. Thus Isabella welcomed Hippolito with a kiss when he returned and he marveled at Livia's skill. Isabella decided that she would still marry the Ward in order to conceal her love affair with Hippolito.

Guardiano told Livia that the duke of Florence was enamored of a girl he had seen on the balcony of Leantio's mother's house. Livia undertook to win her for the duke and summoned Leantio's mother for a game of chess. Under pressure, the mother admitted that she had a daughter-in-law in her home, and Bianca was sent for. She was taken on a tour of the house by Guardiano, who thus led her to the duke.

While the duke spoke of his passion for her, Bianca pleaded for her honor, virtue, and safety. The duke, continuing his token pleading, intimated to Bianca that she did not have the power to refuse him. When she returned to the two chess players, Bianca was half pleased by the duke but also eager to have revenge on Livia.

At home, Bianca's ensuing frustration and discontent infuriated her mother-in-law, who was glad that Leantio would soon return. On his arrival, Leantio anticipated an ecstatic reunion with his wife, but he was greeted coldly by Bianca and angrily repulsed. Before long, Bianca was sent for by the duke and went to the palace with Leantio's mother. Left alone, Leantio abandoned himself to jealousy, but he failed to realize the extent of his betrayal until he, too, was summoned to dine with the duke.

When offered the command of a distant city, Leantio was as powerless to refuse as he was to disrupt the affair between his wife and her noble lover, and he was forced to stand by when Bianca, bored by the banquet, left with the duke.

Livia, who had fallen in love at first sight with Leantio, was determined to woo him from his grief. When she indirectly offered herself as his mistress, he accepted because of the wealth and luxury she promised. Some weeks later, Leantio visited Bianca in her apartment at the court, and they jeered at each other's finery and new place in the world. Bianca told the duke of her husband's visit and disclosed that he had become Livia's lover. Jealous of Leantio, the duke informed Hippolito, who, as the ruler expected, threatened to kill his sister's lover in order to preserve publicly Livia's honor.

The duke's pleasure at the idea of Leantio's death was increased when his brother, the cardinal, threatened him with the fires of hell if he continued to live adulterously. Having vowed that he would reform, he decided that with Leantio dead he could lawfully marry Bianca, so Leantio was murdered. Livia, finding Hippolito with her lover's body was driven almost to madness by grief, fury, and malice. She betrayed him and Isabella and admitted that she had lied to Isabella about her parentage in order to make her Hippolito's mistress. Isabella, who had transgressed, unlike the others, through ignorance, resolved to leave Hippolito and avenge herself by destroying Livia.

The separate revenges plotted by these people resulted in their own deaths. At a masque held ostensibly in honor of the duke's marriage to Bianca, poisoned incense killed Isabella and Livia. Hippolito stabbed himself, and Bianca had the duke poisoned and then drank also from the poisoned cup.

Critical Evaluation:

This Jacobean drama is set in Italy, the background that, in tragedies of the period, implies luxury, vice, and violence. Within this framework, Thomas Middleton dispassionately and ironically records human—especially feminine—motivation and passion. As she dies from drinking a poisoned cup, Bianca exclaims: "Oh the deadly snares/ That women set for women . . ./ Like our own sex, we have no enemy, no enemy!" Yet her judgment, like that expressed in the title of the tragedy, is false. The action of Middleton's play proves quite the opposite: that women should beware men, who set the snares of money and power that destroy women. Livia schemes in behalf of her brothers Fabricio and Hippolito; her motives have nothing to do with selfish exploitation. When she takes a lover of her own choosing, Leantio, she is abused as sinful, and her lover is murdered so that the family "honor" may be restored. Set in the corrupt and libertine atmosphere of Renaissance Florence, the play shows, with cool detachment, the terrible effects of passions mingled with greed.

Middleton skillfully combines two separate stories that conclude with one explosive catastrophe. The Bianca plot was based upon the notorious true history of Bianca Capello, born approximately 1548 of a family of Venetian nobility. In 1563, she eloped with a Florentine, Pietro Buonaventuri, who was not of the noble class; later she married him and bore him a daughter. The powerful Francesco de' Medici soon favored her; she became his mistress, and her husband—doubtless on Francesco's orders—was assassinated in 1569. Francesco and Bianca, in turn, died suddenly of a fever in 1587, under circumstances that, in the popular imagination, appeared suspicious; Francesco's brother, the cardinal, succeeded him as grand duke of Tuscany. This story of lust and betrayal is combined with the Isabella-Hippolito plot. In its theme of adultery and deceit, the second plot corresponds to the first, emphasizing the moral object of the drama: to expose the ruinous effects of amorous plots and counterplots conceived through guile or greed.

In his moral vision, Middleton is different from the other great Jacobean tragedians. Unlike John Webster and Cyril Tourneur, in whose poetic drama horror is heaped upon horror, Middleton avoids melodramatic scenes of sheer terror until the final moments of the play, when the complications of the plot are resolved in a compressed action of mass slaughter. Unlike John Ford, who is masterful in pathetic scenes of sexual aberration, Middleton is a realist who avoids "abnormal" psychosexual behavior. Although Isabella willingly submits to the embraces of Hippolito—and thus commits incest—she is deceived by Livia into believing that her uncle's bloodline is different from hers. As soon as she learns the truth about the relationship, she plots revenge on her betrayers. Yet her passion for Hippolito, so long as she could deny to herself the incest inhibition, was as fierce as the man's.

Middleton is interested in the ruthlessness of men who are dominating, even sadistic, lovers; and in women as men's victims, who often masochistically acquiesce in their own destruction. Bianca, like Beatrice-Joanna in Middleton and Samuel Rowley's *The Changeling* (1621), is a sensual woman who fixes her love on one man and then, driven by sexual urges, on another. Just as Beatrice-Joanna comes to love—or at least lust for—her seducer, the abhorrent De Flores, so Bianca comes to champion the duke over her husband Leantio. It is not riches alone that has tempted her to cancel her marriage vows; it is lust for the more powerful man. Because of her sexual weakness she is without moral resources; and the man, through his sexual power, uses her as property—as a mere physical possession to be bought and sold. Middleton objectively records the actions, without sentimentality or preaching, and allows the audience a chance to judge whether women should indeed beware women.

The moral ending of *Women Beware Women* is conventional. The dramatic structure of the play is unbalanced, and the slow entanglement of destructive passions is abruptly changed to the final, almost farcical, holocaust. The lasting impression left by the play is one of the movement of characters from deliberate scheming to uncontrollable involvement and destruction. The tragedy is memorable, not for its moral ending, but for the nightmare quality of human passions revealed by the force of richly dramatic verse.

Bibliography:

Dawson, Anthony B. "*Women Beware Women* and the Economy of Rape." *Studies in English Literature 1500-1900* 27, no. 2 (Spring, 1987): 303-320. Argues that Middleton presents female characters as trapped in an economic hierarchy that reduces them to commodities for male use. This presentation is complicated by a need to maintain a conventional Elizabethan perception of women as naturally corrupt.

Holmes, David M. "*Women Beware Women* and *The Changeling*." In *The Art of Thomas Middleton*. Oxford, England: The Clarendon Press, 1970. Places the play within the context of Middleton's late work. Asserts that Bianca is vulnerable to seduction because of a repressive upbringing that does not prepare her for a morally corrupt world.

Kistner, A. L., and M. K. Kistner. "*Women Beware Women:* Will, Authority, and Fortune." In *Middleton's Tragic Themes*. New York: Peter Lang, 1984. Asserts that Middleton insists upon the individual moral responsibility of his characters. Characters ignore their awareness of sin in order to satisfy their overriding will, thus bringing on catastrophe.

Ribner, Irving. "Middleton's *Women Beware Women:* Poetic Imagery and the Moral Vision." *Tulane Studies in English* 9 (1959): 19-33. Investigates the play's characterization, action, and imagery; concludes that the play is an incisive social commentary on the destructiveness of avaricious ideals.

Wigler, Stephen. "Parent and Child: The Pattern of Love in *Women Beware Women*." In *"Accompaninge the Players": Essays Celebrating Thomas Middleton, 1580-1980,* edited by Kenneth Friedenreich. New York: AMS Press, 1983. Examines three dominant love relationships of the play, which demonstrate a similar parent-child incest pattern and explain the stylistic shift in the final act. Suggests that a possible source lies in Middleton's biography.

WOMEN IN LOVE

Type of work: Novel
Author: D. H. Lawrence (1885-1930)
Type of plot: Psychological realism
Time of plot: Early twentieth century
Locale: England and Austria
First published: 1920

> Principal characters:
> RUPERT BIRKIN, a school inspector
> GERALD CRICH, a coalmine operator
> URSULA BRANGWEN, a teacher
> GUDRUN BRANGWEN, her sister, an artist
> HERMIONE RODDICE, a wealthy intellectual
> LOERKE, a sculptor

The Story:

Ursula Brangwen and her sister Gudrun first noticed Rupert Birkin and Gerald Crich as the sisters were watching a wedding party arrive at a church. Ursula explained that Birkin, the best man, was trying to terminate his prolonged affair with Hermione Roddice, one of the brides-maids. Some days later, Birkin came to inspect Ursula's classroom with Hermione in tow. Hermione, after arguing fiercely with Birkin, invited Ursula and Gudrun to visit her home. Once alone, Ursula inexplicably wept. Gudrun had been drawn to Gerald, the bride's older brother; when the sisters caught sight of him swimming, Ursula told Gudrun that when he was a boy, Gerald had accidentally killed his brother.

When Birkin and Gerald met on a train to London, they discussed whether love was the "center of life"; Birkin expressed his pessimism about humanity. That evening, Gerald joined Birkin and some bohemian friends at a café and slept with a young model after they had all retired to her former lover's flat. In the morning, Gerald joined Birkin and his friends as they chatted, naked, around the fireplace.

The Brangwen sisters became better acquainted with Birkin and Gerald when they visited Breadalby, Hermione's home. Gerald found Gudrun arousing when the women, in silk robes, improvised a modern ballet. After Birkin and Hermione again quarreled, Hermione tried to break his skull with a paperweight.

Some days afterward, Gerald appalled the sisters when he brutally forced his horse to stand as a train passed. Gerald and Hermione later found Gudrun sketching by the lake. Gudrun clumsily dropped her sketchbook into the water. Gudrun, though blaming Gerald, established a silent intimacy with him. Meanwhile, Ursula had found Birkin repairing a punt, and, on an overgrown island, they discussed true happiness. Ursula found his misanthropic vision of a world rid of humans strangely pleasing. Afterward, having tea with Gerald and Hermione at Birkin's new lodgings, Ursula objected when Birkin compared a horse's will to submit to its master to a woman's will to submit to a man. When she met Birkin alone, however, he avowed that while he did not "love" her, he sought a relationship deeper than love, a "pure balance." They watched as a cat playfully cuffed a female stray, and Birkin suggested that the cat wanted the same equilibrium, like a star in orbit. Ursula still believed he wanted a mere satellite.

When Gerald's father gave the annual "water party" for the townspeople, the Brangwen sisters took a canoe to a clearing on the far shore. There, Gudrun danced as Ursula sang, and when some cattle appeared, Gudrun brazenly danced before their horns until suddenly Gerald intruded and, alarmed, shooed them off. Gudrun, repudiating his protection, struck his face. As night fell, the couples rowed by lantern light, and Ursula reached an understanding, a shared pessimism, with Birkin. They heard screams; Gerald's sister had fallen into the water, and her fiancé had dived in after her. In vain Gerald tried desperately to find the pair in the darkness. Birkin assured him that death was better for them. Toward dawn, they found the bodies, the girl's arms clasped round her lover's neck.

Birkin later dropped in on Ursula at home. The profound sympathy between the young pair became evident as compared with her parents' conventionality. After Birkin left, however, Ursula felt a strange hatred for him, even as she felt his possession of her. Still unable to reconcile himself to any marriage, Birkin began to envision some new, freer relationship with women. When Gerald visited, the tenderness between them induced Birkin to invite him to swear blood-brotherhood, but Gerald demurred.

Gudrun had been invited to tutor Gerald's young sister in drawing, and when they agreed to sketch the girl's pet rabbit, it scratched Gudrun as she took it from its cage. When it also scratched Gerald, he subdued it with a blow, and they shared an appreciation of the fierce energy in the rabbit's "madness."

Near the lake by moonlight, Ursula discovered Birkin talking to himself. Birkin again tried to explain what he wanted: not Ursula's love exactly, but her spirit. They kissed, despite her misgivings. The next evening, Birkin came to her home to propose, but, instead, quarreled with her father and angrily left. He found Gerald, and the two men agreed to wrestle naked. They fought to complete exhaustion, then they clasped hands as Gerald confessed his love for his friend.

Later, while waiting for Birkin in his lodgings, Hermione advised Ursula not to marry him. Ursula decided that all of Hermione's ideas were merely abstractions, but after Birkin arrived, Ursula was mortified by the easy familiarity between Birkin and Hermione. She left abruptly as they planned Hermione's departure for Italy. Soon afterward, Birkin drove Ursula into the countryside to give her three gemstone rings, but when she learned that he intended to join Hermione for dinner, she angrily threw them away and walked off. She immediately relented, and after reconciling, they spent the night in the car in Sherwood Forest.

As Gerald held vigil over his father's demise, Gudrun brought needed comfort, and as he walked her home, they kissed passionately under a bridge. At last his father died, and Gerald hurried to the Brangwen home and stole into Gudrun's bedroom where he silently made love to her.

When Gerald suggested a double wedding, Birkin argued against conventional marriage, insisting that love between man and man was marriage's necessary complement. Again, Gerald resisted. When Ursula told her family that she planned to marry Birkin the next day, her outraged father struck her, and Ursula moved in with Birkin that evening. Gerald suggested the four of them go away together.

The couples traveled separately to the Continent, met in Innsbruck, and proceeded to a hostel high in the Alps. In this brilliant, snow-bound, silent world, Gudrun and Gerald immediately began to drift apart.

Among the guests was a German sculptor, Loerke, who, with his aesthetic theory and scorn for opinion and "life," exercised a perverse fascination over Gudrun. Ursula became repelled, and she left with Birkin for Italy.

Alone in this otherworldly realm, the hostility between Gudrun and Gerald intensified. To Gerald's disgust, Gudrun fell further under Loerke's spell. She decided to leave Gerald, but while she was tobogganing with Loerke, Gerald appeared and began to strangle her. He then wandered off into the snow until he fell, exhausted. After Birkin returned with Ursula, he gazed grief-stricken at Gerald's icy corpse. He told Ursula that things would have been different if Gerald had accepted his love.

Critical Evaluation:

Although at first poorly received, *Women in Love* has come to be considered D. H. Lawrence's most important novel, and it is one of the most remarkable novels of its time, both for its innovative narrative technique and its psychological depth. Although the novel employs a narrative strategy familiar from nineteenth century novels, in developing the relationships among four distinct personalities, Lawrence revolutionizes narrative technique, replacing the traditional concept of character. He includes more basic dimensions of human existence: blood and flesh. His characters are motivated not primarily by conscious, ego-driven wills, but by drives that originate at a deeper, more physical level. Lawrence, who knew the work of Sigmund Freud long before it became widely known in England, believed that "blood" possessed its own consciousness and had its own ways of knowing.

The novel's plot results from the characters' discovery of and attempts to satisfy their most basic demands. These struggles frequently entail reversals and paradoxes that are difficult to account for in strictly rational terms, since their motivation is at a deeper level than the rational mind. Birkin is the chief exponent of this point of view, but while he possesses some of Lawrence's personal traits, and often voices the author's views, he does not function simply as a mouthpiece. Lawrence is careful to show Birkin's flaws and to make him occasionally ridiculous. All the central characters somehow "represent" Lawrence as reflections of the self and antiself. At the same time, all four central characters, in trying to understand themselves and to make themselves understood to others, articulate a philosophy that, while it is persistently challenged and problematized within the novel, also possesses enough cogency to stand as a powerful statement against the hypocrisies and complacencies of Lawrence's era.

Women in Love had its beginnings around 1913 in a work called *The Sisters*, which Lawrence eventually divided into two independent novels, publishing the first as *The Rainbow* in 1915. After *The Rainbow* was suppressed on grounds of obscenity in 1915, Lawrence found it impossible to publish his writing and had to endure poverty as he completed *Women in Love* during 1916-1917. Although the war never enters the novel, the pessimistic atmosphere reflects not only Lawrence's personal crisis but also his sense that Europe was committing suicide. The older generation are fools, and the futureless, godless young contemplate humanity's annihilation. Yet this hopelessness does not prevent Birkin and his friends from seeking authentic interpersonal relationships and radical solutions to questions of marriage and friendship. They stand disdainfully apart from the world, yet seem to grow larger than life in the icy crucible of the Alps.

Lawrence treats aspects of human experience that few novelists of his time dared to touch. He treats sexuality not only in the narrow sense, but also forbidden passions and thoughts. Lawrence offers no simple answers; in the end the tragedy of Gerald Crich's suicide marks the failure of Crich's relationship with Birkin as much as his relationship with Gudrun. Birkin's unsatisfied need for a deep connection with a man as a complement to marriage has a physical dimension that stops just short of open homosexuality. Lawrence explicated its significance for Birkin in a prologue that he ultimately decided to omit from the published version.

Gudrun's spiritual death is almost as final as Gerald's physical death. Always inclined toward aestheticism, her friendship with the sculptor Loerke draws her into decadence and depravity. Loerke's sculpture of Lady Godiva embodies Loerke's philosophy of art as a self-enclosed, autonomous realm without reference to morality or life. Gudrun succumbs to Loerke's sterile influence and finally becomes reduced to a cheap artist's model.

Ursula and Birkin, on the other hand, ultimately reach an understanding that makes their marriage possible. Their relationship is based on polarity; each partner preserves a distinct identity within a balance of opposites. The disastrous opposite to this balance is symbolized by the entwined corpses of Gerald's sister and her fiancé. Ursula's independence and assertiveness make such an end impossible. Her relationship with Birkin is based on more than mere affection; she finds with him a profound bond based on mutual understanding and a shared outlook on the world.

Matthew Parfitt

Bibliography:
Draper, R. P. *D. H. Lawrence.* New York: Twayne, 1964. An accessible introduction to Lawrence's chief works, including useful biographical background and extensive commentary on *Women in Love.*
Kermode, Frank. *D. H. Lawrence.* New York: Viking Press, 1973. Sheds light on the novel's philosophical concerns.
Leavis, F. R. *D. H. Lawrence: Novelist.* New York: Alfred A. Knopf, 1968. Includes a lengthy chapter on *Women in Love* that draws attention to overlooked themes. Reassesses the novel's importance.
Miko, Stephen J., ed. and comp. *Twentieth Century Interpretations of "Women in Love."* Englewood Cliffs, N.J.: Prentice-Hall, 1969. Does not cover recent studies, but provides convenient access to a range of important earlier essays and opinions.
Oates, Joyce Carol. "Lawrence's Götterdämmerung: The Apocalyptic Vision of *Women in Love.*" In *Critical Essays on D. H. Lawrence,* edited by Dennis Jackson and Fleda Brown Jackson. Boston: G. K. Hall, 1988. A brilliant discussion of symbolism and eschatology in *Women in Love,* informed by Oates's own experience as a novelist.

THE WOMEN OF BREWSTER PLACE
A Novel in Seven Stories

Type of work: Novel
Author: Gloria Naylor (1950-   )
Type of plot: Social realism
Time of plot: 1930's-1960's
Locale: A northern urban neighborhood
First published: 1982

Principal characters:
MATTIE MICHAEL, the stable "mother" figure
ETTA MAE JOHNSON, Mattie's long-time friend
LUCIELIA (CIEL) TURNER, Mattie's young friend
KISWANA BROWNE, young would-be revolutionary
CORA LEE, young unwed mother
LORRAINE, a lesbian schoolteacher
THERESA, her lover
BEN, the tenement janitor

The Story:

At twenty-three, Mattie Michael was seduced by Butcher Fuller, a handsome ne'er-do-well. When she became pregnant, her father beat her to get her to reveal her unborn child's father. Mattie, disgraced in her father's eyes, moved from home in Rock Vale, Tennessee, to North Carolina, where her friend Etta Mae Johnson took her in. After Mattie's son was born and Etta Mae had moved on, Mattie started boarding with Miss Eva and her granddaughter Ciel. After several years, Miss Eva died, Ciel's parents came for her, and Mattie was left with the responsibility for paying the mortgage and for raising her son Basil.

Miss Eva had always said that Mattie was too indulgent and protective of Basil, but Mattie would not listen. When Basil, now grown, got into a barroom fight and accidentally killed a man, his lack of moral fiber was apparent. He allowed his mother to put up her now mortgage-free home as bond for his bail. He would not face the slim possibility of going to prison, though conviction was unlikely. He skipped town and disappeared. Mattie, homeless again, found a home through Etta Mae in Brewster Place.

Etta Mae Johnson was in Brewster Place after many years of roaming from place to place, making and breaking off liaisons with men who temporarily supported her. When she reached the age where, as she said to Mattie, "each year there's a new line [on her face] to cover" and her body "cries for just a little more rest," she decided it was time to find a good man, marry, and settle down. She thought she had found that man in a dynamic preacher, Moreland Woods. Woods knew, however, that Etta Mae was a "worldly" woman whom he could use and discard with no fear of entanglement, which he did, leaving Etta Mae resigned to relying for "love and comfort" on her friend Mattie.

Brewster Place was also home to younger women. Kiswana Browne was a twenty-three-year-old college dropout who had left her middle-class life in Linden Hills for Brewster Place to be close to "her people." Her mother, a proud genteel woman, visited Kiswana in Brewster Place to try to persuade the young woman that living in poverty was not the only way Kiswana could show her solidarity with the black masses. Kiswana's rebellion, however, required that she remove all traces of her middle-class background, including changing her name from "Melanie," her grandmother's name, to one she had found in "an African dictionary."

Ciel Turner, Mattie's young friend dating back to their days in North Carolina, had married Eugene and had a baby girl, Serena. When Ciel got pregnant a second time, Eugene felt trapped. He lost his job and blamed Ciel for all his troubles. Ciel, out of love for him, got an abortion, which depressed her and caused her to be unhealthily focused on Serena. The day Eugene decided to leave, ostensibly to take an out-of-town job, Serena was accidentally and fatally electrocuted when she stuck a fork into an electrical outlet. Ciel nearly died of despair, but Mattie helped pull her out of her painful despondency.

Cora Lee as a child had been fixated on baby dolls. By the time she was thirteen, her parents had realized there was something not quite normal in the way Cora Lee demanded and expected a brand new baby doll each Christmas. Thirteen was also when she found out about sex and making real babies on her own. Very soon thereafter, she was having babies by "shadow" men identified, even in her own mind, only as the fathers of her various children. Living on welfare in Brewster Place with seven children, one an infant, Cora Lee spent most of her days watching television and caring for her baby while giving the older children little attention.

Kiswana befriended Cora Lee when Kiswana tried to organize a tenants' association among the Brewster Place community. She persuaded Cora Lee to take her children to a production of a modern version of "A Midsummer Night's Dream." When Cora Lee saw how her older children were enthralled with the play, she realized she neglected them once they stopped being infants, and she vowed to do better by them.

Lorraine and Theresa moved to Brewster Place when their lesbianism was suspected at their former residence. Lorraine, a first grade teacher, was afraid she would lose her job if her sexual orientation became known. The people of Brewster Place, especially a self-righteous busybody named Sophie, began to suspect that the two women were "that way," and some of them began to ostracize them. Lorraine had a run-in with one of the area's thugs, C. C. Baker, who called her a freak. Lorraine, more needy of acceptance than her partner Theresa, befriended Ben, the janitor, who saw in her the same qualities as were in his long-lost daughter.

One night, C. C. Baker and his gang trapped Lorraine in an alley and raped her. Brutalized, she lay in the alley, unseen and unheard, all night. The next morning, Ben, nearly drunk, took his usual early morning seat on a garbage can in the alley. Lorraine, deranged from her brutalization, attacked him with a brick and killed him. She never knew what she had done.

After Ben's death, Kiswana Browne's attempts to organize the Brewster Place residents culminated in a block party to raise money for a lawyer to fight the landlord. Mattie dreamed that the block party managed a miracle: The Brewster Place residents tore down the ugly wall that cut Brewster Place off from the rest of the city. Mattie awoke believing that maybe the block party would bring improvements to the lives of the people of Brewster Place.

Critical Evaluation:

The women of the title are the main characters, and Brewster Place is the set on which they act on, and react to, the circumstances of their lives. Those circumstances are usually disheartening and usually caused by men, who are seen generally as malign forces. Throughout the book, males are shown as causing the adverse condition of women.

Mattie Michael is a pleasant, God-fearing, churchgoing woman with moral strength, who, without the support of other women, might not have survived. Butch Fuller, when he impregnated her, not only destroyed her relationship with her father, he changed the course of her life, possibly for the worse. Her father, in his angry frustration, nearly destroyed her life when he beat her. Her son Basil broke her heart by deserting her without a backward glance. Each time, a woman helped Mattie survive. Her mother rescued her from her father's savage beating by firing a shotgun close enough to his head to get his attention. Etta Mae gave her sanctuary so Mattie could have her child. Miss Eva gave her a home when the one she had became unlivable because of rats. The men in her life gave little or nothing.

Etta Mae had used men all her life and apparently asked no more from them than she wanted. She had been a kind of floating concubine for most of her adult life, having learned at an early age in Tennessee that her sexual charms attracted men, who were willing to pay for them. As she grew older and her looks and energy were diminishing, she wanted to settle down, preferably with a kind man who would take care of her. She thought the Reverend Mr. Moreland Woods was right for her. He seemed "well-off," with his "manicured hands and a diamond pinkie ring," but he turned out to be a hypocritical opportunist, viewing Etta Mae as someone who could satisfy his "temporary weakness of the flesh." Forewarned about him by Mattie, who recognized that Woods was only interested in a "quick good time" with her, Etta Mae finally accepted that her friendship with Mattie might be the only abiding relationship left to her.

While the women are fully drawn characters whose stories explain why they are what and where they are, the only rounded male characters are Basil Michael, Ben, and Eugene Turner, Ciel's husband. He is shown to be a whiner and an emotional abuser who takes flight whenever the going gets tough. Ciel ultimately realizes that he is worthless when he complains that her love for him just "ain't good enough" to compensate for the life he is being forced to live as husband, father, and provider. Ciel then sees him at last as a "tall, skinny black man with arrogance and selfishness" whom she knows she will soon grow to hate.

Ben is the kindest male figure, and he is emotionally crippled and morally bankrupt (as revealed in the story of his spineless passivity regarding his daughter's adversity). He is kind and supportive to Lorraine, and for his trouble, his is killed by her—a woman with whom he had a close, almost father-daughter relationship. The only relationships that work out consistently in the novel are those between women.

This novel portrays women as survivors who must deal with the damage done to them by men. Usually the men are those with whom the women have had a close relationship. The one episode in which a woman encounters males with whom she has no prior connection is the rape of Lorraine by C. C. Baker and his gang. These young men inspire a condemnation unlike any other in the book. They are described as always "moving in a pack," needing one another "continually near to verify their existence." They have fifty-word vocabularies, ninth grade educations, and strive to emulate the "blaxploitative" Shaft and Superfly. They are "the most dangerous species in existence—human males with an erection to validate." They are the most mindlessly brutal characters in the book, evidence of the need for women to band together in support of one another.

Episodic in organization, with flashbacks providing background on the major characters, *The Women of Brewster Place* portrays seven very different African American women. The familiar stereotypes are there: the motherly, religious woman who accepts things and goes on, the hussy with the heart of gold, the welfare mother who has one baby after another by different men, the gossip (Sophie), the middle-class matron. They fall into the two stereotypical categories: the good woman (Mattie, Ciel, Miss Eva, Lorraine) and the bad woman (Etta Mae, Ben's wife Elvira, Cora Lee). The circumstances of their lives individualize them into believable human beings.

In their characterization, the dialogue rings true without resorting to excessive dialect, slang, profanity, or obscenity. Capturing the sound of African Americans in their familiar surroundings, it communicates the moment and the milieu of the story.

The Women of Brewster Place defines the black experience and illustrates the strength of friendship among women, never once suggesting that often-accepted view that women cannot be friends to other women. Men are shown as base. Perhaps Gloria Naylor is trying to balance the literary scales that so often show men as heroic and steadfast.

Jane Lee Ball

Bibliography:
Andrews, Larry R. "Black Sisterhood in Gloria Naylor's Novels." *CLA Journal* 33 (September, 1989): 1-25. Discusses the various relationships that create a bond of sisterhood among the characters in *The Women of Brewster Place*. Two other novels by Naylor are also discussed.
Awkward, Michael. *Inspiriting Influences: Tradition, Revision, and Afro-American Women's Novels*. New York: Columbia University Press, 1989. Naylor's novel is discussed in the context of writings by other African American writers.
Matus, Jill L. "Dream, Deferral, and Closure in *The Women of Brewster Place*." *Black American Literature Forum* 24 (Spring, 1990): 49-64. Discusses the variety of "dreams" of the women and explores Naylor's intent in communicating their postponement.
Montgomery, Maxine L. "The Fathomless Dream: Gloria Naylor's Use of the Descent Motif in *The Women of Brewster Place*." *CLA Journal* 36 (September, 1992): 1-11. Discusses Naylor's use of the descent motif to explore her characters' search for self-knowledge and their nontraditional lifestyles.
Tanner, Laura E. "Reading Rape: *Sanctuary* and *The Women of Brewster Place*." *American Literature* 62 (December, 1990): 559-582. Examines two views of rape, in Naylor's work and in William Faulkner's *Sanctuary*. Explores the impact of Faulkner's male violator perspective and Naylor's female victim perspective.

THE WOMEN OF TRACHIS

Type of work: Drama
Author: Sophocles (c. 496-406 B.C.E.)
Type of plot: Tragedy
Time of plot: Antiquity
Locale: Trachis
First performed: Trachinai, 435-429 B.C.E. (English translation, 1729)

Principal characters:

HERAKLES
DEIANIRA, his wife
HYLLUS, their son
LICHAS, herald of Herakles
IOLE, captive of Herakles
CHORUS OF TRACHINIAN MAIDENS

The Story:

Fifteen long months had passed since Deianira had received word from Herakles, her husband, who, when he left on his last journey, had given her a tablet setting forth the disposition of his estate and stating that it had been decreed that after a year and three moons had passed he would either die or live happily thereafter in untroubled peace. The fated day had arrived, and Deianira was filled with foreboding.

Before she could send her son Hyllus to get accurate news of her husband, a messenger, outstripping the herald Lichas, arrived to announce that Herakles was living and would soon appear. Lichas himself followed shortly with a group of captive maidens and, answering Deianira's question, assured her that her husband, alive and sound of limb, was at that time sacrificing the fruits of his victories to great Zeus in fulfillment of a vow made when he took from towered Oechalia the captive women. Deianira was touched by the plight of the captives. Lichas told her they were from the city ruled by Eurytus, selected by Herakles as chosen possessions for himself and the gods. He added, however, that it was not the taking of the city that had delayed the hero this long time. He had been detained in Lydia. Sold into bondage, he had passed a year as servant to Omphale, the barbaric queen. Before this bondage, Eurytus, an old friend, had taunted and so incensed him that Herakles, encountering Iphitus, one of Eurytus' four sons, without warning hurled him from a cliff. This act roused the ire of Olympian Zeus who, because Herakles had slain a foe by treachery and not in fair fight, drove him out to be sold as a slave to Omphale. Those who had reviled Herakles had been conquered, however, and now Lichas brought the virgins by Herakles' order to Deianira.

A strange pity came over Deianira as she gazed at the captives. One in particular, Iole, held her attention. Lichas pretended not to know who Iole was; and Iole herself spoke no word, bearing in silence her grief and suffering. The messenger, however, informed Deianira that Lichas had not told the truth, which was that Herakles for love of Iole had destroyed Eurytus, the maiden's father; that it was not his adventures in Lydia, his serfdom with Omphale, nor the death of Iphitus which had held him these many moons, but love for this maid. Failing to persuade her father to give up his daughter, Herakles had attacked Oechalia, sacked the city, slain Eurytus, and taken Iole for his concubine. Deianira, cruelly hurt, called upon Lichas to tell her everything. He confirmed the news. Sorrowfully she asked the herald to wait while she had suitable gifts prepared for Herakles in return for those he had sent.

Deianira could not bear the thought of having another share her husband's affections. Judging it unwise to give way to anger, she thought of another course. In an old urn she had long hid a keepsake of Nessus, the centaur whose work it was to ferry wayfarers across the river Evenus, carrying them in his arms. When Deianira, as a bride, was on her way to Herakles, she, too, was carried across by the centaur, but in midstream he lewdly sought to take her. Her screams brought from the waiting son of Zeus an arrow that pierced the centaur's lungs. Dying, he told Deianira that as the last to be ferried across the river she should profit by receiving from him a love philter made by taking the curdled gore from his wound. This would act as a charm so that Herakles would never find any other woman fairer than she. Now, recalling these words, Deianira selected a festal robe and smeared it with the magic ointment. Then she presented the robe to Lichas, telling him he was to instruct Herakles to put it on immediately, before sun or light struck it, and stand before the people with it on as he made his sacrifices to the gods.

No sooner had Lichas departed, however, than Deianira felt uneasy because she had resorted to magic to win back her husband's love. Quickly her fears were realized. She had faithfully followed the instructions of the centaur by preserving the drug unexposed to light or fire or sun until the moment of application. Secretly, indoors, she had spread the unguent on the robe with some wool and, folding the gift, had placed it securely in a chest. Now, by chance, she threw the tuft of wool on the flagstones in the blazing sun, whereupon there boiled up from it clots of foam as it consumed itself and disappeared into nothingness. In consternation Deianira realized that the black-venomed gore, instead of winning anew her husband's love, had been dying Nessus' trick to cause his death, and she would be his murderer. Overwhelmed, she determined to end her own life.

Hyllus returned. He had seen Herakles receive from Lichas the robe and put it on. Then, when the fierce rays of the sun had melted the venom with which the deadly garment was coated, it clung to his body, the sweat burst out, and, before the assembled company, he writhed in dreadful pain. Herakles in his agony called out to Lichas, who told him the robe was Deianira's gift, whereupon the unhappy man seized the messenger by the foot and dashed out his brains against a rock. When, shouting and shrieking, Herakles called on Hyllus to carry him away to die where no one might see him, they had placed him on a ship and brought him to his home.

Hyllus now accused his mother of her vile deed and called down on her the vengeance of the Erinyes. Silently Deianira went indoors and in the bedchamber of Herakles bade farewell to her bridal bed. Then with a sword she pierced her heart and died. Hyllus, told by others that his mother's gift of the robe to Herakles had been instigated by the centaur, realized too late her innocence, and he grieved to lose in one day both mother and father.

Hyllus, still lamenting, left, but returned with attendants bearing his father on a litter. Herakles, fighting off the deadly spasms that shook him, entreated his son to end his miserable life. He recalled his great labors and the fact that he had never met defeat. Now death had come by a woman's wile. Hyllus told him that Deianira had been innocent of murderous intent in her act, that she had wished only to win back his love, that it was the centaur's venom that had brought about his undoing, and that Deianira, not wishing to live without him, now lay cold and dead.

Herakles admitted that it had been foreshown him that he would perish not by any living being but by a dweller in the realms of the Dead. The prophecy had also promised him release from his toils, but he had misinterpreted it as meaning a happy life; instead, it had portended death, for with death comes the end of toil.

Knowing thus that his death was the will of the gods, Herakles faced it nobly. He bade Hyllus bear him to the peak of Oeta, place him on a great funeral pyre of oak and olive, and ignite it. Hyllus consented to carry his father to his destination and prepare the pyre, but he refused to light it. Herakles, not pressing him, asked as one other boon that Hyllus take Iole to wife and care for her. Unwillingly, but moved by filial obedience, Hyllus assented. In these dread matters he saw the will of immortal Zeus.

Critical Evaluation:

The Women of Trachis, recounting the last crisis in the life of Herakles, is the only surviving tragedy of Sophocles that ends in death for both of the chief characters. The tragedy also presents the devotion and love of ideal womanhood in Deianira and the heroic endurance and strength of ideal manhood in Herakles. *The Women of Trachis* has as its tragic protagonist not one person but a family of three. For this reason critics sometimes claim that the play lacks unity, since half is devoted to Deianira and half to Herakles, with neither appearing onstage at the same time. To consider this drama properly, however, one must regard the tragedies of Deianira, Herakles, and Hyllus as one large event instigated by the gods, carried out by human will, and transcended in the end by strength of character.

Although the play lacks the smoothness and facility of *Oedipus Tyrannus* (c. 429 B.C.E.), it is significant, and it treats the major problem of Sophocles' dramatic career, that of human freedom. The problem is this: When events are determined by the will of the gods, as revealed in oracles and prophecies, and by the passionate compulsions of the human animal, freedom lies in learning the truth and accepting it—not passively, but with all the force of one's being. For one to be free one must knowingly seek to accomplish one's destiny in harmony with divine law. In Sophocles that destiny is always hard and terrible, which makes the acceptance of it truly ennobling. This problem and its solution are at the heart of *The Women of Trachis*, which was probably written when the dramatist was in his sixties, an age when he had looked at life fully and accurately. The play is a mature statement of Sophocles' deepest convictions.

The action moves from ignorance to truth, and from misconceptions to a revelation of the total pattern imposed by divine will. Each of the three tragic characters acts from a lack of understanding and then must confront the awful truth. The audience sees this first in Deianira. Her greatest apprehension in the beginning is that her husband, Herakles, will not live much longer. Then she learns that he is both alive and returning home in triumph. She sympathizes with the most miserable of the captive women, Iole, only to learn that Herakles has taken Iole as his concubine. Deianira does not find fault with either Iole or Herakles, but determines to win her husband's love by black magic. The potion is made from Nessus' poisoned gore, the centaur that Herakles killed. After sending the deadly robe to Herakles, she realizes how dangerous it is. When her son Hyllus reviles and curses her for murdering Herakles by slow agony, she knows that she herself has accomplished her worst fear. Her knowledge is subject to reversal upon reversal until the original prophecy and dread have been fulfilled.

Deianira's character is as much a part of this sequence as fate. She is a fearful, devoted, and rather gullible wife. Her only reason for resorting to magic is to regain Herakles' love, and it wins for her his undying hatred, not to mention Hyllus' condemnation. She does not excuse herself but accepts full responsibility for the deed she committed in ignorance, and she atones for it by suicide, choosing the noble method of stabbing herself. In that acceptance of her guilt and in that atonement, she achieves true freedom. Deianira's tragic courage lifts her above the fate to which the weakness of her character brought her.

Herakles, in an ironic twist, is dying not from a foe but at the hands of a rather pathetic woman, which humiliates him tremendously. He bawls and rages in pain, wishing to murder his wife. As he cites his triumphs in killing beasts and monsters, the audience realizes that the beasts have taken their revenge through Nessus' poisoned blood. The centaur, the most lustful of creatures, repays Herakles his lust; it is Herakles' bestial lust for Iole that precipitates his doom. Ironically, the beast-slayer is possessed of the same violence and lechery as the beasts he killed, and his body is mortally infected with the centaur's gore.

Once again the process of revelation begins. As Herakles learns that his death is being caused by Nessus' cunning, it dawns on him that the prophecy of his death is being completed and that Deianira was an innocent agent of the gods. When this is driven home by Hyllus' penitent and intrepid honesty, Herakles addresses himself to the fact of his death in earnest. He chooses the manner of his death freely, just as his wife had done. He determines to be burned alive rather than suffer death by poison passively. In that resolve he shows the same tragic courage as Deianira. He seizes the terrible will of Zeus and makes it his own. The audience is aware that Herakles will be transfigured as a god on his funeral pyre, but the important thing for Sophocles was the heroic determination of Herakles to make his death his own, in which he, too, transcends fate.

The third tragic figure is Hyllus, the son of Herakles and Deianira. Like his parents, he acts in ignorance, must suffer the truth, and make an atonement. Hyllus lays a dreadful curse on his mother, thinking she murdered Herakles out of jealousy and spite. By the time he learns what actually happened, Deianira has killed herself, and he bears some of the guilt for her death. He loves both of his parents. Thus, he finds himself in an unbearable situation. He atones in part by braving Herakles' rage to justify his mother's intentions, which in turn leads to Herakles' recognition of the truth. Herakles, the audience recalls, has recently dashed out the brains of a hapless messenger. Hyllus' father makes two very hard demands on him and binds him to them by oath. The first is that he build the funeral pyre on which Herakles is to perish, thus taking a hand in the death of his father as well as his mother. The second is that Hyllus marry the woman he loathes—Iole, the "cause" of all the trouble. It seems likely that this forthcoming marriage will put an end to the blood-and-lust syndrome that destroyed Hyllus' parents. Hyllus shows his manliness in the fortitude with which he accepts both conditions.

The final statement of the play, "there is nothing here which is not Zeus," expresses Sophocles' faith that while the gods lay down the tragic circumstances of human life and that people fulfill these tragedies through inner compulsion, people can triumph over necessity by strength of character. The divine pattern imposes hopeless suffering, which gives people the opportunity to show their nobility. This is a stern faith, but a stern faith is essential in a hard world.

"Critical Evaluation" by James Weigel, Jr.

Bibliography:
Bowra, C. M. *Sophoclean Tragedy.* Oxford, England: Clarendon Press, 1967. Includes a chapter on each of the seven plays by Sophocles. Discusses the themes and the motives and conflicts of the characters in *The Women of Trachis.* Explains the plot and gives several lines in the original Greek; includes many lines in English translation.
Kirkwood, Gordon MacDonald. *A Study of Sophoclean Drama.* Vol. 31 in *Cornell Studies in Classical Philology.* Ithaca, N.Y.: Cornell University Press, 1958. Analysis of Sophocles' structures and methods of dramatic composition. Considers *The Women of Trachis* in context with the other plays of Sophocles for characterization, irony, illustrative forms, use of diction, and oracles.

Scodel, Ruth. *Sophocles*. Boston: Twayne, 1984. Synopsis of *The Women of Trachis*. Consideration of other works which may have influenced Sophocles. Discusses the structure and the mythological gods and oracles. Includes information on the seven plays by Sophocles, a chronology of Sophocles, a bibliography, and an index.

Seale, David. *Vision and Stagecraft in Sophocles*. Chicago: University of Chicago Press, 1982. Distinguishes Sophocles from other playwrights of his time and demonstrates his influence on later ones. An excellent starting point. Considers the theatrical technicalities in the Sophoclean plays. Contains an extended section on *The Women of Trachis* and a long section of notes following it.

Segal, Charles. *Tragedy and Civilization: An Interpretation of Sophocles*. Cambridge, Mass.: Published for Oberlin College by Harvard University Press, 1981. Treats all the plays of Sophocles. Considers the Odyssean themes in *The Women of Trachis*. Follows and elaborates on the plot and possible meanings.

WONDERLAND

Type of work: Novel
Author: Joyce Carol Oates (1938-   )
Type of plot: Psychological realism
Time of plot: 1939-1971
Locale: Upstate New York; Ann Arbor, Michigan; Chicago; Wisconsin; New York City; and Toronto, Canada
First published: 1971

Principal characters:
JESSE HARTE, an orphan, later Jesse Vogel
DR. KARL PEDERSEN, his adoptive father
MARY PEDERSEN, Dr. Pedersen's wife
BENJAMIN CADY, Jesse's college professor
RODERICK PERRAULT, Jesse's supervising surgeon
HELENE CADY, Cady's daughter, later Jesse's wife
T. W. MONK, a student and poet
SHELLEY VOGEL, Jesse and Helene's daughter
REVA DENK, Jesse's lover

The Story:

One December day, fourteen-year-old Jesse Harte came home to find his family brutally murdered and his crazed, chronically unemployed, and spiritually desolate father coming after him with a shotgun. Jesse barely escaped through a window; his father's subsequent suicide left him to make his way alone as a traumatized orphan. He first went to live with his silent, bitter grandfather, where he took the surname Vogel for a time. That proved to be unacceptable, so he moved on to his uncomprehending cousins, and then to an orphanage.

Eventually, he encountered and came to live with the Pedersen family. The father, Karl, was a dogmatic morphine-addicted doctor/mystic, the mother, Mary, an obsequious alcoholic, the son, Frederich, a blithering piano virtuoso, and the daughter, Hilda, an angry mathematical genius. The Pedersens were all grotesquely obese, and, with them, Jesse swelled accordingly. He took their surname and their ways and strove to become one of them. He never gave himself completely, however, to the doctor's maniacal and philosophical egoism. In the end, after helping Mrs. Pedersen in an aborted attempt to escape, Jesse was disowned, dislocated, and, again, left homeless and nameless.

He once again became Jesse Vogel. He attended college at the University of Michigan, studying medicine. An excellent student, he came under the tutelage and influence of Dr. Benjamin Cady, Dr. Roderick Perrault, and an errant scientist/poet named T. W. Monk. Each of these men espoused a distinct and limited worldview—empiricism, behaviorism, and nihilism, respectively. Cady took a mechanistic view of human life. Perrault believed in the interchangeability of personalities and in the ethical merits of brain transplants, and Monk challenged the premise of Jesse's career with Monk's desire for death, disdain for creativity, and adulation of chaos. While Jesse partially adopted each philosophical outlook in turn, he ultimately proved unable to fully possess or embody any of them.

Nevertheless, he became a brilliant surgeon, married Cady's daughter Helene and fathered two daughters, Shelley and Jeanne. In time, the marriage grew unfulfilling, and Jesse became inexplicably obsessed with Reva Denk, a woman he encountered at a chance moment in the emergency room, where they both witnessed a man's self-castration. Obsessed with Reva, Jesse decided impulsively to begin a new life with her. Once she agreed, however, he equally impulsively reversed his determination and, in a measured frenzy, decided to return at once to his wife and home in Chicago.

Years later, Jesse and Helene's older daughter Shelley ran away with her boyfriend Noel. Shelley taunted Jesse with long letters from various locales across the country, where she and Noel lived and traveled, lost in poverty, illness, aimlessness, and drug addiction. The letters were filled with probing questions, detailed reminiscences, sharp accusations, and enigmatic expressions of love. Jesse set out in search of Shelley and finally caught up with her in Toronto, Canada, among a community of draft dodgers, where he confronted her in an effort to rescue her from her self-inflicted oblivion and bring her home. In an alternate ending published in the hardcover edition of the novel, Jesse and Shelley were floating out in a rowboat on a Toronto lake, and Shelley's death seemed imminent.

Critical Evaluation:

Wonderland is divided into three sections. Book one, entitled "Variations on an American Hymn," follows Jesse's journey from family tragedy through life with the Pedersens; book two, "The Finite Passing of an Infinite Passion" (which phrase is drawn from the Danish philosopher Søren Kierkegaard), depicts his academic career, marriage, and relationships with Monk and Reva; and book three, "Dreaming America," is an account, through letters and prose, of Jesse's search for Shelley. As the titles imply, Joyce Carol Oates is concerned with the nature of American passion and dreams.

Oates used Lewis Carroll's *Alice's Adventures in Wonderland* (1865) and *Through the Looking-Glass* (1871) as thematic sources for her novel. The Alice novels were important influences in Oates's literary development, and she has thoroughly investigated their psychological and dramatic structures. Thus, like Alice, Jesse bursts into new worlds and must deal with characters that verge on caricatures. The Pedersens, Monk, and others in *Wonderland* parallel Alice's Mad Hatter, Red Queen, Cheshire Cat, and other Carroll creations. Oates has taken Carroll's thematic framework and applied it sharply and imaginatively to the American scene.

That scene is Oates's "Wonderland." It is the name of the new shopping mall where the dissatisfied Helene meets her lover. "Wonderland" is the name of a poem by T. W. Monk that describes a dizzying, visceral, primal emergence, and that is set as a prologue to the novel. In a larger sense, "Wonderland" is an Oatesian world of unnatural proportions where, like the Pedersens' obesity and the doctors' fanaticism, ideas, emotions, and aspirations are often ridiculously reduced or horrendously magnified. The portraits Oates creates are exaggerated, narcissistic, and often very comical.

The game of proportions contributes to the novel's schizophrenic character. At times it is recognizable naturalism, detailing life-sized actions, thoughts, and events; at other times it is nearly psychedelic surrealism, full of swirling movements and syncopated rhythms, more evocative of a dream or of a nightmare than of documentary reality. Throughout *Wonderland*, Oates's language and imagery are palpable and graphic. Certain scenes are striking and link the physical manifestations of excess to the emotional phenomena of obsession. Hilda Pedersen gluttonously devours chocolates during a mathematical competition. Helene's obsession with her own reproductive capacities turns to panic during a gynecological examination. A man, who turns out to be Reva Denk's lover, arrives at Jesse's hospital self-mutilated. Later Jesse, having tracked Reva to a small town in Wisconsin and having agreed to marry her and father her child, symbolically lacerates himself with a rusty razor before abandoning her altogether.

Wonderland's more graphic scenes reinforce the thematic presence of science and medicine as means of knowing and experiencing life. There are recurrent perceptions of living organisms as reduced to their simplest form, protoplasm, and as beings that emerge from and consume other beings. The concept of 'homeostasis'—the natural tendency toward balance—which Dr. Pedersen asks Jesse to explain one evening at the dinner table, provides a standard for the desirable pattern of functioning that Jesse, not to mention the gallery of characters that surround him, cannot achieve. Psychological balance is rare in *Wonderland*, for the Oatesian universe is subject to constant and sudden flux and revolution.

Amid this whirlwind, Jesse is virtually lost, for he lacks an inherent personality. Before his character is definitively established—in the novel or in his life—his father's atrocities thrust him into the world scrambling to pick up the shattered pieces of his identity. Jesse embarks on a lifelong search for a father figure, a permanent home, true love, and a viable belief system. In the process, he goes through a series of impressive but ultimately vacant surrogates and unwittingly becomes a reflection or an embodiment of the people and ideas around him. Thus, the other characters take on the dimensions of allegory. They become emotional or philosophical options for him to review and try, but his movement through and experience of them, like his movement from name to name and home to home, leaves him at the novel's end only barely less innocent and passive than he was at its start. Ultimately, his search for identity and his longing for a sense of solidity in his existence are the only reliable facts of his life.

Ironically, however, what Jesse has learned from those who have absorbed or tormented him is how to absorb others as well. The entire third book, "Dreaming America," focuses on an impulse that is opposite to the aspirations prevalent throughout the first two books: Shelley's desire to disappear, to become smaller, to simplify, to be left alone, to refuse to commit to love or family or place or belief. In pursuing that desire, she robs Jesse of the only power—illusory at best—that he has gained in his life.

Wonderland bears certain characteristic markings of the Oatesian novel. Like *A Garden of Earthly Delights* (1967), it follows several generations of a family through stages of rage, searching, and emptiness. Like *The Assassins: A Book of Hours* (1975), it offers critical comment on the lust for knowledge and power. It spans a particular period of American political and economic history, and is set against a backdrop of that history, including such events as the technological revolution, the assassination of John F. Kennedy, and the Vietnam conflict. It moves irregularly, with sudden shifts and changes; rather than a unified story, it is built on numerous episodes, shifting viewpoints, and quick juxtapositions.

Wonderland also stakes its own ground on the Oatesian landscape. It is stylistically unnaturalistic, its commentary verges on the broadly satirical, and its concern for the issues of dislocation and identity are fully focused on a single central character. Oates has also been criticized for the novel's unsatisfactory conclusion; in both versions it has been deemed unequal to the novel's overall sharpness and color. Oates herself has noted that *Wonderland* "is the first novel I have written that doesn't end in violence, that doesn't liberate the hero through violence, and therefore there is still a sickish, despairing, confusing atmosphere about it." There is certainly plenty of violence in the novel, and, given the amount of criticism Oates has received for being such a violent writer (criticism she considers blatantly sexist), it is not certain that Jesse's violent liberation would have assuaged all critics. Nevertheless, in *Wonderland*, Oates meditates vividly and passionately on the American Dream, on the way people navigate the narrow channel between the psychological and material worlds, and on how the individual identity is forged.

Barry Mann

Bibliography:

Creighton, Joanne V. *Joyce Carol Oates.* Boston: G. K. Hall, 1979. Creighton discusses *Wonderland* in the context of Oates's earlier novels and in tandem with *Do With Me What You Will* (1973). She explores the series of father figures that the novel offers and rejects, as well as its parallels to *Alice's Adventures in Wonderland.*

Friedman, Ellen G. *Joyce Carol Oates.* New York: Ungar, 1980. An exploration of alienation through Oates's first nine novels. In the chapter entitled "Journey from the 'I' to the Eye: *Wonderland,*" Friedman looks at the novel's links with *Alice's Adventures in Wonderland* and its treatment of the individual's relationship to the external world.

Grant, Mary Kathryn. *The Tragic Vision of Joyce Carol Oates.* Durham, N.C.: Duke University Press, 1978. Grant's long essay interweaves discussion of several Oates novels and other writings into a meditation on the elements of violence and tragedy in modern America. Her references to *Wonderland* bring out themes of self-mutilation, spiritual homelessness, and the alienation of urban life.

Wagner, Linda, ed. *Critical Essays on Joyce Carol Oates.* Boston: G. K. Hall, 1979. A diverse anthology of seventeen reviews and eleven essays spanning the Oates oeuvre. In addition to excerpts from the other entries in this bibliography, discussions of *Wonderland* are found in a skeptical *Newsweek* review, in an essay by Robert H. Fossum exploring the themes of control and salvation, and in a Joanne V. Creighton piece examining Oates's women.

Waller, G. F. *Dreaming America: Obsession and Transcendence in the Fiction of Joyce Carol Oates.* Baton Rouge. Louisiana State University Press, 1979. Waller's chapter on *Wonderland* discusses the novel as social commentary on some of the more manifest obsessions of modern American life—materialism, sex, and violence—treated with a unique mixture of surrealism and satire.

WOODCUTTERS

Type of work: Novel
Author: Thomas Bernhard (1931-1989)
Type of plot: Social realism
Time of plot: 1980's
Locale: Vienna, Austria
First published: Holzfällen: Eine Erregung, 1984 (English translation, 1987)

  Principal characters:
  THE NARRATOR, a writer
  AUERSBERGER, a composer
  HIS WIFE, a wealthy heiress
  JOANA, a deceased actress and dancer
  JEANNIE BILLROTH, a writer
  ANNA SCHREKER, another writer
  AN ACTOR, appearing at the Burgtheater

The Story:

One evening the Auersbergers gave a so-called "artistic dinner" at their home in the Gentzgasse to honor the Actor who was playing the role of Ekdal in a performance of Henrik Ibsen's *The Wild Duck* at the Burgtheater in Vienna. The nameless narrator observed the guests in the music room from his vantage point in a wing chair (in German, an *Ohrensessel*, literally an easy chair with ears) situated in a dimly lighted anteroom.

The narrator's invitation to this gathering was the result of a fortuitous meeting with his hosts several days earlier in Vienna's inner city. The Auersbergers had assumed the role of the city's patrons of "high culture" during the past two decades, a position that had given them high status in Viennese society. The narrator had been a member of their circle twenty-five years earlier, but he had fled to London when he realized that his fellow artists merely continued to live off their early reputations rather than develop their artistry.

Sitting in his wing chair and speaking only to himself, the narrator directed his greatest malevolence toward Auersberger, who had once been described as a "composer in the Anton von Webern tradition." In all the intervening years he had never progressed musically beyond being a poor imitator of that composer. At the time of the dinner he was known for such works as his four-minute chorus, twelve-minute opera, three-minute cantata, and even a one-second opera. On the evening of the dinner Auersberger contributed nothing of artistic value to the conversation. Indeed, the narrator observed that he just became more and more inebriated, to the point of falling asleep in the presence of his guests, who were also all "well-known" and "celebrated" artists. His wife was described as a light-minded, but charming hostess who bubbled about the "distinguished" Actor while serving more champagne every fifteen minutes.

The narrator expressed great passion for Joana, a dancer and actress whose funeral he had attended earlier that day. Joana had shown great talent thirty years earlier when she first established herself in Vienna. Rather than pursuing her own career, however, she had assisted in making her husband a world-renowned artist. Once his position was secure, he had left Joana, a trauma from which she had never recovered. She succumbed to alcoholism, which eventually drove her to suicide. In reflecting on her life, on the funeral earlier that day, and on Ravel's *Bolero*, of which the Auersbergers were playing a recording that evening, the narrator decided that the evening's gathering was a requiem for Joana.

The guests had been waiting for several hours before the Actor finally arrived after midnight. At that point, the narrator's vantage point shifted from the anteroom to the dining room table. Rather than expose himself to the Actor's pompousness and to hearing pretentious nonsense about the Burgtheater tradition, the narrator employed Jeannie Billroth as his pettifogger.

Jeannie was the spokesperson for and representative of the Viennese literary establishment that evening. For many years she had fancied herself to be the brilliant Virginia Woolf of Vienna. She had successfully maneuvered the cultural and political powers of the city to award her literary prizes for her few novels, which were of questionable merit, and for her service as editor of a minor literary journal. That evening she was supported by her long-time friend and even less competent writer, the high school teacher Anna Schreker, who had assumed for herself the pose of being the local Gertrude Stein and Marianne Moore.

At dinner, Jeannie attempted to draw the Actor into one of her "intellectual conversations," but to no avail. Finally she confronted the tired and aging Actor with the question: "Do you think now at the end of your life that you've found fulfillment in your art?" The Actor was outraged and refused to speak to her any longer, but the narrator was delighted that Jeannie had finally been berated for the repulsive insolence she had exhibited her entire life.

The Actor, reflecting on Jeannie's attack and wondering why he had to contend with the never-ending artificiality of life in the theater, had become meditative. His ideal, he philosophized, had always been to be not on the stage speaking the words others had written but to be at home in nature, to enter deep into and yield himself to the forest: "The forest, the virgin forest, the life of a woodcutter—that has always been my ideal." The narrator found that the Actor's pronouncement had great insight, and as he left the gathering, he resolved to write about this "artistic dinner" at once.

Critical Evaluation:

Thomas Bernhard, one of the most prolific and provocative writers of German literature, published about fifty volumes, representing all the major genres of literature. He is best-known for his ten novels, fourteen plays, and seven volumes of memoirs, and most of his prose and dramatic works were translated into English and the other world languages. In his work and in his life, Bernhard publicly castigated the values, institutions, and cultural and political personalities in post-World War II Austria.

The publication of a Bernhard novel or the premiere of one of his plays was always a noteworthy event in Austria. Indeed, *Woodcutters*, a *roman à clef*, unleashed a tumultuous scandal in Austria because the major characters were so thinly disguised. The Austrian writer Jeannie Ebner was Jeannie Billroth, Maja Lampersberg was Auersberger's wife, the choreographer Joana Thul was Joana, and Bernhard himself was clearly the narrator. Gerhard Lampersberg, the composer portrayed in the character of Auersberger, sued for defamation of character, to which Bernhard responded by prohibiting the sale of all his books in Austria for the next fifty years. Newspaper editors and literary critics entered the fracas with debates on the freedom of expression in the arts and for the press. By the time the entire affair was concluded three months later, even more copies of the novel had been sold than anticipated by the publisher.

It is, however, ultimately less important to know about the historical figures being portrayed or the specific Austrian institutions being criticized than it is to experience the novel as a work of art and a philosophical statement. Bernhard is intent on exposing the manner in which artists can become famous through institutions that award literary prizes, whereupon the artists use that commendation, rather than honest attempts at creative work, to promote themselves. In criticizing the institution of the Burgtheater, Bernhard wants to expose the unjustified dictatorship that cultural institutions can bring about merely by virtue of their long and well-entrenched position in society. Bernhard believes that neither the artist nor artistic institutions should automatically be granted the right to speak and that they should continually be subjected to scrutiny and critical evaluation. Bernhard includes himself as one of those artists whose work must constantly be validated, because he has witnessed too many artists who have fallen prey to dangerous institutions and ideologies.

Yet *Woodcutters* exposes a dilemma. The true and honest artist is here represented most forcefully by the character of Joana. The reader is told that there is absolutely no question that she has extraordinary artistic talent, but it is also clear that she is too sensitive to survive in her society. After living a marginal and precarious life in the artistic world, she is finally forced to live in her mountain retreat—among ignorant woodcutters—with whom she is unable to communicate her art. This environment brings about her eventual destruction through suicide. Thus the Actor—who, after all, must remain a public figure in society—could not survive if he were to pursue his ideal of "The forest, the virgin forest, the life of a woodcutter."

At the conclusion of the novel, the reader is momentarily led to believe that the narrator has experienced euphoria and insight, for he seems to have discarded his long-standing detestation for all whom he had revisited in his thoughts that evening at the "artistic dinner." In his jubilation, however, he fails to provide a convincing statement of purpose. The question remains open whether it is the pessimist Thomas Bernhard who wants to write "something at once, no matter what . . . before it's too late?" That might be the novel that—like Ibsen's drama—would remove the veil of illusion and destroy the private fantasies that every human being needs to make life bearable.

Thomas H. Falk

Bibliography:
Demetz, Peter. "Thomas Bernhard: The Dark Side of Life." In *After the Fires: Recent Writing in the Germanies, Austria, and Switzerland*. San Diego, Calif.: Harcourt Brace Jovanovich, 1986. This comprehensive survey of German literature since 1945 includes a chapter on the important role that Thomas Bernhard has played in defining new directions in literature.
Dowden, Stephen D. *Understanding Thomas Bernhard*. Columbia: University of South Carolina Press, 1991. An excellent and complete introduction to the life and works of Thomas Bernhard. Dowden correctly places *Woodcutters*, along with the five-volume memoirs, in the chapter on the autobiographical works.
Fetz, Gerald. "Thomas Bernhard and the 'Modern Novel.'" In *The Modern German Novel*, edited by Keith Bullivant. New York: Berg, 1987. A critical analysis of the eight major prose works published between 1963 and 1985, concentrating on the uniqueness of Bernhard's contribution to the genre of the modern novel.
Modern Austrian Literature 21, nos. 3/4 (1988). Includes sixteen articles on various aspects of Bernhard's work. Of special interest is David Daviau's article "The Reception of Thomas Bernhard in the United States."
Ryan, Simon. "New Directions in the Austrian Novel." In *The Modern German Novel*, edited by Keith Bullivant. New York: Berg, 1987. An excellent survey of the experimentation in language and writing that has become the hallmark of Austrian literature since the 1960's. This article should be read in conjunction with Fetz's study of Bernhard's novels.

THE WOODLANDERS

Type of work: Novel
Author: Thomas Hardy (1840-1928)
Type of plot: Social realism
Time of plot: Nineteenth century
Locale: Rural England
First published: serial, 1886-1887; book, 1887

Principal characters:
GEORGE MELBURY, a timber merchant
GRACE MELBURY, his daughter
GILES WINTERBORNE, an itinerant farmer
FELICE CHARMOND, a lady of the manor
EDGAR FITZPIERS, a doctor

The Story:

The timber merchant George Melbury had spared no expense in educating his only daughter, Grace. She had been away from home for one year, and he was eagerly awaiting her return. Giles Winterborne, an itinerant farmer and apple grower, also looked forward to Grace's homecoming. Mr. Melbury had wronged Giles's father many years before; to atone for this, he had half promised Giles that he should have Grace for his wife.

When Grace returned, it was immediately evident that she had become much too cultured and refined for the ways of a simple farmer. Yet Grace knew that her father had promised her to Giles, and she meant to go through with it even though she shrank a little from his plainness. Mr. Melbury was the most concerned. He was an honorable man and liked Giles, but he loved his only child above everything else. He could not bear to see her throw herself away when she could marry better.

Giles agreed that he was not worthy of Grace, and so the three vacillated, no one wanting to make a decision. Then through a series of unfortunate and unforeseen circumstances, Giles lost the houses that ensured his livelihood. His loss decided the matter. Although Mr. Melbury could easily have supported them both, it was unthinkable that such a lady as Grace should be tied to a man without a steady income. Yet when her father told her that she must forget Giles, Grace found herself for the first time thinking of her would-be lover with real affection.

The local doctor, Edgar Fitzpiers, was the descendant of a formerly fine family and in his own right a brilliant and charming man. The local folk thought he consorted with the devil, for he performed many unusual experiments. From the first time that Edgar saw Grace, he was enchanted with her beauty and her bearing. At first, he thought she must be the lady of the manor, Mrs. Charmond, for he could not believe that the daughter of a merchant could be so well-educated and charming. Before long, the two young people met, and Edgar asked Grace's father for her hand. Mr. Melbury gladly gave his permission, for Edgar was far above Grace in position. Despite his sorrow at disappointing Giles and at failing to keep his pledge, Mr. Melbury encouraged Grace to accept Edgar. She had always obeyed her father in all things, so she accepted Edgar even as she realized that she was growing fonder of Giles by the day.

When the young couple returned from a long honeymoon, they settled in a newly decorated wing of her father's house. Edgar continued his practice. It grew alarmingly smaller, however, for the country folk who had once looked up to him now considered him one of their own. He decided that perhaps he should accept a practice in a neighboring town.

Before he could make a final decision on this question, Mrs. Felice Charmond entered the picture. The lady of the manor was well known for her many love affairs and her questionable reputation. When she had a slight accident and sent for Edgar, he was attracted to her immediately. The few scratches she had suffered were enough to take him to her house day after day, until even the servants and farmers were talking about them. At last, Mr. Melbury decided he could not stand idly by and see his daughter suffer; he appealed in person to Mrs. Charmond to leave Edgar alone. Grace herself was rather immune to the whole affair, for she did not care enough for her husband to suffer great jealousy.

The climax to the situation came when Mr. Melbury found Edgar after he was thrown from a horse near Mrs. Charmond's home. Mr. Melbury picked him up and placed him on his own mount, but Edgar was drunk and unaware that he was riding with his father-in-law. He berated Mr. Melbury and Grace as ignorant peasants and cursed his ill luck in having married beneath himself. His drunken ravings were too much for the kindhearted merchant, who threw Edgar off the horse and rode away. When he came to, Edgar, who had been injured in the first fall, made his way to Mrs. Charmond and begged her to hide him until he could travel. He must now leave the district; there could be no forgiveness for his many sins.

Mrs. Charmond left her home to travel on the Continent. Before long, there were rumors that Edgar was with her. Grace remained stoic. Unknown to her husband, she was aware that he had had an affair with a peasant girl in the neighborhood before his marriage. She would have let things stand, but an unscrupulous lawyer persuaded her father that a new law would permit her to divorce Edgar. While he was making arrangements for the divorce, Mr. Melbury encouraged both Giles and Grace to renew their old plans to marry. By that time, they were both sure that they loved each other, but they were more cautious than Grace's father. Thus when the word came that she could not be free of her husband, they were resigned to their unhappiness.

Grace and Giles did resume the friendship they had known since childhood, but decorously in all respects, for neither wished a hint of scandal to touch the other. Many months later, Grace heard from her husband that he wanted her to live with him again. Mrs. Charmond was dead, killed by a thwarted lover who afterward committed suicide. Edgar did not mention this fact, but a newspaper article informed them of the whole story. Grace and her father decided she should not meet Edgar as he had asked, so he came to their home.

When Grace heard Edgar approaching, she slipped out of the house and ran into the woods. Stumbling and afraid, she came at last to the hut occupied by Giles. Learning that she did not wish to see her husband, Giles installed her in his hut and went out into the rain to sleep. What Grace did not know was that Giles had been very ill of a fever, and a few days and nights in the cold rain made him desperately ill. When she found her faithful friend so ill, she ran for Edgar, forgetting her desire not to see him in her anxiety for Giles. Edgar returned with her, but there was nothing to be done. Grace held her love in her arms as he died, seeming unaware that her husband was present.

For a long time, Grace would not listen to her husband's pleas to return to him. She wanted to hurt him as she had been hurt, and she told him that she and Giles had lived together those last few days. Even before he learned that her self-accusation was not true, Edgar realized that he truly loved her. When a man trap, set for Edgar by the husband of the peasant girl he had once wronged, almost caught Grace in its steel jaws, Edgar helped his wife to safety. After he told her that he had bought a practice at a great distance from her old home and that he would be a faithful husband, devoting himself to her happiness, she went away with him. She intended to be a good wife, but part of her remained with Giles in the country churchyard grave.

Critical Evaluation:

Written between *The Mayor of Casterbridge* (1886) and *Tess of the D'Urbervilles* (1891), this novel, with its plot full of melodramatic excess, is neither strict tragedy nor comedy, nor does it have the depth or majesty of Thomas Hardy's later works. Rather, in its efforts to combine realism and sensationalism, it exhibits affinities with such earlier novels as *Desperate Remedies* (1871).

The oppressively enclosed society of Hintock, where the so-called woodlanders dwell, is one of contrasting sets of individuals, both rural and urban. Giles Winterborne, Marty South, George Melbury, and the workers are opposed to the exotic Felice Charmond of Hintock Manor and Edgar Fitzpiers, the new doctor. Grace Melbury vacillates between the two groups, finally committing herself, after the death of Giles, presumably to life with Fitzpiers in another area; Hardy leaves the end of the novel rather ambiguous.

The story revolves not only around Grace's decisions and indecisions but also around those of Fitzpiers, who is trapped in marriage with Grace at the same time he is having an affair with Felice; around those of Mr. Melbury, who cannot make up his mind whether to marry his daughter to the apple grower or to the doctor; and around those of Felice, who cannot settle on one lover.

Most events in the novel take place in dense woods, on forest paths, or in remote huts almost hidden by foliage. Trees and undergrowth are so omnipresent as to appear stifling. Hintock dwellers plant, trim, and tend trees, fell them at maturity, and strip the bark to sell. The woods have utilitarian as well as symbolic significance. They are real, and so are Giles and Marty, who accept with stolid, earthlike quality their fate of endless hard work. The woodland here lacks the gentleness and beauty of that in *Under the Greenwood Tree* (1872); it demands a high price from those who make it their living. The characters are compared implicitly to trees and plants: Giles and Marty are the indigenous trees, Felice and Fitzpiers the imported ones that finally uproot themselves and seek climates more favorable to their growth.

After an almost unbelievable network of promises made and broken, infidelities, romantic seductions, and accidental deaths, Grace and the repentant Fitzpiers are left to repair their ill-starred marriage. The last chapter, however, points to no satisfactory or simple solution. Hardy does not extol their renewed love; instead, he focuses on Marty South's devoted soliloquy as she places flowers on Giles's grave. She, too, loved him faithfully. In contrast to other women in the novel, she is the epitome of self-sacrifice, and it is Marty whom Hardy leaves with the reader, perhaps embodying in her the residual human values when he comments, "she touched sublimity at points, and looked almost like a being who had rejected . . . the attribute of sex for the loftier quality of abstract humanism." Marty, however, is more a figure of stoic resignation than of sublimity; and even Giles, despite his loyalty and sacrifice for Grace, does not attain tragic stature.

Bibliography:

Boumelha, Penny. *Thomas Hardy and Women: Sexual Ideology and Narrative Form*. Totowa, N.J.: Barnes & Noble Books, 1982. Comparison of contemporary notions of women with Hardy's view. Includes a chapter on *The Woodlanders*, which notes elements of disparate genres and treats the novel's self-consciousness and its echoes of pastoral elegy. Also points out the realistic treatment of sex and marriage.

Brooks, Jean R. *Thomas Hardy: The Poetic Structure*. Ithaca, N.Y.: Cornell University Press, 1971. Includes a chapter on *The Woodlanders*, which emphasizes the organic connection between plot and place. Stresses social hierarchies in comparison with natural environment.

Lucid explication of characters and themes and of the interconnections of natural, human, and cosmic themes.

Kramer, Dale, and Nancy Marck, eds. *Critical Essays on Thomas Hardy: The Novels*. Boston: G. K. Hall, 1990. Helpful overview. Includes a chapter on *The Woodlanders* that synthesizes earlier criticism and analyzes divisions in characters that reflect Hardy's conflicts. Stresses a strand of "secret humor" that keeps the novel realistic.

Moore, Kevin Z. *The Descent of the Imagination: Postromantic Culture in the Later Novels of Thomas Hardy*. New York: New York University Press, 1990. Approaches Hardy's relationship to and departure from Romanticism. Concludes that *The Woodlanders* represents William Wordsworth's crossroads of British culture, where choices are forced between the culturally antithetical railway and the woodland.

Sumner, Rosemary. *Thomas Hardy: Psychological Novelist*. New York: St. Martin's Press, 1981. Analyzes the character of Grace Melbury as a divided woman, an educated woman in a static village. Points out that Hardy drew Grace with clinical precision. Also treats the "modern" elements of *The Woodlanders* and notes that surface conflicts reflect deeper divisions.

WORKS AND DAYS

Type of work: Poetry
Author: Hesiod (fl. c. 700 B.C.E.)
First transcribed: Erga kai Ēmerai, c. 700 B.C.E. (English translation, 1618)

The details of Hesiod's biography at times overshadow his contributions to the literary tradition. Whether he was a contemporary of Homer (proven unlikely by careful linguistic analysis); whether he ever bested the author of the *Iliad* and *Odyssey* in a poetry contest (equally unlikely); even whether the brother to whom *Works and Days* is addressed actually lived (a fact questioned skillfully by the twentieth century scholar Gilbert Murray)—all are of little importance in comparison to his works, especially his long didactic poem on the joys and vicissitudes of the agricultural life. In *Works and Days* Hesiod explains how the people of his day fit into a cosmos peopled by gods who interact frequently, if indirectly, with them and with the creatures of the natural world. His advice, sometimes philosophical, sometimes extremely practical, shows how one can live a life that can be at some times happy, at all times virtuous.

Perhaps the best way to appreciate the significance of Hesiod's accomplishment is to compare his work to that of Homer. The latter fills his stories with heroes and gods engaged in political and military struggles; personal bravery, cunning, and might serve as measures of greatness. By contrast, Hesiod focuses on the commonplace, on life outside of the limelight of national issues and international conflict. Hesiod is the first in the history of Western civilization to think earnestly about problems of conduct and to embody these thoughts in literary form. Hesiod is the first writer in Greek history to judge deeds by their rightness and not their strength, brilliance, or cleverness. In fact, Hesiod consciously set out to oppose the Homeric ideal in his works, becoming in the process the champion of the commoner and the proponent of righteous living. Numerous scholars have noted the similarities between Hesiod's moralizing and the works of the Hebrew prophets and teachers whose admonitions and prescriptions fill the pages of the Old Testament.

The Western literary tradition has come to venerate the Homeric writings, but the significance of Hesiod's investigation of the moral dimensions of human nature should not be overlooked. The immediate source for Vergil's *Georgics* (36-29 B.C.E.), *Works and Days* is also the first work of a tradition that finds exponents in every century: The pastoral poems of the Greeks and Romans and their European inheritors, and moralistic poems, owe much to this Greek ancestor, who believed that people should be judged by the strength of their character rather than their might in deeds.

Facts of the existence of a writer who flourished more than two thousand years ago is hard to find. Herodotus, liking to exaggerate the antiquity of people, wrote that Hesiod lived "not more than 400 years before my time," putting him about 850 B.C.E. Most scholars, however, are inclined to place him about a century later.

At any rate, Homer and Hesiod have left the only Greek writing of the epic age. It is clear from Homeric influences in Hesiod that Homer came first. In *Works and Days*, the gods are contemporary, directly influencing life in Boeotia. Hesiod speaks about his own environment. From internal evidence (lines 636-640), it is assumed that the author's father migrated across the Aegean from Cyme in Aeolia on account of poverty. He settled at Ascra, a village of Boeotia, at the foot of Mt. Helicon. Ovid, in referring to Hesiod, used the adjective "ascraeus." The poet himself, heir to the traditions of minstrelsy in this colony of Hellas, says that he once sailed to Chalcis in Euboea, where he competed in a poetry contest held by Amphidamas, and won the prize, a tripod with handles, which he gave to the Muses of Helicon.

The poem also contains details of a lawsuit brought against Hesiod by his brother Perses. Apparently by bribery of the judges, Perses was awarded Hesiod's sheep, but the diligent Hesiod accumulated another fortune, whereas Perses lost all he had and was forced to beg further help from the poet. Without hard feelings, Hesiod gave him assistance, with the warning not to ask again, and put his admonitions in a poem of 828 lines, of which the title well sums up its content: Rules for work and days on which luck is favorable.

Works and Days is neither a scientific treatise on farming nor a lesson on economic recovery through diligence, but rather a combination of moral precepts and an agricultural almanac. Under the symbols of Prometheus and Epimetheus (Forethought and Afterthought), Hesiod epitomized himself and his brother.

In epic style, Hesiod begins *Works and Days* with an appeal to the Muses of Pieria, to sing of their father Zeus, who determines one's fame or dishonor, provides the good and the bad, destroys the mighty, and rewards the humble. The poet adds that there are two kinds of Strife on earth, one good and one bad. The good Strife, the elder daughter of Dark Night and of Zeus the Son of Chronos, makes people industrious so that they strive to imitate and surpass their neighbors.

Then, addressing himself to his brother Perses, Hesiod begs him not to follow the other Strife, in marketplace or courthouse. First lay up food for a year, he advises, and then, if necessary, enter disputes of law. This section contains references to Perses' unbrotherly lawsuit to get more than his rightful share of their father's possessions.

Prometheus by craft recovered the fire that Zeus had taken from men, and in revenge Zeus created a woman of water and earth. Pandora ("The All-Endowed") received all the lures provided by the gods to deceive men. She was eagerly accepted by Epimetheus, who had forgotten his brother's warning against gifts from the gods. Before her advent, men lived on earth free from wearying toil and death-bringing diseases. Pandora removed the great lid from the jar, and all the evils flew out and scattered over the earth.

Hesiod then tells another tale about the way gods and humanity came from the same seed. In the time of Chronos there existed a golden race of mortals, living like gods and ignorant of sorrow or old age. Everything good belonged to them: abundant flocks, fruits, the blessings of the gods. After the earth covered them, the gods created an inferior race of silver. After a hundred years of idiotic childhood, they came of age, only to kill off one another in warfare. A third race followed whose delight was war; they died and went to chill Hades. Then came the demigods, the heroes of Thebes and Troy, preceding the present race of iron, whose daily lot is weariness and woe. To them, might is right. They have no reverence for justice and oaths.

At this point in the poem Hesiod tells the first animal fable in Greek literature, the tale of a hawk who flew high into the sky with a nightingale, lecturing her against the folly of trying to compete with stronger people. To Perses, he adds a warning that violence is a bad quality in a poor man. For him, justice is better.

A city that provides honest judgments, says Hesiod, is blessed by Zeus, who protects it from war and famine. Its citizens never have to make sea voyages (which Hesiod hated); their earth provides their living. An insolent city, even one with a single insolent citizen, is plagued by the gods because Justice, the daughter of Zeus, is quick with rewards or punishment. Then follows a series of homilies as encouragement to the lazy and improvident Perses: "Work is no disgrace; it is idleness that is disgraceful." "The idle envy the wealth of the hard worker and try to seize it violently. God-given wealth is better."

After these homilies the poet rhymes a sort of farmers' almanac: Plow when the Pleiades set (in November). After forty days they come back. Then sharpen your sickle. When the autumn rains come, cut your wood. Choose oak for ploughbeams, and bring home two, in case one breaks. Get two nine-year-old oxen to plow. A forty-year-old slave is most reliable in the fields. Have everything ready to start plowing when the cry of the crane is heard. If the cuckoo sings, plant quickly, for it will rain in three days. When winter comes, your slaves will need twice as much food, your oxen half their regular ration. Prune your grapes before the return of the swallow, sixty days after the sun turns. When Orion is overhead, it is time to harvest your grapes. Sun them for ten days, cover them for five, and then press out the wine.

His theories on husbandry extend into domestic life. The ideal time for a man to marry, he says, is at the age of thirty; for a woman, the fifth year after puberty. Marry a neighbor, but be sure the others will not laugh at your choice. Finally, the poet records holy days and the lucky days for different tasks. He concludes that the wise man is the one who works blamelessly before the deathless gods, for he knows the propitious omens and avoids sin.

Updated by Laurence W. Mazzeno

Bibliography:
Athanassakis, Apostolos, trans. *Hesiod: Theogony, Works and Days, Shield.* Baltimore: The Johns Hopkins University Press, 1983. A superior translation of three major works. Includes a concise introduction to Hesiod and his historical period as well as useful notes to the text.
Fränkel, Hermann. *Early Greek Poetry and Philosophy.* Translated by Moses Hadas and James Willis. New York: Harcourt Brace Jovanovich, 1975. Fränkel's work provides an exhaustive scholarly study of the major contributions to literature in ancient Greek society. His third chapter is an interesting exploration of Hesiod's role in the dialogue between the literary genres.
Lamberton, Robert. *Hesiod.* New Haven, Conn.: Yale University Press, 1988. Brief, excellent introduction to Hesiod. Provides line-by-line interpretation of Hesiod's poems and focuses on the meaning of his imagery. Chapter 3 focuses exclusively on the *Works and Days.* Includes extensive bibliography, notes on translations, and index.
West, M. L. *Hesiod: Works and Days.* Oxford, England: Clarendon Press, 1978. The standard scholarly commentary on Hesiod's poem. Includes Greek text and copious notes. A rewarding introduction to the poet and his society as well as to issues surrounding the poem's composition.

THE WORLD AS WILL AND IDEA

Type of work: Philosophy
Author: Arthur Schopenhauer (1788-1860)
First published: Die Welt als Wille und Vorstellung, 1819; augmented editions, 1844, 1859
 (English translation, 1883-1886)

The three volumes of *The World as Will and Idea* comprise Arthur Schopenhauer's major contribution to the literature of philosophy. At the time of the book's writing, the philosophy of Georg Wilhelm Friedrich Hegel, with its vast vision of the dialectic process underlying the tensions and currents of human history, held sway over the thinking of many. The European rationalists, led by the formidable figure of René Descartes, had previously promoted an optimistic view of the almost limitless possibilities of penetrating the nature of reality by means of human reason. Contrary to the Hegelian vision and rationalist hopefulness, Schopenhauer maintained a fierce pessimism about the limitations of human knowledge and certainty. Even though *The World as Will and Idea* sold poorly and aroused little interest at the time of its publication, the thought behind the book, carried forward as it is by Schopenhauer's strongly individualistic and wide-ranging literary style, stands today as a weighty counterbalance to Enlightenment-era optimism and assurance.

In fact, Schopenhauer's philosophy has at times been considered by critics to be an elaborate metaphysical justification for a profoundly pessimistic and gloomy temperament brought about by several factors. While Schopenhauer was still in his teens, his father died, apparently by suicide, and a serious disagreement with his mother continued throughout his adult life. He also experienced early frustrations in both the business and academic worlds; these continued throughout his publishing and lecturing career until late in life, when his collection of essays, *Parerga und Paralipomena* (1851) brought him a following and a measure of fame that increased steadily for the remainder of his life. Even though gratified by his late success, Schopenhauer considered his earlier work, especially *The World as Will and Idea,* his primary philosophical statement, despite its poor reception, and never entertained doubts as to its worth: "Subject to the limitation of human knowledge," he wrote, "my philosophy is the real solution of the enigma of the world."

Volume 1 of *The World as Will and Idea* is divided into four books, two dealing with "The World as Idea" (books 1 and 3) and two with "The World as Will" (books 2 and 4). Volume 2 consists of supplements to books 1 and 2, while volume 3 presents supplements to books 2 through 4. In addition, volume 2 contains an extensive criticism of certain points of the philosophy of Immanuel Kant, who remained, however, the philosopher whom Schopenhauer admired most and was influenced by to the greatest degree. In his original preface, Schopenhauer said of Kant's works that "the effect these writings produce in the mind to which they truly speak is very like that of the operation for cataracts on a blind man." In his preface to the revised version of the book, Schopenhauer repeated his praise: "Kant's teaching produces in the mind of every one who has comprehended it a fundamental change that is so great that it may be regarded as an intellectual new birth."

Two other major influences on Schopenhauer's philosophy were the metaphysical idealism of Plato and, somewhat surprisingly, the Eastern philosophy in the Upanishads, a portion of the Hindu scriptures. To Schopenhauer, the "greatest advantage" the nineteenth century held over previous centuries was the new availability in European languages of the "sacred, primitive Indian wisdom" contained in "Sanskrit literature." In volume 2, he confesses that "next to the impression of the world of perception, I owe what is best in my own system to the impression made on me by the works of Kant, by the sacred writings of the Hindus, and by Plato."

What all three of these influences have in common is a rather pessimistic view of the possibilities of human knowledge of reality. In particular, Kant's conception of the *Ding an sich*—the "thing in itself"—is crucial to an understanding of Schopenhauer's work. The *Ding an sich* is that aspect of existence that lies beyond all human perception, since according to Kant people only know their own perceptions and understandings of objects in the world; they can never know the "thing in itself," the object as it actually is. This insight, Kant's Copernican Revolution of philosophy, shifts the locus of reality from the external world typically thought of as real to the consciousness of the subject perceiving this world. The perceiver is forever cut off from the thing perceived, for immediate experience is only that of the perceiver's perception of the thing. Consequently, people know no other world than that subjective world that is placed before their own perception and understanding; as the Upanishads maintain, the world thought of as real is actually mere appearance. In fact, the word *Vorstellung* in Schopenhauer's title is sometimes translated as "representation" rather than "idea," for that which is present in the consciousness of the perceiving subject is a mere representation of the object itself.

Accepting this line of thought led Schopenhauer to the startling assertion with which he opens his book: "The world is my idea." He goes on to explain:

> This is a truth which holds good for everything that lives and knows, though man alone can bring it into reflective and abstract consciousness. If he really does this, he has attained to philosophical wisdom. It then becomes clear and certain to him that what he knows is not a sun and an earth, but only an eye that sees a sun, a hand that feels an earth; that the world which surrounds him is there only as an idea, i.e., only in relation to something else, the consciousness, which is himself.

The intellect, according to Schopenhauer, organizes the body's perceptions into the world in which it lives, and thus "the whole world of objects is and remains idea, and therefore wholly and forever determined by the subject." On the other hand, this does not mean that the universe of experience does not objectively exist or that it is not somehow created by the perceiving subject. Schopenhauer follows Kant in distinguishing between mere sensory impressions, on the one hand, and the intellectual understanding that converts these impressions into ideas, on the other. The external world must actually exist, for the intellect would lie dormant were it not stimulated into activity by the body's perception of itself and its place in the external universe.

All of this is equally true of every consciousness, including animal consciousness. What sets humans apart from animals is the capacity for "reflective and abstract consciousness," that is, reason, which enables humans to transcend the universe of things and to achieve inner quiet and calm as they contemplate the world of suffering.

In book 2, Schopenhauer carries his argument beyond the philosophy of Kant, who, holding that the "inner nature" of things is forever sealed to human understanding, never identifies the *Ding an sich*. According to Schopenhauer, however, this can only be identified with the will, for the awareness that people possess of themselves as will is quite distinct from the awareness that they possess of themselves as body or thing. People know themselves in two primary ways: as bodily objects, no different in any respect from the world of objects with which they interact, and as self-directing beings whose actions are the embodiment of the will's direction. The operation of the will and the operation of the body thus appear to be one and the same, although they can be contemplated separately for the purpose of analysis; the body is the objectified will. In knowing themselves as such unified beings, such objectifications of the autonomous will, people know themselves to be irreducible, the *Ding an sich*, which thereby stands revealed as the will in their own consciousness.

If this principle is applied not merely to humanity but to all phenomena (Schopenhauer's "great extension"), the universe becomes a much different place from that described by more traditional metaphysics. From its least significant aspect to its greatest, the universe as a macrocosm takes on the character of will ascribed to the microcosmic human. The reality behind the phenomenal universe becomes not rational, not orderly or designed, but nonrational, nondesigned, purposeless, and meaningless, the endless striving and conflict of wills. If this is indeed the state of affairs—if the "thing in itself" behind reality is in fact the will—then all philosophies that purport to find meaning, purpose, or design behind natural and human history (such as the philosophy of Schopenhauer's arch-rival Hegel) are delusory, and the real purpose of philosophy is to reveal the grim and stark nature of the universe and of the human condition. Thus Schopenhauer's profound pessimism would have a metaphysical justification.

In book 3, Schopenhauer uses this doctrine of the will to help explain his theories of art. Schopenhauer places a higher importance on art and the artist than any other modern philosopher, for he believes that it is by means of art that humanity is enabled to separate itself from and transcend the world of will and conflict. In contemplating a work of art, observers enter a disinterested state of will-less perception that is quite different from the ordinary perception of sensory impressions; they escape for a time from the ordinary struggles and desires of life and disappear into or become one with the "permanent essential forms of the world and all its phenomena." In thus adapting Plato's "Ideal Forms," Schopenhauer considers artistic knowledge more valuable than scientific knowledge, for that concerns itself with the shifting and imperfect appearance of reality conveyed by sensory impression, while artistic knowledge penetrates to the archetypal reality behind the appearance. In particular, the artistic expression known as music dispenses with all forms of surface appearance and grants immediate access to its subject, the will itself.

Finally, in book 4, Schopenhauer explores the implications of this will-less perception, this disappearance from the world of strife, particularly as presented in the Hindu formula *Tat tvam asi* ("That art thou"). When the world of sensory impressions is rejected as mere appearance, the recognition of the illusory nature of surface phenomena enables people to perceive the deeper underlying unity between all things. Desire and the individual will are renounced, even to the extent of renouncing the will to live.

This renunciation does not lead to suicide, for suicide would also imply desire or will (the desire or will for death). Rather, this renunciation leads to a peaceful state of freedom from the will's demands, in which the subject "draws less distinction between himself and others than is usually done" and is enabled to rise above the meaningless universe in a state of mystical insight. According to Schopenhauer, to accept this philosophy would lead to humanity's ultimate triumph.

Craig Payne

Bibliography:
Copleston, Frederick C. *Arthur Schopenhauer: Philosopher of Pessimism.* 2d ed. New York: Barnes & Noble Books, 1975. A magisterial survey and criticism of *The World as Will and Idea* from an explicitly Catholic position. Presents Schopenhauer's views fairly and objectively but points out their opposition to Christianity's positive affirmation of life. Includes a biography of Schopenhauer, a summary of the philosophical activity immediately preceding him, and an account of his later influence. Highly recommended.

Gardiner, Patrick. *Schopenhauer*. Harmondsworth, England: Penguin, 1967. Argues that although Schopenhauer's thought includes many problems and inconsistencies, his writings played an important role in the nineteenth century intellectual world. Further, Schopenhauer had greater influence on such novelists as Thomas Mann, Marcel Proust, and Leo Tolstoy than he had on other philosophers of the time. Gardiner also explores Schopenhauer's ideas on the primacy of the will and the nature of the artistic imagination.

Hamlyn, David. *Schopenhauer*. London: Routledge & Kegan Paul, 1980. Discusses Schopenhauer's earlier work, particularly *The Fourfold Root of the Principle of Sufficient Reason* (1813), as it relates to *The World as Will and Idea*. Points to the influence of Kant on Schopenhauer's philosophical idealism and explores his adaptation of the Platonic "Ideas" to fit this philosophy.

Magee, Bryan. *The Philosophy of Schopenhauer*. Oxford, England: Clarendon Press, 1983. An interesting later contribution; well-written and accessible. Recommended as a supplement to Copleston's work.

Taylor, Richard. "Schopenhauer." In *A Critical History of Western Philosophy*, edited by D. J. O'Connor. New York: Free Press, 1964. Excellent article-length overview of Schopenhauer's output; recommended as a source by both Gardiner and Hamlyn.

WORLD ENOUGH AND TIME

Type of work: Novel
Author: Robert Penn Warren (1905-1989)
Type of plot: Philosophical realism
Time of plot: 1801-1826
Locale: Kentucky
First published: 1950

Principal characters:

JEREMIAH BEAUMONT, an idealist
COLONEL CASSIUS FORT, a frontier politician and Jeremiah's benefactor
RACHAEL JORDAN, a woman betrayed by Fort and, later, Jeremiah's wife
WILKIE BARRON, an opportunist
DR. LEICESTER BURNHAM, Jeremiah's teacher
LA GRAND' BOSSE, a river pirate

The Story:

Jeremiah Beaumont was born in Kentucky in 1801. His father was Jasper Beaumont, one of the first settlers in Glasgow County, and his mother was the disinherited daughter of a wealthy planter. Jasper Beaumont never prospered as he had hoped, and his unfulfilled ambitions bred in him a strain of awkward moodiness which was reflected in his son.

Jasper died, debt-ridden, when Jeremiah was thirteen. Before that time, the boy had been put to school with Leicester Burnham. Hoping for a better life than his father's, Jeremiah was diligent in his studies. He was also stubbornly independent, for he refused to become his grandfather's heir because the old man insisted that he take his mother's maiden name, Marcher. When he was seventeen, Dr. Burnham introduced him to Colonel Cassius Fort, a famous frontier lawyer and politician who was looking for a young man to train in his law office at Bowling Green. Jeremiah was eager to accept Fort's offer but could not do so because of his ailing mother. Fort said that he was willing to wait for anyone Dr. Burnham recommended so highly.

The next spring, Mrs. Beaumont died, and Jeremiah went to Bowling Green to study law, not in Fort's office, however, for the lawyer had returned to Congress. Jeremiah's only friend in the town was Wilkie Barron, another law student, from whose mother Jeremiah rented a room. Fort returned from Washington in 1820 and took the young man under his patronage. From him, Jeremiah learned to look on the law not as a collection of dry statutes but as humanity's agent of truth and justice. Times were hard in Kentucky following the Panic of 1819, and the legislature had passed a law allowing a twelve-month stay of sale for debt. Fort was on the side of the Relief Party, as those who supported the measure were called.

Wilkie Barron first told Jeremiah of a scandal linking Fort's name with that of Rachael Jordan, daughter of a planter who had died heavily in debt. Called in to help settle the estate, Fort was supposed to have seduced the girl and fathered her stillborn child. Grieved by that story of innocence betrayed, Jeremiah decided to have nothing more to do with his benefactor. In a letter he informed Fort, who was away at the time, of his decision. Fort wrote in reply, but before his letter reached Bowling Green, Jeremiah had gone to visit Wilkie's uncle, old Thomas Barron, in Saul County. The Jordan place was only a few miles away from his host's. There he met Rachael Jordan, won her confidence, and, after hearing from her own lips the story of her shame, married her. She accepted him on the condition that he kill Fort.

In the meantime, he had become involved in local politics. Wilkie Barron and Percival Scrogg, fanatic liberal editor of a Frankfort newspaper, arrived to take part in a disputed election. After a riot at the polls, in which he and Wilkie fought side by side, Jeremiah was dismayed to learn that his friend was working for Fort. Wilkie advised him to put aside personal grudges for the public good.

Jeremiah and Rachael Jordan were married in 1822. At the time, Fort was away on private business. Taking over the Jordan plantation, the young husband devoted all his energies to making the place productive. Sometimes he felt that he had his father's score to settle as well as his wife's, that his hard work would vindicate his bankrupt father against men like Fort, to whom wealth and fame came easily. Ambitious for the future and foreseeing expansion of the settlements, he formed a partnership with Josh Parham, a rich landowner, and, with Parham's son Felix, surveyed town sites in the unclaimed western lands. The venture in land speculation fell through, however, when Desha, the Relief candidate, was elected governor in 1824. Parham, an anti-Relief man, swore that he would never spend money opening up land in Kentucky while the Relief Party was in office.

Rachael and Jeremiah were expecting their first child when Fort returned from the East. Rachael, begging her husband to give up his intention of killing Fort, persuaded him that his first duty was to her and the unborn child. A week later, Wilkie arrived at the plantation with a handbill in which Fort, announcing his candidacy for the legislature, disavowed membership in the Relief Party. Urged by Wilkie, Jeremiah also became a candidate for office. The campaign was a bitter one. Unknown to Jeremiah, the Relief Party printed a broadside in which the scandal involving Fort and Rachael was revived. Jeremiah, to his wife's relief, was defeated by Sellars, the candidate he opposed.

Two months later, Rachael had a miscarriage. On the same day, a handbill was mysteriously delivered to the house. Signed by Fort, it refuted the campaign slanders against him and accused Rachael of having her first child by a mulatto slave. That night Jeremiah reached his decision to kill Fort. As soon as he could leave his wife in a neighbor's care, he rode to Frankfort. Disguised, he went at night to the house in which Fort was staying, called him to the door, and stabbed him to death. He then rode home and told Rachael what he had done.

Four days later, officers appeared and summoned him to Frankfort for examination in connection with the murder. Believing that there was no evidence against him, he went willingly. His enemies, however, were already busy manufacturing false clues, and, to his surprise, he was bound over for trial. By the time of his trial, bribery and perjury had done their work. In spite of the efforts of Dr. Burnham and other loyal friends, his case was lost when Wilkie appeared to testify against him. Although many believed him innocent, Jeremiah was sentenced to be hanged on August 20, 1826. Meanwhile, Rachael had been arrested and brought to Frankfort, where she and her husband shared the same cell. Jeremiah's lawyers appealed the sentence. When they failed to produce one of the handbills defaming Rachael, the appeal was denied.

Two days before the execution date, Wilkie Barron and several men broke into the jail and freed the prisoners, who were taken secretly to a refuge ruled over by La Grand' Bosse, a river pirate. There, from one of Wilkie's former henchmen, Jeremiah learned that Scrogg and Wilkie had forged the handbill responsible for Fort's death. In despair, Rachael killed herself. Realizing how he had been duped, Jeremiah tried to return to Frankfort and reveal the truth. Wilkie's man overtook him and cut off his head.

Wilkie went into partnership with the Parhams and became rich. Still politically ambitious, he was elected senator. One night in Washington, he shot himself. Among his effects, to be uncovered in an old trunk years later, were some letters and a manuscript in which Jeremiah Beaumont, during his months in prison and in the outlaw camp, had written his story of deceit and betrayal. No one would ever know why Wilkie had kept those incriminating papers. Unable to destroy the truth, he had tried to conceal it. Perhaps at the end, like Jeremiah, he wondered whether the striving, pride, violence, agony, and expiation had all been for nothing.

Critical Evaluation:

Colonel Solomon P. Sharp, Solicitor General of Kentucky, was killed by a masked assassin in 1825. Shortly afterward, Jeroboam Beauchamp, a young lawyer and a member of the political party opposing Sharp, was arrested and charged with the crime. During the trial, it was revealed that Beauchamp had married a planter's daughter whom Sharp had seduced. Found guilty and awaiting execution, Beauchamp was visited in his cell by his wife. The husband and wife stabbed themselves after a dose of laudanum failed to kill them. The wife died in her husband's cell. Beauchamp was hanged. The Kentucky Tragedy, as this story of intrigue and revenge was called, became a popular subject during the nineteenth century, among writers as dissimilar as Edgar Allan Poe, Charlotte Barnes, Thomas H. Chivers, Charles F. Hoffman, and William Gilmore Simms. Robert Penn Warren, reworking the old tale, has filled it with philosophical speculation and symbolic moral overtones. His Jeremiah Beaumont is an idealist confronted by the realities and compromises of the world, a man betrayed not only by an acquisitive and self-seeking society but also by the very idealism that sustains him in loneliness and doubt. The plot, centering on a theme of community guilt and expiation, illustrates the complex moral issues of the era.

Given his lifelong preoccupation with Southern history, it is not surprising that Robert Penn Warren was attracted to the Kentucky Tragedy as a vehicle for the expression of his thoughts and feelings about idealism, fanaticism, politics, love, sex, and violence. In adapting this historical event—almost a folk legend—Warren begins with a story of innocence violated, villainy rewarded, revenge, political corruption, and backwoods violence. The raw material is, therefore, highly dramatic. Warren's first problem is how to tell the story without descending to sentimental romance or lurid melodrama.

First, he mutes the obvious sensationalism of the events through his handling of point of view. An unnamed historian, having pieced together the story from Jeremiah Beaumont's "confession" and other data, narrates the events with scholarly objectivity and frequent moralizing in an ornate prose style. This elaborate, indirect approach, with the highly charged dramatic scenes, gives the book both historical distance and dramatic intensity.

Second, Warren shifts the usual focus of the tale from the sentimental, revenge-seeking woman, Rachael Jordan, to her idealistic but confused husband, Jeremiah. Therefore, the novel takes on a shape not unlike Warren's earlier masterpiece *All the King's Men* (1946). As in the previous book, the novel revolves around the relationship between a young man (Jeremiah), a powerful father figure (Cassius Fort), who combines idealistic good with pragmatic evil and who inspires worship as well as revulsion, and the woman (Rachael) who is the victim both of the older man's attractiveness and of his ruthlessness. Again, the father figure is murdered by the young man to avenge the honor of the woman.

Warren's analysis of the political context of the act further differentiates his handling of the Kentucky Tragedy from previous ones. The results of Jeremiah's act demonstrate the potential dangers of fanatical idealism in conflict with corrupt pragmatic politics. He is finally convicted not because he committed the crime but because his guilt serves the selfish needs of those in power.

Warren's biggest deviation from the original events, however, lies in the novel's resolution. The historical couple attempted mutual suicide; the woman died, and the man was hanged. In Warren's version, an escape is arranged. In the course of their flight, Jeremiah and Rachael learn the truth of their situation, which drives Rachael to suicide and Jeremiah to an attempt at public confession. The important thing to Warren is not Jeremiah's legal punishment but the growth of his personal awareness. Jeremiah, like other Warren protagonists, must finally accept responsibility not only for his own deed but also for the sequence of turbulent events provoked by that first act of violence.

Bibliography:

Burt, John. "The Self-Subversion of Value: *World Enough and Time.*" In *Robert Penn Warren and American Idealism*. New Haven, Conn.: Yale University Press, 1988. Discussion of the novel as romance and of Beaumont as unaware of the world's complexity. The novel's major images reinforce the idea that humanity's best instincts lead to self-destruction.

Guttenberg, Barnett. "*World Enough and Time.*" In *Web of Being: The Novels of Robert Penn Warren*. Nashville: Vanderbilt University Press, 1975. Existential interpretation of Beaumont as an absolutist whose reliance upon the 'idea' has not prepared him for the 'reintegration of self' that is necessary when he perceives reality. The novel develops the conflict between humanity's need for order and the world's incoherence.

Justus, James H. "Dream and Drama: *World Enough and Time.*" In *The Achievement of Robert Penn Warren*. Baton Rouge: Louisiana State University Press, 1981. Discussion of Warren's double point of view, as the narrator at various times supports, undercuts, and simply relates Beaumont's account. Another of Warren's egoist idealists, Beaumont struggles but fails to remake the world to conform to his nebulous ideals.

Kallsen, Loren J. *The Kentucky Tragedy: A Problem in Romantic Attitudes*. Indianapolis: Bobbs-Merrill, 1963. Collects nineteenth century publications which have served as the sources for literary treatments of this historical incident. Supposedly, these documents are Jeroboam Beauchamp's confession, Ann Cook Beauchamp's letters to a friend in Maryland, the transcript of the couple's trial, and a brother's vindication of Solomon Sharp's character. The book also includes a bibliography and discussion questions.

McDowell, Frederick P. W. "The Romantic Tragedy of Self in *World Enough and Time.*" In *Robert Penn Warren: A Collection of Critical Essays*, edited by John Lewis Longley, Jr. New York: New York University Press, 1965. Discussion of the novel's theme as typical of Warren's emphasis upon the self-induced alienation of the individual who cannot distinguish between romance and reality. Beaumont journeys west in search of Edenic innocence; instead, he finds a savage wilderness.

THE WORLD OF THE THIBAULTS

Type of work: Novel
Author: Roger Martin du Gard (1881-1958)
Type of plot: Social realism
Time of plot: Early twentieth century
Locale: France
First published: Les Thibault, 1922-1940: *Le Cahier gris,* 1922; *Le Pénitencier,* 1922; *La Belle Saison,* 1923; *La Consultation,* 1928; *La Sorellina,* 1928; *La Mort du père,* 1929; *L'Été 1914,* 1936; *Épilogue,* 1940; English translation, 1939-1941

> *Principal characters:*
> MONSIEUR THIBAULT, the father
> ANTOINE, his older son
> JACQUES, his younger son
> GISE, an orphan girl reared by the Thibaults
> MADAME DE FONTANIN, a Protestant woman
> JÉROME DE FONTANIN, her husband
> DANIEL, her son
> JENNY, her daughter
> MEYNESTREL, a Socialist leader

The Story:

Monsieur Thibault was furious when he learned that Jacques had lied to him and run away with young Daniel de Fontanin. The Abbé Binot, Jacques's teacher, had even more disquieting news. From a copybook that had fallen into the abbé's hands, it was apparent that Jacques, not yet fourteen years old, had formed an unnatural friendship with Daniel. What was worse, the de Fontanins were Protestants.

Antoine Thibault, already a doctor, went to see Madame de Fontanin to learn what he could about Daniel and his friendship with Jacques. Antoine found her a very attractive, sensible woman, who rejected Antoine's hints of an improper relationship between the boys. They questioned Jenny, Daniel's younger sister, who had come down with a fever. To Antoine's practiced eye, Jenny was suffering from meningitis. When neither Antoine nor the other doctors could help Jenny, Madame de Fontanin called in her minister, Pastor Gregory. He effected a miraculous cure of the girl by faith healing.

Jacques and Daniel got as far as Marseilles. Although Jacques was the younger of the two boys, he was the moving spirit in the escapade. He had revolted against the smug respectability of his father and the dull Thibault household. Monsieur Thibault was such an eminent social worker that he had no time to try to understand his own family. The suspicions of the Thibaults, however, were unfounded; Jacques's feelings for Daniel were no more than a schoolboy crush.

When the runaways were returned by the police, Daniel was scolded and forgiven by his mother. Jacques, on the other hand, was put in a reformatory founded by his father. There, the boy's spirit was nearly broken by brutal guards and solitary confinement. Only by devious means was Antoine able to get his brother away from his father's stern discipline. He took a separate flat and had Jacques live with him, assuming responsibility for his younger brother's upbringing.

When Jérome de Fontanin, Daniel's father, ran away with Noémie, a cousin, Noémie's daughter, Nicole, came to live with the de Fontanins. Nicole was very attractive, and Daniel tried to seduce her. Nicole, however, had before her the unhappy example of her mother, and she resisted him.

Under Antoine's care, Jacques slowly recovered his mental health. During the summer vacation he was greatly attracted to Jenny de Fontanin. Just as Jenny was beginning to care for him and to overcome her aversion to physical contact, Jacques disappeared.

For three years the Thibaults thought Jacques was dead. Only Gise, an orphan girl reared by the Thibaults, hoped that he was still alive. One day, she received from England a box of rosebuds like those she had sprinkled on Jacques just before his disappearance. Convinced that Jacques was alive in England, Gise went to school in England, where she hoped to find him.

Antoine followed a different course. By chance, he discovered a Swiss magazine with a story entitled *Sorellina* or *Little Sister*. Antoine thought he could recognize both the Thibault and de Fontanin families thinly disguised in the story. Disquieted, Antoine hired a detective agency in Geneva to trace the author.

Antoine's own life was quite unhappy. On an emergency case one night, he had met Rachel, an adventuress, and they had become lovers. Little by little, Rachel told him the story of her sordid past, a story that strangely endeared her to Antoine.

She had once been the mistress of the ferocious Hirst, a fifty-year-old man who had been having incestuous relations with his daughter, Clara. Rachel's brother had married Clara, and they had gone to Italy on their honeymoon. A few days later, Clara had written to her father, asking him to join them. After his arrival, the young husband learned the true relationship between father and daughter. To avoid a scandal, Hirst had strangled Clara and her husband and had thrown their bodies into a lake.

Rachel said she was through with Hirst. One day, she said she had to make a trip to the Congo to see about some investments. When Antoine did not believe her, she admitted that she was going back to Hirst, who had sent for her. Antoine sadly accompanied Rachel to Le Havre and helped her embark.

According to a report from the detective agency, Jacques had become an international socialist and an influential writer in Geneva. Monsieur Thibault developed a serious illness. Fearing that his father would die, Antoine went to Geneva and asked Jacques to return, but Monsieur Thibault died without recognizing his errant son. At the funeral, Gise saw Jacques again and realized that she still loved him. Jacques, however, had lost all of his affection for her. Jenny was still afraid of Jacques, and in her frigidity she had even come to hate him. Daniel was busy as a successful artist.

Jacques felt no ties in Paris and returned to Geneva. He worked there during the fateful summer of 1914. Under the leadership of Meynestrel, a group of socialists were involved in trying to unite the workers of England, France, and Germany in an effort to stop the impending war with paralyzing strikes. Jacques was frequently sent on secret missions. One such trip was to Paris just before general mobilization was decreed. By chance, Jacques saw Jenny again. The new Jacques, mature and valuable to the pacifist movement, soon converted Jenny to his views. They fell in love.

Madame de Fontanin's husband had died in Vienna, where he was suspected of embezzlement. In an attempt to clear his name, she went to Austria despite the imminence of war. While she was gone, Jacques became a frequent visitor to the de Fontanin flat. When Madame de Fontanin returned early one morning, she was shocked to find Jacques and Jenny sleeping together.

Jenny planned to leave for Geneva with Jacques. At the last moment, however, she decided to remain at home. Jacques was free to leave on his humanitarian mission. He and Meynestrel had their own plan for ending the war. Jacques took off from Switzerland in a light plane piloted by Meynestrel. He had with him several million pamphlets that called on both Germans and French to lay down their arms. The plane crashed near the French lines, and Meynestrel was burned to death. Jacques, severely wounded, was captured by the French as a spy. While he was being carried to headquarters on a stretcher, one of the orderlies shot him in the temple.

Gassed severely during the war, Antoine realized that his recovery was impossible. On leave, he visited his old country home near Paris, where he found Madame de Fontanin a competent hospital administrator and Nicole a good nurse. Jenny was happy, rearing her and Jacques's son, Jean-Paul. Daniel had come back from the front a changed man, for a shell splinter had unsexed him. Now he spent his time looking after Jean-Paul and helping the nurses.

Back at the hospital in southern France, Antoine received a necklace from Rachel, who had died of yellow fever in Africa. He tried to keep notes on the deteriorating condition of his lungs. He lived until November 18, 1918, but he never knew that the Armistice had been signed before his death.

Critical Evaluation:

Roger Martin du Gard, a dramatist as well as novelist, was born into a professional middle-class family in 1881. He studied to be an archivist and paleographer, served with a motor-transport unit during World War I, and, for a brief period, worked in the theater. Most of his life, however, was spent in seclusion, wholly dedicated to his writing. Literature was Martin du Gard's entire life. His closest friend was André Gide, about whom he eventually wrote a book. His last novel was never finished and remains unpublished, but Martin du Gard's achievement and his influence on French fiction were formidable.

The eight-part novel cycle *The World of the Thibaults* was inspired by the author's desire to emulate for his own time the accomplishment of Leo Tolstoy's *War and Peace* (1865-1869). In fact, the work's style and pessimism is closer to Roger Martin du Gard's countryman Gustave Flaubert than to the Russian author. Although the historical background of the action in the novel is of interest, it is the powerful depiction of human relationships that constitutes the book's chief merit.

In many respects, the most influential character in the vast novel is old Monsieur Thibault, the patriarch of the Thibault family. A complete hypocrite, he announces to the world that his conscience is clear, yet he is concerned only with his own convenience and peace. Cloaking his craving for power and authority under a guise of fervent religiosity and philanthropy, he actually has no sense of either religion or generosity. He possesses no love for his sons, demanding only that they be completely docile. Any contradiction or sign of individuality throws him into a rage. For all of his big gestures, he is a petty man. Everyone automatically hides feelings from him, for one never can tell what his reaction might be. He forces his family into hypocrisy. By avoiding all introspection, Monsieur Thibault unknowingly condemns himself to a life of petty pride and cruelty, a life so alone that he must find his only consolation in public honors and the "knowledge" that he is a "good man." As he grows older, however, the fact of approaching death terrifies him increasingly, and he desperately seeks some kind of immortality, as if he subconsciously realizes how futile his busy life actually has been.

The volumes of the series are crowded with fascinating, well-drawn secondary characters. These include Monsieur Chasle, the middle-aged secretary of Monsieur Thibault, who is suddenly revealed to have his own life, his own preoccupations, fears, and miseries. The reader becomes aware of many other lives lurking in the background, and beyond them still others. In the volume entitled *The Springtime of Life*, the adult Daniel and Jacques experience the bohemian life of Paris, encountering characters such as Mother JuJu, the retired prostitute, and many colorful girls of the streets, as well as the rich Jew Ludwigson, who sells Daniel's pictures. Earlier, in a powerful scene at young Jenny's sickbed, the Rasputin-like pastor Gregory chants and prays and condemns with equal fury and somehow saves the girl's life.

The growth of the relationship between Jacques Thibault and Daniel de Fontanin is shown in many different ways, as the author explores the various paths the boys take in their lives. At first, when they run away together at the beginning of the book, the homely little redheaded Jacques dominates the older, more restrained Daniel. After his first sexual experience, however, Daniel becomes less easily ruled by his friend. When Jacques is sent to the reformatory, their relationship nearly dies, but later it is restored on a quite different level. Martin du Gard skillfully captures the changing attitudes and emotions of young men in the process of maturing.

The strained relationship between Jacques and Antoine is portrayed with particular subtlety. The family reticence, the legacy of the tyrannical father, prevents an early comradeship between the brothers, but gradually, after Jacques returns from the reformatory, the brothers build a new and solid relationship.

A subplot of complexity and great interest is woven into the tale of the young men: It is the story of Madame de Fontanin and her unfaithful husband. She is a most unusual figure in fiction, a good person who is neither boring nor cloying. Although imperfect, she is admirable in most of her thoughts and acts. She possesses no malice, although she suffers and occasionally reacts with anger. The touching scenes of her reunion in Holland with her husband and his dying mistress, whose daughter Madame de Fontanin has cared for, are unforgettable. The complex relationships reveal the subtle and ever changing realities of human emotions. It is as difficult to hate, Martin du Gard seems to be implying, as it is to love.

The death that waits for everyone, as it does for the two brothers in the war, is anticipated when Jacques and Jenny see Daniel and Jenny's dog crushed by an old car. The accident prompts Jacques and Jenny to discuss death, but neither realizes how soon World War I will cause the deaths of millions of young people such as themselves, including Jacques and his brother. The irony is compelling yet not overdone.

Rachel, another of the fascinating secondary characters, tells Antoine that she is afraid of being lonely, a fear shared by most of the characters in the book. There is a gripping horror in Rachel's monologue as she shows Antoine her photographs and tells him about her past life and her lover, the infamous Hirst. The Africa described by Rachel becomes a mythological place of fulfilled desires and strange passions, and Hirst a fabulous man-monster. Nevertheless, the reader is hardly surprised when Rachel leaves Antoine and returns to Hirst. Rachel and Antoine Thibault never could have found permanent happiness together.

The graphic realism of the sickbed and death scenes, and, in the seventh volume, *Summer 1914*, the dramatic buildup of the war, as the European nations are swept relentlessly to destruction, are impressive achievements. Even more impressive, however, is the fact that as the focus of the novel expands, the author never loses sight of the individuals who make up the world. For this vast, panoramic survey of society and the meaning of life, as well as for his earlier novel of the Dreyfus affair and atheism, *Jean Barois* (1913), Martin du Gard was awarded the Nobel Prize in Literature in 1937.

"Critical Evaluation" by Bruce D. Reeves

Bibliography:

Boak, Denis. *Roger Martin du Gard*. Oxford, England: Clarendon Press, 1963. Discusses Martin du Gard's cyclical novel within the context of humanist philosophy. Boak compares Martin du Gard effectively to existentialist writers and sees this work as symphonic with tragic overtones. Reinforces the connection to Pierre Corneille on the basis of related transcendental qualities.

Brosman, Catharine Savage. *Roger Martin du Gard*. Boston: Twayne, 1968. Analyzes Martin du Gard's artistic vision and places him squarely in the nineteenth century tradition because of his use of omniscient narration and authorial interjections, by which he produces a literature of ideas. Calls attention to Martin du Gard's style for its naturalness, simplicity, and spontaneity.

Gilbert, John. "Symbols of Continuity and the Unity of *Les Thibault*." In *Image and Theme: Studies in Modern French Fiction*, edited by W. M. Frohock. Cambridge, Mass.: Harvard University Press, 1969. Gilbert discusses the structural unity of *The World of the Thibaults* and makes a compelling case for the coherence of the cyclical novel, which has elsewhere been judged to be formless.

O'Nan, Martha, ed. *Roger Martin du Gard Centennial, 1881-1981*. Brockport: State University of New York, 1981. This special edition of nine essays is wide-ranging and comprehensive. Almost all articles refer extensively to *The World of the Thibaults*. The themes discussed include the writer as phoenix, the ethics of ambiguity, the psychology of revolution, and fiction as testimony.

Schalk, David. *Roger Martin du Gard: The Novelist and History*. Ithaca, N.Y.: Cornell University Press, 1967. In this uneven study, Schalk investigates the sudden change in Martin du Gard's literary objectives, which led him to incorporate contemporary history into fiction. Overestimates Martin du Gard's historical perspective and offers observations that seem, at times, coincidental. Includes an impressive collection of critical comments from other scholars.

THE WOULD-BE GENTLEMAN

Type of work: Drama
Author: Molière (Jean-Baptiste Poquelin, 1622-1673)
Type of plot: Comedy of manners
Time of plot: Seventeenth century
Locale: Paris, France
First performed: 1670; first published, 1671 as *Le Bourgeois Gentilhomme* (English translation, 1675)

> *Principal characters:*
> MONSIEUR JOURDAIN, a tradesman
> MADAME JOURDAIN, his wife
> LUCILE, their daughter
> NICOLE, a servant
> CLÉONTE, in love with Lucile
> COVIELLE, his valet
> DORANTE, a count
> DORIMÈNE, a marchioness

The Story:

Monsieur Jourdain was a tradesman who aspired to be a gentleman. Thinking, like many of his kind, that superficial manners, accomplishments, and speech were the marks of a gentleman, he engaged a dancing master, a music master, a fencing master, a philosophy teacher, and other assorted tutors who were as vain and ignorant as he. They constantly quarreled among themselves as to which art was the most important, and each tried to persuade Jourdain to favor him above the others.

From the dancing master he learned to approach a lady: to bow, to step backward, and to walk toward her bowing three times and ending at her knees. From the philosopher he learned that all speech is either poetry or prose. Jourdain was delighted to learn that he had been speaking prose all his life. He also learned that he spoke with vowels and consonants. He believed that this knowledge set him apart from ordinary citizens and made him a gentleman.

The primary reason for his great desire to be a gentleman was his regard for one Dorimène, a marchioness. He had himself fitted out in costumes so ridiculous that they appeared to be masquerades, six tailors being required to dress him in his fantastic costumes. Monsieur Jourdain's wife had retained her common sense in spite of her husband's wealth, and she constantly chided him about his foolishness. He considered her a bumpkin, however, and reviled her for her ignorance.

In addition to criticizing his dress and speech, his wife rebuked him for being taken in by Count Dorante, a nobleman who flattered Jourdain's affected gentlemanly customs and at the same time borrowed large sums of money from him. Jourdain begged Dorante to accept the money because he thought it the mark of a gentleman to lend money to a nobleman. Jourdain, engaging Dorante to plead his case with Dorimène, provided money for serenades and ballets and a large diamond ring. Dorante promised to bring Dorimène to Jourdain's house for dinner one evening when Jourdain had made arrangements to send his wife and daughter away. Madame Jourdain, who suspected that her husband was up to some knavery, sent the maid,

Nicole, to listen to the conversation between the two men. Nicole could not hear all of it before being discovered by Jourdain, but she heard enough to convince Madame Jourdain that her husband needed watching.

Jourdain's daughter Lucile loved and was loved by Cléonte, and the Jourdain servant, Nicole, loved Cléonte's servant, Covielle. When Lucile and Nicole passed the two men on the street without nodding, the men swore to forget the faithless ladies and turn to new conquests. After learning, however, that Lucile's aunt had been the cause of their coldness—the old lady thinking it unseemly to speak to men—the four lovers were reconciled. Lucile and Cléonte needed only Jourdain's permission to marry, for Madame Jourdain approved of Cléonte and had promised to intercede with her husband. Jourdain refused to accept Cléonte as a son-in-law, however, because the young man was not a gentleman. Cléonte was honorable, and he possessed both wealth and a noble career, but he shunned hypocrisy and false living, conduct he considered unbecoming a gentleman. The lovers pleaded in vain. At last, Covielle suggested a deception to play on the foolish old man, and Cléonte agreed to the plan.

Dorante, meanwhile, had used Jourdain's money in his own suit for Dorimène's favors. Even the diamond ring had been presented as a gift from himself. Dorante secretly thought Jourdain a fool and enjoyed making him a real one.

At the dinner in Jourdain's home, Dorimène was somewhat confused by Jourdain's ardent speeches to her, for she thought it known that she was Dorante's mistress. She was even more disturbed when Madame Jourdain burst in and accused her husband of infidelity. Convinced that she was being insulted by a madwoman, Dorimène left in tears.

Covielle, disguised, called on Jourdain and informed him that he had been a friend of Jourdain's father, who had indeed been a gentleman. He had not been a tradesman, but had merely bought fabrics and then given them to his friends for money. Jourdain, delighted with the news, felt justified in his belief that he was a gentleman. Then Covielle told Jourdain that the son of the Grand Turk desired to marry Lucile. Jourdain was flattered and promised to give the girl to the Grand Turk's son, even though she had vowed she would marry no one but Cléonte. Jourdain, duped into accepting initiation into the Grand Turk's religion, a ceremony performed with much silly gibberish, believed he was being honored above all men.

When Cléonte appeared, disguised as the son of the Grand Turk, Lucile recognized him and agreed to be his wife. Madame Jourdain chided her for infidelity to Cléonte until Covielle whispered to her that the Grand Turk's son and Cléonte were one and the same; then she, too, gave her consent to the marriage. Jourdain sent for a notary. After convincing Jourdain that their plan was only in jest, Dorante and Dorimène said that they would be married at the same time. In great joy at his exalted position Jourdain blessed them all and in addition gave Nicole to Covielle, whom he thought to be the interpreter of the Grand Turk's son's. Thinking that Dorimène loved him, Jourdain offered his wife to whoever wanted her. She, knowing the whole plot, thanked him and proclaimed him the greatest fool of all.

Critical Evaluation:

The Would-Be Gentleman was first presented at court in 1670 in the Grand Gallery of Chambord, a royal castle on the Loire, which, like all the royal residences, was large and luxurious. The play, by command of Louis XIV, was to be a "turquerie." In 1699, an ambassador from Turkey had visited the king, and enthusiasm was still high for the exotic. Jean-Baptiste Lully wrote the music and Molière added his comedy to it. The expenditures indicate that the initial production was elaborate. It was a great success, and the play has remained one of Molière's most popular.

Twentieth century productions of the play often cut the ballet scenes. The play is, however, actually a combination of comedy and ballet, in which the ballet is an integral, if separable part. Dance has a literary or symbolic function as the extension of Monsieur Jourdain's obsession with display; the more preposterous the ballet, the better Jourdain is shown to like it.

Although in some way no more than light entertainment, *The Would-Be Gentleman* has become one of the best-known French plays and Monsieur Jourdain one of Molière's most celebrated characters. He is something of an archetype in French tradition of the bourgeois who tries to conform to aristocratic manners and circles.

The English translation of the play's title is somewhat misleading, as *gentilhomme* means "nobleman" and the juxtaposition of *Le Bourgeois* and *Gentilhomme* should be understood as a contradiction. It is an idea, according to Molière and the court for which he wrote, worthy only of ridicule. The satire, however, is relatively mild; Monsieur Jourdain is more a buffoon, and the comedy is essentially farce, rather than a profound critique of vicious social traits.

Of the inner circle into which Monsieur Jourdain is trying to gain admittance, the audience never sees more than the marchioness, Dorimène, and the count, Dorante. The marchioness has a minor role, and is not only the object of Monsieur Jourdain's absurd affection, but she remains relatively untainted by his foolish intrigues. Dorante, too, is of noble birth, but if he associates more or less intimately with the bourgeois, it is clearly to exploit the latter's gullible ambitions and to get the marchioness for himself. His duplicity is charming, however, and he cannot be accused of much more than shallowness, since Monsieur Jourdain appears sufficiently wealthy and remains blissfully deceived to the end. All of the other characters within the family circle are notable for their relatively good sense. In large measure, this good sense means knowing one's place in the social hierarchy.

The principal counterpoint, or foil, for Monsieur Jourdain is Madame Jourdain. Her loyalty to her class and her proud insistence that both her father and Monsieur Jourdain's had been merchants, is presented as solid, if contentious, good sense. When she argues that their daughter Lucile would do better to marry a man proper to her sphere in life, an honest, nice-looking, and rich bourgeois, the absurd response of Monsieur Jourdain is that he himself is rich enough for his daughter to require only "honor," so that she can become a marchioness. When she interrupts the banquet Monsieur Jourdain and Dorante are having for Dorimène, Madame Jourdain is told by Dorante that she needs better eyeglasses. The irony here is that she needs them not at all, and that of the others present, only Dorante has an inkling of what is going on, for it is his private scheme to gull Monsieur Jourdain by courting Dorimène with Jourdain's money and lavish gifts. The deceptions and self-deceptions of the play, chiefly of Monsieur Jourdain, are the main source of the humor in *The Would-Be Gentleman*.

From the series of educational vignettes at the opening to the finale, Monsieur Jourdain is a victim of "stage irony." The audience is aware of something of which he himself is unaware, for not only the examples of his self-deception but also the various tricks played on him are quite evident. A critic has theorized that comic characters are essential types more or less constantly at risk of being revealed, as opposed to the process of self-discovery in tragedy: Monsieur Jourdain's wealth permits him the freedom to reveal himself very liberally. He pursues every foolish symbol that the parvenu par excellence feels he must have. What he constantly reveals is that the symbols, worn by him, are empty of meaning. The main action of the play displays that Monsieur Jourdain cannot see beyond display and thus is easily duped.

An extreme example of his obsession with external symbols of status, as well as his foolish single-mindedness in their pursuit, is when the tailor's assistant addresses him by titles of honor. The boy gets a larger tip for each higher title. If he had gone so far as to say "your highness,"

Jourdain was going to give him the whole purse. However, if the symbol of status is more profound, as when the philosophy teacher instructs him on moderating the passions, Monsieur Jourdain is unimpressed and completely uninterested.

"Critical Evaluation" by James Marc Hovde

Bibliography:
Abraham, Claude. *On the Structure of Molière's Comédies-Ballets.* Paris: Papers on French Seventeenth Century Literature, 1984. An original study, which explores the relationship between Molière's text and the music composed by the court composer Jean-Baptiste Lully for the intermezzos in *The Would-Be Gentleman.* Argues persuasively that Lully's music forms an integral part of this ballet comedy.
Howarth, W. D. *Molière: A Playwright and His Audience.* Cambridge, England: Cambridge University Press, 1982. Examines Molière's creative use of theatrical conventions both in his spoken comedies and his ballet comedies. Excellent description of the comic richness of Monsieur Jourdain, a role first played by Molière himself.
Hubert, Judd D. *Molière and the Comedy of Intellect.* Berkeley: University of California Press, 1962. Examines social satire, comic uses of language, and the importance of the intermezzos in *The Would-Be Gentleman.* Stresses the importance of theatricality in Molière's plays.
Moore, Will G. *Molière: A New Criticism.* 1949. Rev. ed. Oxford, England: Clarendon Press, 1968. Remains an influential work, which points out that Molière was not just a playwright but also an actor and a manager of his own theatrical troupe. Explains very clearly the importance of mime and comic gestures in Molière's comedies.
Walker, Hallam. *Molière.* 1971. Rev. ed. Boston: Twayne, 1990. An excellent general introduction to Molière's plays including an annotated bibliography of important critical studies on Molière. Describes the connection between artificiality and self-deception in *The Would-Be Gentleman.*

WOYZECK

Type of work: Drama
Author: Georg Büchner (1813-1837)
Type of plot: Psychological realism
Time of plot: Early nineteenth century
Locale: Germany
First published: 1879 (written, 1836; English translation, 1927); first performed, 1913

Principal characters:
FRIEDRICH JOHANN FRANZ WOYZECK, a military conscript
MARIE, his sweetheart
A DRUM MAJOR, Marie's other lover
ANDRES, another soldier and Woyzeck's friend
A CAPTAIN
A DOCTOR

The Story:

Franz Woyzeck was a conscript fusilier, a poor, simple soldier with a peasant's slow mind and a peasant's superstitions. The only happiness he had in his wretched existence came from his relationship with his sweetheart Marie and their small son. Because his army pay did not suffice for the support of his household, he was forced to earn additional money by performing menial tasks about the camp and in the garrison town where his regiment was stationed.

Having served as a barber's apprentice in his youth, he was often called in to shave his Captain. The officer, a man of speculative, ironic temperament, liked to talk about such topics as time and eternity, matters that were often beyond Woyzeck's comprehension. Sometimes the Captain jokingly reproved the poor fellow for his lack of morals, since he had fathered a child without benefit of a wedding ceremony. Woyzeck always declared that if he were a gentleman with a laced coat and a cocked hat he, too, could be virtuous. He considered virtue to be a privilege of the educated and great, and not intended for miserable creatures like himself.

An eccentric Doctor also paid Woyzeck a few coins to act as the subject of fantastic medical experiments. The soldier was supposed to live on a diet of peas and to hold his water for stated periods of time. When Woyzeck tried blunderingly to explain his views on nature and life, the Doctor was delighted. He thought that Woyzeck's halting remarks showed an interesting aberration, and he predicted that the man would end in a madhouse.

One day, Woyzeck and his friend Andres went into the country to cut wood for the Captain. Woyzeck began to talk wildly about the freemasons, claiming that they had burrowed under the ground and that the earth they had hollowed out was rocking under his feet. Their secret signs having been revealed to him in dreams, he was fearful of their vengeance. Andres, usually a matter-of-fact fellow, became rather alarmed when Woyzeck pictured the Last Judgment in the glowing colors of the sunset. Returning home, Woyzeck tried to explain to Marie the vision he had seen in the sky. She was hurt because in his excitement he failed to notice his son. That afternoon, a handsome, bearded Drum Major had ogled Marie while she stood at her window and talked to a friend outside. She wondered about Woyzeck and his strange thoughts. Marie was hearty and earthy. It was easier for her to understand people's emotions than their ideas.

Woyzeck and Marie went to a fair. As they entered one of the exhibits, the Drum Major and a Sergeant came by and followed them into the booth, where the barker was showing a horse that could count and identify objects. When the showman called for a watch, the Sergeant held up his timepiece. To see what was going on, Marie climbed on a bench and stood next to the Drum Major. That was the beginning of their affair. A short time later, Woyzeck found Marie with a new pair of earrings that she claimed to have found. The simple-minded soldier remarked that he had never been lucky enough to find anything in pairs. While Woyzeck was on duty or doing extra work, the Drum Major visited Marie in her room. Herself full-blooded and passionate, she yielded to him.

Woyzeck had no suspicions of her infidelity. One day, as he was bustling down the street, he met the Captain and the Doctor. The Captain began to talk slyly about beards and hinted that if Woyzeck were to hurry home he would be in time to find hairs from a bearded lover on Marie's lips. Woyzeck became pale and nervous, whereupon the Doctor showed great clinical interest in his reactions. The Captain assured Woyzeck that he meant well by the soldier and Woyzeck went loping home. When he peered steadily into Marie's face, however, he could see no outward signs of guilt. His scrutiny disturbed and then angered her. She defied him, practically admitting that she had another lover, but she dared Woyzeck to lay a hand on her. Unable to understand how anyone so unkind could look so beautiful and innocent, he left the house. Not knowing what else to do, he went to the Doctor's courtyard. There the physician made him appear ridiculous in front of a group of medical students.

The next Sunday, Woyzeck and Andres were together in the barracks, Woyzeck was restless and unhappy because there was a dance at an inn near the town and he knew that Marie and the Drum Major would be there. Andres tried to stop his friend, but Woyzeck said that he had to see them for himself. He went to the inn and through an open window watched Marie and her lover dancing. Andres, fearing a disturbance, finally persuaded him to go back to town. Karl, a fool, was among some loafers near the inn door; he said that he smelled blood.

That night, Woyzeck, unable to sleep, told Andres that he still heard music and saw the dancing. He also mumbled about his vision of a knife in a store window. The next day, when he encountered the Drum Major at the inn, the two men fought and Woyzeck was badly beaten by his swaggering rival. Mad with jealousy, he went to a pawn shop and bought a knife like the one he had seen in his dream. At the barracks, he gave away most of his possessions. Resisting Andres' attempt to get him to the infirmary, he went to Marie and asked her to go walking with him. On a lonely path near the pond he took out his new knife and stabbed her to death.

Then he went back to the inn and danced madly. When a girl named Käthe noticed bloodstains on his hand, he said that he had cut himself. Questioned further, he screamed that he was no murderer and ran from the inn. Wanting to get rid of the incriminating knife which he had left beside Marie's body, he threw it into the pond. His first throw fell short. Desperate, he waded out to hurl the knife into deeper water, got in over his depth, and drowned.

A group of playing children heard adults talking about the murder. They ran to Woyzeck's son and told him that his mother was dead.

Critical Evaluation:

Georg Büchner's untimely death in 1837 was fortunate in one respect: His play *Woyzeck* remained unfinished. Had he lived to polish the play's structure and bring it, as most scholars agree was his intent, to its logical conclusion with Woyzeck's trial, conviction, and execution, the result may have been an interesting, perhaps even pioneering work, but it would not have been the completely unprecedented, startling piece that it is in its unfinished state. Indeed, the unordered succession of scenes and fragments seems out of place in the early nineteenth century, seeming to belong much more comfortably with the tortured expressionism of the early twentieth century.

Because the style and structure of the *Woyzeck* fragments are so perfectly wedded to the work's characterization and theme, the play has, in whatever order it is presented or read, the inevitability of a finished product. Yet whereas one version ends with the court clerk describing the crime with relish as a "beautiful murder," another ends with the children excitedly rushing off to view Marie's body before the authorities move it. The other obvious aspect of the play's being incomplete is the fact that it breaks off shortly after Woyzeck murders Maria, but this very lack of resolution is ideally suited to reflect not only the uncertainties of the twentieth century worldview but, more important, those of Woyzeck's world. The play offers no consoling gesture, just as Büchner offers Woyzeck none. All of society's institutions fail Woyzeck, who is tragic in the twentieth century sense, not because he is a great man brought low but because he started low and never had a chance.

Büchner was caught up in the radical protest politics of his day and his primary thematic intent in *Woyzeck* was no doubt political. Woyzeck's troubles can be traced most directly to his low economic class. His pay is so meager that he is forced to hire himself out for scientific experiments that play havoc with his health. Even with supplemental pay, he cannot afford to marry Marie, whose affection, as long as he thinks he has it, is the one redeeming feature of his life. Since they cannot afford to marry, their child is illegitimate and cannot be baptized. Marie is as much a victim of poverty as is Woyzeck. She worries about her bastard child and is so pathetically eager for something to take her away from her drab surroundings and circumstances that she takes up with a vulgar drum major who can afford to buy her a few trinkets.

Poverty, though, is just one aspect of Woyzeck's world that makes his life so hopeless. No age has been free of poverty, but most ages have offered consolations to the poor, the most obvious being religion, with its promises of the hereafter. Actually, *Woyzeck* is filled with religious imagery and direct quotations from the Bible, but these, rather than healing and consoling, tend toward the apocalyptic and anticipate violence to come. At moments, Marie is acutely aware of her "fallen" state, feels painful remorse, and calls on God for mercy. It is Woyzeck who summons up the apocalyptic imagery, and his wrath most closely resembles the biblical prophets impatient of evil. Had his moral vision been less rigid, Woyzeck might have accommodated himself to the world's imperfections and not been driven to violence; had Marie not come equipped with moral sense, she might at least have enjoyed her dalliance and not been afflicted with remorse. These two not only do not profit from their religious beliefs but are plagued by them.

It was in Büchner's century that there was, at least among many intellectuals, a movement away from religion as a guiding principle and source of truth. What replaced religion for many of these apostates was science. Here, too, however, Büchner was ahead of his time, for *Woyzeck* manifests modern cynicism about the wisdom and worth of scientists and science. Woyzeck's being forced to hire himself out as a guinea pig for the doctor's experiments, who wants to observe the effects of a diet of peas, underscores both the evils of poverty and the inhuman arrogance of science. Indeed, Woyzeck's depression and psychosis were certainly exacerbated by a diet lacking in vitamins and other nutrients. Like the god of religion, the god of science fails Woyzeck.

Referring to Woyzeck as a guinea pig is in keeping with the play's animal motif. Horses, monkeys, and lizards are all present or at least referred to, always with a direct or implied comparison to human beings. The horse can count as well as a person; the monkey sports a uniform and sword just like a soldier; and the death of a lizard, the doctor maintains, would be a greater loss to his experiment than the death of Woyzeck. This underscores the pessimism of the play and also prefigures Charles Darwin, who not long after Büchner's death was to rock the world with the theory that human beings were not higher beings close to a god of creation but animals that, like all animals, had evolved according to laws of nature.

Although Woyzeck is a brilliantly conceived character, the play is not a character study so much as the dramatization of the spirit of an age about to be born. Woyzeck is an Everyman suffering through an age when the old certainties have eroded and the new ones are suspect. Driven to desperation like so many of his fellow human beings, Woyzeck can only lash out and destroy, but that, too, brings only pain.

"Critical Evaluation" by Dennis Vannatta

Bibliography:
James, Dorothy. "The 'Interesting Case' of Büchner's *Woyzeck*." In *Patterns of Change: German Drama and the European Tradition*, edited by Dorothy James and Silvia Ranawake. New York: Peter Lang, 1990. A fine introduction to the place of *Woyzeck* in German drama. Also places Büchner in a context of developing European thought.

Kaufmann, Friedrich Wilhelm. *German Dramatists of the Nineteenth Century.* New York: Russell & Russell, 1972. Kaufmann notes that in plays such as *Woyzeck*, Büchner is dramatizing the collapse of old European values and the process of coming to grips with new realities. Woyzeck himself is an Everyman, condemned by his poverty to a life of misery.

Mills, Ken. "Moon, Madness, and Murder: The Motivation of Woyzeck's Killing of Marie." *German Life and Letters* 41 (July, 1988): 430-436. Discusses Woyzeck's murder of Marie as less an act of jealousy than an act of expiation.

Ritchie, J. M. *German Expressionist Drama.* Boston: Twayne, 1976. Notes the influence of *Woyzeck* on twentieth century German expressionist drama and provides compelling evidence for the play's being ahead of its time.

Stodder, Joseph H. "The Influences of *Othello* on Büchner's *Woyzeck*." *Modern Language Review* 69 (January, 1974): 115-120. An interesting comparison that points to the plot similarities between William Shakespeare's *Othello* (1604) and Büchner's *Woyzeck*, which both concern men driven by jealousy to murder women they love and are then tortured by remorse. Leads the author to conclude that Shakespeare's work was a direct influence on Büchner.

THE WRECK OF *THE DEUTSCHLAND*

Type of work: Poetry
Author: Gerard Manley Hopkins (1844-1889)
First published: 1918

In a letter written to R. W. Dixon, Hopkins explained the background of the poem. In 1875, during cold weather, the German ship *The Deutschland* had set sail for New York but suffered shipwreck on the sands of the Kentish Knock at the mouth of the Thames River. Although Hopkins had resolved not to compose any more poetry after his ordination as a Jesuit priest, his superior had expressed the wish that someone write a poem in the wake of this tragedy. "I was affected by the account," Hopkins wrote in his letter.

He was moved by the loss of 168 passengers and crew, including five nuns from a convent in Westphalia who were exiled from Germany. Although 138 people were rescued by a Liverpool tugboat, many boats passed by and ignored the distress signals because sailors feared risking their lives in the freezing weather. Stranded off the English coast near Harwich for nearly thirty hours, *The Deutschland* eventually sank. With great descriptive power and depth of emotion, Hopkins depicts the scene of tragedy and the anguish of the drowning victims. The blasts of wind ("For the infinite air is unkind"), the blinding snowstorm ("whirlwind-swivelled snow"), the shock of the ship hitting, not a rock or a reef, but "a smother of sand" all bring the passengers and crew into the jaws of death. After twelve hours of desperate waiting, with no help in sight, "Hope had grown gray hairs," and "lives at last were washing away." The heroic efforts of a man to save a woman from drowning are spent in vain before the awesome power of death: "What could he do/ With the burl of the fountains of air, buck and the flood of the wave?" The piercing sounds of women wailing and children crying echo the roaring of the storm and parallel the blinding of the snow, the wildness of the gales, and the swirling of the sea. In the midst of this tempest, roar, and deluge, a tall nun (a "lioness") speaks above the din of terrifying destruction, crying "O Christ, Christ, come quickly" (stanza 24). In asking "what did she mean?" Hopkins recalls Jesus calming the waters when his disciples, terrified on the lake of Gennesareth, cried "we are perishing" (Matthew 8:23-27). Rebuking the winds and the sea, Jesus calmed the storm and saved the disciples, demonstrating God's mastery of nature. Hopkins emphasizes the striking resemblances between the sinking of *The Deutschland* and the tempest on the lake that frightened the disciples. Christ is present in the hour of danger and death to all who believe. While the disciples on the lake were reproached for their lack of faith, the tall nun in the hour of darkness entrusted all to God's providence: "Christ, King, Head:/ He was to cure the extremity where he had cast her" (stanza 28). While the naked eye observes human victims powerless against nature's forces and drowning in perilous seas, the eyes of faith see God's hand in all events. "There was single eye!" observes Hopkins of the nun who saw in death not only suffering but consolation.

The Christian faith of the nun did not leave her "comfortless" or "unconfessed," for the eyes of faith see in shipwreck also a harvest and view the tempest as an agent of "grain for thee" (stanza 31). That is, as the Catholic church has always taught, the blood of the martyrs is the seed of the church. The heroic death of Christians who embrace their cross and remain steadfast in their faith in the hour of trial wins souls for Christ. The eyes of faith also "Grasp God, throned behind/ Death with a sovereignty that heeds but hides, bodes but abides" (stanza 32). Just as Christ the master commanded the winds and the waves, Christ as sovereign rules over death. He comes to claim his own. The five Franciscan nuns accept their crosses with courage and conviction in the knowledge of God's mercy. "The Christ of the Father compassionate, fetched in the storm of his strides" (stanza 33) will not drown them but seal them "in wild waters,/ To bathe in his fall-gold mercies, to breathe in his all-fire glances" (stanza 24).

"The Wreck of *The Deutschland*," then, comes to describe not only the deaths of the passengers and the tragedy of a shipwreck but also the shipwreck of a world devastated by Original Sin. Hopkins alludes in stanza 1 to this greater shipwreck in his reference to fallen man ruining God's original Creation: "And after it almost unmade, what with dread,/ Thy doing." The storm without, on the sea, magnifies the storm within in the soul. In stanzas 2 and 3, Hopkins examines the destructive effects of Original Sin in the human soul and in the world. The fear of God's punishment for sin, His "lightning and lashed rod" and Christ's "terror" that evoke the dread of "the hurtle of hell." Stanza 4 describes the constant decay and impermanence of one's mortal life, which is symbolized by the image of the hourglass marking one's progression from life to death. God is as real and present, however, in a fallen world and in sinful human life as He was to the tall nun in the fury of the disaster at sea. Stanza 5 describes the glory of God in the splendor of the star-filled heavens ("lovely-asunder starlight") and in the beautiful sunset ("the dappled-with-damson west").

Creation in all its beauty declares the mystery of God's presence in a fallen world stained with sin. History also gives witness to God's presence as the Word becomes Flesh and dwells among people. Stanza 7 refers to the Incarnation in its references to "manger, maiden's knee." Just as God manifests Himself in the beauty of nature and in the miracles of history, God is present in the moment of death.

Christ has conquered both sin and death with his "driven Passion and frightful sweat" (stanza 7). He comes as both "lightning and love" and as "a winter and warm" (stanza 9). That is, the wreck of a fallen world or the destruction of passengers at sea do not signify a world devoid of God's grace and love. God is present in the darkness and storm of tragedy. He comes in the wreck of sin and death to call souls to him. Just as he called Saul of Tarsus on the road to Damascus "at once, as once a crash" (stanza 10) or summoned Augustine to repentance and conversion "With an anvil-ding," in a burst of force or energy that erupts like the fire in the forge or the ebullience of spring, God appears in a flash to the drowning victims on *The Deutschland*—not in a "dooms-day dazzle" but "royally reclaiming his own" (stanza 34) in a surge of love and mercy. This divine energy of God's infinite love and goodness overflows on Calvary, where Christ's body bursts with his outpouring blood for man's redemption. Like a ripe fruit whose juices gush upon being tasted—"How a lush-kept plush-capped sloe/ Will, mouthed to flesh-burst,/ Gush!"—God proffers His everlasting mercy throughout the ages to the sinful who are struggling in the wreck of a fallen world. This divine energy Hopkins calls "inscape" or "instress," a dynamic creative power that radiates God's glory in flashes, bursts, explosions, and eruptions in unique, unpredictable, and astonishing ways. The manifold expressions of God's power in the world in wind, lightning, fire, and sea; the myriad forms of beauty in all its colorful variety that infuse nature; and the multiple manifestations of God's mystery and reality all reflect the boundless, kinetic energy of God's being. The passion and sweat of Christ, that burst with the blood of sacrifice, the discharge of the flash of lightning, the day-spring of Easter that swells with life and rebirth all emanate from the divine energy of God's being that overflows in "God's three numbered form" and hurls itself throughout all of Creation in "The heaven-flung, heart-fleshed, maiden furled/ Miracle-in Mary-of flame" (stanza 34). In order to capture the fullness of God's being that is constantly spilling, flinging, hurling, flashing, and erupting with spontaneous energy and generating life, Hopkins writes in a style called "sprung rhythm" which imitates the dynamic surges and bold movements of God's art in the world. Hopkins' verbal power breaks loose in the poem with the same explosive force as God's creative energy. However, sprung rhythm, while not a tame or rigidly controlled movement, is not a wild, undisciplined, or random force. Rather it is as intricate, designed, and harmonious as God's beauty—a complex pattern of words and rhythms that echoes the music of sound and follows the expansion of the heart in the ecstasy of love. Sprung rhythm, in other words, resembles the vibrations, movements, and passions of a heart in love with God and in awe at His beauty, love, and grace. The lifting of the heart ascends in rapture and ecstasy with breathless wonder: "Our heart's charity's hearth's fire, our thoughts's chivalry's throng's Lord." Hopkins' originality in the use of sprung rhythm, his notions of "inscape" and "instress" that inform his poetry, and his use of authentic but unusual diction and syntax with a strong emphasis on alliteration ("lovely-felicitous Providence/ Finger of a tender of, O of a feathery delicacy") all distinguish Hopkins as one of the great pioneers of modern poetry.

Mitchell Kalpakgian

Bibliography:
Boyle, Robert. *Metaphor in Hopkins.* Chapel Hill: University of North Carolina Press, 1960. Chapter 1, "The Heroic Breast," discusses the theme of heroic sacrifice in "The Wreck of *The Deutschland.*" This chapter provides a careful, close reading of the many religious allusions in the poem.
Downes, David. *Gerard Manley Hopkins: A Study of His Ignatian Spirit.* Boston: Twayne, 1959. Discusses Hopkins' poetry in the light of his training and background as a Jesuit priest. Chapter 2 applies many of the moral precepts of St. Ignatius to the poem, comparing individual stanzas to specific exercises in St. Ignatius' spiritual classic.
Gardner, William. *Gerard Manley Hopkins.* New York: Oxford University Press, 1944. This comprehensive two-volume work encompasses a multitude of topics—from "Diction and Syntax" to "Critics and Reviewers" to "Hopkins and Modern Poetry." Chapter 2 focuses exclusively on "The Wreck of *The Deutschland,*" arguing that the poem has a completeness, an intellectual and emotional unity, and a subtlety and variety of verbal orchestrations that are unique in English.
Lahey, G. F. *Gerard Manley Hopkins.* New York: Oxford University Press, 1930. Excellent biography of Hopkins, examining his early life, his years at Oxford, and his friendships with writer Coventry Patmore, Cardinal Newman, and poet Richard Dixon. Chapter 7, "The Artist," presents a succinct discussion of Hopkins' poetry, comparing his techniques to the work of other English poets.
Peters, Wilhelmus A. M. *Gerard Manley Hopkins: A Critical Essay Towards the Understanding of His Poetry.* New York: Oxford University Press, 1948. This book renders a close, careful reading of Hopkins' poetry, analyzing many of the techniques and devices of Hopkins' verse. Chapter 1, "The Meaning of Inscape and Instress," offers an especially valuable discussion of two major concepts that inform all of Hopkins' poetry.

THE WRETCHED OF THE EARTH

Type of work: Politics
Author: Frantz Fanon (1925-1961)
First published: Les Damnés de la terre, 1961 (English translation, 1963)

Frantz Fanon's *The Wretched of the Earth* treats many of the central ideas on the struggle for liberation against colonialism. Fanon, who was a psychiatrist, worked in a hospital in Algeria during the war for independence from France and bases many of the essay's ideas on his observations and experiences in Algeria. He wrote during the era that would ultimately lead to the collapse of most colonialism in Africa. However, his ideas are about liberation in general. Fanon sets forth the idea that Marxist notions of history and of the progression toward freedom need to be adapted to the struggle for independence. Analyzing the movement from colonization to independence, he modifies Marxist ideas. For example, Fanon notes that workers, far from being revolutionary, sometimes have an interest in colonialism and in the maintenance of a colonial economy. In sum, in *The Wretched of the Earth,* Fanon offers ideas that are central to literature on colonialism and on revolution.

Fanon's chapter, "Concerning Violence," lays the groundwork for many of the ideas to come in the rest of the book. Essential in this chapter are Fanon's belief that decolonization is always a violent process. Decolonization is also the process of creating a "new person." The struggle for independence necessarily entails the destruction of the image of the oppressed the colonizers have set forth in an attempt to define the colonized. There is, he argues further, to be no reform of colonialism in the struggle for independence. The destruction of colonialism must be total.

Central to Fanon's ideas throughout the work is the role of violence in the struggle for liberation. Fanon's ideas on violence are complex. First, he notes that only force may meet force: Colonialism is held in place by soldiers and policemen. In addition, the takeover of nations by European countries was a violent phenomenon that tried to obliterate the ways of life of the indigenous people and to kill their spirit and their culture. Hence, from its inception and in its maintenance, colonialism is violent. Moreover, as Fanon knew, the colonialist powers could not be expected to leave peacefully. Therefore, violent struggle was a necessary agent for colonized people to gain independence. While Fanon's discussion of the need for armed struggle might seem obvious, his discussion of violence is complex and thoughtful. He also describes the psychological violence against the colonized that has been perpetuated by the settlers. For example, colonialism hinges in part on the acceptance by the colonized of their inferior status. This inferiority is economic and social. In fact, the one imposed condition of inferiority hinges on the other. Yet, Fanon asserts, the inequality of colonialism sparks in the indigenous people the desire to overthrow the settler. The indigenous people naturally desire to throw off their inferior status. Hence, while psychological violence against the people (which results in their physical and psychological degradation) has helped keep colonialism in its place, Fanon suggests that this very degradation makes clear one of the foremost reasons for the need for violent overthrow of the colonizers. He stresses the need for a revolutionary re-creation of the psychological and economic status of the people. A revolution must entail, according to Fanon, violent thought and deeds. Violence for Fanon seems to be both a psychological catharsis and a historical process, which are necessary for the overthrow of oppressors.

In "Concerning Violence" and in "Spontaneity: Its Strength and Weakness," Fanon discusses some of the problems confronting liberation movements. He clearly has faith in the need for liberation, but he makes evident that liberation is a process, not one quick war that establishes independence. He stresses that in the historical process of attaining liberation, those among the colonized who are part of the struggle must realize the roles they have to play. To do so entails a transformation of the consciousness of many people. Many received ideas have to go. Central in this process are political activists who may bridge the gap between themselves and the common people. Fanon states that many political activists and intellectuals are unfamiliar with the people who live in villages and, thus, have limited their political connections to people who live in towns. This, states Fanon, is a major mistake. Among rural people, Fanon believes, one will find those whose culture has been the least affected by colonialism. Hence, he believes, rural people have been less brainwashed into feeling inferior to the colonizers. Moreover, people from rural areas have clung to their culture, unlike members of the middle classes and intellectuals who may feel they prosper either from the way things are under colonialism or from immersing themselves in European ideas and values. Thus, the common people, Fanon writes, never having lost the value of their own culture, would actively support those who want to reclaim their country, their customs, and themselves from European domination. The role that political activists could play in working with rural people is to keep them involved in the struggle and to illuminate them to the ideas for liberation that motivate the struggle. Fanon is concerned with a major problem of any revolution: the continuance of revolutionary acts. Revolution is a historical process, he points out, and hinges upon the continuance of acts of liberation. Again, a war alone does not a revolution make; the nation's mind must also be freed. Fanon places primary importance on the need for those concerned with liberation to value and work with the nation's peasants.

Fanon's ideas about the peasants as being important as revolutionaries is one of the most essential and innovative aspects of *The Wretched of the Earth*. Traditionally, peasants are often discounted as having no significant role to play in society. After the Russian Revolution, particularly during the Stalinist era, peasants were killed by the millions, mainly starved to death, because of the belief that peasants were antirevolutionary. The idea that farmers and the rural poor are antirevolutionary is refuted by Fanon, who uses Marxist thought to give a central role to the peasants in the march toward liberation.

Other essential ideas are found in Fanon's chapters titled "The Pitfalls of National Consciousness" and "On National Culture." In both chapters, Fanon is concerned with overcoming disunity among colonized peoples. In particular, he cares about how culture and consciousness can be used to fuel liberation. Fanon's comments on intellectuals' concerns with reclaiming their indigenous culture show how oppressed people wage a psychological fight to assert their value—a value denied by colonists. Fanon asserts that the intellectuals' need to affirm their culture is a response to the way colonialism attempts to destroy the image of the oppressed people's past. Colonialism asserts that the colonized people's past is worthless. Nigerian writer Chinua Achebe has described the colonizer's version of the colonized's past as "one long night of savagery." This version of history implies that without European constraints and control, the colonized people would merely be savages. For the indigenous people to learn of their own value independent of the colonialists would be an important ingredient in their valuing themselves enough to reclaim their traditions, their culture, and their country. Fanon points out a barrier that must be crossed before the value of national culture can be transformed into a part of the process of revolution. He states that it is essential that the intellectuals, writers, and artists who assert the value of national culture not merely focus on the glory of the past as if all one needs to do is look to the past and be proud of it. This, Fanon writes, is not enough. Intellectuals and artists must use the past to reformulate the present and the future. One example Fanon offers is the use of the oral tradition during Algeria's struggle for independence. Instead of merely prefacing a story by saying, "This happened long ago," many storytellers emphasized that the story might well be happening in the present. Authorities became so concerned, states Fanon, that they started to arrest storytellers. Thus, Fanon makes clear that the culture of the country needs to be reclaimed and used as a revolutionary agent in struggles for liberation.

Many of Fanon's comments on culture and revolution were later incorporated into African Americans' ideas of the black aesthetic. A product of the 1960's, the black aesthetic often emphasized that cultural productions such as art and literature needed to be socially committed to improving the condition of African Americans in order to hasten liberation from oppression. In addition, some theoreticians of the black aesthetic pointed out that cultural productions needed to inspire the people to become committed to the struggle against racism. Hence, as in Fanon's theories in *The Wretched of the Earth*, an aspect of the black aesthetic was that art should be useful in illuminating the people and inspiring them to try to change their place in society. Thus, one can see the influence that Fanon's ideas about culture in *The Wretched of the Earth* have had.

The penultimate chapter of the book, "Colonial War and Mental Disorders," is one of the most powerful. In this chapter, Fanon gives several case studies from his work in a hospital in Algeria during the war for independence to show the psychological scars left by the violent oppression of the people. He offers many striking cases, including the story of a political activist whose wife was raped by French authorities who were trying to find him. There is also the tale of a man suffering from the psychological aftermath of surviving the mass murder of his village by the French. There is the story of two Algerian boys, both teenagers, who killed a European boy who was a friend of theirs. One reason Fanon tells of these cases is that, he argues, the process of recovering from colonialism and establishing independence needs to take into account the psychological scars of the period of colonialism. Fanon also tells of cases of European authorities affected by their torturing of Algerians. In this section of the book, one clearly sees the emotional tragedies that have resulted from colonialism. Thus, one of the most striking and unique parts of *The Wretched of the Earth* is Fanon's use of his experience as a psychiatrist to make vivid the horrors of colonialism.

Fanon's concluding chapter is important for coming back to the beginning point of the book: the creation of new people by the struggle for liberation. In this section, Fanon does a devastating critique of Europe for its oppression of its colonized people and for failing to live up to the alleged European ideals of liberty and equality. Another point of this critique is that Fanon wants to make clear that newly independent countries should not try to imitate Europe. In refashioning their economies and their cultures, they must strive to remain true to the ideals of liberation. The book ends with Fanon's challenge to the oppressed people to create themselves anew in the spirit of freedom.

After reading *The Wretched of the Earth*, one is struck by the importance and the complexity of Fanon's ideas. Fanon was able to bring unique insights into the analysis of colonialism as a result of his experiences as a psychiatrist. Furthermore, he offers many creative ideas. One rethinks the role of the peasant class in revolutions, the importance for political leaders to connect with the masses, the controversial role of violence in liberation struggles, and the need for art and culture to function as tools of liberation. Whether one agrees or disagrees with Fanon's analysis of these important issues, one cannot deny the imaginative and intricate nature of the arguments he presents. For these reasons, *The Wretched of the Earth* is a classic work on oppression, colonialism, and liberation.

Jane Davis

Bibliography:

Caute, David. *Frantz Fanon*. New York: Viking Press, 1970. Lucid discussion of Fanon's life and works; useful introduction to Fanon's thought.

Gendzier, Irene L. *Frantz Fanon: A Critical Study*. Rev. ed. New York: Grove Press, 1985. An important critical biography of Fanon as a political theorist and psychiatrist. Analyzes important themes in *The Wretched of the Earth*, including the roles of violence and of the peasants.

Hansen, Emmanuel. *Frantz Fanon: Social and Political Thought*. Columbus: Ohio State University Press, 1977. Analyzes Fanon's political ideals in his writings. Examines the themes of the alienation of the oppressed and the connection between violence and liberation.

Perinbam, Marie B. *Holy Violence: The Revolutionary Thought of Frantz Fanon*. Washington, D.C.: Three Continents Press, 1982. Incisive analysis of Fanon's theory of violence in liberation movements. Discusses his use of data from wars in Algeria and Martinique and his intertwining of psychology and politics.

Woddis, Jack. *New Theories of Revolution*. New York: International Publishers, 1972. Intriguing critique of Fanon's ideas on violence. Covers such social themes in Fanon's writings as the role of the peasants and the need for the obliteration of racism.

WUTHERING HEIGHTS

Type of work: Novel
Author: Emily Brontë (1818-1848)
Type of plot: Love
Time of plot: 1757-1803
Locale: The moors of northern England
First published: 1847

Principal characters:
MR. EARNSHAW, the owner of Wuthering Heights
CATHERINE, his daughter
HINDLEY, his son
HEATHCLIFF, an orphan
MR. LINTON, the proprietor of Thrushcross Grange
MRS. LINTON, his wife
ISABELLA, their daughter
EDGAR, their son
FRANCES EARNSHAW, Hindley's wife
HARETON EARNSHAW, Frances' and Hindley's son
CATHERINE LINTON, Catherine Earnshaw's and Edgar Linton's daughter
LINTON HEATHCLIFF, Isabella Linton's and Heathcliff's son
ELLEN "NELLY" DEAN, the housekeeper at Thrushcross Grange
MR. LOCKWOOD, a tenant at Thrushcross Grange and narrator of the story

The Story:

In 1801, Mr. Lockwood became a tenant at Thrushcross Grange, an old farm owned by a Mr. Heathcliff of Wuthering Heights. In the early days of his tenancy, he made two calls on his landlord. On his first visit, he met Heathcliff, an abrupt, unsocial man who was surrounded by a pack of snarling, barking dogs. When he went to Wuthering Heights a second time, he met the other members of the strange household: a rude, unkempt but handsome young man named Hareton Earnshaw and a pretty young woman who was the widow of Heathcliff's son.

During his visit, snow began to fall. It covered the moor paths and made travel impossible for a stranger in that bleak countryside. Heathcliff refused to let one of the servants go with him as a guide but said that if he stayed the night he could share Hareton's bed or that of Joseph, a sour, canting old servant. When Mr. Lockwood tried to borrow Joseph's lantern for the homeward journey, the old fellow set the dogs on him, to the amusement of Hareton and Heathcliff. The visitor was finally rescued by Zillah, the cook, who hid him in an unused chamber of the house.

That night, Mr. Lockwood had a strange dream. Thinking that a branch was rattling against the window, he broke the glass in his attempt to unhook the casement. As he reached out to break off the fir branch outside, his fingers closed on a small ice-cold hand, and a weeping voice begged to be let in. The unseen presence said that her name was Catherine Linton, and she tried to force a way through the broken casement; Mr. Lockwood screamed.

Heathcliff appeared in a state of great excitement and savagely ordered Mr. Lockwood out of the room. Then he threw himself upon the bed by the shattered pane and begged the spirit to come in out of the dark and the storm. The voice was, however, heard no more—only the hiss of swirling snow and the wailing of a cold wind that blew out the smoking candle.

The housekeeper at Thrushcross Grange, Ellen Dean, was able to satisfy part of Mr. Lockwood's curiosity about the happenings of that night and the strange household at Wuthering Heights, for she had lived at Wuthering Heights as a child. Her story of the Earnshaws, Lintons, and Heathcliffs began years before, when old Mr. Earnshaw was living at Wuthering Heights with his wife and two children, Hindley and Catherine. Once, on a trip to Liverpool, Mr. Earnshaw had found a starving and homeless orphan, a ragged, dirty, urchin, dark as a gypsy, whom he brought back with him to Wuthering Heights and christened Heathcliff—a name that was to serve the fourteen-year-old boy as both a given and a surname. Gradually, the orphan began to usurp the affections of Mr. Earnshaw, whose health was failing. Wuthering Heights became riddled with petty jealousies; old Joseph, the servant, augmented the bickering, and Catherine was much too fond of Heathcliff. At last, Hindley was sent away to school. A short time later, Mr. Earnshaw died.

When Hindley Earnshaw returned home for his father's funeral, he brought a wife with him. As the new master of Wuthering Heights, he revenged himself on Heathcliff by treating him like a servant. Catherine had become a wild and undisciplined hoyden who still continued to be fond of Heathcliff.

One night, Catherine and Heathcliff tramped through the moors to Thrushcross Grange, where they spied on their neighbors, the Lintons. Attacked by a watchdog, Catherine was taken into the house and stayed there as a guest for five weeks until she was able to walk again. During that time, she became intimate with the pleasant family of Thrushcross Grange, Mr. and Mrs. Linton and their two children, Edgar and Isabella. Afterwards, the Lintons visited frequently at Wuthering Heights. As a result of Hindley's ill-treatment and the arrogance of Edgar and Isabella, Heathcliff became jealous and morose. He vowed revenge on Hindley, whom he hated with all of his savage nature.

The next summer, Hindley's consumptive wife, Frances, gave birth to a son, Hareton Earnshaw, and shortly thereafter she died. In his grief, Hindley became desperate, ferocious, and degenerate. In the meantime, Catherine Earnshaw and Edgar Linton had become sweethearts. The girl confided to Ellen Dean that she really loved Heathcliff, but she felt it would be degrading for her to marry the penniless orphan. Heathcliff, who overheard this conversation, disappeared the same night and did not return for many years. Edgar and Catherine married and lived at Thrushcross Grange with Ellen Dean as their housekeeper. There the pair lived happily until the return of Heathcliff, who was greatly improved in manners and appearance. He accepted Hindley's invitation to live at Wuthering Heights, an invitation extended because Hindley found in Heathcliff a companion for card-playing and drinking, and because he hoped to recoup his own dwindling fortune from Heathcliff's pockets.

Isabella Linton began to show a strong attraction to Heathcliff, much to the dismay of Edgar and Catherine. One night, Edgar and Heathcliff had a quarrel. Soon afterward, Heathcliff eloped with Isabella, obviously marrying her only to avenge himself and provoke Edgar. Catherine, an expectant mother, underwent a serious illness. When Isabella and Heathcliff returned to Wuthering Heights, Edgar refused to recognize his sister and forbade Heathcliff to enter his house. Despite this restriction, Heathcliff managed to have a tender interview with Catherine. Partly as a result of this meeting, her child, named Catherine Linton, was born prematurely, and she died a few hours later.

Isabella found life with Heathcliff unbearable and left him, going to London, where a few months later her child, Linton, was born. After Hindley's death, Heathcliff the guest became the master of Wuthering Heights, for Hindley had mortgaged his estate to him. Hareton, the natural heir, was reduced to dependency on his father's enemy.

When Isabella died, twelve years after leaving Heathcliff, her brother took her sickly child to live at Thrushcross Grange. Heathcliff soon heard of the child's arrival and demanded that Linton be sent to Wuthering Heights to live with his father. Young Catherine once visited Wuthering Heights and met her cousin Linton. Her father had tried to keep her in ignorance about the tenants of the place, but Heathcliff had let it be known that he wished the two children to be married. About the time that Edgar Linton became seriously ill, Heathcliff persuaded Cathy to visit her little cousin, who was also in extremely bad health. Upon her arrival, Cathy was imprisoned for five days at Wuthering Heights and forced to marry her sickly cousin Linton before she was allowed to go home to see her father. Although she was able to return to Thrushcross Grange before her father's death, there was not enough time for Edgar Linton to alter his will. Thus his land and fortune went indirectly to Heathcliff. Weak, sickly Linton Heathcliff died soon after, leaving Cathy a widow and dependent on Heathcliff.

Mr. Lockwood went back to London in the spring without seeing Wuthering Heights or its people again. Traveling in the region the next autumn, he had a fancy to revisit Wuthering Heights. There, he found Catherine and Hareton in possession. From Ellen Dean, he heard that Heathcliff had died three months earlier, after deliberately starving himself for four days. He was a broken man, still disturbed by memories of the beautiful young Catherine Earnshaw. His death freed Catherine Heathcliff and Hareton from his tyranny, and Catherine was now teaching the ignorant boy to read and improving his rude manners.

Mr. Lockwood went to see Heathcliff's grave. It was next to Catherine Earnshaw's, on whose other side lay her husband. They lay under their three headstones: Catherine's in the middle, weather-discolored and half-buried, Edgar's partly moss-grown, Heathcliff's still bare. In the surrounding countryside, there was a legend that they slept unquietly after their stormy, passionate lives. Shepherds and travelers at night claimed that they had seen Catherine and Heathcliff roaming the dark moors as they had done so often many years earlier.

"The Story" by Peter A. Brier

Critical Evaluation:

Not only is *Wuthering Heights* a powerful love story and a compelling tale of the supernatural, it also offers readers insightful commentary on issues relating to class and morality. Emily Brontë's novel is a complicated exploration of what happens when the established order of a community is thrown off balance. In the case of the Linton and Earnshaw families, it is the appearance of Heathcliff, the dark, mysterious orphan, that sets a chain of events in motion that destroy or threaten to destroy the lives of many of the characters. Although it is never clearly articulated, there is some reason to suspect that Heathcliff could be the illegitimate offspring of Mr. Earnshaw, who brings him into his home claiming to have found the child in Liverpool. Heathcliff poses a threat to the Earnshaw family because he is dark-skinned (therefore different), wild, and possibly a half-sibling to the Earnshaw children, Catherine and Hindley. This complication adds a more frightening aspect to the physical, spiritual, and emotional attraction that develops between Catherine and Heathcliff. Added to the possibility of breaking the incest taboo is the problem of social class: Because of his suspect origins, Heathcliff could never fit into the life of the Earnshaw/Linton families.

Brontë employs great skill in making the landscape, the weather, the houses—even the dogs—reflect the opposing emotional climates of the Linton and Earnshaw homes. The Earnshaw residence, Wuthering Heights, is, as its name implies, subject to extremes in weather; winds, snow, and cold buffet the house and grounds. By contrast, Thrushcross Grange, the home of the Lintons and later of Cathy and Edgar, is refined and filled with light, comfort, and opulence. Even the weather seems less severe there. The Grange stands in splendid contrast to the home shared by young Cathy, Hindley, and Heathcliff, a disjuncture made clear in the scene in which Catherine and Heathcliff spy on the Linton children from outside a window at the Grange. The show of temper between Isabella and Linton as they fight over their delicate dog pales in contrast to the vehemence with which those at Wuthering Heights express their emotions. While Heathcliff is disdainful of these soft children, Catherine is captivated—metaphorically and literally. Significantly, from this chance encounter spring all of the troubles that Heathcliff and the Earnshaw and Linton children will endure. Whereas Catherine grows entranced with the soft life at the Grange and with Linton, Heathcliff falls victim to the destructive envy that will finally drive him to destroy everyone with whom he comes in contact. In his mind, the Lintons represent all that he can never be or have.

Yet it is above all the love and passionate attraction between Catherine and Heathcliff that destroys the two families. It is Heathcliff's misunderstanding of the overheard conversation between Catherine and her nurse, Nelly Dean, that causes him to run away and eventually gives him the economic means to effect his revenge against the Earnshaws and the Lintons.

When Heathcliff returns to Wuthering Heights after many years' absence, he finds Catherine and Edgar married. Heathcliff's anger damages everything it touches, from the ignorant child of Hindley and Frances Earnshaw, the wild Hareton, to Edgar Linton's delicate sister, Isabella. Heathcliff's first overt act of revenge against Catherine and Edgar is to pursue and marry Isabella. From this point until he dies years later, Heathcliff's anger at losing Catherine destroys everyone with whom he comes in contact, including Isabella, his own son, Linton, Catherine's daughter, young Cathy, and her cousin, Hareton.

Even though both he and Catherine are married, Heathcliff does not leave her in peace. Not content simply to torture his own wife, Isabella, Heathcliff attacks Catherine verbally, and his violence causes her to fall ill and die soon after, while giving birth to young Cathy. Heathcliff never recovers from the loss of Catherine, which remains the reason for his brutal treatment of everyone whom he associates with her. His anger also directly causes his own death. Yet, for all of his violence, hatred, and vindictiveness, Heathcliff does not attain peace of mind or release from grief. He only succeeds in bringing Hindley to financial ruin; capturing Edgar Linton's fortune; and creating in young Hareton an untutored, violent beast.

As Heathcliff nears his own death, Brontë again uses the weather to mirror a character's interior turmoil. Heathcliff dies alone while a storm rages around the Heights. He is later found, a window open, the implication being that Catherine finally came to claim him for her own. While this scene is a climax, it does not constitute the resolution of *Wuthering Heights*, for Brontë provides an ending that offers a ray of hope in the promised union of young Cathy with Hareton Earnshaw. Not only does Cathy "tame" Hareton and teach him to read, she also learns to love and value him. The union of these two people represents a transformed version of the passions of Catherine and Heathcliff. The first Catherine could not have Heathcliff in this life, but her daughter can hope to build a satisfying life with Hareton. Although Heathcliff and Catherine's passion could not survive in this life, Brontë implies that the two lovers are finally united beyond the grave.

"Critical Evaluation" by Melissa Barth

Bibliography:
Davies, Stevie. *Emily Brontë: The Artist as a Free Woman.* Manchester, England: Carcanet

Press, 1983. Discusses not only the novel but also Brontë's personal life and tragedies, the fantasy worlds created by her and her siblings, and her poetry. Provides an incisive look at the novel's structure and an in-depth study of the personalities and motivations of the main characters.

Everitt, Alastair, ed. *Wuthering Heights: An Anthology of Criticism*. London: Frank Cass, 1967. A collection of introductory critical explorations of the novel that examine such fundamental issues as structure, narrative strategies, origins, the supernatural, madness, and sadomasochism.

Kavanaugh, James H. *Emily Brontë*. New York: Basil Blackwell, 1985. Offers a late twentieth century critical interpretation of the novel, including a deconstructionist reading. Useful also for its survey of critical approaches to this novel.

Miles, Peter. *Wuthering Heights*. Basingstoke, England: Macmillan, 1990. Provides various readings of Brontë's novel as well as an introduction that traces the history of the most popular interpretations of and reactions to the book. Includes a helpful bibliography, mostly covering the more traditional approaches.

Vogler, Thomas A., ed. *Twentieth Century Interpretations of Wuthering Heights*. Englewood Cliffs, N.J.: Prentice-Hall, 1968. Offers insight into the novel's background, important themes such as childhood and incest, and an informative account of the lives of the Brontë family. Also includes selected portions of important mid-twentieth century critical responses.

XALA

Type of work: Novel
Author: Ousmane Sembène (1923-   )
Type of plot: Social realism
Time of plot: Early 1970's
Locale: Dakar, Senegal
First published: 1973 (English translation, 1976)

Principal characters:

EL HADJI ABDOU KADER BEYE, a businessman
ADJA AWA ASTOU, his first wife
OUMI N'DOYE, his second wife
N'GONE, his third wife
RAMA, his daughter
MODU, his chauffeur
YAY BINETA, N'Gone's aunt
SEREEN MADA, a marabout, or holy man
THE BEGGAR

The Story:

It was a day of celebration. The characters celebrated and congratulated one another on the appointment of an African as president of the Chamber of Commerce and Industry. With an African presiding over the chamber, El Hadji Abdou Kader Beye and his fellow businessmen felt they could acquire greater economic control in Senegal, now that the last vestige of foreign rule had been removed. Seated at the right of the newly appointed president, El Hadji rose amid the jubilation inspired by this propitious moment and reminded his colleagues that, while they had been celebrating, his third marriage "had been sealed" at the mosque. He had become a captain according to traditional standards of nobility. Together, they all left the chamber to accompany El Hadji to his third wife's home, where the wedding festivities were in full progress.

Yay Bineta officiated proudly over the bustling crowd of guests which had already gathered for N'Gone's postnuptial celebration. She watched as the women examined enviously the numerous wedding gifts El Hadji had presented to his new young wife as tokens of love. El Hadji had not disappointed her expectations. Sadly, Adja Awa Astou and Oumi N'Doye observed this grand reception held in honor of their new cowife. After having made a sufficient show of acceptance of this third marriage, Adja departed. Back at her villa, she reflected on her own unhappiness provoked by renewed feelings of abandonment. Her daughter, Rama, who was vehemently opposed to the marriage and to polygamy, tried in vain to console her mother.

At N'Gone's villa, El Hadji's arrival with his entourage of businessmen caused an even greater stir of excitement among the guests. In the middle of the peals of laughter, loud music, and dancing, the lights went out, and the newly wedded couple slipped away to their bedroom, where El Hadji prepared himself to "deflower" his bride.

The next morning, Yay Bineta returned to N'Gone's villa in the company of an old woman. She entered the couple's room and observed El Hadji seated on the edge of the bed, while N'Gone sat gazing with a blank stare. El Hadji revealed that nothing had happened during the night. Struck with dismay at the announcement of this unwanted turn of events in her social victory, Yay Bineta blamed El Hadji, who had refused, beforehand, to take traditional precautions. Yay Bineta insisted that El Hadji go see a marabout to help rid himself of xala, the spell of impotency.

El Hadji could not believe that he had been inflicted with xala. He thought about his wives, Adja and Oumi. He wondered if one of them could have been the author of his affliction. Desirous to become potent again, El Hadji confided in the president of the chamber and, later, in his father-in-law Baboucar. On their advice, El Hadji sought out a number of reputed marabouts, healers and diviners, all of whom provided him with ineffective cures and useless clues for discovering the author of his xala.

While in pursuit of a cure, El Hadji increasingly neglected his business affairs, especially avoiding contact with the other businessmen. Burdened with the expense of the three villas and the financial demands of his wives and children, he continued to spend extravagantly, paying no attention to the declining state of his finances. He suffered immensely, convinced that his colleagues talked secretly about his xala. Previously overcome by his desire to possess the young N'Gone, El Hadji now saw her as a bitter reminder of his own seduction into the third marriage and his present miserable condition. His driver, Modu, also knew about El Hadji's xala. Moved by his employer's profound look of sadness, the chauffeur finally told him about the renowned marabout, Sereen Mada.

Sereen Mada lived in a small village outside the bustling capital of Dakar. Accustomed to the amenities of life in the capital, El Hadji resigned himself to make the painstaking journey. Sereen Mada did not disappoint his guest. As the holy man murmured prayerful incantations over his body, El Hadji felt the return of those pleasurable sensations which had previously deserted him. Modu's boss paid the marabout by check. Happy that he was no longer impotent, El Hadji returned to Dakar. With his virility restored, El Hadji felt he could now consummate his new marriage. He arrived at N'Gone's villa and was greeted by Yay Bineta with the announcement that N'Gone was having her menstrual period and was, therefore, unavailable. Filled with a sense of defeat, he dismissed the idea of wasting his passion on Adja, who fulfilled her conjugal duty with indifference. To her supreme delight, Oumi enjoyed a passionate night with El Hadji.

El Hadji returned to work and discovered that his financial affairs were in great jeopardy. Distraught over the disintegration of his life, El Hadji failed to recognize Sereen Mada, who had come to return his worthless check. Angered by El Hadji's display of disrespect, Sereen Mada quickly restored his xala.

El Hadji suffered the loss of his business, expulsion from the chamber, and the breakup of his marriages to N'Gone and Oumi. In the depths of his despair, he sought refuge with Adja. Days later, followed by a throng of cripples, blind persons, and others inflicted with all sorts of maladies, the beggar approached Adja's villa. In the presence of everyone, the beggar recounted how El Hadji had taken his clan's land by fraudulent means. The beggar, the real author of El Hadji's xala, declared that he could restore his potency. At the mercy of the beggar, El Hadji submitted to the scourge of humiliation inflicted upon him by the beggar's followers, who spat in turn upon his naked body.

Critical Evaluation:

An internationally acclaimed writer and filmmaker, Ousmane Sembène, a self-taught man, is considered one of the most prolific authors of his time. In search of employment, Sembène went to France, where he wrote and published his first work, *Le docker noir* (1956; the black docker), which launched his literary career. Over the next thirty years, he wrote six major novels, published several short stories, and directed and produced five films based on his own literary works. Often referred to as a modern-day griot, a term designating the traditional African storyteller, Sembène dramatizes the sociopolitical issues that affect the African people and their society. Apart from his first work, Sembène's novels are set primarily in Senegal. Placing less emphasis on his former preoccupation with the effects of French influence on African society, the author now concentrates largely on the issues of corruption, poverty, illiteracy, and other social ills perpetuated by the African elite at the expense of the poorer classes. Preceding his most recent work, *Le Dernier de l'empire* (1981; the last of the empire), *Xala* focuses, in particular, on the leadership of postindependence Senegal.

The forcefulness of Sembène's criticism is intensely conveyed through the symbolic connection established between xala and the impotency of the Senegalese leadership. A profoundly powerful work, *Xala* illustrates the use of traditional elements, a technique frequently used by the author in his works, to create a unique narrative style. The sense of a parable is effectively developed through the unanticipated decline of El Hadji's business affairs. The introductory scene evokes a false sense of optimism by the new African masters. The move from the national context to the personal situation of El Hadji serves to confront the hero with the true reality of life in Senegal.

The majority of the story focuses on El Hadji's unhappy married life. The occasional flashbacks interspersed throughout the story recall the familiar stylistic use of the historical past as a means to illuminate events of the present. The symbolic representation of the three wives underscores the relevance of the past to the present. Adja abandons Catholicism and converts to Islam to marry El Hadji. Her return to the old ways and her aspirations to be a model Muslim wife represent, in part, a retrogressive Africa which refuses to confront the changes of modern times. Oumi's exaggerated imitation of French values exposes the excessive materialism adopted by members of the middle class. Representative of the younger generation, N'Gone becomes a pawn in the hands of her elders and, consequently, forfeits the opportunity to act as a progressive agent of change within society.

El Hadji's distant relationship with his three wives focuses special attention on the problem of polygamy. Adja and Oumi feel emotionally and physically abandoned. Rama, the oldest child, attempts to express her dissatisfaction openly. Her small protest is squelched with a slap in the face by her father, who states that she "can be a revolutionary at the university or in the street but not in [his] house." Rama realizes, eventually, that she is powerless to improve her mother's moral plight.

The author proceeds to expose El Hadji and the other businessmen, who are only middlemen dependent on foreign enterprises to survive. The religious leadership is subject to similar criticism in the guise of Sereen Mada, who "only worked for bosses." The assistance that the marabout provides El Hadji serves only to promote the limited self-interest of the latter. Sembène thereby reveals how the state of impotency permeates society.

The inconspicuous presence of the beggar is skillfully intertwined in the web of intrigue. He first appears in the story on the day when El Hadji's xala is revealed. It is only in the final pages of the story that the beggar comes to the forefront as a major character, revealing himself as the author of the xala. The novel's main theme is expressed through the beggar's personal indictment of El Hadji: "You and your colleagues build on the misfortunes of honest, ordinary people." Typically, it is the common people who rise up as a potential force of change and revindicate their dignity and rightful place in society.

Cherie Maiden

Bibliography:

Bayo, Ogunjimi. "Ritual Archetypes: Ousmane's Aesthetic Medium in *Xala.*" *Ufahamu: Journal of the African Activist Association* 14, no. 3 (1985): 128-138. The article presents a complex analysis of symbolic images derived from African traditions and provides a profound reading of characterization and thematic content. The significant cultural features which contribute to Sembène's particular narrative style are highlighted to reveal the subtler dimensions of his social criticism.

Cham, Mbye B. "Islam in Senegalese Literature and Film." In *Faces of Islam in African Literature: Studies in African Literature,* edited by Kenneth W. Harrow. Portsmouth, N.H.: Heinemann, 1991. An illuminating study of the presence of Islamic influences in the Senegalese literary tradition. An entire section is devoted to its impact on Sembène's works, including *Xala.* There are fascinating stylistic, as well as thematic, similarities and differences described through a panoramic view of the artistry of Sembène, his predecessors, and his contemporaries.

Condé, Maryse. "Sembène Ousmane *Xala.*" *African Literature Today* 9 (1979): 97-98. A succinct but comprehensive overview of the dominant themes and issues commonly mentioned with reference to the novel. This review of *Xala* would be an especially beneficial introduction to the reading of the novel.

Iyam, David Uru. "The Silent Revolutionaries: Ousmane Sembène's *Emitai, Xala,* and *Ceddo.*" *The African Studies Review* 29, no. 4 (1986): 79-87. A detailed examination of the major characteristics prevalent in Sembène's literary and cinematic work. Although there is more discussion of the controversial film, *Ceddo,* the insights into *Xala* point out the issues and stylistic techniques present in both media and provide some familiarity with their social and political importance in the development of the artist's creative expression.

Makward, Edris. "Women, Tradition, and Religion in Sembène Ousmane's Work." In *Faces of Islam in African Literature: Studies in African Literature,* edited by Kenneth W. Harrow. Portsmouth, N.H.: Heinemann, 1991. Provides references to current trends in the reading of Sembène's novels. The novelist is considered one of the few writers of his generation to focus on the African woman as a credible and powerful agent of social change. Limited but very insightful commentary on *Xala* within the larger context of Sembène's literary vision.

THE YEARLING

Type of work: Novel
Author: Marjorie Kinnan Rawlings (1896-1953)
Type of plot: Regional
Time of plot: Late nineteenth century
Locale: Florida scrub country
First published: 1938

Principal characters:
JODY BAXTER, a young boy
PENNY BAXTER, his father
ORA BAXTER, his mother
FODDER-WING FORRESTER, Jody's disabled friend
OLIVER HUTTO, Penny's friend
GRANDMA HUTTO, his mother
TWINK WEATHERBY, Oliver's sweetheart

The Story:
The Baxter family consisted of Penny Baxter, his plump wife Ora, and their son Jody. They lived in a simple cabin in the Florida scrub country, where patient, hardworking Penny eked out a meager living by farming and hunting.

Young Jody still saw life through the eyes of a child and found a boy's pleasure in building a flutter mill at the spring when he should have been hoeing the garden patch.

One spring morning, the family discovered that Betsy, their black brood sow, had been killed by a bear. Penny recognized the tracks as those of Old Slewfoot, a giant black bear with one toe missing. Determined to be rid of this offender, he cornered the animal in the scrub, but his old gun would not fire, and the bear escaped.

Unable to afford a new gun, Penny traded a worthless dog to his neighbors, the Forresters, for a new double-barreled shotgun of fine make. The Forrester family consisted of the old parents, six gigantic, lawless boys, and Fodder-Wing, a deformed and disabled boy who was Jody's best friend. Penny was reluctant to dupe his neighbors, but his very living depended upon Old Slewfoot's destruction. He eased his conscience by telling the Forrester boys truthfully that the feist could not be trained for hunting. His words convinced the suspicious Forresters that the dog was even more valuable than they had thought, and they insisted on the trade.

After the old gun had been repaired, it became Jody's great pride. One day, while hunting with his father, he shot a buck which Penny sold at the store in Volusia. After selling the venison, Penny and Jody went to see Grandma Hutto, at whose house they spent the night. In the morning, everyone was made glad by the unexpected arrival of Oliver Hutto, Grandma's son, just home from the sea. Later that day, Oliver went downtown, where he met Lem Forrester. Both of the men were courting a blonde girl, Twink Weatherby. When the two started to fight, all of Lem's brothers joined in against Oliver Hutto. Wiry Penny and small Jody also entered the fight with Oliver, since the odds against him were so heavy. Oliver left the fight badly battered. Jody had been knocked unconscious. To keep people from talking, Twink Weatherby left town on the riverboat the next morning.

A short time later, Penny discovered that his hogs had disappeared. He suspected the Forresters of having trapped them in order to get revenge for the shotgun deal, and he and Jody started to track the hogs. As he searched, a rattlesnake bit Penny on the arm. He saved himself by shooting a doe and applying the liver to the bite to draw out the poison. Even in the excitement, Jody had noticed that the doe had a fawn. While Penny staggered homeward, Jody went to the Forresters to ask them to ride for Doc Wilson.

The Forresters, with the exception of Lem, evidently held no grudge over the trading of the dog and the fight in town, and they did all they could for the Baxters. One of the boys brought Doc Wilson to the cabin. Later they rounded up the hogs and returned them, and Buck Forrester stayed on at the Baxter cabin to help with the work.

While Penny was still desperately ill, Jody returned to the place where his father had been bitten, and there he found the helpless young fawn. He was so eager to have it for his own that his parents allowed him to bring it home as a pet. Rations were scarcer than ever at the Baxters during Penny's illness, but Jody was willing to share his own food and milk with the fawn. Fodder-Wing gave the fawn its name. He called it Flag.

In September a great storm came, destroying most of the Baxter crops. About a month later, Old Slewfoot visited the Baxter land again and killed a fat hog. Penny, who was in bed with chills and fever, was not able to follow the great black bear. Later, wolves killed one of the calves, and, with the Forresters, the Baxters hunted down the whole pack. During the hunt, they found ten bear cubs, left motherless by the plague and by hunters. Two of the Forresters took the cubs to Jacksonville and sold them. Penny and Jody's share of the profits bought the necessities which would tide the Baxters over the coming winter.

The Baxters had planned to spend Christmas in Volusia with Grandma Hutto and to attend the town's festivities on Christmas Eve, but a few days before Christmas, Old Slewfoot again appeared and killed a calf. Penny swore that he would kill the raider, and, after several days of determined hunting, he found and shot the huge bear.

The Baxters joined Grandma Hutto at the Christmas party. During the evening, Oliver Hutto arrived in town with his wife, Twink. To get revenge, Lem Forrester and his brothers set Grandma Hutto's house on fire and burned it to the ground. Without Oliver's knowing that the house had been destroyed by the Forresters, Grandma Hutto, Oliver, and Twink left town the next morning on the riverboat. They had decided to go to Boston to live.

Back in their cabin, the Baxters settled down to a quiet winter of fishing and hunting. Flag, the fawn, had grown until he was a yearling. The fawn had never been a favorite of Ma Baxter because she begrudged him the food and milk Jody fed him, and because he was a nuisance around the cabin.

In the spring, while Jody was helping his father plant corn, Flag got into the tobacco field and destroyed about half of the young plants. One day, while trying to pull a stump out of the ground, Penny suffered a hemorrhage and had to spend many days in bed. Jody had to do all of the farm work. He watched the corn sprouting through the ground. One morning, he found that Flag had eaten most of the tender green shoots. Mrs. Baxter wanted to kill the fawn at once, but Penny suggested that Jody build a fence around the corn to keep Flag out. Accordingly, Jody spent many days replanting the corn and building a high fence around the field. When the new planting of corn came up, Flag leaped the high fence with ease and again nibbled off the green shoots.

Her patience exhausted, Mrs. Baxter took Penny's gun and shot the fawn. Unhappy Jody had to shoot his pet again because his mother's aim was so poor. Jody felt that the family had betrayed him and hated them for it. He left the clearing and wandered into the scrub. With the vague idea of running away from home to join the Huttos in Boston, he headed for the river and set out in Nellie Ginright's dugout canoe. After several days without food, he was picked up by the river mail boat. He returned home, ashamed and penitent, no longer interested in the flutter mill, which he now considered only a plaything for children.

Critical Evaluation:

"There is of course an affinity between people and places," Marjorie Kinnan Rawlings writes in *Cross Creek* (1942). When she first arrived at Cross Creek, deep in Florida's Ocala National Forest, in 1928, Rawlings seemed an unlikely candidate to fit into the frontier landscape that existed in Florida at the time. She was a sophisticated career woman, an educated and accomplished journalist from Rochester, New York, with little knowledge of the outdoors. The inhabitants of her new home, on the other hand, were rural natives who lived close to the earth and close to natural disasters. Yet Rawlings discovered in their hard lives elements of beauty and meaning, which she incorporated into her greatest work, *The Yearling*. The publication of this book in 1938 brought Rawlings the Pulitzer Prize and worldwide recognition as a great original talent.

The affinity between people and places in *The Yearling* is most clearly seen in Penny Baxter, who has chosen to live on Baxter Island because of its isolation. Shunning city life, which makes "intrusions on the individual spirit," Penny moves to the Florida scrub because the "wild animals seemed less predatory to him than the people he had known." He learns to live in harmony with nature and to subsist on what his land has to offer. The challenge is great because Baxter's Island is "ringed with hunger." Penny's struggles to survive made him Rawlings' favorite character. In an interview that appeared in the *Christian Science Monitor* in 1940, Rawlings explains; "Penny expresses my own philosophy—that life knocks a person down; and he gets up, and it knocks him down again. And that the only strong, manly thing for a man to do when he's down is to take the experience calmly and go on—that is, get up and go at it again."

Penny tries to pass on this philosophy to Jody, who, as a child at the beginning of the story, is interested only in the flutter mill. Jody's desperate desire to domesticate Flag shows how immature and out of harmony he is with nature. By attempting to make a pet out of an animal who is an important part of the Baxters' food supply, Jody is bound for disaster. Second, Jody's passionate love for Flag highlights how lonely he is after Fodder-Wing's death: "Flag had eased a loneliness that had harassed him in the very heart of his family." Penny's offhand remark to Jody regarding Flag, " You're a pair o' yearlin's," illustrates how Flag and Jody have merged by the end of the narrative. Jody's childish—though human—attachment to Flag must end so that Jody may move on to the next stage of his development toward independent, strong adulthood. Both boy and fawn engage in prankish behavior that threatens the precarious survival of the family. Therefore, Flag's death is a grim necessity.

When Jody runs away from home after Flag has been shot, he experiences for himself the "terrifying" power of hunger: "It had a great maw to envelop him and claws that raked across his vitals." Suddenly, he understands his father's lessons in survival. Even though he knows that he will be "lonely all his life," he realizes that this truth is a "man's share," and he can continue.

Jody's evolution toward adulthood is accomplished in great circular journeys that take him away from the security and warmth of his center, Baxter's Island, and into the fierce outer world. His quest is mythic in nature, reinforced by the structure of the book, which encompasses the passing of one year. The book begins and ends in April, the time of renewal. Jody is accompanied by spirits in his journey through the dark woods: the memories of Spaniards who had once roamed afield, Fodder-Wing and his love for all living things, and, finally, the dream of Flag—"a boy and a yearling ran side by side, and were gone forever." Rawlings relates that the inspiration for the novel came in her poignant awareness of the passing of innocent youth into adulthood. She conceived of the work as a "tragic idyll of boyhood" and recalled an experience that she had at the age of ten. She had been standing under a tree on a beautiful April morning when she had a "premonition of maturity": "And at the height of my delight, a sadness came over me, and I understood suddenly that I should not always be a child, and that beyond this carefree moment life was waiting with its responsibilities."

Transmuting real-life experiences and people into art was a struggle that Rawlings faced throughout her writing career. Living in the exotic, semitropical locale of rural, frontier Florida among colorful, eccentric, and strong-minded individualists, she was continually tempted, as a trained journalist, simply to record facts. To do so, though, would have been artistic suicide because "Facts are unreliable and treacherous." She recognized that she must learn a harder task—that is, to give facts "the breath of life." A fact is an empty cup that must be filled with "the prismatic fluid of the creative imagination," as Rawlings told University of Florida students in 1938. Her literary editor, Maxwell Perkins, urged her in this direction in order to make her characters more fictional.

She achieved the perfect balance between facts and fiction in *The Yearling*. By placing the story's events in the past, in the 1870's, she allowed herself a measure of distance. She also chose uncomplicated characters for her story. In a letter to F. Scott Fitzgerald in 1936, she tells him that she prefers to write about "the very simple people" because their problems "are only the most fundamental and primitive ones." Finally, she simplified her writing style, perhaps under the influence of her fellow Floridian, Ernest Hemingway, who was living in Key West in the 1930's and whom Rawlings knew. Although she never publicly acknowledged a debt, critic Gordon Bigelow believes that she learned how to write a simple declarative sentence from him.

The big risk that Rawlings took by moving to Florida and giving all to literature culminated in her production of *The Yearling*, a book that transcends the reality of its place to appeal to children and adults throughout the world.

"Critical Evaluation" by Anna Lillios

Bibliography:
Bellman, Samuel. *Marjorie Kinnan Rawlings*. New York: Twayne, 1974. A basic beginner's overview of Rawlings' life and artistic output. The section on *The Yearling* provides good background information regarding its composition and the people who inspired Rawlings.
Bigelow, Gordon. *Frontier Eden: The Literary Career of Marjorie Kinnan Rawlings*. Gainesville: University of Florida Press, 1966. An important study of Rawlings' complete works and a source of interviews and eyewitness accounts of Rawlings' life in Cross Creek. The last chapter, "The Literary Artist," focuses on Rawlings' philosophy of composition.
Parker, Idella, and Mary Keating. *Idella: Marjorie Rawlings' "Perfect Maid."* Gainesville: University Press of Florida, 1992. An entertaining, fascinating look behind the scenes of the Rawlings' household in Cross Creek from the perspective of Rawlings' maid, who worked for her from 1940 to 1950. The most disturbing revelation surrounds the visit of Zora Neale Hurston, whom Rawlings sent to sleep in the servants' quarters.
Silverthorne, Elizabeth. *Marjorie Kinnan Rawlings: Sojourner at Cross Creek*. Woodstock, N.Y.: Overlook Press, 1988. A readable biography that is not too academic. Contains interviews with Norton Baskin, Rawlings' second husband.

THE YEARS

Type of work: Novel
Author: Virginia Woolf (1882-1941)
Type of plot: Domestic realism
Time of plot: 1880-1937
Locale: London
First published: 1937

Principal characters:
COLONEL ABEL PARGITER
ELEANOR,
EDWARD,
MORRIS,
DELIA,
MILLY,
MARTIN, and
ROSE, his children
CELIA, Morris' wife
NORTH and
PEGGY, the children of Morris and Celia
PATRICK, Delia's husband
SIR DIGBY PARGITER, the colonel's brother
EUGENIE, his wife
MAGGIE and
SARA, their daughters
RENÉ (RENNY), Maggie's husband
KITTY MALONE, later LADY LASSWADE, the Pargiters' cousin
NICHOLAS POMJALOVSKY, Eleanor's friend
CROSBY, a servant

The Story:

On a blustery April afternoon in 1880, Colonel Abel Pargiter sat at the window of his club looking out over Piccadilly. Everyone in the street seemed to have somewhere to go, some end in view. The colonel felt that there was nothing for him. At home, in the shabbily genteel house on Abercorn Terrace, his wife was dying of cancer; he had a family of three sons and four daughters to provide for, he was retired, and he was not rich. He decided to visit his mistress, Mira, who lived in a side street near Westminster Abbey. When he arrived, dusk was already falling; it filled the dingy rooms with the secret, furtive atmosphere of lust.

In the same dusk, in the house on Abercorn Terrace, Milly and Delia Pargiter were boiling water for tea. Their younger sister Rose was wearing a green-smudged pinafore, and Milly tried to be severe with her in a grown-up fashion. Twelve-year-old, red-haired Martin came home from school. When the colonel arrived and asked for Eleanor, his oldest daughter, Milly reminded him that it was her day for social service. Eleanor appeared, dropping her books on the table. Since her mother's illness, she had become the family's mainstay, the keeper of accounts, the soother of hurts, and the arbiter of quarrels. Delia went to sit with her mother. She resented Mrs. Pargiter's illness and the ties of sickness and home; in her imagination, she saw

7325

herself on the platform at a political meeting, the great Irish leader, Charles Stewart Parnell, beside her. Morris Pargiter, a young barrister, came home for dinner. The family was at the table when Crosby, the servant, brought word that Mrs. Pargiter had suffered a relapse. She died later that same rainy night.

Rain also fell in Oxford. Edward Pargiter put aside *Antigone* and daydreamed of his cousin, Kitty Malone, a don's daughter with whom he was in love. His friend Hugh Gibbs came in with talk of horses and women. Another friend, Ashley, appeared, but Ashley was jealous of Gibbs, and Edward, unhappy and bored, went off to bed. Kitty Malone, reading history with eccentric Miss Craddock, admired Jo Robson; he reminded her of a young farmhand who had once kissed her under a rick. Mrs. Malone read the letter that told of Mrs. Pargiter's death and thought of her cousin as a young girl. She decided that Edward would not do; young Lord Lasswade would make a more suitable match. Mrs. Pargiter was buried on a day of shadows and sunshine.

It was cool in England in the autumn of 1891. In the north, Kitty, now Lady Lasswade, shivered on the terrace where she sat with her husband. In Devonshire, Hugh Gibbs told his wife Milly, who had been a Pargiter, that the leaves on the trees were still too thick for good hunting. At Oxford, Edward Pargiter, now a don, walked in the crisp air and thought of poetry. Morris, the lawyer, recalled his childhood as leaves crisped under his feet on the flagstones of the Law Courts. Martin was a soldier in India. Delia and Rose had left home to lead lives of their own. Only Eleanor remained, tied to her aging father and the house on Abercorn Terrace, keeping accounts, doing social service work, going to the Law Courts with Celia, Morris' wife, buying children's presents that the colonel would give to his nieces, Maggie and Sara, when he went to dine with his brother, Sir Digby Pargiter. Sir Digby was in politics; his wife, Eugenie, was pretty and frivolous. The colonel had dinner with Digby and Eugenie on the day that Parnell died.

By midsummer, 1907, Martin was back from India; he was still Captain Pargiter but no longer in the army. Sara Pargiter thought of her cousins as she lay in bed and read Edward's translation of *Antigone*. Her mother and father had gone out to dinner and had taken Maggie with them; it was Maggie's first grown-up party. Sara's back was crooked, for she had been dropped as a child. She read Edward's book and listened to the music of a dance down the street. Finally, she fell asleep.

A year later, Sir Digby and Eugenie were both dead, and their house had been sold. Colonel Pargiter had suffered a stroke. Sometimes Eleanor, who still looked after him, reflected on what a terrible thing old age was. Sir Digby and his wife had been fortunate, she thought, dying in their prime. Rose was now forty years old and mannish in appearance and behavior. She returned from suffragist meetings she had been attending in the north. Meeting at the Abercorn Terrace house, she and Martin recalled the time they had quarreled and Rose had cut her wrist with a knife.

After their parents' death, Maggie and Sara went to live in Hymas Place, a crescent of shabby old houses. Maggie and Rose met in a shop, and Rose went to have lunch with her cousins on a day in 1910. Delia had married an Irishman. For a brief time, some of the family—Eleanor, Martin, Kitty, Rose, and Sara—came together at a suffragist meeting. That night while Sara was telling Maggie about the meeting, they heard shouting in the street outside. The king was dead.

After her father's death, Eleanor went on a holiday in Spain and Greece. She was fifty-five years old, too old to begin a new life. She went to visit Morris and his wife Celia, who had two children, North and Peggy. Maggie was married to a Frenchman. The Abercorn Terrace house was sold in 1913, and Crosby went off to live in lodgings in Richmond. She was still loyal to the Pargiters, looking after Martin's laundry and socks.

While returning from his stockbroker's on a spring day in 1914, Martin ran into Sara at St. Paul's and took her out to lunch. They talked about Rose, who had been jailed after breaking windows during a suffragist demonstration. Later, they met Maggie and her baby in Kensington Gardens. That night, Martin dined with the Lasswades. Sitting beside a young girl at dinner, he suddenly felt that he was old and that his life was empty.

The war came. One night in the winter of 1917, Eleanor went to dinner with Maggie and her husband, Renny. There were other guests—Nicholas Pomjalovsky, a Pole, and Sara. In the middle of dinner, a German air raid began. Later, Nicholas tried to explain his hopes for the new world to come after the war. Eleanor felt that here was the man whom she might have married. Maggie confided that he loved only other men. Eleanor, Sara, and Nicholas walked across London in the cold darkness. Eleanor had forgotten the air raid and the wail of the sirens. They wailed again, and guns boomed on a November day in 1918. Crosby was waiting in the queue at a grocer's shop. Someone said that the war was over.

In 1937, Eleanor, now more than seventy years old and just back from a trip to India, went to Delia's party, a gathering of the Pargiter clan, with her niece Peggy, who was a doctor in a London hospital. Peggy's brother, North, had sold his farm in Africa; he took Sara, who had invited him to dinner at her shabby flat. On their way from the theater, Maggie and Renny went with them. Delia was old; Patrick, her Irish husband, was handsome but hard of hearing. Peggy, looking at Delia and Patrick, wondered how people married and had children. She talked to Martin, who was never at ease with her; she was his doctor and knew his dread of cancer. Rose came in; she had grown stout and deaf. Milly waddled beside big, jovial Hugh Gibbs. North thought of animals munching in their stalls. Morris, the barrister, was there, as was Edward, the distinguished bachelor-scholar. Kitty Lasswade, now the widow of a governor general, appeared in time for supper. Nicholas tried to make a speech, and everyone's health was drunk. The young looked at the old, and the old looked at the young. Eleanor wondered if there had been a pattern behind these lives, like a theme or motif in music. Then it was time to go. Eleanor stood at the window and watched a taxi drive up to a nearby house and a young man and young woman get out. The young man was fitting his latch key to the door. The sun was shining; it was a bright new day.

Critical Evaluation:

The entry in Virginia Woolf's diary for November 2, 1932, contains a reference to the novel that was eventually published as *The Years*. In the beginning, it was to be called *The Pargiters*, an essay-novel into which she planned to pour the total sum of her experience in the narrative of the experiences of a single family through several generations. The pattern was not to follow that of family chronicles such as John Galsworthy and Hugh Walpole had written; instead, it was to jump chamoislike across gaps in time between 1880 and 1937. A domestic story, *The Years* lacks the bold technical brilliance of *To The Lighthouse* (1927) and *The Waves* (1931). The work may appear at first reading like a reversion to the style of earlier books such as *Night and Day* (1919), but nothing could be further from the truth. *The Years* is more than the story of the frustrations, ambitions, triumphs, joys, tragedies, and defeats of a middle-class family. In its episodic pattern, the novel represents an effort to record the process of time passing and to capture in fiction that sudden flash of recognition, the moment of perception, that in earlier periods was the function of poetry alone. In the separate divisions of the novel, descriptions of the seasons and the flowing movement of the prose convey the sense of change and recurrence that Woolf in her later novels tried to dredge from the depths of human consciousness.

In her essay "A Room of One's Own," Woolf describes a young man and woman getting into a taxi together to exemplify her artistic ideal: the "androgynous mind" that unites both male and female principles. The same symbol—here the two are alighting from a taxi—is found at the end of *The Years* and strikes one of the few hopeful notes in the book.

The novel covers roughly the time period of Woolf's own life, a sixty-year span that witnessed massive historical changes. It is this period—the period of late nineteenth century colonial expansion, World War I and the ensuing disillusionment, and the depression and cynicism of the 1930's—that is narrated through the lives of three generations of Pargiters. Although social milieu is more important here than in any previous novel, Woolf does not merely provide a historical chronicle but also explores such themes as uniting the one with the many, bringing order to chaos, and seeing with the androgynous vision. The Pargiter family remains a unit despite the infrequent reunions that occur.

Eleanor Pargiter is perhaps the most important character in the novel, a young woman of about twenty years at the beginning, more than seventy years old at the end. As of the mother's terminal illness, Eleanor is the element that holds the family together. Throughout, her thoughts and situation are given more prominence than those of the others, and she is often shown in the contact she has with the other family members. Woolf makes note of her jottings, as when she makes an "I" with lines radiating from that center. This image suggests the ego at the center of each person's perceptions; different events become known from different characters' perspectives. Only the reader is able to see the pattern of the whole.

Eleanor typifies the woman who sacrifices her own ambitions and desires for the good of her aging father. Woolf often commented on this kind of woman, remarking that it was a blessing that her own parents died when she was relatively young, leaving her free to pursue her writing. By the time Colonel Pargiter dies, it is too late for Eleanor to begin her own life.

The themes of earlier books are found in *The Years*, but the imagery has darkened considerably. Characters are often compared to animals or parts of nature that are gross or horrible. Uncle Edward looks like the shell of an insect; Patrick's face looks like a red gooseberry with a few hairs, and his hands are like bear paws; Milly's fat arms draped with beads remind North of pale asparagus. The idea of the animal in human beings is emphasized by observations about people being "nasty creatures" with "uncontrollable lusts." North characterizes marriage as thirty years of "tut-tut-tut and chew-chew-chew." Such radical dehumanization dominates the book but is most prevalent in the last "Present Day" section. It suggests a fundamental pessimism about human possibilities: Because human beings are purely animal, "progress" is an illusion.

The constant association of progress with death and aging emphasizes this pessimistic outlook. Nicholas, for example, who speaks of a New World in 1917, expounds a similar idea in 1937, by which time there is the sense that optimistic words are empty and meaningless: After his attempted speech, Nicholas brings his glass down, and it shatters; two children sing for the party, but their words are incomprehensible; Eleanor realizes that people know nothing, even about themselves. At the end, when the old Pargiter brothers and sisters are grouped together by a window, the next generation regards them as "unreal" as statues. True communication, self-knowledge, and human progress all seem to be lacking.

The book's structure reinforces the theme of decay and entropy: People grow old and die, and little else changes or improves. The first section is divided into ten parts, each treating a day in a particular year from 1880 to 1918. Historical events—the death of Parnell or Edward VII, air raids during World War I, Armistice Day—are used as a means for bringing together different characters. The historical and social situations are always in the background. The second section is entitled "Present Day" and encompasses the final quarter of the book.

Throughout the novel, such natural phenomena as rain, moon, wind, sun, and snow are used to connect places and people. Sometimes these phenomena recur from one year to another, so that each subsequent mention gains associations from the earlier ones. The way the sunlight shines through the trees, for example, is noted both in 1910 and 1914. The same objects and actions are periodically mentioned, giving a large network of recurrences to the book, where everything has a place in an order and where nothing happens by chance. Flames, sparks, and smoke are mentioned often, evoking memories of previous thoughts in the characters' minds. The fraying of the wick under the slow teakettle, the spotted ink-stained walrus, and the cooing of the pigeons are some of the repeated images that provide links between the years.

Eleanor herself finally realizes that some sort of pattern for the whole exists, and this awareness makes her happy, but she wonders "Who makes it? Who thinks it?" Eleanor's vision of the pattern sets a note of hope to the ending of the book that counteracts the dark, dehumanized quality of foreboding prevalent in the 1937 section. Yet it is questionable whether her final optimistic image of the young couple and the new day overcomes the pessimistic tone that dominates most of the rest of the book.

"Critical Evaluation" by Margaret McFadden-Gerber

Bibliography:
Bell, Quentin. *Virginia Woolf.* New York: Harcourt Brace Jovanovich, 1972. A standard biography that provides background, as well as photographs of family and friends, indexes and appendices, and a limited and dated bibliography. Also contains pertinent references to the creation of *The Years*.
Gorsky, Susan Rubinow. *Virginia Woolf.* Boston: Twayne, 1989. A good starting place for any research and commentary. Discusses *The Years* and other works of the author and provides a chronology, annotated bibliography, and an index.
Guiguet, Jean. *Virginia Woolf and Her Works.* Translated by Jean Stewart. New York: Harcourt Brace Jovanovich, 1965. An exhaustive study of most of Woolf's works. Examines *The Years* and other novels individually and in comparison with other works. Also provides a brief biography and an overview of the historical period, as well as a bibliography and indexes.
Majumdar, Robin, and Allen McLaurin, eds. *Virginia Woolf: The Critical Heritage.* Boston: Routledge & Kegan Paul, 1975. The informative introduction provides a brief biography of Woolf. Individual criticisms of her major and minor published works include many references to *The Years*. Also includes a selected bibliography and index.
Marcus, Jane, ed. *New Feminist Essays on Virginia Woolf.* Lincoln: University of Nebraska Press, 1981. A crucial compilation of women's viewpoints. Supplies an extremely useful political complement to earlier criticism of *The Years*.

THE YEMASSEE
A Romance of Carolina

Type of work: Novel
Author: William Gilmore Simms (1806-1870)
Type of plot: Adventure
Time of plot: Early eighteenth century
Locale: South Carolina
First published: 1835

> *Principal characters:*
> SANUTEE, a Yemassee chief
> MATIWAN, his wife
> OCCONESTOGA, his son
> GABRIEL HARRISON, a young settler
> HECTOR, Gabriel's black slave
> PARSON MATTHEWS, a minister
> BESS MATTHEWS, his daughter

The Story:

The English settlers, who at first had to accept aid from the Yemassee Indians when they landed on the South Carolina shores, had become quite powerful by 1715. No longer did they have to be careful not to offend the Indians; instead, they continually set up farms on the wrong side of the boundary lines between white and Indian territory. Sanutee, one of the Yemassee chiefs, had become suspicious of the colonists; he was afraid that they would soon take over all the Yemassee land. In order to keep them from occupying Indian territory, he had made treaties with other tribes and with the Spanish, who were willing to help the Indians defeat the English. Sanutee's life was made unhappy by his son, Occonestoga, who had been tempted by liquor to become a close friend of the whites. Sanutee was too proud of his ancestry and his position to call a drunkard his son, and it was only by constant pleas that his wife, Matiwan, was able to keep him from completely disowning Occonestoga.

One of the recent settlers was Gabriel Harrison, a strange young man whose commanding presence and jolly manner made him both admired and disliked. Among those who liked him were Bess Matthews, the daughter of old Parson Matthews, and Walter Grayson, an honorable young farmer. Parson Matthews disliked Harrison because he was too gay and worldly in his manner, and Walter's brother, Hugh, disliked Harrison because he was also an admirer of Bess. Harrison had brought with him a fine African slave named Hector, who was his constant companion, and a strong and faithful dog named Dugdale. With these two companions, Harrison wandered about the district.

One day in the forest, Harrison came upon Sanutee fighting with a stranger over the carcass of a deer. He arrived in time to save Sanutee's life, but the proud Indian expressed no gratitude. Harrison learned that Sanutee's opponent was a sailor named Dick Chorley, who had recently arrived on the coast. Although Chorley said that he had come to trade, Harrison rightly suspected that he was really a Spanish agent who had come to arm the Yemassee against the English. Harrison sent Hector to spy on Chorley and Sanutee, who had been joined by Ishiagaska, another Yemassee chief.

Hector, hiding in the brush, overheard Chorley's declaration that he had come to South

Carolina to arm the Yemassee. Displaying the wampum belt of an Indian treaty, he asked the Yemassee tribe to join the tribes who were willing to fight the English. Before Hector could return to tell Harrison what he had learned, the slave was captured and taken aboard Chorley's ship. Harrison guessed what had become of Hector. He found Chorley in the Parson's cabin and, by threats, forced the seaman to sign an order freeing Hector. His action angered the Parson, who refused to suspect Chorley of treason. He denied Harrison the right to wed his daughter Bess.

In the meantime, the Yemassee chiefs were called to a council and asked to sell more land to the English. Most of the chiefs were willing to sell, but Sanutee, who arrived late at the meeting, made a stirring speech against the sale. Interrupted by his drunken son, the old Yemassee almost killed Occonestoga. When he heard that the chiefs intended to sell the land over his protests, Sanutee left the meeting and went to arouse the people against their chiefs. With the aid of an Indian prophet named Enoree Mattee, he so infuriated the crowd that they repudiated the other chiefs and punished them by having the tribal mark cut from their skins, so that they became outcasts from the tribe. Only Occonestoga escaped this punishment.

Occonestoga hid in the woods. One day, he saved Bess Matthews' life by killing a rattlesnake that was about to strike her. For his deed, Harrison rewarded the young Yemassee with his friendship. Soon afterward, he sent Occonestoga back to the Indian stronghold to learn what the Yemassee were planning. Occonestoga secretly made his way to his mother, Matiwan, who hid him in her tent. By chance, Sanutee discovered the boy and ordered that he be killed after having the tribal mark cut from his skin. In desperation, Matiwan killed her son before the sentence could be carried out, for the tribal mark could not be cut from a dead man.

Harrison, realizing that Sanutee was about to lead the Yemassee against the whites, did his best to get all the settlers to go to the blockhouse for protection. Parson Matthews insisted that the Yemassee had never been more friendly, and he refused to leave his cabin. Harrison, while scouting in the woods, was captured by Yemassee. With the aid of Matiwan, who had heard of his kindness to her dead son, he escaped. In his attempt to save Bess before the Yemassee could seize her, he was almost recaptured. Hector and his dog Dugdale arrived just in time to save him.

Meanwhile, Chorley had led a party of Yemassee and sailors to the Parson's cabin and had captured both Bess and her father. Harrison was able to rescue them and lead them to the blockhouse before the Indian attack began. A furious struggle took place, with men and women fighting side by side to hold off the Yemassee. Both the Grayson brothers became friendly with Harrison because of the bravery he had shown in saving their families, and together they fought valiantly to save their community. At last, the Yemassee were forced to withdraw.

Harrison made plans to send many of the settlers to Charleston, where they would be safe until troops could be mustered to defeat the Yemassee permanently. After winning the Parson's permission to marry Bess, consent freely given after his heroic defense of the colony, Harrison astonished the group by announcing that he was in reality Charles Craven, the new governor of the province. He had come to the region in disguise so that he could see for himself the true state of affairs on the frontier. He made Hugh Grayson commander of the garrison forces. When he offered Hector his freedom, the old slave refused to be parted from his kind master.

In Charleston, Craven raised a considerable fighting force and returned to battle with the Yemassee on the banks of the Salkehatchie River. When the Yemassee attacked the camp of the white people, the governor's troops, firing from ambush, defeated them. Sanutee fell, mortally wounded, and Craven saw Matiwan run upon the field and fall weeping by her husband's body. The last of the Yemassee warriors was dead.

Critical Evaluation:

In early American frontier novels, the Indian was inevitably characterized in one of two ways: either as a noble savage, a natural primitive untainted by civilization's corrupting influences, or, more commonly, as a savage barbarian who took pleasure in cruelty and violence toward innocent white settlers. Even America's most famous author of historical romances, James Fenimore Cooper, divided his Indians into absolutely good and bad types and developed his novels accordingly. Perhaps only William Gilmore Simms in *The Yemassee* succeeded in creating believable, human Indians with mixed qualities, natures, and potentials; that is the primary reason why *The Yemassee*, in spite of severe artistic flaws, must be acknowledged as one of the best nineteenth century frontier novels.

Through the first third of the book, the action is seen primarily from the Indian viewpoint. Simms carefully describes the Yemassee tribe as they plan and attempt to execute an uprising against the white settlers. Their motives, however, spring not from innate hostility or from cruelty but from a realization that the powers and needs of the white settlers make the conflict—and their own ultimate defeat—inevitable. Thus, Simms imports to the Yemassee a kind of doomed, almost tragic grandeur.

It is in his presentation of the intimate life of the Yemassee that Simms is most impressive. Unlike Cooper, Simms describes the natives in their own environment and shows their daily routines, tribal mores, rituals, and politics in minute, careful detail. This Indian culture is presented with respect, and individual tribe members are presented as fallible but admirable human beings.

The most vivid portraits are those of Chief Sanutee, his wife, and their son. Sanutee is a proud, intelligent, brave but flawed leader, who understands and accepts the unavoidable dissolution of his tribe, but who, nevertheless, inspires his people to heroic resistance. His wife, Matiwan, shares her husband's courage and insight, but her compassion elevates her above racial identity to become a kind of Earth Mother figure. Their son, Occonestoga, contaminated by contact with the white culture's whiskey and promises, finally finds his courage and nobility in a time of crisis, although too late to salvage his tribal status. Few scenes in nineteenth century fiction are as powerful as the one in which, during the ritual that is to strip Occonestoga of his tribal identity, Matiwan kills her own son before the assembled Yemassee to save his honor and dignity. Had Simms been able to sustain the insights and intensity of the first third of the book, *The Yemassee* might have been a great novel. Unfortunately, once the focus of the novel shifts to the white culture, the characters, both Indians and whites, become stock characters, and the novel degenerates into a clichéd adventure story.

Simms's sympathetic treatment of the Yemassee, however, does not mean that he considered them the equal of white people. Even Sanutee "well knew that the superior must necessarily be the ruin of the race which is inferior." As a staunch upholder of the Southern position in the pre-Civil War American South, Simms firmly believed in racial superiority and what he and others called an "organic society." In Simms's view, the Indian was doomed because he was an inferior race and culture and, unlike the black, could not be placed into a useful position in the white people's world. However tragic and seemingly unjust the displacement or destruction of the Indians might be, it was, to Simms, a necessary price.

Bibliography:
Cowie, Alexander. Introduction to *The Yemassee*, by William Gilmore Simms. New York: American Book Company, 1937. Summarizes Simms's life and literary career and relates *The Yemassee* to general characteristics of his fiction and literary theory. Contains a contem-

porary news account of the 1715 Yemassee uprising.

Ridgely, J. V. *William Gilmore Simms*. New York: Twayne, 1962. This critical biography discusses theme and setting of Simms's works and argues that Simms's own preface to *The Yemassee* forgives historical inaccuracies by claiming the writer's license "to weave the facts of history into a wholly fictional main plot."

Rubin, Louis O., Jr. "The Romance of the Colonial Frontier: Simms, Cooper, the Indians, and the Wilderness." In *American Letters and the Historical Consciousness*, edited by J. Gerald Kennedy and Daniel Mark Fogel. Baton Rouge: Louisiana State University Press, 1987. Discusses the genre of frontier romance and evaluates Simms's portrayal of Native Americans.

Trent, William P. *William Gilmore Simms*. New York: Houghton Mifflin, 1892. This early critical biography discusses the writing, publication history, and critical reception of *The Yemassee*. Finds the white characters weak, but praises Simms's portrayal of Native Americans, calling Matiwan "the loveliest and purest Indian that I have met with in fiction." Claims chapter twenty-five (Matiwan's rescue of Occonestoga) is as great as the best of James Fenimore Cooper or Charles Brockden Brown.

Wimsatt, Mary Ann. *The Major Fiction of William Gilmore Simms: Cultural Traditions and Literary Form*. Baton Rouge: Louisiana State University Press, 1989. Discusses the backgrounds and traditions of the romance genre (influenced by Sir Walter Scott) that Simms used for his long fiction.

YOU CAN'T GO HOME AGAIN

Type of work: Novel
Author: Thomas Wolfe (1900-1938)
Type of plot: Autobiographical
Time of plot: 1929-1936
Locale: New York, England, and Germany
First published: 1940

> *Principal characters:*
> GEORGE WEBBER, a writer
> ESTHER JACK, the woman he loves
> FOXHALL EDWARDS, his editor and best friend
> LLOYD MCHARG, a famous novelist
> ELSE VON KOHLER, a woman also loved by Webber

The Story:

As George Webber looked out of his New York apartment window that spring day in 1929, he was filled with happiness. The bitter despair of the previous year had been lost somewhere in the riotous time he had spent in Europe, and now it was good to be back in New York with the feeling that he knew where he was going. His book had been accepted by a great publishing firm, and Foxhall Edwards, the best editor of the house, had been assigned to help him with the corrections and revisions. George had also resumed his old love affair with Esther Jack, who, married and the mother of a grown daughter, nevertheless returned his love with tenderness and passion. This love, however, was a flaw in George's otherwise great content, for he and Esther seemed to be pulling different ways. She was a famous stage designer who mingled with a sophisticated artistic set. George thought that he could find himself completely only if he lived among and understood the little people of the world.

Before George's book was published, he tried for the first time to go home again. Home was Libya Hill, a small city in the mountains of Old Catawba. When the aunt who had reared George died, he went back to Libya Hill for her funeral. There he learned that he could never really go home again, for home was no longer the quiet town of his boyhood but a growing city of money-crazy speculators who were concerned only with making huge fortunes out of real estate.

George found some satisfaction in the small excitement he created because he had written a book which was soon to be published. Even that pleasure was not to last long, for when he returned to New York and the book was published, almost every citizen in Libya Hill wrote him letters filled with threats and curses. George had written of Libya Hill and the people he knew there. His only motive had been to tell the truth as he saw it, but his old friends and relatives in Libya Hill seemed to think that he had spied on them throughout his boyhood in order to gossip about them in later years. Even the small fame he received in New York, where his book was favorably reviewed by the critics, could not atone for the abusive letters from Libya Hill. He felt he could redeem himself only by working feverishly on his new book.

George moved to Brooklyn, first breaking off his relationship with Esther. This severance from Esther was difficult, but George could not live a lie himself and attempt to write the truth. In Brooklyn, he did learn to know and love the little people—the derelicts, the prostitutes, the

7334

petty criminals—and he learned that they, like the so-called "good" men and women, were all representative of America. His only real friend was Foxhall Edwards, who had become like a father to George. Edwards was a great man, a gifted editor and a genius at understanding and encouraging those who, like George, found it difficult to believe in anything during the years of the Great Depression. Edwards, too, knew that only through truth could America and the world be saved from destruction, but, unlike George, he believed that the truth could not be thrust suddenly upon people. He calmly accepted conditions as they existed. George raged at his friend's skepticism.

After four years in Brooklyn, George finished the first draft of his new book. Tired of New York, he thought that he might find the atmosphere he needed to complete his manuscript in Europe. In London, he met Lloyd McHarg, the embodiment of all that George wanted to be. George yearned for fame in that period of his life. Because his book had brought him temporary fame, quickly extinguished, he envied McHarg's world reputation as a novelist. George was disillusioned when he learned that McHarg found fame meaningless. He had held the world in his hand for a time, but nothing had happened. Now he was living feverishly, looking for something he could not name.

When his manuscript was ready for publication, George returned to New York, made the corrections Edwards suggested, and then sailed again for Europe. He went to Germany, a country he had not visited since 1928. In 1936, he was more saddened by the change in the German people than he had been by anything else in his life. He had always felt a kinship with the Germans, but they were no longer the people he had known. Persecution and fear tinged every life in that once proud country, and George, sickened, wondered if there were any place in the world where truth and freedom still lived.

There were, however, two bright horizons in his visit to Germany. The first was the fame which greeted him on his arrival there. His first book had been well received, and his second, now published, was a great success. For a time, he basked in that glory, but soon he, like McHarg, found fame an elusive thing that brought no real reward. His other great experience was his love for Else von Kohler. That was also an elusive joy, for her roots were deep in Germany, and George knew he must return to America to cry out to his own people that they must live the truth and so save America from the world's ruin. Before he left Germany, he saw more examples of the horror and tyranny under which the people existed, and he left with a heavy heart. He realized once more that one can never go home again.

Back in New York, he knew that he must break at last his ties with Foxhall Edwards. He wrote to Edwards, telling him why they could no longer travel the same path. First, he reviewed the story of his own life, through which he wove the story of his desire to make the American people awake to the great need for truth so that they might keep their freedom. He told Edwards, too, that in his youth he had wanted fame and love above all else. Having had both, he had learned that they were not enough. Slowly he had learned humility, and he knew that he wanted to speak the truth to the downtrodden, to all humanity. Because George knew he had to try to awaken the slumbering conscience of America, he was saying farewell to his friend, for Edwards believed that if the end of freedom was to be the lot of humanity, fighting against that end was useless.

Sometimes George feared that the battle was lost, but he would never stop fighting as long as there was hope that America would awaken to truth. He eventually discovered the real enemy in America. It was selfishness and greed, disguised as a friend of humankind. He felt that, if he could only get help from the less fortunate people of the nation, he could defeat the enemy. Through George, America might go home again.

Critical Evaluation:

In May, 1938, having broken with his first editor and mentor Maxwell Perkins ("Foxhall Edwards" in the novel), Thomas Wolfe deposited an unfinished manuscript of perhaps a million words on the desk of his new editor, Edward C. Aswell of Harper and Brothers, and left for a tour of the West. In Vancouver, he contracted pneumonia, in Seattle it worsened, and finally, after he had been moved to The Johns Hopkins in Baltimore, it was found that the illness had triggered the release of previously latent tuberculosis bacteria in his lungs which had gone to the brain; he died on September 15, 1938.

Thus, it was left to Aswell to assemble, organize, and edit Wolfe's admittedly unfinished material into publishable fictions. The major results of Aswell's efforts were the two massive novels that chronicle the life and artistic development of George Webber, *The Web and the Rock* (1939) and *You Can't Go Home Again*. Consequently, the episodic, fragmentary, sometimes even arbitrary structure of these books and the unevenness and occasional excessiveness of the writing must in part be the result of the compositional problems—though these flaws also exist in his two prior works. There is no way of knowing what the final form of the novels would have been had Wolfe lived to complete them to his own satisfaction.

It has been said that Wolfe wrote only one book during his career, a thinly disguised autobiography. In a sense this is true, but, like Walt Whitman, the American author who seems most like Wolfe in artistic intention and attitude, Wolfe saw his own experience as the focal point for the experience of a nation still in the process of becoming. Thus, as the major character in Wolfe's novels strives for experience, personal meaning, and a means of artistic expression, he is also trying to seize and formalize the nature and direction of nothing less than American society itself.

You Can't Go Home Again is the most external and social of Wolfe's four major novels. The title sets the theme and action line of the novel. George cannot go "home" to any of the old places, experiences, or ideas that have formed him, because every time he attempts to do so, he either finds a corruption that has destroyed the thing he would return to, or he finds that he has gone beyond that particular experience and has neither the need nor the desire to repeat it. Metaphorically, "home" is the naïve, idealized vision of America and of his potential place in it that he had held as a young man but now learns no longer exists and perhaps never did. When George returns to his hometown of Libya Hill to attend his aunt's funeral, he finds the old rural values gone and a new corrupt speculative fever running rampant. Then he sees the collapse of this greedy dream in the beginnings of the Depression. He cannot go back to his physical home because it no longer exists, and he is repelled by what has replaced it. Libya Hill, however, is only a microcosm, a foreshadowing of what he is to encounter. As America enters into the Depression, George comes into painful contact with the results of the American economic and social system as he intimately observes both its victims and its victimizers—and he seeks to disassociate himself from both.

It is Europe and especially Germany, however, that brings George to his final understanding. The notion that artistic success and fame will bring him satisfaction is destroyed by his meeting with the famous novelist Lloyd McHarg (a fictionalized Sinclair Lewis), who finds that only bitterness, loneliness, and alcoholism come from his success. George then completes his education in Germany when he is exposed to the horror of the newly powerful Nazi regime. The Nazi horror, thus, is the logical extension and end result of the greed and corruption George has observed in America, perhaps even the America of the not too distant future.

Yet *You Can't Go Home Again* is not a despairing book. It ends with an exhortation. For all the evil and pessimism he has encountered in his education, George continues to feel that humanity in general and America in particular still have the potential to assert their positive capacities and realize the ideals they once possessed. That is what, as an artist in Whitman's bardic tradition, George sees his place in America to be—as a spokesman for that vision.

Bibliography:
Clements, Clyde C. "Symbolic Patterns in *You Can't Go Home Again.*" *Modern Fiction Studies* 11, no. 3 (Autumn, 1965): 286-296. Defines and explicates these symbolic patterns: reminiscence (family and hometown), progression (business ethic, love, and art), and projection (fame in exile and the father).

Holman, C. Hugh. *The Loneliness at the Core: Studies in Thomas Wolfe.* Baton Rouge: Louisiana State University Press, 1975. Analyzes the ambivalent attitudes of Wolfe, via his hero George Webber, toward the South and its place in modern America.

Idol, John Lane, Jr. *A Thomas Wolfe Companion.* New York: Greenwood Press, 1987. Explains Wolfe's avowed purpose in writing this novel and describes how Max Perkins, his editor, pieced it together and published it after Wolfe's death. Identifies the novel's main themes: discovery, growth, illusion and reality, hope, sorrow, dreams and their loss, ambition, freedom, honesty, and loneliness. Discusses its structure (rejection follows discovery), summarizes its episodes, and analyzes its characters, all identified in a glossary.

McElderry, Bruce R. *Thomas Wolfe.* New York: Twayne, 1964. Explains how closely this novel follows *The Web and the Rock,* summarizes its continuing action and the maturing thoughts of the hero, and shows how significantly the work differs from Wolfe's earlier, more autobiographical novels. Praises its satiric, demonic, and comic episodes.

Snyder, William U. *Thomas Wolfe: Ulysses and Narcissus.* Athens: Ohio University Press, 1971. Demonstrates how events in Wolfe's life, chronologically charted, caused his swings between depression and elation. Labels these events love denied, love unavailable, fame denied, love gratified, fame gratified. Parallels these events and elements in *You Can't Go Home Again.*

YOU KNOW ME AL
A Busher's Letters

Type of work: Novel
Author: Ring Lardner (1885-1933)
Type of plot: Satire
Time of plot: c. 1915
Locale: Chicago
First published: 1916

Principal characters:
JACK KEEFE, a ballplayer
AL BLANCHARD, his correspondent
FLORRIE, Jack's wife
ALLEN, Jack's brother-in-law, also a ballplayer
MARIE, his wife

The Story:

When Jack Keefe, a pitcher, was brought up from the minor leagues by the Chicago White Sox, he began writing a series of letters to his hometown friend, Al. It was a peculiar friendship, however, for Jack was basically incapable of any of the emotions real friendship requires. He patronized Al and used him. Jack was a braggart and a chronic self-excuser, and the letters gave him a chance to exercise his ego. Al apparently never saw through Jack.

So sublimely self-confident that he felt every trifling detail of his life was important, Jack wrote full accounts of his adventures. Having neither modesty nor shame, he even included episodes in which he appeared foolish. When Jack reported to training camp on the West Coast, he immediately annoyed the manager by his overeating, refusal to take orders, and laziness. Though a powerful right-handed pitcher, he was an indifferent fielder and careless about base runners. The manager tried to handle Jack with irony, but it was lost on him. Whenever he had a bad day, he alibied that his arm was sore. Any hit made against him was the fault of the fielders, the umpires, or the scorers. Jack also believed that he was irresistible to women. In training camp, he met a girl from Detroit named Violet, and he planned to romance her when the White Sox were playing in Detroit.

Jack did well enough in spring training to be included on the White Sox roster, however in his first starting assignment against the Tigers, he played miserably. The manager left him in the game as punishment, and sixteen runs were scored against him. Ty Cobb stole four bases. As usual, Jack complained that his arm was sore. By now, the manager was thoroughly disgusted with him, and Jack was sent down to San Francisco. He sulked and said he would quit baseball, but he went. Violet called him a busher.

In San Francisco, he won eleven straight games and became engaged to a girl named Hazel. Recalled by the White Sox at the end of the season, he pitched well enough to be used in the City Series between the White Sox and the Cubs. Hazel asked him for one hundred dollars to pay her fare to Chicago for their wedding. He sent her thirty, and she married a boxer instead. Jack then attempted to marry Violet, but she married another ballplayer. Jack married Florrie, the sister-in-law of a White Sox left-hander named Allen.

When Florrie refused to spend the winter in Bedford, Jack's hometown, they rented an apartment across the hall from Allen and Marie, Allen's wife. There were many quarrels between the two families, most of them occasioned by Jack's stinginess. Jack had always been convinced that all left-handers were crazy; his trouble with Allen only served to strengthen his conviction. Allen was taking his wife Marie along to spring training. Florrie wanted to go too, but Jack felt that he could not afford to take her. Since he felt that he was underpaid, he tried to get a raise from the club, even though he had already signed a contract. Charles Comiskey, the owner of the White Sox, had already had contract trouble with Jack and refused to grant him any concessions. Jack then tried to join the Federal League, a third major league that was hiring players away from the American and National Leagues; however, the Federal League would have nothing to do with him because he had signed a contract with the White Sox. Then his team learned about this attempted defection. Hog-fat after gorging himself on food and liquor all winter, he was sold to Milwaukee as a disciplinary measure. Florrie left him. Jack, protesting that he would not go to the minors again, borrowed money from Al to return to Bedford. The White Sox were forced to keep him because of a technicality in the waiver rule.

The manager limited Jack's diet, and he got into good enough shape to be given another chance with the White Sox. Florrie and Jack were reconciled because she was pregnant, and she soon presented him with a son. At first, Jack worried because the baby appeared to be left-handed. Florrie named the baby Allen after her brother-in-law, but Jack insisted that the baby was named for Al. Although he continued to display the same old patterns of bragging and complacency, Jack turned out to be a doting father in his own fashion. After a successful season, he was selected to pitch in the City Series, a cause of fresh strife with Florrie because she wanted to attend the games, and he wanted her to stay home with the baby. Jack was not concerned about the money for a baby-sitter as much as he was worried about the welfare of his son. When the team bribed Florrie to stay home, she used the money to hire a baby-sitter. Jack then decided to leave her but changed his mind when he learned that she would have custody of the child. After another argument with Allen and Marie, Jack moved his family out of the apartment which they shared and for which Allen paid the rent.

The White Sox wanted Jack to join the world tour the team was making with the Giants, but he did not want to be away from the baby. The real reason for taking him was to keep him in shape, but Jack believed that baseball fans in other countries wanted to see him. They coaxed him to Canada because Christy Mathewson was going that far. Then they told him that President Wilson was afraid Japan would declare war if Jack did not go there to play. Convinced at first, he later began to worry about the dangers of the ocean voyage and backed down, but when he was told that Allen would be taken in his place, his vindictiveness triumphed over his fear. He sailed away boasting of triumphs to come.

Critical Evaluation:

Ring Lardner first gained a reputation as a sportswriter. From the beginning, however, he often treated sports with irony and humor. Lardner admired thinking, hardworking athletes and made fun of those players whose talents were paired with flawed thinking. Later, Lardner left sportswriting to satirize wrongheadedness in other aspects of American culture in highly popular newspaper columns, essays, and works of fiction. During the 1920's and early 1930's, Lardner was one of the highest-paid and best-known writers in America. A master of irony and the precise use of language, Lardner's best works continue to impress readers with their insights into the ambiguities and contradictions of American society.

You Know Me Al is generally recognized as Lardner's best attempt at long fiction. Lardner used the device of letters from a would-be big-league pitcher, Jack Keefe, to his hometown Indiana friend, Al Blanchard, in order to expose the narrator's character flaws and the shortcomings of the popular association of the American Dream with material, romantic, and athletic success.

The phrase "you know me" was a common expression among friends in the early twentieth century, usually intended to elicit respect or support for the speaker's accomplishments, personality, or behavior. In Lardner's novel, however, the phrase becomes an ironic refrain that underscores the ineptness of the narrator, generally included after a particularly foolish outburst or confrontation. Such dramatic irony (that is, a discrepancy between what characters think they are saying as opposed to what they are actually revealing) is a main tool used by Lardner to achieve humorous and satirical effects.

An important motive for Jack's writing of letters is his desire to impress his hometown friend about his ballplaying skills, his income, and his success with women. Jack's building up of himself is often undercut by the inclusion of details that suggest a different or opposite picture. For example, Jack boasts of his natural pitching talents, his gifted right arm, and his athletic physique. Jack also notes that the manager and coach badger him into learning more about pitching, fielding, and especially thinking. Although his natural talent often results in wins, his other weaknesses lead to nearly as many losses. For example, Jack's hatred of a romantic rival causes Jack to hit him with a pitched ball when the bases are loaded. Although by novel's end, he has had a somewhat successful season with the White Sox, earlier he has been sent down to San Francisco to learn more about the game and, for a time, he is traded to another team because of his shortcomings.

In the same way, Jack's boasts of financial acumen and increased income often prove empty. Like many others caught up in the material aspects of the American Dream, Jack measures success by the money he earns and the things he can afford. He hopes to get rich through sports. In truth, however, he always fails to win the salary demands he places on the owner, settling for figures that in earlier letters to Al he has insisted he would never accept. Although he tries to control his spending and his family budget, Florrie, his wife, clearly takes advantage of him repeatedly. Other women in his life do too, so that his relatively comfortable salary is squandered on entertainment, clothes, and overpriced furniture. Once, after overspending, he even has to ask Al for some financial help.

Another part of Jack's dream is to marry a pretty girl and raise an ideal family. Jack sees himself as a great ladies' man. All three sweethearts he romances in the novel, however, take advantage of him and ridicule him. Violet and Hazel eventually reject Jack's romantic advances and marry other, more promising athletes. The rapidity of the changes in Jack's romantic fortunes ironically underscores his naïve notions of romance. On October 7, he finds out Hazel is married. By October 9, his attempt to renew a relationship with Violet has ended in disaster. He meets Florrie on October 12 and writes on October 14 that they will be getting married, this in spite of his admission that Florrie is not as pretty as Violet or Hazel. By October 17, he is married and claiming to be "the happiest man in the world," even though he goes to great length to list in detail every expense of the marriage and honeymoon. The reader understands that Jack's romantic success off the field is as mixed as his athletic success on the mound.

Lardner's ironic portrait of Jack is not bitter or hateful. Jack's foolishness is partially redeemed by his devotion to his child and his wrongheaded attempts to do the right thing. Although a braggart, he is not malicious. His mistakes are the mistakes of his American society—ignorance, thoughtlessness, prejudice, laziness, inconsistency, and an overawe of material success.

Besides a reliance on dramatic irony, Lardner's novel is rich in the skillful use of language. The narrator's voice in the letters is highly conversational, full of idiomatic and slang expressions, often ungrammatical, and showing little acquaintance with the conventions of punctuation. Lardner shows his concern for realism, however, by having Jack spell correctly the long words in his vocabulary, those an up-and-coming athlete like Jack might look up in order to impress his friend. In contrast, misspellings often occur with common words, which a narrator like Jack might have the confidence to think he knows. The language and writing style of the letters realistically and humorously show Keefe's relative lack of education and his roots in the rural lower classes of early twentieth century America. The letters are always easy to read and clearly express the narrator's emotional confusion and personality. So effective was Lardner in accurately catching the voice of his fictional characters' semiliteracy in this and other books that the voice has been dubbed "Ringlish."

"Critical Evaluation" by Delmer Davis

Bibliography:
Elder, Donald. *Ring Lardner*. Garden City, N.Y.: Doubleday, 1956. The first full-length biography of Lardner, with extensive details about the writing, contents, and publication of Lardner's Jack Keefe stories. Excellent analysis of Lardner's use of language.
Evans, Elizabeth. *Ring Lardner*. New York: Frederick Ungar, 1979. A good, short critical introduction to Lardner's writings, themes, strengths, and weaknesses. Includes an evaluation of Lardner's fiction.
Patrick, Walton R. *Ring Lardner*. Boston: Twayne, 1963. A helpful, brief critical interpretation of Lardner's literary contributions, with meaningful analysis of the several Jack Keefe stories and novels.
Robinson, Douglas. *Ring Lardner and the Other*. New York: Oxford University Press, 1992. Treats Lardner's works with critical seriousness. Probes Lardner's psychological reactions to his upbringing and emphasizes that his status as a minor writer resulted from a conflicted childhood and adulthood. Sees *You Know Me Al* as a pivotal revelation of Lardner's interest in characters whose faults inhibit success in sports and in life.
Yardley, Jonathan. *Ring: A Biography of Ring Lardner*. New York: Random House, 1977. The most complete biographical account of Lardner. Revealing critical analyses and comments on all of Lardner's works, including *You Know Me Al*.

YOUMA
The Story of a West-Indian Slave

Type of work: Novel
Author: Lafcadio Hearn (1850-1904)
Type of plot: Psychological realism
Time of plot: 1840's
Locale: Martinique
First published: 1890

Principal characters:
> YOUMA, a young slave
> GABRIEL, another slave, in love with Youma
> MAYOTTE, a white child entrusted to Youma's care
> MONSIEUR DESRIVIÈRES, Gabriel's master
> AIMÉE, wife of M. Desrivières and Mayotte's mother
> MADAME PEYRONETTE, Youma's owner and Mayotte's grandmother

The Story:

Youma was a slave and the godchild of Madame Peyronette, who lived in the city of Saint Pierre. Youma's mother had been the nurse of Madame Peyronette's only daughter, Aimée, and the two children, white and black, had grown up together almost as sisters. Even when Aimée was sent to a convent to have her manners polished according to Creole custom, the vacations she spent at home were always in the company of the young black slave.

As the girls grew to womanhood, Aimée begged her mother on several occasions to give Youma her freedom, but Madame Peyronette felt that she was safeguarding Youma by keeping her in slavery. Privately, Madame Peyronette had decided first to find Youma a good husband and then, after she was safely married, to grant her freedom. Before Madame Peyronette could carry out her plan, Aimée married Monsieur Desrivières, son of a wealthy old Creole family. Upon her marriage, Aimée asked that Youma be permitted to serve for her in the new household, a request speedily granted by her mother.

Thirteen months after Aimée's wedding, a baby girl was born to her and her husband. The child was named Marie; the blacks called her by a diminutive, Mayotte. Tragedy struck the household a year later when Aimée, who had been caught in a chilling rain while riding in an open carriage, fell ill and died within twenty-four hours. Before she died, Aimée begged Youma to assume the duties of a nurse for little Mayotte. Youma, recalling the kindnesses she had received at the hands of Aimée, vowed to do the best she could for the motherless child.

Monsieur Desrivières went to his sugar plantation at Anse-Marine, in another section of the island, for he could not remain in the same house after his wife's death. Not long after, little Mayotte, being in delicate health, was sent by Madame Peyronette, in Youma's care, to the plantation. The grandmother thought that the climate at the plantation would be better for Mayotte.

The little girl and Youma loved the life at the plantation; for both, it was an experience in people. Little Mayotte was irked at times because she was not permitted to mingle freely with the little black children. This was not caused by difference in race but by fear that she was in danger of sunstroke while participating in their games. To pass the time, Mayotte and Youma went on walks in shaded places or sat on the verandas while Youma told folktales of her race.

One afternoon, Youma warned Mayotte that if she heard so many tales during the day she would see zombies at night. Mayotte laughed and asked for another story, but that night, she screamed to Youma that something was in her room. As Youma stepped into the room to calm the child, she felt a tremendous snake under her foot. Keeping the snake imprisoned beneath her foot, Youma called for help as the serpent wrapped itself about her legs and body. When Monsieur Desrivières and the servants arrived with a light, they found Youma holding down a large and poisonous reptile. One of the slaves, Gabriel, swung a cutlass and lopped off the snake's head. Fortunately for Youma and the child, Youma had stepped on the snake immediately behind the head, and it had not been able to strike at her with its fangs.

The incident earned for Youma the respect of everyone at the plantation. Gabriel, in particular, showed his admiration by bringing gifts of fruit and spending the hours of early evening listening to her tell stories or sing to little Mayotte. He even made a rustic bench which he placed beside the little pool where Youma took Mayotte to play in the water. Finally, Gabriel gave her a pair of earrings; when she put them on, he knew that she was willing to marry him. Gabriel, wishing to marry Youma, was told that Madame Peyronette's permission was necessary, since Youma belonged to her. When asked, Madame Peyronette refused to give permission; she felt that it would be wrong to permit Youma, who had been brought up almost as a white girl, to marry Gabriel, who, although a fine man, was only a field hand.

Gabriel and Youma were grievously disappointed at the denial of their request. When Gabriel, a resourceful fellow, proposed that he and Youma elope and cross the channel to a British-held island where slavery had been abolished, Youma was ready to join him in the plan until she remembered her promise to care for Mayotte. With that promise in mind, she refused to desert her charge.

Within a few days of the refusal, Youma and Mayotte were sent back to the city. Not long after (the year being 1848), word spread through the West Indies that a republic had been proclaimed in France and that slavery would soon be abolished in Martinique. There were only twelve thousand whites on the island and more than a hundred and fifty thousand blacks. The whites, knowing full well of the troubles in Haiti years before, were extremely cautious in dealing with the black people. Even so, rumors began to spread that the whites were conspiring to retain slavery. An outbreak began over the imprudent whipping of a slave on the very eve of emancipation. Thousands of slaves poured into the city from the country.

Madame Peyronette, Youma, and Mayotte, after taking refuge with another family in a large, well-built stone house near the army barracks, believed that they would be safe from the mob. When the hordes of slaves poured into the city, however, a crowd gathered in front of the house and finally broke in. Since the whites on the second floor were temporarily out of their reach, the slaves set fire to the house. When some of the whites tried to escape by leaping out of windows, the mob killed them immediately.

Youma, in an effort to save Mayotte and herself, went out on a balcony and identified herself as a slave. Gabriel, who happened to be in the crowd, tried to save them, but the bloodthirsty mob refused to let the white child be spared. Youma, rather than leave Mayotte to die alone, stood on the balcony with the child until the walls of the house collapsed and killed them both.

Critical Evaluation:

Youma is an ambivalent narrative centering on the dilemma of a young Creole nurse torn between her ingrained sense of selfless loyalty and duty on the one hand and, on the other, a suddenly emerging, contrary impulse toward love and personal happiness. Hearn begins his account with a long and careful expository introduction in which he defines the traditional role of the *da*, the slave nanny of a white child. He describes the typical black *da* as so devoted to her white charge that he virtually gives away the climax. Then follow fourteen numbered, untitled chapters. In chapter 4, Youma's love interest, stalwart Gabriel, is first mentioned. His attraction to sweet little Mayotte's beautiful *da* develops in chapters 5 and 6. In the pivotal chapter 7, which ends the first half of the novel, Youma's and Gabriel's owners deny the couple permission to marry. This subtly rationalized but arbitrary cruelty precipitates the personal part of the tragedy. Paralleling Gabriel's no longer quiescent hatred of slavery in general and the heartless behavior of two slave masters in particular is the mounting discontent of the field and town blacks, who are fanned into riotous action by the winds of emancipation blowing through the islands.

Of central thematic importance is the nursery story that Youma tells Mayotte one afternoon. It is about a witch named Dame Kélément and seems, voodoolike, to evoke, once articulated, the appearance of the serpent that night. Youma's bravery, in steadfastly holding the serpent down with her bare foot, is in turn what fatally impresses the cutlass-wielding Gabriel. That same courage enables Youma to stand immobile with helpless Mayotte in the fire, refuse to escape despite that fact that Mayotte will die in either case, and immolate herself in the flames. When Gabriel sees how calm she is, he is reminded of her identical courage when threatened by the serpent.

Helping to unify the narrative is Hearn's skillful sprinkling in of local-color details. Hearn spent two years on the island of Martinique, freely observed the inhabitants of all classes there and made friends with many, admired their way of life, quickly added a considerable understanding of their Creole dialect to his already thorough knowledge of French, and even climbed Mount Pelée. In 1890, he published *Two Years in the French West Indies*, containing many sketches of island life. A curious feature of dialogue in *Youma* is its tantalizing mixture of standard French and native patois, sometimes but not always translated. For example, Gabriel praises Youma thus: "*Quaill! ou brave, mafi!—foute! ou sévè!*" Hearn translates only *sévè*, as "severe," meaning "courageous" in context. Hearn's own prose is often similarly quaint. It sometimes reads like a deliberately archaic translation of a foreign text. For example, "'Gabou' . . . realized for her some figure of the *contes*." Employing a palette of diverse colors in his descriptions, Hearn combines the vividness of African primary colors—especially in the complexions, dress, and jewelry of the slaves—with the West Indian pastels of flowers, houses and fields, beaches and water, and vaporous mountain slopes. Notable is Hearn's startling, if infrequent, use of similes and metaphors. For two examples: "those strange Creole words which, like tropic lizards, change color with position," and "spidery shadows of palm-heads on the floor."

A key element in *Youma* is the heroine's scary story, reluctantly told to the child. Hearn devotes fully eight pages to it and even annotates two native words in it, although he leaves many others unexplained, for example, in the serpent's song which ends thus: "Bennepè, bennemè—tambou belai!/ Yche p'accoutoumé tambou belai!" Significantly, in the story the serpent does not offer the slightest harm to the little girl, whereas the real serpent attacks Youma. In the folktale, the serpent is transformed back into a man, who then returns the girl safely to her mother. The real serpent, however, goes so far as to wrap its flesh around Youma's thigh. It must be concluded that the episode's symbolism is ambivalent. Is the evil snake under Youma's foot intended to symbolize fatal rebellion? Or perhaps fatal sexual love? Hearn does not say.

The pervasive tone of *Youma* is ironic. The island could be a latter-day Eden, with its slumberous climate, creamy seas, fertile soil, gentle rains, and exotic fruits and flowers—and serpents. The white rules combine a fancy, indolent lifestyle, austerely aristocratic manners, a brave love of family, and a fierce determination to keep their slaves in their place. The slaves are muscular and lissome, intelligent and highly articulate, but also dominated by voodooism. A curious touch is the fact that the French army, garrisoned in Saint Pierre, is mysteriously ordered not to interfere when the slaves go on their murderous rampage. The dominant religion of the island is Christianity, but one entwined in native superstitions. During the climactic fire, one "négresse" gesticulates like a cannibal at a helpless white mother and her baby. Yet Gabriel's last sight of Youma, with Mayotte in her arms and the fire "serpentined" behind her, reminds him of a statue of the Virgin Mary seen at the anchorage chapel. A final irony comes in the last paragraph of *Youma*, in which Hearn tersely explains that at the very hour of the fire a ship was bearing news to the island of emancipation and universal suffrage for the slave population.

"Critical Evaluation" by Robert L. Gale

Bibliography:
Bisland, Elizabeth. *The Life and Letters of Lafcadio Hearn.* 2 vols. Boston: Houghton Mifflin, 1906. Contains a significant letter from Hearn to a friend vouching for the historical truth of elements in *Youma,* including the house, the incident of the serpent, the girl who died, and the circumstances of her self-sacrificial act.
Colt, Jonathan. *Wandering Ghost: The Odyssey of Lafcadio Hearn.* New York: Alfred A. Knopf, 1991. Defines *Youma* as a prosaic and sentimental story and then, curiously, links the heroine's memory of her deceased mother to Hearn's yearning for his lost mother.
Kunst, Arthur E. *Lafcadio Hearn.* New York: Twayne, 1969. Praises *Youma* as admirable in conception, balanced in development, and restrained in effect. Commends such distractions as sex symbolism, dreams, historical notes, and folktale elements.
Stevenson, Elizabeth. *Lafcadio Hearn.* New York: Macmillan, 1961. Criticizes *Youma,* despite its early respectful reviews, for its slow start and digressions, insufficient passion, and lack of plot development.
Yu, Beongcheon. *An Ape of Gods: The Art and Thought of Lafcadio Hearn.* Detroit: Wayne State University Press, 1964. Summarizes the plot of *Youma* and analyzes the two main characters as idealistically treated and yet, fortunately, not made into noble savages.

YVAIN
Or, The Knight with the Lion

Type of work: Poetry
Author: Chrétien de Troyes (c. 1150-c. 1190)
Type of plot: Arthurian romance
Time of plot: Sixth century
Locale: Britain
First transcribed: Yvain: Ou, Le Chevalier au lion, c. 1170 (English translation, c. 1300)

Principal characters:
YVAIN, a knight of King Arthur's Round Table
LAUDINE DE LANDUC, whom he married
LUNETE, a damsel in Laudine de Landuc's service
KING ARTHUR
QUEEN GUINEVERE
SIR GAWAIN, Yvain's friend and King Arthur's nephew
SIR KAY, the cynical seneschal
HARPIN OF THE MOUNTAIN, a giant slain by Yvain

The Story:

At the season of Pentecost, King Arthur held his court at Carduel in Wales. After dinner on that feast day a knight named Calogrenant told a tale of adventure that was not altogether to his credit, and for which he was mocked by Sir Kay the seneschal. Calogrenant revealed that seven years before he had journeyed beyond the forest of Broceliande. After a night's lodging in the tower of a courteous vavasor he continued on his way until he encountered a giant seventeen feet tall who was guarding some wild bulls in a clearing. The giant told the knight that if he sought some marvel he was to look for a spring in a mysterious wood, for water from the spring poured on a nearby stone would bring down upon him a storm such as few men had ever seen, with bolts of lightning that would blind him and thunder that would shake the earth. All befell as the giant had foretold. After the storm had ceased a knight appeared and challenged Calogrenant to a duel because of the great damage caused by the wind and rain. The two fought and Calogrenant was overthrown. So shamed was he in that encounter that he had never told the story before.

One of those who listened to his tale was Yvain, a valiant knight who swore to avenge the shame of Calogrenant, his German cousin. Yvain was also mocked by Sir Kay. While they spoke, King Arthur came from his chamber and to him Queen Guinevere told the tale as she had heard it. The king thereupon swore an oath that he must see these wonders for himself and that any of his knights who wished could accompany him on the venture. Yvain, thinking that the quest should be his alone, left the court secretly and rode over mountains and through valleys until he came to the forest of the magic spring. When he poured a basin of water on the stone, a great storm arose. After the storm the strange knight appeared and he and Yvain battled until their lances splintered and their armor had been pierced in many places. At last Yvain dealt the enemy a blow that shattered his helmet and split his skull, but even then the knight did not fall down at once but galloped off to take refuge in his castle. Yvain, riding in close pursuit of his foe, was trapped when a portcullis fell before him as well as behind him after he rode

7346

through the gate. There the maid Lunete found him and saved his life with the gift of a magic ring, which made him invisible while the nobleman's vassals searched for the knight who had given their lord his mortal wound. While he was thus protected, Yvain saw the Lady Laudine de Landuc, the mistress of the castle, a lady so fair that he fell in love with her on the spot. The maid Lunete, seeing how matters stood, concealed Yvain and ministered to him, and between times she spoke to her lady, urging her to put aside her anger and grief and to take a new husband who would be master of her domain and defender of the magic spring. Lunete was so cunning in her speech that her lady finally agreed to do as the damsel suggested. Then Yvain was brought from the chamber where he was hidden. Falling on his knees before the Lady Laudine he begged forgiveness for killing her lord in fair fight. The lady, impressed by Yvain's comeliness and bravery, was soon reconciled, and the two were wed with great rejoicing.

As he had sworn, King Arthur came with his knights to see the magic spring, and Sir Kay mocked the absent Yvain, who had sworn to avenge his cousin's name. Then the king poured a basin of water on the stone and immediately the rain began to fall and the wind to blow. When the storm had subsided, Yvain appeared to challenge King Arthur's knights, and Sir Kay begged the first encounter. Yvain quickly unhorsed the braggart seneschal and then revealed himself to King Arthur and the other knights. All were delighted to find Yvain safe and hale. For a week thereafter Yvain and his lady entertained the royal party with feasting and entertainment of all kinds.

At the end of that time, as the king was preparing to depart, Sir Gawain urged Yvain to return to Britain with them and to take part in all tournaments so that none could say that so brave a knight had grown weak and slothful in marriage. The Lady Laudine agreed, but on the promise that Yvain would return to her a year hence. Before he left, she gave him a ring set with a stone that would keep its wearer from all harm as long as he would keep his sweetheart in mind.

So successful was Yvain in all the tournaments that were held throughout the land that he forgot his promise until the Lady Laudine sent a damsel to denounce him as a hypocrite and liar and to demand the return of the ring. Yvain, overcome by remorse at the thought of losing his lady's love, went mad and lived, naked and distracted, like a wild beast in the forest. A hermit living there gave him bread and water and so succored him until one day the noble lady of Noroison and her two damsels found the naked man asleep under a tree. The lady and her maids attended the knight and anointed him with a soothing, magic ointment to restore his wits. On his recovery Yvain pledged himself to the lady's support and to champion her against Count Alier, who was plundering her lands. So fierce was his attack on the marauders that the count yielded himself and gave his oath that he would live in peace from that time on. Afterward, having refused to accept the lady's hand or to take her as his mistress, Yvain rode away in search of new adventures.

As he was wandering through the wood, he came upon a lion and a fire-breathing serpent that held the beast by the tail. Yvain drew his sword and slew the scaly monster. From that time on the grateful lion became the knight's inseparable companion. At last, Yvain returned to the magic spring where all his adventures had begun. There he found the maid Lunete held prisoner in a nearby chapel by orders of the Lady Laudine. The damsel was to be burned the next day, and she wept that she had no one to defend her against charges brought by a wicked seneschal who had persuaded her mistress that the maid had acted falsely in the sad affair of the Lady Laudine's marriage to Yvain. The knight, without revealing himself, promised to act as her champion before he rode away to find lodgings for the night. At last he came to the castle of Sir Gawain's brother-in-law, only to learn that the baron was threatened with the death of his four sons, prisoners of a dreaded giant, Harpin of the Mountain, unless the father would give his daughter over to the lewd embraces of the ogre's lackeys. In spite of the fact that Yvain had not much time, he rode out and slew the giant, with the help of the lion, because of his friendship for the baron's kinsman, Sir Gawain. Refusing to give his name, he said he wished to be known only as the Knight with the Lion. Then he rode as fast as his horse would carry him to the chapel in the forest, where the pyre had already been prepared on which the maid was to be burned. Although wounded in his encounter with the giant, Yvain fought the seneschal and his two brothers. Again, with the lion's help, he was victorious, and the false knights whom he slew were burned on the funeral pile prepared for Lunete. When confronted by the Lady Laudine he again refused to reveal his identity, so ashamed was he of his inconstancy, but called himself the Knight with the Lion. Lunete had recognized him, however, and she accompanied him for some distance when he rode away. Although she promised to keep his secret, she declared that she would bring about a reconciliation between him and his lady if it were ever in her power to do so.

Disconsolately, Yvain departed to seek other adventures, but he was unable to travel far because of the wounds he and the lion had suffered in their battles with Harpin of the Mountain and the three false knights. At length he came to a fair castle where the lord's retainers helped him from his horse and attended gently to the lion, which Yvain was carrying on his shield. There they stayed, attended by maidens skilled in surgery, until both the man and the beast were completely healed. Then they continued on their way.

About that same time, the lord of Noire Espine died and his older daughter claimed the whole of his estates, saying that she would give no share to her sister. When the younger daughter went to King Arthur's court to plead her case, she learned that her older sister had been there before her and that Sir Gawain had promised to act as her champion. Granted forty days in which to find a champion of her own, the maid set out in search of the famed Knight with the Lion.

Along the way she fell ill, but the quest was taken up by a friend whose search brought her at last to the magic spring while Lunete was saying her prayers in the chapel close by; Lunete was able to point out to the traveler the road Yvain had traveled many days before. So the maid came finally to the castle where the knight and the lion had been nursed back to health. Told that the two had departed only a short time before, she rode after them as fast as she could. Overtaking the knight and his beast companion, she told her story, and Yvain promised to help the younger sister in her need.

Before he could act for the maid, however, he was to engage in still another desperate adventure. Toward nightfall he and the damsel came to the town of Pesme Avanture, where, as they approached the castle, all the people called out to them to turn back; but Yvain paid no heed to their warnings. Entering the castle, the knight found three hundred maidens working at all kinds of embroidery; they were, they told him, hostages for the king of the Isle of Damsels, the ransom he had paid to escape doing battle with two half-devils born to a mortal woman and an imp. Yvain and the damsel were courteously received by the lord of the castle, however, and that night everything was done in their honor. When Yvain prepared to depart the next morning, the owner of the castle told him that he could not go without fighting the sons of evil. The prize, if he won, would be the hand of the baron's beautiful daughter and suzerainty of all her father's demesne. Although Yvain tried to refuse the terms of the offer, the lord assured him that no knight who had lodged in the castle could avoid or renounce the battle. Although the lion was shut away from Yvain, the beast managed to scratch his way beneath the threshold of the room where he was confined, and he arrived on the scene of the conflict in time to save sorely wounded Yvain by rending one devil outright and so disconcerting the other that the knight was able to lop off the evil creature's head.

With this victory, Yvain released the wretched hostages from their imprisonment. Over the protests of the lord of the castle, he renounced the hand of the daughter and rode away with the damsel to the court of King Arthur. Great was the joy of the younger sister when the Knight with the Lion arrived in time to champion her cause against her avaricious sister, defended by Sir Gawain. The struggle lasted all day and into the dusk. By that time both knights were exhausted, but neither knew the identity of the other until Yvain at last proposed postponement of the contest until the next day. Then Sir Gawain, recognizing his friend's voice, granted him the victory, while Yvain, in turn, refused this boon and reversed the decision. King Arthur finally solved the problem by granting them equal prowess in arms and conferring upon the younger sister her rights after the older one had incautiously admitted her attempt to dispossess her sister.

As soon as Yvain was cured of his wounds, he set out once more for the magic spring, accompanied only by his faithful lion. Again he poured water on the stone and brought down such a storm that the Lady Laudine feared her castle and the town would be washed away. Meanwhile, the damsel Lunete spoke to her mistress in such winning fashion that the lady, losing all the resentment she held against her husband, promised to restore him to her favor and love. So Yvain and his lady were reconciled after many troubles and trials, to the great happiness of Lunete and all their vassals.

Critical Evaluation:

Yvain is the most elegant and sophisticated of Chrétien de Troyes's romances, exploring the very nature of courtliness through the adventures of its hero, Sir Yvain of King Arthur's Round Table. An important part of his twelfth century romance is chivalric discourse, whereby the principal characters discover the principles of courtly behavior as much through conversation as through deeds of arms. This code was essentially a set of ethics to which well-born knights and ladies adhered. Above all, it was grounded in social responsibility. When in perfect balance, courtly behavior allowed one to reconcile one's own desires with the necessities demanded by one's social position. When Yvain fails to keep the one-year deadline imposed upon him by his wife, Laudine de Landuc, he is guilty of sacrificing his personal commitment to Laudine to his social duty as a knight. In this respect, he is the counterpart of another of Chrétien's heroes, Sir Erec, who neglects his knightly renown to languish in the arms of his wife, Enide. When Yvain, overcome by grief for having failed to keep his promise, neglects his own knightly responsibilities, he is rightly termed mad. His stripping of his knightly armor is an outward sign of his inward rejection of courtly standards. Yvain ceases to be a knight, and it is appropriate that he is nourished by a hermit during this period of penitence and renunciation. The episode with the lion marks his reentry into the world of knighthood.

Yvain's rescue of the lion shows his new maturity and understanding of proper behavior, since it shows a heart that can pity as well as be brave. It also shows that Yvain is once again capable of right thinking, as he reasons out that it would be better to save the lion, rather than the serpent, when he finds them in combat. Chrétien's general pragmatism does not desert him here; he adds that, if need be, Yvain is prepared to do battle with the lion as well. The lion, one of the most delightful beasts of medieval romances, is the model of a true knight, bowing in homage to Yvain and continuing along with him as a faithful retainer. It is precisely through the lion's perfect courtly behavior that readers understand that Yvain is now worthy of such loyalty: He has matured in courtliness and is now ready to be finally reconciled with Laudine.

The similarities between the lion incident and the classical Greek fable of Androcles and the lion suggest a possible source; what is interesting is the way Chrétien uses the story of a man helping a wounded lion, who later repays him in time of need for his own purposes. The battle with the snake—traditionally a symbol of evil—becomes a struggle between villainy and nobility. It is, in essence, the chivalric battle. Greek fable has been translated to medieval Christian iconography.

What separate *Yvain* from other chivalric romances are the attention paid to the psychological states of the characters and the way this is probed through conversation. This is most notable in the exchange between Yvain and Laudine, in which Yvain persuades her to marry him even though he has just slain her husband. The way has been prepared for Yvain, however, in a remarkable internal dialogue Laudine has already had with herself, in which she takes both her own part and the part of her husband's slayer. By demonstrating to herself that the unknown knight who killed her husband meant her no malice or harm, Laudine has readied herself to be won later by Yvain's actual plea on his own behalf.

This kind of psychological resolution of a difficult problem is relatively rare in medieval literature. Typically, psychological issues were explored through allegory, in which allegorical figures such as Mercy or Good Deeds reveal the internal pressures brought to bear on the characters. Romances, on the other hand, are primarily adventure tales, filled with enchantments and acts of prowess. They are stories of action in which the cause of the action is a given, much as a gunshot signals the start of a race. The classic example of this in the Arthurian legends is the love potion that seals the fate of Sir Tristam of Lyonesse and the Belle Yseult. Ignorant of its powers, Tristam and Yseult drink a potion prepared for the wedding night of Yseult and King Mark of Cornwall. Their love is therefore determined, and they follow this fated passion unquestioningly to their deaths. *Yvain* has all the adventures and wonderments common to romance, but it also incorporates the characters' own discussion of their feelings and motives in a way that became increasingly pronounced in later literatures.

While Laudine's easy acquiescence may strike twentieth century readers as little more than opportunism, Chrétien's language allows us to see the very real problems confronting Laudine. She can no more act independently than can Yvain. If she refuses Yvain, her self, her dependents, her possessions—in short, everything that makes up her honor—are in jeopardy. It would be improper, as her clever handwoman Lunete points out, to indulge in a purely private sorrow at the risk of all else and all others. Appropriate courtly behavior demanded that one take responsibility not only for one's self, but also for one's retainers. The adultery between Queen Guinevere and Sir Lancelot was mischievous not so much because it was a personal betrayal of King Arthur, but because it unsettled and ultimately destroyed the court. In addition, Lunete reminds Laudine that none of her other retainers would be brave or competent enough to withstand attack. Chrétien demonstrates the rightness of Laudine's behavior by giving readers the example of a happy and faithful marriage. Courtly to the finish, *Yvain* remains a jewel among medieval romances.

"Critical Evaluation" by Linda J. Turzynski

Bibliography:
Frappier, Jean. "Chrétien de Troyes." In *Arthurian Literature in the Middle Ages*, edited by Roger Sherman Loomis. Oxford, England: Clarendon Press, 1959. A good starting point for a study of Chrétien. Deals mainly with sources and characterization.
Lacy, Norris J. *The Craft of Chrétien de Troyes.* Leiden, The Netherlands: E. J. Brill, 1980. Describes all of Chrétien's romances and argues that the meaning can be determined by a comparison of similar episodes. Chapter 3, which covers characterization and symbolism, suggests that the lion in *Yvain* is a symbol of Christ.

Loomis, Roger Sherman. *Arthurian Tradition and Chrétien de Troyes*. New York: Columbia University Press, 1949. Shows how Chrétien's romances were influenced by Irish and Welsh mythology. Although Loomis' conclusions have been challenged, his work is still very stimulating.

Noble, Peter S. *Love and Marriage in Chrétien de Troyes*. Cardiff: University of Wales Press, 1982. Examines the theme of love and marriage in all of Chrétien's romances, concluding that Yvain's situation is different from that of Erec in Chrétien's earlier romance. Laudine is not at fault; rather, Yvain is entirely blameworthy, and he must undergo his trials alone—he, not the marriage, needs testing.

Topsfield, L. T. *Chrétien de Troyes: A Study of the Arthurian Romances*. Cambridge, England: Cambridge University Press, 1981. This allegorical or symbolic interpretation of Chrétien's work shows how Yvain's first quest is successfully accomplished when love makes him whole. The tension in the poem is not between knighthood and love, but between the rival worlds of Laudine and Arthur.

ZADIG
Or, The Book of Fate

Type of work: Novel
Author: Voltaire (François-Marie Arouet, 1694-1778)
Type of plot: Social satire
Time of plot: Antiquity
Locale: Babylon
First published: Zadig: Ou, La Destinée, histoire orientale, 1748 (English translation, 1749)

> *Principal characters:*
> ZADIG, a wealthy young man
> MOABDAR, king of Babylon
> ASTARTÉ, his queen
> SÉMIRE, Zadig's first betrothed
> AZORA, Zadig's first wife
> CADOR, Zadig's best friend
> ARIMAZE (THE ENVIOUS), Zadig's enemy
> MISSOUF, an Egyptian woman
> SÉTOC, an Arab merchant
> ALMONA, Sétoc's wife
> NABUSSAN, king of Serendib
> ARBOGAD, a happy brigand
> ITOBAD, a rich lord
> OGUL, another lord and a voluptuary

The Story:

Zadig, a charming young man with a good education and great wealth, lived in the time of King Moabdar in Babylon. Despite the fact that he was a very sensible young man, or perhaps because of it, he never boasted of his own abilities or tried to find fault in others. He expected that with the advantages he modestly enjoyed he would have no difficulty in being happy. Nevertheless, he was mistaken in this belief.

In rescuing the beautiful Sémire from kidnappers, Zadig was injured by an arrow in his left eye. The great doctor Hermes predicted that he would lose the eye because wounds in the left eye never heal. When Zadig's eye healed, the doctor wrote a book proving that it could not have happened. Unfortunately, Sémire, to whom Zadig had been betrothed, decided that she did not like one-eyed men. In her ignorance of Zadig's recovery, she married Orcan, the young nobleman who had sent the kidnappers to seize her.

Zadig married Azora, the wisest girl in the city, who took a frivolous interest in handsome young men. When she chastened a widow for changing the course of a stream in order to escape from her vow to stay by her husband's tomb as long as the stream flowed there, Zadig arranged to have Azora told that he had died. He then had a friend named Cador make friendly overtures to Azora and, having done so, to complain of a pain in the spleen for which there was but one cure: rubbing the place with the nose of a man dead no more than twenty-four hours. When Azora came to the place where Zadig presumably was buried, he leaped up to keep her from cutting off his nose with a razor. He said that her act proved she was no better than the widow she had criticized. Finally, when living with Azora became too difficult, he left her.

One day the queen's dog and the king's horse were lost. Zadig was able to describe the missing animals and their location, but when he said that he had never seen them he was imprisoned. When he explained that he had been able to tell from marks on the ground what the animals were like, he was released. He had learned a lesson, however, and kept quiet when he saw an escaping prisoner. Nevertheless, he was fined for looking out of his window.

A rich and jealous neighbor named Arimaze, who was called "The Envious," found a broken tablet on which Zadig had written a poem. Half of the tablet could be read as a poem criticizing the king; just as Zadig was about to be condemned for insulting the monarch, a parrot dropped the other half of the tablet in the king's lap. Both the king and the queen, and especially the queen, began to hold Zadig in high esteem. Zadig was awarded a goblet for having been generous enough to speak well of a minister who had incurred the king's wrath; such an act was new in the king's experience, and he valued Zadig for it.

Zadig became prime minister of Babylon and by sensible decisions won the hearts of the people. He cured a great lord who was too conceited for his own good by having a band, an orchestra, and a choir sing his praises all day long until the lord in desperation called a halt to the chorus of praise. He also settled a religious dispute that had gone on for fifteen hundred years concerning the question of whether one should enter the temple of Mithra with the right foot or the left foot. He jumped in with both feet.

Zadig was popular with the ladies of Babylon, but he succumbed only once and did so without pleasure. He was too much in love with Queen Astarté. The wife of Arimaze, enraged because Zadig rebuffed her, allowed her husband to send her garter to the king so that he might be deceived into believing that Zadig and the queen were already lovers. The queen warned Zadig that the king meant to kill him. Zadig escaped to Egypt.

Upon arriving in Egypt, Zadig found an Egyptian beating a woman. When Zadig intervened, the jealous Egyptian assumed that Zadig was a rival lover, and a fight ensued, ending in the Egyptian's death. The woman, Missouf, far from being grateful, screamed that she wished Zadig had been killed instead. When four men seized her, he allowed her to be taken, not realizing that the four men were couriers from Babylon who had mistaken Missouf for the queen, who had also disappeared.

Since Zadig had killed a man, the Egyptians condemned him to be a slave, and he was bought by an Arab merchant named Sétoc. At first the merchant valued Zadig's service more than he did Zadig, but he finally came to see the value of Zadig's intelligence and common sense. The incident that revealed Zadig's ability was one in which he was able to prove a Hebrew guilty of not returning a loan made to him by Sétoc; Zadig pretended he would bring into court the stone on which the loan had been transacted, whereby he trapped the Hebrew into a description of the stone that proved he really was the man to whom the loan had been made.

Zadig next convinced an Arabian widow that she should not leap upon the burning funeral pyre of her husband. He did this by making her realize that there were still attractive young men in the world. By pointing out that they all admitted the existence of a superior being, he settled a dispute between an Egyptian, an Indian, a Chaldean, a Celt, and others concerning the nature of the universe and its operation. He was saved from execution by the priests when Almona, the young widow, pretended that she would allow the priests to make love to her if they signed a pardon; when the priests came to her, they were greeted by judges who condemned them. Sétoc was so much impressed by her cleverness that he married her.

Zadig showed that one can judge an honest man by making candidates for the comptroller's position engage in a dancing contest. Only one candidate resisted the money Zadig had placed in a passageway, and only he danced lightly and with grace, the others being fearful of jostling the money from their pockets. Having performed this service for King Nabussan of Serendib, to whose kingdom Zadig had been sent by Sétoc, Zadig then undertook to show which of the king's hundred wives were faithful. Only one resisted the temptations of money, youth, and power to which Zadig exposed them.

After settling a revolt of the priests against Nabussan, Zadig, guided as always by the sayings of Zarathustra, set forth to find news of Queen Astarté. He met a happy brigand, Arbogad, who reported that King Moabdar had been killed in an uprising, but the robber had no news of the queen. Zadig also met an unhappy fisherman who had lost his money, his wife, and his house during the revolt in Babylon. Since some of the money owed the fisherman was for cream cheese he had sold to Zadig and Queen Astarté, Zadig, without revealing his identity, gave the fisherman half the money he had.

Next, Zadig met several women hunting for a basilisk that was to be used to cure Ogul, their lord and master. Zadig was overjoyed to find Queen Astarté among the women. She informed him that his friend Cador had helped her escape from the king, that the king had married Missouf, and that she had frightened the king out of his wits by speaking to him from within a statue in the temple in which she was hidden. The revolt in Babylon had resulted from the king's madness, and he had been killed. Queen Astarté had then been captured by the prince of Hyrcania and had escaped from him only to be captured by the brigand Arbogad, who sold her to Ogul. Zadig cured Ogul and thus managed to free Queen Astarté and to win more honor for himself. He told Ogul that a bag contained medicine that would go through his pores only if he punched it hard enough. The resultant exercise cured the lord.

Returning to Babylon, Zadig entered a jousting tournament and a battle of wits in order to win Queen Astarté as his wife. Despite the trickery of Itobad, who stole his armor and pretended to be the victor after Zadig had won the tournament, Zadig managed to win both contests— partly through the encouragement of the angel Jesrad who was disguised as a hermit—and he married Queen Astarté. As king, Zadig was a just and compassionate ruler under whom Babylon became a prosperous and happy empire.

Critical Evaluation:

François-Marie Arouet, known to his contemporaries and posterity as Voltaire, represented classicism in the age of the Enlightenment. He was true to the ideas of logic and nature and presented works of philosophical optimism. The core of meaning in *Zadig* is similar to that of his more popular novel *Candide* (1759). *Zadig* is aptly subtitled *The Book of Fate*. The reader is shown many chance occurrences and their results. Voltaire's theory is that coincidence is really a trial, reward, punishment, or foresight. There are no chance happenings in the larger picture of life, and his philosophy implies that people should consider possible meanings of seemingly random events instead of dismissing them as accidental and therefore unimportant.

Zadig is a testament, as is the rest of Voltaire's writing, to his belief in a system of universal justice and morality that applies to all people of any year or century. His philosophy, cloaked in wit, sarcasm, and satire that was relevant to his own time, still sparkles with truth more than two centuries after it was written.

The question posed in *Zadig* is why do bad things happen to good people? The plot takes Zadig through his troubles, constantly asking himself why the bad things keep happening, and forcing the reader to consider the same quandary. Zadig himself is reinforced as a wonderful specimen of maleness and humanity, a person pure of heart, a competent and clever judge, and a brave and winning fighter. Zadig is repeatedly punished for his good and honest nature. Evil is, however, only rewarded in the short term. Just when Zadig is in trouble because his poem was haphazardly broken in half in such a way that it appeared insulting to the king, he is relieved from trouble by a parrot that transports the other half to the king, an even greater unlikelihood. The miracle of chance has elevated his status. Had it not been for the earlier unjust and unlikely charge, he would not have been in the circle of the king at all. Although he was introduced to the palace by this unexpected occurrence, he ends up as the court prime minister. He also meets the queen, Astarté, with whom he will eventually live happily ever after. But first there are more chance incidents, many of them bad things happening for no particular reason. Bad events are just as necessary as good events are, in propelling Zadig toward his eventual destiny.

Zadig is subtitled "an oriental tale," and, indeed, Zadig's ability to go where fate directs and to accept whatever happens without question or offense is a philosophy more Eastern than Western. Zadig embodies the nature of Chinese Taoism, which is to take the path of least resistance, as a leaf floats down a stream, and to go around rocks instead of attempting to go through them. This was a fairly unusual thought in the eighteenth century.

Near the end of *Zadig*, the hero happens upon a hermit who is a disguised angel. The hermit is reading from "the book of fate." The tale that follows is ancient and dates back to the Koran, which was popular in Europe from the thirteenth century on. The hermit does bad things to people who treat him very well, and is kind to one who treats him badly. How and why this is possible is the root of Voltaire's book and, incidentally, Zadig's problems. When questioned by Zadig, the hermit explains that the people he has hurt will learn from their trials and will profit spiritually or monetarily from them. The hermit's conclusive statement is that, "there is no evil out of which some good is not born." Zadig attempts to argue, modestly fending off the inevitable moral of this story, but the hermit disappears and leaves Zadig not completely understanding and accepting but unable to disagree.

Zadig becomes a parable, or a parody of a proper story. It is more a didactic argument for living morally and well than it is a plot- and character-oriented novel. All the scenes and people are designed for the purpose of expressing philosophical optimism. The story line is a vehicle in the vein of the classic "hero's quest." Here the holy grail turns out to be that Zadig marries Astarté and becomes king of Babylon. Zadig's greatest assets—wit and the ability to solve problems—keep him constantly moving in the direction of a pleasant resolve, although certain difficulties must necessarily be encountered before fate grants him the big payoff. His troubles are punctual and specific, are traditional and random. These occurrences in the life of Zadig are Voltaire's reconfiguration of authentic oriental stories, which are strung together and sensibly made to order by a single hero character.

Over time, there has been debate over whether Voltaire should be regarded as creator and originator of ideas or whether he had the extreme competence to realign and reassert classical philosophies that he respected and that fit into his own scheme of life. Either way, he promised in the opening section of *Zadig* that it would be "a work that says more than it seems to say," and this is accomplished almost as a joke on the reader. *Zadig* was originally written to entertain Voltaire's aristocratic friends. It was only at their insistence and because of their enthusiasm that he had it published, though he thought of it as a trifle. Yet this trifle has come to be known as one of Voltaire's best-loved and most accessible and humorous tales. The unlikely event that this "throwaway" piece would become so popular was not accidental or unlikely at all; rather, it was the actualization of its contents. The longevity and acclaim of *Zadig* are testimony to the philosophical optimism that it slyly and diligently expresses.

"Critical Evaluation" by Beaird Glover

Bibliography:

Aldridge, A. Owen. *Voltaire and the Century of Light*. Princeton, N.J.: Princeton University Press, 1975. A biography of Voltaire with extended discussions on his writings, including *Zadig*. Seeks to combine literature with the history of ideas and present Voltaire's personality along with his philosophical framework.

Gay, Peter. *Voltaire's Politics: The Poet as Realist*. Princeton, N.J.: Princeton University Press, 1959. Places Voltaire's political ideas in the context of his times. Includes criticism, clarification, exposition, and analysis and attempts to avoid twentieth century controversies.

Sherman, Carol. *Reading Voltaire's Contes: A Semiotics of Philosophical Narration*. Chapel Hill: North Carolina Studies in the Romance Languages and Literatures, 1985. Systematically scrutinizes *Micromégas* (1753), *Zadig*, *Candide* (1759), and *L'Ingénu* (1767), line by line. Written in a dry, academic style. Includes charts and graphs that dissect the stories.

Topazio, Virgil W. *Voltaire: A Critical Study of His Major Works*. New York: Random House, 1967. The essential handbook on Voltaire. Covers his poetry, dramas, and novels. Gives insight to his life and the mood of the century in which Voltaire was working. An excellent and eminently readable study on Voltaire.

Wade, Ira O. *The Intellectual Development of Voltaire*. Princeton, N. J.: Princeton University Press, 1969. Traces Voltaire's development from his early poetry through his philosopher status and devotes considerable time to his stay in England and the writing done there. Includes Voltaire's thoughts on science and biblical criticism.

ZAÏRE

Type of work: Drama
Author: Voltaire (François-Marie Arouet, 1694-1778)
Type of plot: Tragedy
Time of plot: During the reign of Osman, Sultan of Jerusalem
Locale: Jerusalem
First performed: 1732; first published, 1733 (English translation, 1736)

> *Principal characters:*
> OROSMANE (OSMAN), sultan of Jerusalem
> LUSIGNAN, a prince in the line of the kings of Jerusalem
> ZAÏRE and
> FATIMA, slaves of the sultan
> NERESTAN and
> CHATILLON, French gentlemen
> CORASMIN and
> MELEDOR, officers of the sultan

The Story:

Fatima and Zaïre were slaves of Orosmane, sultan of Jerusalem, but their lot was not an unpleasant one. Although Orosmane had the power to treat them as mere chattel and to use them for his pleasure in his seraglio, he treated them with respect and consideration. Nevertheless, Fatima was disturbed to find that Zaïre was not only resigned to her fate but appeared actually to enjoy it. When she asked Zaïre to explain why she no longer wept or looked forward to the return of Nerestan, who had gone to France to seek ransom for them, Zaïre replied that she found it difficult to yearn after a mode of life she had never known. Since childhood she had been confined to the seraglio under the care of Orosmane, and she had grown fond of her life and even of her master.

Fatima then reminded Zaïre that Nerestan, who had conducted himself so nobly in the battle of Damas as part of the Christian army fighting against the Turks, had been captured by Orosmane but, because of his courage, was later released on his word to return with ransom for the Christian prisoners, including Fatima and Zaïre.

Zaïre replied that two years had passed since Nerestan's departure and that perhaps Nerestan had made the promise to return with ransom for ten slaves only because there was no other way for him to escape a similar servitude. She admitted that she had admired Nerestan at the time of his promise, but she had decided to think of the matter no longer. Zaïre then confessed to Fatima that Orosmane was her slave, that he loved her, and that she loved him. She quickly added that this love did not mean that she had consented to become his mistress. The truth was that Orosmane's love for her was so strong and pure that he planned to wed her.

Fatima, delighted to hear that Zaïre would be elevated from the place of a slave to that of sultana, had but one misgiving—Zaïre was forgetting that she was a Christian. Zaïre replied that she did not even know who her parents were; she had only Nerestan's surmise, because of the cross she had worn since childhood, that she was a Christian. Since she had been a slave from her childhood, it was only natural that her faith reflected the customs of the place where she was reared. With Fatima, Zaïre admitted, the situation was different; Fatima had been captured in adulthood, and had deliberately embraced Christianity before becoming a slave. Although

7357

Zaïre regarded herself as Muslim, she admitted that she was impressed by the Christian faith, but she assured Fatima that her love for Orosmane was so strong that she no longer considered becoming a Christian.

Orosmane then entered and expressed his love for Zaïre and his intention to marry her. As he professed his love, a servant entered and announced the arrival of Nerestan, who entered and told the sultan that he had come with ransom for the prisoners and that he was willing to remain as Orosmane's slave. The sultan, impressed by Nerestan's honor, replied that he would release not ten but one hundred prisoners. The only ones who would have to remain were Lusignan, a French nobleman who claimed the hereditary right to rule in Jerusalem, and Zaïre.

Nerestan protested that Orosmane had promised to release the prisoners, and Zaïre in particular, if the ransom money were brought from France. Orosmane, however, permitted no discussion of his decision. He dismissed Nerestan and ordered Zaïre to prepare to assume her place as his sultana.

After the others had gone, Orosmane remarked to Corasmin, one of his officers, that Nerestan had sighed and fixed his eyes on Zaïre. When Corasmin warned his master against jealousy, the sultan replied that he could not be jealous on Zaïre's account since she was truth itself.

Chatillon, a French gentleman released at Orosmane's command, praised Nerestan for having arranged the release of the prisoners, but Nerestan refused to be gratified by Chatillon's praise because of Orosmane's refusal to release Zaïre and Lusignan. Chatillon agreed that without Lusignan, the great Christian leader and soldier who had fought so valiantly in defense of Caesarea, there was no joy in his own release.

Nerestan then related how, as an infant, he had been carried from the smoking ruins of the city of Caesarea to the seraglio. Zaïre had been a fellow captive. Chatillon tried to encourage Nerestan by suggesting that Zaïre might charm Orosmane into releasing Lusignan, but Nerestan knew that Lusignan would not accept liberty under such circumstances.

Zaïre then entered and told Nerestan that she regretted not being able to return to France with him, but her love for Orosmane made that impossible. She assured him that she would use her new status to protect the Christians and to relieve the wretched. As evidence of her intentions she offered Lusignan's freedom, granted at her request by the sultan.

After Lusignan's release, Nerestan told him how he had been a slave in Solyma almost from his birth and how he had been able to escape to fight with Louis against the Turks. Lusignan, greeting Chatillon, an old friend who had been captured with him at Caesarea, reminded the Christian knight that he, Lusignan, had seen his own wife and two sons die there, and that another son and a daughter had been taken from him. Chatillon remembered that he had baptized the daughter just before the Saracens swept her and her brother away.

When Nerestan remarked that he had been captured at the age of four, the age of Lusignan's son when he was taken, and when Lusignan noticed that Zaïre wore a cross that he had given to his wife as a present, it was revealed that Nerestan and Zaïre were Lusignan's long-lost children. Zaïre, deeply moved by this discovery, vowed to be a Christian from that moment.

Believing them to be friends from the time they were slaves together, Orosmane permitted Zaïre to meet with Nerestan. Unknown to the sultan, however, Zaïre's declaration as a Christian had inspired Nerestan to urge her to give up Orosmane altogether, even after Nerestan learned that Zaïre had hoped to wed the Turk. Zaïre was torn by emotional conflict; she knew Orosmane's virtues and loved him as a person, but she could not tolerate disappointing the hopes and faith of her brother and father, particularly after learning from Nerestan that her father was near death.

When Zaïre asked Orosmane to defer their nuptials, the sultan was amazed; her excuse, that Lusignan was dying, seemed to him insufficient. After Zaïre left in tears, Orosmane raged to Corasmin and revealed his fear that he had cause to be jealous of Nerestan. He resolved not to allow himself to be governed and deceived by Zaïre.

Orosmane confronted Zaïre again and told her that he no longer loved her, but when she wept and protested her love, he repented. Yet, when she left him, he wondered again about her virtue. When guards intercepted a letter sent to Zaïre by Nerestan, Orosmane interpreted the references to secrecy and to faithfulness as signs of a lover's passion, and he accepted Corasmin's suggestion to send the letter on to Zaïre in order that they might observe her behavior. In suppressed fury and jealousy he once more confronted Zaïre and asked her for the name of his rival. Although she insisted that she had no other master, he could no longer believe her.

Orosmane had one last faint hope that the romance was one-sided, instigated by Nerestan, but his slave's report that Zaïre had received the letter with trembling and weeping and that she had promised to meet Nerestan that night, confirmed his fear that she loved another. Zaïre, trying desperately, in the meantime, to reconcile her duty to her family and Christianity with her love for Orosmane, hoped that he would understand and pity her.

Orosmane intercepted Zaïre at the place of her meeting with Nerestan and, calling out that she had betrayed him, stabbed her to death. When Nerestan arrived and revealed that Zaïre was his sister, the Turk was overcome with grief and remorse. After ordering Corasmin to free all the Christians, he killed himself with his dagger. Nerestan, understanding the depth of Orosmane's remorse and sensing that his love had become perverted by jealousy, lamented the sultan's death.

Critical Evaluation:

Although *Zaïre* was one of the most popular plays of the eighteenth century, it lost a considerable amount of prestige as time continued. François-Marie Arouet remains best known for his novels *Zadig* (1748) and *Candide* (1759), which were created many years after his greatest theatrical successes. Of the fifty-two plays Voltaire wrote, twenty-seven were tragedies. He considered himself first a poet and dramatist and only second a fiction writer and historian. Of the incredible body of work he produced in his eighty-four years, it would probably surprise and perhaps even sadden him to know that his novels outlasted his plays in literary esteem.

Zaïre was a daring and creative achievement in 1732. While adhering to the classical theatrical tradition, Voltaire still was the most accomplished innovator of his time. Before *Zaïre*, French characters had never appeared on the tragic stage. Written in twenty-two days, *Zaïre* was popular because it included a strong love interest that had been absent from Voltaire's earlier tragedies. His original hit, *Oedipe* (1718), had been fourteen years earlier, and Voltaire had been reproached because there was not enough "love" in that play and the succeeding ones. Of *Zaïre* he writes, "they shall have it this time, I swear to you, and it will not be mere gallantry. I am resolved that there shall be nothing so Turkish, so Christian, so amorous, so tender, so furious, as what I am now putting into verse to please them."

The controversy, and probably the popularity of this play, came essentially from its juxtaposition of romantic love and religion. Voltaire employs the tenet that religion comes to a person as a result of birth and education. Zaïre, who was born a Christian but was from infancy a slave to the sultan and exposed exclusively to the influence of the Muslim faith, faces the dilemma of either forsaking the religion of her father or continuing with the religion she has been taught. If she chose to be a Christian, she would have to leave both the only life she knows and Orosmane, the greatest love of her life; her life in France would presumably be humble. If she chose to be a Muslim, she would wed the loving Orosmane and elevate her status from that of slave to that of the sultan's only wife. Zaïre must consider which is better: religion for the sake of her father and brother, who have only just become known to her, or a romantic love that is everything to her. She does not fully confess a choice but opts toward confidence with her family and against telling the truth of her circumstance to her true love. She is unfaithful to him through a breech of honesty, while Orosmane is guilty of plain jealousy, of supposing that the only thing she would possibly keep from him would be desire for another man. In choosing to consult her brother, Zaïre is acting against the sultan's wishes, and in leaning toward her religious birthright, she loses the trust of her lover and, more dramatically, her life.

This created a stir in Voltaire's day because religion was not regarded as something to be tampered with or explored objectively as to its value or liability in particular situations. The love relation is what made this play accessible and enjoyable to the theatergoers, but the ultimate cause of the tragedy is religious dogma. Without making his effort too visible or overbearing, Voltaire is questioning the merit of keeping the tradition of religion intact at the expense of personal happiness. Yet he did no more than question and refrained from an answer one way or the other. The great novelty was that he did not present one religion as better or more worthwhile than another. This sort of religious tolerance was not approved of in eighteenth century France and was difficult for many to accept. Both religions are equal in *Zaïre*, where the emphasis is on the opposing strength and importance of love. The two characters who are in love fail miserably at the act of communication; they deceive each other, and both act in selfishness, showing that romantic love, theirs in particular, is not flawless.

Voltaire withholds a conclusion or resolution to the questions he posed. Neither religion is better, neither lover more unselfish than the other, and it remains undecided whether religion or romantic love is better. Nothing was offered as a solution to the tremendous ethical dilemma, a point that critics consider to be perhaps the greatest problem in the play.

In accord with Aristotle's classical structure, this entire action takes place in the period of one day. In accord with Voltaire's later and more acclaimed writings, a chance occurrence changed the mood of that single day. The reunion between Zaïre and her family could only happen on this day, the day of her wedding to Orosmane. Everything hinges on this single contrived event. Voltaire presents a different philosophy here than in his more memorable *Candide* and *Zadig*, in which horrible and unlucky events occur at random but later prove to have occurred for a higher and ultimately beneficial purpose. In *Zaïre*, happenchance destroys the hero and heroine, a much more pessimistic viewpoint than Voltaire's later "philosophical optimism."

"Critical Evaluation" by Beaird Glover

Bibliography:
Aldridge, A. Owen. *Voltaire and the Century of Light*. Princeton, N.J.: Princeton University Press, 1975. A biography of Voltaire that contains a significant amount of criticism on his writings, including *Zaïre*. Seeks to combine literature with the history of ideas and to present Voltaire's personality as well as his philosophical framework.
Howells, R. J., et al., eds. *Voltaire and His World: Studies Presented to W. H. Barber*. Oxford, England: Voltaire Foundation, 1985. Critical analysis of the body of Voltaire's theatrical and poetic work. Compares Voltaire to his contemporaries and gives a perspective on the Age of Enlightenment and Voltaire's place in it.
Noyes, Alfred. *Voltaire*. London: Sheed and Ward, 1936. An extensive study of Voltaire,

including an extended criticism of *Zaïre* and discussion of Voltaire's life at the time he wrote that work. Includes reproductions of several portraits of Voltaire at different times of his life.

Russell, Trusten Wheeler. *Voltaire, Dryden and Heroic Tragedy*. New York: Columbia University Press, 1946. Concentrates on Voltaire and the influence on him of the English author John Dryden. Draws correlations between verses from Voltaire's plays and those of Dryden, Shakespeare, and other playwrights.

Topazio, Virgil W. *Voltaire: A Critical Study of His Major Works*. New York: Random House, 1967. The essential handbook on Voltaire and an excellent and eminently readable study. Covers his poetry, dramas, and novels, and provides insight into his life and times. Includes a comprehensive chronology.

EL ZARCO, THE BANDIT

Type of work: Novel
Author: Ignacio Manuel Altamirano (1834-1893)
Type of plot: Historical
Time of plot: 1861-1863
Locale: Province of Morelos, Mexico
First published: El zarco: Episodios de la vida mexicana en 1861-1863, 1901 (English translation, 1957)

Principal characters:
NICOLAS, an Indian blacksmith
EL ZARCO, a bandit
MANUELA, a woman in love with El Zarco
DOÑA ANTONIA, her mother
PILAR, Doña Antonia's godchild, in love with Nicolas
MARTÍN SÁNCHEZ, a rancher and El Zarco's enemy
EL TIGRE, El Zarco's lieutenant

The Story:

During the War of Reform, and after, bands of robber outlaws took advantage of the troubled times to overrun those districts of Mexico where the local authorities, in a land still disturbed by civil war, were powerless to make effective reprisals against them. Roaming the countryside in armed bands, the *plateados*, as they were called, waylaid and murdered travelers, kidnapped wealthy estate owners for ransom, and levied tribute on the villages and haciendas. For their amusement, they often wantonly burned the cane fields and inflicted brutal tortures on their prisoners.

One town terrorized in this fashion was Yautepec, a pleasant village of the *tierra caliente* in the province of Morelos. By day, the people maintained lookouts in the church towers to give warning of approaching marauders; at night, they barricaded themselves in their houses, so that after sunset the little town in the middle of its circling orange groves resembled a place of the dead. The bandits, some five hundred strong, had their headquarters at Xochimancas, a nearby ruined hacienda from which they made forays to ravage the whole district. Their leader was El Zarco, a man of savage temper and cruel disposition whose bloody exploits caused respectable, decent people to fear him. The bandits sometimes entered the town and rode boldly through the streets.

On an evening in August, 1861, Doña Antonia sat in the inner courtyard of her house with her daughter Manuela and Pilar, her godchild. The two girls were plaiting flower garlands for their hair. After a time, Manuela began to tease Pilar because her friend was making a wreath of orange blossoms, the flower of weddings; Manuela was twining a circlet of roses. When Manuela complained of her dull life, her mother rebuked her sharply, saying that Manuela ought to forget fiestas and dances, and take a husband who would protect her. Doña Antonia's choice was Nicolas, the sober and industrious blacksmith of the estate at Atlihuayan. At this suggestion, Manuela began to speak scornfully of the Indian, as she called him, and declared that she would rather have El Zarco as a suitor. She added that Nicolas might be good enough for Pilar, but she herself would never have him. Pilar blushed but said nothing.

Before Doña Antonia could reprove her daughter further, Nicolas, a nightly caller, arrived with the news that, on the previous night, the *plateados* had robbed and killed an English family traveling to Acapulco, and that a cavalry detachment was being sent from Cuernavaca to pursue the bandits. Alarmed at this latest outrage, Doña Antonia decided that she and Manuela would go to Mexico City until times grew better; they would travel with the troops as their escort for part of the dangerous journey. Nicolas thought her decision a wise one for Manuela's sake.

Later, while Nicolas was on his way back to Atlihuayan, another rider was traveling toward Yautepec. The horseman was El Zarco. In the village, he turned down a dark lane that led to a stone wall surrounding Doña Antonia's orange grove. Drawing rein beneath a giant sapota tree, he whistled twice. An answering whistle came from the darkness under the tree where Manuela was waiting for her lover.

El Zarco had met Manuela in Cuernavaca during a brief period when he and his men were aiding the government forces, and the two had been strongly drawn to each other. After he had established himself at Xochimancas, the bandit learned that Manuela and her mother had returned to Yautepec. Through his spies in the village, he had arranged to see her regularly. El Zarco found her wholehearted devotion flattering to his vanity. Manuela, refusing to believe the stories of his violence and cruelty, saw him only as a handsome, brave *caballero*. Now, unwilling to leave Yautepec, she told him of Doña Antonia's plans and asked him to take her away. Before they parted that night, they had arranged for him to carry her off to Xochimancas. In parting, El Zarco gave her several small boxes for safekeeping. After his departure, she saw that one was bloodstained. The boxes contained a diamond ring, two bracelets, and earrings. Putting them on, she went to a pool in the garden and looked at her reflection by the light of a lantern. She buried the jewels with other gems and money that El Zarco had already entrusted to her.

The next night, Manuela fled with El Zarco to his hideout, leaving behind a note in which she told her mother good-bye. Heartbroken, Doña Antonia asked Nicolas to go with her to beg the cavalry troop from Cuernavaca to hunt down the bandits and rescue Manuela. When the commander refused, Nicolas charged the officer with shirking his duties. The blacksmith was placed under arrest and ordered held for trial.

Pilar, upset by the news of Nicolas' arrest, tried to visit him in prison but was turned back by his guards. Nicolas, hearing her pleas, realized that it was Pilar and not Manuela whom he truly loved. The authorities of Yautepec and the manager of Atlihuayan were indignant over the treatment Nicolas had received. When the commander set out to take his prisoner to the capital, a large party accompanied the troops to see that the blacksmith received full justice. Through the intercession of the owner of Atlihuayan, Nicolas was finally released. He returned to Yautepec in time to see Doña Antonia on her deathbed, for the poor woman was dying of grief over her daughter's disgrace. After her death, Nicolas continued to ride into the village each evening, but now he went to visit Pilar.

Meanwhile, at Xochimancas, Manuela lived a different and sordid life of lawlessness and violence. Forced to associate with the disreputable women of the *plateados*, ogled and showered with lewd compliments from the men, she was at first terrified by her new surroundings. She realized that she had been attracted to El Zarco by infatuation and greed, not love. In particular, she was horrified by the condition of a French prisoner, tortured daily to extort from him a greater ransom. At a fiesta to celebrate one of El Zarco's raids, she was forced to dance with El Tigre, a repulsive creature who told her that El Zarco would tire of her eventually and turn her over to one of his lieutenants. El Tigre intended to be the man.

A short time before, El Zarco had killed the father and son of a rancher named Martín Sánchez. Swearing revenge, Sánchez sold his property and bought arms and equipment for twenty men whom he recruited to track down the bandits. After he had made several successful raids on the outlaws, other men were roused from their apathy and fears to join him. In an encounter at La Calavera, in which Nicolas took part, El Zarco was wounded and taken prisoner. With him was Manuela.

In spite of Martín Sánchez's protests, El Zarco cleverly arranged to have his trial held in Cuernavaca. While the prisoners were being taken there, bandits fell on the escorting troops and set El Zarco and Manuela free. Sánchez, determined to end lawlessness in the region, obtained from President Juarez authority to hang, without trial, any bandit who fell into his hands.

The day of Pilar and Nicolas' wedding arrived at last. After the mass had been said, they started by coach for Atlihuayan with friends invited to the feast that was to be held there. On the way, they met a troop of horsemen led by Martín Sánchez, who asked the party to drive on without stopping. At that moment, Manuela appeared from behind the horsemen and begged the help of Nicolas and his bride. El Zarco and El Tigre, she said, had been captured and were to be executed. Martín Sánchez told how he had saved the wedding party from an ambush. Pilar, filled with pity for Manuela, wanted to take her into the coach, but Manuela cried out that she would rather die with El Zarco than see Pilar in her wreath of orange blossoms. Saddened, the wedding party rode on.

Shot down by a firing squad, El Zarco's body was then hung from the branch of a tree. Manuela, seeing her lover dangling there, gave a loud cry and fell to the ground. Blood ran from her mouth. Several men tried to lift her, but she was already dead.

Critical Evaluation:

Ignacio Manuel Altamirano, who was of Aztec background, became a lawyer and served as a soldier in the War of Reform (1858-1860) and in the resistance to the French occupation of Mexico (1862-1867). In addition to writing novels, he produced poetry, newspaper articles, and essays. He was also an active politician associated with the Liberal Party. In 1889, he became Mexico's consul to Spain. The fact that he never forgot his humble origins is reflected in his active promotion of literacy programs for the lower classes, peasants, and indigenous peoples. His political platform presupposed that Mexico's success depended on its becoming a more intellectually developed country, which would become aware of its glorious past as its masses became educated.

Altamirano also promoted the study of European cultures in order to incorporate the Mexico of the turn of the century into the most innovative intellectual currents. He spoke French fluently, a feat for one who had learned Spanish at fourteen years of age. He was an avid reader of European literatures, which provided him the classical structure for his own literary craft. Contemporary critics praised his works; they considered him a true Mexican novelist who had moved away from the old literary molds inherited from Spain.

In fact, Altamirano displayed no major involvement in Spanish literature, since Spanish culture was associated with the Conservative Party, Altamirano's political opponents. His novels exhibit the carefully studied neoclassical literary design much in vogue in eighteenth century Europe. He also was considered to be an acclaimed literary critic and a chronicler of Mexican literature, both colonial and contemporary.

As a politician, however, he also understood that his literature served a strong pedagogical purpose in promoting Mexico's political positions. *El Zarco, the Bandit* is the product of a sophisticated political theorist. Its plot is partially founded on historical events that he had witnessed as a soldier. His strong interest in Mexican history made him a forerunner in the promotion of a national literature. The novel continues the Romantic tradition of recapturing folklore; it also seeks to validate Mexican motifs as material worthy of literature. This radical position illustrates Altamirano's strong desire to incorporate autochthonous types, settings, and events into a literature formerly dominated by foreign influences. Because the Mexican illiteracy rate was high, it is probable that Altamirano intended for his literature, full of local color, to be appreciated by international readers.

The peculiar untamed environment of the *tierra caliente* of Southern Mexico, and its native characters, stand out in *El Zarco, the Bandit*. In rural settings, Altamirano sets characters against one another in a struggle for the survival of the fittest. Although the struggle is physical, as reflected in the many armed confrontations between outlaws and innocent peasants, it is also moral. The characters in *El Zarco, the Bandit* fall into two distinct groups: The evil of the robbers contrasts with the honesty and the patriotism of the civilians who fight the outlaws. This primal view of human behavior is the central focus of the plot. This archetypal construction makes *El Zarco, the Bandit* read like an epic narration. The novel tells of the clash between good and evil and the consequent destruction of evil. At first, the land in the *tierra caliente* is claimed by the outlaws. When the hardworking peasants triumph, the suggestion is that the land itself will also be tamed by the forces of good.

Altamirano incorporates an important difference in *El Zarco, the Bandit*, however, from what one may expect of an archetypal story. The hero, Nicolas, is an Indian and physically unattractive. Nicolas, a hardworking blacksmith, is a strong and able man, a jack-of-all-trades, and he also has a good heart. El Zarco, who is blond and blue-eyed, has no useful skills, except his ability to kill. The contrast of the racial backgrounds of El Zarco and Nicolas defies what might politely be called traditional symbology. The unattractive Indian is an uncommon protagonist in the newly developed Mexican literature. Traditional colonial literature presents natives as a destructive entity; indigenous groups appear aligned with nature and both are depicted as untamed forces. In *El Zarco, the Bandit*, however, the blond antagonist (whom the reader supposes to be of Spanish descent) is evil. At a time when European influence in Mexico was despised by peasants and light-skinned people were the target of outlaws, the novel presents a struggle between two typical figures of the New World, the European newcomer and the indigenous laborer.

Another important function of the ethnic contrast is its use to build suspense as several related issues find themselves linked in the plot. The most significant issue is that of interracial love. Nicolas, unaware that El Zarco has been visiting Manuela furtively, expresses his desire to court her. Manuela, who, like El Zarco, is white, openly disdains Nicolas, whom she considers to be a dirty, ugly Indian. Nicolas finds love, however, in Pilar, also an Indian and in love with him. Suspense grows as characters come to know their own feelings and to recognize the emotions of the other characters.

Altamirano's *El Zarco, the Bandit*, with its emphasis on history as a means of understanding modern Mexico, precedes the literature of the Mexican Revolution. Like writers of that movement, Altamirano shows a consistent interest in promoting Mexican folklore and in documenting accounts of armed confrontations. His writing has a strong political and moral purpose. The message is clear: Mexican society, without a detailed account of all the forces involved in its formation, may appear chaotic. Once patterns of behavior are established, however, it is obvious that Mexican society can be examined by objective means. A close understanding of Mexico as a complex country will help to make possible the building of a more stable society.

"Critical Evaluation" by Rafael Ocasio

Bibliography:

Castagnaro, Anthony R. *The Early Spanish American Novel*. New York: Las Américas, 1971. Focuses on the development of the Latin American novel since the nineteenth century. Establishes Altamirano as a precursor of the genre in Mexico.

Duncan, Cynthia. "Altamirano, Ignacio Manuel." In *Dictionary of Mexican Literature*, edited by Eladio Cortés. Westport, Conn.: Greenwood Press, 1992. A survey of Altamirano's works; a good introduction to this author.

Nacci, Chris. *Ignacio Manuel Altamirano*. New York: Twayne, 1970. Good introduction to Altamirano's life and works. Presents an overview of his works, with strong biographical and historical background.

Reyes, Lisa. "The Nineteenth-Century Latin American National Romance and the Role of Women." *Ariel* 8 (1992): 33-44. Provides a comparative study of major nineteenth century novelists' treatment of women in their works. Stresses the influence of the strong Latin American patriarchal social structure on the emerging novel.

THE ZOO STORY

Type of work: Drama
Author: Edward Albee (1928-   )
Type of plot: Absurdist
Time of plot: Late 1950's
Locale: Central Park, New York City
First performed: 1959; first published, 1959

> *Principal characters:*
> PETER, a man in his early forties
> JERRY, a man in his late thirties

The Story:

Peter, a successful upper-middle-class man in the publishing business, was reading on a bench in Central Park in New York City on a sunny summer afternoon. Another man, Jerry, an aimless, rootless outsider who described himself as a "permanent transient," declared that he had come from the zoo and insisted on talking to Peter. Peter did not want to be bothered. He tried to brush off Jerry and get on with his reading, but Jerry confronted him to examine his life. In the course of their conversation, the audience discovers that Peter was married; had two daughters, two parakeets, and two television sets; lived in a nice neighborhood; and had an executive position in textbook publishing. When Peter questioned Jerry about his life, Jerry accused him of trying to make sense out of things and bring order to a chaotic world. Although these two men were nearly the same age, in their late thirties or early forties, they seemed to have very little in common, at least on the surface.

Jerry told Peter that he had had only short-term relationships with women. After discussing the difference between fantasy and reality, Jerry abruptly brought the conversation back to the reason for his trip to the zoo. He proceeded to tell Peter a long, detailed story about his landlady and her dog, who were the gatekeepers of his dwelling. Jerry lived in a rooming house, and the landlady's dog attacked him every time he came in. He was fascinated with and challenged by the dog's hatred and wanted to find a way to make contact with it. He decided that he would first try to kill the dog with kindness. If that did not work, he would simply kill it. He fed the dog hamburgers, but the dog's hatred did not diminish. He then decided to give the dog a poisoned hamburger, but still nothing happened. The dog did not die, nor did it come to love Jerry. For a brief moment, Jerry and the dog looked at each other, but then the dog withdrew from contact with him. Even its hatred seemed gone forever.

Not able to make contact with people, Jerry had tried to make contact with a dog, but even this had failed and proved nothing. Whenever they met, they regarded each other "with a mixture of sadness and suspicion, and then we feign indifference." An "understanding" had been reached: The dog no longer rushed Jerry, and Jerry no longer fed or poisoned the dog. Jerry then announced, "The Story of Jerry and the Dog, the end," bringing to an effective and dramatic close the important second part of the play.

Upon hearing this story, Peter shouted that he did not understand and did not want to hear any more. Jerry told Peter that he would explain what happened to him at the zoo, but first he must explain the reason for his visit. Jerry went to the zoo to find out about the way people existed with animals and the way animals existed with one another and with people. After telling Peter that in the zoo everyone was separated from everyone else, Jerry began to punch Peter and move him off the park bench.

Jerry told Peter that he was crazy and wanted the bench on which Peter was sitting. Peter screamed furiously to the police and yelled at Jerry to get away from his bench. Jerry told Peter that he needed the bench, called Peter a vegetable, and prodded him to defend the bench. They began to fight for the bench. Jerry took out a knife and threw it at Peter's feet. Peter picked up the knife to defend himself. Jerry charged Peter and impaled himself on the knife. Although Jerry was dying, he thanked Peter for not going away and leaving him, and for giving him comfort. With his dying breath, Jerry told Peter that he had been dispossessed, as he had lost his bench, but that he had defended his honor. Jerry had made contact with another human being, even if it had cost him his life. Jerry told Peter that he really was not a vegetable, but was an animal. The entire human condition for Jerry was a zoo story of people (and animals) forever separated by bars. The play ended with Peter howling "OH MY GOD!" as he left Jerry, uttering the exact same words, to die.

Critical Evaluation:

Slightly before his thirtieth birthday, when it began to look as if Edward Albee would not be successful as a writer, he sat down at a wobbly table in the kitchen of his Greenwich Village, New York City, apartment and typed out *The Zoo Story*. It was first produced in Berlin on September 28, 1959, along with Samuel Beckett's *Krapp's Last Tape* (1958). Later, the play appeared in twelve other German cities, and it was finally presented in Greenwich Village at the Off-Broadway Provincetown Playhouse on January 14, 1960. Critics hailed the debut of an extraordinary dramatic talent, and Albee quickly emerged as the leader of the American wing of the "theater of the absurd." He was singled out by many critics as the crucial American dramatist of his generation. The production of his play *Who's Afraid of Virginia Woolf?* in 1962 won him several national awards and marked the peak of his popularity and fame.

Albee's creative masterpieces are both subtle and complex, and they reflect the tension between realism and the theater of the absurd. The action and dialogue of *The Zoo Story* are dislocated, arbitrary, and absurd up to the moment of Jerry's death. Jerry spends his dying breath telling the audience what the play means. Jerry explains to Peter the farce and the agony of human isolation. It is because human isolation is so great, and because the "contact" that would end it is so painful and difficult to obtain, that Jerry went to the zoo. What he discovered is that the entire human condition is a zoo story of people (and animals) forever separated by bars. From his experience with the dog, which symbolizes the vicious aspects of society, Jerry learned "the teaching emotion," that combination of kindness and cruelty that forms, for him at least, life itself.

At the same time, Albee engages his audience in harsh social criticism as he attacks the American way of life, the way in which Americans are assumed and expected to live. In the play, Albee explores the relationship between the observed world and its inner reality. He uses the images of nonreason in his attack on the American way of life without accepting the absurdist vision that generated them. Albee is a defender of society's outcasts who are forced to live in a savage society and who have been victimized by the stupidity and bias of the privileged elite.

Albee's multiple and complex themes deal with deeply philosophical subjects also handled by notable European playwrights Eugène Ionesco, Samuel Beckett, and Jean Genet: the breakdown of language, the attempt to live by illusion, the alienation of the individual from others, and the terrible loneliness of every living human being. Critics have pointed out that Albee is working, at least partly, from an existentialist position. Jerry's life can be seen as a struggle for existence in the jungle of the city, against the forces that threaten his highly individualistic, nonconformist character, as well as his protest against the consequent isolation that a conformist society punishes him with for daring to assert such individualism. The confrontation with Peter as a representative of that society becomes a kind of crisis or climax to his entire life. The park bench is the arena for the conflict of values and the attack on the conformist, middle-class emptiness and complacency of Peter's life. Jerry feels compelled and challenged to combat the isolation in his life and to make contact with Peter the only way possible. Jerry qualifies as an existentialist hero because he makes his choice freely. His decision at the end of the play to impale himself on the knife is a deliberate act. He knows full well what he is doing.

The Zoo Story is considered to be a modern morality play with the theme of human isolation and salvation through sacrifice. Albee has chosen traditional Christian symbols that serve as an expanded allusion to Christ's sacrifice. Jerry, in his natural state, is alone, a prisoner of self. He must prove his kinship with all other things and creatures, "with a bed, a cockroach, with a mirror," by defying self, thus being in touch with his humanity and the spark of divinity within him. The only way Jerry can smash the walls of his isolation and reach his fellow creatures is by an act of love, a sacrifice so great that it altogether destroys the self that imprisons him and ultimately kills him.

Jerry's death is a deliberate act of protest against the physical and psychological violence of the city; the injustice and indifference of the system; empty, conformist, materialistic American middle-class values; the feeling of life being lived in a void; and the isolation of humanity. The play suggests an uncomfortable conclusion, that the price of survival under these conditions may be the murder of a fellow human being. For Jerry, all humans are divided into two classes, vegetable and animal. The former comprises those who merely subsist, and the latter those who are willing to fight and kill, as animals do, for survival. At the end of the play, the "teaching emotion" plays itself out in full dramatic focus. Peter leaves his vegetable existence and becomes an animal. By the courageous and noble act that cost him his life, Jerry momentarily connects with Peter, who now has the possibility to live authentically for the first time and become an apostle who will carry the message of humans' caged animality and isolation in the contemporary world.

Milton S. Katz

Bibliography.
Amacher, Richard E. *Edward Albee*. Rev. ed. Boston: Twayne, 1982. In chapter 3 of this book, "Ancient Tragedy and Modern Absurdity," the author analyzes the classical plot of *The Zoo Story* and discusses the problems of biblical language, the face of the television screen, and the existential position found in the play. He concludes with an interesting and informative discussion of the play as a classical Greek tragedy.
Hayman, Ronald. *Edward Albee*. New York: Frederick Ungar, 1973. Contains a relatively brief and easy-to-follow analysis of the plot and themes in the play. Hayman concludes that *The Zoo Story* is not a homosexual play, an absurd play, or a religious play as other critics contend; it is an outstanding moral play.
Rutenberg, Michael E. *Edward Albee: Playwright in Protest*. New York: DBS, 1969. A discussion of Albee as an astute social critic, deeply moral and committed to the cause of human dignity in an ethically moribund age. Chapter 1, on *The Zoo Story*, analyzes the play as a defense of society's outcasts who have been victimized by the stupidity and bias of the successful elite.

Way, Brian. "Albee and the Absurd: *The American Dream* and *The Zoo Story*." In *Edward Albee*, edited by Harold Bloom. New York: Chelsea House, 1987. A perceptive and well-articulated analysis of the tension between the realist and absurd dimensions in the play and of Albee's brilliance, inventiveness, intelligence, and moral courage in writing it. This book has a useful Albee bibliography along with a number of other excellent essays.

Zimbardo, Rose A. "Symbolism and Naturalism in Edward Albee's *The Zoo Story*." In *Edward Albee: A Collection of Critical Essays*, edited by C. W. E. Bigsby. Englewood Cliffs, N.J.: Prentice-Hall, 1975. An interesting analysis of *The Zoo Story* as a modern morality play whose theme is human isolation and salvation through sacrifice. Albee uses traditional Christian symbols because the sacrifice of Christ is perhaps the most effective way that the story has been told in the past.

ZOOT SUIT

Type of work: Drama
Author: Luis Miguel Valdez (1940-   )
Type of plot: Historical
Time of plot: Early 1940's
Locale: Los Angeles
First performed: 1978; first published, 1978

Principal characters:
EL PACHUCO, the narrator
HENRY REYNA, the protagonist, accused of murder
GEORGE SHEARER, a lawyer to Henry
ALICE BLOOMFIELD, a reporter
DELLA BARRIOS, Henry's girlfriend
THE PRESS

The Story:

A large newspaper hung in place of a curtain. Its large bold print read ZOOT SUITER HORDES INVADE LOS ANGELES and US NAVY AND MARINES ARE CALLED IN. The narrator, El Pachuco, dressed in his traditional zootsuit, ripped through the newspaper with the use of his switchblade. Speaking in English and Spanish, he told the audience how every Chicano fantasized about putting on a zoot suit. He also cautioned the audience that the play was fact and fantasy.

El Pachuco was next singing at a barrio dance. The members of the Thirty-eighth Street Gang were present, including Henry Reyna, a twenty-one-year-old Chicano who was the leader of the gang, and his girlfriend, Della Barrios. A rival group, the Downey Gang, came into the dance hall. Harsh words were exchanged. At that moment, the police arrived and detained those at the dance hall. Lieutenant Edwards and Sergeant Smith arrested Henry. It was Monday, August 2, 1942.

Alone in a room at the police station, Henry and El Pachuco had a conversation. El Pachuco was commenting to Henry about the problems facing zoot suiters. He told him that the war was not overseas but in his own home turf. He reminded Henry of Chicano pride. Lieutenant Edwards and Sergeant Smith believed in Henry's guilt and interrogated him. They wanted Henry to confess to the murder of Jose Williams at Sleepy Lagoon, but Henry did not talk.

Sergeant Smith beat Henry unconscious. The scene shifted to Henry's home on the Saturday night of the dance. Henry tried to reassure his mother, who feared his wearing the zoot suit because of all the trouble with the police. Henry paid no attention although the newspaper headlines reported a Mexican crime wave.

The scene shifted back to the present. Henry and his friends were angry and worried because they had been accused of murder. They all agreed not to squeal on one another. George Shearer, an attorney, was hired to defend the boys. Henry, at first, did not trust him, but George spoke convincingly of his sincere belief in the justice system. Henry then began explaining the events of that Saturday night. According to Henry, his brother Rudy, who was quite drunk at the time, got into an argument with Rafas, the leader of the Downey Gang. Henry defended his brother. After a near fatal fight, Henry and Rafas both claimed that their insult had been revenged.

As George prepared the boys' defense, Henry was introduced to Alice Bloomfield, a reporter.

They argued in their first encounter, but she and George reassured Henry of the fair justice system. When the trial began, however, George realized the difficulty he faced as the judge denied and overruled his objections.

The first person on the witness stand was Della, who recounted the events after the Saturday night dance. She testified that the Downey Gang went to Sleepy Lagoon and beat up Henry. Instead of going home, they went to the Williams' ranch and were attacked. As the gang members headed back to their cars, Della saw a man repeatedly hitting another on the ground with a stick. Della's story became twisted by the prosecution's cross-examination. With all the objections being overruled, Shearer was not able to present his case adequately. The boys were found guilty and sent to prison for life while Della was ordered to a state girls' school. El Pachuco called for a break.

Henry and his friends were doing time at San Quentin. Henry decided to drop his appeal. He felt hopeless, but Alice was able to talk him back into the appeal. After a visit from George, Henry argued with a guard and was sent to solitary confinement for ninety days. Alice did not know about the solitary confinement and believed Henry was dropping the appeal. In solitary confinement, Henry again talked to El Pachuco, who told him not to hang on to false hope. Henry turned against El Pachuco. Alice continued to give Henry optimistic news. Feeling happy, Henry kissed her. While Henry awaited word of his appeal case, his brother Rudy joined the Marines.

More than a year later, Henry and the boys were acquitted on the charges of murder. On his return home, Henry's parents threw him a celebration party. He made amends with Della. The party did not last long, however, as the police began to harass his friend Joey. Henry, filled with rage, was held back by his father who did not want him to confront the police. Ready to strike his father, Henry instead embraced him, and, one by one, the whole family joined in the embrace. As the play ended, various versions of Henry Reyna's fate were offered.

Critical Evaluation:

Luis Miguel Valdez is one of the most prominent figures in Chicano theater. In 1965, Valdez formed El Teatro Campesino, a theater group founded to help striking farmworkers in Delano, California. The popularity and immediacy of Chicano theater grew as college campuses modeled similar productions in one-act plays. The vital social and political themes generated by these acts led Valdez to write his most widely acclaimed play, *Zoot Suit*, in 1978. Soon after, the play made its debut at the Mark Taper Forum in Los Angeles, where it received overwhelming reviews, and later traveled to Broadway. In 1981, Valdez produced *Zoot Suit* as a feature film.

Set in the 1940's, the narrative lies between "fact and fantasy." The narrator, El Pachuco, cautions the audience that the work is only a play. The play has, however, a true historical backdrop: the 1942 Sleepy Lagoon murder trial. Henry Reyna, a twenty-one-year-old member of the Thirty-eighth Street Gang, finds himself accused of murder, and after a blatantly biased court trial, he is given life imprisonment. With the help of the Sleepy Lagoon Defense Committee and Alice Bloomfield, reporter-turned-advocate, the District Court of Appeals reverses the decision in 1944. After spending more than a year in prison, including the last three months in solitary confinement, Henry Reyna is released. The trial, however, is what creates the passion within the play. The boys of the Thirty-eighth Street Gang are looked upon as social delinquents, as foreigners, and as criminals. At no point during the proceedings do the boys or their attorney, George Shearer, get a fair opportunity for presenting their case. The trial is presented in only two scenes of Act I, but it propels much of the conflict of the play. Valdez recounts a period—a period that has been well-documented in the Los Angeles daily newspapers—of police brutality, civil unrest, and violation of basic human rights within the Chicano community. The dramatic action of *Zoot Suit* allows the reader to enter a world that many may find too familiar in contemporary American society.

The central figure of *Zoot Suit* is the narrator, El Pachuco, the speaker who is dressed in a zoot suit—a long, draped coat, a hat, a four foot watch chain hanging from his waist, and three-soled shoes with metal taps. El Pachuco is the commentator and remains present onstage throughout the play. He reminds the audience of the fantastic element of the play but also reminds the audience of the history that informs the play. El Pachuco interacts with characters and the audience. He sings a song in Act I, scene vii as the couples dance. El Pachuco speaks directly to the audience in English and Spanish, even *caló*, or Chicano dialect. He informs the audience of background information and provides commentary as he participates in the dramatic action. He is also able to stop the action to emphasize statements made by others.

The most poignant role El Pachuco plays is in his relationship with Henry Reyna. In Act I, scene iii, El Pachuco acts as a consoler to Henry after his arrest for the murder of Jose Williams. Then, in Act I, scene vi, El Pachuco becomes the voice of caution to Henry when George Shearer, an Anglo attorney, wants to represent Henry and the boys. The relationship between them develops more on a psychological level in Act II, scene v. It appears that El Pachuco acts as the conscience of Henry, who, in this act, thinks aloud. The frustration and anger built up inside Henry is vocalized in El Pachuco as he antagonizes Henry. In a tense moment, Henry lashes out at El Pachuco, who laughingly reminds him and the audience not to take the play so seriously. El Pachuco, in addition to being a chorus, is something of a trickster figure.

Henry Reyna takes on a symbolic role as well. Henry Reyna, the Chicano from the barrio, is part of the generation in the 1940's who faced harassment and persecution because of its dress, the zoot suit. He endures a humiliating court proceeding and is sentenced unjustly. Henry knows he cannot fully participate in a world that does not see him as an equal. His dreams of enlisting in the navy are dashed. Still, Henry Reyna is representative of young Chicanos who seek justice despite the odds. *Zoot Suit* offers no resolution to Henry's situation. Rather, it points to various fates, possibly Valdez's comment that Chicano youths have many paths to choose, be they good or bad.

One of the innovative stylistic achievements of this play is the backdrop of newspapers. The Press, personified, heightens the emotional context as it brings to light the events that took place in 1942 at Sleepy Lagoon. The Press continues an antagonistic role as prosecutor in the trial against Henry Reyna and his friends. As indicated throughout the stage directions, the reader is made aware of the newspapers' use in the play, especially when Dolores Reyna, Henry's mother, folds newspaper sheets as she would clothes. The influence of the press is shown to be pervasive.

Language and its variety in dialect provide a richness in tone to *Zoot Suit*. Spanish and English are used, sometimes in a mix. Spanish reaffirms the cultural affinity in the Chicano community. When George and Alice speak Spanish, the two are seen as more approachable and trustworthy. *Caló* is a direct presentation of the zoot suiter or the pachuco. Its private usage is indicative of the pachuco. *Caló* sets the zoot suiters apart from the others in the Chicano community, the separation in this case being an article of distinction, not alienation.

Zoot Suit belongs not only to Chicano literature, but also to contemporary American drama.

Carmen Carrillo

Bibliography:

Davis, R. G., and Betty Diamond. "*Zoot Suit*: From the Barrio to Broadway." *Ideologies and Literature* 3, no. 15 (January-March, 1981): 124-132. Analyzes the social and historical influences on the play. *Zoot Suit* is traced from the historical event through the creative interpretation made by Valdez. The differences between history and the drama are noted and explored.

Huerta, Jorge A. "Luis Valdez's *Zoot Suit*: A New Direction of Chicano Theatre?" *Latin American Theatre Review* 13, no. 2 (Summer, 1980): 69-76. Explores the influence *Zoot Suit* has had on Chicano theater. Tracing the history of Chicano theater, *Zoot Suit* is analyzed as a turning point at which Chicano concerns were brought to wider public attention.

Lubenow, Gerald C. "Putting the Border Onstage." *Newsweek* 109 (May 4, 1987): 79. Explores the influence *Zoot Suit* has had on the perception of Hispanics. A short biography of Luis Valdez is also included.

Martin, Laura. "Language Form and Language Function in *Zoot Suit* and *The Border*: A Contribution to the Analysis of the Role of Foreign Language in Film." *Studies in Latin American Popular Culture* 3 (1984): 57-69. Explores the usage, function, and meaning of the language in *Zoot Suit*.

Oroña-Córdova, Roberta. "*Zoot Suit* and the Pachuco Phenomenon: An Interview with Luis Valdez." In *Mexican American Theatre: Then and Now*, edited by Nicolás Kanellos. Houston: Arte Público, 1983. In this interview with the author, the historical influences on the play are discussed. The development of the play and its social messages are also discussed.

ZORBA THE GREEK

Type of work: Novel
Author: Nikos Kazantzakis (1883-1957)
Type of plot: Psychological realism
Time of plot: Mid-twentieth century
Locale: Crete
First published: Vios kai politela tou Alexe Zormpa, 1946 (English translation, 1952)

> *Principal characters:*
> ZORBA, a Greek miner, a man of passion and vigor
> THE NARRATOR, called "the Boss," Zorba's employer
> MADAM HORTENSE, an aging and vibrant harlot
> THE WIDOW
> PAVLI, a young man in love with the widow

The Story:

The Narrator, a bookish man, decided to experience life by going into mining operations on Crete. While the Narrator was waiting with his crates of books for the weather to clear so he could board his ship, Zorba entered the café and started a conversation. Enchanted by Zorba's dynamic personality, "the boss," as Zorba called him, agreed to hire him as personal cook and foreman at the mine. Although in his sixties, Zorba possessed tremendous strength and a boundless appetite for physical pleasures.

They arrived at the village near the site of the Narrator's mine, where they were welcomed by an aging woman who revealed to them her colorful past life as a courtesan. She drank copiously while reminiscing about pleasures and love affairs, and about being the mistress of French, Italian, and Russian admirals and princes. She was now ready, however, to live a life of reflection and repentance.

Zorba's infectious exuberance revived the broken harlot. As they danced, she regained her old sensuality and flirtatiousness. The night continued with music, dancing, food, wine, and lust. Zorba and Madam Hortense satisfied their sexual desires. The Narrator witnessed all with wonder but could not see himself engaging in such behavior.

He was profoundly moved by Zorba's physicality but continued his meditations on philosophy and psychology, always searching for analytic explanations. The Narrator was amused by Madame Hortense's reminiscences but touched at the same time by the power of experience reflected in her memory. He saw the same attachment and sensibility in Zorba, but in him the Narrator could see it in concrete action. As Zorba aged, he grew more passionate, not less. The Narrator was experiencing a sensual dimension of life absent from his abstract speculations.

As the Narrator discovered more about Zorba's past life, he realized that Zorba had a full life as a lover, husband, father, landlord, and beggar. Zorba, however, had never lost his sense of freedom, which was untouched by conventional or Christian morality. His pure animal pleasure was his guide and his theology.

The Narrator and Zorba met the beautiful Widow in the town's tavern, where she was often harassed by the young men of the town. Zorba rescued her from her predicament. This encounter triggered a long dialogue between Zorba and the Narrator.

Zorba theorized that a man would burn in hell for allowing a woman to sleep alone, and he encouraged the Narrator to visit the Widow, who was being courted by other men. There were indications that the Widow was attracted to the Narrator. She returned the umbrella he had lent her along with a bottle of rose water and dainty Christmas cookies. He tried to hide these gifts, but Zorba discovered them and said they were conclusive evidence of her interest. The image of the Widow came to haunt the Narrator. He felt that the mere thought was taking away his freedom. If he had to choose between falling in love with a woman and reading a book about love, he would have chosen the book.

At the mining site, Zorba worked diligently to restore the dilapidated mine, often exposing himself to danger. Progress was slow and discouraging. They needed wood. In a series of delightful and humorous encounters with the leaders of a monastery, Zorba reached an agreement to harvest their forest. He persuaded the boss to give him time and money to invent a means to carry the timber down the hill. When the boss agreed to finance his project, Zorba began dancing to express his emotions.

On Christmas Eve, Zorba gave a passionate lecture about the significance of Christmas and maintained that the Virgin Mary and the Widow were one and the same in God's eyes. The Narrator buried his nose in a Buddhist manuscript, refusing to submit to Zorba's temptations, although Zorba's tutelage was insidiously affecting his repressed sensuality.

Zorba went to the city to buy materials for harvesting the trees. He ended up getting drunk and sleeping with prostitutes. He wrote a confession to the boss detailing his experiences. While the Narrator was reading the letter, Hortense arrived and asked if Zorba had mentioned her in it. Feeling pity for her, he began making up fictitious messages full of promises of marriage, gifts, and happiness. Madam Hortense left full of hope and anticipation.

The Narrator, immensely affected by Zorba, Madam Hortense, the Cretan air, wine, and food, began to think Zorba was right, that the young Widow was destined for him. Meanwhile, young Pavli presented her with a passionate letter. She spat on it and threw it in his face. That same night the Narrator, drunk but resolute, knocked on her door. Word got around that he had spent the night with her. Upon hearing this, Pavli drowned himself in the ocean. His body was found next morning by his distraught father and a band of Pavli's friends. They blamed the Widow's liaison with the Narrator for Pavli's death.

A funeral procession lumbered to the church. At the sight of the Widow and the body of young Pavli, the crowd was stirred to a frenzy. They stoned her and finally decapitated her. Zorba tried to stop them but was unsuccessful. The horror-stricken Narrator watched the ghastly proceeding.

The Narrator later experienced a kind of epiphany, a realization that life had to be lived and not merely studied. All his books of poetry, philosophy, and religion were mere shadows compared with a moment of Zorbatic living. He accepted the Widow's murder as a new beginning to his life.

When Hortense came to ask Zorba about all the promises he had supposedly made in his letter, Zorba realized that he would have to go along with her wishes. They got married in the moonlight, with the Narrator serving as a witness. Madam Hortense was in ecstasy but soon became fatally ill and died in Zorba's arms. The villagers came and looted all her belongings.

Both the Narrator and Zorba felt that they had had enough of Crete. They separated, but the Narrator continued to hear stories about him. Zorba traveled through the Balkans, leading a life of pleasure with wine, women, food, and dancing. Finally he settled down in Serbia and died there, leaving behind a young wife and child.

Critical Evaluation:

Zorba the Greek is based on Nikos Kazantzakis' own experiences while trying to mine low-grade coal during World War I. He engaged a workman named George Zorba to supervise his operation in Peloponnesus. This experience, as well as an earlier scheme to harvest wood from forests, gave Kazantzakis most of the material for his essentially autobiographical novel, which he wrote between 1941 and 1943. The work, which was dedicated to the memory of his comrade, George Zorba, established Kazantzakis' reputation in the English-speaking world.

Zorba the Greek is not an action-packed story, though some episodes have great passion and dramatic intensity. The novel is essentially a long debate between two men of opposite dispositions. One is a scholar-ascetic who prefers to read about life rather than to experience it; the other is a naïve, trusting, and biologically sophisticated man who represents paganism. The two men represent the undying conflict between the two philosophical poles, Dionysian and Apollonian.

To some extent, the novel concerns the transformation of the Narrator. Although Zorba is the main character, Kazantzakis focuses attention on his effect on the Narrator. Nothing changes in Zorba, but he changes everything he touches.

Kazantzakis assigned great importance to Zorba's character and to his philosophy, which was Kazantzakis' synthesis of his favorite ancient and modern philosophies, from Plato to Carl Jung. He would have placed Zorba alongside such luminaries as Homer and Plato. Zorba is not a simple phenomenon. He has a dynamism and complexity that can be interpreted in such different contexts as Friedrich Nietzsche's Dionysian-Apollonian schema or the Buddhist conception of the nothing. Zorba in Nietzschean terms is the Dionysian man, the exuberant extrovert whose sole epistemological meaning is sensual experience and passion. He abhors abstraction and the sterile asceticism of the intellectual life. When words get in the way, he dances to express himself. He is a brute soul, deeply rooted in the earth, and with all the astute physical awareness of a wild animal.

The Narrator, by contrast, is pallid and book-bound, and he struggles in Platonic and metaphysical valleys of doubt. He is on earth but does not feel it. He is overwhelmed by the titanlike character of Zorba and watches him with delight and envy. The Narrator, who represents Kazantzakis in his youth, can feel the conflict of life and death, whereas Zorba sees only the wonder of life.

When asked what he believes in, Zorba summarizes his philosophy by saying that he does not believe in anything or anyone except himself—not because he is better than others, but because Zorba is the only being he has in his power. A rugged individualist, he needs no one to reaffirm his existence and beliefs. He mingles freely with people and departs with no nostalgic sentimentalism. The Narrator also believes in individualism, but he soon realizes that his individualism is hollow compared to Zorba's thrilling dances, delightful indulgences, and childlike fascination with nature. It is Zorba's primitive joy of living that motivates the Narrator to pursue the Widow.

Although the plot revolves around the character of Zorba, it is transformed by the Narrator's abstract mentality. The novel sings the praises of paganism and animal vitality but is firmly in the grip of Kazantzakis' German-educated, analytical mind. It is this underlying methodical analysis that gives the story its dynamism. The intellectual Narrator can never be Zorba, who remains a demigod to be observed and admired.

The Narrator discovers that Crete is more primitive than the mainland. Because everyone is affected by the environment, even the monks who live in the hilltop monastery, Crete seems to the Narrator to be the last bastion of the ancient Greek gods. Perhaps one of them is personified in the person of Zorba, whose passionate dances, playing of the stringed *santui*, and frenzy of sexual love are all characteristic of a savage god on a savage island.

Chogollah Maroufi

Bibliography:

Anapliotes, Giannes. *The Real Zorbas and Nikos Kazantzakis.* Translated by Lewis A. Richards. Amsterdam: A. M. Hakker, 1978. A comprehensive history of Kazantzakis' friendship and adventures with the real Zorba, George Zorba, in 1917, during World War I, when they were engaged in coal-mining and tree-harvesting operations.

Bien, Peter. "The Mellowed Nationalism of Kazantzakis' *Zorba the Greek.*" *Review of National Literatures* 5, no. 2 (Fall, 1974): 113-136. Discusses Zorba's character as an uncommitted patriot who admires Cretan food, oil, wine, and women but does not want to sacrifice his life for Crete.

Elsman, Kenneth R., and John V. Knapp. "Life-Span Development in Kazantzakis's *Zorba the Greek.*" *International Fiction Review* 11, no. 1 (Winter, 1984): 37-44. Analyzes Kazantzakis' novel within its social and political contexts and examines the different transformations and developments of the novel's characters.

Givelski, Paskal. "From Homer to Kazantzakis." *Macedonian Review* 22, no. 2 (1992): 147-150. A useful review and analysis of the connection between Kazantzakis' tragic figures. Gives background to aid in understanding characters in *Zorba the Greek*, such as the village Widow and Pavli, both of whom meet their ends tragically.

Levitt, Morton. "The Companion of Kazantzakis: Nietzsche, Bergson and Zorba." In *The Cretan Glance: The World and Art of Kazantzakis.* Columbus: Ohio State University Press, 1980. An excellent discussion of Zorba's philosophy as encompassing elements from Friedrich Nietzsche, Henri Bergson, Karl Marx, Sigmund Freud, and Carl Jung.

ZULEIKA DOBSON
Or, An Oxford Love Story

Type of work: Novel
Author: Max Beerbohm (1872-1956)
Type of plot: Satire
Time of plot: Early twentieth century
Locale: Oxford, England
First published: 1911

Principal characters:
ZULEIKA DOBSON, a charmer
THE WARDEN OF JUDAS COLLEGE, her grandfather
THE DUKE OF DORSET, an Edwardian dandy
KATIE BATCH, the daughter of his landlady
NOAKS, a poor student

The Story:

Left an orphan, lovely Zuleika Dobson became a governess. Because the older brothers of her charges always fell in love with her, however, she lost one position after another. She moved unhappily from job to job until one enamored elder son taught her a few simple tricks of magic. Then she became an entertainer at children's parties, where she interested older men if not the children. Before long, she received an offer to go on the stage. During a long European tour, she crowned success with success. Paris raved over her. Grand dukes asked her to marry them. The pope issued a bull against her. A Russian prince had magic devices of hers, such as the demon egg cup, cast in pure gold. Later, she traveled to America and was pursued by a fabulous millionaire. Zuleika, however, ignored her admirers. She wanted to find a man who was impervious to her charms, feeling that with someone like that she could be happy.

Between theatrical seasons, Zuleika visited her grandfather, the Warden of Judas College at Oxford, where, as usual, every man who saw her fell in love with her. One night, her grandfather had at dinner the wealthy, proud, handsome Duke of Dorset. He, too, fell in love with Zuleika at first sight, but his pride and good manners kept him from showing his true feelings. During dinner, he was only casually attentive and on one occasion actually rude. Zuleika was captivated. Thinking that the Duke did not love her, she fell in love for the first time in her life. Later that evening, the Duke discovered that his shirt studs had turned the same colors as Zuleika's earrings—one black, the other pink. Abashed, the Duke fled.

The next morning, Zuleika paid a visit to his flat, where she was let in by his landlady's daughter, Kate. When the Duke, unable to restrain himself, confessed his love, Zuleika was disappointed. On her arrival, she had envied Kate the chance to be near him; now she could never feel the same toward him again. The Duke was astounded by her strange attitude and tried to induce her to marry him by reciting his titles and listing his estates, houses, and servants. He told her of the ghosts who haunted his ancestral home and of the mysterious birds that always appeared the day before one of his family was to die. His recital failed to impress Zuleika; in fact, she called him a snob. The Duke was chagrined when he realized that Zuleika did not want him as a husband. He was cheered, however, because she expected him to take her to the boat races that afternoon.

On their way to the races, the Duke and Zuleika met many people. The men immediately fell in love with her. The Duke, whose good looks had always attracted attention, passed unnoticed.

Piqued by his inability to keep her to himself, he threatened to commit suicide. The idea charmed Zuleika; no one had ever killed himself for her, but as the Duke climbed the railing of the barge, she changed her mind. Catching his arm, she begged him to wait until the next day. If he would spend the day with her, she would try to make up her mind and answer his proposal.

The Duke could not see her that night, for he was presiding at a dinner of an ancient Oxford club called the Junta, which was so exclusive that for almost two years the Duke had been the only member. Each year, he had faithfully nominated and seconded prospective members, only to find each time a blackball in the ballot box. To keep the club from becoming extinct, he had finally voted in two more members. That night, the club was having guests, and the Duke did not feel that he could miss the dinner.

The Junta had been founded by a man named Greddon, whose lovely mistress was named Nellie O'Mora. At each meeting, Nellie was toasted as the most bewitching person who had ever lived or ever would. Rising to propose the toast, the Duke was overcome by confusion. Unwilling to break with tradition or to slight his opinion of Zuleika, he resigned his position as president. His resignation was a wasted gesture. Neither the other members nor the guests could offer the toast, for they were also in love with Zuleika. The Duke then confessed that he intended to die for her the next day. Not to be outdone and wishing to imitate the Duke in all things, the others decided to die with him. Later that night, when the Duke met Zuleika on the street, he was overcome by love and caught her in his arms, saying that he wanted to live to be with her. She chided him for breaking his promise. Still later, he returned and stood under her window. She emptied a pitcher of water on him. The drenching convinced the Duke that he was no longer bound by his promise.

As news of the intended suicides spread swiftly through the colleges, the other undergraduates also determined to die for Zuleika. The next morning, the Duke tried to dissuade them, particularly his friend Noaks, a rough and unattractive boy whom Zuleika had noticed when she first came to Oxford. To keep his friends from dying, the Duke was ready to change his own plans. Then a telegram arrived from his old butler, telling him that the birds had appeared the night before. The Duke was now convinced that he must die. The moment finally came that afternoon at the boat races. Calling out Zuleika's name, the Duke jumped from the barge into the river. Immediately, hundreds of young men ran, jumped, fell, and tottered into the water, calling her name as they went under.

That night, Oxford was empty except for elderly officials and dons. Zuleika had hoped that perhaps there was one man who had not loved her, that perhaps one young man was left in Oxford. Noaks was still in his room because he had been afraid to die with the others. Zuleika found him hiding in his room, ashamed, whereupon he became engaged to Katie Batch, who before had loved only the Duke. Katie embarrassed Zuleika by telling her that the Duke had died only to keep his ducal promise and not for love of Zuleika, because it was Katie he had really loved. Noaks, humiliated by Zuleika's charge of cowardice, jumped from the window. The last undergraduate in Oxford had perished.

Discouraged because she could find no man insensible to her charms, Zuleika returned to her grandfather's house. Then, struck by a sudden idea, she ordered a special train to take her to Cambridge. Perhaps there would be another chance at another university.

Critical Evaluation:

Sir Max Beerbohm was rivaled only by Oscar Wilde in being one of the wittiest writers of the aesthetic movement, and his popularity continued throughout his lifetime until his death in 1956. He excelled as a critic, essayist, and caricaturist. Some consider *Zuleika Dobson* his only novel, but Beerbohm himself resisted the term novel, preferring to call the work a fantasy. Whether a novel or a fantasy, *Zuleika Dobson* is definitely a satire.

Beerbohm, who was educated at Merton College, Oxford, lamented the fact that there was no book-length satire about Oxford. He saw the lack of women at Oxford as a stumbling block to good satire, an omission he corrected when he invented Zuleika Dobson, femme fatale extraordinaire, who extinguishes Oxonians with a single glance. Beerbohm began the work in the 1890's, abandoned it, and then revised it for publication in 1911.

As Beerbohm imagined her, Zuleika Dobson is a force of nature, one of those fictional characters that assume life and become real. She owes something to Becky Sharp, the anti-heroine of William Makepeace Thackeray's *Vanity Fair* (1847-1848), and she is certainly the reverse of literary governesses such as Charlotte Brontë's Jane Eyre. She is, rather, someone true to herself, a Venus borne into an unsuspecting Oxford on the steam of a locomotive rather than on the foam of the sea. Beerbohm introduces her in a single paragraph that employs negation to describe what she is not, thereby leaving much to the imagination of the reader.

Zuleika's suitor, the Duke of Dorset, embodies the idea of noblesse oblige and practices such a perfection of manners that his early attempts to rebuff Zuleika are scarcely noticed by her or anyone else. Like Charles Dickens' Mr. Turveydrop in *Bleak House* (1852-1853), the Duke's deportment is "lustrous" and ever at the alert. Beerbohm goes a step beyond Dickens with the Duke, whose nobility affords him added occasions to shine. When he commits suicide for love of Zuleika, he dons the blue mantle of the Order of the Garter before leaping into the Isis. Beerbohm is satirizing not only his duke's snobbery but also the whole aesthetic movement with its refined sensibilities and exquisite tastes. Indeed, the mass suicide of the whole of Judas College is described by Beerbohm as "sacramental," ordained by the gods and a privilege to witness. The unpleasantness and tragedy of a mass suicide is completely exploded by Beerbohm's mock-aesthetic descriptions and observations.

The canny materialism and opportunism of Zuleika are worthy foils for the aesthetic dandyism of the Duke and his college fellows. She has collected jewelry from suitors in America and Europe and much portable property as well. When she decamps for Cambridge at the end of the book, the reader feels her career has just begun and foresees that she will go from strength to strength in the conquest of new suitors and acquisition of fresh wealth.

Max Beerbohm injects into *Zuleika Dobson* several entr'acts in which he tells the reader the history of Judas College, considers the life of Clio, the muse of history, and ponders on the busts of Roman emperors in front of the Sheldonian Theatre. The beauty of Oxford's "dreaming spires" is legendary and so widely celebrated that Beerbohm takes pains to portray the city as too gorgeous, too historic, and too cultured. The stately Roman emperors are seen to sweat in alarm when Zuleika comes to town; Judas College is celebrated as the namesake of the apostle "most remembered and cited" by Christians. Beerbohm even notes Easter week rituals that commemorate Judas by distributing thirty pieces of silver among poor students of the college.

Beerbohm identifies himself as the servant of Clio, the muse of history, but then proceeds to poke fun at Edward Gibbon's *The History of the Decline and Fall of the Roman Empire* (1776-1788) and a number of other historians, thus puncturing their pedantry while showing off his own knowledge. He accuses Clio of being satiated with pulp fiction and therefore addicted to facts, dry facts, very dry facts. In a few short pages, he reduces truth, history, and facts to dull fare and elevates fantasy to a higher level of writing. In this he is very like his creation Zuleika when she reduces the scholars and pedants of Judas College to lovesick swains willing to die for her.

Zuleika Dobson is full of classical allusions, literary quotations, odd bits of history, snatches of Greek and Latin and name-dropping of every sort. Beerbohm casts these gems before the reader in the wittiest possible combinations, then dismisses them as being of no importance, not worth mentioning, really too much. Like Zuleika, he takes Oxford's measure and describes its charms, then lightly casts them away.

Max Beerbohm appears to convey no serious message in *Zuleika Dobson*, to ask no important reform of society as satire often does, preferring, rather, to tease and entertain. Yet his delightful wit elevates *Zuleika Dobson* to a *tour de force*. Stylistically, he flirts with aesthetic excess in his use of archaisms and cultural lore, and he simultaneously mocks aesthetic sensibility and proves to be its most accomplished practitioner.

"The incomparable Max," as George Bernard Shaw dubbed him, always knows just how far to take a joke, how many bizarre words and examples to enumerate to keep his satire at its peak while never letting it lapse into excess. He shares this perfect ear with James Joyce and Mark Twain, although the subject matter and sensibilities of these three writers differ greatly.

Zuleika Dobson is a stunning example of style over substance. When Gibbon's historiography is laid aside by the weary reader, *Zuleika Dobson* will still be read with pleasure. Perhaps Max Beerbohm was as certain of his own ultimate triumph over worthy pedantry and pretentious snobbery as Zuleika Dobson was over the Duke of Dorset. At the very least, Beerbohm saw humor and style as supreme values and employed them with great élan in *Zuleika Dobson*.

"Critical Evaluation" by Isabel B. Stanley

Bibliography:
Behrman, S. N. *Portrait of Max: An Intimate Memoir of Sir Max Beerbohm*. New York: Random House, 1960. Written by an old friend of Beerbohm, the book sheds light on the characters in *Zuleika Dobson* that were modeled on acquaintances.

Felstiner, John. *The Lies of Art: Max Beerbohm's Parody and Caricature*. New York: Alfred A. Knopf, 1972. Examines Beerbohm's extravagance, wit, and style, all of which culminate in *Zuleika Dobson*. Draws comparisons between *Zuleika Dobson* and James Joyce's *Ulysses* in their extravagant use of language. Traces other literary influences on Beerbohm.

Lynch, Bohun. *Max Beerbohm in Perspective*. New York: Haskell House, 1974. A critical look at Beerbohm's work, which takes issue with the form and execution of *Zuleika Dobson*. Examines the satirical aspects of Beerbohm's depiction of Oxford.

McElderry, Bruce R. *Max Beerbohm*. New York: Twayne, 1972. The best book with which to begin a study of Max Beerbohm. Gives close scrutiny to the role of Oxford in *Zuleika Dobson* and examines the episodic form of the novel and the interludes that punctuate the action of the story.

Riewald, J. G. *Sir Max Beerbohm, Man and Writer: A Critical Analysis with a Brief Life and Bibliography*. The Hague: Martinus Nijhoff, 1953. The first and perhaps the best longer critical study of Beerbohm. In an extended criticism of *Zuleika Dobson*, Riewald examines distortions of space and time in the work and makes a case for its being a fantasy rather than a novel.

Revised Second Edition

CHRONOLOGICAL INDEX

IV

CHRONOLOGICAL INDEX

CHRONOLOGICAL INDEX

CHRONOLOGICAL INDEX

CHRONOLOGICAL INDEX

CHRONOLOGICAL INDEX

CHRONOLOGICAL INDEX

GEOGRAPHICAL INDEX

GERMANY

GREAT BRITAIN

GEOGRAPHICAL INDEX

GEOGRAPHICAL INDEX

GEOGRAPHICAL INDEX

TITLE INDEX

TITLE INDEX

AUTHOR INDEX

AUTHOR INDEX

AUTHOR INDEX